ENTERTAINMENT AND SOCIETY, 2ND EDITION

This textbook for upper-division courses in Entertainment Studies introduces students to the ways that society shapes our many forms of entertainment and in turn, how entertainment shapes society. *Entertainment & Society* examines a broad range of types of entertainment that we enjoy in our daily lives—covering new areas like sports, video games, gambling, theme parks, religion, and shopping, as well as traditional entertainment media such as film, television, and print. The textbook begins with a general overview of the study of entertainment, introducing readers to various ways of understanding leisure and play. The book then traces a brief history of the development of entertainment from its live forms through mediated technology. Subsequent chapters introduce discussion of audience research and media effects, and then provide focused overviews of particular areas of live and mediated entertainment.

The second edition of this textbook features updated examples and pedagogical features throughout including text boxes, case studies, student activities, questions for discussion, and suggestions for further reading.

Shay Sayre is Professor Emeritus of Communications at California State University, Fullerton.

Cynthia King is Associate Professor of Communications at California State University, Fullerton.

ENTERTAINMENT AND SOCIETY

Influences, Impacts, and Innovations

2nd Edition

Shay Sayre and Cynthia King

Routledge
Taylor & Francis Group

NEW YORK AND LONDON

First published in 2003 by Sage Publications Inc.

Second edition published 2010
by Routledge
711 Third Ave., New York, NY 10017

Simultaneously published in the UK
by Routledge
2 Park Square, Milton Park, Abingdon, Oxon OX14 4RN

Routledge is an imprint of the Taylor & Francis Group, an informa business

© 2010 Taylor & Francis

Typeset in FranklinGothic by
Keystroke, Tettenhall, Wolverhampton

Printed and bound in the United States of America on acid-free paper by
Edwards Brothers, Inc.

Library of Congress Cataloging-in-Publication Data
A catalog record for this book has been applied for

British Library Cataloguing in Publication Data
A catalogue record for this book is available from the British Library

ISBN10: 0-415-99806-9 (hbk)
ISBN10: 0-415-99807-7 (pbk)
ISBN10: 0-203-88293-8 (ebk)

ISBN13: 978-0-415-99806-2 (hbk)
ISBN13: 978-0-415-99807-9 (pbk)
ISBN13: 978-0-203-88293-1 (ebk)

This book is dedicated to Dr. Mary Joyce, who inspired students until her untimely death from cancer in 2008

CONTENTS

FOREWORD

Jennings Bryant

In his epic *Wit and its relationship to the unconscious*, Sigmund Freud (1905/1958) proclaimed, "we do not know what it is that gives us pleasure and what we laugh about" (p. 107). Three-quarters of a century later, Fischer and Melnik (1979) argued that "theories of entertainment per se are practically nonexistent" (p. xi).

How things have changed. The past three decades have witnessed a remarkable proliferation of diverse yet convergent digital media technologies that have rendered entertainment messages ubiquitous in modern society. Accompanying these dramatic changes in technology and entertainment access have been equally important advances in entertainment science. These intellectual developments have greatly amplified the quality and quantity of entertainment theory, as well as the empirical evidence undergirding the theory.

The resulting phenomenon has numerous dimensions, the sum total of which has led some scholars to suggest that we're living in the *entertainment age* (Zillmann and Vorderer, 2000). Others have emphasized the dysfunctional aspects of the entertainment explosion and have lamented that we are *Amusing ourselves to death* (Postman, 1985).

One result of these technological developments has been the rapid evolution of a vast and exceedingly complex entertainment industry. Today entertainment is a vital part of every known media message system, with even traditionally hidebound newspapers routinely developing entertainment divisions. As a result of the demand for entertainment message system, entertainment has become a trillion-dollar industry worldwide (Emanuel, 1995). Many economists have begun to recognize that entertainment is a driving force in the new world economy (Wolf, 1999).

The concomitant proliferation in entertainment scholarship has evoked abundant changes in the academy. Fortunately, some of these intellectual advances have not only helped enlighten us about the nature and consequences of the many tectonic shifts taking place in the entertainment industries, they have enabled students of media to have a much better understanding of entertainment uses and processes.

A few of the myriad changes to just one discipline that studies entertainment—communication—may be instructive.

- First, consider the changes to major professional associations that serve the communication discipline. For example, the Association for Education in Journalism and Mass Communication (AEJMC) created an entertainment studies interest group in 2000; the International Communication Association (ICA) launched a game studies interest group in 2005 that is extremely entertainment oriented; and, in 2008 the Broadcast Education Association (BEA) launched its Research Symposium Series with a focus on entertainment theory and research.
- Or consider changes to communication journals: traditional communication journals like *Communication Theory* have devoted special issues to entertainment research. Moreover, newer communication journals like *Media Psychology* frequently devote half of an issue's articles to entertainment scholarship. In fact, in 2008, in one issue (Vol. 11, No. 4) of *Media Psychology*, all six of the articles focused on entertainment theory.

- The proliferation of edited scholarly books devoted to entertainment theory and research has been remarkable, and several volumes—such as Tannenbaum's (1980) *The entertainment functions of television*, Goldstein's (1998) *Why we watch: The attractions of violent entertainment*, Zillmann and Vorderer's (2000) *Media entertainment: The psychology of its appeal*, Shrum's (2004) *The psychology of entertainment media*, Bryant and Vorderer's (2006) *Psychology of entertainment*, and Vorderer and Bryant's (2006) *Playing video games: Motives, responses, and consequences*—have become academic "best-sellers."

Such developments indubitably have laid waste to Fischer and Melnik's (1979) claim that "theories of entertainment per se are practically nonexistent" (p. xi). Moreover, the widespread acceptance of the myriad theories of entertainment presented and refined in these volumes casts considerable doubt on Freud's century-old dictum that "we do not know what it is that gives us pleasure and what we laugh about" (p. 107).

Despite the unquestioned role of entertainment as an earmark of postmodern, postindustrial society, and despite the plethora of recent scholarship in entertainment, only one comprehensive and up-to-date *textbook* in entertainment is available to students, and you are holding that one in your hands. Shay Sayre and Cynthia King's second edition of *Entertainment and society: Influences, impacts, and innovations* is a wonderful compilation and synthesis of what we know about entertainment and how it affects citizens and societies today.

There is much to love about this textbook, including its approachability and wonderful use of current photos, illustrations, and examples. But what I like best about this book is that it does not compromise on theory and research or on practical applications of entertainment theory to the modern marketplace. In doing so, it fuses entertainment theory with popular culture and explains how both impact consumers and society today. This is no mean feat.

More specifically, Part 1 introduces and clearly explains the principles of entertainment theory and how entertainment functions in modern media-rich societies. Included are foci on entertainment media, genres, and processes. Additionally, the side effects of consuming entertainment messages on diverse audiences are examined. Part 2 builds on these undergirding principles, examining topics like the entertainment economy, branding, ethnicity, globalization, ethics, and regulatory issues, among many others, in a lucid and highly useful manner. Part 3 offers a fascinating look at innovations in media entertainment and popular culture, including an all-too-rare examination of the classical performing arts and the relevance of entertainment to travel and tourism. This final part concludes with an insightful and provocative examination of the future of entertainment in emerging media and society.

This is a very satisfying textbook. It will scratch some itches that almost everyone has. It is non-compromising in its treatment of theory and research, but it effortlessly applies such to a wealth of popular culture environments. And its reading will provide a truly enjoyable adventure in discovery and self-reflection. The readers of this invaluable volume are extremely fortunate to have Shay Sayre and Cynthia King as their talented and dedicated guides to the entertainment age.

Jennings Bryant
Tuscaloosa, Alabama
2009

References

Bryant, J. and Vorderer, P. (eds). (2006). *Psychology of entertainment*. Mahwah NJ: Lawrence Erlbaum Associates.

Emanuel, E.F. (1995). *Action & ideas: The roots of entertainment*. Dubuque IA: Kendall/Hunt Publishing Company.

Fischer, H.-D. and Melnik, S.R. (eds). (1979). *Entertainment: A cross-cultural examination*, New York: Hastings House.

Freud, S. (1958). *Der Witz und seine Beziehung zum Unbewussten* [Wit and its relation to the unconscious]. Frankfurt: Fisher Bücherei. (Original work published 1905.)

Goldstein, J.H. (ed.). (1998). *Why we watch: The attractions of violent entertainment*. New York: Oxford University Press.

Postman, N. (1985). *Amusing ourselves to death: Public discourse in the age of show business*. New York: Penguin Books.

Shrum, L.J. (ed.). (2004). *The psychology of entertainment media: Blurring the lines between entertainment and persuasion*. Mahwah NJ: Lawrence Erlbaum Associates.

Tannenbaum, P.H. (ed.). (1980). *The entertainment functions of television*. Hillsdale NJ: Lawrence Erlbaum Associates.

Vorderer, P. and Bryant, J. (eds). (2006). *Playing video games: Motives, responses, and consequences*. Mahwah NJ: Lawrence Erlbaum Associates.

Wolf, N.J. (1999). *The entertainment economy: How mega-media forces are transforming our lives*. New York: Times Books.

Zillmann, D. and Vorderer, P. (eds). (2000). *Media entertainment: The psychology of its appeal*. Mahwah NJ: Lawrence Erlbaum Associates.

INTRODUCTION TO THE SECOND EDITION

Many developments have occurred in the entertainment industry since our first edition was released in 2003. By way of an update, this edition redefines and reclassifies the ways in which entertainment shapes our lives.

Because we are an entertainment society, we offer this text as a basic interpretation of contemporary living. An interdisciplinary approach to the study of entertainment means that we cover topics from media, American studies, sociology, business, law, and communication perspectives. Our discussion draws from social scientific and humanistic theory, as well as research from marketing, cultural anthropology, psychology, economics, and communication disciplines.

This text traces the numerous ways that developments in entertainment have been shaped by the social, cultural, technological, political, and legal realities that exist today. Our focus is on how these everyday realities are shaped by the entertainment industry and our entertainment consumption.

Written as an introductory text for courses that approach entertainment as an integral part of popular culture, this book covers a wide range of topics that have direct relevance to twenty-first-century living. Readers familiar with these disciplines will also benefit from the book because it applies general concepts of entertainment to a wide variety of applications and disciplines.

In each chapter, we highlight recent developments in special *Spotlight on* sections and conclude chapters with *A Closer Look* at one aspect of recent entertainment developments related to the topic under discussion. *Flash Fact* boxes call out current statistics and dilemmas. In this edition, we provide three main sections with a total of 17 chapters, which are outlined here.

Part 1: Influences: Theoretical Frameworks and Guiding Principles (Chapters 1–5)

In this first part of our text, we present topics related to understanding the role of entertainment to our modern society. Chapter 1 defines entertainment and traces its origins from early performances to new media. We look at the role of theory and research that influenced the industry, and discuss the importance of an attention economy to contemporary society.

Chapter 2 deals with our convergence culture—the melding of entertainment, advertising, and technology. We discuss postmodernism, its role in convergence, and its impact on society. In Chapter 3, we look at the nature of entertainment audiences. We characterize fans, active and passive viewers, and audience segments; and we discuss the nature of entertainment audience research.

Chapter 4 covers the elements of drama and storytelling, including tragedy, comedy, mystery, horror, reality TV, and sports drama. Chapter 5 deals with entertainment effects and theories, research methods, and the ways in which media impacts our culture.

Part 2: Impacts: Societal Causes and Effects (Chapters 6–12)

This part deals with the impacts of entertainment business, marketing, technology, and ethics in our information age. Entertainment's impact on our culture and the societal causes and effects of entertainment on our global environment are also covered in this section. Chapter 6 presents an overview of our attention economy, mergers and acquisitions, technological influences, and the dynamics of the hospitality, performance, film, and music industries.

In Chapter 7, we discuss the essence of branded entertainment and theming. The marketing mix, sponsorship, imbedded advertising, themed spaces, and symbolic reality are covered in depth. Chapter 8 overviews multiple aspects of entertainment law and Chapter 9 provides the philosophical principles of entertainment ethics. Chapter 10 looks at how religion incorporates entertainment into its doctrine and its ceremonies around the world. And how we, as social beings, use social media and role models to connect with other people.

In Chapter 11, entertainment's effect on ethnicity and culture is traced. We see how stereotypes and superheroes shape our beliefs and our values, and discuss the impact of American media on global attitudes and practices. Chapter 12 investigates the ways in which addiction and violence are manifested in entertainment practices.

Part 3: Innovations: Contemporary Trends and Practices (Chapters 13–17)

Innovations for mass media, live performance, and tourism are featured in this final part of the text, along with the trends and practices of the entertainment industry and their implications for the future. Advocacy in entertainment through politics, social activism, and education are explored in Chapter 13. Chapter 14 revolves around mass media—print, broadcast, and the Internet—including what's new and what's coming. Performing arts—drama, opera, theater, music, and dance—are presented in Chapter 15 for their contribution to entertainment. We also look at dance, comedy, festivals, band concerts, the circus, rodeo, dog shows, bullfighting, and sports as they have evolved for today's amusement.

In Chapter 16, we explore tourism, natural and constructed attractions, and recreation for their roles in entertaining audiences. Finally, Chapter 17 jumps into the future to see how new media, interactivity, and technology will shape the way we live and experience entertainment in the years to come.

PART 1

INFLUENCES: THEORETICAL FRAMEWORKS AND GUIDING PRINCIPLES

1 ENTERTAINMENT EVERYTHING

Along the highway of life, everything is a roadside attraction.
—Tom Robbins

In this new millennium when most of our encounters are paid-for experiences, Americans view entertainment as a fact of life. The average American spends more money on entertainment than on gasoline, household furnishings, and clothing, and spends nearly the same amount on entertainment as on dining out. According to Pricewaterhouse Coopers, spending on global entertainment and media will exceed $1.8 trillion by 2010 (see Figure 1.1). We have transitioned into an "experience economy" where we each become part of the commercial marketplace.[1] The entertainment industry packages experiences by providing access to simulated worlds and virtual realities. Because a large proportion of human activity is centered around it, entertainment is an important element of society. Entertainment drives social behavior, and as such it deserves to be studied for its contributions, its significance, and its effects.

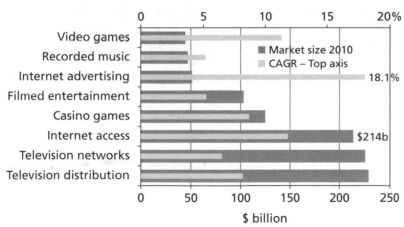

Global Entertainment and Media Industry – 2010
Grow at 6.6% Compound Annual Growth Rate (CAGR) to $1.8 trillion

Figure 1.1   Global Growth

Source: www.metrics2.com/blog/2006/09/19/global_entertainment_media_industry_will_grow_to_1.html

Entertainment and Society

As the title suggests, this text focuses on how our society influences trends and developments in entertainment and how entertainment, in turn, can influence its audiences and larger society. When we talk about "society," we are referring to many factors including culture, business, law, politics, technology, and even religion. It is often easy to see how entertainment such as music, movies, and video games reflects our different cultures. The stories that are told, the way characters dress and talk, often mirror real people and events. For example, you can tell the difference between a French film and an American one, not only because of the language that is spoken, but also because of differences in storylines, settings, cinematography, and even subtle mannerisms that reflect the culture that produced them.

Throughout the following chapters, we look at how culture is communicated through entertainment ranging from hip-hop music to Las Vegas tourist attractions. We also explore the ways that entertainment can shape culture, from more superficial trends such as the "Hannah Montana" effect, to more serious accusations that exported entertainment from the United States is "Americanizing" cultures around the world. You will learn that religion, which is closely tied to culture, has also played a significant role in the evolution of entertainment. We will trace the origins of many forms of entertainment including music, sports, and storytelling to religious teachings and rituals. Likewise, we will consider potential impacts of contemporary entertainment on the faith and morality of audience members.

We also examine how changing laws and economic factors have influenced entertainment trends. We trace how deregulation and economic uncertainty led companies like Sony and Disney to grow into mega-corporations with holdings spanning all facets of entertainment—from film studios to record labels to sports franchises. We will also explore the influences of technological advances including the ways the Internet has changed traditional industries such as music and radio and paved the way for MySpace, Facebook, YouTube and other web-based entertainment providers. In addition, we will introduce the concept of convergent technology that combines entertainment, news, and advertising.

In turn, we will reveal how these new forms of entertainment have changed the way business is conducted and triggered new laws and regulations. We will see how government leaders have used entertainment such as sporting events and national anthems to rally national pride, and how opposition activist groups have similarly used music, film, and other entertainment genres to garner public support for their causes. In some cases, the societal influences and impacts of entertainment are very blatant. In other cases, they are more subtle. In the remaining chapters we will explore these relationships in great depth. In this chapter, however, we wish to begin by centering our attention on the concept of entertainment.

What It Is and What It Isn't

The word *entertainment* has a Latin root meaning "to hold the attention of," or "agreeably diverting." Over the years it has come to refer to a constructed product designed to stimulate a mass audience in an agreeable way in exchange for money. Entertainment can be a live or mediated experience that has been intentionally created, capitalized, promoted, maintained, and evolved. In other words, entertainment is created on purpose by someone for someone else. Entertainment is easily located, accessed, and consumed. And of course, entertainment is also attractive, stimulating, sensory, emotional, social, and moral to a mass audience.

And it is a business with specific components, as explained here. Entertainment may exist as a *product, service, or experience*. Entertainment **products** can be tickets to *live* performances and events; or they can be *mediated* programs and films that we receive in print or electronically. Television and movies are industries completely dedicated to creating entertainment as a product.

The travel and hospitality industries offer **services** to tourists and visitors; venues also offer services to audiences of sports, attractions, and activities. Services are designed to

Stagediving as entertainment

make entertainment pleasant for its consumers and audiences. What makes entertainment different than products and services is its **experiential** component. Unlike products and services, experiences are *perishable*—they last only as long as we are participating or watching—and *intangible*—they are of the moment and have ever-changing content.

The crucial time-bound aspect of entertainment is its perishability. As with fruit, experiences are time-sensitive, and they diminish in importance as time passes. Unlike souvenirs we purchase as mementoes, experiences cannot be taken home—they survive in our memory rather than in our shopping bags. We can purchase a book, but the experience of reading is nonetheless mental. And while the book jacket and graphics may seduce us into buying the book, the experiential pleasure of that book lies in its verbal consumption. Not investments like gold or consumables like popcorn, experiences are intangible, with ever-changing content. The value of an experience is based on an audience member's willingness to pay for it. When was the last time you paid for an experience? Was it worth the price?

Constructing Experiences

Entertainment is always constructed, meaning that it is put together with conscious intent. Entertainment is produced with design and awareness of what it is and what it does. We identify six characteristics of its construction.

- Entertainment is provided by highly trained experts and experienced professionals who act with a team of contributors.
- Most entertainment products are the result of multiple inputs from a range of people.
- Entertainment is usually controlled by a single dominant person or central figure such as a producer, director, writer, and so forth who organizes and makes decisions.
- Entertainment is a web of symbols that are shaped, molded, and polished to add to the audience's experience.

- Most entertainment products rely on technology to maximize their effectiveness.
- Finally, marketing promotions tell audiences how to experience entertainment before they actually access the product.

Of course entertainment products are designed to give pleasure. But a primary purpose for entertainment is to attract audiences to them. To draw, grow, and maintain audiences, entertainment must stimulate agreeable effects for them. As a capitalist product, entertainment is developed to make money—there is always a bottom line to consider. Secondarily, entertainment may elicit strong emotions, may teach us what we don't know, and can help us escape from real life experiences into simulated or vicarious ones.

If it sounds to you as if entertainment is everything, you're almost correct. It is part of our everyday life, but there are a few things that it is not. **Entertainment is** *not*

- *art*, although it may aspire to and attain the level of art at times
- *ordinary life*; it has a different feel, time, and emotion associated with it
- *truth* because it uses whatever will be more stimulating and whatever will make for a better experience
- *intellectual thought*, rather it is more like simple and familiar thought with a touch of surprise
- *moral* because entertainment won't be judged as good or bad for people, just entertaining.

Entertainment Participants

Two groups of experiential participants are celebrants and critics. For *celebrants*, entertainment is experienced and developed in growth stages. We begin as ignorants with no exposure, and, like illiterates, we are unable to interpret the experience. As novices we learn about entertainment and eventually become aficionados who appreciate it at a higher level. Some of us become *fans* with strong attachments for the product. A few of us go behind the scene to become researchers; others become epicureans who prefer the best product available.

People who make judgments or evaluate the product and can explain their judgment criteria are called *critics*. *Simple critics* report their experience without explaining why; *true critics* understand different audiences and can explain, argue, and defend their judgment well enough to convince others to agree with them. People who generate original ideas that explain entertainment products and principles are *theorists*. They examine entertainment products from five perspectives: gender, economics, culture, media (the influence of their technological forms), and production. You'll be introduced to theories later in the chapter.

Entertainment's four constituents are *producers* who understand the process of putting products together, *creationists* who are actively involved in creating a particular product, *promoters* who sell the products, and *consumers* who pay for entertainment's many products, services, and experiences. *Fans* dedicate themselves to following entertainment providers and stars, and they experience fandom as a primary activity of leisure time. As we will learn in succeeding chapters, consumers are audiences and fans who develop and give away loyalty to a variety of entertainment brands. Audience relationships are the most valued by the industry for their loyalty and support.

The World at Play

The story of entertainment and its impact on modern society begins with the advent of *free time* or *leisure*. Leisure is time that is left over once we finish working. By its very nature, leisure is socially stratified—the rich are able to buy more free time than the poor. Because it was enjoyed only by people who could afford not to work, leisure activity was once confined to a few rich and powerful men.

Centuries later in America, leisure time was an outcome of the Industrial Revolution when workers had increasing amounts of free time and could afford to pay for recreational activity. Pre-mediated entertainment traces its beginnings to performance and games. Whether they were practiced as religious, mystical, or cultural rituals, these leisure activities developed into the theater, games, and sporting events we enjoy today.

Rock climber as participant

Time On Our Hands: Forms of Leisure

The way we pass our free time takes various forms, and terms for these forms help us understand their role in society. As mentioned above, we refer to free time—time to use as we please—as *leisure*, which comes from a Latin word meaning "to be free." Leisure is activity performed for its own sake, an activity carried on apart from work, that is a function of social class. Contemporary leisure is time used for going places and doing things. All sorts of consumption activities containing elements of amusement and diversion are now considered to be entertainment. We engage in three types of leisure experiences: recreation, entertainment, and amusement.

Recreation consists of activities or experiences carried on within leisure either because of satisfaction, pleasure, or creative enrichment. The recreation industry was developed to provide a way out of the boredom–fatigue cycle by enriching the play activities of youth and expanding recreational activities for adults. *Entertainment* refers to a

FLASH FACT

On an average day, 96 percent of people 15 and over engaged in some sort of leisure activity such as watching TV, socializing, or exercising. Men spent more time (5.7 hours) than did women (5.0 hours). Watching TV was the leisure activity that occupied the most time of Americans, accounting for about half of leisure time, on average, for both men and women. Socializing (visiting friends, social events) counted for about 45 minutes per day for both sexes. Men were more likely than women to participate in sports, exercise, or recreation every day. Time spent reading, playing games, or using a computer for leisure varied by age, with people 75+ averaging the most time per week.

Source: Bureau of Labor Statistics, www.bls.gov/news.release/atus.nr0.htm

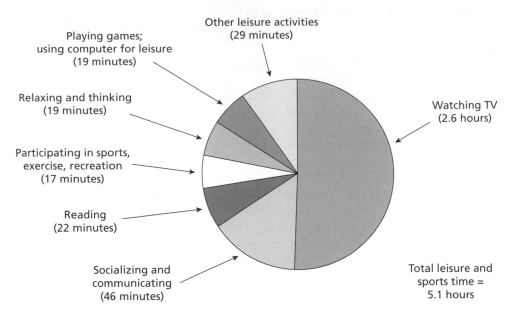

Leisure time on an average day

Playing games;
using computer for leisure
(19 minutes)

Other leisure activities
(29 minutes)

Relaxing and thinking
(19 minutes)

Watching TV
(2.6 hours)

Participating in sports,
exercise, recreation
(17 minutes)

Reading
(22 minutes)

Socializing and
communicating
(46 minutes)

Total leisure and
sports time =
5.1 hours

Figure 1.2   Forms of Leisure Time

Note: Data include all persons ages 15 and over. Data include all days of the week and are annual averages for 2006.
Source: Bureau of Labor Statistics

diverting performance, especially a public performance, as a concert, drama, including the pleasure received from comedy or magic. *Amusement* is a pleasant diversion such as a game or spectacle, especially the individual satisfaction derived from play.

Every form of leisure we enjoy today falls into one of the above three categories. For instance, physically active adults may prefer recreational activities; other adults amuse themselves by gardening, or seek escape through mediated entertainment, or simply enjoy leisurely shopping as a diversion from work. By listing your activities for a week, you'll get some insight into your personal entertainment category preferences. Average leisure time spent on an average day for persons over 15 is charted in Figure 1.2.

Although the leisure triad is used in some industry categorization, a better way to view the entertainment industry is as being content-based. Entertainment content comes to audiences in three distinct ways: as live performance (theater, musical concerts), as media (movies and TV), and as interactive experiences (recreation, amusement parks, travel, and gaming). In this text, the term *experience* characterizes all forms of entertainment content.

Time On Our Hands: The Notion of Play

As leisure time continued to proliferate, people concentrated on expanding the *notion of play*. According to Huizinga,[2] play existed even before culture itself, accompanying and nourishing culture from the beginning of civilization. He asserts that all the great archetypal activities in human society are permeated with play. To characterize play as a cultural function that separates it from the context of ordinary life, he defined its main characteristics.

Play:

- is a *voluntary* activity—no one forces us to play
- is set *apart from reality*—it is an interlude in the day that provides temporary satisfaction
- is *limited* in terms of its locality and duration—it has a beginning and an end
- is controlled or governed by *rules*
- has a sense of persistent social community—sports fans are such a community
- promotes a sense of symbolic *secrecy*—it is different from everyday life
- is a *sacred and profound* activity—it involves rituals, ceremony, and a venue for symbolic representation.

Some aspects of contemporary play may assume different characteristics than those set forth by Huizinga. For instance, as an *extra-mundane activity*, play was thought to provide people with the rewards that they could not find in work or in the consumption of the ordinary world. Yet today, much of our consumption of the ordinary world is filled with all forms of entertainment and play.

Contemporary play is an outgrowth of *hedonism*. As a facet of cultural movement, hedonism is a shaping force behind our individual pursuits of pure pleasure and immediate gratification. Hedonistic consumption designates a conceptual framework of leisure experiences. Hedonism is expressed in activities such as game playing, shopping, and activities that are self-indulgent as well as pleasurable. As we investigate the development of entertainment, try to identify new aspects of play that add dimensions to its original conceptualization.

Wakeboarding is a leisure-time experience

Play Theory   Play, viewed as an outgrowth of leisure-time activities, gets its definition from the word *ludenic*, derived from Latin, which refers to games, recreation, contests, theater, and liturgical presentations. According to William Stephenson,[3] the spirit of play is essential to the development of culture—stagecraft, the military, debate, politics, marriage rules, and so forth are all cultural aspects grounded in play.

Play can be characterized by four classes: agon, alea, mimicry, and ilinx. *Agon* is the principle of games involving two sides, such as football and chess. *Alea* refers to games of dice, roulette, lotteries, and chance. *Mimicry* includes acting and pretending. *Ilinx* is activity that produces dizziness such as that caused by swings, ferris wheels, and dance. Each of these classes can be found in contemporary forms of entertainment as shown in Table 1.1.

Stephenson identified three ways of playing: *Wan* is a quietly sensual Chinese way of playing, such as evidenced in the *Kama Sutra*. *Paideia* is primitive, pure play of carefree gaiety and uncontrolled fantasy. *Ludus* is formal play, the type found in games with rules, conventions, and skill development. Play's dimensions can be conceptualized on a scale that moves from paideia (improvisation and freedom) to ludus (rules and orders). The opposite of work, play teaches loyalty, competitiveness, and patience. Through play, we learn to construct order, conceive economy, check monotony, and establish equity.

Table 1.1 Classifications of Play

	Agon	Alea	Mimicry	Ilinx
Dimensions PAIDEIA	competition	chance	simulation	vertigo
	Racing	Rhymes	Imitation	Whirling
Kite flying	Wrestling		Illusion	Riding
	Athletics	Heads/tails	Magic	Swinging
	Boxing			Waltzing
Solitaire	Chess			Carnival
	Billiards	Betting	Tag	Skiing
Crossword	Football	Roulette	Disguises	
puzzles	Sports in general			Mountain climbing
LUDUS				Tightrope walking

Source: Collins, R. (1961). *Man, play and games.* New York: Free Press, as adapted by Miller, D.L. (1970). *Gods and games: Toward a theory of play.* New York: Harper & Row

Distinguishing play and leisure from work, play theory suggests that work deals with reality and production, while play provides self-satisfying experiences. This theory goes on to explain how play is pleasure, and pleasure is a concept at various levels: physiological pleasure as when a good meal satisfies our hunger; an association with objects and the relationship between self and things (like riding a bicycle); objects themselves (favorite possessions); and communications-pleasure (enjoying a film).

Performance-based Entertainment

In the twenty-first century, play assumes a global manifestation in two forms—*activity where we are spectators* watching others perform in an arena or on stage, and *activity of participation* such as games and travel where we become part of the experience. In the best of times or the worst of times, entertainment has played a role in the leisure-time activities of global audiences. Providing amusement to fill leisure time, the circus and its performers were the forerunners of organized performance. We can trace the origins of Western entertainment back to the days of Pompey's Rome where pachyderms and performance were interspersed with chariot racing to provide what has come to be known as the circus. In keeping with the preferences of the day, Roman circuses featured athletes who fought to the death, dueling with animals, and combative equestrians to entertain the masses. Caesar's audiences cheered for gladiators who fought wild animals and each other; his Circus Maximus accommodated 250,000 spectators. For many of us, one of our first entertainment experiences was at the circus.

Some of the most famous names in circus performance—animal trainer Clyde Beatty, clown Emmett Kelly, and the Escalante Family of aerialists—owe much of their notoriety to a woman circus publicist, Shirley O'Connor.[4] The owner of a Hollywood-based public relations and advertising firm, the 82-year-old O'Connor spent 36 years promoting the famous Ringling Brothers and Barnum & Bailey Circuses where her husband was a ringmaster. Performers such as the Sheep-Headed Man, Flipper Boy, and the Two-Faced Man were brought to the public every year as part of the traveling circus during its various routes across America.

Today, hybrid circus offshoots such as Cirque du Soleil have replaced clowns and calliopes with dancers and violins. And although the Big Top still travels to perform in

America's major cities, traditional circuses are remnants of a by-gone era. How many kids in your neighborhood would ever think of running away to join the circus?

Laughter and Drama

Clowns' predecessors were called *jesters*, physically small fellows charged with making royalty laugh. These one-line comedians were predecessors of late-night techno-jesters such as Jay Leno and Dave Letterman.

News comedy on Comedy Central finds John Stewart's *The Daily Show* providing an ironic perspective that often reveals more of the truth than some serious presentation. He is especially relevant if you are interested in politainment and finding the truth behind all the political marketing smoke.

John Stewart receives an Emmy in 2007 for *The Daily Show*

Theater, one of the greatest contributions to leisure-time entertainment, was first performed in outdoor amphitheaters for thousands of Greeks. Dramatic festivals were so popular in Athens that, when they were held, business was suspended and even prisoners were allowed to attend. When brought to a raised stage, performances became professional productions. Some of the first stage performers began as clowns. Grimaldi, a satirical character played by a woman, revolutionized male-dominated stage performance. And after the Follies became the hit of Paris, women entertained audiences on stage with dance and song. In the American West, burlesque shows in saloons were a primary pastime for range-weary cowboys.

Often rivaling live actors were *puppets*, whose origins date back to India about four thousand years ago. Early puppets were tribal ritual masks with hinged jaws or jointed skulls used primarily for religious ceremonies. They evolved into figures with moving limbs and by the sixteenth century, marionette operas were very popular in Europe. In the 1700s, hand puppets were used for children's shows.[5] In America, puppet stars appearing on early television included marionette Howdy Doody, ventriloquist's dummy Charlie McCarthy, hand puppet Lamb Chop, and the Muppets.

Playing with Rules

Games are a form of play characterized by rules, competition, and one or more elements of physical skill, strategy, chance, and make-believe.[6] Gaming began in 2000 BC in China as *Wei-qi* and in Japan as the game of *Go*. Lotteries—in the form of *Keno*—helped to finance the Great Wall of China three thousand years ago. From the outskirts of medieval European cities to modern America, gaming has played an important role in the socialization of people.

Entertaining ourselves by playing games is an important aspect of amusement. In eighteenth-century England, *parlor games* such as blindman's bluff and charades were alternatives to social dancing. The *board game* backgammon is traced to Rome before the birth of Christ. Coming to the West from India, chess was popular as far back as AD 700. *Card playing* began in Spain about 1300, and within one hundred years the four standard card suits (club, diamond, heart, spade) were solidified in France. By the early twentieth century, Monopoly and Scrabble were popular, and, by 1970, Dungeons and

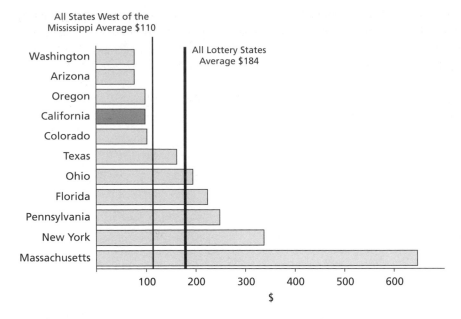

All States West of the
Mississippi Average $110

All Lottery States
Average $184

Figure 1.3   U.S. State Lottery Sales, 2005–6 (Per Capita)

Dragons hit the marketplace. Billiards, shuffleboard, and shooting contests began in New England as sporting games. In the past several decades, arcades have emerged as an important part of the *gaming industry* when they moved from dingy street fronts to regional malls. Now a multi-billion-dollar profit center, arcades were transformed by video arcades that now gross billions of dollars annually.

Since their beginnings in Asia, *lotteries* have provided public funding from food to weapons. Italy was the first country to award prize money for winners, showing Americans how to derive winnings from playing the lotto. Lottery profits helped fund the Colonial army in the Revolutionary War as well as most of the Ivy League colleges. New Hampshire began the first state-owned lottery in 1964, and today 38 states have followed the practice. Lotteries provide 250,000 jobs and lottery products are sold in over 240,000 retailers nationwide. Enthusiasts can even play online at megawin.com. State lottery sales per capita in 2005–6 are shown in Figure 1.3.

One of the most popular forms of games are *spectator sports*. Home of the Olympic Games, Greece amused spectators with four-horse, nine-mile chariot races with up to

Sign at the Beijing Olympics

40 participants. The Roman emperor Claudius devoted 93 holidays to sporting games; by the fourth century, almost every other day was dedicated to state-supported entertainment. In 2008, Beijing hosted the Olympics for global competition in summer sports.

As global audiences of spectators and participants of urban and rural performance increased, public entertainment venues played an important role in the development of modern society. But by the time the first radio broadcast was ready for transmission, audiences were ready and willing to allow some aspects of performance into their homes; thus began the rise and autonomy of mass media.

Mass Mediated Entertainment

Unlike live performance, mediated activity takes place primarily in the home. Total spending (including advertising) in the U.S. on media of all types was about $930 billion in 2007.[7] The withdrawal of audiences from public venues into private spaces not only changed the nature of entertainment, it also changed how we lived our lives. With the arrival of electronic mass media, play shifted from an activity of participation to an activity of visual spectacle. Cable and satellite enhanced media entertainment enables users to choose from a plethora of programming to fit every taste and preference in American society.

Since AMC introduced the concept of "first run movies" in 1959, the film industry has made celebrity the common currency of popular culture.[8] We feed on celebrity activity using every medium available to us. When we tire of chasing celebrities, we use the Internet to log on to our favorite web sites for entertainment, education, and ecstasy. As the millennium turned, entertainment became a $480 billion industry, finding itself at the forefront of economic growth and cultural evolution.[9]

Today, technology drives many forms of entertainment, competing with but not depleting live performance. In fact, the emergence of *theming* (as motifs communicated through mediated popular culture) has enhanced everyday experiences such as shopping and dining. The marriage of performance and technology is evident in concerts where philharmonic orchestras play to films, such as a recent Los Angeles concert performed in tandem with Looney Toon classic cartoons.

Most of the time, our experiences are not confined to one medium or delivery system; instead, we have portable electronic devices that go with us everywhere. A term used to explain the merging of entertainment, advertising, and technology is *convergence*. Convergence, which is described in detail in Chapter 2, is a dynamic that is transforming the way in which media, music, and advertising industries merge to reach their markets. This phenomenon is also referred to as the "Madison and Vine" effect.[10]

 **FLASH FACT**

The first quarter of 2008 was a watershed period for video on the Internet, with the launch of two major initiatives: Apple's rental of major-studio movies on iTunes, and Hulu's offering of ad-supported streaming of hundreds of TV shows—and even major-studio feature films. Which model do you think will pay-off best for content owners of all types—movies, TV shows, and news and sports?

Source: www.adamsmediaresearch.com/index.asp

Media predominance and convergence are exemplified in our everyday lives. As we continue to free ourselves from work, we become ever more engaged in experiential play of all forms. We begin our day with a workout at the gym, we catch a glimpse of the morning newspaper on our iPhones, we listen to downloaded music on iPods, or tune into radio talk shows while driving to work; during the day, we use social networks to connect with friends, play a few games online, eat in a themed restaurant, shop in a mega mall, then see a NetFlix DVD before we go to bed. On weekends, theme parks, restaurants and tourist destinations are popular venues for entertaining consumers and travelers, blurring distinctions between the real and the simulated experience. If you can experience Venice in Las Vegas, why make the trip to Italy?

The Role of Theory and Research

The dramatic worldview, enculturated by mass media, can be explained with a variety of theories developed from the disciplines of communication, sociology, marketing, philosophy, and psychology, which we cover in depth in Chapters 4 and 5. Because theories ground discussions of entertainment's impact on society, they are presented to provide you with a better understanding of how entertainment has become so pervasive and important in the twenty-first century.

Mass media provide a mechanism through which people seek their self-identities and engage in actual or vicarious behaviors of everyday life. Through media and their symbols, we make sense of our lives through the frame of a dramatic structure. This text views all types of leisure time and dramatic entertainment as play—experiences that give people pleasure. Play provides something in common for us to talk about with other people, and sometimes play helps shake up society by being in the forefront of change.

Media and entertainment research, conducted to monitor and understand how society and individuals react to and integrate play into our lives, is presented throughout

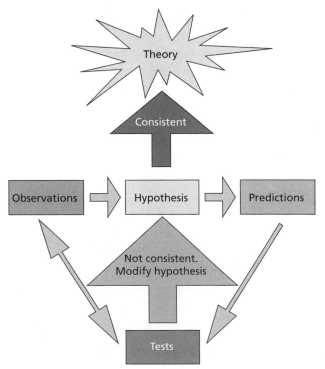

Figure 1.4 **Theory**

the text in various forms. Statistical data provide the "what" of audience participation, while qualitative interviews offer answers to the "why" aspect of entertainment's impact on audiences, consumers, and fans. Still in its infancy, entertainment-based research strives to answer the important questions revolving around how we interact with new technology and merging genres of property creation, performance, and distribution. Much of this research focuses on such integration or convergence.

Experiencing Entertainment

Our lives have become a series of experiences based on our interests and available leisure time. We experience entertainment in a variety of ways based on our participation and what we derive from the experience. We can experience entertainment in four ways— passively absorbing, educational learning, complete engagement, and esthetic appreciation. These realms of entertainment are explained below.

- *Passive* entertainment occurs when people simply absorb an experience through their senses without much participation; listening to music on an iPod or reading a novel are passive experiences.
- *Educational entertainment* requires active engagement of one's mind, the type of engagement that occurs with problem solving. Dedicated television channels and public broadcasting combine entertainment with learning about our world.

Absorbing music: passive

Learning from television: educational

Engaging in video gaming: escapist

Appreciating warm ocean breezes: aesthetic

- *Escapist entertainment* experiences involve much greater immersion than other types of entertainment or educational experiences. Intended to provide a respite from real life, escapist experiences are offered by theme parks, casinos and virtual reality games.
- *Esthetic entertainment* occurs when we immerse ourselves in a cultural experience with a visual component, such as standing on the rim of the Grand Canyon, visiting an art gallery, or lounging in a Starbucks café looking at passers-by.

Our dedication to any or every aspect of entertaining experiences is dictated by our available time. How much time do you spend on each of these realms of entertainment?

Time Is Attention

With a plethora of experiential options at our fingertips, we are of primary interest to entertainment providers who compete vigorously for our attention. Economist Michael Goldhaber uses the term "the attention economy" to describe this condition. As a *scarce resource*, attention is the most sought-after commodity of entertainment marketers. Consumers today have more choices than ever in everything from TV programs to travel destinations to sports. Nowhere is this more evident than on the Internet. A few keystrokes will direct Net surfers to numerous web site options for information on countless products, services, and experiences and brands. And yet, although our choices may be plentiful, our time and money are limited. It seems like everyone wants some of our time and money but, to get it, they must first break through the clutter and get our attention.

Attention has two types of value: instrumental (ways to get our attention) and terminal (attention to self). Like money, attention has *instrumental* value because it can get you other things that you might want. Persuasion is often described as a process, and attention is always the first step. Thus, many of those who want your attention may actually really want something else. For example, advertisers are vying for your attention so that they can try to persuade you to buy their products or services. A nonprofit organization may want your attention to persuade you to volunteer or to give money. Your friends may want your attention to persuade you to do them a favor, and so on.

Attention, however, also has what is called *terminal* value, meaning that many people value it for its own sake. Consider what kids will do to get their parents' attention or, worse yet, what people are willing to do or say to get on tell-all, show-all talk shows. Even the phrase "pay attention" suggests that attention has inherent value. We value both the attention we give and the attention we receive.

The Entertainment Principle

Attention may be valuable, but money can't buy it, at least not directly. Even if you paid people thousands, even millions of dollars, they could not guarantee you their attention. Most of us can recall books we have tried to read, lectures we have tried to listen to, and programs we have tried to watch. We may have the best of intentions but, no matter how hard we try, there are times when our minds still begin to wander or, worse yet, we fall asleep.

And this, naturally, is where entertainment comes in. If something is boring, we don't pay attention to it. Entertainment captures attention. As a result, an attention economy is also an entertainment economy. Whether you are making a film or an advertisement, if you do not hold the interest of your audience—that is, if you do not entertain them—they will stop paying attention.

SPOTLIGHT ON PLAY AT WORK — Virtual Summer Jobs

Rather than flipping burgers or bagging groceries during summer vacation, some college students are working as traders in the fantasy web world of Entropia Universe, buying and selling virtual animal skins and weapons. Although these products exist only online, the earnings are real. One student has earned $35,000 over four summers of online commerce.

These students represent a new breed of entrepreneurs seeking their fortunes online in imaginary worlds. With the shrinking pool of available summer jobs, tech-savvy young gamers are using their computer skills to capitalize on a growing demand for virtual goods and services. Some typical jobs are avatar fashion designers, architects, and real estate developers in Second Life. Personal avatars shop in virtual malls, buy property, hang out with friends, or stay at home watching TV, waiting for computerized commands from their real-life counterparts.

Summer employment among teens has dropped to its lowest level in 60 years, according to labor market studies. Yet money-making opportunities in virtual worlds has grown steadily. Gartner Media estimates that by 2011, 80 percent of Internet users worldwide will have an avatar, making animated online personas a commonality. Driving employment are companies such as IBM and Adidas that have moved into Second Life.

Entropia Universe has 722,000 players and allows virtual money earned online to be withdrawn from actual banks with an Entropia ATM card. Daily averages of Second Life player spending on virtual clothing, jewelry, homes, cars, and real estate hovers around $1.5 million. The site's 1.5 million players use credit cards to purchase Lindens, Second Life currency—270 Lindens equal one dollar US. Virtual merchants convert their profits into dollars using a money exchange run by Linden Lab, which pays out proceeds with actual checks or through Pay Pal accounts.

Two student successes include the following real people:

- Ariella Furman, 21, college senior at Temple University, Philadelphia, is a filmmaker who writes scripts and shoots scenes with avatar actors who are controlled by other players. She has contracts with media tech companies such as Popchal and electric Sheep Co. doing videos for clients like IBM and the World Bank. Projected summer income: $2,000–4,000 per month.
- John Elkenberry, 25, college senior at Eastern Michigan University in Ypsilanti, is a land developer for Digeridoo Designs building entire Second Life neighborhoods. Some of his clients are Microsoft, CNET, and Intel, and he built a theme park for Splenda no-calorie sweetener. Projected summer income: $3,000–4,500 per month.

Source: *The Wall Street Journal*, May 16, 2008, W12

Ironically, although you may not be able to pay people to get their attention, you may be able to get them to pay you for it. People will pay you for entertainment. And as long as you keep people entertained, you will have their attention. Consumers pay for newspapers, magazines, and books to read, movies to watch, and music to listen to. But you had better have something really good to offer if you expect individuals to give you their attention *and* their money.

Keeping audiences entertained is not easy. What entertained audiences yesterday will not necessarily entertain them today. Each new book, movie, video game, or shopping mall must be bigger, bolder, better than the last. Of course, bigger, bolder, and better is usually more expensive, but audiences do not want to pay any more for entertainment today than they did yesterday. Although audiences will pay for entertainment, and even pay well, entertainment providers—those who produce the magazines, the movies, and the music—still often find it difficult to make a profit from the sales of that content alone. Newspapers and magazines, for example, rarely make money from publication sales. Their profits usually come from advertising revenues—from advertisers who pay to take advantage of the attention that the publication captures.

In fact, the content that actually captures your attention is often provided for free. Broadcast television and radio have always been "free" for their audiences. And often performances such as concerts or sports events may even be "free." However, that free entertainment is provided in an effort to capture audience attention for advertisers. Similarly, concert venues and theaters often do not make a profit from ticket sales alone. Instead, they may make their money through concession sales—the drinks, popcorn, and T-shirts you buy while you are there. Thus, although corporations may not be able to buy our attention directly, they do so indirectly by covering the costs of the entertainment "bait" that will capture our attention for them.

One of the most attention-intensive modern-day activities is surfing the web. The number of people communicating through the web—and trying to get attention through it— is continuously rising. The growth in the web's capacity to send multimedia or virtual reality signals allows marketers to capture user attention through these means. Social sites such as Facebook, YouTube, and MySpace all rely on advertising to furnish members with a free venue for proclaiming themselves in an entertaining fashion.

 FLASH FACT

Among girls ages 15–17, 70 percent have a regularly used profile page on social web sites such as MySpace, Bebo, and Facebook, compared with 57 percent of boys the same ages. A similar study by Nielsen Online shows that women ages 18–24 account for 17 percent social network users, while men in the same age group account for 12 percent (The Pew Research Center, 2008).

Source: www.diversityinc.com/public/3483.cfm

FADE TO BLACK

"How shall I spend my leisure time?" "What sorts of experiences shall I buy?" Providing answers to these two questions has propelled the largest industry on earth. From the beginning of time, people have looked to forms of entertainment to relieve the stresses of everyday toil. But only recently has entertainment become the primary activity of a population. Although we cannot avoid or escape encounters with entertainment, we are selective about which forms to use, how often we use them, and how much we are willing to spend on them. As this book explores these and other modes of experiential entertainment, we focus on how "free time" has morphed into "all the time." Transformed by mass media and seduced into a desire for experience, consuming audiences have entered the world of hyper-capitalism that is fueled by sought-after fantasy and fun.

As we will see in the coming chapters, playfulness and pleasure seeking are everywhere. How does this proliferation of entertainment affect us? Profoundly. We have become an "If it's not fun, we don't want to do it" society. This book takes you on a journey around and through our entertainment-everything culture.

SPOTLIGHT ON GLOBAL ENTERTAINMENT   Entertainment Everywhere

Entertainment is a global infusion, with each country and culture developing their own ways to amuse themselves and others. Asian, South American, and African forms of entertainment often provide the basis for Western offshoots. Some of the entertainment forms originating in countries around the world, profiled here, can be explored in depth through the associated web address. Japanese animation (anime) appears on our TV screens and manga comics fill our bookshelves. The drawing below is from *Baron the Cat Returns*. Hits such as Pokemon, Hello Kitty, and Doraemon are popular in Western cultures as well as those in Asia. Find out more on www.japan-zone.com/modern/tv_anime.shtml.

Celebrated in many places throughout South America, Carnaval is a four-day celebration that begins on Saturday and ends on Fat Tuesday (Mardi-Gras). Dates change every year, but it's always a noisy, energetic celebration of music and dance and exhibitions. Learn about all the festivals at www.gosouthamerica.about.com/od/carnavalinsouthamerica/Carnaval_in_South_America. htm.

In the last decade, ethnic theme parks in China have proliferated. Happy Valley, one of the newest and most elaborate, features giant bugs on which children can ride. A complete overview of parks can be found at www.metafilter.com/62799/Chinese-Amusement-Parks.

Bollywood, the informal term popularly used for the Mumbai-based Hindi-language film industry in India, produces popular movies that enjoy a huge fan base. For a closer look, log on to www.bollywoodworld.com.

Dance in Africa expresses an entire complex of living. African dance is basic, vital, and complete with rhythmic action, composure, body decoration, and props. Traditional dance is the integrated art of movement, controlled by music and language, that is a source of communication across tribes. Read about the history and origins of African dance at www.diamanocoura.org/.

A CLOSER LOOK AT THE MEDIA

Profiles of Entertainment-focused Media

Billboard. **Weekly Magazine**

Devoted to the music industry, the magazine maintains several internationally recognized music charts that track the most popular songs and albums in various categories on a weekly basis. www.billboard.com

Entertainment Tonight (CBS). **Evening Half-hour TV Magazine**

The network's answer to its print counterpart (see below), this program is dedicated to star-gazing. Reporters speak with stars and show us clips and trailers of up-coming events in music, TV, video, and film. http://www.etonline.com/

Entertainment Weekly. **Weekly Magazine**

Presented as an insider's view, this quasi-tabloid gives us "Sound Bites" and tips on a "Hot Sheet" each week, plus reviews and goings-on at the movies, on TV, in books and music, and on video. Stars are featured on the cover and color photographs enhance the editorial commentary throughout the magazine. Graphics in this in-your-face glossy publication challenge your visual acuity and take you on a colorful merry-go-round of entertainment activities. http://www.ew.com/ew

Entertainment Media News **Web Site**

Provides news about celebrities, entertainment, movies, and TV, and a blog on mobile technology. http://www.entertainmentmedia2.com

ESPN. **24-hour Sports Network**

From football to frisbee, galloping to golf, or racing to rowing, this network provides sports enthusiasts with live games, match re-caps, and previews of upcoming events. http://espn.go.com/

Fade In: The First Word in Film. **Monthly Magazine**

Graphically sophisticated, this magazine presents interviews, features such as "The Top 100 People in Hollywood (you need to know)", behind-the-scenes stories and previews of films, print media, and soundtracks. http://www.fadeinonline.com

Interview. **Monthly Magazine**

Thick, matt-finished pages present conversations with film stars, designers, politicians, and just about everyone who is anyone. Sprinkled liberally among the interviews are movie news, music latests, comedy corner, *View*man, and fashion details. Up-scale ads and great commercial photography make this a pictorial delight for readers who enjoy off-the-wall reading material. Anti-feminist critic Camille Paglia, for instance, philosophizes about blondes and why they have more fun. http://www.interviewmagazine. com/

Rolling Stone. **Bi-monthly Magazine**

A hip, trendy publication that's been around long enough to be trusted as "all the news that fits" into the world of music, movies, and television. Random news ribbons color page borders, and, like static electricity, photos and copy come together to spark the latest developments in entertainment gossip. http://www.rollingstone.com/

Travel Channel. **Television Network Devoted to Destinations of Interest**

Whether you're interested in desert islands, mountain resorts, or ocean cruises, this channel has it all. Advertisers are providers of vacation hotels, airlines, and rental cars who often make special offers for channel viewers. http://travel.discovery.com/

Variety. **Weekly Trade Publication of Film Industry**

Founded in 1905, this international entertainment weekly provides timely industry news as well as special issues, such as "Scrapbook of the Century" with 100 of the most famous mega-stars, moments, and mavens. If you want to read what members of the film industry read, this publication by Cahners Business Information is a must. http://www. variety. com/

Wired. **Monthly Magazine**

For some of the best ads and editorial in the age of technology, this magazine is the one to buy. From its forward-looking cover to its glossy photographic text, *Wired* brings the present up to date. This publication presents features such as "Design is a Chain Reaction," columns like Zip Drive and Schwag Bag, and departments such as Rants and Raves, Electric Word, Fetish, Must Read, Infoporn, Street Cred (consumer reviews), Best, New Money, and Verge (creative sparks). http://www.wired.com/

DISCUSSION AND REVIEW

1. How does Huizinga's notion of play differ from contemporary play?
2. What social theory best describes the communication aspect of entertainment?
3. What roles have theorists and critics played in entertainment development?
4. How is the way we experience leisure time reflected in the significant growth of the entertainment industry?

EXERCISES

1. Argue for or against the statement that "all of life is a paid-for experience" by citing authors who agree and disagree in written arguments. After presenting both sides, pick one and defend your choice.
2. Go online and find out which games and forms of entertainment fit into each of the four classifications of play: agon (competition), alea (chance), mimicry (simulation), and ilinx (vertigo).
3. Keep a two-week diary of all the forms of entertainment in which you participate and classify them according to the "leisure time" categories presented in this chapter. What is the ratio of your "paid-for" to "free" activities? What conclusions can you make from this exercise?
4. Describe experiences you have had in each of the four realms of entertainment discussed in this chapter—absorbing, learning, involvement, and appreciation. Which ones involve the concept of convergence?
5. Go to www.newsbusters.org, a site dedicated to criticizing what it calls "liberal media bias." What evidence of conservative bias does the site reveal? Why are the site's parodies so popular?

BOOKS AND BLOGS

Aron, C.S. (1999). *Working at play: A history of vacations in the United States*. London: Oxford University Press.

Cooper-Chen, Ann (ed.) (2005). *Global entertainment media: Content, audience, issues*. London and Mahwah, NJ: Routledge/Lawrence Erlbaum Associates.

O'Connor, S.C. (2000). *Life is a circus*. Philadelphia: Xlibris Press.

Rifkin, J. (2000). *The age of access*. New York: Penguin Putnam.

www.MediaFuturist.com—provides news about the future of entertainment, music, and technology.

www.mckinseyquarterly.com/Media_Entertainment—offers entertainment business news and editorial.

www.newsbusters.org—critiques media from a conservative perspective.

www.buzzburster.com/—a media, music, and entertainment news blog.

www.ethnicmajority.com/media_home.htm—discusses diversity in the entertainment and media businesses.

www.clickclickexpose.com/—provides resources for gay media.

www.digitalentertainmentawards.com/finalists2.html—presents digital entertainment and media excellence awards.

2 OUR CONVERGENCE CULTURE

Today we live in the imaginary world of the screen and networks.
All our machines are screens. We too have become screens.
We live everywhere in an "aesthetic" hallucination of reality.
—Jean Baudrillard

As the dissemination of information becomes more efficient and easily accessible, culture changes. People want to access information at all times. Technology is at the forefront of this movement, both satisfying and creating needs.[1] Cultural convergence is more than just a buzzword—it is an emerging pattern of relations bringing together entertainment, technology, advertising, brands, and consumers in creative and often surprising ways. As described so well by Henry Jenkins of Harvard, convergence is a paradigm shift for media and technology.[2] Convergence is all around us—Internet is available on cellphones, on TV, and in cars. The world has become a digital playground where traditional analog media outlets are continuing to struggle to keep in stride with their digital, interactive counterparts.

Convergence is a phenomenon involving the interlocking of computing and information technology companies, telecommunications networks, and content providers from the publishing worlds of newspapers, magazines, music, radio, TV, movies, and entertainment software. In its simplest three elements, convergence is content *creation*, *distribution*, and *consumption*. For example, journalists and bloggers create news and editorial in print and online (creation), which we receive via cellphone or computer (distribution), blurring the distinction between reader and publisher (consumption).

Convergence is a process rather than an endpoint, which is distinguished by changing consumer flows through the media landscape. Convergence is the tectonic shift that has changed the relationship between existing technologies, industries, markets, genres, and audiences. This chapter takes you into the world of cultural convergence to explore the facets of genre blending, fusion journalism, globalization, cultural imperialism, and postmodernism. The multiple merging of technology, history, and media content production characterizes our contemporary society and determines our future.

Principles of Convergence

The ways we experience entertainment, advertising, and culture are rapidly changing, blurring aesthetic and technological distinctions between media platforms of advertising, content and consumer as creator. Here, expression is valued over impression; engaged audiences draw together information across multiple media experiences, creating new opportunities for brands and properties. Convergence includes ways that advertisers look for new ways to engage audiences, content creators search for new audiences, and audiences seek new ways to connect with culture. Convergence culture requires a renegotiation of the expectations of media content producers, advertisers, and audiences.

Convergence Levels

Convergence has occurred at three primary levels:

- *Technologies*—creative content has been converted into digital forms for delivery through broadband or wireless networks for display on computer-based devices from cellphones to PDAs to DVRs. Here, technologies overlap where multiple products come together to form one product with the advantages of each initial component. The mutual remediation of telephone, television, and computer offer combined immediacy of voice exchange, real-time world monitoring, and three-dimensional graphics that come together to promote a new version of intimacy.[3]
- *Industries*—companies across the business spectrum from media to telecommunications to technology have merged or formed alliances to develop new business models that can profit from the growing consumer need for "on-demand" content. Big media companies enter new media environments through mergers, acquisitions, and strategic partnerships, such as international media entrepreneur Rupert Murdoch's acquisition of social networking site MySpace to leverage his News Corporation into an established online community.
- *Media*—removal of entry barriers across the IT, telecoms, media, and consumer electronics industries, creating one large converged industry. Industry analysts see media convergence of traditional media such as print and broadcast replacing new media associated with digital publishing. Because of reduced barriers for production and distribution, new media have empowered us to become involved directly or collaboratively with creating new content over the Internet.

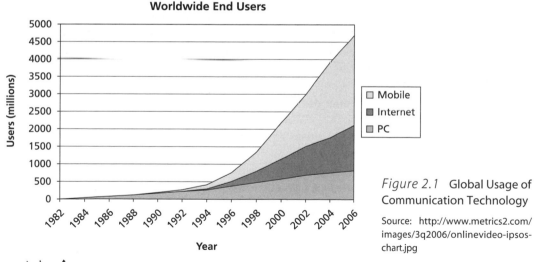

Worldwide End Users

Figure 2.1 Global Usage of Communication Technology

Source: http://www.metrics2.com/images/3q2006/onlinevideo-ipsos-chart.jpg

FLASH·FACT

The Chinese are the world's most avid mobile music listeners. Chinese ages 16–21 spend approximately 14 hours each week listening to music via cellphones. They listen to music mostly at home (49 percent), in cars (32 percent), and traveling on public transport (30 percent); 31 percent of Chinese transfer tunes from a PC or laptop, compared to 22 percent who download to phones from mobile services.

Source: TNS Global Technology

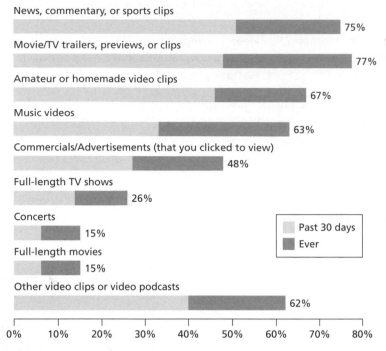

Types of Digital Video Files Streamed

News, commentary, or sports clips — 75%

Movie/TV trailers, previews, or clips — 77%

Amateur or homemade video clips — 67%

Music videos — 63%

Commercials/Advertisements (that you clicked to view) — 48%

Full-length TV shows — 26%

Concerts — 15%

Full-length movies — 15%

Other video clips or video podcasts — 62%

Past 30 days
Ever

Figure 2.2 Streaming Video

Source: Ipsos Insight © Ipsos Insight 2007

With the emergence of new media, societal and industrial models compared new standards with failures of the old ones. The development of multimedia (CD-ROM content, PC games, virtual reality devices, etc.) allowed us to experience all of the pre-existing media types as they converged together into a collage of media elements. When it was introduced in 1991, the World Wide Web seemed the logical extension of this convergence theory. All the power of past media was now accessible through a global network. The Internet became the conduit new-media industry. History taught us that media travel through a cycle of invention, access limitations, and information overflow. Convergence theory applies to the convergence of revenue models and profit motives, and the ebb and flow of market tides that change as media mature. Figure 2.2 shows the various formats in which audiences stream digital video to their electronic devices.

Convergence Concepts

According to Wikipedia, *convergence* denotes the approach toward a definite value, as time goes on; or to a definite point, a common view or opinion, or toward a fixed or equilibrium state. We focus on three **key concepts** that underpin convergence relationships. They are: participatory culture, experiential marketing, and transmedia entertainment.[4] Futuretainment is also included here for its close relationship with all forms of convergence.

Participatory Culture   Participatory culture involves new ways we interact with media content, media producers, and each other as they explore the resources available to them across the media landscape. As consumers, we become active participants who shape the creation, circulation, and interpretation of media content. Such participation deepens our emotional investment in media, expanding our awareness of both content and brand.

In his book *Convergence culture*, Henry Jenkins discusses two cultural trends: the tendency of modern media creations to attract audience participation in the form of fandom and interactive storytelling; and the phenomenon of a single franchise being distributed through and impacting a range of media delivery methods.[5] As an example, he focuses on the reality TV show *Survivor*, which appeared in 2000 as the first of its kind on American television (reality began in the U.K. with *Big Brother* in the 1990s). An outgrowth of the show produced "Survivor spoilers" who sought to discover contest sites before they were announced. Showing how devoted viewers were able to discover or predict the outcome of the show by collaborating in online discussion groups, these fans ultimately influenced the production staff. This example of participatory culture exists when media consumers create new modes of engagement with media content that are not necessarily endorsed by the creators.

Fox Network, noticing the impact of fan involvement, launched *American Idol* to involve audiences in choosing the winner by text messaging their votes on cellphones (popular in Europe, but first introduced in the U.S. in 2002). Verizon, the show's sponsor, leveraged this property across multiple forms of media in classic convergence behavior.

The best example of conversion, according to Jenkins, is the *Matrix* phenomenon. Described as an example of a new trans-media storytelling, *Matrix* has spawned convergence in the form of a rabid fan base who research philosophy behind the story, create elaborate fictions and short movies of their own in this world. The *Matrix* multiplayer online game provided these fans with a new way to participate in their shared fantasy.

Trans-media star in film and video games

A controversial writer on convergence, Steven Johnson (*Everything bad is good for you*), coined the term "Sleeper Curve" to defend accusations that *Survivor* and *Idol* are "TV junk food." Johnson claims that a universe of popular entertainment is forcing pop-culture consumers to make snap decisions and create long-term strategies in role-playing video games and virtual environments. According to Johnson, even in "crappy" television, the "content is less interesting than the cognitive work the show elicits from your mind."[6] So, rather than becoming mindless viewers, audiences are actually participating in decision-making activities that revolve around TV content.

Another example of mass media convergence culture is the increased collaboration between content providers and sponsors. One example is the Coca-Cola cups placed on the *American Idol* judge table. Another type of branded entertainment is much more subtle. When we watch *American Idol*, we learn about the contestants as individuals rather than generic artists. They become real people with personalities, motives, and family ties who we watch improve or fail. Such intimacies allow us to participate with media in a way that traditional advertising does not. Bonding advertising to content is discussed in detail later in Chapter 7.

Experiential Marketing Experiential marketing refers to key ways to capitalize on participatory culture and a transmediated media environment. Creating unique brand extensions and strategies that play out across multiple media channels enhance our identification with both products and brands.

The commodification of everything—meaning that everything is for sale—has empowered marketing and advertising to levels never before experienced. In order to get audiences into entertainment venues, tourists to travel, spectators to watch sports, and so forth, promotion is necessary. **Marketing** is the means by which the whole culture is searched for potential meanings that can be changed by entertainment into paid-for experiences. Spending more than $1.5 trillion a year on marketing (advertising $15 billion and promotions more than $450 billion of the total), U.S. businesses pay to solicit our patronage by transferring cultural values onto experiences that we will buy. What used to be spent marketing products is now spent marketing entertainment in all of its forms. Selling products is secondary to selling the experience of those products by weaving bits and pieces of culture into products and selling them as lived experiences. We buy a Jeep branded by Eddie Bauer so we can fantasize about rugged overland adventures (if we ever leave the freeway!).

Branded entertainment, also known as *branded content* or *advertainment*, is the combination of an audio-visual program and a brand that can be initiated either by the brand or by the broadcaster. Branded programming is the merging of brand strategy and program context to generate engagement between a brand and a target audience. Rather than a focus on product placement or overt brand editorial, branded content allows a brand to build a deep relationship with a program property (show, film) beyond the 30-second commercial. It is where a brand creates entertainment that would not have existed without that brand, and where consumers choose to be involved.

The purpose of a branded entertainment program is to give brand the opportunity to promote their brand image to their target audience by creating positive links between the brand and the program. When you have Internet access from home, but you go to the local Starbucks café to surf the web, that's branded entertainment. Branded entertainment is discussed in more detail in Chapter 7.

Transmedia Entertainment   Transmedia entertainment is the flow of stories, images, characters, and information across various media platforms to deepen our sensory experiences. One example of transmediated information involves news delivery. With our modern landscape, the potential of the written word is limitless. We have redirected print journalism for the Internet and beyond with convergent journalism, which invigorates and transforms how we create and experience media. A vital new resource, news media convergence has broad theoretical and conceptual issues surrounding it.

News programming has entered the entertainment arena head on—we call it **infotainment**. Recognizing that news is not enough, journalists have turned to infotainment news strategies. Today's editorial decisions are often based as much on a story's ability to entertain audiences as it is to inform them. **Fusion journalism** has three forms: newsroom convergence, newsgathering convergence, and content convergence, which are discussed below.[7]

Newsroom convergence allows journalists from different media to share the same workspace instead of occupying separate offices or buildings. One example of this phenomenon is the News Center in Tampa, Florida, which contains the combined staffs of the Tampa Tribune, WFLA-TV, and TBO.com; all are owned by Media General, Inc. This sharing of newsroom facilities encourages cross-platform cooperation and more effective reporting.

Newsgathering convergence occurs when reporters, editors, and photographers collaborate on story production. For instance, news crews can share a helicopter to report on a hurricane; a TV newscaster might use a newspaper's graphics; a TV reporter's broadcast coverage can be expanded for use on the station's web site. Such fusion allows journalists to multitask in multimedia in groups or teams for effective news delivery.

Content convergence is where the final story is presented in different media formats that combine text, images, audio, video, blogs, podcasts, and slideshows. One hybrid medium combines TV audio and video with resources of the web and the portability of newspapers. Reporters and editors are "content producers" who choose the most effective and entertaining way to present news stories.

We have expanded our needs from local and national nightly news hours to news networks that broadcast around the clock. News programming has three sub-genres: investigation, dramatization, and analysis. Investigative **news magazines** have become prime time favorites. *Twenty-Twenty*, *60 Minutes*, and *48 Hours* are representative shows of this type. More sensational versions of the news exist in the form of **tabloid news** that dramatizes events with actors and staged sets after the fact, often confusing audiences who are unaware of the show's fictitious nature. **New analysis** of politics, finances, current events, and celebrities crowd the airwaves in half-hour and hour segments. *Wall Street Week*, *Meet the Press*, and *Entertainment Tonight* are among the most popular of this genre.

Enjoyed for its similarity to dramatic fiction, news programming is a popular choice among television viewers. But when drama becomes reality, the presentation changes. In fiction, drama is used to advance the plot. In news, drama unfolds and replays to update viewers. In 2008, the Democratic primary contest between Obama and Clinton invaded our homes and captured our attention daily until the nominee emerged.

What differentiates news drama from fiction is the inescapable presence of news images. We can easily pop out a DVD or TiVo shows we don't want to watch. We cannot, however, erase the ever-present reality of disaster from consuming the airwaves. Events are replayed unrelentingly. Late-night hosts substitute their comic formats with political discussions, network season premieres are postponed, and sensitive programming is removed from viewing schedules. Viewers are forced to rehash and review the events over and over again. This uncanny blending of fiction and reality situates news programming as both compelling and troublesome in times of such catastrophic crisis.

News has morphed into comedy, giving viewers alternate takes of current events. The *Daily Show* and the *Colbert Report* on Comedy Central offer opposing political philosophies that both entertain and inform viewers with infotainment.

John Stewart and Stephen Colbert appear on MTV Network's *Upfront* in 2008

Futuretainment: New Media, Religion, and Education

Convergence trends are tied closely to new media, but they have implications for all forms of futuretainment. Perhaps the most obvious trend is the multipurpose nature of new media itself.

New Media   Emerging new media entertainment products seemingly do it all—you can send email, surf the Internet, call a friend, play a video, and listen to music all with one handheld device like the Apple iPhone. Products and services that infuse entertainment into other tasks will continue to thrive. "Museums of the future could be a cross between a theme park and a piazza, crammed with gizmos, fantasy, exclusive restaurants and a dizzying array of merchandise."[8]

For many years now, mediated entertainment such as TV and film has been able to stimulate our optical and auditory senses with sights and sounds. Some forms of new media, however, even engage our senses of touch and smell. The view the wearer sees is projected on the screen behind him. Wearers become immersed in the computerized scene and use the gloves to pick up and move simulated objects. Many virtual reality games and rides now allow audiences and players to feel motion and tactile sensations— the rumble of an engine, the sinking feeling of a fall, or the slam of an impact. New media may also include aromas, such as Disney's "Soaring Over California" attraction at the California Adventure theme park, where audiences smell orange groves and pine forests while enjoying a simulated hang-gliding experience across the countryside. Makers of emerging forms of entertainment will likely continue to experiment with ways they can simulate and manipulate reality by stimulating our senses. Experts claim that complete virtual world experiences of the sort featured on the *Star Trek*'s holodeck are not far off.

Religion   Even religious groups are infusing their worship with entertainment. Author and motivational speaker Ken Davis blended entertainment with religious inspiration in his recent video *Is It Just Me?* advertised as "guaranteed to have you laughing as well as leave you encouraged with a simple message of God's love."[9] Many new services offer resources and advice for ways to incorporate entertainment into religious teachings and gatherings. For example, boasting "comedy so clean you can eat off it," the Christian Comedian Index began "providing a resource for Christian event planners" in 1999.[10] Aspects of religitainment are presented in Chapter 10.

Education   Following along futuretainment lines, teachers and educational programs are increasingly looking for ways to combine entertainment with instruction. The Netherlands boasts an Entertainment-Education Foundation dedicated to studying ways to infuse education with entertainment (and vice versa), such as the radio soap operas produced to promote safer sex in Africa and other countries. Not surprisingly, many of the ideas discussed involved traditional and new media entertainment. Edutainment is discussed in detail in Chapter 13. And you'll find more on futuretainment in Chapter 17.

Convergence Trends and the Blender Effect

Entertainment providers are always experimenting and looking for new ways to attract and maintain audiences' attention. They introduce new ideas, try new twists on old genres or story lines, combine genres in different ways, and add new elements in an effort to keep drama fresh and engaging. Such ideas may be born of nothing more than one individual's creativity and ability to think outside the box and uncover new possibilities. In many cases, however, these ideas are inspired or facilitated by larger societal trends or technological advances.

Many forms of contemporary entertainment introduce novelty by violating our expectations or established traditions. As suggested earlier, drama and dramatic genres tend to reflect certain norms that audiences come to expect—for example, good guys usually win, bullies never prosper in the end, romantic comedies end happily ever after. Indeed, norms can be found in most forms of entertainment—video game characters can come back to life, plays have intermissions, bars and clubs have music playing, and so on. However, many entertainers and audiences thrive on breaking the rules and violating established norms. Such manipulations—time and genre blending—reflect the postmodern nature of contemporary entertainment.

Time Manipulation   One way in which entertainers have experimented with drama is to play with the time order in which a story is told. Instead of starting at a single point in time and continuing forward in a direct, linear order, a story may begin at the middle or the end and progress backward and forward from there. Increasingly, a drama may progress forward or backward in time without offering any cues, so the audience may not be able to accurately piece the sequence of events together until the end, if then. This technique is reflected in many popular films, such as *Pulp Fiction*, *Sliding Doors*, *Vanilla Sky*, and *The Lake House*.

Technology has also allowed audiences the ability to manipulate the time order of entertainment. On the Internet, hyperlinks allow individuals to sift through content, moving forward or back at their own pace, and TiVo, DVD, and better VCR technology have made it easier for audiences to move forward and back within a program or film. Video games also often allow players to shift to different times, scenes, or universes. Many forms of entertainment have also manipulated time by blending history and culture from different centuries within a single scene. Movies such as *Shrck* and *A Knight's Tale*, for example, told stories reminiscent of the Renaissance era, but they also included elements of popular culture, such as music, dance, hairstyles, and some fashion influences from the late twentieth and early twenty-first centuries. Similarly, TV shows such as *Hercules* and *Xena* often blend together references from different eras.

Genre Blending   Many new entertainment offerings are a result of combining genres. Comedy, for example, has been blended with horror in films such as the *Scream* and *Scary Movie* series, and it has been combined with action in films such as *Rush Hour*. Genre blending is not limited to film and TV; it is also found in music, where artists experiment with blending different styles together—rock and jazz, techno and hip hop, pop and classical music—and even in cuisine, with "fusion" blends of different ethnic foods, such as Thai pizza or Mexican sushi.

Although not all genres, styles, or tastes may mix well together, genre blending is a popular strategy because it introduces a bit of novelty while still relying on elements that have proven successful in the past. Manipulations of time and genre often force audiences to confront ideas about reality. By violating our norms and expectations, such entertainment often begs the question of what is real and what isn't. Is there an objective reality out there, or is it all in our heads—or perhaps just a matter of perspective? Many audiences are fascinated by such questions.

Intended and Unintended Consequences of Convergence

As with all aspects of progress and change, there are consequences, some are intended, some are not. Two consequences of convergence—globalization and cultural imperialism—are discussed here for their role in convergent culture.

Globalization

Globalization is a process of interaction and integration among the people, companies, and governments of different nations, a process driven by international trade and investment and propelled by information technology. This process has effects on the environment, culture, political systems, economic development, and prosperity in societies around the world.

The earth is listening

For thousands of years, people—and now corporations—have been buying from and selling to each other in lands at great distances, with people and corporations investing in enterprises in other countries. But policy and technological developments of the past few decades have spurred increases in cross-border trade, investment, and migration so large that many observers believe the world has entered a qualitatively new phase in its economic development. This current wave of globalization has been driven by policies that have opened economies domestically and internationally as many governments adopt free-market economic systems. Taking advantage of new opportunities in foreign markets, corporations have built foreign factories and established production and marketing arrangements with foreign partners. A defining feature of globalization, therefore, is an international industrial and financial business structure. Advances in information technology have been the other principal driver of globalization.

Globalization is deeply controversial. Proponents of globalization argue that it allows poor countries and their citizens to develop economically and raise their standards of living, while opponents claim that the creation of an unfettered international free market has benefited multinational corporations in the Western world at the expense of local enterprises, local cultures, and common people.[11] Recent global opinion polls reveal that many people fear globalization; according to a 2007 BBC poll, globalization and the power of the U.S. pose a more serious threat to the world than war or terrorism. The economic impacts of globalization are covered in Chapter 6.

Cultural Imperialism[12]

Travel almost anywhere in the world today and, whether you suffer from habitual Big Mac cravings or cringe at the thought of missing the newest episode of MTV's *The Real World*, American tastes can be satisfied practically everywhere. This proliferation of American products across the globe is more than mere accident. As a byproduct of globalization, it is part of a larger trend in the conscious dissemination of American attitudes and values that is often referred to as *cultural imperialism*.

Cultural imperialism is the practice of promoting, distinguishing, separating, or artificially injecting the culture or language of one nation into another. It is usually the case that the former is a large, economically or militarily powerful nation and the latter is a smaller, less important one. Cultural imperialism can take the form of an active, formal policy or a general attitude.

FLASH FACT

Cultural imperialism in Miami? With 40 percent of the city's population Hispanic, non-Hispanics say they feel like strangers in their own country. With two Spanish-language newspapers, two TV stations, six radio stations, and political domination, Hispanics seem to have taken over. But is this phenomenon more evidence of a hybridization of cultures than cultural imperialism? What do you think?

Source: R. Rauth, The myth of cultural imperialism, Foundation for Economic Education, retrieved from www.ilw.com/articles/2008,0812-rauth.shtm

Cultural imperialism involves much more than simple consumer goods; it involves the dissemination of American principles, such as freedom and democracy. Though this process might sound appealing on the surface, it masks a frightening truth: many cultures around the world are gradually disappearing due to the overwhelming influence of corporate and cultural America.

American corporations are accused of wanting to control 95 percent of the world's consumers. Many industries are extremely successful in that endeavor. For example, with over 30,000 restaurants in over 100 countries, the golden arches of McDonald's are now, according to Eric Schlosser's *Fast food nation*, "more widely recognized than the Christian cross." Such American domination often hurts local markets, as many foreign industries are unable to compete with U.S. economic strength. Because it serves American economic interests, many corporations conveniently ignore the negative impacts of their domination. The Jingoists belief in the concept of social Darwinism where the stronger, "superior" cultures overtake the weaker, "inferior" cultures in a "survival of the fittest," may be an arrogant belief of the United States. America tries to convince the world of its superiority through marketing, which has successfully associated American products with modernity in the minds of global consumers. Selling the image of America through Nike and Gap (which ironically are manufactured outside the U.S.) causes consumers worldwide to clamor for American products.

By pitching diversity, American corporations have developed a successful global strategy. Advertising campaigns such as McDonald's international "I'm lovin'it" campaign and Coke's 1971 "I'd like to teach the world to sing in perfect harmony" illustrate an attempt to portray American goods as products capable of transcending political, ethnic, religious, social, and economic differences to unite the world—peace through consumerism perhaps?

Viacom's MTV has successfully adapted this strategy by integrating many different Americanized cultures into one unbelievably influential American network (with over 280 million subscribers worldwide). MTV has spawned over twenty networks specific to certain geographical areas such as Brazil and Japan which further spread the association between America and modernity by catering to local taste.

By using popular local icons in their advertisements, U.S. corporations successfully associate what is fashionable in local cultures with what is fashionable in America. According to Naomi Klein's *No logo*, American cultural imperialism has inspired a "slow

Excited fans in front of MTV studios, which provide Western music on a global scale

food movement" in Italy and a demonstration involving the burning of chickens outside of the first Kentucky Fried Chicken outlet in India.

Compounding the influence of commercial images are the media and information industries, which claim to be the source for "fair and balanced" information. Satellites allow over 150 million households in approximately 212 countries and territories worldwide to subscribe to CNN, a member of Time Warner, the world's largest media conglomerate. The Internet acts as another vehicle for the worldwide propagation of American influence, according to critics. Yet as a global medium, the Internet also distributes multiples of opinions from users worldwide and can hardly be termed an American propaganda tool in today's web world.

And America isn't the only guilty party. In 2008, the Danes accused Sweden's Ikea (the low-priced furniture store) of insulting them by choosing household objects with the lowest value and giving them Danish names. According to a Swedish retailer, doormats and rugs such as Köge, Sindal, Roskilde, Bellinge, Strib, Helsingör, and Nivå are all "seventh class" citizens in the hierarchical world of Ikea furnishings. An Ikea spokesperson said the naming was purely coincidental. Ikea advertises globally, using the same localized tactics as American marketers to appeal to its target audience.

Bottom line—is America's media and brand presence a global threat or a global opportunity for emerging capitalism? There are arguments for both viewpoints. What is your opinion on the issue?

SPOTLIGHT ON CULTURAL IMPERIALISM   An Olympic Phenomenon

Pro-Tibet protesters at San Francisco Olympic torch rally

Never in previous Olympic history has the Olympic torch passed through nineteen countries before the opening ceremony. However, in Beijing on August 8, 2008, the torch had made its way around the world, encountering a variety of protests against China. Protests represented a range of political issues, particularly those related to China's human rights record—the recent unrest in Tibet, the war in Darfur, China's support to regimes in Myanmar and Zimbabwe, North Korean defectors, territorial disputes with Vietnam over Spratly and Paracel Islands, Falun Gong persecution, and the political status of Taiwan—that resulted in violence at various locations. Protests, which ranged from tens of thousands of people in San Francisco to very few in Pyongyang, made protecting the torch the newest Olympic sport.

European protests were described as "despicable" by the Chinese government. Accusing Britain and France of tarnishing the Olympic spirit, China vowed to protect the torch at any cost. Prompted by the chaotic torch relays, Jacques Rogge, president of the International Olympics Committee, described the situation as a "crisis," saying that any athlete displaying Tibetan flags at Olympic venues would be expelled from the games.

Viewed from China, the fraught progress of the torch took on the appearance of an international ambush. The Chinese government had originally dubbed the tour of the torch "the journey of harmony," a slogan that spoke at least as much of China's view of its rising global profile as it did of the Olympic ideal itself. The games were supposed to be China's graduation party, final confirmation of its arrival at the top table of world powers. The Chinese nationalist bloggersphere argued that Tibet was not an issue and that the real motive behind ruining China's Olympic party was that the West was never comfortable awarding China that amount of authority in the first place. But Tibet underlies just how wide the political gap is between China and the West, "two partners who have no difficulty singing in harmony from the same capitalist hymn sheet."

Calls to withdraw the thirty officers of the "Holy Flame Protection Unit" went unheeded, and the torch continued its journey to Beijing. Many governments purported that such parading would go down in history as an act of cultural imperialism.

Source: www.guardian.co.uk/commentisfree/2008/apr/10/olympicgames2008.tibet

What do you think?

*   *Do you agree with the notion that China's torch display was a manifestation of cultural imperialism? Why or why not?*

Postmodern Convergence

Many people talk about postmodernism, but few people agree on just what it means. For that reason, we present our own notion of the term. The use of the prefix *post* implies that it follows modernity, the epoch of late nineteenth and early twentieth centuries that came into being as the capitalist-industrialist state. Property, labor, manufacturing, and services grounded modernism. Central to the shift from modernity to postmodernity is a type of social order brought about by new forms of technology and information where simulation takes priority over reality.[13]

In other words, postmodernists duplicate rather than create. They dwell upon the future rather than the past, and replace a desire for truth with a quest for meaning. In a contemporary society, we prioritize access to entertainment and experiences over the ownership of things—we'd rather experience than purchase. Because we can apply postmodern criticism to every genre of entertainment, it is appropriate for study in its own right. After we define the postmodern condition, we present specific postmodern examples in the cultural spaces and places of marketing and media, architecture and museum exhibitions. The impact of postmodernism on entertainment and on society often alters our perceptions and our reality. By understanding the nature of this phenomenon, we become better consumers of entertainment and of our mediated society.

SPOTLIGHT ON VIRTUAL REALITY   Postmodern Video Games

Playing *Grand Theft Auto IV*

Recent trends in video gaming conform to a postmodern aesthetic. These trends are the result of a greater cultural consciousness and a social context. Four aspects of postmodernity can be directly applied to videogames; they are explained here.

Time Control (Temporal Mastery)
Allowing participants to rewind time for up to ten seconds, *Prince of Persia: The Sands of Time* (2003) uses the Prince's dagger that contains charges from an hourglass to achieve control over time. First-person shooter game *FEAR* (2005) and racing game *Burnout Revenge* (2005) bring the third dimension to gaming.

Open-ended vs. Linearity
Linear storytelling, called the "grand narrative," takes readers from point A to point B. Postmodern participants have the ability for decision-making. This open-endedness challenges the notion of good vs. evil and the gaming platform becomes more character-driven and character-oriented. Players are able to develop characters from scratch and choose their good/evil balance. *Black and White* (2001) offers player omnipotence, which is the right to power, status, control, and authority that results in a "meta-narrative" (stories about stories) at the psychological rather than plot level.

Emergent Gameplay
Players are finding new ways to tamper with a game's mechanics beyond what was originally programmed. Consider the following examples:

- *Machinima*—cut scenes in games rendered using game models instead of motion video or actors.
- *Cat and Mouse*—used in online car racing games where racers play on teams of at least two cars. Each team picks one very slow car with the goal of having it cross the finish line last. Here, team members in faster cars aim to push their slow cars into the lead and ram their opposing teams' slow cars off the road.

- *Lurikeen Invasion*—an imaginary political movement based on the power of the lurikeen class that was inspired by the diminutive form of the smallest avatar in *Dark Age of Camelot*. Players created characters ending in "keen" (i.e. cokekeen, iamkeen) on a single game server, becoming so popular that Mythic Entertainment had to re-design the guild statistics webpages.
- *Real Economy Interaction*—traders in massively multiplayer online games with economic systems play purely to purchase virtual objects or avatars that they sell for real-world money on auction web sites or game currency exchange sites. The object here is to make real money regardless of the original game designer's objectives (i.e. *World of Warcraft, Everquest*).
- *Glitch or quirk-based strategies*—in first-person shooter games, glitches or physics quirks can become viable strategies or spawn their own game types. Rocket jumping is popular in *Quake* where a player fires a rocket at the ground while jumping, allowing the weapon's splash damage to propel him to otherwise unreachable areas.

Pastiche, Intertextuality, and Genre Hybridity
Manifested in blank parody. One example is *Grand Theft Auto: Vice City*, an archetypal example where storylines borrow from popular culture films (*Pulp Fiction*) and television shows (*Miami Vice*).

Activision Publishing's 2004 *Vampire* game is an extremely intelligent example of postmodern entertainment that almost academically addresses the elusive relationship between reality and fiction/fantasy—and in this context its postmodern means of quotation and allusion actually make real sense.

Source: David Halpert, davidsmag.wordpress.com/2008/04/28/postmodernism-and-the-video-game-part-one/

What do you think?

- *What games can you suggest that have postmodern qualities?*

Our Postmodern Society

Postmodernism is a way to describe our society. Theming, as presented in Chapter 7, is a prime example of postmodern expression. Here, the displacement of time and space are combined with representations of what's real with symbolic or virtual reality to produce a postmodern condition. Many forms of mass media are considered to be postmodern, especially the contemporary cinema of David Lynch, Steven Soderberg, and Oliver Stone.

Postmodernism has been best defined in a variety of ways, including:[14]

- a nostalgic, conservative longing for the past, coupled with an erasure of the boundaries between the past and the present. Example: Johnny Rockets Café.
- an intense preoccupation with the real and its representations. Example: Las Vegas.
- a pornography of the visible. Example: Violent cinema such as *Kill Bill*.
- the commodification of sexuality and desire. Example: Abercrombie & Fitch advertising.
- a consumer culture which objectifies a set of masculine cultural ideals. Examples: Purchasing the biggest televisions, the fastest cars, and guns that are designed to murder people rather than shoot game.
- intense emotional experiences shaped by anxiety, alienation, resentment, and a detachment from others. Examples: Video games and Internet or computer entertainment.

Evidence of postmodernization is everywhere, you just have to know how to recognize it. To that end, we highlight five central features of postmodernism in the entertainment arts. They include:[15]

- *Disappearance of the boundary between art/entertainment and everyday life.* What this means is that amusement is an integral part of our lives, and that we cannot really separate what is performance and what is reality Our cities are centers of consumption, play, and entertainment, saturated with signs and images to the extent that anything can be represented. Leisure activities such as visiting theme parks, shopping centers, malls, museums, and galleries converge to fill our spare time.

- *Collapse of distinction between high culture and popular (mass) culture.* People of all classes attend similar performances, watch similar television shows, play similar sports and take similar vacations. Few true "high brow" activities are practiced today. Mass culture dominates the attention of audiences from all lifestyles in what can be called a "hypermarket of culture."[16]

- *Playfulness and the celebration of "surface" culture.* We enjoy what is often called "kitsch" or the mundane, such as hanging dice, *Reader's Digest*, airport paperbacks, soap operas, and tabloids. Barbie collectors and fan clubs meet and tell stories about their dolls; Beanie Babies are hoarded the moment they are discontinued, then traded as icons. SciFi movies such as *Revenge of the Killer Tomatoes* are featured at film retrospectives. We embrace and love the mundane.

- *Decline of originality.* Ideas, rather than being new, are most often a re-shuffling of what already exists. We draw from all eras of the past and combine materials to come up with different forms like Disneyland and Club Med. We succumb to fads—take a look, for example, at the explosion of SUVs on the roads of America—and jump on band wagons. We flock to the same tourist places and attend the same movies, both of which are created in the image of some other popular or successful place or film.

- *Assumption that art/entertainment can only be repetition.* Cities like Las Vegas are reproductions of other places so we might experience them without actually visiting the true location. We duplicate and fabricate exactly; most aspects of our existence are McDonaldized (franchised). Inner cities are becoming gentrified by the dot com generation who develop them as sites of tourism and consumption like those in most other major metropolitan areas; San Francisco's South of Market area is an example of this phenomenon. If you woke up not knowing where you were, then ventured out into any global metropolis, you would have trouble identifying the location because the franchises, sports, and musical messages you encounter are like those of all other cities. You'd probably wonder, "Where am I?"

SPOTLIGHT ON POSTMODERN FILM   Viewing *Shrek*

Dreamworks constructed this film by using the same computer-animated imaging systems that Disney uses, and it follows a typical Disney-style story line. However, *Shrek* diverges from Disney's genre by adding blatant irony and subversity. The fact that *Shrek* seems to be a typical fairy-tale is just what provides the congruence necessary for its irony to work.

One instance of subversion is the idea of beauty. Princess Fiona, under a curse that transforms her into an ugly ogre at night at sunset until she is kissed, defies the usual notion of a princess. Ironically, once Shrek finally kisses her, she becomes a full-time ogre-princess. Here, true love is portrayed as a green, orange-haired, overweight ogress. Rather than a kiss that turns a frog into a handsome prince as in *Beauty*

Shrek strikes all the right postmodern chords as the movie progresses and it becomes obvious that the film is a celebration of postmodern culture. By deconstructing a traditional fairy-tale theme by breaking it down, poking fun at it, and finally reconstructing it, the movie exists as a sub-genre of fairy-tales. Our ideas of beauty and genre are torn down and rebuilt in a new light.

Characteristics that identify Shrek as the postmodern hero are:

- his rejection of the big narrative, the fairy-tale, the overarching story, which he flushes down the toilet
- his hero status with those of difference, those fairy-tale characters that have been most effected by the darker side of modernism
- his heroism, which is juxtaposed and contrasted to the King Farquad who in Hitler Nazi fashion tortures the gingerbread man and other characters.

It becomes clear that what has marginalized Shrek has been his difference. The remainder of the movie becomes a celebration of the liberating capacity that postmodern devotees proclaim as antidote to the horror of modernity.[17]

and the Beast, this movie's kiss turns a princess into an ogre. Also a warrior, Fiona takes on Robin Hood and subverts traditional gender roles.

The film also uses "intertextuality" by referring to other fairy-tales, adding humor and depth to the story. A musical score combining current hits with classical music and clever pop-culture references create a "pastiche" typical of postmodernism.

What do you think?

- *What other films can you name that invoke postmodern thought?*

The unique aspect of postmodernism is that no style dominates, and we have endless improvisations and variations on these such as parody and playfulness. People everywhere combine traditions, and borrow rituals and myths from the past and from other cultures. Global cultural symbols are in the public domain, and styles from different periods and cultures coexist; high-tech art may reside alongside of antique columns and baroque ornamentation with effects that are sometimes shocking and fascinating.

Hyperreality

Assuming responsibility for the postmodern condition, the media take control of and permeate our lives, bombarding us with instructions, solicitations, education, politics, and news. The intensification of media messages creates a state of being fast-forwarded, of confronting a very "hyperreality" every day of our lives. Time is fragmented into a series of perpetual presence with no sense of time, and reality is a series of visual images.

Postmodernists are also convergence advocates, realizing that interaction with all forms of mediated communications is our reality. Taking Shakespeare literally, postmodernists claim that commerce has made the whole world a stage and all experience a simulation. And in fact, for many children spending between five and six hours each day watching television, using the Internet, and playing games makes media more real than any of their other activities. To some people, an event is not even real until it has appeared on TV, been featured in the news, or hit the Internet. Indications of hyperreality can be found in most realms of our lives. Here we present a few examples—movies, promotion, lifestyle, architecture, and museums—that demonstrate the pervasiveness of the postmodern condition in entertainment and life.

Postmodern Lifestyles

With postmodernism, traditional distinctions and hierarchies are collapsed, multiculturalism is acknowledged and globalism is embraced. We celebrate difference rather than sameness. What this means is that all stories, religions, histories, news interpretations, and so forth can coexist because they all have relevance, and no single perspective dominates. For instance, while you are watching a football game, you see an ad for beer, get a weather report, learn that a bomb has exploded killing hundreds, get a preview of the newest movie release, and experience replays of fumbles and touchdowns. How can viewers attribute importance when each mediated experience receives equal weight and significance?

Key components for capturing the essence of postmodernism are its notions of identity and possessions. French philosopher Jean-Paul Sartre identified three aspects of personal identity: "being, doing and having."[18] During most of the twentieth century, **having** possessions preoccupied us. We used cars and clothing and logos to helps us define ourselves. The transition to an entertainment economy will see a shift from having to **doing** as the most important marker of our personal identity. Where we travel, what events we attend, what clubs we enjoy, and in what sports we participate will become significant parts of self-concept (our **being**) for citizens of postmodern, post-capitalist countries.

Play, according to Sartre, allows us to exercise our desire to exist in the world. By using our resources to purchase play instead of objects, we capture the essence of freedom and fantasy. Sartre assumes that play and reality are separate. Yet in our entertainment society, our reality is often defined though our play activities, and so they become overlapped and indistinguishable from one another. Fashion as play is one example. Today, there is no single fashion standard. Fashions exist without rules and with multiple choices.[19] We can wear hiking boots with a full-length period skirt and see-through branded T-shirt, and wrap ourselves with a mink pelt from the 1940s. We combine eras and fabrics without regard to rules of ensemble.

Fashion has always played a role in personal identity. We embrace logos for what they say about us. Yet in New York or Istanbul, you can get exact copies of brands and logos for a fraction of the cost.

L'Oreal Melbourne Fashion Festival 2008

At a shop in Greenwich Village that sells faux designer purses, you can buy a slick shoulder bag for $18 and the clerk will affix any logo you want to it. A watch shop near the world's largest covered bazaar in Istanbul boasts a sign saying: "Authentic Fake Watches." Rolex, Tag Heuer, Cartier—you name the brand—are available for $25 (less if you bargain) and can pass for the real thing on your wrist.

Because they are ceasing to be significant for personal identity purposes, logos are being replaced by fashions of outrageous designs, mismatched fabrics, and copies of designer outfits, making dress an affordable and entertaining activity. Style enables us to create, maintain, or change our identities at will; we may step in and out of reality by simply changing our clothes!

Postmodern Architecture

Our **built environment** is essential for any discussion of postmodernism. All sorts of places have come to construct themselves as the objects of tourists gaze, as sites of pleasure. Architectural space in postmodernism is localized, specific, context-dependent, and particularistic. Postmodernity can be visualized best by looking at buildings designed by Frank O. Gehry. Architect of the famous Guggenheim Museum Bilbao (Spain), which is a showcase of contemporary art, Gehry explains his creations as "wrappings." Critics have not been good to Gehry, describing Bilbao as "a luxury liner from an art deco tourist poster, docked beside an oil refinery that's died and gone to heaven,"[20] and his Seattle Experience Music Project was called "open-heart surgery gone awry."[21]

The features that render Gehry's work as postmodern are its strange feeling of the absence of inside and outside, the bewilderment and loss of spatial orientation, the messiness of an environment in which things and people no longer find their "place."[22]

But Gehry is but one of many architects combining past and present to provide the interaction of design and art that house activity spaces and workplaces. In particular, the campuses of the University of California at Irvine and Santa Cruz integrate architectural styles and creations by a variety of designers to provide interest and diversity in educational environments. Today, form does not necessarily follow function; rather it manifests hyperreality by entertaining audiences.

SPOTLIGHT ON POSTMODERN ARCHITECTURE   Frank Gehry's Postmodernity

Canadian-born Frank Gehry is best known for his sculptural approach to building design and for constructing curvaceous structures, often covered with reflective metal. His most famous work is the Guggenheim Museum in Bilbao, Spain, which is covered in titanium.

After graduating from the University of Southern California School of Architecture, he studied city planning at the Harvard Graduate School of Design.

The tortured, warped forms of Gehry's structures are considered expressions of the deconstructivist (DeCon) school of modernist architecture where buildings are not required to reflect specific social ideas or the belief that form follows function.

Considered a modern architectural icon and celebrity, Gehry's buildings, including his private residence, have become tourist attractions. Many museums, firms, and cities seek Gehry's services as a badge of distinction, regardless of the product he delivers. Three recently constructed U.S. structures exemplify his postmodern style:

Seattle's **Experience Music Project** (2000) represents his style at its most extreme. The "swoopy" exterior forms—red, blue, purple, silver, and gold indicative of guitar finishes—were designed by a 3D computer modeling program originally designed to develop Mirage fighter jets.

Dancing Building

Experience Music Project

The 293,000-square-foot **Walt Disney Concert Hall** in Los Angeles (2003) features a wavy, steel exterior designed to look like a ship with its sail at full mast. Gehry wanted to create the feeling of traveling along a ceremonial barge to music.

Prague's **Dancing Building** (1996) was originally named *Fred and Ginger* after Fred Astaire and Ginger Rogers—the house vaguely resembles a pair of dancers.

Gehry has been criticized for repeating himself, and that the disjointed metal panoply that has become his trademark is perhaps overused. Much of his recent work seems derivative of his landmark Bilbao Guggenheim. To learn more about the architect, rent film director Sydney Pollack's documentary *Sketches of Frank Gehry* that was released on DVD by Sony Pictures Home Entertainment in August, 2006.

Gehry's design reflects a postmodern approach to entertainment for the following reasons:

- Gehry blurs the boundary between entertainment and life in his architectural presentations.
- Both high-brows of architecture and popular culture fans can enjoy the experience of Gehry's buildings' forms and shapes.
- Gehry has taken shapes from reality and fantasy to create an amalgamation of the past and future.
- Gehry's forms are repeated and fabricated from materials that have been used many times before for similar and dissimilar purposes.

Disney Concert Hall

Shopping Architecture **Retailers** have also embraced architecture as a means to get customers into their stores and to entertain them while they buy. Two New York stores, Prada and Toys "R" Us, are good examples of how architecture is being used to re-infuse brands with a sense of excitement. Believing that shopping is the last remaining form of public activity, Prada architect Rem Koolhaas believes in retail design "epicenters." Epicenters become devices to renew the brand by counteracting and destablizing any received notion of what the brand is, does, or will become.[23] The store he designed in SoHo at 575 Broadway cost $40 million to merge hard-edge late modernism with technology such as glass-enclosed dressing rooms that turn translucent at the touch of a button. The elevator, a cylinder of glass perched on a hydraulic piston, was fabricated in Italy for a cool $11 million. Merchandise is displayed in metal cages hung from the ceiling that move around so the store is constantly redesigned—another expensive solution to a fairly simple problem. The image below shows the Tokyo flagship store for Armani.

Much less pretentious, the Toys "R" Us Times Square store features a 60-foot-high ferris wheel that blends entertainment and the hard sell. It has fourteen passenger cars, each with an individually themed cab—one car is based on Mr. & Mrs. Potato Head and another on a Tonka truck. Mr. Monopoly has a car, as does Barbie. Much of the store is divided into environments with special themes. The store's glass facade, which is sometimes transparent and sometimes covered with a series of images on automated panels that roll down like shades, is a continuously changing billboard. Because both of these stores can be more fully appreciated when they are empty, retail architecture seems to have become more of a private indulgence than a public space.

Armani Ginza Tower
flagship store in Tokyo

Museums as Postmodern Experiences

Guggenheim Museum in Bilbao, Spain

Venues of performance and exhibition, museums provide us with transformations of historical time to the space in which we live. Nearly fifteen thousand museums entertain millions of Americans each year, and one in every twenty-eight Americans is a member of at least one museum. Museums in the U.S. average 865 million visitors each year, or 2.3 million visits a day. The largest museum in existence is the Smithsonian Institution with more than 140 million items.[24] Although museums have never been more important as entertainment alternatives, they are also suffering from an identity crisis. They encompass a universe of places so different in size, budget, and orientation that it's hard to say what links them together beyond the need for visitors. That common need, however, is the prime motivator to offer more than just "dead stuff" for public consumption. To meet the need, museums are modifying their traditional role of education to one of entertainment.

The final evolution of the modern museum into a postmodern museum has occurred only since 2005 with the rapid expansion of the Guggenheim Museum franchises in Berlin and Bilbao and coming soon to Paris, Salzburg, and Geelong. An alliance between the Hermitage Museum (St. Petersburg, Russia) and MoMA (New York) was recently established to create an independent for-profit e-business to curate international exhibitions drawn from both collections. Opened in Washington DC in April, 2008, the Newseum is dedicated to the story of journalism and includes displays of the Berlin Wall, an antenna from the World Trade Center's ruins, a blogger's slipper, and Mark Twain's inkwell. The postmodernization of these museums reflects two specific aspects of postmodern culture—the postmodern corporatization of the museum and the notion of museum as ritual entertainment.

Museum as Corporation and Ritual   The postmodern **corporatization** of the museum combines modern corporate ideals of efficiency and rationalization with postmodern audience (target markets) marketing drives in relation to exhibitions, merchandise sales, food and beverage outlets, and commercial advertising. The key element of postmodern

Topkapi Palace Museum, Istanbul

museum corporatization is that it aims for a wider audience base through specific audience-targeting. This is reflected through aggressive advertising and marketing campaigns, which in turn reflect the nature of the postmodern museum as entertainment provider. In a curious postmodern twist the audience-targeting strategies of the museum cause it to be an audience-driven entity, entrenched in commercialization and fulfillment of the postmodern audience's demand for an essential postmodern museum experience, being "ritual entertainment."

Postmodern audience-driven **ritual entertainment** is an evolution of the modern museum ideal of aesthetic contemplation which is an evolution of the early museum ideal of art as ritual. Ritual entertainment embodies both the early museum ideal of art as ritual and the postmodern audience-driven ideal of museum as comprehensive entertainment center. Consequently, we find the interesting situation of an audience expecting both value for its entertainment dollar and some form of sedated pleasure and spiritual nourishment. The postmodern museum as audience-driven entity is left with little choice but to accede to these demands by providing the complete museum entertainment experience—symptomatic of a certain Disneyfication of the postmodern museum. For example, while a modern museum may have introduced bookshops and cafés to increase its bottom line, the postmodern museum regards parties, hired-out functions, and the promotion of other forms of the arts as part of its responsibility as a comprehensive entertainment center. This audience-driven necessity to provide an all-encompassing experience by the postmodern museum reflects the blurring of boundaries between postmodern art spaces.

Impact of Postmodernism

Our mediated culture reflects the postmodern condition. Movies and television shows include representations of sexuality, violence, and nostalgia for a past where melodrama defines the relation between the sexes. The problem with postmodern cinema is that audiences may view them not as postmodernity but as mirrored reality where the stars' identity becomes our own. As we continually seek entertainment that presents unique visions of reality, we may be held hostage to the creations of directors such as David Lynch and Quentin Tarantino without proper defense mechanisms. An understanding of post-modernism as a societal critique helps to defray the confusion and promotes informed viewing.

SPOTLIGHT ON POSTMODERN DIRECTORS   The Work of Lynch and Tarantino

David Lynch   Quentin Tarantino

Two directors stand out for their postmodern approach to filmmaking: David Lynch and Quentin Tarantino. **David Lynch**'s film *Blue Velvet* (1986) and gothic soap opera *Twin Peaks* (1990 ABC) are examples of mediated postmodern philosophy. Located in small-town America, both film and video contain all the terrors and simulated realities characteristic of postmodern definition. Both texts display an absence of boundaries between past and present, and a treatment of time that locates viewers in a perpetual present. Lynch, called the quintessential postmodern director, puts the un-presentable (brutality, insanity, homosexuality, sado-masochism, drug and alcohol abuse) before viewers in ways that challenge the boundaries that ordinarily separate private and public life.[25]

In *Blue Velvet*, nostalgia for the past is presented as 1950s and 1960s rock 'n' roll, suggesting that the music of our comfortable youth may lead to destruction and violence. Here, the past as sacred and profane is moved to the present and future where the hyperreal is always real. The film exists both as a parable of sin[26] and redemption and as pornographic cult.[27] Characteristic of reader-response theory, Lynch locates the meaning of his film in the viewer's experience with the text. Viewers see his work as either cinematic art or as trash—reviewers are equally split in their opinions. One reviewer even equated the film to religious, symbolic art.

Twin Peaks, a TV soap opera, had all the ingredients of traditional soft-core fare: sex, violence, murder, and adultery. In just a short time, the program became a cult phenomenon, watched faithfully by people who would not normally watch primetime TV.

Lynch's voyeuristic visions look into the future and see technology and violence, so he takes refuge in the fantasies and nostalgia of the past. His dreams are postmodern solutions to life in the present. He implies that small towns are no longer safe from urban evils. His 2001 film, *Mulholland Drive*, is two hours and twenty-five minutes of macabre thrill, highly charged erotica, and indelible images focused around Hollywood and the film industry.

Carrying on the postmodern tradition, **Quentin Tarantino** rose to fame in the early 1990s as a stylish auteur whose bold use of nonlinear storylines, memorable dialogue, and bloody violence brought new life to familiar American film archetypes. Tarantino scripted *Reservoir Dogs* in 1992, a dialogue-driven heist movie that set the tone for his later films.

Following the success of *Reservoir Dogs*, Tarantino retreated to Amsterdam to work on his script for *Pulp*

Fiction. When finally released, the film won the Palme d'Or (Golden Palm) at the 1994 Cannes film festival. It featured many critically acclaimed performances, and earned Tarantino and Avary Oscars for Best Original Screenplay, and was also nominated for Best Picture.

Kill Bill I and *II,* films he both wrote and directed, were highly stylized "revenge flicks" in the cinematic traditions of Chinese martial arts, Japanese film, Spaghetti Westerns, and Italian horror based on a character (The Bride) and plot that he and actress Uma Thurman had developed during the making of *Pulp Fiction.*

Tarantino's movies are known for their sharp dialogue, splintered chronology, and pop culture obsessions. Often they are viewed as graphically violent and, certainly in his key films, *Reservoir Dogs, Pulp Fiction,* and *Kill Bill,* there are copious amounts of both spattered and flowing blood. However, what affects people most is the casualness, and even macabre humor, of the violence, as well as the tension and grittiness of these scenes. His films reflect a truly postmodern outlook on life.

Question

- *What other postmodern directors can you name?*

Postmodernism is the present, the hyperreal condition in which we conduct our daily routines. With it comes the freedom to choose and create our own reality from the plethora of choices brought to us on our phone, our computer, and our television—or experienced in person. As the lines blur between fantasy and reality, the division between work and play also become interwoven. Postmodernism is technology at its pinnacle, and we can expect to continue the experience well into the future.

FADE TO BLACK

As we have seen, convergence has allowed all forms of entertainment, media, and marketing to blend together for hyperreal communication. As Internet technology proliferates, we may not know who is writing what we read or who is reading what we write. Using online personas in cyberspace through virtual communities like Second Life helps undermine the notion of real self, perpetuating postmodernism. Men and women casting about for new live experiences open their minds to being everywhere at once and play into the aspect of life as a paid-for performance. The change in our roles as productive workers into creative performers represents a change in our social relationships.

People like Ralph Lauren and Martha Stewart prepare costumes and sets that we use as backdrops for our life performances. We can outfit ourselves in Quicksilver and become surfers, or wear Armani and become professionals. Our image managers allow us to act out whatever fantasy we like and amuse ourselves by theatricizing of our lives. Lauren and Stewart can do this because the theater is typical of what goes on in society all of the time. As actors on our own stage, we are all entertainers and we are all audiences.

If this sounds a bit hard to swallow, check out the magazine racks, TV guides, and fashion outlets for evidence of the presence of those who help us create a reality designed as fantasy or vice-versa. Welcome to hyper-everything.

A CLOSER LOOK AT POSTMODERNISM

Essay from a Postmodern Critic

The Fashion of The Christ: An Extreme Makeover for The Son of Man

Undeniably, the Christian core of this nation is under attack. From the heights of *Brokeback Mountain* to being peered at by a Queer Eye indeed. The liberal elites force their agenda down audiences' throats and then give themselves Academy Awards for the effectiveness of their iniquity. With the glowering specter of such broadsides against common decency as Spongebob Gaypants, how are the young to be brought to Jesus? How can a moldering old religion be made relevant to a generation of lost souls constantly jacked into the violent pornography on their video iPods?

A partial answer may lie in a simple **change of wardrobe**. Traditional depictions of Christ are of two primary sorts: the living Jesus in some kind of old-fashioned robe wearing sandals and sporting an unruly beard and indifferently-styled hair. The other image is of Christ crucified shown in those depressing crucifixes painted by Giotto in the fourteenth century.

While these images are no doubt theologically useful, neither is likely to appeal to a cadre of kids whose sense of style has been carefully coiffed by a blinged-out 50 Cent. The youth of today view a midriff-bearing, go-go booted Jessica Simpson as the all-American girl. What could be more off-putting to an image-conscious "metrosexual" than a Lord and Savior who looks the part of a bleeding-hearted, LSD-addled old hippie? Likewise, the young ladies who are trained to respond to the Vin Diesels of the world are bound to find a scrawny fellow with handmade underwear and a hat made from thorns a bit unlikely for the role of Holy Warrior of the Armageddon.

In other words, in order to stay relevant, J.C. needs a makeover now

First of all, **Christ's hair**. If we must have length, the least we could do is go *all one length*: something more surfer hunk and less Willie Nelson junk. Perhaps something chin length would be appropriate, and make sure Jesus gets a good shampoo, conditioner, and blow-dry: we want a Holy head with body and sheen.

Next, the **beard** has got to go. Period. And no goatees and no stubble. We need a clean-shaven Jesus who shows a little self-respect. How are we supposed to believe in Him when He doesn't believe in Himself enough to run a razor across His cheeks every once in a while? To finish off the spa treatment, Jesus should get a nice facial massage and an eyebrow pluck. The little things that are noticed the least make the biggest difference. Teeth whitening would be nice, but chances are His glowing, Godly beauty will do enough to shine through here.

Next, the Heavenly **body**. I know that the lean look was meant to convey a certain asceticism, a reflection of the paucity of faith of this world and the sinfulness He died on the cross to correct. But really. **Get Jesus to the gym**. How can a Christ with no pecs and no six-pack be fit to fight the devil? You can sure bet

An updated, casual and savvy Jesus for today's teens

Satan and all his minions project a much buffer image than that!

Last in the appearance department would have to be the Son of God's **clothes**. A strict adherence to tradition does us no favors in a decontextualized postmodern age. Ask your average adolescent if she knows what people wore in AD 33 and she will look at you like you just walked out of a Steppenwolf concert. That is because she does not know and she does not care. Jesus needs something forceful and fit from Armani for more formal occasions, something double-breasted and white, with a baby-blue Fubu tracksuit and a few gold chains for gatherings at the flag pole. He could even go with Abercrombie and Fitch or The Gap for church mixers and prayer groups.

Finally, whatever the Christian community in this country does to get good PR, it should NOT show Jesus dying! Generation Y does not like to dwell on the negative; that's for passé, Morrissey-loving Gen-Xers. Today's youth need an upbeat Jesus, one who can be envisioned enjoying a cappuccino at the local coffee shop or maybe snowboarding at Aspen. We need an X-treme sports Jesus, a Christ with an MP3 player blasting Jars of Clay. We need a successful Lord, one who represents our values.

Skeptics may scoff at what is being presented here, but it is not out of line with the contemporary MegaChurch. What works for value-conscious Baby-Boomers would work equally well for style-conscious young people. We fighters in the culture wars must act boldly; if we want to save souls, we must use any means necessary.

Source: Annie Prada-Klein, postmodernvillage.com/East WesterlyReview (issue 18)

DISCUSSION AND REVIEW

1. Discuss the main areas where convergence has impacted your life. What other types of convergence would you like to see in the future?
2. In what ways is your life postmodern? What elements of the past, present, and future occupy the same time and space in your daily entertainment activities?
3. Compare news magazines, CNN, and the *Daily Show* for their similarities and differences when reporting on political events. Which format is more effective for conveying the real fact? Why?
4. Discuss the differences between globalization and cultural imperialism. What unintended consequences resulted from these phenomena?

EXERCISES

1. Log on to the Museum of Jurassic Technology web site, www.mjt.org/, and describe the museum in terms of the postmodern condition as presented in this chapter. What is the museum's purpose? Would you visit its location on Venice Blvd. during a visit to Los Angeles? Why or why not?
2. View Oliver Stone's movie *Wall Street* and analyze it using the postmodern terms from this chapter. Is the film a work of art or trash? Why?
3. Locate and read Jean Baudrillard's *The ecstasy of communication*. Summarize the subject of his essay. Do you agree with his postmodern perspective? Why or why not?
4. Play a video game that has postmodern features and explain them according to the criteria presented in this chapter's *Spotlight on virtual reality*.

BOOKS AND BLOGS

Baudrillard, J. (1987). *The ecstasy of communication*. New York: Semiotext(e).

Cross, G. (2000). *An all-consuming century: Why commercialism won in modern America*. New York: Columbia University Press.

Featherstone, M. (1991). *Consumer culture and postmodernism*. London: Sage.

Jameson, F. (1991). *Postmodernism*. Durham NC: Duke University Press.

Root, D. (1996). *Cannibal culture: Art, appropriation & the commodification of difference*. Boulder CO: Westview Press.

http://www.postmodernvillage.com/html—current film reviews, journal articles, games, and other postmodern fascinations. Check it out.

http://www.elsewhere.org/pomo—a parody of the postmodern school of academic writing using a system for generating random text.

http://www.sklar.com/page/article/shadrach—a postmodern analysis of Beastie Boys' "Shadrach."

3 UNDERSTANDING ENTERTAINMENT AUDIENCES

*The mediatisation of developed societies disperses the
theatrical by inserting performance into everyday life.*
—Ben Kershaw

The essential feature of the audience experience as we see it today is that *everyone has
become an audience all the time*—it is constitutive of everyday life. This audience concept
is called **diffused audience**. The proliferation of entertainment in our lives has, for all
intents and purposes, merged mass and live audience functions into a continuum of
message reception. All messages all the time. In order to be well-received, messages must
entertain. We will refer to everyone who receives entertainment messages as active
makers of meaning who engage in watching or listening for pleasure. This diffused audience is the audiences of the twenty-first century. The level of pleasure audiences derive
from media, performance, sports, and other leisure activities is an indication of entertainment's social and psychological value. We need entertainment to maintain our feeling
of belonging and our feeling of well-being.

When we think about an audience, most of us visualize a group of people watching
something on a field, screen, or stage. But, like snowflakes, no two audiences are the
same, and most often they react differently, even to the same experience. Your grandmother may clap her hands over her ears when you put a hip-hop channel on Sirius radio,
a type of music you enjoy. And your mom might approve of the music but not the volume

Baaba Maal and his Senegalese dancers combine traditional African music with musical styles
from around the world at the Womad Festival in the U.K.

at which you have it set. Girls may scream at a scary movie, while boys may love the fright, and perhaps the opportunity to calm their frightened girlfriends.

Audience members appreciate performance, game, or travel experiences in unique ways, challenging marketers to interpret desires and reach expectations that satisfy their target audience. To understand audiences, we must first dissect them into groups we understand. This chapter will help you see how audiences are conceptualized for maximum understanding as we look at the nature of live and mediated audiences—who they are and what they want. Audiences are members of both groups and segments, yet we like to think of our own participation as individual. Audiences have value for their ability to make or break entertainment, and as such have great power in today's commercialized society. We begin by characterizing participants of all entertainment performances of live action.

Audiences as Participants

Entertainment is everywhere we want to be! In fact, entertainment is present in almost every sphere of human activity of global developed societies. As audiences of everyday performance, we constantly engage in a variety of activities that are akin to entertainment. The notion of performance-in-everyday-life conceptualizes all of society as theater in four ways.[1]

- We all pretend or role-play. In all our social activities, a particular illusion is created that is difficult to sustain outside that activity. When we're on a sailboat, we wear sailing clothing, use sailor jargon, and act the way we think sailors act.
- We all play separate roles and our roles change with the nature of the performance. When seas are calm, we play the socialite or the captain; when seas turn rough, we assume a role of serious navigator or vigilant crew member.
- Images of people in everyday life reveal performance as pervasive. We see people enjoying themselves in every aspect of our lives. Whether on shore or on the water, we act according to the role required.
- Mediated and live performances prevail at all times and are present in every aspect of our lives. Internet, television, and radio broadcasts invade the windy peace of sailing—nowhere can we avoid media.

Table 3.1 provides a partial list of audience and activity types found in everyday performance. Can you think of any other audience groups that are missing from this list?

It may be obvious from this list that most of our social and personal roles fall into a diffused audience category of some sort. Given the nature of capitalism, we all become audience members all of the time because we are constantly consuming some form of entertainment activity. And as we engage in a variety of spectacles, we are simultaneously performers and audiences. For instance, as tourists we perform consumption roles, buying up souvenirs and taking photographs of our travel experiences. At the same time, we are audiences for the entertainment provided by our hosts, such as theme parks, tours, demonstrations, and so forth.

Actual Audiences

Actual audiences can be differentiated according to the duration that they are involved with an entertainment activity and the degree of engagement they have with that activity.

Table 3.1 Performances in Everyday Life

Audience type	Consumption activities
Activists	protesting, speaking out
Constituents	voting
Consumers	shopping
Diners	eating out
Enthusiasts	membership in club sports and activism
Fans	idolizing film and rock stars or celebrities
Jurors	determining guilt or innocence
Listeners	enjoying radio and music
Members	clubbing or praying in a group
Mourners	attending a funeral
Participants	engaging in entertainment or activities
Patients	seeking medical help
Patrons	supporting the arts
Players	gaming and gambling
Readers	enjoying mystery and romance novels
Shoppers	browsing, buying
Students	learning, studying
Surfers	surfing the Internet, perusing channels
Tourists	sight-seeing, buying souvenirs
Travelers	flying, riding
Viewers	watching TV or film
Visitors	visiting theme parks, zoos, museums
Voyeurs	seeking pornography
Worshipers	embracing religion

Both elements are determinants of financial success or failure of entertainment events. Today's audience members have special characteristics that differentiate them from audiences of the past: autonomy and demassification.

Audience Autonomy Audience autonomy characterizes today's audience members. Once upon a time audiences were at the mercy of many entertainment providers. TV and radio audiences could choose from only a limited selection of programs offered at specific times. If you wanted to see or hear a specific program, you had to be sure to watch or listen at a specific time. If you wanted to watch or listen at 2 p.m., you had to make do with what was on at that time. Live entertainment was similarly limited by time and place. Thus, we all experienced the same entertainment, at the same time, en masse. Entertainment producers and programmers dictated the entertainment we could have and when we could have it.

Recently, however, control has shifted from entertainment producer to entertainment consumer. Audiences are no longer held hostage by the dictates of entertainment pro- grammers. Inventions such as the VCR gave audiences even more control so that today people can have almost any entertainment they desire when they desire it. They can program television systems to find, record, and play programs they want to watch. Entertainment offerings on the Internet are typically available 24 hours a day, and new search engine technology allows users to build tailored, individualized profiles that can be used to alert them to new content, such as web site postings or new music related to their own interests. Individuals are also not restricted by where they can access entertainment. They can enjoy movies, games, music, and the Internet not only in theaters, arcades, automobiles, offices, and living rooms but also on the bus or a park bench, thanks to high-quality resolution technology.

Demassification   Demassification refers to the development of specific genres for specific audience segments, as opposed to mass media designed for everyone. New forms of entertainment are increasingly individualized. For many years now, entertainment has been tailored to niche audiences. Music, movies, TV programs, magazines, video games, and nightclubs are all designed for specific groups of people. Simply by virtue of the increased number of entertainment options available at any given time or place, individuals have more control over their entertainment experiences, and these trends are likely to continue.

Music fans backstage with the Police band (second, third, and sixth from left) prior to their concert at the Cricket Wireless amphitheatre in San Diego in 2008

Look Who's Watching

Audience members form groups because of a merging of common interests. Rather than being defined traditionally according to their socio-economic background, new audiences function as *taste cultures*. **Taste cultures** are dependent upon entertainment products—outcomes of form, style, presentation, or genre that match the lifestyle of an audience segment. Rap music can be called a taste culture, gaining its identity from the music, fashion, and lifestyle of the genre. Within every taste culture, three types of audiences predominate. They are labeled as spectators, participants, and fans.

Audiences are both spectators and participants. As **spectators**, audiences are amused by actors and their props. Fans are spectators who watch athletes compete against one another. Spectators watch movies and TV to catch a glimpse of celebrities and stars. Spectators can also be *passive* listeners or watchers, or they can be active. Most of us have been audience members with an active role in determining the activity's outcome. We may cheer or boo live performance, and we may TiVo electronic content. Either way, we have the power to determine what we want to see and hear. And if we don't like what we see or hear, we turn it off.

As **participants**, we challenge opponents by playing games of skill and chance. As travelers, we participate in exploring the unfamiliar; as tourists we become actors in our

The Myth of Web 2.0 Non-Participation

THE CONSUMERS

Passively consuming content

Passively consuming content and post personalising it

THE SHARERS

PARTICIPATION—DEGREE OF RESONANCE IN THE CO-CREATIVE COMMUNITY

Forwarding and **sharing** content

THE CRITICS

CONTENT – YouTube Video, Podcast, Blog Posts, Flickr Images, etc.

Publically **rating** content

Publically **commenting** on content

THE EDITORS

Submitting content created by others

Editing content created by others incl. mashups

THE CREATORS

Submitting **original** content

TYPICAL ACTIVITY OF PARTICIPANTS IN THE CO-CREATIVE COMMUNITY

Indicative Number of People

Perceived Level of Influence

Low – Content Input into the Creative Community – High

Figure 3.1   Active Audiences

Source: © Gary Hayes. Personalizemedia.com 2007

own performances. Participants come in two forms, passive and active. Passive participants include symphony goers who experience the event as pure spectators. In contrast, active participants, such as skiers or golfers, personally affect the performance experience. Active participants often become fans, close followers of a team, musical group, film star, or performer. As shown in Figure 3.1 audiences are actively participating in media and entertainment creation.

Audiences are essential for the success of all types of performance. Without audiences, there would be no performance. Can you imagine scheduling a concert and no one coming? Attracting, engaging, and satisfying audiences are necessary activities for every aspect of entertainment. Yet, as important as audiences are, we don't understand as much about what motivates and affects audiences as we'd like to. Especially when we can't see them, such as in the case of mass media audiences—viewers, readers, and listeners. Because our knowledge about audiences is fragmented, the term itself has an abstract and debatable character. In this chapter, we discuss audiences as they evolved historically from *live* to *mass mediated* to *entertainment* audience segments. Then we look at new audience trends, the influence of audiences on program content, and audiences' impact on society.

Fans get an autograph from Brutus the Buckeye at an Ohio State football game

Characterizing Audiences

A new trend in **audience characterization** that is suitable for entertainment application is dependant upon the relationship between source and receiver of communication messages and assumes a differentiation of audience and purpose. Three models best describe this relationship: transmission model, ritual model, and attention model.[2]

- In the *transmission* model, audiences are seen as receivers of messages from communicators for the purpose of influence. Here, the audience is **a target** for meaning transfer typical of what takes place through education, public information, and advertising messages. In this relationship, the sender is trying to persuade the receiver to take action. Entertainers use this model to promote specific events.
- In the *ritual* model, communication is shared, increasing the commonality and close relationship between sender and receiver.[3] Here, audience members are essentially **participants**. Audiences are playful or morally committed. Hockey season ticket holders take up the ritual of attending, and are not dependent upon persuasive messages to create action. Entertainment communication is to provide schedule information, offer merchandise, and target fan blogs.
- With the *attention* model, the sender does not seek to transmit information, but simply to capture the attention of an audience. In this capacity, audience members are **spectators**, measured by ratings and box office receipts. Fame and celebrity results from this model where no meaning transfer takes place. Brad Pitt and Angelina Jolie capture viewer attention on entertainment programs and in films, and their attention can be measured and sold to advertisers. The entertainment business prefers audiences yielded by this model over the other two models.

So whether audiences are live or mediated, passive or active, they all engage in some form of experiential activity on a daily basis. Their role in influencing the direction of entertainment cannot be underestimated, and is discussed in the next section.

Audiences of Live Action and Performances

The oldest form of audience participation is viewing spectacles or live action. Our presentation begins with audiences who attend arts performances, such as opera, orchestral concerts, ballet, theater, circus, magic, and musical concerts. This section provides a look into audiences' motives and their value to providers of performing arts.

Before the advent of mass media, all audiences experienced entertainment live. Culture was transmitted orally, engaging people in active support or participation in all forms of entertainment. We call them **simple audiences** because it suggests "the persons within hearing" and a certain immediacy in the experience of being a member of an audience.[4] Simple audiences benefit from direct communication. Today we think of audiences as people who plan, attend, and enjoy live action performances such as concerts, plays, films, festivals, political meetings, public celebrations, carnivals, funerals, legal trials, religious events, and sports matches. These events deliver ceremonial or sacred qualities that attendees cannot obtain elsewhere. Contemporary ceremony involved in attending a theater performance, for instance, involves making reservations, dressing up, socializing during intermission, applauding after each act, and buying a souvenir program.

Communication between theatrical performers and audience is direct; the physical and social distance between them is also characteristic of what goes on in concerts, courtrooms, football games, and political meetings. This social separation is reinforced by the contrast between the status of performers and aura of performance—the stars and fans syndrome. Early researchers thought such social separation would produce passivity

Street parades highlight the Chinese New Year celebration in San Francisco

in live audiences similar to what we see from mass media audiences who become mesmerized by television commercials. Such an outcome was not forthcoming, mainly because of the exchange and engagement of meaning making that occurs between audience and performers during live forms of entertainment.

An audience is comprised of unique individuals. Yet, live audiences often behave as a single entity, arriving, clapping, laughing, and exiting together from assigned seats. Unlike mediated audiences who view, watch, or listen by themselves, live audiences depend upon social interaction for a substantial portion of the entertainment experience. Live audiences also occupy localized or specialized spaces dedicated to an activity, such as stadiums and theaters, which are reserved for the activity and sit vacant at other times. We call such venues *performance spaces*. They are most often public spaces, even when performances are by invitation only. The use of public space reduces audience–audience and audience–performer distances and enables a wide range of socio-economic groups to attend performances together.

Performance Consumption

Important for understanding live audiences is their role in consuming performance; that role revolves around what we call the **consumption system**. The system relevant for attending performing arts includes behavioral triggers, consumption motives, and consuming activities that are embedded in long-term memory and experiences of everyday lives. *Behavioral triggers* include such factors as:

- social class, occupation, ethnicity, gender identity, experience, involvement, and personality. For instance, a person's love of rock music with symphony is a taste typical of outgoing upper-middle-class baby boomers in affluent Western societies.[5]
- social interaction that occurs while attending, which include (1) the number of companions, (2) type of relationship between them, (3) content, frequency, and timing of

interaction, and (4) knowledge of similarity in tastes and preferences.[6] A person may attend with another person because of his/her in-depth knowledge of the performance form.

- attributes of performing arts, such as theater or opera.
- time, money, energy, health, mood, and so forth. An audience member may be relaxed because she has a reliable baby sitter during her theater date.

Consumption Motives

Research indicates that people have multiple **consumption motives** for attending performances. Some of those motives and desired consequences include:[7]

- *enrichment* motives such as emotional stimulation, intellectual enhancement, and experiencing extraordinary states of being. Getting an A in your mid-term exam is an example.
- *reduction* motives including a recovery of energy through relaxation and escapism from work and responsibilities. Kayaking is such a motive.
- *communion* motives that give the participant a sense of attachment with others, friendship, and connecting with celebrities. Joining a fraternity is an example.
- *distinction* motives such as feeling unique, experiencing the power of choice, feeling superior to others and comparing oneself to others through fashion or reaction to the performance. Driving a Porsche may be your way of feeling superior and experiencing a distinction motive.

How we consume live action involves five factors (made from observation of baseball spectators that views consumption as play[8]) that are useful for predicting consuming experiences of performance audiences:

- *acquiring* practice that helps audience members seek information such as a critic's review prior to attending; planning for future events such as buying a season subscription; making choices such as deciding to have dinner after a show.
- *experiencing* practice that helps audience members make sense of events such as the translation crawler presented during an Italian opera; passing judgment through personal assessment of the performance quality; appreciating a performance though emotional responses to it.
- *integrating* practices such as being an informed consumer by attending pre-concert talks; contributing to the performance through laughter or applause; personalizing the event for your own enjoyment.
- *self-expression* practices such as bonding with fellow audience members; making yourself distinctive by sitting in a box seat; exhibiting status by wearing expensive jewelry.
- *socializing* practices by sharing the experience with others during intermission; dancing with others at a rock concert or telling jokes after the show.

Audience Evolution   Attendance motivations may evolve and change as attendees become more avid audience members. Some consumers consume leisure conspicuously by using performance attendance to communicate status. Status of this type is associated with three types of effects:[9]

- *Veblen effects* (abnormal market behavior where consumers purchase the higher-priced goods) occur when one pays $400 to see Madonna in concert.

- *snob effects* occur when one acquires a scarce ticket to see Elton John perform in the Acropolis in Athens.
- *bandwagon effects* occur when a person attends a rave because everyone else is attending.

Sociologists study classical performance audiences and their lifestyles for their reasons to attend. Based on the premise that identity is derived from association, audiences frequent events that fit their desired social status. Ticket prices and expected attire have promoted self-selection by audiences who are attracted to status-driven entertainment. With the encroachment of popular culture into even the highest-brow performances however, audiences are becoming homogenized.

A unique combination of factors are involved in buying or consuming performance experiences. Each consumer responds to a particular aesthetic that lends to or prohibits enjoyment of a performance—some like classical concerts while others prefer to attend raves. Experiences are a result of multiple motives, often unconscious—attending an opera for its status may be an unconscious motive. Some consumers enjoy the ritual behavior that accompanies performance—formal attire and behavior are expected at opera performances. Attendance is often determined by situation-specific opportunities—short-run performances limit our attendance options. Experiences are strongly influenced by social interaction—post-performance conversation or intermission criticism are two occasions. Finally, recollections of events influence repeat consumption—if you enjoyed the event, you will probably attend another.

Live Action Fandom

Sport as entertainment is usually more closely tied to watching rather than playing. Not surprisingly, research suggests that people watch sports for many of the same reasons they enjoy other forms of entertainment. Table 3.2 presents eight basic motives, as identified by Wann, that fans have for watching sports. Although "entertainment value" is

Table 3.2 Fan Motivations for Watching Sports

Self-esteem enhancement	Fans are rewarded with feelings of accomplishment when their favorite players or teams are winning.
Diversion from everyday life	Watching sports is seen as a means of getting away from it all.
Entertainment value	Fans enjoy the drama and the uncertainty of sports.
Eustress	Sports provide fans with positive levels of arousal. It is exciting to the senses. It gets your adrenaline going.
Economic value	Some fans are motivated by the potential economic gains associated with gambling on sporting events.
Esthetic value	Sports are seen by many as a pure art form—people appreciate the beauty and "ballet" of athletic performances.
Need for affiliation	The need for belonging is satisfied by aligning with a sports team, particularly if important reference groups, such as friends and family, are also fans.
Family ties	Some fans feel sporting events can promote family togetherness by providing opportunities for families to spend time together.

Source: Adapted from Shank, M.D. (2002). *Sports marketing: A strategic perspective* (2nd. ed.). Upper Saddle River NJ: Prentice Hall, pp. 188–93

isolated as a single factor on this list, virtually all the motivation factors that are identified reflect general leisure or entertainment functions.

Although some individuals consider themselves general sports fans, most fans are more strongly devoted to certain sports than others. Why do some people prefer football or hockey, whereas others prefer golf or auto racing? Research suggests that differences in one's motivations for watching sports may explain differences in sports preferences. Some evidence suggests that individuals are motivated by esthetics, self-esteem, and economics. *Esthetically* motivated people express preferences for individual and non-aggressive sports, those motivated by *self-esteem* prefer team sports; and those motivated by *economics* preferred aggressive sports. Research also shows that men generally prefer more aggressive sports than women do.

Although sports preferences may be influenced by internal personality factors and other characteristics, they are also affected by external socio-logical influences. Individuals tend to reflect sports preferences that are con-sistent with the preferences of their family, friends, and local and national culture. Preferences are also shaped by situational factors, such as one's geographical location. For example, individuals who live near the water are more likely to show a preference for water sports. As with all industries, sports producers and marketers con-

International sports fans with their faces painted in country colors

duct extensive research on these factors so that they can better target and tailor their sporting events and products to appropriate audiences.

Sports lovers follow their teams with something akin to religious zeal, as evidenced not only by the amount of money they are willing to spend on game tickets and sports merchandise, but also by the quirky traditions and ritualistic behavior they exhibit at all levels of sports, from little leagues to the pros. Like followers of different religious denom-inations, fans for different teams worship according to their own unique traditions. They chant war cries and wear "lucky" caps. In Wisconsin, fans pledge team allegiance by adorning their heads with cheese slices. Fans around the world don war paint from head to toe in team colors. Dennis Perrin, author of *The American fan*, equates this **fanaticism** with primal behavior:

> In Indiana basketball tribalism is particularly extreme. So manic are the fans that one might view them as insects at a feast. . . . To sit in a crowded small-town gym as the boys run the floor is to experience the insect collective at fever pitch . . . and should the game go to overtime, the conscious mind fades and it is hours before one's mammal senses return.[10]

Athletes themselves have their own traditions. Consider some of the pre-game rituals of key NBA players. For Larry Bird such rituals meant locking his eyes on the retired number 4 jersey of Boston Bruins hero Bobby Orr hanging from the Boston Garden rafters while the national anthem played. For Bailey Howell it meant brewing a cup of tea and then sipping—pinkie extended—until the cup was empty. For Kareem Abdul-Jabbar it meant sitting by his locker and reading a book, often in the buff. At Florida State, football tradition includes taking a piece of sod from the opponent's football field following key victories and burying it in a cemetery next to the practice field.

Through their dedication and rituals, fans in a sense move beyond serving as mere spectators to become active participants. This participation makes them feel as though they are part of the team, and this sense of belonging enhances their enjoyment. Psychology offers several explanations for this phenomenon. According to social identity theory, people are motivated to behave in ways that will boost their self-esteem. It is reasoned that sports fans feel that they can get this boost by identifying with a sports team.

Fans identify with their team by *Basking in Reflective Glory (BIRGing)* and *Cutting Off Reflective Failures (CORFing)*. When our team wins, we like to bask or BIRG by proudly wearing team sweatshirts and displaying team posters. By identifying with winners, we feel that we are winners. When our team wins, "we win." In contrast, when our team loses, we CORF. Our rhetoric changes; "we" don't lose, "they" do. We disassociate ourselves from our team. When our team is struggling, we may also CORF by *blasting*, or criticizing and downgrading other teams. Sports fans tend to reflect *in-group, out-group biases*, where characteristics of the in-group (the fan's team) are automatically seen as good, and characteristics of the out-group (the competition) are automatically bad.

Fans also demonstrate a process called *deindividuation*, where people lose their self-awareness and have decreased concern for how those around them evaluate their actions. People seem to lose or change part of their identity, taking on the team identity when engrossed in sports. They are swept up in the moment and act as a group rather than as individuals. Among athletes, this loss of individualism can be advantageous because team members are willing to sacrifice their bodies for the good of the team. It is also in this state that mob violence or rioting may occur among both athletes and fans.

SPOTLIGHT ON FANDOM   Enthusiast, Fan, or Fanatic?[11]

Most Americans have experienced a sports spectacle. Although emotional reactions to sports vary, some sports enthusiasts experience hormonal surges and other physiological changes while watching games, much as athletes do. Self-esteem rises and falls with the game's score. Tracing the role of sports for society, scientists say that sports re-create the same emotions as tribal warfare did for our ancestors. Sports heroes have been cast as warriors and symbols of self. When the team gains respect for winning, the enthusiast who wears the team's shirt or hat shares in that respect.

Research indicates that people who are **highly identified** with their team show extreme arousal compared to the average fan. Men and women who are **diehard** fans are much more optimistic about their own sex appeal after a team victory. Teams love diehard fans for their support both emotionally and financially.

The role of spectators for sports teams is important because it determines the success or failure of a particular franchise over time. Building loyal enthusiasts (or fans) is an important function for sports marketers. To determine an individual attachment to a team and how ardently s/he roots for it, the following test is used in projects to determine fan behavior. Survey respondents report their levels of commitment by circling an appropriate number for each of the seven questions. Take the survey below to determine your level of sports enthusiasm.

Instructions

Name your favorite sports team _____.

Answer the following questions based on your feelings for the team named above. Circle the number for each item that best represents you.

1. How important to YOU is it that this team wins?

    Not important 1 2 3 4 5 6 7 8 Very important

2. How strongly do YOU see YOURSELF as a fan of this team?

    Not at all a fan 1 2 3 4 5 6 7 8 Very much a fan

3. How strongly do your FRIENDS see YOU as a fan of this team?

    Not at all a fan 1 2 3 4 5 6 7 8 Very much a fan

4. During the season, how closely do you follow this team via ANY of the following:

    (a) in person or on TV, (b) on the radio, and/or (c) TV news or a newspaper?

    Never 1 2 3 4 5 6 7 8 Almost every day

5. How important is being a fan of this team to YOU?

    Not important 1 2 3 4 5 6 7 8 Very important

6. How much do you dislike the greatest rivals of this team?

    Do not dislike 1 2 3 4 5 6 7 8 Dislike very much

7. How often do YOU display this team's name or insignia at your place of work, where you live, or on your clothing?

    Never 1 2 3 4 5 6 7 8 Always

Scoring

What does your score mean? Add up the total of your responses. A score below 18 is considered to be a low identification. Between 18 and 35 is moderate. Above 35 is considered "highly identified." From 49 to 56 is diehard.

Shoppers as Audience Members

A distant relative of live action is shopping, a live activity that requires audience participation. We usually think of shoppers as people who are looking to buy something for a good price. But since the advent of malls and megastores, shopping has become recreational. Its offshoot—browsing—is an activity that enhances purchase satisfaction. Shopping is often a social activity, offering a break from routine, sensory stimulation, exercise, amusement, and fantasy. People with time on their hands shop to relieve boredom and loneliness, to explore new products, and to meet friends. For many, the act of buying becomes a means of self-realization. The browsing and buying shopper becomes both audience and performer in the consumption spectacle.

Malls make browsing enjoyable and buying easy. Prices are firm and transactions are usually made with credit cards. Unlike shopping in malls and department stores, bargaining at swap meets or in bazaars is much more akin to what the buy-and-sell process is all about. In these venues, purchases are negotiated, and most of the challenge for shoppers lies in buying below the asking price. Most of us have experienced the triumphant feeling of bartering for bargains at a fair or garage sale. In countries like Mexico, India, Indonesia, and Turkey, shoppers can still enjoy the thrill of bartering for many of the goods for sale. I had the ultimate test during my encounter with Turkey's most skilled rug salesmen, and came away feeling satisfied with my negotiated price. Most Americans don't challenge the tagged or computerized price rung up on digital cash registers—we pay the asking price. Yet bargaining, the act of looking for bargains (also known as comparative shopping) has become this decade's most prolific source entertainment. A more thorough discussion of shopping and shoppers is in Chapter 16.

Mass Media Audiences

Mass media audiences do not interact with one another or with the performers, and are thus hidden from view. Mass audiences, then, are detached individuals, anonymous to each other but with their attention converging on something of interest outside their personal environment.[12] It's everyone on his/her own electronic device and never connecting on a personal basis.

Audience Issues

Two significant issues have surfaced recently that change the nature and activity of mediated audiences: **audience reception** and **audience involvement**.

Audience reception, formerly confined to fixed locations, now occurs via a plethora of devices created to deliver entertainment to audiences in every place and at all times. Broadband and wireless technology yield continuing access to a variety of entertainment formats. Think of how many ways you receive music, video, film, news, games, and information. Now think of all the places you can be when you receive these transmissions. Anticipating all the ways and places you will be challenges entertainment promoters trying to reach new and current audiences.

FLASH FACT

As teens continue to embrace social media, Internet content creation by teenagers grows, with 64 percent of online teenagers ages 12–17 engaging in at least one type of content creation, up from 57 percent of online teens in 2005. Content creation is not just about sharing creative output; it is also about participating in conversations fueled by that content. Nearly half (47 percent) of online teens have posted photos where others can see them, and 89 percent of those teens who post photos say that people comment on the images at least some of the time.

Source: Pew/Internet @ www.pewinternet.org, 2007

Audience involvement has changed from mere active enthusiasm to major determinants of programming outcomes. Audiences of video games and television fans are creators of plots, episodes, games, and their own short films. *Star Wars* fans have created hundreds of new episodes available on web sites. Teens create video games for major game developers, becoming more than simply players. Blogs and web sites like MySpace enable audiences to develop narrative for invisible readers worldwide.

SPOTLIGHT ON BASEBALL AUDIENCES   Show Us the Monkey

Football, basketball, hockey, and wrestling fans have all appeared to wholeheartedly embrace the new sportainment approach. In baseball, however, the response has been less enthusiastic. Although many diehard fans seem to prefer a more traditional game atmosphere, some critics argue that baseball is too outdated for contemporary audiences, who seek fast-paced action. Although baseball still maintains a reasonably strong fan base, professional teams continue to search for ways to increase support.

Disney applied some of its magic to the Anaheim Angels baseball team, with mixed results. Disney signed a deal to buy the Angels in 1996 for $140 million and then spent $90 million to renovate Anaheim Stadium. Edison signed on as a corporate sponsor with an agreement rumored to call for the company to pay Disney about $1.4 million for 20 years in exchange for its name on the stadium. Disney initiated its takeover with the slogan "Kiss your big 'A' goodbye," referring to the landmark big "A" marquee at the stadium.

Not surprisingly, the ballpark now has a family entertainment theme similar to Disneyland, which is located just a few minutes up the road. Gigantic bats and batting helmets frame the main entrance to Edison International Field, serving as an imposing backdrop for the games. The outfield is garnished with "Home Run Extravaganza," a landscaped fountain area resembling Disney's old West "Thunder Mountain" ride. Angels home runs are celebrated with fireworks, music, and 80-foot geysers. And when the kids grow fidgety in their seats, they can drag their parents out to "The Perfect Game Pavilion" beyond center field, where they can match their base-running speed to that of Angel Darin Erstad, try to hit a home run like Tim Salmon in a homer contest, or order up a peanut butter and jelly sandwich at the "Rookie Table Restaurant."

And, at first, these changes seemed to work. Headlines read "Disney's Magic Works on Angels"[13] and "Disney's Wonderful World: First-place Angels Aren't the Only Attraction at the Ballpark."[14] "It's awesome," nine-year-old Jason Anderson said between bites of a ketchup-dripping corn dog.[15] Of course, the Angels were winning then. And even so, not everyone was charmed by the Disney transformation. Disney's approach provides a stark contrast to the nearby Los Angeles Dodgers, who continue to host traditional ball games, playing organ music and selling Dodger dogs in their 1950s stadium. Many longtime Angels fans criticized the cheerleaders and rock music Disney offered as an alternative.

Then came the rally monkey. According to sportswriter Bill Shaikin, "The irony is delicious. Disney, the team owner that put cheerleaders and bands on the dugout roof and fake rocks in the outfield, finally found something to stir the interest of Angels fans, purely by accident. It is, well, a picture of a monkey jumping up and down."[16]

During an Angels game, all of the announcements, video clips, and between-inning entertainment are overseen by Rod Murray, Angels director of entertainment, and his staff. They prepare for each game as one would for a play. Everything is run according to a script, complete with dialogue for announcers and cues for music and video. The Angels are known for producing top-quality video clips, which are shown during the game, and each player has a theme song that is played as he comes up to bat. Baseball games, however, are unpredictable, so the crew must be flexible and creative.

The legend of the rally monkey began in June 2000 as the Angels were losing to the San Francisco Giants. Video crew members Dean Faulino and Jason Humes were working hard to whip up some crowd support. They found a video clip from the 1994 hit movie *Ace Ventura, Pet Detective*, starring Jim Carrey, that showed a monkey jumping up and down. They fixed the clip so it would run in a loop, superimposed the words "Rally Monkey" over it, and flashed it on the JumboTron. The Angels rallied, scoring two runs in the last inning to win, and the crowd went wild.

Fans began to demand the monkey, and the "Show me the monkey!" battle cry was born. The monkey became an Angels game regular, rallying the team to come-from-behind victories in 18 of their next 31 wins. To avoid copyright infringement, the Angels hired Katie, the capuchin monkey featured in *Friends*, to film a series of Rally Monkey promos. A master of mass merchandising, Disney did not anticipate fan demand for the monkey. Angels staff scrambled to find souvenir monkeys to sell at games. The first shipment of 96 stuffed monkeys sold out within hours. "We've been going crazy just trying to keep up with the demand," said Timothy Fisk, who was charged with the duty of locating wholesalers. "Our biggest problem is finding the exact one shown on the scoreboard."[17] Less than one month after the craze began, 3,500 toy monkeys had been sold at Edison Field. The Angels Rally Monkey shows that entertainment, particularly spontaneous entertainment like sports, can often be more of an art than a science. Even entertainment veterans like Disney may find it difficult to anticipate what audiences will enjoy.

Mass Media Audience Types

We also study the collective response to media. Some audience groups are studied as *interpretive communities*[18] that bring meaning through the environment in which messages are seen, read, or heard. Mystery novel readers, soap opera viewers, and talk show listeners are examples of interpretive communities of audiences. Interactive media have created "virtual communities" that function in much the same way as their interpretive counterparts. Audience participants of such communities take an active role in the mediated experience.

By considering mediated audiences in different ways, we are able to make some distinctions for entertainment considerations. One researcher distinguishes between three types of audiences.[19]

- Audience as a **group or a public**. Listeners of news radio are one such public.
- Audience as **gratification set.** These are audiences that form and re-form because of a particular preference—such as rock concerts. Such people with a particular need seek out media to satisfy that need. For example, reading tabloids for gossip about celebrities gratifies film fans. Gratification sets are driven by social status or by cultural categories, and as such are of primary interest to entertainment programmers.
- **Media audiences**. Particularly important for advertisers, media audiences are defined by **channel** (media delivery format such as television) or **content** (genre such as mystery), which refer to their roles as media consumers. Viewing audiences—as products of the media, channel or content—have immediate practical significance and clear market value.

Active and Passive Media Audiences

The degree of audience activity or passivity is also of interest to the mediated entertainment businesses. Mass audiences, such as viewers of advertising commercials, are thought to be **passive** because they are incapable of collective action. However, we know that viewers have the power to zap commercials and select programming, making them individually active. Audience actions provide feedback for media communicators, and interactive technology has enhanced the activity potential of mediated audiences.

Today we attribute varying levels of activity to all types of mediated audiences, casting aside the notion that people sit and take in information without the power to act for or against content. In fact, the instigation of TV viewer rating levels by concerned parents is a vivid indication of mass mediated audience activity. By understanding audiences as **active**, we acknowledge their power of choice in the competitive world of media entertainment programming.

TiVo and interactive technology have given media audiences not only the power to determine what they watch, but more importantly to control outcomes. *American Idol* and other reality-based shows rely on audience feedback to evaluate contestants and determine winners. The most significant trends in audience development are control and creativity; viewers take charge, dictate outcomes, and—most importantly—create new content as never before in the history of mediated entertainment.

SPOTLIGHT ON AN ETHICAL DILEMMA   Audiences as Culture Jammers

We know from past studies that audiences create their own interpretation of mass entertainment. The way in which logos and other symbols of commercial persuasion are subverted by disgruntled viewers is characterized as "semiotic democracy." People who are fed up with advertising often choose to ridicule ads, or they become oppositional and join the battle to redefine the ad's meaning.

An advertising campaign parodying the dairy industry's popular "Got Milk?" ads by the animal rights group People for the Ethical Treatment of Animals

Persuasive Games, an Atlanta-based company that creates online games, has come up with a game about Kinko's that can be billed as an anti-advergame. "Disaffected" puts the player in the role of employees forced to service customers under the particular incompetencies common to a Kinko's store. Six months after the game was developed in 2006, it had been downloaded more than 150,000 times. Obviously others have had a bad Kinko's experience!

Such skepticism about and mockery of commercial persuasion are not new, but online games ridiculing companies and brands are beginning to take center stage. Sometimes referred to as *brandalism, subvertising,* or *adbusting,* culture jamming may also be legally suspect. Anti-branding tactics may be vandalism or trademark infringements that break laws. In fact, such "semiotic disobedience" is actually an attempt to disobey the meaning of the sign (logo) itself by redefining its meaning.

For instance, the game called *McDonald's Videogame* lets players decide how much rain forest to clear in order to raise more cattle for slaughter. McDonald's golden arches, then, become symbols of ecological destruction rather than fast food. And the absolute™ brand becomes a symbol of death, as shown in the ad above.

So are these games legally protected parodies that facilitate cultural dialog, or are they blatant attempts to slander a protected trademark?

Source: Rob Walker's "Consumed" column in *The New York Times Magazine*, Sept. 3, 2006

What do you think?

Log on to adbusters.com and view some of the advertising parodies provided there. In your opinion, are these spoofs and the two games discussed above legally suspect, or are they simply a way to get back at advertisers? Defend your answer.

Media Choice Factors

Two factors that influence entertainment choices for audiences are spectacle and narcissism. Spectacle is the notion that everything in the world is treated as something to be attended.[20] Everything in the world is an event or a performance. As such, every object, event, and person is made to perform for those watching. This spectacle/performance paradigm[21] highlights the *dimensions of a diffused audience*:

* We spend most of our time consuming media of all types.
* Media constitute everyday life.
* Society is performative.
* People are increasingly narcissistic.

Acknowledging the importance of diffused audiences for entertainment, we focus on the impact audiences have on paid-for performance.

Spectacle Spectacle pervades life, the aim of which is to see and be seen. Spectacle has come to dominate leisure activities at work, home, and leisure. Since capitalism has commodified everything, whole areas of free time, private life, leisure, and personal expression are restructured around activities of consumption.[22] Our society is a consumer society where we gaze upon objects and services for sale. We long to possess much of what we see, and we view much of the world and its contents as if it can be owned. We are consumers of images. Our world is constantly becoming more estheticized, more like a cultural object that invites our gazes. Everything performs for a diffused audience; we are all involved in a symbolic world of spectacle. We are all looking at one another, and as such are conscious of people looking at us.

Narcissism Narcissism is the notion that people act as if they are being looked at, as if they are at center stage for some audience. The word narcissistic originated in the Greek myth of Narcissus who falls in love with his own reflection. Today, narcissism describes a personality type characteristic of people in Western societies, especially those in positions of influence. Constructed only by images others have, a narcissist cannot easily separate him or herself from others.

SPOTLIGHT ON NARCISSISM   Self-love as a Personality Type

- the tendency to live in the present with no sense of past or future
- dependence on others combined with a fear of such dependence
- worship of celebrity
- an inner emptiness
- a pseudo self-insight related to personal therapies and self-helps
- nervous self-deprecatory humor
- fiercely competitive yet fearful of competition
- decline of the spirit of play
- intensely acquisitive and demanding immediate gratification.

What do you think?

- *How many of these characteristics do you recognize in people you know? In yourself?*

Some of the attributes ascribed to a narcissistic personality type include:[23]

Some critics write of *a narcissistic society*[24] with a dedication to self-gratification that results in a projection of self into the world. Here, the self is central to a diffused audience. There is no boundary between self and the world of people and things, so what stands outside self is merely a reflection of self. Narcissism requires an active audience that reflects the self. The self is connected to an imagined performance and self becomes a performer under continual scrutiny. We are all watching and being watched. The importance of appearance and style links narcissism to performance. This phenomenon is evident in New Age contemporary spirituality that is founded on "self-development" and "getting in touch with our feelings." How many of us would rather look good than feel good?

The technology of *immersive theaters* and virtual reality now places audiences in a lifelike representation of the three-dimensional world, which is modeled after our narcissistic desires. Using the powers of ego, we are building a universe of simulation where imagination is in control. These technologies are places where human narcissism meets metaphysics—where our inflated selves, unable to reconcile ourselves to the real world, create imitation worlds that are better suited to our desires.[25] Tricks of art and technology enable audiences to participate in stories that results in "absolute fakes"[26] that are intended to be better than what they imitate. One visitor to Epcot Center suggests that it's more fun to experience different cultures in one safe location than to travel around the world in fear. The real danger is that audiences may come to prefer interaction with images to their real surroundings, interfering with their relationship to reality or even becoming sources of addiction.

Diffused Audiences

Diffused audiences, then, are constructed around the relationship of spectacle and narcissism. People, objects, and events are constituted as performances, which command audiences. Mutually reinforcing, spectacle and narcissism both demand and produce performances where people are seen as and see themselves as performers. We are constantly cast in the role of audience member in some form of entertainment. We define entertainment, then, as *any activity in which people participate for pleasure or amusement*. Often our roles shift, taking us from audience member to actor, host, producer, artist, and so forth. The activity created by shifting between audience member and performer occupies most of our time. The importance of the active audience to entertainment's success is precisely why we study audiences and why we need to understand the needs and motivations of ourselves and of others as we assume the role of audience member. The most important member roles in today's entertainment economy are discussed below for their impact on society.

Avatars like those used on virtual sites such as Second Life

Media Fans and Enthusiasts

Some media audience members become emotionally and psychologically attached to certain forms of entertainment or specific entertainers. Extremely devoted followers of a media star, performer, performance, or text are considered *media fans*. Occasionally people form attachments to screen or television stars and carry that relationship beyond the content of the film or show. Known as *para-social relationships*, these attachments relate to the degree of emotional involvement with a media person. One example is the bond created between a woman and the star of daytime soap opera. Fans of soap operas who form attachments to a specific star may fantasize about the person as if he or she were part of the viewer's life. Researchers measure para-social interaction to describe the degree of commitment that exists between television viewers with their favorite news persona.[27]

Enthusiasts are also people who engage in an organized form of audience participation. Certain characteristics distinguish them from fans: enthusiasts' activities are not based around media images and stars, and their activities are usually more organized.[28] Clubs, sports, and music generate dedication and support from enthusiasts. The distinction is based upon the type of entertainment rather than the level of support manifested by both fans and enthusiasts. Extreme dedication may evolve into a cult or subcultural activity typical of the "Deadheads," a group of followers of the 1960s musical group Grateful Dead, who could be readily identified by their tie-dyed shirts and "hippie"-style clothing. The entertainment industry courts fans and enthusiasts, as they are the audiences who support every type of leisure activity.

SPOTLIGHT ON FAME   In Search of Our 15 Minutes

Survivor Castaway winner and finalist at the CBS Panama Exile Island finale/reunion show in 2006

Few network shows have done more, both directly and indirectly, to give every American his or her now requisite 15 minutes of fame—and humiliation—than *Survivor*. Scott Herzog, contestant on *Survivor China*, wanted to be a contestant for global recognition.

For some audience members, the desire to be noticed, to walk into a room and have others care about what they're doing, is primary to their existence. Once considered a shallow motivation by psychologists, fame is the study focus of social scientists who are measuring its psychological effects and characterizing its devoted seekers. According to psychologist and author of *The Fame Motive*, fame-seeking behavior is rooted in a desire for social acceptance.

The urge to achieve social distinction is evident worldwide, even among people for whom prominence is neither accessible nor desirable. In media-

rich urban centers, the drive to stand out tends to be more oriented toward celebrity than in rural areas. Surveys in Chinese and German cities found that about 30 percent of adults reported regularly daydreaming about being famous; another 40 percent expected to get, in Andy Warhol's phrase, "their 15 minutes of fame."

Yet only a small percentage of people actually expect to get meaning out of fame. Some therapists have traced such longing for renown to lingering feelings of rejection or neglect. To feel like they are more than mere mortal animals, people try to view themselves as valuable contributors to the world. But research strongly suggests that aiming for a target as elusive as fame, which is dependent on the judgments of others, is psychologically treacherous. Witness reality television, which creates instant stars, then casts them into oblivion. For them and for most people, coming to grips with the realization that they are not going to be famous is a very difficult task indeed.

Source: Benedict Carey for the *New York Times*, Aug. 22, 2006, D1

What do you think?

- *What media contribute most to the preoccupation with fame?*
- *Define fame in your own words. Did your definition include a presumption that fame brings happiness? Historically, what indicators can you name that suggest otherwise?*

Audience Theory and Research

Mass audiences have only been studied seriously for the past 100 years, primarily since the advent of radio. These audiences are studied for the **effects** media have on them. Large media audiences are thought to be in control of their mediated experiences.[29] Mass audiences are studied in conjunction with mass communication theory and research. Expectancy-value theory is useful for understanding this large group.

Media effects theories help us to understand how media influence behavior. Effects are particularly important to psychologists concerned about television violence and programming aimed at children. Media affect both groups and individuals as they engage in mediated entertainment. A common effects theory is **uses and gratifications theory**, which is used to explain how people use media and what they expect from that usage. Research on individuals can be generalized to larger populations.

Meaning-oriented theories are used to understand how people interpret media. Scholars believe that messages contained in mass media have multiple meanings and are open to the interpretation of the individual viewer, listener, and reader. This approach is known as **reader response theory**. When two people watch a film and have different views from each other and from reviewers, differences are welcome. The film does not have a meaning of its own, only the meaning given to it by viewers and reviewers, regardless of how diverse or oppositional they might be.

Audience as Rating Point

As a tool for quantifying mediated audience, **rating systems** measure viewership. Television audiences are most valued for their viewing presence. Nielsen Rating systems measure who watches what shows. Programs with the largest audiences command the highest advertising revenues. Thus, successful networks and independent stations provide entertainment to please their audiences. Networks feed the masses with beverage spots and car commercials. Niche stations tempt smaller markets with medicines and exercise equipment. One thing we viewers can never forget is the reality of the bottom line. Programming has become a popularity contest, and the winning shows get the best commercials.

Measurement devices, while not theories, are necessary for determining numbers of viewers who watch or read media vehicles. Often referred to as "markets," media audiences are useful for economic analysis. Researchers use information about mediated audiences to measure sales, determine advertising reach, assess market opportunities, test products, and evaluate performance. Audience demographics are valuable for advertisers who must match audiences with brands and programming. Used with television, radio, newspapers, magazines, and the Internet, audience quantification is important for determining advertising rates. Since advertising is the primary revenue source for mass mediated entertainment, attracting large audiences is a very competitive business. In addition to audience size, audience satisfaction and trust are also measured and evaluated for use in program planning.

Nielsen and other syndicated research companies provide audience data to advertisers who make media buying decisions based upon numbers of people watching, reading, or using a particular medium. People meters are used to gather television audience information; hits are units of measure for the Internet.

In 2005, Nielsen/NetRatings combined panel and census-based measurement systems that are being used in Italy.[30] The new methodology links the panel with its site-centric solution that comes up with what NetRatings calls an "Integrated Audience" number that delivers detailed reach and frequency metrics, audience demographic profiles, and other metrics for pre- and post-campaign analysis tools. There has long been a debate about the precision of each approach to audience measurement.

Entertainment Audience Research

Unless we know what people want, what they'll support, and how loyal they are, we cannot deliver the best sources of entertainment. Sociologists, anthropologists, and humanistic marketplace researchers[31] are currently involved in trying to understand audience members as entertainment consumers. Watching people as they enjoy media and as they browse store aisles is a primary activity for consumer researchers. Some current trends are outlined here.

Watching People Watch and Listen   Researchers who study entertainment audiences attempt to "get inside" the heads of viewers by watching them as they interact with media and with performance. Called ethnographic research, this type of study investigates how people in a natural viewing environment watch and listen to entertainment.[32] Watching people's viewing habits over an extended period of time in the homes of 200 families in Wisconsin and California, one researcher[33] found that people use TV for both informational resources and personal relationships that facilitate communication. Some families talked about programs and often interacted during shared viewing times. Others watched in isolation, each watching his or her own set in a separate viewing space. As a result of such studies, we know quite a bit about the effects of TV on viewers, and particularly about the impact TV violence has on children.

The results of audience research tell us that performance interactions involve complex symbolic work on the part of watchers, viewers, and listeners themselves. Yet researchers disagree on how best to proceed in investigating the audience. Some are interested in viewing content itself.[34] Others are concerned with what made certain entertainment forms popular.[35] Entertainment media remain a crucial field of study because people construct a sense of identity and enter into relations with others through their various interactions with communicative forms. And this is important because of the enthusiastic engagements of ordinary members of the public. In addition, audience theory helps to uphold the rights of people to take part in popular commercial cultures, and to hold up the capacity of people to think against the grain of media texts. Our pleasurable and private engagements are an important component of modern living and have a symbolic rather than informational focus. Entertainment, researchers have found, allows us to participate in a plurality of popular narratives out of which we construct a sense of selfhood and imagined community.[36]

Watching People Spend   As entertainment flourishes, audiences are studied for their ability to generate revenue. Rather than focusing on how people interact with performance, marketers want to understand why people choose a particular type of entertainment for the purposes of audience solicitation. As consumers of popular culture, audiences as *market segments* are sought-after commodities by producers of every type of entertainment available around the world today. Entertainment marketers tend to view audiences as spectators whose attention is captured, measured, and cashable in the form of subscriptions, box office receipts, and payments from advertisers.[37]

Marketers often define audiences as targets in terms of their lifestyle; in doing so they tend to construct ready-made identities that may or may not reflect reality. Sailing is an example of a consumer lifestyle. Under conditions of intense competition for audiences, marketers may attempt to control their relationships with those audiences using promotional incentives. Film trailers, for instance, are edited to attract specific audiences who may be disappointed at the actual film content that was not portrayed in a particular trailer.

A market audience is conceived as:[38]

- a **commodity**, a commercial transaction
- **numbers** yielding revenues
- **spectators** whose attention-giving or withholding is the key feature of their relationship to content.

The current meaning of the concept of audience as market is extended to consist of buyers and users of entertainment and technology as much as receivers of messages.[39] And with this shift comes the expansion of power to entertainment consumers. Audiences as market segments are a powerful influence on entertainment content because of their ability to make or break specific entertainment entitics. Entertainment users today have no particular loyalty to their entertainment suppliers, who

Lifestyle segmentation is used by advertisers to target consumers of outdoor recreation

are just agencies for making connections personally chosen by individual consumers. Given the number of messages about entertainment options sent to consumers daily, audiences have more chance to escape exposure to unwanted information marketers send. Much greater ingenuity is now required to catch attention and to engage an audience than every before.

Audience Preferences

Knowing about what consumers think, need, and want is crucial for successful marketing, and gathering that information is the business of large research-oriented companies. They poll audiences to determine whom they like so advertisers can use celebrities in all forms of entertainment to sell branded products. Image transfer—using a celebrity's image to transfer to a brand—is a practice regularly used by advertisers. In order to match the celebrity with the brand, researchers query audiences about their celebrity preferences, which are measured and matched with specific demographics and target segments.

Because celebrities sell, consumer ratings are important for creating successful campaigns. The Davie Brown Index (DBI) determines a celebrity's ability to influence brand affinity and consumer purchase intent. The company uses a database of 1.5 million members of their domestic research panel to rate over 1,700 celebrities on their relevance to a brand's image, awareness, and appeal to gage celebrity influence on consumer buying behavior.

Celebrity Index scores are based on several metrics, including appeal, aspiration, breakthrough, endorsement, influence, trust, and trendsetter.[40] By combining the DBI score with consumer awareness and average attractiveness score, advertisers can

Table 3.3 Consumer Celebrity Awareness (%)

Celebrity	DBI	Consumer awareness	Average attribute score
Donald Trump	74.2	83.2	60.8
Paris Hilton	69.8	82.7	50.5
Sean "Diddy" Combs	60.4	60.9	59.7

determine who best suits the brand they want to advertise. For instance, the three celebrities in Table 3.3 are compared for their general appeal. We see that, although Paris Hilton has an 82 percent consumer awareness score, she ranks low in attractiveness to consumers. So advertisers are not likely to have her endorse products where trust and credibility are issues. The index also rates video game characters and superheroes. Game characters Mario and Pac Man both had high consumer awareness—in fact Mario scored higher (95 percent) in appeal than Matt Damon and Michael Jordan, and Pac Man (94 percent) was more appealing than Ben Affleck![41] Spiderman was voted most loved superhero.

Forbes Magazine is also in the rating business, collecting opinions from millions of readers on line. In June 2008, its top ten list of most popular celebrities from all fields included: Oprah (talk show host), Tiger Woods (golfer), Angelina Jolie (actor), Beyonce Knowles (singer), David Beckham (soccer player), Johnny Depp (three Oscars for acting), Jay-Z (singer), Police (1970s rock group), J.K. Rowling (author), and Brad Pitt (actor). *Forbes* also provides an Infamy Index based on the amount of press coverage received. In 2008, most press coverage for scandal or inappropriate behavior went to Britney Spears (behavior),

Britney Spears received the most press coverage in 2007

Michael Veck (fraud), Roger Clemens (steroids), Eliot Spitzer (immorality), and Rev. Jeremiah Wright (inflammatory speech). Advertisers steer clear of anyone who scores high in the Infamy Index for obvious reasons.

In today's era of human billboards, determining where the star ends and the product and pitch begin is hardly possible. And the more a brand is seen in association with a popular celebrity, the more audience members and consumers allow lines to blur between brand and its star-studded associations. The hidden element—padding the product cost to cover expenses for celebrity endorsements—is mostly overlooked by those of us who embrace the notion of meaning transfer when purchasing products.

Audience Segments

Marketers view audiences in terms of their ability to bring revenue to a performance or venue. The classification process is called *segmentation*. Although there are many different ways to segment audiences—demographic, psychographic, geographic, and behavioral segments—marketers prefer to aggregate audiences into three consumer groups: present customers, competitive customers, and emerging users.[42] For each group, a special combination of messages and incentives about the performance is prepared to attract them to a specific event.

Building Profiles

Measuring audience reaction to advertising, such as gender differences in computer use, is an offshoot of a new technology by a company that specializes in tracking and analyzing remote control clicking behavior on interactive TV to customize advertising. By gathering patterns of use, the company builds profiles called "silhouettes" of the users based on the ads they respond to. This new biometric monitoring penetrated 40 percent of American households in 2005, and was accompanied by $11 billion in advertising. Traditional demographic targeting used by advertisers will be rendered obsolete when this new technology enables cable advertisers to make specific targeting strategies based on actual consumer use.

Current high-speed shifts in media consumption and consumer behavior are nothing sort of spectacular. Digital advertising has exploded. Social networking sites are all the rage as marketers look to obtain eyeballs in places they've never gone before. The effect of media convergence is clear—marketers are now empowered to get granular with their audiences and track them across an ever-expanding group of media platforms. One platform is the Internet. In the online world, consumers now essentially determine their own segmentation based on individualized habits, determined through behavioral targeting. Behavioral targeting enables consumers' online browsing habits to drive which ads they see. It is also an additional way for marketers to target users further down the purchasing funnel and helps marketers better predict how users will act—thus making advertising efforts more cost effective.

Bob Dylan performs on stage in London

The revelation and acceptance of both media convergence and behavioral targeting can help savvy marketers make appropriate marketing decisions and avoid marketing mishaps. Since consumers are now in control, generating their own content, time-shifting TV programming with their DVRs and initiating (or not) video ads online, marketers need to segment their audience with increased efficiency.

Audience Aggregates

Here is an example of how segmentation works for marketers. A new play with music by Sting is opening at a Performing Arts Center. To promote the event, three separate strategies are developed, one for each audience aggregate.

- *Present customers*—those who are season ticket holders or regular theater-goers—are sent an informational piece announcing the performance.
- For *competitive customers*—those who attend other forms of entertainment—promotional trailers are developed and aired on television as advertisements.

Incentives, such as group discounts, first-time vouchers, and so forth, are used to entice members of this audience segment to try a performance at the Arts Center.

• *New and emerging customers*—on-going programs are developed to introduce this audience to theater and develop them into loyal audience members.

By using informational messages for present customers, incentives for competitive customers, and a combination of messages and incentives for emerging customers, marketers can allocate promotional resources in an efficient way to maximize audience attendance. This planning strategy, called Integrated Brand Communication, is successful for promoting products as well as entertainment performances and venues. As a marketing director, would you allocate the biggest budget to retaining current customers or developing new ones? Why?

Because audience expectations are high and because they demand a quality product, performance producers must develop brand equity and establish lasting relationships with consumers in much the same fashion as product manufacturers have had to do to develop loyalty from their consumers. Although the concept of audience has changed, audiences' importance to the entertainment business continues to increase. Let's face it, marketing has become the biggest of businesses. Its impact on our everyday lives is profound, and to become informed audiences, we must understand the nature of entertainment in all of its forms.

SPOTLIGHT ON VALUES AND LIFESTYLES   Consumer Lifestyles as Audience Segments

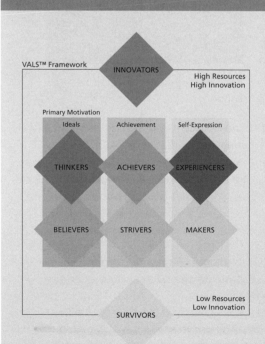

Marketers categorize consumers according to their values and lifestyles using a system developed by SRI Consulting Business Intelligence in California. Its Values And LifeStyles (VALS) system, developed for North America, segments consumers by self-orientation and resource dimensions. There are three self-orientations. **Ideal-oriented** consumers are guided in their choices by abstract, idealized criteria rather than by feelings or desire for approval and opinions of others. **Achievement-oriented** consumers look for products and services that demonstrate success to their peers. **Self-expression-oriented** consumers are guided by a desire for social or physical activity, variety, and risk taking.

Each of eight resource segments specify distinct attitudes, behaviors, and decision-making patterns. Those segments and their application for entertainment audiences are presented here.

Figure 3.2   SRI's VALS system

Innovators are successful, sophisticated, take-charge people with high self-esteem. Because they have such abundant resources, they exhibit all three primary motivations in varying degrees. They are change leaders and are the most receptive to new ideas and technologies. Innovators have season tickets in box seats and take exotic trips and safaris.

Thinkers are motivated by ideals. They are mature, satisfied, comfortable, and reflective people who value order, knowledge, and responsibility. They tend to be well educated and actively seek out information in the decision-making process. Thinkers attend operas and orchestral concerts and are ecotourists.

Motivated by the desire for achievement, **Achievers** have goal-oriented lifestyles and a deep commitment to career and family. Their social lives reflect this focus and are structured around family, their place of worship, and work. Achievers live conventional lives, are politically conservative, and respect authority and the status quo. Image is important, and they aspire to reflect the best image. Achievers prefer sitting in seats to sporting events where they can be seen.

Experiencers are motivated by self-expression. As young, enthusiastic, and impulsive consumers, Experiencers quickly become enthusiastic about new possibilities but are equally quick to cool. They seek variety and excitement, savoring the new, the offbeat, and the risky. Their energy finds an outlet in exercise, sports, outdoor recreation, and social activities. Experiencers like adventure travel and have avatars on Second Life.

Like Thinkers, **Believers** are motivated by ideals. They are conservative, conventional people with concrete beliefs based on traditional, established codes: family, religion, community, and the nation. Believers express moral codes that are deeply rooted and literally interpreted. They follow established routines, organized in large part around home, family, community, and social or religious organizations to which they belong. Believers watch network TV and attend PG-rated movies.

Strivers are trendy and fun loving. Because they are motivated by achievement, Strivers are concerned about the opinions and approval of others. Money defines success for Strivers, who don't have enough of it to meet their desires. Strivers take budget cruises and attend local band concerts.

Makers are motivated by self-expression. They express themselves and experience the world by working on it—building a house, raising children, fixing a car, or canning vegetables—and have enough skill and energy to carry out their projects successfully. Makers are practical people who have constructive skills and value self-sufficiency. Makers go camping in national parks and play in their own bands.

Survivors live narrowly focused lives. With few resources with which to cope, they often believe that the world is changing too quickly. They are comfortable with the familiar and are primarily concerned with safety and security. They are loyal to favorite brands, especially if they can purchase them at a discount. Free outdoor concerts are attractive forms of entertainment for Survivors.

Source: SRI Consulting Business Intelligence, Menlo Park CA

What do you think?

- *How does the VALS system help entertainment marketers to reach specific audiences?*
- *Go to www.sric-bi.com/vals/presurvey and take the survey. In which segment did you place? Does that segment description above fit you?*
- *What are the limitations of such a system for reaching audiences?*

Newest Audience Segment

One group, believed by some people in the entertainment industry to be the most powerful audience segment of all, is called the **prosumers**. This group is turning the heads of entertainment marketers worldwide. Euro RSCG, a big international agency, completed a nine-country study of prosumers that said prosumers can represent 20 percent or so of any particular group or audience segment. They can be found everywhere, are at the vanguard of consumerism, and what they say to their friends and colleagues about brands and experiences tends to become mainstream 6–18 months later. They also vary by category: a sports prosumer, for instance, will not necessarily be a prosumer of music.

Prosumers are creative consumers

Prosumers—producing consumers—often reject traditional ads and invariably use the Internet to research what they are going to buy and how much they are going to pay for it. Half of prosumers distrust companies and products they cannot find on the Internet. If they want to influence prosumers, companies have to be extremely open about providing information.

Further, marketing to the prosumer has taken on conflicting spins: the business sector sees the prosumer as a means of offering a wider range of products and services, whereas activists see the prosumer as having greater independence from the mainstream economy. Either way, prosumers present a challenge for marketers of entertainment and experiences.

The *cluetrain manifesto* (a futurist publication) noted that "markets are conversations" with the new economy "moving from passive consumers . . . to active prosumers." For instance, Amazon.com emerged as an e-commerce leader, partly because of of its ability

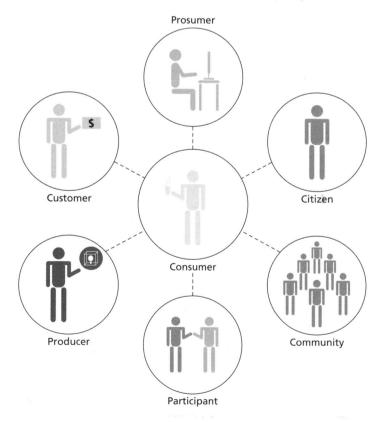

Figure 3.3 Prosumers: Being Prosumers means that Audience Members are Part Consumer and Part Producer

Source: http://dasmano.typepad.com/logic_emotion/2007/12/index.html

to construct customer relations as conversations rather than simple, one-time sales.[43] The emergence of producer consumer and the rise of the Consumer-to-Consumer (C2C) economy has been enabled by easier access to the Internet (open source software, blogs, message boards, and so on) and the availability of selling forums (eBay, for example).[44] To accommodate prosumers, entertainment marketers must establish and maintain a dialog with audiences that provides more than a simple schedule of coming attractions.

FADE TO BLACK

Entertainment audiences, then, are groups of people who constantly engage in message exchange and gain pleasure from using entertainment in a variety of everyday contexts. They have evolved from simple, direct association with the performers into isolated masses of media spectators. As entertainment and media pervade our society, audiences assume different roles and become involved in performance once again. Only this time audience members have dual roles, that of performer and of audience. The diffusion of roles enables us to be participants in the spectacle of life.

Generally, we may characterize the main dimensions of entertainment audiences by their:[45]

- degree of activity or passivity
- degree of interactivity
- size and duration (how many and for how long)
- locatedness in space (where they encounter an event)
- group character or cultural identity
- heterogeneity of composition
- social relations between sender and receiver
- message vs. social/behavioral definition of situation
- degree of social presence.

Because we are all audiences of some form of entertainment, we have experienced the joys and disappointments inherent in all of its manifestations. By paying attention to audience needs and wants, we can learn how to provide entertainment experiences that are enriching and satisfying. Through audience study, we can also begin to understand how to attract and keep loyal participants in all types of entertainment spectacle.

A CLOSER LOOK AT GROUPS   The Straight Edge Subculture

Music has become a powerful social influence today, and many subcultures have developed as a response to societal events that confuse or dismay them. One such group, the Straight Edge movement, began as a sub-creation of the punk rock music scene and has become a global phenomenon.

Straight Edge is a group, scene, and subculture very much like any other; it provides identity for members through self-expression, lyrics, tattoos, signs, symbols, and ideology. One symbol is the letter X, which resulted from attending punk rock concerts where alcohol was served. Establishments drew a large

While we're screaming for attention
No one told
That's all we want.

As the song ("As the Line Between Machinery and Humanity Blurs," written by a Straight Edge band Atreyu) states, this youth culture doesn't want to be controlled, babysat, or mediated by television; it has grown tired of the cold mechanical nature and idealistic images of today's media.

black X on the tops of the hands of adolescents to signify their under-age status to servers. Over time, X emerged as a symbol of solidarity among these rockers who chose not to drink. Today the X is displayed in numerous forms on clothing, on hands, and in band logos. The symbol identifies the community and gives concert-goers a sense of belonging and identity. Members also form their identity through tattoos and piercing, which serve as symbols of their devotion to the edge. By transforming their lives into artwork, Edgers become living symbols of their own identity. According to one 22-year-old Edger from Southern California, piercings help remind him that he is in control of his own life at all times, and they "help keep things in proper order."

Straight Edgers describe their culture as a way of life: a longing for uniqueness and a strong desire to be heard. Straight Edge is about enthusiasm of beliefs, integrity, and individual involvement rather than natural talents or inherent traits. Members live a clean lifestyle without drugs, smoking, and sex; many are vegans or vegetarians. A web site (https://www.myessays.com/details.php?eid=5345) explains that Straight Edge is not an Internet phenomenon; it is hardcore, and it is about music. It's about fellowship and about being drug free. Members agree: the prevailing theme for this lifestyle is that death, dying, and destruction of integrity in this world have forced a need for positivism. Adolescents enter the scene to escape realities and harshness of the world and reject forms of addiction as an avenue of escape. Their philosophy is depicted in H2O's 2002 song, "All We Want":

> *And that's all we want*
> *Is to be wanted*
> *No one told*
> *And the kids are going crazy now*

Small, grassroots, or garage labels organize the work of promoting, selling, and publicizing their own releases. Straight Edgers themselves typically run independent hardcore music labels; they call these labels DIY, "do it yourself." These vehicles provide the only acceptable way to produce CDs and make them available to the hardcore scene. Victory Records, Indecision Records, and Equal Vision Records are the three largest and most influential independent labels of the past decade.

All DIY record labels use fan zines to advertise and get the word out; they consist of band interviews, CD reviews, and record label advertisements. Content includes music, philosophy, attitudes, vegetarian recipes, and animal rights topics. Distributed to local record stores and concert venues, these zines are advertising supported and free to readers. *Maximum Rock & Roll*, a printed extension of a punk radio show, focuses on scene reports and advertisements for record companies. Such fan zines are important for transmitting the Straight Edge culture to its audience.

Internet-based web zines are also popular, allowing bands to directly communicate with their audience with publicity and venue concert listings. The site www.revhq.com provides an extensive catalog of Straight Edge CDs and merchandise through mail order.

Source: Michelle Weber, graduate student, California State University, Fullerton, 2005

What do you think?

- *What symbols do members of this subculture use to communicate with one another?*
- *Would you describe the Straight Edgers as a cult or a fan community? Why?*

DISCUSSION AND REVIEW

1. Explain the difference between the audience of a commercial for Pepsi and the audience attending a concert in terms of active vs. passive attention. Are both activities sources of entertainment? Why or why not?
2. Compare and contrast audiences of rock concerts with those who probably attend an operatic performance using the following dimensions: degree of activity or passivity, event location, group character, social relations between audience and performer, and performance message. In which dimension is the most distinctive difference between the two groups?
3. In what major ways do football fans and football enthusiasts differ? Which group poses a potential threat to other audience members? Why?
4. What are the main differences between media audiences and audiences of live performances? What role does social interaction play for each type of audience?
5. What role do prosumers play in the way audiences experience media? Give three examples of how prosumers can influence or create content intended for viewers.

EXERCISES

1. Record the number of audience participation activities in which you engage during a 48-hour time period as listed in Table 3.1. From your record, develop a description of the term audience as it applies to your activities. How well does your definition fit into the chapter discussion of entertainment audiences?
2. Audiences who vote for contestants on programs such as *American Idol* are much more involved than past active audience members. After going online to vote for your favorite performer in a current version of *American Idol,* write a definition of an involved audience. How well does your definition fit into the chapter discussion of entertainment audiences?
3. Go online and find the equivalent of a VALS system from Japan, the U.K., or Germany. What can you determine from the differences in the two systems? How do marketers of entertainment use these systems to promote experiences?

BOOKS AND BLOGS

Ang, I. (1985). *Watching* Dallas: *Soap opera and the melodramatic imagination.* London: Routledge.
Fiske, J. (1987). *Television culture: Popular pleasures and politics.* London: Methuen.
Gray, A. (1992). *Video playtime.* London: Routledge.
Jenkins, H. (2006). *Fans, bloggers and gamers: Exploring participatory culture.* New York: NYU Press.
Leitch, W. (2008). *God save the fan: How preening sportscasters, athletes and convicted quarterbacks have taken the fun out of sports.* New York: Harper Collins.
Ross, K. and Nightengale, V. (2003). *Media and audiences: New perspectives.* London: Open University Press.
Sayre, S. (2008). *Entertainment marketing and communication: Selling branded performances, people and places.* Upper Saddle River NJ: Prentice-Hall.
www.audiences.blogspot.com—This blog is about the intersection of tech-enabled social networking and emerging media audiences.
www.personalizemedia.com—discussions of our digital, immersive, and evolving media worlds.
www.nielsenmedia.com—defines the global standard in online audience measurement.
www.sportsfanatics247.com—a social networking site for sports fans.

RAMA AND STORYTELLING

The office of drama is to exercise, possibly to exhaust, human emotions. The purpose of comedy is to tickle those emotions into an expression of light relief; of tragedy, to wound them and bring the relief of tears. Disgust and terror are the other points of the compass.
—Laurence Olivier[1]

Sigmund Freud maintained that humankind's mental life began in fantasy; the oldest primary mental process was the pleasure-pain principle described as the "waking tendency to shut out painful experiences."[2] The *pleasure principle* dictates that we strive to seek pleasure and to avoid pain. It seems reasonable to assume, then, that an important criterion for entertainment is to bring pleasure. Many forms of entertainment bring direct pleasure; going to a movie, a ballgame, or an amusement park might all result in pleasure. Yet many people seem to be entertained by experiences that, at least at first glance, would seem far from pleasurable—long, painful sports workouts or movies that bring tears of sadness or screams of terror. What is it about these experiences that makes them entertaining?

Consider another approach. What makes something entertaining rather than just simply interesting? Compare a television sitcom or drama to a documentary or a classroom lecture. Often (we hope) you might find a lecture interesting, but is it entertaining? Have you ever heard a lecture or speech that was not just interesting, but also entertaining? If so, think of what made it entertaining. You may recall a lecture that was really inspirational, shocking, or funny—one that made you feel like your head, heart, or gut was going to burst. The key word here is *feel*. We feel happy when we win a game, perhaps angry or upset when we lose one. We may feel scared when we see a horror film and sad when we hear "that song." Interesting experiences or information are often designed to make us *think* but, with entertaining experiences, a more significant emphasis seems to be placed on making us *feel*. And, to make us feel, entertainers create drama.

Dramatic Formula

Drama is the driving force of many forms of entertainment. Genres such as suspense, tragedy, comedy, and mystery are typically considered to be specialized forms of drama. Although dramatic genres are traditionally associated with books, films, TV programs, and live performances, elements of drama can be found in most forms of entertainment, from video games and sporting events to music and dancing. Thus, it might be argued that good entertainment hinges on good drama.

According to Webster's dictionary, drama creates "a state, situation, or series of events involving intense conflict of forces."[3] These events enable audiences to experience the entire range of human emotions. Drama produces conflict and its resolution by depicting events that affect the welfare of dramatic characters: the protagonists (good guys) and antagonists (bad guys). The events that are depicted create a narrative or story in which good and bad things happen to different characters. As audiences witness these events, they form judgments about the characters and events that transpire. They may love some characters and events and hate others.

According to a **disposition theory of drama**, our reactions to dramatic events depend on our opinions about the characters involved.[4] We feel good when good things happen to characters we like and when bad things happen to characters we dislike. Conversely, we experience negative emotions when bad things happen to characters we like and when good things happen to those we dislike. A drama must include both "lovable" and "hate-able" characters, and audiences may feel amused, sad, terrified, angry, excited, or triumphant depending upon what happens to whom. Thus, a winning dramatic formula relies on the strategic use of character and story development to manipulate audience emotions. This basic formula has proven to be successful throughout the ages. In Roman and Greek drama, for example, masks were used for the portrayal of characters. Each mask had its own shape and color to denote the character or emotion being depicted. The most well-known of these are the masks of Comedy and Tragedy, which still symbolize drama today. One measure of the quality of a dramatic presentation, then, is its ability to evoke desired emotional reactions from its audiences.

Drama relies on character and story development to manipulate audience emotions

One common emotional reaction to drama—whether found in a book, comedy sketch, or ballgame—is suspense. **Suspense** is the emotional experience of anticipation and uncertainty about upcoming events. Thus, suspense occurs before the audience is certain about the final outcome. As the outcome is revealed, the audience's emotional state changes to feelings such as joy or sorrow. Uncertainty will trigger suspense, however, only if the audience cares about the fate of the characters involved.

Do we feel with or for dramatic characters?

This necessity raises an interesting question. Why do audiences care about the welfare of dramatic characters, particularly fictional characters? Dolf Zillmann proposed two mechanisms by which audiences relate to dramatic characters.[5] The first mechanism is **identification**. Audiences begin to identify with protagonists so that they feel what the protagonist feels to the point where they almost believe they are the protagonists. The notion of identification is often criticized, however, because cues often prevent the audience from feeling as the protagonist does. For example, the protagonist walking through the forest may feel peaceful, but the audience who sees the monster lurking behind the tree and hears the scary music feels afraid.

Another proposed mechanism is **empathy**. Audiences are thought to feel for, rather than with, dramatic characters. Onlookers feel happy and triumphant for the protagonist when things go well, and they feel scared, sad, or angry when things are going poorly.

Positive feelings for the protagonist trigger hope and happiness for the character's good fortune and distress for the character's misfortune. Conversely, audiences should feel counter-empathy for the antagonist, resulting in distress regarding the character's triumphs and pleasure for the character's demise.

Most audiences are familiar with the standard three-act "boy meets girl; boy loses girl; boy wins girl back" dramatic plot. Story lines can be varied for different genres by substituting "girl" or "boy" with "life-threatening illness," "secret military jet," or "gruesome space alien," but the basic formula remains the same. In the first act the characters are introduced; in the second act the major conflict emerges sprinkled with minor conflicts; and in the third act the conflicts are resolved. It is not difficult to understand why audiences would find empathizing with feelings of love, joy, and triumph entertaining, but what is entertaining about suspense and conflict? Or, in simpler terms, why must the boy lose the girl at all? Imagine a drama in which a boy simply meets a girl and they live happily ever after. Sound entertaining? Probably not. Conflict and uncertainty are the essence of drama. That is what makes drama exciting and interesting. In life, we often find that hard-fought victories are more enjoyable than those that come easily. Our enjoyment of dramatic representations of such victories is no different. There are many theories that attempt to explain exactly why audiences find drama and suspense so appealing.

Elements of Story and Drama

Many theorists have elaborated on this simply story format, outlining detailed frameworks and elements that they suggest are essential for all good stories and drama. Melanie Phillips and Chris Huntley set about writing a text of screenwriting tips and ended up developing a comprehensive theory of story they called Dramatica.[6]

According to this theory, every complete story is a model of the mind's problem solving process. The authors maintain that:

> To fully explore any issue, an author has to examine all possible solutions to that issue and make an argument to prove to an audience that the author's way is best. If you leave out a part of that argument or diverge from the point, your story will have plot holes or inconsistencies. Once you have covered every angle in your argument, you've mapped all the ways an audience might look at that problem and, therefore, all the ways *anyone* might look at that problem. In short, you have created a map of the mind's problem solving process.[7]

When a story fully develops this model of the mind, they call it a **Grand Argument Story** because it addresses the problem from all sides. Characters, plot, and theme are outlined as essential elements of the "story mind." Characters represent the mind's motivations which can be positioned from two different views: the Objective view from the outside looking in, and the Subjective view from the inside looking out. The objective view is like looking at another person, watching his thought processes at work. For an audience experiencing a story, the objective view is like watching a football game from the stands. All the characters are most easily identified by their functions on the field. The Subjective view is as if the Story Mind were our own. From this perspective, only two characters are visible: Main and Obstacle. The Main and Obstacle Characters represent the inner conflict of the Story Mind. In fact, the theory suggests that a story is of *two* minds. In real life, we often play our own devil's advocate, entertaining an alternative view as a means of arriving at the best decision. Similarly, the Story Mind's alternative views are made tangible through the Main and Obstacle Characters. To the audience of a story, the Main Character experience is as if they were actually one of the players on the field. The Obstacle Character is the player who blocks the way.

The theory also outlines four pairs of oppositional archetypal characters commonly found in stories. First, there are the *Protagonist* (chief proponent and principal driver to achieve the story's goal) and the *Antagonist* (opponent to the protagonist's successful attainment of the goal). Next, there are *Reason* (calm, acts based on logic) and *Emotion* (frenetic, reacts based on feelings) characters. The third set of characters are the *Sidekick* (faithful supporter) and the *Skeptic* (cautious disbeliever) and the last pair are the *Guardian* (teacher, helper, story conscience) and the *Contagionist* (distracter, creates obstacles, represents temptation). In many stories the characters are more complex than these simple archetypes, and a single character might serve multiple functions. Dramatica suggests, however, that if you look closely you can find elements of these archetypes represented in all complete stories. These archetypes can be further broken down and recombined into many recognizable "stock" characters. Examples of these are explored at the end of this chapter in *A Closer Look*.

According to Dramatica, the **plot** of a story describes the internal logic or sequence of events that lead the characters from their situations and attitudes at the beginning of the problem to their situations and attitudes when the effort to solve the problem is finally over. However, the presentation of the story does not necessarily have to follow this logic in sequential order. For example, a story about a man's life doesn't have to presented in order from birth to death. You can see this technique used in *Pulp Fiction* and the television series *Lost*. The narrative may jump forward or back but, in a cohesive story, it adheres to a consistent plot—the underlying structure of what happens, when, and to whom.

SPOTLIGHT ON BROADWAY

Appealing to Younger and Diverse Audiences

Traditional Broadway musicals were developed for adults because they had the money to pay for tickets. Today, musical ticket pricing and titles are structured to appeal to younger, more ethnically diverse audiences. Combining hip stories with edgy music,

writers and producers are addressing the interests of this new target audience. Popular Tony-winning shows, such as *In the Heights* and *Spring Awakening*, are directed at college students.

By connecting with potential theater-goers through YouTube, MySpace and TV commercials, marketers are exposing youth to stage happenings. *Wicked* was advertised on Facebook for about $1,000 a week, and *Legally Blonde* was advertised on iTunes which works closely with the theater industry by making Broadway tracks available for download.

And because so many musicals become successful movies, the line between Hollywood and Broadway is blurring. Young audiences flock to see stars such as Julia Roberts and Ashley Parker Angel on stage. To help with the high costs of attending, shows such as *Rent* are selling "lottery tickets" two hours before show time for $25.00.

Broadway shows attract audiences that are much more ethnically diverse then in past years. *In the Heights*, a show about Latinos in Upper Manhattan, and *Passing Stage*, about an African American kid from LA who strives for artistic recognition in Europe, get cheers and foot-stomping from audience members. Kevin McCollum, producer of *Heights*, *Rent*, and *Avenue Q*, believes that "Broadway should reflect every aspect of America."

Broadway's need to replace its aging patrons means attracting a younger consumer base. Most young adults today have not grown up with theater, so they need a connection with music to bring them in. It worked for *Passing Strange*, which was the first musical to see its cast recording available online before the CD went on sale.

In 2007, there was a 26 percent increase in attendance by non-whites, and the percentage of patrons under 24 rose 22 percent over the previous year according to the League of American theaters and Producers.

Source: reportermag.com and latimes.com

Theme is more difficult to describe. Some authors will say that theme has something to do with the topic or the mood or feel of a story. Others will say that theme is the message of the story. Some will put forth that theme is the *premise* of a story that illustrates the results of certain kinds of behavior. Taking each of these a bit farther, a story's topic might be blue collar workers and its mood or feel might be "anger." A message might be "nuclear power plants are bad." A premise could be "greed leads to self-destruction." Clearly each of these might show up in the very same story, and each has a somewhat thematic feel to it. It might be argued that this is because each is just a different angle on what theme really is.

According to Dramatica, theme is perspective. Perspective is relationship. Theme describes the *relationship* between what is being looked at and from where it is being seen. This is why theme has traditionally been so hard to describe. It is not an independent thing like plot or character, but is a relationship *between* plot and character. The plot in a movie is usually fairly straightforward. For example, the plot in Pixar's *Wall-E* might be briefly summarized as "robots falling in love and saving the polluted, abandoned earth." Clearly, people might argue about the best way to summarize the details of the story, but all can agree that the plot is a description of the story line. Descriptions of the theme, however, may vary more widely. The theme of *Wall-E* might be differently described as "a lighthearted story of the power of love" (mood or feel), as a criticism of "human laziness, ignorance and greed" (message), or as a warning that "technological advances can distance us from nature" (premise). Dramatica theory offers a more complex analysis of characters, plot, and theme than can be detailed here, but a general understanding of these principles is helpful for classifying entertainment and understanding its appeal.

 FLASH FACT

Similar archetypal characters are found in stories and legends from very different cultures. The blood drinking risen dead, the angel, the tragic hero trying to overcome past evils, the coyote, Xena, and even Gruff Grandpa are examples of characters that could, at any moment, appear disguised as aliens. TV Tropes Wiki came up with 35 different archetypes. How many more can you name?

Source: http://tvtropes.org/pmwiki/pmwiki.php/Main/ArchetypalCharacter

Drama's Appeal

There are many theories that attempt to explain exactly why audiences find story and suspense so appealing. *Excitation transfer theory* provides a physiological explanation for why the standard dramatic formula works.[8] According to this theory, emotional reactions are accompanied by physiological excitation or arousal. When we are afraid, happy, or angry, our body reacts. Our blood pressure rises and our heart rate increases. According to this theory, our body reacts in the same way regardless of which emotions we are experiencing. In fact, it has been suggested that the emotions we feel are simply our subjective interpretations of these physiological reactions. Although we are not consciously aware of it, our bodies may react first, and then we may analyze the situation to determine how we are feeling. The theory further postulates that the physiological excitation that accompanies emotional reactions may linger long after the emotions themselves have subsided. This residual excitation may then transfer onto the next events we witness or experience. We misattribute this arousal to the new event and, as a result, our feelings are intensified.

Physiological reaction to a scary movie

Figure 4.1 demonstrates the excitation process. Event A begins at Time 1. By Time 2 the thoughts and emotions associated with Event A may have subsided, but the physiological arousal that is generated takes longer to decay or go away. Thus, arousal is still high from Event A when Event B begins at Time 2. The shaded area indicates the extent to which Event A increases the arousal activity and thus, presumably also intensifies the accompanying cognitive and emotional reactions for Event B. The dotted lines show how arousal reactions would have been if each event happened separately.

In other words, if we hear a joke soon after we receive a scare, we may laugh a little louder and find it a little funnier than we normally would. The standard dramatic formula

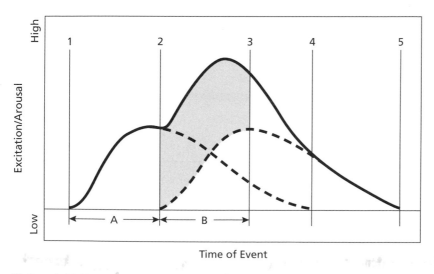

Figure 4.1 The Excitation Transfer Process

is said to capitalize on this phenomenon. The more conflict and suspense there is in the drama, the more excitation there should be to transfer, making the happy ending that much more enjoyable. This theory can be used to explain the appeal of most forms of entertainment. Sporting events, books, video games, films, even roller coasters are all made up of series of "scenes" or events. As the events unfold, the excitation generated from one event, whether positive or negative, transfers to the next, enhancing the overall experience.

Excitation transfer theory suggests that the more intensely the audience reacts to threats or conflicts in drama, the more they should ultimately enjoy the happy ending. Some scholars, however, have questioned whether that is the *only* value of the intense, negative emotions that drama can evoke. They question why audiences would tolerate what is often long periods of negative emotional circumstances, only to experience relief through excitation transfer in the last few minutes or seconds, if at all.

Another popular theory used to explain the appeal of entertainment is **escapism**. According to this notion, entertainment can serve as an escape or diversion from the worries and shortcomings of everyday life. If the enjoyment of drama primarily hinges on its ability to distract audience members from real-world problems, it may not matter what emotions the drama creates—fear, anger, sadness, joy, amusement—as long as it makes them forget their own concerns. A different suggestion is that drama serves an **informative and self-reflective function**. In almost direct opposition to escapism, this theory suggests that some audiences may enjoy drama because it allows them to reflect on their own feelings and experiences.[9] This notion suggests that individuals enjoy drama that parallels their own lives because it allows them to replay events they have experienced, evaluate their actions, and get ideas for how to act and react in the future. For drama to serve this function, it needs to be realistic; indeed, some might argue that if real life appears to include a great deal of conflict and suffering, so should drama.

Mood management theory similarly suggests that audiences often seek out media (and presumably other forms of entertainment) that will enhance their moods. This theory rests on the premise of **selective exposure**—namely, that audiences will seek information and experiences consistent with their feelings and beliefs and will avoid those that are inconsistent. This theory is a popular explanation for the appeal of tragedy. Indeed, there is evidence that people, particularly women, are more likely to select sad songs or movies when they are sad, and to avoid them when they are happy. Note, however, that the basic theory is not called mood enhancement, but mood management, reflecting the notion that people may sometimes seek to change rather than enhance their moods. Thus, although some individuals may prefer sad music or stories when they are upset, others may search for something more upbeat to cheer themselves up.

Genres

Although the general theories discussed in the previous section are applicable to most forms of drama, different story types, or genres, possess unique characteristics and appeals. Like theme, genre is difficult to define. Genre sometimes refers to the setting of a story, as in *Westerns* or *Science Fiction*. Other times, it describes the relationships between characters such as *Love stories* and *Buddy pictures*. Genre might pertain to the feeling an audience gets from a story as in *Comedy* and *Horror stories*. Even styles of storytelling can have their own genres like *Musicals* or *Character studies*. Thus, some genres might be defined in four different ways: the underlying **dramatic structure** (storyform—example Tragedy) through the **subject matter** (encoding—example Westerns) and **style** (weaving—example Musical) or via **audience expectations/reactions** (reception—examples Comedy, Horror).

Here we review some of the unique qualities of popular genres including tragedy, comedy, mystery, action/horror, and reality programming.

Tragedy

As with all drama, tragedy depends on the audience's dispositions toward the dramatic characters. In contrast to traditional drama, however, where good usually triumphs, the essence of tragedy is bad things happening to good people. If audiences do not perceive a character as noble or good, they will not interpret the character's misfortune as tragic. Thus, the formula for good tragedy is to create very good, noble characters who meet terrible fates. A common theme in tragedy, as found in many of Shakespeare's plays and sonnets, is love lost. Lost love is also a popular theme in contemporary tragedy, including films such as *Titanic*. Tragic elements are also found in many award-winning television dramas (such as *Grey's Anatomy* and *Lost*), in popular novels (such as Danielle Steele novels), and, of course, in countless love songs.

Similar to how individuals enjoy other forms of drama, they may welcome tragedy as an escape from their own problems or, as mood management theory suggests, individuals may prefer tragedy when they are upset because it matches their mood. Following the old adage that misery loves company, it may be that those who are sad or upset find dramatic tragedy comforting because it makes them feel that others share and understand their pain and despair. Several other explanations have also been offered. Dating back to Aristotle, the **catharsis doctrine** provides one of the oldest explanations for the appeal of tragedy and dramatic distress.

Catharsis is described as the therapeutic release of emotions that cause tension or anxiety. It is argued that, instead of acting on their emotions, individuals who harbor fears or anger resulting from certain life experiences may be relieved of their feelings by vicariously living through similar experiences found in games or depicted in drama. Thus, this theory suggests that audiences may enjoy conflict and tragedy because it provides them with an opportunity to purge rather than enhance any negative feelings that they have been experiencing. **Social comparison** theory offers a related explanation.[10] This theory states that people feel better when they can make favorable comparisons between themselves and others. According to this theory, people may feel better about their lives when they can compare themselves to individuals who "have it worse." Thus, another reason why individuals may enjoy conflict and tragedy drama is because it provides them with ample opportunities to make favorable life comparisons.

Although good characters often die, in many cases one or more protagonists remain to cope with the aftermath of the tragedy. Thus, tragedy may also provide a particularly valuable **informative function** by demonstrating successful coping strategies for people facing similar personal tragedies. Finally, another thought is that people simply enjoy experiencing the range of human emotions. We tend to assume that emotions such as anger, sadness, and fear are unpleasant, but the success of such genres as tragedy and horror suggest that some individuals may actually enjoy these emotions. Of course, experiencing these emotions through drama allows a certain amount of safety or detachment. Audience members are free to feel sorrow or fear without actually having to cope with the situations that created those emotions. The feelings drama creates have been called **meta-emotions**, suggesting that it may not be the emotions themselves that audiences enjoy as much as it is that they appreciate drama's ability to "safely" but effectively simulate such intense emotions.

Humor and Comedy

Comedy abounds as a source for entertainment. In fact, comedy accounts for almost one half of the top television programs and films of all time (see Figures 4.2 and 4.3). In addition to the standard dramatic outlets of film, TV, and print media, comedy is also popular in radio shows and in live performances. Comedy is typically considered to be a form of drama. Serious drama, such as action, mystery, and tragedy, are said to differ from other forms of entertainment because of the importance they attach to an overarching plot.

By contrast, genres such as situation comedy, erotica, and horror may derive their appeal more from discrete scenes. Enjoyment of these stories may not require detailed background and plot development. Nonetheless, the events and dialogue in individual scenes still typically reflect basic principles of drama. Comedy includes conflict and its resolution as well as character and plot development; however, whereas most drama takes time to develop, a comic skit can be developed more quickly, making it popular for venues such as radio programs and live performances.

Comedy, by its nature, is lighthearted and not serious. Freud argued that audiences rely on cues that signal the play context of humor and comedy, and he outlined features of jokework that can serve as these cues.[11] Freud differentiated between nontendentious and tendentious humor. **Nontendentious** humor relies on jokework, including innocuous plays on words, irony, and exaggeration that does not victimize, humiliate, or disparage. This is the humor of innocent "Knock, Knock" jokes and "Why did the chicken cross the road?" riddles. In contrast, tendentious humor emphasizes the victimization of one party by another.

Disparagement Humor   Humor that pokes fun at others is often called **tendentious** or **disparagement humor**. Like other forms of drama, disparagement humor has been explained by disposition theory. If the audience is positively disposed toward an individual, they are more likely to laugh at his or her jokes. In other words, the more a comedian or comic character is liked, the funnier the audience will find the humor. It is argued that

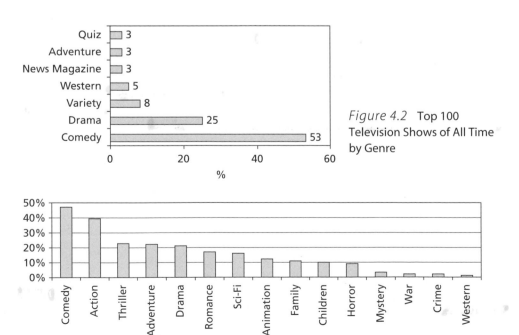

Figure 4.2   Top 100 Television Shows of All Time by Genre

Figure 4.3   Top 100 Films of All Time by Genre

people find it funny when a joke is targeted at someone that is disliked. People are not as amused, possibly even insulted by jokes that target liked individuals.[12] According to Freud, although nontendentious jokes and riddles may produce a few smiles and polite giggles, they are rarely capable of producing the intense amusement that tendentious humor elicits with ease. He further maintained that very little of what we label as humor is truly innocent. Instead, much of even the most simple wordplay and jokework includes tendentious undercurrents of hostility and taboo topics.

Incongruity Resolution   Although disposition theory may explain why we laugh at some forms of humor, **incongruity resolution** provides another rationale.[13] Riddles and other forms of humor often pose a question or some confusion (incongruity) that is then explained by the punch line (the resolution). Some humor of this type may be tendentious or disparaging, but often it is innocent and victimless. Consider the verbal joke "What is black and white and red all over?" "A newspaper." The incongruity of how something can be black and white and red all over simultaneously is resolved when the punch line "A newspaper" triggers recognition of the wordplay on *red* and *read*. Similar to mystery, the belief is that, if a joke or riddle is too easy or obvious, audiences will not find it very amusing; however, if it is too difficult to figure out, they may not get it at all. Thus, in true Goldilocks fashion, the goal is to create a riddle that poses just the right amount of challenge. The irony found in many comedies reflects the notion of incongruity resolution. Many comedies contain ironic elements—an immigration department for "illegal aliens" from outer space run by *Men in Black* (1997, 2002) or a *Wedding Planner* (2001) who can't find a groom—and it is these incongruities that form the basis for the humor.

One thought is that the incongruity creates tension and uncertainty. When the punch line or resolution is provided, this tension is released in the form of laughter. Theory also suggests that laughter reflects triumph and feelings of *mastery* and *superiority*. Laughter has been equated with the roar of triumph over one's enemies in battle. Therefore it has also been speculated that individuals who understand a joke laugh in triumph, feeling superior to those who don't get it. Feelings of superiority have also been tied to disparagement humor, which is thought to stimulate feelings of superiority over the individuals who serve as the butt of the joke.

Misattribution Theory   Nonetheless, it is argued that even tendentious humor relies on nontendentious elements—jokework such as plays on words, irony, and exaggeration—to serve as the cues for audiences to laugh. It was Freud's contention that audiences do not truly understand exactly what it is about tendentious humor that makes them laugh. He argued that although audiences may believe that they laugh at the jokework and wordplay, the fact that innocent jokework does not create the same level of mirth suggests it is the tendentious elements—the hostility and taboo topics—that truly inspire amusement. These speculations inspired the formulation of a **misattribution theory of humor**.[14] As the name suggests, this theory postulates that individuals misattribute their enjoyment of hostile humor to the innocent, nontendentious humorous cues. The logic is that it is not considered socially acceptable to laugh at others' misfortune. Thus, even though deep down audiences might be intrigued, even amused, by blatant hostility, they are not free to admit or express that enjoyment due to fear of social censure. In comedy, however, the nontendentious humorous cues that accompany hostility may unconsciously provide audiences with the justification they need to laugh openly.

Humorous Cues and Parody   Thus, it would seem that it is these lighthearted cues that differentiate drama from comedy. Although both drama and comedy are governed by disposition theory, the victimization and demise of a villain in a dramatic presentation might produce feelings of exhilaration, even triumph, but laughter would be inappropriate. Comedy, however, includes humorous cues that create a lighthearted context for this victimization, informing audiences that laughter is not only tolerated but encouraged. Tendentious and disparaging humor is prevalent in commercial entertainment. Slapstick comedy found in movies and cartoons, for example, tends to focus on physical humor, such as people slipping and hitting each other. This tendentious form of humor can actually be quite violent, yet it includes cues such as music and facial expressions that let the audience know it isn't serious.

For example, *Scary Movie* (2000) poked fun at some of the biggest contemporary horror and suspense hits including *Scream* (1996), *I Know What You Did Last Summer* (1997), *The Sixth Sense* (1999), *The Blair Witch Project* (1999), and *The Matrix* (1999). The success of this film resulted in the development of a Scary Movie franchise of film spoofs. These comic parodies often follow a similar story line of characters and events and are often as violent as their dramatic counterparts; however, there is additional jokework and exaggeration that signal to audiences that they should not take these events too seriously. Thus, although audiences may have held their breath in suspense and screamed in fear in the original thriller, in the parody the same story line may have audiences holding their sides and hooting with laughter.

In an interesting postmodern twist, two of the *Scary Movie* screenwriters, Aaron Seltzer and Jason Friedberg, collaborated on *Date Movie* (2006), a parody of the related genre, romantic comedy. Following the traditional dramatic formula, boy meets girl, but before they can have their *Big Fat Greek Wedding* (2002), they'll have to *Meet the Parents* (2000), hook-up with *The Wedding Planner* (2001), and contend with a woman who wants to put an end to her *Best Friend's Wedding* (1997). Consistent with the premises of incongruity resolution, a good parody balances a fine line in providing sufficient context so that audiences will recognize the characters and story lines that are being parodied while still infusing enough new twists to keep the film fresh and the audience engaged.

Situation Comedies: Fading Laughter[15]   A situation comedy (*sitcom*) is a radio or TV comedy series that involves a continuing cast of characters in a common environment or "situation" such as a family, home, or workplace. *Sam and Henry*, which debuted on WGN radio of Chicago in 1926, is often credited as being the first situation comedy. The show was inspired by the idea of bringing the mix of jokes and story line found in comic strips to the new radio medium. A similar program, *Amos & Andy*, which debuted on CBS in 1928, became the first syndicated sitcom, and it remained one of the most popular programs through the 1930s. When TV emerged, situation comedies were among the first programs developed for that new medium as well. In the United Kingdom, the BBC broadcast *Pinwright's Progress* from late 1946 until early the following year. *Mary Kay and Johnny* was likely the first American sitcom, a 15-minute show which debuted on the DuMont Television Network in November 1947. According to the 12th edition of the *Merriam-Webster Collegiate Dictionary*, the term sitcom was coined in 1951, at the time *I Love Lucy* was produced.

FLASH FACT

Television commercials use the same comedic and dramatic techniques as full-length versions of the genre. GEICO Insurance developed a fictional comedy campaign with the caption, "Even a caveman can do it." The cavemen were such likable characters that a full-length sitcom was developed for them. Some commercials are directed by famous film directors such as Woody Allen, George Lucas, and Francis Ford Coppola. One of the most famous science fiction commercials was produced by Apple Computer in 1984. Shown only once during the Superbowl, the spot was directed by Ridley Scott to introduce the Macintosh.

Traditionally, situation comedies featured individual episodes that were mostly self-contained. The regular characters remained largely static, and events of the episode resolved themselves by the conclusion of the episode. Most sitcoms took this format. Events of previous episodes would rarely be mentioned in subsequent episodes. While school friends or beloved relatives might appear, often they would only be seen once in the series, and they would rarely be mentioned in subsequent episodes (apparent in *The Brady Bunch* and many other programs). More recently, sitcoms have introduced some ongoing story lines. *The Beverly Hillbillies*, for example, frequently had continuing stories during its successful 1960s–1970s run, and *One Day at a Time* frequently featured ongoing issues and four-part episodes. The trend toward more serial style sitcoms became firmly entrenched with *Friends*, an immensely popular U.S. sitcom of the 1990s–2000s, which had an overall story arc similar to that of soap operas. In addition to using traditional sitcom stories, which were introduced and resolved in the same episode, the show always had two or three ongoing stories taking place at any given point in the show's run. *Friends* also used other soap opera elements such as regularly resorting to an end-of-season cliffhanger and gradually developing the relationships of the characters over the course of the series.

Sitcoms in America began to decline in popularity in the early 1980s, giving way to the evening soap opera format. In 1983, *Kate & Allie* was the only sitcom to finish in the top ten most-popular TV productions in the U.S. However, in 1984, the "Cosby Show" brought new life to the genre. Cosby's success was echoed by other shows centered on comedian personalities such as Tim Allen on *Home Improvement*, Paul Reiser on *Mad About You*, and Jerry Seinfeld on *Seinfeld*.

During the 1989–90 TV season, 11 of the top 19 shows were 30-minute sitcoms, but by 1998 the sitcom again showed signs of decline. This time the decline was attributed not to lack of interest but to rising production costs and increased network preference for reality television. Actor salary demands and rising audience expectations regarding production quality had begun to drive up sitcom production costs considerably. By 2005, those costs had risen to an average of $1,250,000 an episode compared to only $700,000 for a reality program episode. Not surprisingly, in the 2005–6 TV season, only one of the top 20 shows was a 30-minute sitcom, while nine shows were what could be labeled "reality" programs.[16]

Although the 30-minute sitcom may currently be out of vogue, audiences who enjoy a good laugh need not fear. Comedy can still be found in abundance on television, most notably on the reality programs that have replaced more traditional, scripted shows. Most reality programs are not strictly designed as comedies, but almost all of them include humorous elements. In many cases, the producers of sitcoms and reality programs start with a similar premise such as "what kind of things might happen when two very different people get married?" Both begin by choosing characters and situations they believe have good story potential. In the case of reality programming, however, instead of relying entirely on their own imagination or personal experience, the writers can observe the "characters" to see what happens, but the writers still must work to cobble together coherent, entertaining stories from what they see.

Comedic elements are found in almost all entertainment genres. Humor is often incorporated into more serious drama as *comic relief. The Oxford companion to the English language* (1992) defines comic relief as "an amusing scene, incident, or speech introduced into serious, tragic, or suspenseful drama to provide temporary relief from tension."[17] One theater historian notes that "an audience may concentrate better on crises if it has relaxed at moments in between. Anyone who has watched a chick struggling out of its shell realizes how often Nature's way is 'strain—rest—strain—rest.'"[18] Thus, comic relief may serve as a break in serious drama, providing audiences an opportunity to mentally and physically relax and settle down after tense or tragic scenes. Comic relief has been used to varying degrees by most dramatists, including Shakespeare. Today, the prevalence of humor in more serious drama is evidenced by the number of popular films of various genres that are cross-listed under comedy. Indeed, of the 47 top-grossing films of all time listed as comedy, 40 percent (19) were cross-listed with more serious or suspenseful genres, including action, adventure, drama, crime, thriller, mystery, and/or horror.[19]

A New Role for Comedy   New technology is providing new media and new challenges that are creating an environment in which comedy thrives. Many new media (such as the Internet) and handheld devices (such as cellular phones and palm organizers) are thought to be better suited to shorter, less complex entertainment content.[20] Although many other dramatic genres require time for character and story development, comedy can be developed quickly and easily. Consider cartoons in which a single still image, often without any text, can convey an entire comic plot. Thus, comedy becomes a natural choice for new media.

People need only check their own e-mail inboxes to recognize the proliferation of humor and comedy on the Internet. At the turn of the century, organizations such as Shockwave.com began enjoying great success with so-called "performance animation," including Flash-generated cartoons, often lasting just a few seconds, that can be down-loaded and e-mailed to others. These animations often feature recurring characters—such as a disco-dancing alien, jiggling to the song "I Will Survive," who gets flattened by a falling disco ball.[21] According to Errol Gerson, a senior agent in the new media department of the Los Angeles-based agency Creative Artists Association (CAA), "This interactive programming is going to be a new entertainment format. It fits the Web audience profile, giving people a short laugh every now and then."[22] The wild success of YouTube's video sharing web site provides perhaps the best evidence of comedy's dominance in new media. On any given day, a look at the most popular YouTube videos is likely to include short film parodies, slapstick home videos, celebrity blunders, or other humorous fare.

Current technology restricts the length and complexity of the material that can be transmitted through new media devices, but it is thought that, even if and when these obstacles are overcome, brevity will still rule the day for many of these new media. It is reasoned that, when individuals have time for more involved entertainment, they would prefer viewing a big screen from a couch or a theater seat to sitting at a desk squinting at their computer or iPhone. Thus, it would appear that humor and comedy are well-positioned to continue their reign in the media entertainment kingdom.

Mystery

In standard suspense stories, there are typically only two major outcomes. The protagonist either defeats the opponent or does not. Either the heroine defuses the bomb or the building explodes. Suspense is enhanced by the magnitude of the potential consequences and by the intensity of the audience's preference for one outcome over the other. In a mystery, however, uncertainty is enhanced by introducing numerous possibilities. Mysteries are often retrospective. The outcome may be known (something is stolen or someone is killed). The suspense revolves around the uncertainty of who did it and/or how it happened. Thus a good, suspenseful mystery is one in which several equally viable possibilities are presented. It is argued, however, that the involvement of too many suspects and situations may overwhelm audiences to the point where they lose interest. Mystery can be found not only in books, plays, and films but also in board games, video games, and promotional contests. Magic acts are shrouded in mystery, and themed dinner theaters that put on live mysteries, where guests can actively solve and even participate in a mystery, are gaining in popularity.

Some mysteries are designed so that, although the solution is not overly obvious, audience members should be able to solve the mystery as they go, ultimately having their suspicions *confirmed* at the end when all is revealed. Other mysteries keep the audience guessing the entire time, maximizing *uncertainty.* Still others lead the audience on, making them feel they know who did what and how, only to *surprise* them in the end. Audiences are thought to vary in terms of the types of mystery outcomes they enjoy.[23] Although some individuals might prefer having their suspicions confirmed, others may prefer mysteries that surprise them or keep them guessing. Researchers speculate that thrill and sensation seekers, who value confronting problems more than they value solving them, might prefer uncertainty-maximizing mysteries because solutions terminate the thrill of the unknown. In contrast, the surprise model should be favored by individuals who love to take on a challenge and who are not disturbed when they are outwitted. And finally, the confirmation model might prove more satisfying to persons of low self-esteem because they may feel better about themselves when their hunches are validated. It is also possible that individuals may prefer different types of mysteries at different times, depending upon their moods.

Action and Horror

Action and horror are also found in traditional forms of entertainment, including books, films, and even music, and they are equally popular in video games and amusement park rides and attractions. Action and horror genres are both typically characterized by high levels of violence. This type of drama typically follows the standard dramatic principles, including exciting conflict between good and evil. Not surprisingly, disposition and excitation transfer theories offer reasonable explanations of the appeal of these dramas.

It has been suggested that these genres also provide catharsis, allowing audience members to purge their own anger and fear.[24] Horror and other threatening drama are thought to give individuals an opportunity to face and master their fears by forcing them to confront and vicariously conquer their "demons." Evidence suggests that audience reactions to violent drama may also reflect socialized gender roles. Violent drama, particularly horror, is thought to provide adolescent males the opportunity to demonstrate their manhood by acting fearless. At the same time, young female viewers can display the appropriate fear response to gain "protection" from their male companion. Indeed, research indicates that females find males more attractive when they appear brave and fearless while watching horror, whereas males find females more attractive when they appear afraid and turn to the males for comfort.[25]

FLASH FACT

According to the Internet Movie Database (IMDb.com), the top nine horror movies of all time are: *Psycho* (1960), *Aliens* (1979), *The Shining* (1980), *Les Diaboliques* (1955), *Jaws* (1975), *Das Cabinet des Dr Caligari* (1920), *Bride of Frankenstein* (1935), *Faust–Eine deutsche Volkssage* (1926), and *The Thing* (1982) The only recent movies to make the top 50 horror films of all time are *Grindhouse* (2007) and *Shaun of the Dead* (2004). Note that one French and two German films are among the leaders.

The Watchers Perhaps not surprisingly, adolescent males are the dominant audience for graphic violence, particularly horror. Studies find that males enjoy horror films more than females do, and females are more distressed by horror films than males are. Research also suggests personality differences in preferences for violence and horror.[26] The personality variable that has been researched most often in association with exposure to horror and thrillers is *sensation seeking*, the desire to seek out experiences that produce "sensation" and arousal. Sensation seekers, in particular, seem to enjoy the thrill caused by the fear that scary films create. Differences in *empathy*, the degree to which individuals relate to and feel for others, may also play an important role in determining the appeal of graphic horror. Research has found that nonempathic individuals find horror more appealing. The reasoning here is that highly empathic individuals relate closely to the victims and, thus, may become too distressed to enjoy the films. Low levels of wandering imagination (daydreaming about unreal situations), fictional involvement (transferring one's feelings into the actions and feelings of movie characters), and emotional contagion (becoming emotionally caught up in the film) are good predictors of the appeal of horror. Again, the logic is that an individual who does not daydream or let his or her imagination wander never forgets that the horror isn't real, and therefore does not get upset by these events, whereas an individual who gets very emotionally involved in drama may find horror and graphic violence too upsetting.

Individuals who enjoy violence and horror appear to do so for different reasons. Johnston identified four motivations that adolescents report for viewing graphic horror films:[27]

> The **gore watcher** personality is characterized by low empathy, low fearfulness, and high adventure seeking. This combination of personality traits makes gore watchers seek high arousal originating from graphic portrayals of blood, death, and even physical torture. Gore watching motivations may reflect a curiosity about physical violence (the ways that people are killed), a vindictive interest in killing (victims get what they "deserve"), and an attraction to the grotesque (viewing blood and guts). Gore watchers, particularly males, tend to identify more with the killer than the victims.
>
> **Thrill watchers** enjoy the thrill of being startled and scared. Unlike the gore watcher, who focuses on blood and mutilation, the thrill watcher focuses more on the suspense. The personality of the thrill watcher is characterized by high levels of empathy and high levels of adventure seeking.

Independent watchers view horror films to test their maturity and bravery. They have low levels of dispositional empathy, show no preference for either violence or suspense, and report positive feelings both before and after viewing horror films.

Problem watchers report being angry and lonely. The personality of the problem watcher is characterized by sensation seeking, which can take the form of substance abuse and low dispositional empathy. Problem watchers' identification with the victim may be a reflection of their own perceived helplessness. Unlike the other three viewing motivations, only problem watchers reported feeling bad both before and after viewing graphic horror.

From classic eighteenth-century gothic horror to twentieth-century "shoot-'em-ups," most violent action and horror films followed standard dramatic principles, concluding with good ultimately triumphing over evil; however, evil has had more success in recent tales of violence and horror. Gone are the serious and silent, but inevitably doomed, killers of traditional action and horror. Originally, horror and other violent thrillers followed a traditional formula where, at the end of the story, the evil is unequivocally destroyed. Various film critics, however, argue that many films no longer follow this tradition. Starting in the early 1970s with the success of *Rosemary's Baby* and *The Exorcist*, a new thriller formula emerged that portrayed defenseless victims in terrifying no-win situations where the evil/antagonist triumphed over the forces of reason and rationalism.[28] Typically, these films contain teaser endings in which, although at first it may appear that the villain or monster has been destroyed, a final scene reveals that the evil has survived. Many popular film series—such as *Halloween, Friday the 13th, A Nightmare on Elm Street*, and the Hannibal Lecter films—contain teaser endings. Not only do the villains and demons of contemporary violent action and horror films often survive for the sequel, today characters such as Hannibal Lecter (from *Silence of the Lambs, Hannibal*, and *Red Dragon*), and Freddy Kruger (from the *Nightmare on Elm Street* films) are quite sophisticated and witty. Although these developments suggest alternative character and plot options for those who seek to create entertainment, there is also concern about the impact that these trends may have on audience members. These possibilities will be explored in the next chapter.

Reality Programming

Although most drama is at least loosely based on reality, typically the stories are scripted rather than spontaneous and, even in impromptu performances, actors are given characters and basic scenarios to act out. More recent reality programming involves real people and real events. TV programs such as *The Real World* and *Survivor* put so-called "regular" people in different living situations and just let the cameras roll. The early popularity of these shows was astounding, including popular sub-genres such as game shows (*Who Wants to Be a Millionaire* and *Weakest Link*), shock/stunt shows (MTV's *Jackass*), tell-all talk shows (*Maury, Sally, and Jerry*), and slice-of-life programs that follow people supposedly just living their lives (*Real World* and *Big Brother*). Many programs include elements of more than one of these sub-genres.

Reality programming, however, is really not new. Radio broadcasts have always relied on real people and events for much of their entertainment, and game shows were among some of the first TV programs ever produced. Television and movie producers have also experimented with other reality programming over the years in TV shows such as *Candid Camera* and *Cops* and films such as *Faces of Death*.

Cast of *Big Brother's All Stars Finale* at CBS studio

The formula of reality programming is, in essence, the same as it is for all drama. There are "good" and "bad" characters that audiences root for and against. Drama, of course, is driven by conflict, so program producers usually create situations in which conflict is likely to occur. Individuals with strong personalities are forced to live together or compete against each other. Audiences appear to enjoy these programs even in cases where they suspect events might be staged. In fact, even though these shows continue to be more spontaneous than most programming, the term *assisted reality* has recently emerged, acknowledging the fact that "reality" often needs the help of writers, producers, and editors to enhance its dramatic appeal.[29] Even scripted programming, however, has shifted to reflect a more "realistic" feel and look. TV programs such as *ER* and films such as *The Blair Witch Project* and *Traffic* use camera angles, panning, and sound quality that make scenes appear as if they were recorded with home video cameras. Programs such as *The West Wing* and *One Tree Hill* have incorporated current events and real public figures into their story lines, again blurring the line between fact and fiction.

The Appeal of Reality Programming   In some cases the "realistic" nature of these programs may make them perhaps more believable, and thus more entertaining, but in other cases the events are so extreme and unusual, it is difficult to believe that is their main appeal. One factor that may increase their interest is their spontaneity. In theory, even the program producers do not know what will happen next. When you watch *Survivor* in any given episode, for example, you don't know whether you will get comedy, tragedy, or action/adventure. This uncertainty may enhance suspense and thus enhance program enjoyment. Some analysts believe that audiences are attracted to the voyeuristic nature of these programs. Consistent with the notion that drama serves an informative and self-reflective function, audiences may look to these programs for ideas on how to act or behave. Or, in cases of some of the more extreme programming, they may provide a sort of catharsis where people can vicariously live out experiences they would not dare to attempt.

Part of reality television's appeal may relate to its ability to place ordinary people in extraordinary situations. For example, on the ABC show, *The Bachelor*, an eligible male dates a dozen women simultaneously, traveling on extraordinary dates to scenic locales. Reality TV also has the potential to turn its participants into national celebrities, outwardly in talent and performance programs such as *American Idol*, though frequently *Survivor* and *Big Brother* participants also reach some degree of celebrity.

Some commentators have said that the name "reality television" is an inaccurate description for several styles of program included in the genre. In competition-based programs such as *Big Brother* and *Survivor*, and other special-living-environment shows like *The Real World*, the producers design the format of the show and control the day-to-day activities and the environment, creating a completely fabricated world in which the competition plays out. Producers specifically select the participants, and use carefully designed scenarios, challenges, events, and settings to encourage particular behaviors and conflicts. It really is unscripted drama.

Even in docusoap series following people in their daily life, producers may be highly deliberate in their editing strategies, able to portray certain participants as heroes or villains, and may guide the drama through altered chronology and selective presentation of events. Some participants have stated afterwards that they altered their behavior to appear more crazy or emotional in order to get more camera time.

Several former reality show participants have spoken publicly about their experiences and the strategies used on reality shows

The Reality Principle   If not truly "real life," reality programming perhaps more than other genres attempts to maintain this illusion of authenticity. To Freud, the pleasure principle may explain much of our motivation for entertainment; however, fantasy and make-believe cannot produce real gratifications. Although the world of make-believe might be pleasant, our pleasure is tempered because we know it is not real. The land of make-believe cannot sustain us. In the real world, we must work and struggle to survive. Nonetheless, real, authentic experiences, although imperfect and often unpleasant, are valued because they are genuine. Thus, the individual is forced to strive not only for what is pleasant, but for what is real even if unpleasant. This is the *reality principle*.

Stephenson[30] distinguishes play and leisure as separate from reality and work: "Leisure time is our free time, time for recreation, hobbies, or self-cultivation. Work deals with reality, with earning a living, with production. Play, on the contrary, is largely unproductive except for the self-satisfaction it provides." Stephenson also outlines characteristics of play, as follows:

> Playing is pretending, stepping outside the world of duty and responsibility. Play is an interlude in the day. It is not ordinary or real. It is voluntary and not a task or moral duty. It is in some sense disinterested, providing a temporary satisfaction. Though attended to with seriousness, it is not really important. . . . Play is secluded, taking place in a particular place set for the purpose in time and space: it has a beginning and end.[31]

The qualities that Stephenson outlines characterize entertainment as "pretend" in that it doesn't have any real impact on us, that it is somehow separated from everything else in our lives. But therein lies the dilemma. Although we may use entertainment to escape the turmoil of our lives, we seem to find it difficult to truly enjoy experiences that seem "pretend" and unrealistic. It is perhaps this tension that has led the lines between drama and reality to become increasingly blurred. Although individuals do enjoy fictional drama, audiences appear to increasingly demand more "real" entertainment. Consistent with the principles of the attention economy detailed in Chapter 1, some people enjoy broadcasting their personal dramas to the world as much as other people enjoy viewing them.

Reality Show Audiences   Humanity's love affair with attention is what makes reality programming work. Analysts contend that "the tastes of the younger generation of viewers, a group more interested in visceral 'realistic' programming than artificial jokes from fictional characters in ersatz living rooms, seem to be taking command of an industry that is more than ever driven by the need to cater to the tastes of young adults."[32] Brian Graden, the president of programming for MTV, offers a similar explanation for why the trend in spontaneous reality programming originally exploded: "For these young people, the odd artifice of a layer of writers and actors is the abnormal thing. These shows are being watched by young audiences who grew up watching O.J. and Monica as entertainment. They have had a much different video access than any previous generation."[33] Graden observes that many in today's 25-and-under generation have actually grown up as videotaped subjects, endlessly filmed by parents who have wielded video cameras at every major (and often minor) event in their children's lives. For young viewers, reality shows on network TV are out of the same tradition that produced *Jackass*, *The Man Show*, and other outrageous fare on cable TV. According to Jeff Zucker, the president of entertainment for NBC, the shift in taste is not unlike what happened in TV comedy in the mid-1970s when Lorne Michaels brought *Saturday Night Live* to NBC—to the dismay of older fans of Bob Hope and Jack Benny and to the delight of comedy fans under the age of 30. "The young viewers are looking for high-octane television, stuff that is full of adrenaline," said David Goldberg, the president of the American branch of Endemol, the Dutch company responsible for reality formats such as *Big Brother* and *Fear Factor*.[34]

And if young people are hooked on these programs, whatever else is said about them does not matter. More than ever, network television is steered by youth culture. Advertisers prefer young viewers, and networks will do anything to deliver them. "We have to start reaching this next generation of viewers," Zucker said. "Our economic future depends on it."[35]

People who enjoy watching reality television often are just as enthusiastic about participating in the program. In the American version of *Big Brother*, the contestant who neither cracks under the scrutiny nor is vetoed by the fans receives the $500,000 prize. This format is so popular, audience contestants flocked to CBS interviews located in 16 cities at their own expense. The desire to relinquish privacy and endure ruthless scrutiny drives men and women to surrender themselves to viewing audiences. Human knowledge, not factual data, is required of these contestants striving for cash rewards.

Such kwik-gloss concepts of pop culture give participants more than just their "15 minutes of fame"[36]—many contestants are featured in magazines and receive product endorsements. As contestants get rich, viewers get to watch everyday life as entertainment. Actually, they get fooled into thinking it's everyday life. The deception is that as much planning goes into reality TV as into any other kind. And there is nothing ordinary about the "ordinary people" featured; they have been carefully selected, edited, and packaged. As one critic put it, we're actually watching "rats trapped in a very public maze."[37]

After four segments of *Survivor*, viewers understand that reality TV shows are just another kind of game show. Still, some viewers will do just about anything to be on television. One group of people who thought they were trying out for a reality show called *Cannibals* signed waivers taking responsibility for their possible beheading; three out of four actually ate pieces of what they were told was human flesh (it was pork).[38] For viewers unwilling to risk all for the sake of reality, quiz shows provide a safer and more manageable opportunity for on-screen participation.

Survivor: Micronesia, Fans vs. Favorites

Will Survivor *Survive?* Producers of the reality program *Survivor* have used many techniques to maximize and sustain the program's "dramatic" appeal, including staging post-competition events such as reunions and interviews which furthered "character" and "plot" development and the potential for more spontaneous conflict and controversy. In 2006, the new "twist" for season 13 was dividing the tribes by ethnicity: African American,

Table 4.1   Reality Programming Formats and Shows

Genre	Number of shows	Example
Documentary	25	*Family Plots* (2004) A&E Network show about a mortuary in San Diego
Historical recreation	12	*Frontier House* (2002) PBS show set in American frontier of 1883
Dating	23	*Boy Meets Boy* (2003)
Law enforcement	5	*American Fighter Pilot* (2002)
Makeover	13	*The Swan* (2004)
Life change	5	*Trading Spouses* (2004)
Docusoaps starring celebrities	7	*Osbournes* (2002)
Hidden camera	6	*Punk'd* (2003)
Reality game shows	25	*I Survived a Japanese Game Show* (2008)
Spoofs	8	*Superstar USA* (2004)
Talent searches	20	*Can you Be a Porn Star?* (2004)
Fantasy fulfilled	5	*Pimp My Ride* (2004)

Asian American, Hispanic, and Caucasian. Although this strategy did draw significant criticism and concerns about racism, in sparking such debate it likely accomplished its intended effect, which was to draw renewed attention back to the aging show. The season's premiere show was ranked first in its time slot, with the highest rating it had received since the start of the 2005 season. These ratings were far lower than ratings the show had received earlier; however *Survivor* was still ranked in the top 20 TV shows at the end of the season.

That same year ratings for other previously popular reality shows such as *The Apprentice* also began to slide. However, just as with other genres, even as some reality shows die out, new ones emerge. The finale of VH1's *Flavor of Love* drew 6 million viewers in 2006, making it the highest-rated show in the history of that network. Similarly, UPN's number-one-rated show in 2006 was the reality show *America's Next Top Model*. In the 2007–8 broadcast season, thanks to multiple night airings, *American Idol* and *Dancing with the Stars* reality competition shows captured all of the top five rating slots, and reality programming dominated nearly half (nine) of the top 20 shows overall.

Network executives had expressed concern in the media that reality TV programming was limited in its appeal for DVD reissue and syndication. This concern has lessened, however, as shows including *Laguna Beach*, *The Amazing Race*, *Project Runway*, and *America's Next Top Model* have all ranked in the top DVDs sold on Amazon.com in 2006. Reality concepts have also enjoyed success in recent stunt and prank films such as the *Jackass* movies, and *Borat!*. The generation of reality programming that brought in the new millennium may die out, but, as do many entertainment trends, it may continue to influence generations of entertainment to come.

Reality Program Sub-genres First-generation reality entertainment such as the show *Candid Camera* was nothing more than edited highlights of un-staged events fortuitously captured on film or simple, staged events documented with hidden cameras. A typical staged event showed a wallet presumably lost on the sidewalk. When a passer-by bent down to pick it up, the wallet was snatched away by an attached string. The reactions of multiple passers made up an episode of the show, complete with laugh track.

Today's reality programs, however, have evolved into much more sophisticated productions, many with very different, distinguishable features. To explore these developments, we have categorized reality TV into sub-genres discussed below: game shows, documentary style, self-improvement/makeover, dating shows, and doctor reality.

GAME SHOWS In game shows, participants are filmed competing to win a prize, usually while living together in an enclosed environment. Participants are removed until only one person or team remains, who/which is then declared the winner. Probably the purest example of a reality game show is the globally syndicated *Big Brother*. *Survivor* is another game technique; the final season had ethnic minority teams competing.

We question whether talent-search shows such as the *Idol* series and *America's Got Talent* are truly reality television, or just newer incarnations of shows such as *Star Search*. There is no element of plot on these shows; on the other hand, there is a good deal of interaction shown between contestants and judges, and the shows follow the traditional reality-game-show conventions of removing one or two contestant(s) per episode and having the public vote on who gets removed.

A sub-set of gaming, dating-based competition shows follow a contestant choosing suitors. Over the course of the season, the suitors are eliminated one by one until the end, when only the contestant and the final suitor remains. *The Bachelor* is the best-known member of this category.

In another game sub-set, competitors perform a variety of tasks based around that skill, and are judged, and then kept or removed, by a single expert or a panel of experts. The show is invariably presented as a job search of some kind, in which the prize for the winner includes a contract to perform that kind of work. Examples include *The Apprentice* (which judges business skills), *America's Next Top Model* (for modeling), *Who Wants to Be a Superhero*, and *Project Runway* (for clothing design).

Sometimes just getting on the show can get a contestant the job. The owner of UFC declared that the final match of the first season of *Ultimate Fighter* was so good that both contestants were offered a contract. Many of the losers from WWE's *Tough Enough* and *Diva Search* shows segments have wound up being picked up by the company. Sporting competition among participants who are athletes attempting to establish their name in that sport include the *Contender*, a boxing show, and *Ultimate Fighter*.

DOCUMENTARY STYLE   We call reality television shows where the viewer and the camera are passive observers following people going about their daily personal and professional activities a documentary style. The "fly-on-the-wall" style of filming can be seen on MTV's *Laguna Beach*. The epitome of this style of show is *The Real Housewives of Orange County* with unscripted situations, real-life locations, and no tasks given to the cast. When "plots" are constructed by editing or planned situations, shows resemble soap operas. Some documentary-style programs place cast members, who in most cases previously did not know each other, in artificial living environments.

Another subset of fly-on-the-wall-style show is celebrities going about their everyday life such as *The Osbournes*. In shows like *Dancing with the Stars* and *Skating with Celebrities*, celebrities are given a specific task.

SELF-IMPROVEMENT/MAKEOVER   Some reality TV shows cover a person or group of people improving some part of their lives. In *Trading Spaces* a group of people are covered over an entire season, but usually there is a new target for improvement in each episode. Despite differences in the content, the format is usually the same: first the show introduces the subject or subjects in their natural environment, and shows us the less-than-ideal conditions they are currently in. Then the subject(s) meet with a group of

The cast of MTV's *Laguna Beach*

experts, who give the subject(s) instructions on how to improve things; they offer aid and encouragement along the way. Finally, the subject(s) are placed back in their environment and they, along with their friends and family and the experts, appraise the changes that have occurred. Examples of self-improvement or makeover shows include, *The Biggest Loser* (weight loss), *Extreme Makeover* (entire physical appearance), *Queer Eye for the Straight Guy* (style and grooming), and *Supernanny* (child-rearing). The show *This Old House* shows people renovating a house; *Pimp My Ride* and *American Hotrod* show vehicles being overhauled. Such shows are generally not considered true reality TV because there is no potential for human drama in the format.

DATING SHOWS   Some shows, such as *Blind Date*, show people going out on dates. Sometimes a competition element is included, with more than one suitor for each potential match. And for those whose relationships didn't work out, the cable network Oxygen offered a new reality show called *Breaking Up with Shannon Doherty*.

DOCTOR REALITY   There was a new wrinkle in reality TV in 2006 as Arizona-based Medicis Pharmaceutical, the maker of cosmetic treatment Restylane, recruited women to compete for the title of *Hottest Mom in America*, a contest the company hoped to film and sell to a TV network. Designed for suburban moms, the contest winner receives a college scholarship for her child and becomes an official Restylane spokeswoman. By intertwining the reality show with a viral marketing campaign, the company offered its popular beauty treatment to women who are not necessarily affluent. Two episodes are filmed in each city—Dallas, Miami, Chicago, New York, Los Angeles, and Toronto—and the winners face off at the finale. Judges include a local media celebrity, a physician, a young adult, and a child between ages 10 and 12. Thirty-second spots advertised auditions in each city. Unlike these in *Extreme Makeover*, *Hottest Mom* stars are women with fulfilling family and professional lives who merely want "a little help" to look good.[39]

Genre Revisited

Just as individual characters can possess characteristics of more than one archetype, a single story may possess characteristics of more than one genre or sub-genre. In reality programming, a show such as *Survivor* is a game show, but also a documentary of the lives of the contestants during the competition. Reality programs may also possess elements of mystery, comedy, horror, or tragedy. Similarly a scripted program may be a romantic comedy or a horror mystery. As discussed in Chapter 2, genre blending has become increasingly popular in contemporary entertainment. Nonetheless, genre categorizations provide an important function in helping us understand the varying appeal and impacts of different types of stories. See Table 4.2 for summaries and examples of each of the major dramatic genres reviewed here.

Drama Is Everywhere

It is easy to see these principles of drama, storytelling, and genre reflected in traditional "story"-based entertainment such as books, TV, and film. If you look closely, you will also find elements of story and drama in most forms of entertainment. At amusement parks, such as Disney's Magic Kingdom, attractions are themed based on popular fairy-tales and action adventure films. Scenery along a ride route depicts story characters in scenes that trace the story's "plot." Similarly video games include characters and story lines that run

Table 4.2   A Review of Major Genres

Dramatic genres each have their own unique characteristics and formulas. This chart provides descriptions and examples for a few select genres.		
Genre	*Formulas and characteristics*	*Examples (from film, television, etc.)*
Tragedy	Features a tragic ending, where bad things happen to good people.	*Romeo and Juliet, Titanic,* many country songs
Comedy	Disparagement and putdowns with light-hearted cues. Irony, incongruities, and resolutions.	*Meet the Parents, The Three Stooges, The Simpsons,* Jay Leno's monolog on *The Tonight Show*
Mystery	Begins with what happened and traces back to "whodunit." Introduces numerous possibilities.	*The Usual Suspects, CSI* television series, *Clue* (board game and movie), Mary Higgins Clark novels
Action/Horror	Aggressive battles between good guys and bad guys. Good guys usually win in the end.	*Star Wars,* war films, *Dracula, Jaws,* Stephen King novels and films
Reality	Unscripted story shaped by strategic selection of cast and situations to simulate different genres listed above.	*Dancing with the Stars, Jackass: The Movie,* Howard Stern radio show

the range of dramatic genres. Recall the notion that entertainment makes us feel. Drama and story are the vehicles that evoke our emotions, thus making them an integral feature of entertainment. Elements of story and drama can even be found in sports and music. Sports revolve around players, similar to characters. Fans may develop positive and negative dispositions toward a player, toward a team, or even toward a specific sport more generally. Consistent with disposition theory, audiences enjoy the victories of favored players or teams, and the defeat of despised opponents. According to sports marketers Rick Burton and Dennis Howard, "One of the reasons for professional sports popularity is that it produces winners and losers, heroes and villains." Even when viewed as an individual exercise such as running or biking, sports produce emotions and performances that are frequently hard to generate in most other pursuits.[40]

Sports as Drama

Although sports have much in common with other forms of entertainment, they also have some unique characteristics. One important way in which sports differ from other entertainment forms is their immediacy:

> There's good reason why sports is a TV staple: It's human drama at a base level, it's cheap to produce and it's live. One can't minimize the power of immediacy in this time-shifting era when sports are the last remaining live coast-to-coast events—The Oscars, the Emmys, even *Saturday Night Live* are delayed to the West Coast. Only sports has the nation, and sometimes the world, watching the same thing at the same time, and if you have a message that's a potent messenger.[41]

Sports are spontaneous. Most dramas have scripts and most music has a score, but the action in sports is spontaneous and uncontrolled by its participants. Although other forms of entertainment include elements of surprise, they usually follow general expectations. We expect to be scared by a horror film, to laugh at a comedy club, and to cry along with a sentimental country music song. With sports, like some reality programming, our emotions are much more difficult to anticipate; however, our reactions are often equally—if not more—intense. At the beginning, we feel eager anticipation, uncertain as to whether the game or contest we are about to watch will be a fast-paced thriller, a drawn-out tragedy, or perhaps even an unexpected comedy. As the game unfolds, if it is a close match, we might ride a roller coaster of emotion—from elation to anxiety to despair and back again. In a more one-sided contest in which one team or player completely dominates over the other, we might experience one long, rolling wave of triumph or disappointment, depending on which side we are rooting for. Although reality programming has introduced many new forms of live, unpredictable entertainment, these programs have rarely succeeded in evoking the intense, spontaneous audience reactions that sports generate with ease.

Because of its spontaneity, however, sports producers face challenges that are different from those of most entertainment providers. No one goes to a game hoping that their team will lose, yet it is the threat of losing that fosters the suspense audiences crave. In traditional drama, the producer controls the content, setting the tempo and sequence of events to create suspense and outcomes that will satisfy their audiences. In sports, however, those that are selling the entertainment, including sports franchises and sports media, have little control over these factors. Nonetheless, sports producers are always looking for ways to maximize the drama and entertainment value of a sporting event. In some cases these efforts are obvious, such as in professional wrestling, which some might argue has become as much a soap opera as it is a sport. Rather than protest such comparisons, professional wrestling has seemingly embraced them, as reflected in the sport's title change from the World Wrestling Federation to World Wrestling Entertainment in 2002.[42] One way this shift has been accomplished is by focusing as much if not more attention on what the wrestlers do outside the ring as what they do in it. This focus allows for more character development and greater control to maximize dramatic appeal (see *Spotlight on Wrestling Mania*).

 FLASH FACT

Viewers followed the drama of the Olympic games from Beijing in record numbers. NBC reported 209 million viewers in over 16 days, making it the most watched television event in U.S. history, With a nightly average of 28.1 million, Nielsen reported that half of the viewers were women over 18.

According to the official Chinese Olympics web site, a total of 680 million or 56 percent of mainland China's audience watched the event each day on TV. Over 16 days, the Olympic Channel attracted 1.3 billion viewers in China, representing 90.5 percent of China's audience. The European Broadcasting Union said that over 120 million video streams were downloaded of the games from its members' web sites. The event was the most widely viewed Olympic games ever, pleasing advertisers who spent over $1.5 billion to place their brands on air.

Source: http://en.beijing2008.cn/news/official/noc/oca/n21 4576451.shtml

In other sports such efforts may be more subtle, but they reflect similar dramatic techniques. To promote sports as drama, "character development" is enhanced by profiles on the athletes provided in game programs, sports articles, and game commentaries. Fans are given not only the athletes' sports performance statistics, but also personal information about their lives and families. Over the years, the sports themselves have changed and evolved to promote spectatorship. Rules for football, baseball, and basketball were modified in the 1970s to favor dramatic offensive action, thus enhancing spectator appeal and fitting more efficiently into the requirements of television programming.

Rules and schedules are continuing to change. To better fit within fans' typical leisure-time schedules, baseball includes more night games, and the World Series begins on a weekend. The pitcher's mound was lowered to make the curve and slider pitches more effective—and more exciting to watch. In basketball, rule changes were designed to facilitate scoring because fans tend to find high-scoring games more exciting. Similarly, in the National Football League, to emphasize higher scoring and forward drive, the goal posts were moved back to the endline, kickoffs now begin at the 35-yard line rather than the 40, and the penalty for offensive holding was reduced from 15 to 10 yards. In addition, sudden death overtimes were instituted to intensify the pace and maximize the excitement of tiebreakers. And schedules were changed to increase the number of games played by better teams in bigger television markets.

Sports franchises must work to keep audiences entertained even when the action is slow or the home team is suffering a long losing streak. Most of the techniques used today to enhance the dramatic value of sports are not new, just improved. Cheerleaders, mascots, and music help sustain momentum during game lulls, as they always have, but with twists that add pizzazz. Players are no longer simply announced over the public address system as they take the field or court—they are introduced with theme songs and elaborate video presentations. Teams have flashier team colors, logos, and uniforms, and new stadiums are designed to maximize entertainment with luxury boxes, jumbo video screens, VIP clubs, novelty stores, a vast array of dining options, and better camera angles for the television viewing audience.

SPOTLIGHT ON WRESTLING MANIA   Sports as Drama

Shamelessly drawing on classic dramatic devices, professional wrestling is dramatically entertaining

Nowhere is the concept of sports as drama more evident than in professional wrestling. Wrestling as entertainment has survived in some form for more than 100 years, first as a carnival spectacle and later as a television spectacular.[43] Many of the characteristics of theater can be found in professional wrestling. The ring is like a stage, and the ropes, turnbuckles, and chains that form the ring are stage props. The theme of the drama—the vengeance of justice—is expressed in a plot of confrontation between good and evil. The wrestlers are portrayed as heroes or villains. These characters are developed through a combination of the wrestler's name, costume, and behavior. In soap-opera fashion, however, these roles are subject to change at any time. Good characters go bad, and bad characters reform. Romances, alliances, and conspiracies frequently realign. Interestingly, the amount of time spent on the actual wrestling during these matches has decreased in recent years, with more and more time is spent on the posturing, taunting, and drama that takes place between the wrestlers and other characters. Consider this report of one World Wrestling Federation live broadcast:

Baseball legend Wade Boggs was in the house; the nation's No. 1 author, a man in a leather mask named Mankind, was scheduled to wrestle; the women's chocolate-pudding match was good to go. Yet all was not right: not for the WWF and not for Vince McMahon, its chairman and mastermind. On the previous week's broadcast, his real-life daughter, Stephanie, had been "tricked" into marrying his arch nemesis, the wrestler Triple H. Now McMahon was running into the ring with a sledgehammer, out for blood. Stephanie had a surprise for him. She was in love with Triple H, she told him. And further, they were taking control of the company. She said, "Triple H outsmarted you by making business personal. That's something you know all about."[44]

And, like more traditional drama, most of the action is at least loosely, if not entirely, scripted. Most wrestling fans accept that the wrestling matches are faked, but this does not prevent fans from enjoying them. In fact, the number of wrestling fans has been growing. According to one report, in 1999, two Monday night wrestling programs each lasting two hours attracted 35 million viewers. Although males ages 12–34 make up the vast majority of viewers, the number of female viewers has been increasing.[45] Besides watching wrestling on TV, fans attend live events, subscribe to wrestling magazines, visit wrestling web sites, and buy T-shirts, theme music, and autobiographies of wrestling superstars. Audiences, however, are forever fickle and, by the end of 2002, program ratings and event attendance suggested World Wrestling Entertainment might be losing some of its audience. As with all forms of entertainment, the popularity of professional wrestling may fluctuate over the years, and the sport will continue to change and evolve as it attempts to attract and retain audiences.

What do you think?

- Is professional wrestling more sport or drama? Watch a wrestling match and see what comparisons and contrasts you can draw between wrestling and other sports, and wrestling and other forms of drama, such as an action film or a soap opera.
- Why do you think professional wrestling became so popular at the beginning of the twenty-first century?

Music and Emotion

Recall the notion that entertainment makes us feel. Drama and story are the vehicles that evoke our emotions, thus making them an integral feature of most all entertainment. It is argued that music is a form of entertainment that can most directly evoke emotion. Song lyrics tell stories of love, hard times, or triumph. Within minutes, music can calm us, inspire us, or sadden us. Lyrics aside, even just the beat and tone of music can communicate emotion and story. Slow, low sounds often suggest sadness, while fast, high sounds can suggest happiness or surprise. Loud, low tones may sound angry and so on. Many people who do not speak Italian still enjoy Italian opera because the heart of the story is conveyed more by the music and tone of the vocals than by the songs' lyrics. In fact, one classic music composition, *Peter and the Wolf*, actually uses different instruments representing animal characters (French horns for the wolf, flute for a bird, strings for Peter, and so on) to tell a story and at the same time teach children about music.

What is particularly amazing about music is that it conveys story and emotion using only the sense of sound whereas other popular forms of entertainment engage multiple senses. Television and film use both sight and sound to tell stories, and other forms of entertainment such as amusement park rides and video games, for example, often engage sight, sound, touch, and sometimes even smell. Video games and other forms of entertainment (such as films, books, and other drama-based entertainment) also require more cognitive effort if they are to be interpreted or appreciated. Audiences can enjoy music without exerting a great deal of energy or attention. Individuals may choose to devote a significant amount of their energy and attention to music, dancing and singing along to tunes cranked up full blast, but they do not have to. People can also enjoy music even if their attention is focused elsewhere—for example, on working, driving, or dozing. To truly enjoy a book, film, or video game typically requires much more energy and attention.

Music's single sensory input (sound) and effortless emotional connection makes it a popular supplement for storytelling in other forms of entertainment. Films include soundtracks to cue audiences' emotional reactions—playing scary music to stimulate fear, melancholy songs to evoke sadness, and so on. At sporting events, music is played to rally the players and fans. Music is also played in restaurants, bars, retail stores, theme parks, and other leisure settings to set a mood and facilitate and enhance patrons' enjoyment without detracting from their social activities and interactions.

FADE TO BLACK

Drama is a driving force in most forms of entertainment. Drama drives the excitement and emotion in entertainment that makes us feel. There are many speculations regarding the appeal of drama. It may distract us from our problems, help us purge negative emotions, make us feel better about ourselves, and give us ideas for our own lives. Different dramatic genres are characterized by their own twists on the standard dramatic formula, and much research has explored who likes these different genres and why.

Drama is everywhere. It can be found in books, movies, television shows, video games, and music. Even unscripted entertainment such as reality programs and sports reflects traditional dramatic principles. The spontaneity and unpredictability of these genres crreate the suspense and excitement that contemporay audiences crave.

A CLOSER LOOK AT ARCHETYPES   Stock Characters

A **stock character** is a fictional character largely based on cultural *types* or *stereotypes* for its personality, mannerisms, and other characteristics. Most stock characters are related to literary archetypes, but they are often more narrowly defined. Stock characters are a key component of genre, providing relationships and interactions that people familiar with the genre can easily recognize. Stock characters are sometimes parodied, exaggerating any stereotypes associated with these characters. Listed in the following sections are some common stock characters and situations. See if you can come up with additional examples for each from recent books, films, and so on that feature aspects of one or more of them.

Stock Characters

The Reluctant Hero: This hero is usually an ordinary person thrust into extraordinary circumstances beyond his/her control that will require a great deal of effort and peril on his/her part. This hero has reservations about fulfilling their heroic obligations for various reasons, such as disbelief in their importance, or the desire to live a simple life. Examples of the reluctant hero include Frodo Baggins of *The Lord of the Rings*, Cloud Strife in *Final Fantasy VII*, Luke Skywalker in *Star Wars*, and Richard Rahl of the *Sword of Truth* series of books.

The Comic Sidekick: Cowards who bring some humor into the plot, such as Jack on *Will & Grace* and Donkey in *Shrek*.

The Nerd Girl: She doesn't dress fashionably and may be intensely interested in some specialized area or notable for her intelligence. Deb in *Napoleon Dynamite* is a classic Nerd Girl (she wears her hair in an unusual way, dresses in loose, unfashionable clothing and is into photography). Darla Simmons in *Martin Mystery* is another example. The Nerd Girl is often kind and goodhearted, and may be quite attractive, or have the potential to be so with some "tidying up" (like Hermione Granger in *Harry Potter* and Ami Mizuno in *Sailor Moon*).

The Wacky Neighbor: Lives close to the main character and has eccentric qualities which often serve as a convenient plot device. Examples: Cosmo Kramer of *Seinfeld*, Ned Flanders of *The Simpsons*, Wilson of *Home Improvement*, and Gladys Kravitz of *Bewitched*.

The Wise Old Man: An elderly character who offers advice and guidance to the protagonists. Examples include Gandalf from *The Lord of the Rings*, Yoda from *Star Wars*, and Pai Mei from the *Kill Bill* movies.

Stock Situations

The Bitter Rivals: Two rival factions that are constantly fighting and feuding with each other with both sides equally to blame for the feud. Such examples include the Montagues and the Capulets from *Romeo and Juliet*, the Jets and the Sharks from *West Side Story*, and the Hatfields and the McCoys.

The Dysfunctional Nuclear Family: A normal family with a simple-minded father, a reasonable mother, a troublesome son, an anxious daughter, and a peculiar younger child. Famous examples would be the Simpsons, the Griffins, the Jetsons, and the Incredibles.

The Middle Child: This character tends to be good natured and intelligent, but can be insecure and lack confidence. Jan and Peter Brady from *The Brady Bunch* are perhaps the best-known television examples; more recent characters include Malcolm from *Malcolm in the Middle* and Lisa Simpson from *The Simpsons*.

The Girl Threesome: A group of three girls where one is blonde, one is a brunette (and/or Black), and one is a redhead. They are usually heroines and have different tempers, but may also serve as "hangers-on" as the friendship group of the main Heroine. Examples: *Charlie's Angels*, the Powerpuff Girls, *Josie and the Pussycats*, and Buffy Summers, Cordelia Chase, and Willow Rosenberg of *Buffy the Vampire Slayer*.

The Ill-fated Lovers: Passionate, sensual, and naïve. They love fiercely and irrationally, usually against societal or parental approval, or against the crushing inevitability of time. Examples include Romeo and Juliet, their modern analogs, Tony and Maria of *West Side Story*, Zack and Kelly of *Saved by the Bell*, Buffy Summers and Angel of *Buffy the Vampire Slayer*, J. D. and Elliot of *Scrubs*.

DISCUSSION AND REVIEW

1. Review theories regarding the dramatic formula and theories regarding the appeal of drama. Consider some of your favorite stories (books, films, TV, etc.) and use these theories to explain why you like them.
2. Examine examples of songs, films, TV programs, and so on that reflect different genres. Identify examples of each genre and use the theories in the text, as well as your own ideas, to pinpoint what differentiates good from bad examples of each genre—i.e., what qualities make a good horror film, comedy, reality program, etc.?
3. How do traditional theories of drama explain the appeal of unscripted entertainment such as reality program or sports? What are the similarities and differences between unscripted and scripted entertainment? Speculate on the types of audiences that might prefer either unscripted or scripted entertainment.

EXERCISES

1. Do an informal poll. Ask as many people as you can what their favorite films and TV programs are. Note the genres of those shows (comedy, mystery, etc.) and look for patterns in who likes what including demographic differences such as age and gender and any personality differences you can identify. Compare what you find to the trends explored in the chapter.
2. Look on the Internet to find a listing of the top films for last year. Break them down into the genres listed in Figure 4.3. How do your findings compare? What conclusions can you draw?
3. Take another look at the genres in Figure 4.3 and Table 4.2. See if you can come up with general formulas and characteristics for the ones not specifically discussed in the text.

BOOKS AND BLOGS

Bryant, J. and Zillmann, D. (eds). *Responding to the screen: Reception and reaction processes.* Mahwah NJ: Lawrence Erlbaum Associates.

Phillips, M. and Huntley C. (2004). *Dramatica: A new theory of story.* Glendale CA: Write Brothers.

Zillmann, D. and Vorderer, P. (eds). *Media entertainment: The psychology of its appeal.* Mahwah NJ: Lawrence Erlbaum Associates.

5 ENTERTAINMENT EFFECTS

Even the most conservative estimates indicate that preschool children in America are spending more than a third of their waking hours watching television. What are the effects upon the vulnerable and developing human organism of spending such a significant portion of each day engaged in this particular experience?

—Marie Winn, *The Plug-in Drug*, p. 4

The effects of entertainment can be examined in much the same way one might examine the effects of a prescription drug. Indeed, some critics even contend that entertainment (such as movies, television, music, and video games) may have drug-like effects. When researchers are testing a new drug, they examine both its intended effects (how well it does what it is supposed to do—e.g., relieve a headache, clear up acne, or cure an infection) as well potential, unintentional side effects (e.g., nausea, weight gain, sun sensitivity, and so on). Researchers have examined effects of entertainment, particularly media entertainment, in a similar manner, often relying on methods and techniques similar to those used in medical research.

The most obvious intended effect of entertainment, of course, is to entertain. Performers, writers, and producers create stories, movies, games, songs, and experiences with the intention of entertaining audiences. And audiences expose themselves to these experiences with the intention of being entertained. Thus, research that focuses on the intended effects of entertainment usually explores how "effective" different forms of entertainment are at entertaining audiences. In Chapter 4, we introduced some of this research, which reveals how drama is used to create emotional, psychological, and even physiological reactions that form the crux of the entertainment experience. As is the case with drugs, not all forms of entertainment have the same effects on all audiences. Research finds that some forms of entertainment "work better" for some audiences than others.

Entertainment also creates a number of other effects, both intentional and unintentional. Chapter 3, for example, relates a variety of the effects or "gratifications" that audiences seek from entertainment, including distraction from life's problems and information about societal norms. As you will see in later chapters, entertainment often has other intended effects. A corporate sponsor of a sporting event hopes that the event will not only entertain audiences but also capture attention and ultimately result in an increase in sales of its products. And many books, films, or songs are written not only to entertain but also to educate and persuade audiences about specific topics or issues that are important to the writer. For example, books like *Uncle Tom's cabin*, movies like *American History X* (1998), and songs like NWA's (Niggaz With Attitude) "F . . . the Police" may entertain audiences, but they also promote certain views about race relations.

Like drugs, entertainment may also have some unintentional "side effects." If entertainment can intentionally affect our emotions, thoughts, and physical reactions, as suggested in Chapter 4, some argue that these effects may also unintentionally extend beyond the entertainment experience to affect our more general feelings, thoughts, behavior, and physical well-being. Although books, sports, movies, music, and video games are often accused of initiating negative effects such as encouraging violence, drug use, racial stereotyping, and eating disorders, they have also been credited with some positive impacts such as relieving stress, educating children, increasing awareness of social issues, and improving physical health.

Effect Types

This chapter explores media and entertainment effects, both intentional and unintentional, that extend beyond the effect of being entertained. Most of these effects can be categorized into one or more of the following effect types:

- *Psychological effects*. Researchers are interested in many psychological effects of entertainment. Can what we see, hear, and do for entertainment influence our more general thoughts and opinions? For example, can movies like *American History X* or *Blood Diamonds* influence people's opinions about race relations, prejudice, and police action? Much of this psychological research focuses on the impact of entertainment on our knowledge and opinions about societal issues or certain groups of people, including our own self-images.
- *Behavioral effects*. Can our entertainment choices affect our more general behavior? Can movies and music influence not only our opinions but also our actions toward other people? Can they make us more introverted, more aggressive, or more fashionable? Corporate sponsors of films, sporting events, concerts, and other entertaining activities spend a great deal of money because they believe that pairing their brands with these entertainment options will encourage people to buy and use their products and services. Behavioral effects research focuses on how entertainment such as films, music, video games, and sports might influence behaviors ranging from our meal choices to our career choices.
- *Physiological effects*. Researchers have even examined physiological effects of entertainment. As discussed in Chapter 4, some research has examined how the suspense found in entertainment can influence our heart rate, breathing, and other physical reactions. Research has also examined other physiological effects. Some research even suggests that humor and other forms of drama may boost our immune systems, increase our pain tolerance, and aid in healing.

History of Media Effects Theories

Given that so much contemporary entertainment is media-based, it is perhaps not surprising that much of effects research has focused on the media. Although not all media research focuses on entertainment (some research examines news or informational media), most of the theories and studies can be easily adapted. Furthermore, as the lines between news and entertainment and even between live and mediated communication become more blurred, these distinctions may become even less relevant.

Media effects research has gone through several stages of development or paradigms. As research advances, different ideas or hypotheses are tested, and gradually a uniform theory or paradigm emerges. A **paradigm** serves as an overarching view of a field that summarizes and is consistent with existing research. However, as research continues, new insights are made that may conflict with that view, and often our thinking begins to change. Old ideas are replaced with new ones. Sometimes thinking can change quite radically, resulting in what is often called a **paradigm shift**.[1] Our theories and ideas about what is true are fundamentally altered, and a new paradigm emerges.

Powerful Effects Theories

The idea of **powerful effects** or **mass society theory** reflects what many media scholars consider to be the first media effects paradigm. The first research on the impact of the media emerged when mass media themselves emerged, beginning in the second half of the nineteenth century with the "mass" circulation of newspapers and magazines and continuing through the first half of the twentieth century with the invention of silent films, talkies, and radio. These times were characterized by the industrialization and urbanization of society in the United States and Western Europe. The fabric of these societies was changed as immigrants traveled and settled in different countries and regions in search of better opportunities and quality of life. In the United States, some leaders saw these changes as threats to the "American" way of life. They felt that the media undermined traditional values by sensationalizing and oversimplifying content to pander to the limited language levels and the perceived low tastes of the immigrants. These fears were reinforced by the successful media propaganda campaigns by totalitarian governments in Europe, such as Adolf Hitler's regime in Nazi Germany. In the United States, demands were made for media control to prevent such abuses.

These ideas—that the media are all-powerful and that the average person is defenseless against this influence—served as the overarching view of the powerful effects or mass society paradigm. One prominent proponent of the powerful impact of the media was Walter Lippmann. In his famous book *Public opinion*, Lippmann argued that we see the world not as it really is but as "pictures in our heads"—pictures shaped not by our personal experiences but by the mass media.[2] The views of this era are often summarized by the **hypodermic needle theory** or the **magic bullet theory**. Like a dangerous drug or bullet, media messages were thought to be mindlessly absorbed by audiences, as though injected or shot into their systems.

FLASH FACT

About 48 communications theories are considered relevant to the study of how people relate to and are affected by the media. Micro, meso, and macro levels describe theories that are clearly focused on a particular arena of study. Upwards of 57 scholarly communication journals publish studies that emphasize theory. The most important organization of academic study is the International Communication Association, which holds annual conferences that bring together researchers in the discipline.

Limited Effects Theories

Mass society theory is an example of a **grand theory**—a simple, all-encompassing theory that tried to describe and explain all aspects of a phenomenon (in this case, the effects of the media). However, it became readily apparent that audiences were not becoming brainwashed en masse by subversive media messages. Media effects proved to be too complex for a single grand theory, and eventually the paradigm collapsed.

Paradigm shifts typically do not happen suddenly; rather, they develop over an extended period of time. Nonetheless, these shifts are often sparked by key events or research findings. This was the case in mass media research with the shift from a powerful effects paradigm to a limited effects paradigm. One crystallizing event happened on Halloween in 1938 when Orson Welles broadcast his dramatized version of H.G. Wells's science fiction novel *War of the worlds* over the radio. This radio dramatization portrayed the Earth under Martian attack in docudrama style. Thousands of people fled from their homes in panic, believing the attack to be real. Mass society theorists claimed this phenomenon as proof of their theory. Further research, however, called this conclusion into question. Scientists at Princeton University found that although one million people might have been frightened into taking some action, the other five million people who heard the show did

Radio listeners in 1938 heard Orson Wells say that the world was being invaded by Martians

not. These researchers concluded that different factors led some people to be influenced whereas others were not, calling into question the mindless, universal impacts predicted by mass society and powerful effects theories.[3]

Scientific Perspective   This research reflected a new, emerging **limited effects** paradigm based on a more scientific approach to the study of media effects. Although the theories that developed within this paradigm still suggested that the media can have psychological, physical, and physiological effects on their audiences, these effects were argued to be "limited" by many factors. These theories provided conditional rather than universal explanations of media effects, isolating the impacts of specific media phenomena for specific audiences. Yale psychologist Harold Lasswell, who studied World War II propaganda, outlined a systematic approach to media effects with his model of mass communication: *Who, Says what, In which channel, To whom, With what effect*, and thus, a new era of research was born that focused on isolating and examining each of these facets.

This approach was championed by Paul Lazarsfeld, who argued that mere speculation and anecdotal evidence alone could not explain the complexities of media effects.[4] He and his colleagues advocated the use of well-designed studies based on survey research, polling, and other social scientific methods. Based on Lazarsfeld's work, researchers began to isolate individuals and groups who tended to be more or less susceptible to media influences and identified individual differences (e.g., intelligence, age, education), social categories (e.g., religion, political affiliation), and personal relationships (e.g., friends, family) that accounted for differences in media impact. The collection of theories that came out of this first era of systematic and scientific study of media effects have been labeled limited effects theories.

Two-step Flow Theory   One popular example of a limited effects theory is Lazarsfeld's own **two-step flow theory** of mass media and personal influence.[5] In their study of the 1940 presidential election, Lazarsfeld and his colleagues found that the media's influence on voting behavior was filtered through **opinion leaders**—that is, people who regularly consumed media content on topics of interest to them, interpreted media content based on their own beliefs and values and then passed along their thoughts to **opinion followers**, people who have less exposure to the media. Thus, according to this theory, media impact flows through a two-step process: first to opinion leaders and then indirectly through the opinion leaders to everyone else. Opinion leaders are still important today, particularly in influencing trends in entertainment; however, because television and other advances have given people greater exposure to the media firsthand, opinion leaders are not thought to play as critical a role in filtering the media's influence for the rest of society as they once did.

Cumulative and Cultural Effects

Beginning during World War II, the limited effects approach dominated thinking about media for several decades. As this research progressed, however, it reached a level of complexity that led some theorists to argue that yet another new paradigm had developed. They speculated that one reason that research had not revealed more powerful effects of the media was because of the narrow, short-term focus of many of the more scientific media studies. As a result, new approaches began to expand the scope and duration of media studies. Whereas some research continued to follow a more classically scientific, quantitative approach, other investigations began exploring the impact of the media from a more subjective, cultural approach. Investigations of both types began to once again consider potentially more powerful **cumulative** media effects—effects that accumulate gradually from long-term repeated media exposure. Given the diversity of contemporary theories and approaches, many mass media scholars argue that, today, there exists not one but several paradigms of effects research. Many of these theories and research methods have implications not just for media entertainment but for all forms of entertainment.

SPOTLIGHT ON DIFFUSION THEORY   Application to Nigeria

Developing economies are looking inwards to solve imaging problems. Nigeria's image project intended to use diffusion of innovation theory to re-image the country in the eyes of visitors and residents alike. In this instance, diffusion refers to the process in which an innovation, or the Nigeria image project, is communicated over time through opinion leaders and mass media to citizens and other stakeholders and publics such as potential investors.

Because of low literacy among citizens of Nigeria, many people could not access media content and had to rely on literate persons or opinion leaders for information about the project. After implementing a promotional campaign on Nigeria as a tourist destination, researchers asked survey respondents if they knew about the image project. Eighty percent

said yes, 63 percent said they read about it online, and 38 percent said they heard about the project from second hand sources. About 20 percent said they had never heard about the project.

Asking whether or not Nigerian input was gathered for the image project, all opinion leaders (church leaders, medical doctors, and journalists) responded "no." Because innovation says that people are more likely to cooperate and bring change if they are consulted about the process and have a stake in it, the theory was not well-used for Nigeria's image program.

Information and knowledge gaps among citizens of Nigeria account for the lack of awareness of the image project. Project goals to attract potential investors and re-orient citizens to think Nigeria first, and to promote Nigerian ideals and culture in different parts of the world, were not successful. Social marketing, a strategy that applies diffusion of non-profit services, has been successful in Turkey and South Africa and was recommended for use in a new image campaign for Nigeria.

Source: www.collegehandouts.com/files/applying_commu-nication_theories_to_country_branding.doc

What do you think?

- *How would you use the diffusion of innovations theory to communicate a positive image to Nigerian citizens?*

Research Methods

Researchers have studied the impact of media and entertainment in many different ways. In general, quantitative media scholars tend to study media from a detached, objective, and clinical perspective similar to the way biologists, chemists, or medical researchers conduct research in their fields. In comparison, qualitative or cultural theorists tend to study media effects from a more involved, subjective approach using techniques similar to those of anthropologists or literary scholars, whose theories evolve from more personal insights gained by immersing themselves in their studies, sometimes as participant observers. This difference in perspective is reflected in the varying methods that are used to study media and entertainment effects.

Quantitative Measures

In **quantitative analyses**, psychological, behavioral, and physiological effects are *quantified*—counted and statistically analyzed to determine how media and different forms of entertainment may affect people. These studies often look for statistical differences in the thoughts, behaviors, or physical conditions of those who have been exposed to certain forms of entertainment and those who have not. Some quantitative measures are based on **direct observations** whereas others are based on **self-reports**. Observations might be quantified by watching people and counting the number of times or the length of time that they perform a specific action—for example, counting the number of beers fans drink at a ballgame when their team is winning versus when their team is losing. Self-reports can be similarly quantified by asking people (verbally or on a survey) to estimate the number of times or length of time that they perform a specific action, such as asking them how many beers they drank at the ballgame.

Quantitative researchers interested in the effects of video games on a child's behavior toward other children might collect their data through observation or self-reports, or both. They might first observe children playing video games or survey them about their video game playing habits and then either observe how those children interact with other children (whether children play well and share with other children or keep to themselves) or use reports of behavior obtained either by asking the child questions about his or her interactions with other children or by asking the child's teachers or parents.

Observational and self-report measures each have relative advantages and limitations. Observations are usually preferred, but researchers may be restricted in what they can observe, so studies are often limited to self-report measures. For example, we cannot directly observe opinions and attitudes. Instead, we must rely on estimates usually obtained through self-reports on surveys and questionnaires. We may ask people to rate their opinions on scales from 1 to 5 to reflect their agreement with listed statements. Answers to theses questions provide us with quantifiable opinion measures.

Qualitative Measures

Qualitative and ethnographic studies of media effects include observations, self-reports, and historical data. Instead of converting this data into numbers and statistics, qualitative studies analyze the phenomena they study in their natural textual, auditory, and/or visual forms or through narrative descriptions. Behavioral observations, for example, are documented through videotape, audiotape, or transcribed descriptions. Results of the analysis are presented as excerpts and summaries of these observations.

Two popular qualitative strategies for acquiring self-reports are **in-depth interviews** and **focus groups**. In-depth interviews allow researchers to probe individuals' thoughts, opinions, and self-reports of behavior with less structure but more detail than a structured survey or questionnaire. Researchers begin with very general questions and then adapt their probing based on what the interviewee says. For example, in-depth interviews exploring the influence of video games on children's social behavior might start with asking children what games they like to play and why, and then progress to asking them to talk about what other things they like to do for fun, probing to discover their interest and play interactions with other children. Focus groups are very similar to in-depth interviews, but, instead of interviewing people one on one, people are interviewed in a group, which allows the interviewees to interact with each other and respond to each other's comments. Rather than statistically analyzing who says what, qualitative researchers review the entire interview sessions looking for trends and isolating and reporting specific comments that represent key findings for their study.

In historical analyses, researchers may examine the relationship between media and societal trends by documenting historical issues and events and relating them to media offerings of the time. One advantage of qualitative studies is the depth and richness of their analysis, but the subjective nature of this research leads some critics to be skeptical of their findings.

Entertainment Exposures

Laboratory Research Experimental research most closely follows the clinical, quantitative tradition. In true experiments, researchers select a sample group of participants from a population they are interested in studying (e.g., citizens of a certain city, fifth graders, single women) and bring the participants to a lab or controlled environment and then expose them to different media. For example, in one of Albert Bandura's classic Bobo doll studies,[6] children were selected to be part of a sample group. That group was then divided in two.

One group, the **experimental group**, was shown a film of someone beating up an inflated Bobo doll, and the other group, the **control** or **placebo group**, saw another version of the film where the same individual played nonviolently with the Bobo doll. After

Albert Bandura found that children who saw an adult hit a doll in a film imitated the violent behavior

they saw the film, the children were placed in a room with a Bobo doll to see what they would do. Sure enough, the children who had seen the more violent film were more aggressive toward the Bobo doll than the children who had seen the nonviolent film.

Experimental studies are carefully structured to give researchers maximum control over who is exposed to what. Ideally, experimental researchers want **random selection**, meaning that individuals who are picked for the study are selected at random from the larger population, and **random assignment**, meaning that participants are randomly assigned or placed into different groups or conditions (in the Bobo doll experiment, violent or nonviolent film conditions). This randomness is necessary to help assure that the different groups are relatively equal to each other and to the larger population that is being studied before the experiment begins. If, for instance, the experimental group was older than the control group, or tended to generally watch more television than the control group did, then any differences found in the study might be due to those differences rather than the "treatment" they received. Similarly, if everyone who participated in the study was on average older or watched more TV than the rest of the population, then the researchers wouldn't know if the impact they found in their sample group would affect children in the general population in the same way. Researchers can try to "match" groups to make sure they are equivalent, but, because people can differ in so many ways (age, personality, demographics, and so on), random selection is typically considered to provide the best assurance that these differences are not concentrated in one group more than another.

This need for control makes it very difficult to conduct true experimental media and entertainment research. First, it is difficult to obtain a truly random selection of a population. It is often very difficult to find and persuade people to participate in these studies, so researchers are limited to voluntary and convenient sample groups—people who are willing and readily available to participate. Because most research takes place at universities, studies often focus on college students. This is fine if we are only interested in the effects of media or other forms of entertainment on *college students* who are *willing* to participate (often only those who want extra credit); however, usually researchers are also interested in effects on other populations.

Another challenge is that, after you obtain a sample, it is often difficult to create random assignment. We may be able to convince individuals to come to our labs to watch one film, play video games, or listen to an hour or two of music that we select for them. However, just as one dose of a drug may not have much effect, one "dose" of media or other form of entertainment may not be enough to have much effect, either. It is much more difficult to control what people do and see for long periods of time, particularly when it comes to entertainment.

Even perfectly controlled laboratory studies are open to criticism. One concern is the impact of the "laboratory" environment itself. People typically do not watch movies or listen to music for pleasure while seated at desks in college classrooms. That, however, is often the environment in which effects studies are conducted. Thus, there is some question as to whether individuals will act and react the same way in the lab as they would in a more natural environment, particularly when they know they are being watched. To create more natural settings, many modern research facilities include complete theaters and even mini "homes" that simulate or imitate natural environments (see the image on p. 118). Thus, for a study on video games, researchers might create a lab that looks like a living room with a home game system, an office or bedroom set up for computer games, or even a room set up to look like a video arcade. People are then brought into the lab and asked to play video games as they normally would at home, work, or the arcade. Even in the most realistic labs, however, individuals may still not behave as they normally would,

Modern entertainment research "labs" include more naturalistic settings such as mini theaters

because they usually still know that they are being observed. Thus, although laboratory research allows for control, it is less *ecologically valid* than other forms of research, meaning that the study environment is less representative of the real world.

Field Research   To overcome the artificiality of the laboratory environment, some researchers turn to field studies. In these studies, rather than having the people come to the researchers, the researchers go to the people. Researchers go to theaters, concerts, video arcades, bars, sporting events, and other natural environments to observe how audiences are affected by entertainment experiences. For example, researchers might go to a video arcade and look for trends in what types of children (age, gender, ethnicity, and so on) play which types of video games, and then they might try to determine if playing different games changes the way the children think or their behavior—such as making them more or less assertive, aggressive, or shy with other children. Some of these investigations follow in the quantitative tradition, where researchers document individuals' media and entertainment experiences and the resulting effects, collecting data for systematic, statistical analysis. In other studies, however, individuals take a more qualitative approach, interpreting information obtained through field observations or interviews more subjectively.

Although these studies have the advantage of being more based in the real world, typically they are not based on random selection or random assignment. It is natural for people to choose their own entertainment, as well as when and where they will experience it. Assigning people to specific groups in a field study would be difficult and artificial. Even in field studies where more control is established (for example, if individuals were randomly selected to go see specific movies or concerts or play certain video games), people are still usually aware that they are being observed or studied, so there is still no way to be sure that people will react as they normally would. Nonetheless, although field studies usually provide less control than laboratory studies, they are usually more ecologically valid, or more representative of the real world.

Self-reported Exposure   Rather than controlling the media or entertainment "treatments" that people receive, as is done in a laboratory study, or by directly observing individuals' media or entertainment choices, as is done in a field study, researchers often must rely on self-reports of exposure. Increasingly, researchers are interested in studying more long-term, cumulative effects. Because it is difficult if not impossible to control or even observe what people naturally see, hear, and do for weeks, months, or years at a time, researchers often simply ask individuals what they typically watch, see, or do and then look for differences in their attitudes or behaviors based on what they report. Thus, researchers may ask on a survey what kind of video games a child typically plays and how often and then see if children who regularly play certain games think or behave differently than those who do not.

But, of course, in self-report studies, as in many field studies, we cannot control the "treatments" or entertainment that people receive. As a result, any differences we find between people who select different entertainment may not be due to the entertainment itself but to any number of other factors. For example, when a survey study finds a correlation between exposure to violent video games and aggressive tendencies, it may not be that playing these video games makes children become more aggressive, but rather that children who are more aggressive tend to choose more aggressive games. Or, there may be other factors that are involved. We might find that a survey suggests that individuals who attend rock concerts are more likely to develop emphysema than individuals who go to classical concerts. Does this mean that live rock music causes emphysema? Hardly. It might simply be that people who attend live rock concerts smoke more cigarettes than do people who go to classical concerts and that it is the smoking that is causing the emphysema. If researchers also include survey questions about other potential influences (such as smoking, in this case) they can try to statistically separate and identify the effects of each (e.g., the impact of attending live concerts versus the impact of smoking), but it can be difficult if not impossible to ask questions for every possible factor that might influence differences in these effects.

Content and Text Analysis   If we want to truly understand how audiences are affected by media entertainment, we also need to understand the nature of the media itself. A pharmaceutical researcher would not test the effects of a new drug without knowing the contents of the drug. Similarly, media researchers cannot truly test or explain the effects of different forms of media entertainment without knowing the content or *text* of that media, including words, images, and sounds. Most content analyses include very systematic, quantifiable measures of media content, where researchers actually quantify the amount of different types of content—for example, measuring column inches devoted to certain topics in magazine articles, counting the minutes of violence in movies, or the number of women or minorities that play certain roles in TV programs.

It can be difficult, however, to develop objective, quantitative measures of media content. How, for example, do you create a measure of the amount of violence in a film? Does violence include instances when one character pushes another or holds a gun to someone's head but doesn't pull the trigger? Do you measure violence by the length of time that fighting occurs or by the number of people that are killed or injured? The measures that are used in a study usually depend upon what the researchers are specifically interested in studying. Nonetheless, researchers need to be very careful about clearly defining the measures they use because those methods need to be objective and reliable—that is, when different people use the same measure to analyze the same content, such as the violence in a film, they should come up with the same results.

In other research, content or text is analyzed from a qualitative perspective. In these studies, instead of trying to objectively count content, researchers subjectively demonstrate trends by selecting excerpts or examples and interpreting them from a specific theoretical approach or perspective. Different researchers might isolate different examples or trends depending on their own opinions or perspectives. For example, Jean Kilbourne has created a series of documentary movies called *Killing Us Softly* that makes the argument that advertising depicts unrealistic and sexist portrayals of women by showing examples of advertisements and pointing out distortions in those messages.

Researchers have analyzed the content of many forms of media entertainment, including films, TV programs, magazines, video games, sporting events, song lyrics, and the images in music videos. Therefore, when individuals self-report high exposure to certain forms of media, researchers gain a better sense of what exactly

Analyzing the content of a film or magazine can serve as an important first step to understanding its potential impact on readers

they have been exposed to. In formal content analyses, however, evaluations are typically limited to objective measures of content. Although this analysis might be combined with surveys or other data for further evaluations, content analyses alone do not attempt to interpret or evaluate the meaning or potential impact of that content. In other words, content analysis can tell us only how often guns are shown in prime-time television programs or how many women in fashion magazines are showing their midriffs; it does not tell us what those depictions mean or what impact they may have on their audiences. Exceptions to these limitations, however, are found in qualitative analyses of media content, such as Jean Kilbourne's studies, which often do include interpretations of the meaning and impact of the trends they find.

Both quantitative and qualitative analyses of media content often serve as a starting point for more media effects research. For instance, a study on how the media influences stereotyping might first analyze content to look for stereotypical depictions. Researchers might analyze the content of films or TV programs to see if certain ethnic groups are disproportionately portrayed as criminals or deadbeats. If such stereotyping does appear to exist, then the researchers might do further research to see if individuals who report watching more films or television are more likely to hold the stereotypical views portrayed by the media. Content analyses can thus provide useful insights into understanding the impact of media entertainment. Although content analyses are informative, critics contend that these studies are not sufficiently objective because of the difficulty researchers have in creating clear, informative measures of media content.

A Final Note on Research Methods

Quantitative and qualitative analysis, observational data and self-reports, laboratory and field studies, and content and text analyses—each method and approach has relative strengths and weaknesses for studying media and entertainment effects. Many studies now incorporate a mixture of approaches to take advantage of the strengths of each. But there is no such thing as a perfect study; every investigation is open to criticism. Researchers, however, do not abandon their investigations simply because they cannot design a perfect study. Instead, they recognize that the value of their research does lies not in the individual results of a single study but in the cumulative findings of many studies over time. The following section reviews some of these findings and the theories that have been used to explain them.

Theories of Media Effects

This section presents discussion of both limited and longer-term effects of mass media on their audiences.

Limited Effects

Both the United States and Germany provided generous government funding for media research during and following World War II to learn how to use the media to effectively generate and counter war propaganda. This era was characterized by the limited effects perspective or paradigm. Many of the emerging theories and the resulting research followed the quantitative, scientific tradition, relying on carefully structured and controlled experiments.

Attitude Change Theory The United States Army established an Experimental Section inside its Information and Education Division and staffed it with Carl Hovland and other psychologists who were experts in attitude change. In what are commonly called the *Hovland Studies*, these researchers developed *attitude change theory*, which sought to explain how peoples' attitudes were formed, shaped, and changed through communication, and to understand the relationship between attitudes and behavior.[7] This research followed the social scientific tradition; they tested their ideas experimentally, as medical researchers might, by exposing individuals to different media or messages and testing differences in their effectiveness. Typically, these studies were done in laboratories. And, thus, this research is often criticized for being artificial.

Nonetheless, this research, which sought to explain why the media do not affect everyone the same way, made important contributions to our understanding of media effects. One concept that emerged was the notion of *cognitive dissonance*. People are said to experience cognitive dissonance, a kind of mental discomfort, when they are confronted by information or media that conflict with their own experience, ideas, or opinions. Because dissonance is uncomfortable, people are thought to engage in screening processes that can help them avoid or reduce their discomfort. Researchers propose three interrelated selective processes regarding information or media that individuals consume, remember, and interpret.

- *Selective exposure (selective attention)* refers to the tendency for people to expose themselves to or to pay attention to only those messages consistent with their preexisting attitudes or beliefs. People tend to read newspapers and magazines, watch TV programs and movies, and to listen to music and radio commentators that reflect their own views.

- *Selective retention* suggests that people best remember messages that are consistent with their preexisting attitudes and beliefs. Research finds that when individuals are exposed to media that present multiple views on an issue, they better remember the information that is consistent with their own views.
- *Selective perception* maintains that people will interpret messages in a manner consistent with their preexisting attitudes and beliefs. For example, if your favorite public figures, politicians, athletes, actors, or musicians change their position or style, they are perceived to be experimenting or responding to the demands of their public, but when those you don't like do the same thing, they are assumed to be sellouts.

SPOTLIGHT ON THEORY   Cognitive Dissonance and
                                          Changing Your Mind

A funny thing about cognitive dissonance is that it works differently with each of us. How often have you changed your behavior or your views to conform with the views of others? Or revert to views you had but no longer have? Often our drive towards self-consistency arises because we work extraordinarily hard to present a consistent front to the world rather than admitting a change of mind.

People often voice their opinions about a film, then, a few weeks later, tell you the exact opposite without any obvious compunction. One explanation for this phenomenon comes from an experiment by Cooper and Worchel (1970),[8] which found that people change their own attitudes when paid a small fee for participating in the study, but had consistent views when they were paid a large compensation for their participation. The meaning? When people think their inconsistent behavior has negative consequences, they actually defy the laws of cognitive dissonance.

Along with avoiding consequences that activate cognitive dissonance, we tend to behave according to outcomes associated with that behavior. If we foresee negative consequences, we won't admit to our own inconsistencies; if there are no unfavorable consequences, we cop to the fact that our decisions are often based on the outcome.

Are people's choices random? Studies show that, when choosing between two films they rated, viewers will change their opinion if they think it will align them with the critics and make them look smarter to their friends. Perhaps it's because we all have a hard time admitting that we're wrong.

Social psychologist Eliiot Aronsen[9] says our brains work hard to make us think we are doing the right thing, even in the face of overwhelming evidence to the contrary. According to Aronsen, cognitive dissonance is the "engine of self-justification." When our ideas, attitudes or beliefs are inconsistent (such as smoking could kill me but I smoke two packs a day), we incur a state of uncomfortable tension. We won't rest easy until we find a way to reduce this discrepancy. By holding two ideas that contradict each other, we can't make sense of our reasoning. Discrepancy causes discomfort.

Advertisers take advantage of this theory by producing commercials that make buyers happy about their purchases, even if they have doubts. "Should I have paid this much for a hybrid?" a Prius buyer wonders. But Toyota commercials that show how hybrid buyers are smarter than buyers of other cars make us feel good about spending the extra dollars to save fuel consumption. Smart folks, these advertisers.

These selective processes were proposed when the limited or minimal effects paradigm dominated media studies. If people filter out information or experiences that are inconsistent with their beliefs, we would not expect to see much attitude or behavioral change. If the only information or experiences audiences expose themselves to, retain, and perceive are those consistent with their existing attitudes and experiences, the most we might expect is reinforcement of those attitudes and experiences.

This concept is supported by Thomas Klapper's **reinforcement or phenomenistic theory**.[10] According to Klapper, the media may contribute to changes in attitude and behavior, but these changes are usually instigated by larger societal changes that are only reinforced through the media. Rather than conducting experimental, laboratory studies, Klapper's research relied more on field-based survey studies. Through these surveys, Klapper measured media exposure as well as other influences (such as church, family, and school) and found that these other influences tended to be much stronger predictors of attitudes and behaviors.

Supporters of the reinforcement view argue that critics should not be overly concerned about the impact of the media because people only read, watch, and listen to news and entertainment that is consistent with what they already think and do anyway. Because this research relies on voluntary, self-reported media use rather than experimentally controlled exposure, studies involving this theory are subject to many of the criticisms of field and self-report studies described previously in the research methods section. In addition, because Klapper's reinforcement research was conducted prior to the invention of television, some theorists speculate that Klapper might have found more powerful effects for the impact of television and other new media.

Agenda-setting Theory   Another theory that reflects the limited effects paradigm is **agenda-setting theory**. News research has found that, by focusing more on some issues than others, the media may help set the agenda by influencing how important certain issues are perceived to be.[11] In these studies, measures of actual media content obtained through content analysis were compared to survey measures of media exposure and to other influential factors and opinions on key issues. These studies have found that the more media exposure people report, the more their rankings of issue importance reflect the amount of coverage those issues get in the media. When more news stories focus on health care, we think health care is a more important issue, and when more stories focus on education or the death penalty, we think those are more important issues. However, perhaps owing to the selective processes described previously or perhaps simply because it is extremely difficult to change opinions, this research suggests that the media may influence the relative importance we ascribe to issues, but it does not necessarily influence our specific attitudes toward those issues. Thus, if the media start focusing more on the death penalty, people may begin to rank the issue as more important, but their opinions (either for or against the death penalty) are likely to remain the same, even if the media coverage appears to be biased one way or the other. Thus, the crux of agenda-setting theory is embodied by this paraphrase of Barnard Cohen's statement:[12] *The media may not tell us what to think, but they are stunningly successful at telling us what to think about.*

Setting the agenda on terrorism

Although the research on agenda setting has focused on news media, we might expect the same effects for entertainment media. Like news, entertainment media often go through different trends, where certain topics or genres proliferate the media. Often these trends reflect or respond to trends in the news media. For example, shortly after the September 11, 2001, attack on the World Trade Center in New York City, fantasy and heroic themes dominated film, television, and even music. It is reasonable to think that these offerings might similarly affect people's perceptions of the relative importance of different issues. As with all survey-based effects studies, however, agenda-setting research can reveal only correlations or similarities between media or entertainment and perceptions of issues; it cannot prove that the media or entertainment directly create or influence those perceptions.

Social Cognitive Theory   Another approach to media effects that reflects the scientific tradition is supported by social cognitive theory. Albert Bandura proposed **social learning theory**, later revised to **social cognitive theory**, which applied popular psychological theories of observational learning to mass media.[13] He proposed that people model the behaviors they see in the mass media. Bandura and his colleagues maintain that observers can acquire or learn new behaviors from the media in the same manner that they can learn from observation in any other context. In other words, you can learn to dance, flirt, smoke, and so on from watching someone else do it in a movie just as easily as you could learn from watching your cousin do the same things in your own backyard. Many of us may never have actually shot a gun, but we have a general idea how to do it from watching others, typically in television programs or in the movies.

Modeling may occur either through direct *imitation*, where individuals directly replicate behavior they observe in the media, or through *identification*, where individuals do not directly replicate behavior, but they behave in ways that reflect related, generalized responses. For example, a child who sees the cartoon *Road Runner* character hit Wile E. Coyote over the head with a frying pan might directly imitate the behavior by hitting a sibling over the head with a frying pan or indirectly imitate or identify with the aggressive action by kicking or punching the other child instead. People, however, obviously do not replicate *all* behavior that they see in the media. Consistent with a limited or conditional effects approach, social cognitive theory outlines the key conditions that are necessary for effects to be modeled:

- *Attention.* To acquire new attitudes or behaviors, an individual must first take notice of (or attend to) what the role model says or does. If people aren't paying attention to behavior that is being modeled on TV or in some other form of entertainment, they cannot replicate it.
- *Retention.* An individual must symbolically encode and retain the modeled behavior. If we do not remember what we have seen, we cannot replicate what was shown.
- *Physical reproduction.* The individual must be capable of performing the behavior. If we do not have the necessary resources (strength, money, gun, time, and so on) we cannot replicate it.
- *Reinforcement.* The individual must be reinforced for the behavior, either directly or vicariously (by watching others be rewarded).

The need for reinforcement results in two modeling effects that the media may have: inhibitory and disinhibitory effects. **Inhibitory effects** occur when the media inhibit or decrease the likelihood of imitating a behavior we otherwise might have engaged in. When we see a model, such as a movie character, punished for a behavior, we are less likely to imitate that behavior. For example, our natural inclination may be to help a stranger who has fallen on the street. However, this reaction may become inhibited and we may become less willing to help if we watch movies that show people being sued or shot when they try to help a stranger. **Disinhibitory effects** occur when the media disinhibit or increase the likelihood of imitating a behavior. When we see models rewarded for their behavior, we are more likely to imitate that behavior. Thus, if we see behaviors that might not normally seem that appealing, such as smoking or starving oneself, reinforced or rewarded in the media, we may be more inclined to imitate them.

Such effects are not necessarily negative. Behavior modeled in the media might inhibit a child's natural aggressive tendencies if aggressive models are punished. Likewise, media models might encourage positive behavior, such as modeling and rewarding outgoing sociable behavior to help individuals overcome shyness. Nonetheless, the potential for modeling effects forms the basis for complaints against media depictions that appear to glorify undesirable behavior (such as drug use and criminal activity) and to discount desirable behavior (such as doing well in school).

Social cognitive theory is one of the most common theories used to understand the impact of entertainment media. Many studies have applied social cognitive theory to TV programs, feature films, and video games, typically in laboratory-like settings, making this theory one of the few in the scientific tradition to focus more on entertainment than news media. Some of these studies will be addressed more specifically later in the chapter. One reason this theory is so popular is because it intuitively makes sense. The idea that people may imitate their favorite television or film characters, athletes, or musicians is readily accepted. Typically, when we think of this form of learning, we think of children who run around karate kicking like Ninja Turtles or wearing lightning bolts on their foreheads and casting spells like Harry Potter. Most of us, however, can also think of our own anecdotal examples of adults who have imitated the dress, talk, or actions from a movie or music video.

Priming and Association Theories   Leonard Berkowitz and his colleagues proposed a theory that focused on extremely short-term, temporary media effects.[14] **Priming theory** holds that witnessing, reading, or hearing an event or idea through the mass media can *prime* or stimulate related thoughts or ideas. These thoughts are believed to stay with us for a short time after our media experience and influence our reactions and behaviors in consistent ways. Thus, according to this theory, if someone hits our car as we are driving out of the movie theater parking lot, our reaction may vary considerably depending on the movie we have just seen. If we have seen a violent action film, we might react more aggressively than we normally would, because the film has made aggressive thoughts and ideas more salient or prominent in our minds. Many studies on priming have examined the role of media violence on subsequent violent behavior. If we have just seen a romantic comedy, however, we might be more understanding than we normally would be because the film may have made more warm and lighthearted ideas more salient or prominent. In another example of priming theory, a study found that heterosexual male participants who read a "boy meets girl" story smiled more, talked more, and leaned forward more when talking to a female after reading the story than did those who read a control story.

Research has examined priming effects of many forms of entertainment, including film, TV, radio, video games, and sporting events. In most cases, research suggests that ideas or concepts from entertainment can influence later thoughts and behaviors. These effects, however, tend to be extremely short-lived. The primed ideas and thoughts quickly begin to fade as we become preoccupied with other ideas and activities. Research suggests that priming can occur automatically without us even knowing about it. One study found that when participants were unknowingly exposed to hostile words (flashed so quickly on a screen that individuals didn't consciously register them), they made more hostile and negative evaluations of a person than did those not exposed to the hostile words. This subconscious priming provides one explanation for the effectiveness of music, lighting, and other cues in films, plays, and other forms of entertainment. For example, certain melodies, tones, or music tempos have come to be associated with fear, excitement, joy, and so on. Thus, playing a certain type of music may trigger related thoughts and feelings, priming audiences' reactions for the events that follow. If we concentrate on the music itself, we may recognize how our reactions are being manipulated, but often, when we are absorbed in the entertainment experience, we become less aware of the specific cues that are being used to prime our reactions.

Like social learning, the priming function of entertainment has intuitive appeal. We have all had the experience of having a sudden craving for something we just saw in a film, perhaps a sudden desire to eat a burger or go swimming. An athletic coach, for example, might find that the team plays better after watching an inspirational sports film or listening to energetic, aggressive, or triumphant music. Although priming is typically considered a short-term effect, other *association theories*, such as classical conditioning, suggest effects of entertainment cues that may be last longer. The reasoning is that by repeatedly pairing specific cues with certain concepts or events, the two become associated or connected in people's minds, and we become conditioned to the point where merely witnessing the cue will trigger thoughts about the primed concepts or events.

Celebrity endorsements and product placements in films are often made on the premise of association. Companies hope that, by pairing their products with popular celebrities or films, the positive thoughts people have about the celebrities or the films will become associated with their products to the point where, when we see these products, we will have the same positive thoughts even without the presence of the celebrity or the film. Critics, however, condemn entertainment for some of the associations they believe may be formed. Certain rock music videos are criticized, for example, because repetitiously pairing degrading and aggressive lyrics with images of women in some videos is feared to create a lasting association in viewers' heads, so that any women or images of women that these individuals later encounter begin to cue degrading and aggressive thoughts and behaviors.

SPOTLIGHT ON INTERPRETATION   Theory from an Islamic Perspective

The field of theoretical investigation in communication for the past 50 years has been based on Western, especially American, methods and orientations. A survey of textbooks used in university journalism schools in Third World countries showed that educational materials originated primarily from the U.S.

Arab universities have modeled their communication programs on Western standards using Western books. A worldview assumption about the nature of the world suggests that ideas from inside the culture rather than outside define the communication experience of that culture. Normative communication theories used to describe desired criteria of media system structures suggest that Arabic communication patterns are based on different interpretations of Western theories.

Arab-Islamic worldview originates from two sources: secular traditions and values from interaction with foreign cultures. These secular-religious components maintain symbiotic relationships to operate as an interactive whole. An Arab-Islamic conception of communication may be understood by four dichotomous themes that may not conform to Western thought.

Individualism–Conformity

Individualism in Arab-Islamic cultures contains both individual and group identification, which has produced two patterns of communication. Secular traditions see communication as a process of liberating the individual from conformity to a collective system of asserting a code of dignity. Islamic communication denotes a process of facilitating a person's harmonizing the inner self with the collective self of the community.

Transcendentalism–Existentialism

For Arabs, reality has two domains, the ideal, which is perfect, and the profane, which is imperfect. The transcendental world is a guide for dealing with the mundane. Words are important for the meanings they convey and their musical beauty.

Intuitive–Rational Processes

For Muslims, revelation is the most primary source of knowledge. Here, individuals surrender to the revealed message of God as an absolute truth. A feature of communication is that it is inwardly oriented first.

Egalitarian–Hierarchial

All Muslims are equal before God, but religion grants males the responsibility for females. In Arab secular traditions, authority is vested in the father, tribal leader, elderly, male child, and the rich, resulting in paternalistic communication. State leaders count on poets and speakers to defend national interests, much as Westerners rely on today's media to do.

A new communication perspective, independent of Western theoretical tradition, has been a challenge for Arabs. Their worldview, with its secular-Islamic components, has yielded communication patterns based on the four sets of values described above. Yet with the indigenous system, where male-dominated and extended family ties are the strongest, communication thrives at the oral level. However, the Internet and satellite TV have phased out the orally based system. Imported media have brought about a disruption of traditional social and communication arrangements in the Arab world. News and entertainment outlets, such as Al Jazeera, Orbit TV, and radio networks, have changed the way communication is received.

Most media personnel in the Arab world are poets, novelists, and literary experts, contributing to the classical character of their mass communication. However, the paternalistic approach to communication has receded in an evolving private media environment. Radio listening is the most preferred medium because of its similarity to oral traditions. Also, a media code of ethics now guides communication work, including references to freedom of expression that call for penal actions against violations of religious, moral, and security interests.

So although Arab media draw on Western-oriented communication production and distribution modes, their discourse lends itself more to inherited norms and practices. In this time of critical Western–Arab-Islamic disharmony, the elaboration of a normative culture-based perspective of communication management and rituals may serve to narrow gaps of misunderstanding and misperception between the U.S. and its Muslim neighbors.

Source: http://www.javnost-thepublic.org/media/datoteke/ayish-2-2003-5.pdf

Physiological Effects

Physical forms of entertainment, such as dancing, sports, and games like tag or hide and seek, can have obvious short-term physiological impacts, such as increased heart and breathing rates and muscle strains or bone breaks, as well as long-term impacts, such as weight loss and lowered blood pressure, arthritis, and tendonitis. As we discussed in Chapter 4, research suggests that relatively passive forms of entertainment, such as watching a movie or listening to music, can also have short-term physiological impacts. When a film or song excites us, our hearts may start to beat faster, and our breathing may become irregular. Some research also suggests possible short- and long-term health benefits for such forms of entertainment, particularly for humor and comedy.

Folk wisdom suggests that humor can relieve pain as well as stress, ward off illness, and aid in healing. These speculations have led to a growing body of scientific, experimental research on the health benefits associated with humor and comedy.[15] Humor and comedy have been found to increase feelings of relaxation and decrease levels of stress-linked hormones. Research suggests that laughter can increase the flow of oxygen and nutrients to tissues and promote the movement of immune elements throughout the system to help fight infection. Exposure to comedy and upbeat drama was also found to increase pain tolerance. Some studies, for example, have found that patients in hospitals or senior homes who watch more comedies ask for less pain medication than patients who watch serious dramas. Interestingly, increased pain tolerance has also been observed after exposure to tragic films.

It is unclear why some forms of media entertainment, including comedy, appear to increase pain thresholds, although several explanations have been offered. One thought is that the positive emotions stimulated by media entertainment simply serve to counteract the negative perceptions of the pain. A similar notion, based on the distraction principle, is that any engaging film serves to distract individuals from their pain to the point where they may even continue to cognitively reflect on the film even after the film has ended, and thus remain distracted from the pain. Others postulate that the physiological arousal—whether positive or negative—generated by entertainment such as a film serves to increase one's pain threshold directly or through the release of special hormones, although research has failed to confirm this relationship.

Inconsistencies in methodology and findings make it difficult to draw any firm conclusions about the health impacts of comedy and other forms of entertainment. Nonetheless, given the overwhelming concerns about negative media effects, it is encouraging to see even limited evidence for positive effects of comedy and other forms of media entertainment.

Cumulative and Cultural Effects

The distinction between **social scientific** and **cultural and critical theories** is not clear cut. Contemporary theories in both traditions acknowledge the potential for more powerful but conditional media effects, and both reflect a shift in focus from limited, short-term effects to cumulative, long-term influences. Today, most researchers in both traditions recognize that meaning is subjective; thus, there is no objective Truth (with a capital T) of the media's impact. Different audiences will interpret and thus react differently to the media. For the social scientist, this is an important qualification, one that makes research difficult. However, ultimately, most social scientists are relatively comfortable with the idea that some level of objectivity can and should be obtained for understanding how audiences are differently affected.

Cultural and critical media studies, however, typically embrace the subjective nature of the media's influence. Cultural researchers maintain that the media and other experiences have more global, profound influences, not only on individual perceptions and behavior but on our society and culture. They believe that these effects cannot be easily isolated or quantified. They question the need for and advisability of "quantifying" subjective concepts like media content or individuals' opinions. From the cultural perspective, an objective, detached approach to media or entertainment research is unnecessary if not impossible. This difference in perspective leads many scholars to suggest that cultural studies of effects reflect a distinct paradigm. As researchers in both traditions increasingly share ideas and methodologies, scientific and cultural perspectives exist perhaps more as a continuum than as separate approaches, with different theories and theorists falling more to one side than another yet still reflecting aspects of each.

Dependency Theory   Many limited effects theories, such as agenda-setting and social cognitive theory studies, suggest that the effects of the media and entertainment, although limited to specific effects or conditions, tend to build over time. Melvin DeFleur and Sandra Ball-Rokeach argued for more powerful, cumulative media effects with the introduction of **dependency theory**.[16] Introduced in 1975, this theory argued that people were becoming increasingly dependent on the media to understand their world, to be told how to behave, and as a means for escape when that world became too overwhelming. According to this theory, we rely more heavily on the media for some situations and issues than others. In the case of a crisis or a national disaster, we turn to the media. Again, consider the September 11 terrorist attacks. For most of the world, including even most of those in New York City, our knowledge and experience of the event was largely limited to what we saw and heard from the media. We turned to the media not only for information about what had happened but also for comfort and companionship—to share our grief. We even used the media to escape, turning to videos, games, or music to distract ourselves from what had happened.

Simple logic would dictate that, if our only exposure to an issue or event comes from the media, any resulting thoughts, attitudes, and behavior would necessarily be shaped by the media. Most of us do not know, however, if our perceptions or actions are any different than they might have been if we had received information from sources other than the mass media, such as direct experience or personal accounts. According to dependency theory's conditional effects model, the media may have only limited effects when they are only one of many sources for our information and experiences, but the effects may be very powerful (although not necessarily different) if media are the primary or sole source of information and experience.

The researchers that proposed dependency theory come from a social scientific tradition of structured, empirical testing, but the spontaneity and magnitude of the types of issues and situations that are media dominated, such as crisis and national disasters, make it difficult to control and isolate the effects of the media and compare them to societal influences. For example, it would be difficult to empirically test the impact of media coverage for September 11 because it would be virtually impossible to maintain a control group of people who were not exposed to the media coverage. Interestingly, and perhaps not surprisingly, however, the rationale behind dependency theory is also reflected in some of the cultural theories whose research methods depart from the strict social scientific tradition.

Diffusion of Innovation   Studies examining the diffusion of innovation examine how the media and other forms of communication, including entertainment, introduce us to information about new discoveries in technology and culture, including products to make our lives easier, inventions, and other innovations.[17] The term **diffusion** refers to the idea that information about new ideas and other innovations slowly spreads throughout society propelled by the media and word of mouth. This theory proposes that media can play an important role in triggering awareness, interest, and ultimately adoption of new ideas, trends, inventions, and innovations. This process is said to be guided by four steps: interest, evaluation, trial, and acquisition.

Imagine that you are considering buying a new mobile phone. While flipping through a magazine, you might come across an advertisement for a new, small, sleek phone. You glance at the ad briefly and recognize the phone as one used by Brad Pitt in a movie you recently saw. Later, you see a TV advertisement for the phone. Now, you are really becoming *interested*. You then begin *evaluating* the phone. You might look up information about the phone on the Internet and talk with some of your friends who have bought similar ones. You might go to a dealer to look at the phone. A friend who has just purchased the phone might let you make a *trial* phone call to test the reception quality. Finally, after you discover there is a sizable mail-in rebate, your mind is made up, and you *acquire* the phone by purchasing it. Evidence for diffusion is found not only for technological advances, but also for fashion trends. For example, Ray-Ban claims that sales of the Predator 2 sunglasses worn by Will Smith and Tommy Lee Jones in *Men in Black* tripled to almost $5 million after the release of the movie in 1997.

SPOTLIGHT ON *TOMB RAIDER*   The Diffusion of Ericsson

To help Lara Croft save the world from evil domination, Paramount Pictures teamed up with Ericsson, one of the world's leading mobile communications companies. For *Tomb Raider* (2001) Ericsson equipped Lara Croft (played by Angelina Jolie) with products on her car dashboard, her head, and even in a holster on her hip. Many of the

products she uses are actually available for consumer purchase, such as the Ericsson Bluetooth Headset seen hooked over her ear.

Croft's home base boasts an Ericsson Cordless Web Screen, which offers voice communication, Internet access, e-mail, voicemail, and her own top-secret address in one easy-access, virtual-touch screen device. Ericsson launched the Web Screen later in the year of the movie's release. The bright-orange R310 phone mounted to the dashboard of her Land Rover was developed in real life for professional adventurers and extreme sports enthusiasts.

Reflecting the diffusion of innovation process, the rugged R310s were even used behind the scenes by the crew throughout filming. Therefore, they were exposed to varying climates, from the heat of Angkor Wat, Cambodia, to the frozen Siberian tundra. Ericsson, of course, generously supplied the filmmakers with these products in the hopes of encouraging diffusion to film audiences.

Symbolic Interaction(ism)   Another theory that focuses on more cumulative and cultural effects is symbolic interactionism. **Symbolic interaction** or **symbolic interactionism**, also borrowed from psychology, maintains that symbols are learned through interaction and that, once learned, these symbols mediate and influence further interaction. For example, we designate the color red to represent danger and, once designated, this meaning guides our interactions, how we react and behave—whether it's the red of a traffic signal or the red of a cocktail dress. According to communication scholars Don Faules and Dennis Alexander, communication is "symbolic behavior which results in various degrees of shared meaning and values between participants."[18]

Symbolic interaction is a cultural study because the theory dictates that different experiences and interactions create different symbolic meanings, and these differences both create and reflect cultural differences. The word *cultural* is used here to reflect not merely ethnic or socio-economic differences, but any factors that work to create shared symbols—workplaces, sporting events, restaurants, concerts. Any environment that facilitates interaction creates the opportunity for the development of shared meanings and subcultures of employees, fans, patrons, or audiences. Researchers have thus examined how different factors, such as the media and other experiences, shape and reflect shared meanings and cultures. Rather than relying on quantitative, structured surveys and behavioral measures, symbolic interaction is usually documented through less structured, qualitative data collection through text analyses, artifacts, and in-depth interviews and focus groups.

Symbolic interaction theory has interesting implications for the study of entertainment because entertainment itself is rich with symbolism. Almost all forms of entertainment rely on shared symbols to connect with audiences. In a live play, audiences recognize that an actor wearing a leotard and mask is a lion, and a white glowing globe hanging from the ceiling is the moon. Music relies heavily on symbolism and shared meanings. Even without words, the tone and beat of a melody can convey emotions—fear, anger, sadness, excitement, or joy—to audiences. Research that examines the symbolic interaction of media and entertainment focuses not only on the shared meanings that develop within these experiences (while watching a movie or play, listening to music, or playing a video game) but also on how these experiences influence interactions in our everyday lives.

Social Construction of Reality   A related perspective on the influence of the mass media is borrowed from sociologists Peter Berger and Thomas Luckmann's social construction of reality theory.[19] This theory argues that people who share a culture also share an "ongoing correspondence" of meaning. Some things have direct, objective meanings that almost everyone shares, such as the meaning of a stop sign. Things that possess objective meanings are called *symbols*. Other meanings, although more or less commonly shared, are more subjective. Things with more subjective meanings are called *signs*. For example, a car may be a symbol of transportation, but a BMW or a Ferrari is a sign of wealth or success. The meanings of both symbols and signs are negotiated. People learn them through experiences and interactions but, for signs, the development of meaning is more complex.

Over time, people collect what they have learned about different symbols and signs to form **typification schemes**—collections of meanings assigned to some phenomenon or situation. Typification schemes form the basis for people's interactions and interpretations in their everyday lives. For example, when you enter a library, you automatically recall the cultural meaning of various elements. You recognize this facility as a library as opposed to a restaurant, nightclub, or even a bookstore by the arrangement of the rows of books, posted signs, furniture, and so on. This recognition causes you to invoke your "library typification scheme." You know to study quietly and speak in whispers. You may know not to bring in food or drink. You may expect to wait longer for assistance or request help more politely and formally than you might at a bookstore. Many of these rules may not be published on the wall. You applied them because they were appropriate to the reality of the setting, or at least to your "social construction" of that reality. In other cultures, even quite similar subcultures, behaviors in this setting might be quite different. Indeed, on some college campuses, libraries can be loud, sociable, informal environments.

Social construction of reality can be applied to the study of media and entertainment effects in much the same way that symbolic interaction can be applied. They both explore how our entertainment experiences can shape our everyday perceptions. As is the case with symbolic interactionism, research on the social construction of reality tends to rely on qualitative data analysis,

U.S. reality for many non-Americans is created from photos of the elaborate lifestyle in Beverly Hills, especially on Rodeo Drive

where media content or entertainment experiences are subjectively analyzed and compared with societal trends and perceptions. For example, what do politicians mean when they say they are going to "get tough on crime"? The meaning of this statement is shaped for both the politicians and the voters by their previous experiences. For many people crime signifies (is a sign for) gangs, drugs, and violence. This is their socially constructed reality, even though there is ten times more white-collar crime in the United States than there is violent crime. For many people, direct experience with crime is relatively limited. Most of what people know about crime comes from what we have read or seen in news media or, even more often, on TV programs or in the movies.

Thus our "construction of reality" is thought to be based on these mediated experiences. And, because both news and entertainment media tend to focus more on violent crime than on white-collar, nonviolent crime, that is the "reality" that shapes our understanding of the concept of crime. Our understanding of getting "tough" is similarly socially construed. Thus, for those raised on a Hollywood diet of action films, getting tough on crime might signify more heavily armed police forces and the use of lethal force and vigilante justice. To the politician, however, "tough" might only mean longer jail sentences. Even though, realistically, voters may know that a politician would not support more radical, vigilante responses to crime, the politician's statement may still appear "tougher" thanks to the lingering images perpetuated by the entertainment media.

SPOTLIGHT ON SOCIAL CONSTRUCTION OF REALITY   A Chinese Perspective[20]

Almost all of us have been guilty of possessing ethnocentric attitudes and beliefs, meaning that our views are so deeply grounded in our own culture and beliefs that sometimes we may not even know that other views exist. Americans have often been accused of ethnocentrism by people from other countries who feel that their cultures are inaccurately represented in American films, music, and other forms of entertainment. Ethnocentrism can emerge in almost any culture because our reality is always socially constructed, based on our own direct experiences and the "stories" we are told by our friends, family, and mass media.

Much of China's ethnocentric attitude toward the world comes from its belief that China is the center of the world. Seen in countless narratives, national superiority is evidenced in words for their civilization such as Middle Kingdom (*zhong guo*), under heaven (*tien xia*), and center or source (*zhong yuan*). The arrogance of Chinese attitudes toward people who are physically different can be seen in folktales that reveal historical and projected realities. Folktales, both written and oral, are stories that have been handed down from generation to generation that contribute to contemporary Chinese attitudes about race and nationalism.

Three forms of the relationship between folktales and reality were identified by Rohrich:[21] fictive reality,

which is a construct of the imagination; historical reality of factual data; and projected reality, which results when the present is incorporated into folktales. The social construction of race can be traced directly to folktales.

Racism in ancient folktales has both historic and fictive realities that reflect the nature of past Chinese beliefs about foreigners. For example, Chinese mythology characterizes those living outside the country as "barbarians." The most popular source of ancient beliefs comes from Pu Songling's tales of the seventeenth and eighteenth centuries. Pu, born in 1640 in the Qing dynasty, became keenly aware of prejudices against frontier people living along China's borders. Pu's tales describe how officials were appointed on the basis of physical features rather than abilities.

Folktales, serving as a source of primary research, provide an understanding of Chinese society. Such tales, rather than being purely fictive constructs, incorporate actual customs, beliefs, and social relations that represent historical realities. Using folktales, one can see how these ancient stories were a way of conceptualizing race as a social construction rather than a biological given, much like the social reality constructed by American media.

Source: profile.nus.edu.sg/fass/geokong/folktale.pdf

Cultivation Analysis Dependency theory, symbolic interaction, and social construction of reality are all consistent with **cultivation analysis**, which maintains that television cultivates or constructs a reality of the world that, although potentially inaccurate, becomes culturally accepted because we believe it to be true. George Gerbner and his associates[22] developed cultivation analysis as an explanation for the impact of TV violence on perceptions of crime, and this analysis has since been applied to television's cultivated effects on perceptions of beauty, sex roles, religion, the judicial process, marriage, and other concerns. In every case, the premise is the same—that repeated, heavy exposure to television cultivates a distorted perception of the world we live in, making the world seem more the way television portrays it than it is in real life. One of the popular conclusions from this research is **mean world syndrome**—the idea that because television portrays unrealistically high levels of violence, people who engage in heavy TV viewing perceive the world as a much meaner, more dangerous place than it really is. Like agenda-setting research, cultivation analysis relies on quantitative analysis of TV content combined with self-reports of media use and resulting perceptions. Thus, in the mean world study, researchers analyzed TV content, found that television portrayed an inordinate amount of "mean" violence, and surveyed people; they found that those who watched a lot of television (and thus a lot of violence) perceived the world to be a meaner place.

The term *cultivation* reflected Gerbner's perspective that television did not influence views by directly offering facts and figures about societal trends; instead, it influenced indirectly through the accumulation or cultivation of consistent images. Television never directly says, "There is lots of violent crime committed by people of color, so you should be afraid of these people." However, because television tends to show a bias toward portraying minorities as violent criminals, we form our own conclusions that reflect this bias. Cultivation theory does not suggest that television can radically alter societal views; rather, it suggests that television serves to stabilize social patterns by reinforcing existing power relationships and societal beliefs. The term *mainstreaming* is used to describe the process in which television helps move people toward a shared understanding of how things are.

Cultivation analysis has typically been limited to studying the influence of television. Gerbner felt that television was fundamentally different from other mass media because it is so pervasive. However, much has changed since the early days of this research. In the past, TV offerings were more limited and homogeneous. Today, offerings are more diverse. Thus, some scholars question whether TV images are universal or consistent enough to influence perceptions in predictable, "mainstream" ways. Other scholars have more fundamental criticisms of cultivation analysis, arguing that the correlational, survey-based, methodological approach provides no control over media exposure. Again, because the research relies on self-reports of media use, a popular counter-explanation for mean world syndrome and other cultivation effects argues for reverse effects. In other words, it is not that watching TV makes people afraid of the mean world, it is that people who think the world is a mean place stay home and watch TV because they are afraid to go outside. Nonetheless, Gerbner and cultivation research are among the most widely cited references with regard to media effects. Cultivation theory provides a valuable theoretical and methodological approach for studying entertainment effects—not only for TV programs, but also for other pervasive forms of entertainment, such as music videos or content on the Internet.

Narcotizing Effect   Still other theorists propose yet other potential effects of long-term, cumulative heavy media or entertainment exposure. Rather than changing opinions or mobilizing people to act, some theorists claim that, over time, the media can lull people into passivity. This narcotizing effect, sometimes called **narcoticizing disfunction**, is supported by studies finding that when people become overloaded with information, they begin to withdraw. One thought is that when people obtain an abundance of information on a subject—for example by watching several movies, reading several books, or surfing the Internet—they become lulled into feeling as though they have actually done something about the issue. They may begin to use passive news or entertainment offerings as substitutes for active involvement. So people may continue to watch films about racial injustice—like *Guess Who's Coming to Dinner?* (1967), *Mississippi Burning* (1988), *American History X* (1998), and *Crash* (2005)—that make them feel involved instead of actively becoming involved in civil rights groups, writing letters, signing petitions, or attending rallies. Another thought is that people simply begin to feel overwhelmed by the

What different predictions would social learning, priming, agenda setting, excitation transfer and a narcotizing effect make for films such as *Guess Who's Coming to Dinner?* which confront issues of race?

ominous or conflicting views that the media present. Feeling confused and helpless, people become paralyzed and do nothing.

Critical Cultural Theory   A major influence on modern media and entertainment theory comes from **critical cultural theory**, which echoes some of Gerber's cultivation sentiments, maintaining that the media operate primarily to justify and support the status quo, supporting certain groups or elites at the expense of ordinary people or select groups of people. Modern neo-Marxist theorists believe that people are oppressed by those who control the culture, the superstructure—in other words, the mass media. In the opinion of traditional Marxists, these oppressors are right-wing political elites who use the news and entertainment media not only to convey their own ideologies but also to keep the masses pacified and distracted. It is reasoned that elites try to keep people happy and entertained so that they are less likely to protest or challenge the existing power structure.

Critical scholars approach their studies from a variety of perspectives. Feminist critiques examine ways in which the media and entertainment reinforce patriarchy and male domination in society. Gay and lesbian critiques examine the ways in which the media marginalize lesbians and gay men. African American critiques focus on ways in which the media subjugate African Americans, and so on. Critical scholars approach their studies qualitatively, relying on subjective analyses of media content and its impact. Modern critical theorists possess a number of different conceptions of the relationship between media and culture, but all share several identifying characteristics:[23]

- They tend to be macroscopic in scope, examining broad, culture-wide media effects.
- They are openly and avowedly political. Based in neo-Marxism, their orientation is typically from the political left.
- Their goal is minimally to instigate change in government media policies, at the most to effect wholesale change in media and cultural systems. Critical cultural theories assume that the superstructure, which favors those in power, must be altered.
- They investigate and explain how elites use media to maintain their positions of privilege and power. Issues such as media ownership, government–media relations,

and corporate media representations of labor and disenfranchised groups are typical topics of study for critical cultural theory because they center on the exercise of power.

This section has reviewed many different theories that have been offered to explain how entertainment, particularly media entertainment, affects its audiences. Although there is some overlap, many of these theories suggest very different effects. For review, take a look at Figure 5.1 and see if you can match the theory to its predicted impact for images such as the one that is depicted.

Match the Theory to the Effect	Effects
What perceptions or impacts might media news and entertainment images like the one pictured here have on audiences? 	1. Reinforces criminal stereotypes. 2. Inhibits/reduces criminal behavior. 3. Makes crime seem like a more serious issue. 4. Marginalizes minorities and strips their power. 5. Temporarily triggers violent thoughts and actions. 6. Handcuffs convey subservience/submission, uniforms convey dominance/power. **Theories** A. Agenda-setting theory B. Critical theory C. Cultivation analysis D. Priming theory E. Social/cognitive theory F. Symbolic interaction/social construction of reality

Answers. 1-C. Repeated depictions of certain groups create and reinforce stereotypes. **2-E.** Crime is punished, not positively reinforced or rewarded. **3-A.** Media tell us what issues are important. **4-B.** Images perpetuate the power of the elites over the rest of society. **5-D.** Images stimulate related violent behaviors and thoughts. **6-F.** Images create and reinforce signs and symbolic meaning.

Figure 5.1   Matching Theory to Effect

FADE TO BLACK

Many theories and methods have been invoked to study media and entertainment effects, and each possesses various strengths and weaknesses. Content and text analyses may be best for identifying cultural themes and images that might have significant impacts. Experiments and limited effects theories may be best for demonstrating whether media and entertainment are capable of producing specific, isolated effects and for ruling out possible effects. Field studies may be best for assessing the presence and extent of these effects in the environment. Cultural, qualitative, and ethnographic studies may be best for examining the complexity of these effects and for understanding how the media's impact fits within our larger social fabric.

Theories variously suggest that media and entertainment may influence our thoughts, behavior, and even our health. The movies we watch, the music we listen to, and the games we play and observe may all serve in different ways to reinforce or discourage stereotypes, destructive behavior, the value of education, and other perceptions and behaviors. Debate continues, yet together these theories and methods have provided researchers, industry professionals, and audience members with a comprehensive array of tools and perspectives for understanding how, when, why, and to what extent media and entertainment effects may occur.

A CLOSER LOOK AT 9/11 Causes and Effects: The Media and Terrorism

Many people have speculated about the relationship between Western media and entertainment and the September 11, 2001, terrorist attacks on the World Trade Center in New York City. There is consideration of both how media and entertainment may have played a role in precipitating the attack as well as how they may have influenced how people reacted to the attack.

First, there are concerns about the images of Western culture that are portrayed by news and entertainment programs—sensationalized images of crime, violence, sex, and lifestyles of the rich and famous. Americans seem to have so much, and yet many Westerners portrayed in the news and entertainment media appear to be ungrateful, godless criminals who do not care about anyone but themselves. Meanwhile, even before September 11, U.S. books and films also portrayed Middle Easterners in very negative ways, often as the enemy, as villains and terrorists. Given these images, some argue it is no wonder that individuals from other cultures might view Westerners, particularly Americans, as violent, unscrupulous hedonists who hate Middle Easterners. Indeed, such views reflect the very accusations that Al Qaeda and other terrorist groups have made against the Western world—accusations that they have used to rally support for their causes and to justify their attacks.

Books, films, and other forms of entertainment have also been accused of aiding terrorists by giving them ideas for attack strategies. People have noted parallels, for example, between Tom Clancy's book

Debt of Honor (published the year after the failed bombing of the World Trade Center in 1993) and the September 11 attacks. In the book, the antagonist flies an airplane into the Capitol building during a joint session of Congress and into other targets, similar to the actual 2001 attacks on both towers of the World Trade Center and the Pentagon (as well as an attack probably planned for the Capitol or the White House but that was prevented when the fourth plane crashed in a Pennsylvania field).

Video games have been similarly accused of providing ideas and perhaps even practice for would-be terrorists. Following the attacks, Microsoft announced the elimination of the World Trade Center from the skyline of its upcoming *Microsoft Flight Simulator 2002*—a game said to be so realistic that some student pilots use it for training. Other video game makers also planned to purge images of destruction involving New York from new releases following the terrorist attacks at the World Trade Center. Activision indefinitely postponed release of its PlayStation game *Spider-Man 2—Enter: Electro* a day before it was to hit stores because the superhero battles villains atop skyscrapers resembling the World Trade Center.

Shortly after the attack, Hollywood executives met with Karl Rove, a senior advisor to U.S. President George W. Bush, and unanimously endorsed the government's request for film and TV projects promoting America and "American values." Rove had, in fact, enumerated seven specific themes, from tolerance to volunteerism, that he hoped the entertainment industry would address. Thus, the events of September 11 show us not only how the media and entertainment may influence our society but also how societal events influence media and entertainment offerings.[24]

Terrorists, of course, are not the only ones who may be affected by entertainment images. Even the most law-abiding citizens may inadvertently begin to adopt stereotypical views, such as suspecting all Middle Easterners of being terrorists because that is how they are depicted in books, games, TV programs, and movies. Our experience with entertainment media may also influence our perception of news coverage of events such as those that occurred on September 11. Many people were unable to resist the coverage of the U.S. terrorist attack. As horrific as it was to watch on television or read about in the newspaper and in magazines, many people found it nearly impossible to turn away. Some people say that they watched hoping for information or because they felt fearful of a future attack and wanted to be prepared; others say that they were watching in an effort to digest and process the event.

Some critics, however, contend that the media intentionally created seductive and addictive images almost like an action movie. Whether that was the intention or not, some say that viewers did seem to view the news coverage as if it were a movie—a self-contained story that would include a beginning and an ending. However, news coverage is not the same as a movie. In a movie, audiences expect and typically are given all the information they need to understand the story—all of the characters are introduced, background and details are provided. It is difficult if not impossible, however, to gain the same depth of information from a news report. In real life, stories are much more complicated. When did the battle between the United States and terrorists like Osama bin Laden and his followers really begin, and will it ever really end? In real life, it is difficult to pinpoint a beginning and an ending, and to collect all of the information necessary to truly understand events as they unfold.

Although this may seem obvious once you stop to think about it, years of entertainment (watching movies and television, playing games, reading books) combined with the recent trend of making news more entertainment-like, may train people to interpret news as if it were entertainment. As a result, viewers may watch more passively and less critically, assuming that watching a couple of hours of CNN will tell us the complete and accurate "story" of what is happening in our world.

The events of September 11 offer almost limitless opportunities to explore the relationship between the media, entertainment, and the real life they portray and imitate. As with all media effects, however, we will probably never completely understand the impact of Western media and entertainment on the terrorist attack and its aftermath.

What do you think?

- Do you think entertainment such as movies, books, TV programs, and video games in any way influenced the terrorist attack? If so, how?
- What theories might explain these effects?
- What role, if any, do you think entertainment may have had in how people reacted to the attack?
- What do you think about the entertainment industry leaders' reactions to the terrorist attack? Should they have done anything differently? Should they do anything differently in the future?

DISCUSSION AND REVIEW

1. Review the different types of effects that entertainment may have on audiences and give specific examples of each.
2. Explain the different paradigms of effects research, including examples of theories and studies from each of them. Speculate on how these paradigms might continue to evolve.

3. Explain and compare and contrast each of the following pairs: quantitative vs. qualitative research, self-report vs. observation, laboratory vs. field research, content and text analysis. Which methods do you like best and why?

4. Consider your own (or others') images of different groups—women, African Americans, Asians, Hispanics, Middle Easterners, blondes, the elderly, lawyers, people who work on computers. How do you envision "typical" individuals of these groups? What do they look like? How do they behave? What images or stereotypes immediately come to mind? Use theories from the chapter to explain how these images may form.

EXERCISES

1. Consider each of the following: smoking in movies, hip-hop music, and *Harry Potter* or *Lord of the Rings* books. What kind of effects might each of these have on people? How might they affect attitudes and behavior? Now design research strategies to study these effects.

2. Pay attention to new trends you see in fashion, hairstyles, toys, gadgets, catch phrases, and so on and see how many you can trace back to entertainment—from movies, music videos, magazines, and so on, or actors, musicians, athletes, and so on. Use theories from the chapter to explain how these trends form.

3. Search through a database of social science research (EBSCO Complete, PsychAbstracts, and so on) for effects studies. Try using the word "effect" or "effects" and other keywords you are interested in, such as "media violence," "video games," "heavy metal music," "horror films," and so on. Read through a few articles and see if you can find any of the theories and methods discussed in this chapter. Comment on what you find.

4. Researchers have noted some interesting trends in entertainment media. One trend is lighthearted but still very violent movies, including action films such as the *Rush Hour* movies and horror films such as the *Scream* and *Scary Movie* series. Another trend is reality programs like *Survivor* and *Big Brother*. List any other trends you notice (consider not only TV and film, but music, video games, books, and so on). Speculate about what effects these trends might have on audiences.

BOOKS AND BLOGS

Bryant, J. and Zillmann, D. (1994). *Media effects: Advances in theory and research*. Hillsdale NJ: Lawrence Erlbaum Associates.

Jeffries, L.W. and Perloff, R.M. (1997). *Mass media effects* (2nd ed.). Prospect Heights IL: Waveland Press.

Fischoff, S. (1999). Psychology's quixotic quest for the media-violence connection. *Journal of Media Psychology*, 4: 4. Available online at www.calstatela.edu/faculty/sfischo/

Lowery, S.A. and DeFleur, M.L. (1995). *Milestones in mass communication research*. White Plains NY: Longman.

www.mhhe.com/mayfieldpub/westturner/student_resources/theories.htm—defines communication theories.

www.sociosite.net/topics/texts/berger_luckman.php—discusses social construction of reality theory.

www.healthyminds.org/mediaviolence.cfm—discusses the psychiatric effects of media violence.

PART 2

IMPACTS: SOCIETAL CAUSES AND EFFECTS

6 THE ATTENTION ECONOMY: BUSINESS AND TECHNOLOGY

Entertainment—not autos, not steel, not financial services—is fast becoming the driving wheel of the new world economy. . . . An infusion of entertainment content, what I call the E-Factor, is increasingly playing a fundamental role in determining which stores we shop at, what airline we fly, the restaurant where we eat, what clothes we wear, which pots we cook with, which computer we use. Is there a line between "real" business and entertainment? Not anymore.

—Michael J. Wolf[1]

Entertainment is the fastest-growing sector of the global economy. In the United States, entertainment ranks ahead of clothing and health care as a percentage of household spending (entertainment 5.4 percent, clothes 5.2 percent, health care 5.2 percent). Each year Americans spend at least 120 billion hours and more than $150 billion on legal forms of entertainment. Because "entertainment" spans a diverse set of industries, it is difficult to place a dollar figure on the revenue entertainment generates. Some figures estimate that, in the United States, entertainment is a more than $480 billion industry, including domestic and international business. That figure does not include tourism or consumer electronics such as TV sets and VCRs which, many would argue, are bought primarily for entertainment.[2] And, as mentioned in Chapter 1, spending on global entertainment and media is estimated to exceed $1.8 trillion by 2010.[3]

The question, then, is: Why is the entertainment sector outpacing growth in other industries? The simplest answer is: because it can. Economies grow with supply and demand, and, in the case of entertainment, we've seen rapid growth on both ends. Technological advances have increased both the quantity and the quality of entertainment choices (the supply). Meanwhile, because other sectors of the economy were doing well, people had more money to spend on entertainment "extras" (demand). However, even as world economies began to slow down at the beginning of the twenty-first century, entertainment industries remained relatively healthy.

Entertainment has blurred beyond its traditional boundaries into other sectors. You can find entertainment in hotels, restaurants, and shopping malls, on news programs, on web sites, and in classrooms. We are entering an age when entertainment touches every aspect of our lives. And, once again, the question is: Why? This chapter explores how economic and technological forces are shaping and are shaped by the evolution of entertainment.

Economic and Technological Forces

As noted in Chapter 1, today entertainment is big business, indeed it is a multitude of businesses that can be segmented into several different industries. Thus competition and the drive to maintain profitable enterprises have been driving forces in the way entertainment has evolved. In their search for ways to improve the quality, quantity, and diversity of entertainment offerings, entertainment artists and entrepreneurs are often among the earliest adopters and promoters of many of society's most significant technological advances. Consider landmark advances in communication technology such as the printing press, radio, film, and TV. Although most of these innovations were developed first and foremost to convey important news and information, they were all quickly employed to create revolutionary forms of entertainment— books, movies, and serial radio and TV programs. It is entertainment even more than news and information that has come to define and drive the industries that have been built around these technologies. As we will see in this chapter, large entertainment conglomerates such as Sony develop communication hardware, such as televisions, music players, and game consoles as well as the entertain-

ment content (programs, songs, video games, etc.) that plays on these devices. Although many entertainment companies are thriving, once again technological advances, in this case, digital technology and the Internet, are transforming their industries.

The Attention Economy

For several decades economists and futurists have argued that we have moved into a period completely different from the past era of factory-based mass production of material items. During that era, talk of money, prices, returns on investment, laws of supply and demand, and so on all made excellent sense. Today's economy is said to be driven more by the production and exchange of information than by the production and exchange of material goods. The statistics documenting the information proliferation in our society are impressive. For example, a typical weekday edition of the *New York Times* contains more information than the average seventeenth-century Englishman encountered in a lifetime. In a mere ten-year span from 1980 to 1990, the worldwide production of books increased by 45 percent. And it is estimated that a new site emerges on the World Wide Web every minute.[4] Many names for the new era have been invoked: the Information Age, the Third Wave, the move toward cyberspace. Beginning with the advent of TV and large mainframe computers and continuing with personal computers, the Internet, and wireless products, this era is fueled by revolutionary technological advances in electronic data and communication technology.

Some theorists, however, argue that it is not this abundance of information, but the competition for attention that this abundance creates, that drives the economy. Economist Michael Goldhaber uses the term "the attention economy" to describe this evolving era. He explains why he does not see information itself as a driving economic force:

> Information . . . would be an impossible basis for an economy, for one simple reason: economies are governed by what is scarce, and information, especially on the Net, is not only abundant, but overflowing. We are drowning in the stuff, and yet more and more comes at us daily. . . . What would be the incentive in organizing our lives around spewing out more information if there is already far too much?[5]

It is this overabundance, however, that leads to growing competition for what *is* increasingly scarce, which is, of course, our attention. It is argued that this competition for attention has fueled the rise of infotainment. Whether you are writing a script, a news story, or an advertisement, your goal is to capture attention. Drama and intrigue offer a better guarantee of engaging audiences than do facts and thoughtful analysis. And, thus, as introduced in Chapter 1, this attention economy has transformed into an entertainment economy.

Commerce and Entertainment: A Symbiotic Relationship

The entertainment business as we know it today would not exist without the corporations who have supported it, typically through advertising. Some estimates say 40 percent of the revenue stream for the entertainment industry comes from advertisements. Today, advertising serves as a primary source of revenue not only for newspapers, magazines, TV, and radio stations but also for web sites and sporting events. With the emergence of product placements, even the film industry has managed to generate a revenue stream from advertising.

Advertising attention at Piccadilly Circus, London

Integrated Marketing Communication   Early radio programs were usually sponsored by a single company in exchange for a brief mention before and after the broadcast aired. However, radio station owners soon realized that they could earn more money by selling sponsorship rights in small-time allocations to multiple businesses throughout their radio station's broadcasts, rather than selling the sponsorship rights to single businesses per show. This practice was carried over in the late 1940s and early 1950s to TV where advertising was clearly compartmentalized into program breaks, entirely separate from entertainment content. During this era, advertisers could rely on television to provide them with large, captive audiences for their sales pitches. Beginning in the 1980s, however, with the rise of viewing technologies like cable TV, the remote control, and the VCR, companies had to become increasingly creative to prevent viewers from tuning out their messages. It is this competition for attention that has created incentives and opportunities for a systematic coordination of different marketing and branding activities, and to reach desirable audiences through unconventional (and thus less escapable) means such as product placement and corporate sponsorship at live events.

FLASH FACT

Marketers shelled out 71 percent more—$941 million—to integrate brands into TV shows in 2005 vs. 2004, PQ Media says.[6] EMarketer reported that online video ad-spending on brand integration was $505 million in 2008. According to a producer of "lonelygirl15" and its spinoffs on MSN, Disney, Paramount, and Procter & Gamble, the vast majority of the shows' revenues are derived from brand integration.[7]

Scholars and researchers have suggested that **Integrated Marketing Communications** (IMC) may end up being one of the defining concepts of not just post-twentieth-century marketing but even of post-twentieth-century culture. Described by marketing executives as a "holistic" strategy that is "gaining momentum," one survey found that nearly 75 percent of advertising firms stated they used IMC.[8] Although definitions vary, IMC can be understood as an attempt to coordinate several functions and modalities of marketing activities: advertising, public relations, marketing activities (may include point of purchase and packaging), sales promotion (such as couponing), and other "below the line" operations such as sponsorship and product placement.

Matthew McAllister has isolated some of the developments that have emphasized IMC philosophies:[9]

- the erosion of traditional media's ability to reliably deliver audiences through traditional advertising
- the complicity of media companies in IMC activities, both in terms of generating advertising dollars through attractive marketing and multi-platformed deals, and in terms of their own marketing, via partnering with firms to market media company brands (both Time Warner and Disney, for example, are simultaneously major collectors of advertising revenue, and major spenders of advertising moneys)
- the fragmentation of audiences through different media choices, and the increased collection of information about specific audience members' consumer and media-use behavior through database marketing
- the prevalence of digital media, which not only add to the increased outlets to reach consumers but also, in form, encourage the blurring of different textual categories that were traditionally distinct, such as commercial forms versus programming forms. This includes both new digital delivery systems—such as the Internet (which also integrates commercial activity, such as the ability to buy)—but also new digital production techniques, as especially seen in the enhanced graphics and visual techniques on TV
- the collection and "bundling" of marketing activities facilitated by the concentration of ownership in global advertising organizations (such as Omnicom and WPP Group, the two largest ones).

IMC has been the rise of marketing concepts designed to blend explicitly commercial with the non-commercial (or less commercial): product integration and branded entertainment. According to McAllister, "we now see Integrated Marketing Communications designed to be, and often manifested as, Integrated Marketing Culture; infusing our culture with marketing foundations."[10] In other words, it is argued that marketing has become so integrated into the fabric of entertainment and other aspects of popular culture that it begins to shape and define that culture. To hype the fall 2006 TV season, CBS plastered pictures of its shows' stars on postage stamps and across the insides of elevator doors. It laser-coated its eye logo on more than 35 million eggs, and carved the name of a new program, *Jericho*, into a 40-acre Kansas cornfield. Advertising is intruding on more previously untouched corners of life, including novels, hotel shower curtains, school buses, and the bellies of pregnant women. Golfer Fred Couples has been followed around the course by a gaggle of women paid to wear the name Bridgestone Golf, his sponsor.[11] See *Spotlight on IMC* and Chapter 7 on branding for more discussion on the pervasiveness of the integration of marketing into entertainment.

SPOTLIGHT ON IMC   Beyond Product Placement: Integrated Marketing in *Movie Extra*

Will Ferrell

On July 10, 2008, *Movie Extra* featured the 2003 Will Ferrell movie *Old School*. This broadcast reveals how sophisticated and pervasive promotional efforts have become integrated into entertainment offerings:

• *Televised movie as ad carrier:* The movie is the bait to attract audiences for the advertising, ads that are shown during commercial breaks, or pods. In addition, TBS promotes programs during commercial breaks. There was about 14 minutes of ads and program promotions per hour during this telecast's ad breaks; not excessive, but more on this later.

• *Product placement in the televised movie:* At one point before a commercial break, Will Ferrell's character (Frank the Tank), drunk, asks his wife: "Honey, you think KFC's still open?" It did not lead into a KFC commercial, but it did lead into a Taco Bell commercial.

• *Bugs and snipes as promotions:* Graphics that pop up on the screen promoting upcoming TBS shows to watch. They usually appear before and after commercial breaks, and may last nearly one minute on the screen. They often complement the promotional spots that air during commercial breaks, such as a snipe and commercial for TBS airing of the movie *Fun with Dick and Jane.*

• *Movie as direct-sale commodity:* Similar to above, these are graphical "Bottom thirds" which appear on the screen that tell viewers to "Buy 'Old School' on DVD @ tbs.com!" In this sense, each network is now its own store. And since movies on TBS are often edited for content, the airing of the movie serves as a promotion for sales of different versions of *Old School*, including the "unrated" version.

The above represent the commercial commonplace; similar promotions may appear in virtually any program in the new televisual, hypercommercial environment: promotions and commercials that are graphically woven throughout the program. But the *Movie Extra* adds other layers of promotion on top of these.

These interstitial-added, extra-textual layers include:

• *Interstitial program as cross promotion: Movie Extra* is a play on words. It adds extra, interstitial content to the movie, but also signifies a partnership with *Extra*, the syndicated entertainment news TV program. In this case, the brand of the program serves to promote *Extra* the syndicated program. *Extra* is also distributed by Warner Bros., so this also adds a synergy incentive as both Warner Bros. and TBS are Time Warner properties.

• *Interstitial program hosts as cross promotion:* The two *Extra* hosts are also personalities on other cable TV programs, such as *Celebrity Extreme*

Dodgeball and *Foody Call* on The Style Network, and Fine Living Channel's *What You Get for the Money*, so they can cross-promote their other shows.

- *Interstitial program as integrated campaign:* Before commercial breaks, the two *Extra* hosts claim to give us "the hottest buzz." In this case, though, this buzz is not random, but focused on one movie: "this summer's hottest comedy," *Step Brothers*. *Step Brothers* was released on July 25, or about two weeks after the airing of this program, and of course both *Step Brothers* and *Old School* are the same basic movie: a "Frat Pack" driven comedy featuring Will Ferrell as a developmentally arrested male. The *Extra* commentary on the film mostly uses movie clips and interviews with the stars.

- *Ads as integrated campaign:* More traditional ads for *Step Brothers* also air during the commercial break for *Old School*, thus hinting at an incentive

for the integrated tie-in. The clips in the ad are the duplicates of what airs in the interstitial programming.

- *Product placement in integrated ads/program:* Finally, there is product placement in the *Step Brothers* clips that are integrated in both the interstitial programming and in the traditional movie ads: one character is clearly using a Vaio computer in bed; John C. Reilly wears a Kawasaki T-shirt; Ferrell is wearing a Mountain Dew T-shirt, in the same scene that Reilly is drinking a Pepsi. It is framed as a key scene, too ("You have one month to find jobs"). There's no ad for Mountain Dew, but there are ads for Taco Bell, which used to be owned by PepsiCo and offers Mountain Dew as a fountain drink.

Source: Excerpted from McAllister, Matthew (2008). Integrated marketing culture? Paper presented at the annual meeting of the Association for Education in Journalism and Mass Communication, Chicago IL

Convergence and Consolidation

Nowhere is competition for attention more fierce than within the entertainment industries themselves. This competition has resulted in some interesting trends. In the 1990s, the trend was bigger is better. Entertainment-related organizations merged, diversified, and expanded their businesses creating mammoth corporations with holdings spanning every industry niche—film studios, TV networks, music labels, sports franchises, and Internet service. Starting in 2002, however, the tide began to shift, and some of these same companies were slimming back down and returning to more narrow specializations. Nonetheless, industries continue to converge in innovative ways to extend brands, infuse them with entertainment, and tailor them for audiences and consumers around the world. This section will review these trends and explore the factors that have influenced them.

Mergers and Acquisitions

Unlike the configuration of stations and single owners of early television, today's entertainment providers are giant conglomerates. During the 1990s, mergers, acquisitions, and joint ventures proliferated among cable companies and programmers, and between cable companies, programmers, and a host of interested parties from fields like telephone, computer, film, and electric utility industries. **Convergence** became an industry watchword. A foundation concept for the National Information Infrastructure and the Information Superhighway, convergence accurately describes what is taking place in today's mediated technology. By the end of the 1990s there were eight transnational corporations, or TNCs: General Electric (holding NBC Universal), Liberty Media, Disney, Time Warner, Sony, News Corporation, Viacom, and Bertelsmann. Nearly all the major Hollywood studios are owned by one of these conglomerates, which in turn control the cable channels and TV

Table 6.1   Match the Parent Company With Its Corporate Holding

In some cases, the parent company may outright own the entity; in other cases, it may only hold a major stock interest.

Parent corporation	*Corporate holding (as of August, 2008)*
1. Time Warner	A. ABC Television Network
2. Liberty Media	B. Random House Books
3. Bertelsmann	C. MySpace
4. Disney	D. Blockbuster (video stores)
5. General Electric	E. Universal Studios Theme Parks
6. News Corporation	F. AOL
7. Sony	G. DirectTV
8. Viacom	H. *Days of Our Lives* (TV soap opera)

Answers: 1F, 2G, 3B, 4A, 5E, 6C, 7H, 8D

networks that air the movies.[12] See if you can match the corporations with their holdings in Table 6.1.

In the 1990s, companies such as America Online (AOL) and Time Warner merged, wedding old and new media technology for news and entertainment. Meanwhile, Disney's assets grew to include motion picture studios, a TV network, cable networks, a book publishing company, a magazine division, TV stations, retail stores, theme parks, sports teams, and merchandise. In many cases, combinations of these eight major media conglomerates even share ownership of various assets. In the near future, cable and telephone industries may merge or synthesize into an entirely new media system.

More Choices   Although many factors fueled the growth of these mega-corporations, the competition for attention certainly played a significant role. Thirty years ago our entertainment options were more limited. TV included only three networks and handfuls of local channels, and there were fewer radio stations, magazines, musical groups, amusement parks, and so on. As a result, companies that owned only one of these operations could capture a large portion of the entertainment market. With the emergence of cable TV, specialty magazines, the Internet, and other developments, however, entertainment choices began to multiply. Thus, rather than compete with each other for audience attention, companies began to merge and consolidate.

Synergy   In spite of these partnerships, however, the competition for attention remains fierce. This battle is reflected in the growing costs in production, marketing, and promotional budgets. In 1987, it cost $28.4 million to develop, release, and market an average feature film. In 1997, it cost $75.6 million. These numbers reflect an average 10 percent increase in costs every year, significantly higher than the rate of inflation.[13] Such high costs make it difficult for smaller companies to compete. Large companies with diverse holdings also gained leverage through synergistic partnerships. For example, when Disney launches a new film, it engages its publishing, merchandising, TV, and theme park divisions both to promote the film and to develop related products.

Consider the film *The Lion King*. Advertisements on Disney-owned TV networks promote the film; the film promotes interest in *Lion King* toys, books, spinoff videos, TV programs, theme park attractions, and even the theater production of *The Lion King*. Ultimately, each element reinforces and promotes the others. These cross-promotional efforts are not subtle. Indeed, nowhere are such efforts more blatant than at Disney's family-oriented theme parks, where the company's family-oriented films are brought to life with film-themed roller coasters and interactive multimedia shows, each with its own themed souvenir shop strategically located so that patrons must walk through it as they exit the attraction.

After exiting Disney theme park attractions based on Disney themed films, patrons are funneled into Disney themed gift shops

Diversification   Media mega-corporations also enjoy another advantage. As already noted, to keep audiences' attention in today's market, you must continuously offer something new—bigger, better, more entertaining than what you offered yesterday. It is difficult to keep up with technological advances, and perhaps even harder to predict what audiences will like. Companies must take risks investing in new technology and new ideas, not knowing which ones will succeed and which will fail. It is hard for small companies with limited resources to take such gambles. By "not putting all their eggs in one basket," so to speak, it was argued that large companies with diverse holdings were better equipped to handle the uncertainty and fickleness of the entertainment industry.

Are monopolies "unfair competition"?

Deregulation   Another reason that entertainment companies began to merge and consolidate was simply because they could. Ironically, in years past, before we had so many different choices for entertainment—particularly media entertainment—many of these mergers and acquisitions would have been illegal. For years, the United States government had antitrust legislation with strict rules limiting ownership because leaders feared that monopolies—both horizontal and vertical—would threaten fair competition. **Monopolies** occur when a single company controls a significant portion of an industry. Industries typically have multiple levels. Some companies may produce the raw materials or resources that are used, other companies may build or develop those resources into products and services, and still other companies may distribute the products and services to audiences and customers. In the film industry, for example, writers develop scripts, studios produce the films, and theaters, rental and retail stores, and cable and TV stations "distribute" the films to audiences.

Horizontal monopolies occur when a limited number of companies dominate a single level of an industry—for example, if one company or a very limited number of companies controlled all of the studios, all of the movie theaters, or all of the TV stations. **Vertical monopolies** exist when a single company controls a slice of all levels of an industry—for example, if one company owned a talent agency that represents screenwriters, a film studio, and movie theaters, retail stores, TV stations, and so on. Although monopolies were traditionally considered a threat in any economic sector, in the media, where many forms of traditional entertainment are found, they were considered particularly dangerous.

In the United States the media have always been considered "watchdogs" that help police the activities of government and industry. Early technology limited the number of outlets for key media. Bandwidth allowed for only a few TV and radio stations, and even the number of movie theaters and print news publications was limited. Thus, in addition to concerns about monopolistic problems such as price fixing and restricted consumer choices, people feared that, if only a few companies owned all the media outlets, the lack of competition might cause them to abandon their watchdog function and instead control news content and entertainment content for their own benefit.

Media industries, including entertainment, may have wanted to merge and consolidate, but the government would not allow it. In the 1980s, however, deregulation in all industries began to remove some of these restrictions. And, thanks to the introduction of cable, the Internet, and other advances, these barriers broke down even further as the proliferation of new media outlets reduced fears that a single entity might control public information. Although regulations are less strict than they once were, proposed mergers and acquisitions are still closely examined and sometimes denied because of monopolistic concerns. In spite of this scrutiny, feelings about today's mega-corporations are mixed. Advocates argue that consumers gain cheaper, better-integrated entertainment choices. Critics, meanwhile, argue that mega-corporations limit competition, which results in price fixing and reduced entertainment and news quality and selection. Nonetheless, even most critics would grudgingly agree that these mega-corporations are exceedingly successful at one thing—capturing our attention.

Divestiture and Fragmentation   At the start of the new millennium, however, there were already signs that the strain of maintaining such vast empires might be taking their toll on some of these mega-corporations. In 2002, although some corporations continued to merge and grow their empires, others began to *divest* or sell off some of their holdings.[14] Vivendi Universal entered negotiations to sell off most of its publication unit and was receiving pressure from interested buyers to sell its U.S. Universal entertainment holdings. Disney was looking for buyers for its sports franchises, the Anaheim Angels and the Mighty Ducks. AOL Time Warner was also considering selling "non-core" assets including the company's three Atlanta-based sports franchises and its 50 percent holdings in the Comedy Central and Court TV cable channels, and Robert Murdoch's News Corp. was working on a deal to get rid of the corporation's stake in Madison Square Garden, MSG Network, the New York Knicks, the New York Liberty WNBA team, and the New York Rangers.

In December 2002, *Washington Post* writer Frank Ahrens noted this rapidly changing trend: "Only two heady years ago, the buzzwords in the media industry were 'merger' and 'strategic acquisition,' which were supposed to lead to 'combined revenue' and 'synergy.' Today, the operative phrases are 'sales' and 'non-core assets,' which the companies hope will lead to 'debt reduction' and 'strategic fit.' "[15] Analysts pointed to slumping stock prices and a change in the synergistic value of some of these assets as the impetus for this downsizing. For example, in the case of sports franchise ownership, owning both a TV network and a sports franchise was first seen as a way to gain leverage over cable systems for distribution of game broadcasts, but, once that distribution was secured, dual ownership was no longer much of an advantage. As a result, many companies' calculations suggested that there was more money to be made in selling the franchises than in keeping them, and, in a time of slumping economies, corporations become eager to take advantage of opportunities that might improve the bottom line for shareholder reports.

Technological Influences

Converging technologies make it unlikely that there will be a complete reversal where entertainment conglomerates fragment all of their various holdings back into independent companies under separate ownership.

In addition, changes to FCC regulations in 2003 further relaxed restrictions on the number and variety of media outlets that one corporation can own, changes that were strongly supported by conglomerates such as Disney, Viacom, AOL Time Warner, News Corp. and other corporations eager to increase their holdings.[16] Today, the relationships between entertainment corporate entities are changing as quickly as those of the celebrities they create. In 2003, Vivendi merged with NBC, which was then bought out by General Electric. Also in 2003, Sony partnered with Bertelsmann on Sony BMG music, but then in 2006 Bertelsmann announced a proposed sale of its music holdings to Vivendi (owned by General Electric).[17]

Thus, while it is likely that we will continue to see more splintering and downsizing, we may also see additional strategic mergers and holding shuffles as big media companies continually search for a balance between diversification and streamlining. *Mother Jones* magazine reported that, by the end of 2006, there were eight giant media companies dominating the U.S. media, from which most people got their news and information:[18]

- Disney (market value: $72.8 billion)
- AOL Time Warner (market value: $90.7 billion)
- Viacom (market value: $53.9 billion)
- General Electric (owner of NBC, market value: $390.6 billion)
- News Corporation (market value: $56.7 billion)
- Yahoo! (market value: $40.1 billion)
- Microsoft (market value: $306.8 billion)
- Google (market value: $154.6 billion).

Of this list, Yahoo!, Microsoft, and Google are newer media companies compared to the other "traditional" five players. Note that many of these companies also made the list of global entertainment providers from more than a decade ago. So, while the corporate landscape does change quickly, many of the larger players have remained fairly constant. Given the difficulty of defining what qualifies as entertainment, however, as well as the ever-changing landscape of mergers, acquisitions, and splits it is difficult to create a definitive list of today's top global entertainment conglomerates.

The Hospitality Industry: Strategic Alliances

The competition for attention that has fueled industry restructuring has not been limited to media entertainment, it can be seen in almost all forms of leisure and recreation. Mergers and acquisitions began to explode in the hospitality industry in the mid-1990s. In the hotel industry alone, merger activity doubled from $3 billion in 1995 to a record

$8.8 billion in 1996. Fueled by rising profits, big companies became even bigger and smaller companies merged to stay competitive. Although the tourism industry in the United States saw a big dip in revenue after the World Trade Center terrorism attack in 2001, tax law changes soon after in 2003 led to even more consolidation in the industry creating conglomerates on scale with those found in media entertainment.

FLASH FACT

In 2005, Harrah's Entertainment merged with Caesar Entertainment, paying $1.87 billion in cash and $3.27 billion in stock and assuming $3.86 billion in Caesar's debt. Harrah's now maintains 40 properties in 12 states, controlling 17,600 rooms in Las Vegas alone.[19] And of the writing of this text, Delta Airline was posed to merge with Northwest Airlines.[20]

Like media entertainment, we are seeing vertical as well as horizontal expansion in the hospitality industry, and convergence and consolidation are not limited by corporate ownership. With mega-corporations such as Disney demonstrating the synergy and competitive advantage of controlling all elements of the travel experience (hotels, restaurants, attractions, and transportation such as Disney cruise lines), even independent players now rely on partnerships and "strategic alliances" for survival. In a strategic alliance, a hotel will partner with tour companies, restaurants, and local attractions. They might offer reciprocal referrals and discounts, pool resources for promotional campaigns or create all-inclusive tour packages. Often, even competing companies will join forces on projects such as destination marketing campaigns designed to increase business and revenue for everyone.

Public/private alliances involving the hospitality industry have increasingly become the centerpiece of urban revitalization and economic development strategies. Local governments and hospitality companies also often jointly invest in infrastructure such as

San Diego convention center was built to attract conference business

better roads and landscaping resulting in a nicer environment for residents and a more desirable destination for travelers. Another recent trend is the growth of convention/ conference centers in second-tier and third-tier cities such as Valencia, Spain, or Cincinnati, Ohio, in the United States. Counties and development offices in these areas have invested considerable amounts of taxpayer dollars in convention centers, leveraging industry partnerships to increase a destination's visibility and attract additional visitors to compete with larger, more popular cities such as Barcelona in Spain or Chicago in the U.S. As a result of these efforts, these revitalized areas are becoming increasingly popular as low-cost, high-quality alternatives for business conferences, sporting events, and family vacations.

Live Performances: Ticket Wars

Audiences watch concerts, sporting events, and theatrical performances in venues ranging from small bars and clubs to forums and amphitheaters seating tens of thousands of fans. These events generate serious revenues. In North America, ticket sales for live concerts reached $1.5 billion dollars in 1999, breaking a $1.4 billion record set in 1994. Promoters began raising their prices in 1994 to reduce the gap between a ticket's face value and the prices charged by scalpers and ticket brokers. By 1999, the average ticket price of the top 50 tours in North America reached $43.63, according to Gary Bongiovanni, editor-in-chief of Pollstar Inc., a music industry trade magazine and online service in Fresno, California. That is an increase of more than $10 per ticket from 1998—a 30 percent jump in one year. Ticket prices are also linked to audience demographics, he adds. Elton John tickets carry higher prices than Blink 182 tickets because John's audience represents a higher income level.[21] In 2008, Eric Clapton's June 2 date at the Mohegan Sun Arena in Uncasville, Connecticut, went on sale for $125 to $195, compared to $85 to $150 at the same venue in 2006; the Eagles' three late May dates at Madison Square Garden were $50 to $190, compared to $25 to $180 when they played there in 2005.[22] Artists resisting the economic pressure to increase prices included Tom Petty and Bruce Springsteen, who generally kept their tickets below $100. Dave Matthews Band topped out at $75, Pearl Jam was between $42 and $77 and the Warped Tour was in the $23–$37 range.

In the past, critics argued that ticketing agencies were inflating ticket prices. This criticism centered on exclusive arrangements ticketing agencies often make with venues. If a band or other act wants to book a venue, it must do its ticketing with a specific agency. A single company, Ticketmaster, controls at least 90 percent of America's ticket market and sells 60 million tickets annually.[23] It was founded in 1978 by two University of Arizona computer students who created a barcode-based system for ticketing that helped the company become the industry leader in the U.S., after buying out its only competitor, Ticketron, in 1991. As of the writing of this text, Ticketmaster boasted a roster of more than 9,000 clients, operated call centers in 20 countries and had 6,500 retail outlets.[24]

The concern is that these exclusive arrangements, and Ticketmaster in particular, have created a monopoly that eliminates competition that would keep ticket prices lower. Conversely, others have argued that centralized ticketing actually keeps prices lower (see *A Closer Look* later in this chapter). Recently, however, new online ticket resell brokers have joined the fray, challenging this centralized model. Ticket resale web sites allow ticket holders to hold auctions for their tickets. The sites charge the buyer, seller, or both a percentage of the sale price. Today, finding a ticket for a Green Bay Packers playoff game or a Rascal Flatts concert is a click away on StubHub.com or other Internet resale sites.

FLASH FACT

StubHub, a secondary resource for concert ticket sales, reported these statistics for 2007:

- Gross sales of online concert tickets increased over 91 percent.
- The Hannah Montana "Best of Both Worlds" tour was the highest grossing tour in the history of StubHub, based on dollar volume, surpassing legendary acts like Van Halen, Bruce Springsteen, and The Police.
- Celine Dion's Las Vegas tour topped the average ticket price category at a whopping $352 per show.

Source: www.stubhub.com

Ticketmaster sued one of its own clients, the Cleveland Cavaliers, for using Flash Seats, a company started by Dan Gilbert, the team's majority owner, to resell tickets. Ticketmaster claimed that it had exclusive rights to handle all Cavaliers ticket sales, including secondary ticketing, because of its primary ticketing contract with the team. The Cavaliers responded with a lawsuit accusing Ticketmaster of anticompetitive and monopolistic practices.

Flash Seats recently acquired Dallas-based ticketing company Vertical Alliance, whose clients include the NBA's Houston Rockets, Boise State University, and Texas A&M University. That acquisition gives Flash Seats the ability to provide customers with both primary and secondary ticketing, said Sam Gerace, chief executive officer of the company. The company believes it's poised to compete with Ticketmaster, which it accuses of using bullying tactics to keep Flash Seats from adding clients. Flash Seats says Ticketmaster forces teams to use its secondary ticketing site because it has contracts with those clubs for primary ticketing.

"You have to look at the secondary market as something that is a real threat to Ticketmaster," said Joe Bonner, a securities analyst at Argus Research Corp. who tracks Ticketmaster's parent company, New York-based IAC/InterActiveCorp. "They missed the boat. StubHub has been around a few years now already. They weren't as proactive as they probably should have been."[25] "It's the equivalent in the ticketing industry of the fall of the Roman Empire," said Eric Baker, founder and CEO of Viagogo.com, a European ticket resale web site.[26]

Ticketmaster denies such assertions. "We're in a transformation in some sense," said Eric Korman, Ticketmaster's executive vice president. "We're taking a very profitable 30-year-old company that's a leader in ticketing and entertainment marketing and looking to expand that." Those moves include the acquisition of Rolling Meadows, Illinois-based TicketsNow, which works with more than 800 professional ticket resellers. Ticketmaster also has made deals to become the official resale source for several professional sports leagues and the purchase of Irvine, California-based Paciolan Inc., which provides sports and entertainment venues with the software needed for automated ticketing. Korman acknowledges the company is an underdog in reselling tickets. The ticket resale market was essentially created by Internet upstarts, and Ticketmaster's resale site, TicketExchange, lags behind its younger competitors.

Many experts argue that the advent of secondary ticketing means more tickets are available to the public, which will drive down prices. Ticketmaster points to the Police tour as an example, in which an overabundance of tickets in places such as Chicago and Minneapolis caused prices to plummet, in some cases below face value. Others, like

Sucharita Mulpuru, a senior analyst at Forrester Research Inc., believe the opposite, saying secondary markets will inflate prices for popular events such as Hannah Montana concerts.[27]

While secondary ticketing has proved challenging for Ticketmaster, the bigger question is the future of the Ticketmaster model, with teams and artists seeking to take control of their destiny in the primary and secondary markets. In December of 2008, concert promoter Live Nation, Ticketmaster's biggest client, said it would begin selling its own tickets in 2009. Live Nation accounted for about 15 percent of Ticketmaster's roughly $1 billion in revenue in 2006.

This Ohio State fan is an ideal target for ticket scalpers

Ticketmaster was successful because it had deals with major venues, but now that the technology is available for companies such as Live Nation to sell its own tickets, it is unclear where that leaves Ticketmaster. "If you're a great team and by the nature of who you are—like the (Los Angeles) Lakers—you sell a lot of tickets, why should you do any revenue share with Ticketmaster?" Mulpuru said.[28]

Experts say they don't see any companies encroaching on Ticketmaster overnight because of its long-term contracts.[29] Ticketmaster executives believe they can sell tickets more effectively than if teams and entertainers do it in-house because of the company's reach and experience in marketing live entertainment to consumers. Nonetheless, it is undeniable that the ease and accessibility of online transactions is profoundly changing the traditional ticketing model, and once again we are seeing an industry being transformed by digital and online technology.

The Filming Industry: Collapsing Windows

Convergence is also challenging a standard practice in the filming industry known as "**windowing**." Movie success or failure used to be determined during the first weekend of its run. Today, box office receipts do not necessarily determine the film's overall revenue generation. A series of exhibition "windows" such as DVD, pay-per-view, and fiber-optic video-on-demand are used to maximize profits. Windowing, a second-degree price discrimination model, emerged as the underlying economic principle applied to film distribution. According to windowing, profits can be maximized by segmenting consumers into clearly distinct groupings, and charging them their "reservation prices."[30] To extract the highest prices, classes of customers must be clearly identified and correspond to various exhibition windows and the profit objectives. The sequential order of exhibition after the theater is DVD, pay-per-view, pay cable, network TV, and syndication. Recently, however, video-on-demand has come to the front of the line as a primary exhibition window for films.

Because consumers have different demographic and psychographic makeup, movies have different levels of popularity as they move through the windows, and must be handled to match a specific pattern. Less popular films have shorter windows, and low-budget movies may even bypass theaters completely by going directly to DVD or cable.

Windowing also provides opportunities for TV stars and personalities from other media to appear in movies. Each subsidiary window is important to a film's overall success. Windows for domestic and international distribution are discussed in more detail below.

The DVD Market The **DVD market** has become the viewing preference of choice by consumers because of its versatility and freedom from programming time constraints of network and local channels. And although the theatrical motion picture industry still has over 70 percent share of sales, DVDs can act as major distributors for themselves. The distribution process works much like it does for magazines, paperback books, and records. Although rentals account for most consumer transactions, first sale copyright provisions permit distributors to collect payments only the first time the cassette or DVD is sold. Sales prices to retailers are high, but, since retailers receive rental revenues, they pass along the high prices to encourage consumers to rent rather than purchase. Consumers can pick up titles with their groceries and their drugs, making the rental business a lucrative market for many retailers. Netflix and other subscription services combine online ordering with postal delivery for a convenient alternative to retailers like Blockbuster.

The International Market The **international market** is the second most important subsidiary with over 80 trading partners of the U.S. The size and power of the American market causes it to dominate world distribution. To combat some of the competition, many countries restrict production to local companies or provide them with tax breaks and favorable loan rates. Governmental tactics have been circumvented by American producers who establish their own companies abroad to escape the penalties levied at foreign production. Foreign co-productions have become commonplace and the export market continues to grow.

For years, this movie windowing system worked within a fairly stable framework: a movie would be released and run in the theaters for as long as it was profitable. Later—often much later and with great fanfare—the film would be edited and released on TV. Over the course of that era, a large gulf existed between the theatrical experience, which was loud and environmental, and the home experience, which was severely watered down.

With the arrival of home video systems, the home viewing experience has been consistently improving. Movies showed up at home relatively unedited. Over the course of the next two decades, consumer formats got better, as did the TVs the consumers were watching. Studios and electronics manufacturers began to pitch the high-quality viewing experience to be had in the home, and DVD sales took off.

Selling movies that did well in the theaters makes studios happy, and the time between a film's big screen release and its appearance on DVD began to shrink. It used to take six months or more before a film would be made available for home viewing. The average time is now less than four months.[31]

Will we see the demise of movie theaters in favor of viewing on mobile devices and at home?

Some studios are even talking about using different windows for different kinds of pictures. For example, a picture for an older audience might have an expanded window of a more traditional six or seven months, whereas a younger audience that has more of that immediate need for gratification might have a window of only four months.

Combating Piracy   Another reason that some of these windows are shrinking is concerns regarding piracy: movies are often available for download on the Internet before they even arrive in the theaters. To combat illegal downloads, Disney head Robert Iger suggested simultaneous release dates for both theater and home—an idea that has also intrigued other industry executives such as Time Warner chairman Richard Parsons. A related idea is to sell DVDs in the theater. So you've seen the movie and, just as when you go to a play on Broadway or a concert, you can buy the DVD, that's when people are feeling best about it, and you cut the theater owner in to the video sale.

At least one film has given the simultaneous release concept a try. The film *Bubble*, which was directed by Steven Soderbergh and bankrolled in part by maverick rich guy Mark Cuban, hit theaters and DVD at the same time in January 2006, but didn't find much success. As of the writing of this text, a simultaneous release had not been tested with a big studio film. Nonetheless, Soderbergh argues that windowing is an outdated system:

> Name any big-title movie that's come out in the last four years. It has been available in all formats on the day of release. It's called piracy. Peter Jackson's *Lord of the Rings*, *Ocean's Eleven*, and *Ocean's Twelve*—I saw them on Canal Street on opening day. Simultaneous release is already here. We're just trying to gain control over it.[32]

FLASH FACT

Consumer spending on DVDs and Blu-ray in the first six months of 2008, purchases and rentals combined, was up 1.6 percent from spending in first-half 2007, according to *Home Media Magazine*'s market research department. The first-half 2008 tally: $10.77 billion, compared with $10.6 billion a year ago.[33]

The Music Industry: 360 Deals[34]

Digital advances and concerns about piracy are also changing traditional business models for other entertainment industries. In the music industry, labels are rethinking the way deals with bands are negotiated. In the past, artists signed contracts that would allow that label the exclusive right to represent the artist's music. Representation included selling music at retail, as well as generating income from song placement in movies, TV shows, and advertising. That was it. Seven album cycles were the standard time frame for these deals, leaving many artists contractually obligated to a particular record label for their entire career. In exchange for exclusivity, artists were given additional benefits. Often, a significant signing bonus, funds to record their music, and tour support were extended. These funds were deducted against the artist's future royalties. Once records began to sell, the artist would earn a fraction of the income generated, but usually had a team of executives who aided their career development.[35]

Recently, however, musicians such as the pop-punk band Paramore are signing deals in which artists share not just revenue from their album sales but concert, merchandise, and other earnings with their label in exchange for more comprehensive career support. Since signing one of these new deals with Atlantic Records, Paramore has built a passionate audience that has snapped up more than 350,000 copies of its recent second album, *Riot!*, more than doubling the sales of its debut. And the band began selling out theaters on recent tours.

Commonly known as "multiple rights" or **"360" deals**, the new pacts are said to have their origins in a deal that Robbie Williams, the British pop singer, signed with EMI in 2002. They are now used by all the major record labels and even a few independents. Madonna has been the most prominent artist to sign on (her recent $120 million deal with the concert promoter Live Nation allows it to share in her future earnings), but the majority of these new deals are made with unknown acts.

It is difficult to tabulate the number of acts working under 360 deals, but, worldwide, record labels share in the earnings with such diverse acts as Lordi, a Finnish metal band which has its own soft drink and credit card, and Camila, a Mexican pop trio that has been drawing big crowds to its concerts. In the United States, Interscope Records benefits from the marketing spinoffs from the Pussycat Dolls, including a Dolls-theme nightclub in Las Vegas. "Five or eight years ago an eyebrow would be raised," said the music producer Josh Abraham, whose recent credits include recordings by Slayer and Pink. "Now it's everywhere. You can't talk about what a deal looks like without seeing 360."[36]

Like many innovations, these deals were triggered by economic and technological changes. After experiencing the financial havoc unleashed by slipping CD sales, music companies started viewing the ancillary income from artists as a potential new source of cash. The argument went that, if labels invest the most in the risky and expensive process of developing talent, why shouldn't they get a bigger share of the talent's success?

In return for that bigger share, labels might give artists more money up front and in many cases touring subsidies that otherwise would not be offered. More important, perhaps, artists might be allowed more time to develop the talent and following needed to build a long career. And the label's ability to cross market items like CDs, ring tones, VIP concert packages, and merchandise might make for a bigger overall pie.

The industry's hunger for 360 deals might subtly shift the ways labels view the scouting and cultivation of talent, a process known as A&R, or artist and repertory, development. Rap acts, for example, might lose out, since their recordings can be expensive to produce and very few become touring successes. On the other hand, rappers can attract lucrative endorsements for products from sneakers to computers to soft drinks; many have started apparel lines. With an eye to a piece of that potential revenue, Atlantic recently signed the Brooklyn rapper Maino to a 360-style pact.

And labels may take a closer look at the progeny of the Grateful Dead: hard-touring jam bands that don't necessarily sell many CDs or score radio hits but do draw obsessively loyal fans who gobble up tickets and memorabilia. "We used to look at jam bands as bands that absolutely we shouldn't sign," Mr. Kallman said. "Now all of a sudden I'm saying: 'Guys, you absolutely must find the next hottest jam band. I need the next Phish. Urgently.'"[37] Though the concept could be applied to anyone, even fleetingly famous pop stars, the real potential of a 360-style pact does not emerge unless an act is popular long enough to attract either loyal fans who reliably buy tickets, or attention from business partners who might help market spinoffs like a fragrance or sneaker line.

Not everyone is sold on the concept. Many talent managers view 360s as a thinly veiled money grab and are skeptical that the labels, with their work forces shrinking amid industrywide cost cutting, will deliver on their promises of patience. "That's a hard speech for many people to buy into," said Bruce Flohr, a longtime talent executive who signed the Dave Matthews Band to RCA Records and now works for ATO Records, an independent label. "You can speak to me that you're going to work a record for 18 months. You're going to work a record for 18 months when it's selling 420 copies six months from now? Come on—really?"[38]

Even inexperienced performers may resist sharing their take from the box office, particularly at a time when plunging CD sales have pushed artists to rely even more on their concert earnings. But record executives argue that such deals could free them from the tyranny of megahits because there would be less pressure to make back the label's money immediately. In the 1990s the arrival of computerized data from SoundScan, which tracks retail sales, meant the industry had an instant scorecard that tempted companies to push for Hollywood blockbuster-style opening weeks. The demand for quick payoffs persisted, even though a review of the last 15 years of Billboard data shows the albums that immediately seized spots on the upper half of the Billboard Top 200 chart would go on to sell fewer copies, on average, than the releases that slowly worked their way up.

If 360s mean that labels might practice more patience in developing raw talent, however, today's open, online culture presents significant challenges. Internet fans can render judgment on burgeoning artists almost instantly, long before the musicians have a chance to hone their songs or road-test their performance skills. Indie-rock bands run a gauntlet of blogs that might include a round of breathless hype that vaults them to Next-Big-Thing status then a thorough backlash, all before they even release an album.

While most labels now monitor blogs for new acts to sign, many executives insist that, once they commit to developing a new act's career, they can discount much of the online banter. "It's not just like, 'Oh my god, they're not hip in Williamsburg anymore, so therefore it's over,'" said Steve Ralbovsky, a longtime A&R executive who signed artists including Kings of Leon at RCA Records and now runs his own unit, Canvasback, at Columbia Records. "You just have to realize there's a world apart" from the blogosphere. Like so many other emerging changes in the entertainment business, an ultimate verdict on the impact of 360 deals for labels, artists, and fans remains to be seen.

SPOTLIGHT ON 360 DEALS   Atlantic and Paramore

Paramore on tour

Particulars of a 360 deal might differ from label to label, but Atlantic's deal with Paramore provides an example of how one might be structured.

In 2005 Atlantic Records and a small partner, the Florida company Fueled By Ramen, signed Paramore with plans to build a brand-name rock band, one that now not only racks up sold-out shows but sells merchandise from flip-flops to tube tops. The band members, who were mostly teenagers when they signed, felt drawn to a comprehensive approach that allowed for slower growth, lead singer Haley Williams said during a recent chat on the band's tour bus.

Atlantic's document offers a conventional cash advance to sign the artist, who would receive a royalty for sales after expenses were recouped. With the release of the artist's first album, however, the label has an option to pay an additional $200,000 in exchange for 30 percent of the net income from all touring, merchandise, endorsements, and fan-club fees. Atlantic would also have the right to approve the act's tour schedule, and the salaries of certain tour and merchandise sales employees hired by the artist. But the label also offers the artist a 30 percent cut of the label's album profits—if any—which represents an improvement from the typical industry royalty of 15 percent.

As Paramore developed, Atlantic and Fueled By Ramen underwrote many of its touring expenses, including, early on, the purchase of a van and payments to Ms. Williams's mother to continue the band members' high school education on the road, said John Janick, Fueled By Ramen's top executive. Paramore's handlers wanted the band to hone its craft off the industry radar, forgoing the push to get radio play for any singles from the band's first album, 2005's *All We Know Is Falling.* Instead, Fueled By Ramen tried to drum up support on web sites like Purevolume.com, where users explore new music. "The band was so young, and they were trying to figure out who they were," Mr. Janick said.

"If we weren't so mono-focused on the selling of recorded music, we could actually take a really holistic approach to the development of an artist brand," said Craig Kallman, chairman of Atlantic Records. "What's the healthiest decision to be made,

not just to sell the CD but to build the artist's fan base?"

Paramore's debut sold more than 140,000 CDs: no flop but far below typical expectations for a band considered a label priority. "We were given all the time in the world, and all the support we could ever ask for, to basically do nothing but play shows," Ms. Williams said. Without the 360 approach, she said, "I don't know that we would've been given that lenience."

There are tradeoffs, however. As a result of their contact, the band's chance to develop away from the spotlight of the mainstream marketplace has now ended. With its gathering fame, the band has already confronted a handful of tough decisions about how to maintain its identity. Ms. Williams said she rejected an overture from a shoe company that wanted to feature her—alone—in an ad campaign.

Still, to grow, the band will have to expand its reach. Josh Farro, Paramore's guitarist, sounded wary. Until now "we didn't want to get lumped into that whole machine, MTV and all that stuff," he said. "We felt like it was just too soon. And we'd rather build a solid fan base." He added, "We have such crazy fans, and those are the ones that are going to stick with us forever."

Source: Excerpted from Leeds, Jeff (2007). Not many big bands—Madonna, Pussy Cat Dolls, Paramore. *New York Times,* Nov. 11. Retrieved on Aug. 29, 2008 at http://www.nytimes.com/2007/11/11/arts/music/11leed.html?pagewanted=1&_r=1

What do you think?

- *Are 360 deals better for the artists? The record labels? The fans?*

Following the Rules: The Dynamics of Attention

A review of successful, contemporary entertainment reveals some of the key dynamics involved in capturing an audience's attention. This section highlights some of these dynamics in eight areas, including the importance of novelty and reinvention, exiting on top, people power, time considerations, solitude and shared community, hits and phenomena, alpha consumers, and barriers to entry.

Novelty and Reinvention

Perhaps the most important principle to remember is that what captures attention today may be ignored tomorrow. Audiences are fickle, so entertainers must constantly reinvent themselves and their entertainment. Journalists know that novelty captures the attention of news audiences. Indeed, the name "news" reflects an emphasis on delivering information that is new or different. Similarly, companies market their products as new and improved to gain and retain customers. Entertainers are no different. They know that novelty captures attention. Elvis Presley both shocked and delighted audiences when he introduced dirty dancing to rock and roll. Movies such as *Jurassic Park* and *The Matrix* attracted attention with "new and improved" special effects. Although some audiences may have longer attention spans than others, all audiences eventually get tired of the same old thing and start looking for something new.

According to former Disney executive, Mike Berry, in the world of attention and entertainment, the rule "If it ain't broke, don't fix it" does not apply.[39] If something seems to be working, it is easy to become complacent. Writers, musicians, and other entertainers— even hotels and theme parks—may be tempted to stick with formulas and styles that have worked in the past, following the same routine until it "breaks" and they begin to lose their audiences. Berry warned that those who follow this policy may find it difficult if not impossible to win those audiences back again. Instead of waiting until it's "broke," Berry recommended continuously looking for ways to reinvent the old and make it new again.

Companies in the video game industry have learned the importance of reinvention the hard way. Although Atari was the first to put a game console on the market, it was Nintendo who dominated the market in the 1980s. In the 1990s, however, Nintendo began to lose market share first to Sega with its release of the game *Sonic the Hedgehog*, and then to Sony PlayStation's CD-only game console. Today competition in the gaming market is fierce. Not only do companies regularly introduce new games long before players have mastered the old ones, these new games often can be played only on new game consoles.

When Nintendo launched the GameCube in November 2001, the company faced stiff competition not only from existing systems like Sega and Sony but also from Microsoft, a new player in the console gaming industry, which launched its new console, the XBox, on November 15, 2001, beating Nintendo to the market by three days. Recognizing the importance of novelty and reinvention in this competitive marketplace, the head of Nintendo software development, Shiguru Miyamoto, tried to position the GameCube as a dynamic machine that would evolve instead of stagnate:

> In first thinking about Nintendo GameCube 3 years ago, we envisioned a system that would allow us to create entertainment which would surpass the common definitions of video gameplay. The engineers have given us just that—a machine that not only excels today, but will continue to break boundaries for years to come.[40]

Yet it wasn't the GameCube, but the Wii that transformed the gaming experience and helpd keep Nintendo on top in the home console market. In October, 2009, VG Chartz reported the Wii holding 48.4 percent of the worldwide console market followed by Microsoft's Xbox at 29.1 percent and Sony's PS3 with 22.5 percent. In the portable device market, Nintendo was also the leader with their DS claiming 68.3 percent of the market, followed by Sony's PSP at 31.7 percent (see Figure 6.1). Competition among these companies is also fierce for the games themselves. *FIFA Soccer 10* (PSP) topped the world chartes in 2009, followed by *FIFA Soccer 10* (X360), *Halo 3: ODST* (X360), *Wii Fit Plus* (Wii), and *Wii Sports* (Wii). Nintendo, Sony, and Microsoft also faced a growing threat from Apple which began developing games and promoting the iPhone and iPod Touch media players as game devices.[41]

It is not enough just to keep up with cutting-edge technology, companies also must keep up with their audiences. Brian O'Rourke, In-Stat analyst, predicted that "Microsoft may outship Nintendo in the next generation of consoles due to its head start in launching, its strength in the North American market, and its appeal to older gamers, a demographic that seems to widen with each new generation of consoles."[42]

In music, bands and recording artists whose success spans multiple decades (for example, the Beatles, the Rolling Stones, and Aerosmith) are often described as "reinventing" themselves. Some critics argue that, if you listen to the varied sounds of these musicians, you can hear the precursors to many contemporary music trends, including such styles as rap and techno. In fact, rap stars Run-DMC and Public Enemy petitioned for rights to do remakes of some Beatles songs.[43] Other examples of reinvention include artists such as Madonna, Prince, and Sting, who have experimented with different sounds, looks, and names over the years, and bands such as Nirvana and Pearl Jam, who shifted from more traditional hard rock to leading the grunge/alternative movement. Even though audiences have been more receptive to some changes than others, these efforts at reinvention emphasize the value of novelty.

Product	Total global sales ($ million)	Percentage game sales
Wii	53.97	48.4
XBOX 360	32.42	29.1
PS3	25.03	22.5
NINTENDO DS	111.49	68.3
PSP PlayStation Portable	51.8	31.7

Figure 6.1   Video game hardware sales as of October, 2009

Source: VGChartz.com

Consumers are drawn to entertainment offerings that are novel and different but, unfortunately, after the novelty wears off, attention may be lost. When consumer businesses begin behaving like entertainment businesses, they are likely to be treated like entertainment businesses. Thus, consumer products and services are also facing shorter life cycles guided by hits and fads. As Gillette and other companies have shown, even products as commonplace as razors must regularly reinvent themselves if they want to survive in the marketplace. This trend presents a problem for many enterprises. Consider the history of entertainment-infused themed restaurants, such as Rain Forest Café and Planet Hollywood. Both had early success and then quickly faded. Kurt Barnard, of *Barnard's retail trend report*, believes that novelty presents a problem for all themed stores and restaurants because "once you've seen it, you've seen it," he says, "A theme store cannot reinvent itself every four weeks."[44]

Video gaming with passion

Exit on Top

To keep attention, you need to stay dynamic, and you have to be willing to take risks. For every novel concept or idea that succeeds, hundreds of others fail. And for the few that do make it, success is often short-lived. As a result, entertainers and entertainment companies sometimes resemble day traders on the stock market as they try to "buy low," hoping to discover the next big entertainment trend, and then "sell high" at the pinnacle of success, right before attention begins to fade. This philosophy is reflected in many popular TV sitcoms, such as *Seinfeld, Home Improvement*, and *Friends*, that went off the air while still receiving peak audience ratings. In explaining his decision to end his series, *Home Improvement* star Tim Allen said, "I don't like second encores. I don't like people who stay onstage too long."[45] And for good reason. Actors are most marketable when their program ratings are high, because that is when their ability to capture attention is maximized. Often actors leave successful programs to pursue new and different acting opportunities. Although it may be risky to leave a highly rated and high-paying program, actors who wait to look for new projects until after their program ratings drop risk not having any new or different opportunities to pursue. Furthermore, some believe that, if you discontinue the show while it is still popular, it will do better in syndication (reruns) than if you wait until audiences have already "burned out" on the program.

The same logic applies to music. When radio stations play a song too frequently, audiences will often get sick of it. To guard against this problem, many stations do extensive marketing research, polling listeners to try to determine when audiences are beginning to "burn out" on a song. Of course, stations tend to play the most popular songs most often, and songs that are good, but perhaps not great, are played less frequently. As a result, top ten songs sometimes come onto and go off playlists quite quickly because of audience burnout, whereas many lower-rated songs may remain on playlists longer because they are played less frequently.

People Power

Just as reporters know that readers find stories more interesting when they appeal to human interest, advertisers and marketers know that people pay more attention to personal stories and individual testimonials—who did what and how others have been or might be affected—than to more impersonal facts or statistics. Similarly, filmmakers know that moviegoers often select a movie based more on the stars in the film than on the film's subject matter or plot. As you learned in Chapter 4, entertainment is driven by drama, and drama is driven by human interest. In books, films, even sporting events, an audience's attention is held by audience members' interest in what is happening to whom and by the anticipation of what will happen to whom next.

People are valuable in an attention economy, some more than others. The more attention you capture, the more valuable you are. Consider Michael Jordan. In his last year with the Bulls alone, Jordan made millions because of his ability to capture the attention of sports fans worldwide. But his salary pales in comparison to the many millions of dollars he made from corporate sponsors because of his ability to capture the attention of their consumers.

Movie stars and athletes are not the only ones capturing attention. When you think of the company Microsoft, who do you think of? If you are like many people, you think of Bill Gates. The old adage that companies are only as valuable as the people who run them has renewed meaning. Economic theorist Michael Goldhaber demonstrates this point by making a comparison between Bill Gates and the late John D. Rockefeller, who served as leader and chief owner of the Standard Oil Trust almost a century ago. Goldhaber maintains that Rockefeller's wealth consisted chiefly of oil fields, oil wells, tanker cars, refiners, and other material things that would have been worth just as much if someone else had bought him out. Microsoft's value, on the other hand, is less tangible—it depends on new concepts and software that is yet to be completely designed. Rockefeller could have sold his interests and still kept about the same net worth, which is what monetary net worth is supposed to mean. But the share value of a company such as Microsoft, which depends on concepts and ideas, depends more on the brainpower behind those ideas.

This logic suggests that if Gates were to decide to sell out and buy control of the XYZ Corporation instead of staying at the helm of Microsoft, Microsoft stock would plummet, and XYZ's stock would rise. According to Goldhaber,

> Despite the fact that the arena in which he made his mark happens to be business, it is already true that Gates' actual wealth, and that of many like him, is less in money or shares of stock than in attention.[46]

Thus, Goldhaber argues that business becomes a lively spectator sport. Just as we care about record breakers in football or basketball, we are interested in who heads lists such as the Forbes 400. And he argues that for some on those lists, the main motive for trying to earn still more boils down to wanting attention, wanting to be recognized as number one.

Although attention cannot be bought, it can be transferred. Attention will often "rub off" on things that are associated with it. Celebrity product endorsements (Michael Jordan for Gatorade, Paris Hilton for Carl's Jr.) and corporate sponsorships of entertainment venues (The Staples Center in California, Heinz Field in Pennsylvania) and events (Tostitos Fiesta Bowl, Hard Rock Café's sponsorship of Rockfest, a traveling rock festival) are based on the premise that the corporation will get to share the attention given the celebrities or events. Michael Jordan serves as one of the most convincing examples of the power of these alliances. *Fortune* magazine estimated that Michael Jordan had a $10 billion effect on the U.S. economy while he was playing in the National Basketball Association (NBA) from 1984 to 1998:[47] Jordan's name was a powerful marketing tool. By 1998, Jordan videos had made over $80 million. He had written or been the inspiration for 70 books totaling over $17 million in sales. Michael Jordan cologne had sales of $155 million, and his Hanes underwear exceed sales of $10 million annually. His debut feature movie, *Space Jam*, made $230 million in theaters and $209 million in video sales. These items alone combined to total $701 million in revenue. Jordan's impressive corporate alignments include companies such as Coke, General Mills WorldCom, CBS.SportsLine. com (web site), Quaker Oats (Gatorade), Oakley (sunglasses), and Rayovac (batteries and lighting). Bill Schmidt, Gatorade's marketing director, explains Jordan's value: "We've gone into countries where they don't have a clue about what a sports beverage is, but they know Michael. He's instant validation. We manage him like a brand."[48]

One of the corporations that most greatly benefited from the Jordan effect was Nike. Nike's Air Jordan brand made more than $130 million in shoe sales the first year. Over his career, it is estimated that Jordan will gross about $2.6 billion for Nike. But Jordan's value to Nike goes well beyond sales. According to footwear analyst Jennifer Black, his impact on Nike's overall image is almost incalculable:

> I've been doing this for 18 years, and I have not seen anything like the power of the name, and the ties to consumer, and the sales generated by him. Is it worth double the number he's done in sales? Maybe.[49]

Because attention is so valuable, events or individuals that are good at capturing attention are also highly valued. In fact, Goldhaber argues that attention can serve as currency, making money virtually obsolete. He reasons that the right attention from the right people can get you everything that money can buy, and even some things, such as attention itself, that money cannot buy. Michael Jordan is clearly not the only athlete with big dollar endorsements. Close on his heels is Tiger Woods, who in 2000 signed a five-year, $105 million contract extension with Nike. It was the largest endorsing deal ever signed by an athlete at that time.[50] Companies offer celebrities free clothes to wear, food to eat, cars to drive, stays in hotels—all with the hope that consumers will give the same adoration and attention to the company's products and services that they give to the celebrity that endorses them. With the right sponsorships and endorsements, a celebrity like Michael Jordan could probably manage quite well without money. Of course, in today's economy, he gets plenty of that, too.

As one of the most successful celebrity endorsers of all time, Tiger Woods has been used to capture attention for everything from razor blades to cars

While celebrities do financially profit from their endorsements, some stars also choose to align themselves with brands for more personal or political reasons. Recently, Stephon Marbury, a talented, but widely criticized point guard for the New York Knicks, received high-profile praise for putting his name on a line of cheap athletic wear and shoes, dubbed Starbury. Marbury's signature Starbury One basketball shoes retail for a mere $15. Marbury says his motivation was rooted in discussions he had with Knicks GM Isaiah Thomas about the civil rights movement and Marbury's eventual legacy. The campaign is marketed as an effort to promote social justice by making apparel more affordable. Critics, however, have questioned the motives and practices of both Marbury and Steve and Berry's University Sportwear, Starbury One's manufacturer. Take *A Closer Look at Sneakers for Social Justice* in Chapter 13 for a more detailed discussion of these issues.

Starbury One

FLASH FACT

Going into the Beijing Olympics, Michael Phelps had an estimated $5 million in sponsorships. After winning eight gold medals in the Beijing Olympics, Phelps was featured in Visa commercials and on Kellogg's cereal boxes. Air-time value for Speedo, which he wore during the games, was $3.6 million. While impossible to gage, experts estimate his potential worth up to $30 million a year—which puts him in the same league as Tiger and Michael.[51]

Time Won't Give Me Time

Once upon a time, analysts predicted that, as technology increased, so would our leisure time as computers and other advances continued to do more and more of our work for us. Today it might seem comical, but critics once worried about what people would do with all of their free time. Of course, in reality, many of us may feel like we have less free time than ever. And time is what we want. Surveys show that if given the choice at work between more money and more time off, most people would take the time. This preference is even reflected in our gift giving. For example, although chocolate and roses still are ranked first as Valentine presents, studies found that more than one-third of those surveyed give their Valentines gifts of time, such as catered meals, dry cleaning services, or certificates to a day spa.

Even though it may feel like we have less leisure time, studies comparing the total number of free hours that people report having today compared to past decades suggest that the amount of free time has actually remained fairly constant. One reason we may feel like we have less time is because of the many demands for our attention. In addition to work, family, friends, and school, we have organizations wanting us to spend time paying attention to them, listening to their sales pitches, buying their products, using their services, and signing their petitions. It is estimated that the average consumer is bombarded with as many as 3,000 advertising messages each day, all competing for attention.[52]

Similar to television programming, we budget our time into slots. But we only have so much time, so the more things we try to squeeze in, the smaller and smaller each time slot becomes. Because leisure time is a priority, most of us still manage to schedule in a fair amount of it, but instead of enjoying that time in a few long uninterrupted blocks, we break our free time up into smaller but more frequent time segments. And our entertainment preferences reflect these changes. We prefer short books or magazines to long ones. Instead of going to the movie theater or a video arcade and pumping quarters into a machine for several hours one Saturday afternoon, we watch movies and TV shows on our laptops and play games on our PDAs, sneaking in a few minutes here and there during our lunch breaks, between classes, and while we wait at the doctor's office. Instead of taking one two- or three-week vacation every year, we take a one-week vacation and several long weekends. Starting in the 1990s, for the first time, more than half of all holiday trips were weekend trips, according to the Travel Industry Association of America.[53]

When you parcel your time in this way, you want to make the most of it, so you cram in all you can. Tourist organizations respond by packaging deals with airfare, rooms, meals, and sightseeing tours so travelers can maximize their time and money. Similarly, many entrepreneurs have found that they can build successful enterprises by making the chores we have to do more fun. Ventures such as comedy traffic schools, work seminars at mountain or beach resorts, and "shoppertainment" centers attract audiences by infusing entertainment into otherwise mundane tasks. Such time-sharing strategies allow individuals to get double duty—work and play—out of a single time segment, often for only a marginal increase in cost. Consider the costs—in terms of both time and money—of going to traffic school and a comedy show, or a two-day work seminar and a weekend trip to the mountains, separately versus the costs of the combined offerings. Granted, comedy traffic schools and work retreats do not compare to the pure entertainment value of your favorite stand-up comedians and weekend getaways, but a little entertainment is usually better than none at all.

This time-maximizing mentality is also reflected in the increasing popularity of simulated experiences and venues. Video games simulate all types of real experiences, including skiing, golfing, kayaking, flying planes, and even building cities. Water parks simulate beaches, complete with sand and waves. Perhaps the best examples of simulated environments are Las Vegas and Disney attractions, where you can tour Paris, China, Egyptian pyramids, and other wonders of the world without even leaving the country. The image below shows Paris Las Vegas, a themed casino that brings the sights, sounds, and tastes of Paris to the Nevada desert. Consistent with other entertainment trends, these attractions offer a better-than-nothing alternative for those who do not have the time or money to experience the real thing. However, these simulated experiences are often preferred even when the time and money costs are equivalent to, or even higher than, costs for more authentic experiences. Instead of going outside and playing football, kids play it on Sega. People who live at the beach drive to water parks. International tourists visiting California bypass the authentic boardwalk at Santa Monica Pier located only minutes away from the airport to travel an hour inland to the boardwalk at Disney's California Adventure.

Although such behavior might seem puzzling, simulated environments do offer some advantages. Perhaps the biggest advantage is that they are more controlled. Simulated attractions extract and maximize the best, most popular attributes from the experiences they imitate. Real environments can be unpredictable. You go skiing, and a blizzard leaves you trapped in the lodge, or you go out on the slopes and break your leg on your first run. You go to the beach only to find that a ruptured sewage line has contaminated the water. You travel to Paris, France, as did one of the authors of this text, and all the museums are closed because government workers decide to go on strike. At the video arcade, however, broken bones are mended at the push of a button; at the water park, a set of chemically

Las Vegas, Nevada. The ultimate simulated environment. Pictured here is the Eiffel Tower of Paris, France, recreated at the Hotel Paris

treated waves arrives onshore every ten minutes, and nothing ever closes in Las Vegas. Although there are never any absolute guarantees in entertainment, because our time and money (not to mention our life spans) are limited, we look for ways to minimize our risks. And simulated, controlled entertainment experiences do just that.

Solitude and Shared Community

It is sometimes argued that in modern society people have become more isolated from one another. Today, few families regularly gather around the dinner table to spend quality time together. Fast food and microwave meals make it easy for family members to fend for themselves and continue with their busy schedules. At work, face-to-face meetings are replaced by teleconferencing or e-mail exchanges. Many people no longer go to a communal workplace at all, but instead telecommute from home offices. Many of the chores that used to bring us into contact with others, such as shopping and banking, and even education and exercise, can be conducted at home via the phone, the Internet, videos, or cable TV. Thanks to increased urban and suburban sprawl, those who do venture out of their homes often find themselves spending more solitary hours sitting in traffic.

Although most of us welcome the conveniences of modern life, such isolation can make us feel a bit lonely. As a result, two opposing trends have emerged in entertainment. On the one hand, because we spend more time alone, there is an increased demand for entertainment that people can enjoy when they are by themselves, such as video games, home videos, books, and magazines. On the other hand, there is also increased demand for shared entertainment experiences that help bring people together. Mega-plex shop-pertainment centers create a renewed sense of community where people can come together in one place to socialize, run errands (buy shoes, switch cellular service providers, grab lunch) and have fun (listen to some live music, play video games, go to the movies).

When physically isolated from others, individuals can interact through virtual entertainment. Indeed, the most popular online video games are ones where players get to interact with each other. Online chat rooms, networking sites, and special interest and hobby club web sites also provide avenues for entertaining social interaction.

Hits and Phenomena

Every entertainer and entertainment business mogul shares the same aspirations to create the next big hit or phenomenon. In movies, it's the next *Jaws, Star Wars*, or *Titanic*; in TV programs it's the next *Seinfeld* or *American Idol* (see *Spotlight* below); in books it's the next *Harry Potter* or *Men Are from Mars, Women Are from Venus*; in toys it's the next Razor Scooter. Hits are not limited to entertainment, they are also found in other goods and services, such as Kinko's and the iPhone. According to entertainment industry strategist Michael Wolf, hits are driven by "high concepts," which are compelling ideas that can be expressed in simple thoughts.[54] It's *Seinfeld*, the show about nothing. It's expressing gender differences as different planets. It's the phone that changes everything by doing everything.

Wolf relates hits and phenomena to German philosopher Friedrich Hegel's concept of a "world historical person." Such a person is said to be so in touch with the times he or she can express the longings and desires of mass humanity. Leaders such as Abraham Lincoln, Martin Luther King, and Adolf Hitler are classic examples of world historical persons who shaped, reflected, and virtually embodied their eras. People feel connected to these individuals and they follow their lead. Similarly, according to Wolf, hits or phenomena might be considered to be world historical products in that they similarly express society's longings and desires. He argues that "hits transform mere commerce into a consumerist culture statement." People define themselves by the music they listen to, the programs they watch, the books they read, the clothes they wear. Hits are fueled by our desire to fit in, to be part of a group. If we haven't seen the latest blockbuster film and aren't wearing the "right" clothes, we feel left out. Our purchases and our entertainment choices give us a sense of belonging. They identify us as rebellious, goth teenagers, yuppie bikers, or soccer moms. Such labels help individuals define the lines between "us" and "them."

By definition, not everything can be a hit; in fact, hits are rare. As with all other products, entertainment marketers are looking for a *unique selling proposition (USP)*—something that sets them apart from and above the competition. In the case of most hits, the USP is not just a fancy gimmick, it delivers on its promise. In the competitive soft drink market, Mountain Dew was able to break from the pack by tying into extreme sports. Given that both soft drinks and extreme sports are youth-oriented, many soft drink brands might have liked to make this connection; however, the high caffeine content of Mountain Dew made the brand uniquely suited to capitalize on the "extreme" concept.

SPOTLIGHT ON SALES   Selling an Idea to the Networks

Simon Cowell's *American Idol*, created for the benefit of his record label, became an international hit. But only after being rejected by every American TV network.

Coming into the U.S. music reality show realm, *American Idol* followed Britain's *Popstars* and *Fame Academy*. After introducing yet another similar show, *Pop Idol* in the U.K. with four judges, Cowell believed he could combine fun with candid and final fan voting to choose a winner in almost a soap opera format. At the time Cowell tried to market the show in the U.S., however, ABC had already experienced a failed music show, *Making the Band*, and had declined. WB network tried a similar format with a show called *Pop Stars* that found only a niche audience. It said no to *Idol*. NBC's reality executives also passed, and CBS's reality division rejected the idea during an initial phone call.

That left Fox. Pitching the idea with fervent passion, Cowell's colleague impressed Fox with the notion that the format would essentially be all audition, complete with a lot of really woeful early performances. In this show, the audience would rule. Needing fresh summer programming, Fox accepted the show. The

network, however, agreed to air the program only if it could be a fully sponsored broadcast.

As talks with Fox dragged on, execs at News Corporation (Fox's owner) were witnessing the success of Britain's *Pop Idol*. The daughter of the corporation's founder, Rupert Murdoch, loved the show. With a call to the top decision maker at the Fox network, Murdoch ordered a buy. In spite of faltering advertising sponsorship, Fox closed the deal as a 15-episode series like it had been in Britain. As part of the deal, Fox wanted Cowell's charismatic figure on the judging panel.

The success of *American Idol* inspired many similarly formatted competition programs

Cowell worried both about his lack of knowledge about American music and whether American television would insist that he water down his critiques of the contestants. Although the name was changed to *American Idol*, the British format was retained to the letter. Fox believed that American audiences were ready to rebel against what Cowell called "the terrible political correctness that invaded America and England."

The other judges were smoothly selected. Randy Jackson, former Journey band member, and Paula Abdul, who had her own solid musical and dance career, came on board. The judges were limited to three to avoid ties. As the show progressed, Cowell unleashed his lash on every offending wannabe. He told one girl to get a lawyer and sue her vocal coach. Others he labeled with terms such as wretched, horrid, and pathetic. As it turned out, *Idol* was an instant hit, with opening ratings of ten million viewers, the most-watched show on American television on its first night. The second night it added a million viewers. Among coveted audience members in the 18–35 group, *Idol* finished first and second for the week.

Cowell embarked on a round of publicity, doing 50 interviews with American radio stations in one day alone. Within a matter of weeks, Fox was making arrangements to bring *Idol* back in the regular season. The show became more than fresh programming, it became a business-changer for all of network television.

Source: Bill Carter for the *New York Times*, Sunday Business Section, April 30, 2006

What do you think?

- *What other shows follow the* Idol *formula? Are they as successful?*
- *What could the American political system learn from this interactive concept of audience involvement?*

Alpha Consumers

Hits are set into motion by *alpha consumers*. Alphas are the trailblazers among different audiences and consumer groups. They are the first to try the latest market offerings, and they waste no time passing along their verdict to their peers: "I love it; you gotta get one," "Don't waste your money," or "Wait until it comes out on video." In a hit-driven society, marketers are anxious to reach alphas and eager to get their blessing. Reflecting the shift from mass to target marketing, efforts are focused on drawing the attention of key alphas or alpha groups who, it is hoped, will then capture the attention of the rest of the herd. In music, bands usually build followings by word of mouth. The bands or their agents try to secure gigs at venues such as Britain's King Tut's Wah Wah Hut in Glasgow, where other successful bands such as Oasis, Radiohead, and the Verve were discovered by key alpha fans. Recognizing the importance of the alphas, music label executives also frequent popular live music venues, scrutinizing the reactions of the alpha audience to try to determine a band's "hit" potential.

The production and marketing budgets of established entertainment conglomerates continue to grow as they battle to create the next entertainment phenomenon. Some experts, however, argue that the new focus on alpha consumers combined with key technological innovations can actually reduce the barriers to entry for new players on the entertainment market. The Internet has become a popular, low-budget option for reaching alpha consumers. Hits from relative unknowns such as the film *The Blair Witch Project* and the *South Park* precursor *The Spirit of Christmas* were born through this insider-based marketing strategy based on Internet buzz and circulation. Today, posting rough work on sites such as MySpace and YouTube is more than just a long shot chance taken by aspiring musicians and filmmakers hoping to be discovered. Even the most popular entertainment artists are learning that maintaining an Internet presence is almost a requirement for both initial and continued success.

A movie, book, or any other product or service can often enjoy relative success when it is embraced wholeheartedly by one or more subcultures. Such phenomena are sometimes called *cult classics*. Popular among self-proclaimed "anticool" counter-culture teenagers and twenty-somethings, movies such as *The Rocky Horror Picture Show*, *Harold and Maude*, and *Clerks* are good examples of cult classics. It could be argued that Sue Grafton's alphabet mystery books (for example, *A is for Alibi*), popular among female mystery aficionados, and even Ben and Jerry's ice cream, fit the definition of cult classics in the sense that these classics have extremely loyal fans who identify with each other and with the "brand" in very personal ways.

Typically, however, for something to truly become an entertainment phenomenon, it must attract more than just a cult following. Major hits cross group boundaries, appealing to a wide range of audiences or consumers. The theatrical version of Disney's *The Lion King* became a hit when it became popular not just among regular theater-goers and their youngsters but among audiences of all ages and backgrounds. Similarly, the video game *Tetris* became a hit when moms, dads, and even grandparents began buying their own game units so they wouldn't have to fight their kids for the chance to play. Just as individual alphas can influence their individual groups, an entire group can become an alpha that in turn influences other groups. However, it is not always the same groups that are the first to discover new hits. Whereas middle-aged mothers led the way to the film *Bridges Over Madison County*, their daughters led them to *Titanic*.

Barriers to Entry

Today, audiences have more options than ever—more movies, music, TV stations, video games, amusement parks, and so on. With all these choices, the challenge to break through the clutter to become a hit might appear more daunting than ever.

And, in some ways, it is. Although novelty does have its appeal, we hesitate to try new things unless we are confident that we will like them. There are no guarantees in entertainment, but we still look for ways to minimize our risks. So we are more likely to go to movies that feature actors or directors or producers from films we have liked in the past. As a result, movies that do well at the box office invariably are followed by sequels. We see a similar pattern in publishing, where the same authors appear on best-seller lists year after year. Thus, success tends to breed success in these industries, and the rich do tend to get richer. And yet, as already noted, many hits, such as *The Blair Witch Project* and *South Park*, as well as J.K. Rowling's *Harry Potter* book series and products like Razor Scooters, did not come from well-established producers or writers. Some analysts argue that, even though more established producers do have a competitive advantage, technological advances have lowered production, marketing, and distribution barriers to allow at least a few unknowns the opportunity to enter the market.

FADE TO BLACK

The competition for attention has provided a new, empowered role for entertainment in today's economy. Entertainment trends both influence and are influenced by economic trends. And these trends evolve at a very rapid pace. This book was first conceived during the late 1990s, when the economy was booming and investors were pouring their money into new technology, new products, and new entertainment resorts. At the start of the new millennium, however, while the first edition of the book was being written, the economy began to take a significant downturn.

This downturn was exacerbated by the terrorist attacks of September 11, 2001. Travel and tourism were hit hard as people canceled trips and stayed closer to home. The television industry lost advertising revenue as regular programs were replaced with ad-free news broadcasts of the crisis. Several film productions were shelved, such as *Spiderman*, which included footage of the World Trade Center's twin towers. Nonetheless, while some industries suffered setbacks, others prospered. Film box office overall ticket sales were up 44 percent the weekend after the attack ($54.1 million compared with $37.8 million from the same weekend the previous year).[55] Video rental revenue rose 30 percent to $156 million in the week after September 11 and remained high in the weeks that followed.[56] Audiences' entertainment preferences might have changed, and their spending power might have changed, but the demand for entertainment had not.

At the time of publication of the second edition of this text, the world economy was facing new opportunities and challenges. In response to concerns about the impact of piracy and illegal file sharing on corporate revenues, entertainment companies began to experiment with new online distribution models. Reflecting the times, Hollywood vacillated between capturing the horrors of international conflicts in films such as *Flight*, *Hotel Rwanda*, and *Blood Diamonds* and small town triumphs in football flicks such as *Invincible*, *Marshall*, and the *Gridiron Gang*. It is difficult to say from month to month, much less from year to year, what entertainment or the economy will look like. But one can predict that entertainment trends will continue to reflect and shape larger economic and societal trends.

A CLOSER LOOK AT TICKETING AGENCIES

Is More Always Better? The Case of Pearl Jam vs. Ticketmaster[57]

The Accusation

In the spring of 1994 the rock band Pearl Jam brought an antitrust suit against Ticketmaster. In a memorandum filed with the Antitrust Division of the U.S. Department of Justice on May 6, 1994, Pearl Jam argued that Ticketmaster has a "virtually absolute monopoly on the distribution of tickets to concerts." *Time* magazine called the legal battle "Rock 'n' Roll's Holy War." According to Pearl Jam and other Ticketmaster critics, the company keeps ticket sales organized and revenue high, but often

at the expense of fans. The service charges that Ticketmaster adds to tickets range from $3 to $6 and can add more than 30 percent to a ticket's face value.

Ticketmaster and its supporters defend these fees as a lower-cost alternative, suggesting that these fees are reasonable compared to the time and transportation expenses that would accrue if people went to the box office. Indeed, although people may grumble, if they really felt that purchasing tickets from the box office was the best option, that is what they would do. And, if that were the case, then Ticketmaster would be out of business. Critics, however, maintain that, if Ticketmaster were competing not just with the box office but also with other ticket agencies, these fees would be lower.

One reason these surcharges are purported to be so high is that Ticketmaster pays a small fee to venues or promoters for every ticket sold in order to maintain exclusive contracts that give Ticketmaster sole control over those sales. Ticketmaster was said to have even loaned promoters money to meet the guarantees of stadium acts and to have given money to venues for promotion and marketing. Several lawsuits called Ticketmaster dividends to venues "kickbacks." Critics argue that these exclusive arrangements unfairly limit competition, leaving musical artists, venues, and music fans completely at Ticketmaster's mercy. They contend that fans would be better served if more ticket agencies were allowed to compete for their business.

Is Ticketmaster a Monopoly?

The question of whether or not Ticketmaster maintains a "virtually absolute" monopoly is open to debate. Patent law creates monopolies (single seller positions) in inventions and innovations; copyright confers monopolies in literary and artistic works. Pearl Jam has a legal monopoly on any songs and performances the band creates, meaning that no one else can legally try to sell Pearl Jam's work without permission. The question, then, is whether or not Ticketmaster has a monopoly on tickets. On the macro level, other companies can try to compete with Ticketmaster. Indeed, others have tried, but most have failed. Ticketron, the largest competing ticket service, sold out to Ticketmaster in 1991 after losing millions of dollars a year since 1988.

Pearl Jam and others, however, charge that Ticketmaster engages in anti-competitive practices, such as exclusive venue contracts, that give it monopolistic power. Defenders counter that the money Ticketmaster loans or gives to arenas or promoters actually benefits both venues and fans by serving as a guarantee that the show will be performed. Some even speculate that Ticketmaster started these loans and promotion subsidies in response to people who complained after shows were canceled. The concern, however, is that such policies are anti-competitive because small-scale ticket services are often unable to duplicate them. They do not have the resources to loan or give money to venues as guarantees, particularly if they are trying to gain a competitive advantage by charging less for their tickets. Another question then becomes whether concert-goers would rather spend more money or pay less and risk a show cancellation because the venue couldn't meet its guarantees. Ticketmaster's policy is predicated on the belief that people would rather pay more. The company's success would seem to support that

preference. Still, critics maintain that Ticketmaster simply leaves people no other choice.

Would Competition Lower Ticket Prices?

Would more competition lead to lower prices? Many Ticketmaster critics believe that it would. Ticketmaster supporters, however, claim that it would not. They maintain that other ticketing agencies *were* given an opportunity to compete, but they folded because Ticketmaster beat them out with better pricing and value. The thinking is that Ticketmaster can offer better pricing because of its high volume of sales. To let smaller agencies compete, it is argued, Ticketmaster would have to raise its fees to match the higher costs of the smaller agencies and risk being sued for price fixing for keeping ticket prices artificially high. Critics, however, counter that if Ticketmaster is so confident that it can offer the best pricing and value, it should be able to maintain high-volume sales without relying on exclusive arrangements with venues that eliminate the possibility of even small-scale competition. Ticketmaster again emphasizes that these agreements are the only way it can offer venues guarantees . . . and the argument continues back and forth in similar fashion.

Who Will Win the War?

The justice department eventually ruled in favor of Ticketmaster, ending the two-year dispute between Pearl Jam and the ticketing agency. Ticketmaster also won a second legal battle against charges of monopolistic control brought against the company in a class action suit launched by consumers who had purchased tickets from Ticketmaster in 1998. This case was appealed all the way to the Supreme Court, which ruled in January 1999 that the consumers did not have proper legal standing to launch the suit. However, some critics contend that Ticketmaster's victories to date are more the result of legal technicalities then any ultimate verdict on current ticketing practices, and debate continues regarding whether or not Ticketmaster maintains monopolistic control of the event ticketing market.[58]

What do you think?

- *Is Ticketmaster a monopoly? Does Ticketmaster provide the best value for concert-goers, or would music fans be better served by having more ticket agencies competing for their business?*

DISCUSSION AND REVIEW

1. Review the logic for the pronouncement that we have entered an entertainment economy. Do you agree with this assessment? What predictions would you make for the future regarding the relationship between entertainment and the economy?
2. Thanks to rapid technological advances and shifting economic forces, the businesses of entertainment often change quickly. Scan recent business and entertainment news to see if you can identify any changes or new developments that reinforce or possibly even contradict trends or information presented in this text. Are convergence and consolidation still dominant forces or are other factors now at work?
3. Review the principles of the dynamics of attention. Think of some of your favorite brands again, or think of your favorite films, games, bands, and so on and evaluate how they compare to these principles. Rules are often meant to be broken, so look for both consistencies as well as possible inconsistencies that may violate these principles.

EXERCISES

1. For one week, try to pay attention to the ways different individuals and organizations use entertainment to capture your attention. Examples might range from a friend or a teacher cracking a joke, to an entertaining advertisement, to a corporate-sponsored festival, to a giveaway for a new car during an intermission at a sporting event. List as many as you can identify.
2. Does success breed success? Do an Internet search to find a list of the 100 top-grossing movies. Determine how many of the films had sequels that followed. Count how many of the top-grossing films are sequels themselves. Look at the film directors. How many directors have more than one film on the list? Go to the bookstore and take a look at the current bestsellers. How many of the authors have had best-sellers before? Study top-selling video games, toys, and so on in the same manner. Examine the brands to see if there are any trends in which companies are producing "hits."
3. As noted in the chapter, an entertainment economy can change very quickly. Skim through the chapter again, and look for any claims that you think might already be outdated. Do some research to discover updated information on the statistics and information presented in this chapter (for example, statistics on entertainment's impact on the economy, the eight large conglomerates and their leaders, top-ranked films in different countries and who "owns" them). Make comparisons. Have there been any significant changes?

BOOKS AND BLOGS

Adler, R.P. (1997). *The future of advertising: New approaches to the attention economy.* Washington DC: The Aspen Institute.

Goldhaber, M.H. (1997). Proceedings from "Economics of Digital Information," conference hosted by the Kennedy School of Government, Harvard University, Cambridge MA, January 23–6.

McChesney, R.W. (1999). The new global media: It's a small world of big conglomerates. *The Nation*, Nov. 29. Retrieved from www.thenation.com/doc.mhtml?i=19991129&s=mcchesney.

Wolf, M.J. (1999). *The entertainment economy: How mega-media forces are transforming our lives.* New York: Random House, Times Books.

Entertainment news: http://www.eonline.com/, http://www.tmz.com/, http://www.latimes.com/entertainment/news/

Entertainment and technology: http://www.etcenter.org/, http://www.businessweek.com/technology/entertainment/

7 BRANDED ENTERTAINMENT AND THEMING

Disneyland, Mall of America and Las Vegas foster surrogate experience and surrogate environments that have become the American way of life. Distinctions are no longer made, or deemed necessary, between the real and the false.

—Ada Louise Huxtable

In a world where everything is for sale, entertainment providers must employ sophisticated marketing tactics to engage audiences and consumers of experiences. Branding has become the most important component of marketing because of its importance for making personal connections with performance audiences and media consumers. Everyone involved in the entertainment industry must understand the importance of marketing for the success of a product, service, or experience.

This chapter takes us through an experience-based approach to marketing, branding, advertising, and other facets of branded entertainment. We introduce basic marketing principles and provide examples of successful strategies that engaged audiences and consumers.

We also take a closer look at the places we shop and visit through the perspective of themed experience, from the staged indoor worlds of malls and restaurants to outdoor amusement parks, and entire cities; all places where theming has become a way of life for Americans.

Branding, Marketing, and Entertainment

Branding is *the* concept in twenty-first-century marketing principles. Branding looks to provide a product, a service, or an experience with an identity, which can be called its own and exist for the infinite future. Branding turns a generic experience into an entity with a name and with attributes, which can evoke associations and feelings, and which has a distinct personality. Before considering the importance of branding, we begin with an overview of marketing principles around which branding centers—the marketing mix.

The 4Ps Marketing Mix

Old-school marketing focused on the mix of 4Ps—product, place, price, promotion. Today, that typology has been reconfigured to address experience-based activities. Philip Kotler developed the 4Ps approach to marketing in the 1960s, decades before entertainment branding was differentiated from product branding. Products were tangible items, price was its cost, place was where it was sold, and promotion was how it was advertised. Using his basic 4P approach, we have tailored those mix elements to entertainment, which are explained here.

Product Product can be understood as the value of audience-based experiences. Where a consumer product's value lies in its consistency and brand association, an

Table 7.1   Applying the Marketing Mix to Entertainment Venues

Mix element	Concert	Theme park	Museum
Product/Experience			
Content	music	rides	exhibits
Packaging & design	venue lighting, sound, seats, lobby, lounge	theme, location, food	architecture, exhibits, café, shop
Service	ushers, servers, ticket window	security, staff/ characters	docents, staff
Branding	Lincoln Center	Six Flags	MOMA
Image/position	state-of-the-art	friendly	global/local
Price/Expenditure			
Normal	seat location	adult/kid	adult/student
Promotional	group rate, package price	group rate, corporate sponsor	group rate, member rate
Place/Ticket delivery			
Reservation system	box office, Internet	Internet	tourist office, hotels
Promotion			
Ad media	radio, print ads	radio/TV ads	print ads
Merchandising	radio contests, T-shirts	souvenirs, clothing	tote bags, books
PR	event calendar	feature story	event calendar

entertainment property's value is the form the experience takes—what audience members get when they attend a performance or watch a movie. *Audience value* is the audience's assessment of their experience as weighed against the ticket price, time investment, and as compared with other entertainment options.

EXPERIENTIAL COMPONENTS OF PRODUCTS   The experiential components of an entertainment product are design, venue, service, and brand identity. *Design* is how the experience is packaged, such as a three-day weekend at a spa. *Venue* is about the style and ambience of the place where entertainment or an activity take place. Most audiences prefer safe, comfortable, and easily accessible venues. *Service* includes the attitudes and actions of every person involved with delivering the experience. Front-desk receptionists, ushers, servers, ticket-takers, and so forth are all part of the service element of an experience. *Brand identity* is the primary focus of marketing communications that identifies an experience by making known a particular set of values, a logo, an image, and an expectation of the entertainment to be delivered.

Price   Price is the value that an audience member is willing to pay for experiential content—what we pay to experience something. With travel, price is often considered a personal investment rather than an expense. *Promotional pricing* is a common feature for entertainment venues by differentiating price according to time and demographics. For instance, matinees may be cheaper than evening shows, and senior or student rates may also be offered to accommodate the needs of these groups. Theme parks offering coupons for entrance discounts are another example of promotional pricing.

Place   Place is the location of the entertainment experience. Most often offered in a venue, attractions, performances, and shopping are housed in a physical space where audiences come together to enjoy the activity. Access convenience is a major factor in venue location and development—freeways, restaurants, and parking are aspects of convenience important for venue selection.

Promotion   Promotion is the information, persuasion, and incentives made available to audience members. Marketers use media, advertising, direct mail, sales promotions, merchandising, PR, and the Internet to inform consumers about entertainment and travel opportunities.

Every element in this 4P marketing mix is an organizational expenditure that has direct implications for revenue. Table 7.1 shows how the marketing mix can be adjusted for specific aspects of entertainment experiences.

The 4Cs Marketing Mix

Another way to express the industry structure—4Cs—is addressed here for its value to understanding contemporary principles. Entertainment veteran Al Lieberman characterizes the entertainment industry with a set of criteria called the 4Cs: content, conduit, consumption, and convergence.

- *Content* is the entertainment product delivered to the consumer.
- *Conduit* refers to where and how the performances is delivered—the venue.
- *Consumption* is the result of advertising and promotional activities that result in the purchase of tickets and performance attendance.
- *Convergence* is the experience created when live performances are converted to a digital format as described in Chapter 2.

Missing in Action: People

But what's missing from both of these mixes? The most important element—(P) people or (C) consumers. Both Kotler and Lieberman ignored consumers in their marketing mixes. For entertainment marketing success, this fifth P or C involves three groups of participants who are crucial for selling an event: audiences, employees or staff, and community.

- *Audiences*, as we discovered in the last chapter, are groups of entertainment content consumers who are an inseparable part of the marketing equation. Happy audiences keep the lights on—unhappy audiences shut the place down.
- *Employees and staff* include workers who deal directly with audience members and non-contact workers who provide support.
- *Community* consists of residents of neighborhoods where venues (amusement parks, outdoor theaters, casinos) are located.

Now that we are grounded in marketing, let's look at the role of branding for marketing success.

Branding

We are all branding experts, as our lives are filled with brands for everything we use or see in our daily lives. To many audience members, brands are not just *in* the culture, they *are* the culture. Brands are tools with which people construct their personal and social identities. One example of the bond formed between consumers and brands is the Harley Davidson culture. Wearing brand tattoos clarifies a biker's identity as part of the group, similar to Internet brand tribes like Apple users. Brands as a type of cultural infusion are here to stay. Consequently, entertainment franchises must adopt an unusual but relevant view of what their brands are and what they mean.

Because competition for attention is so fierce, if you are able to capture an audience, you want to do all you can to keep it. Organizations will often try to leverage the attention they have captured through branding. Branding is critical to almost all industries. Companies such as Nike, Coca-Cola, and Microsoft have worked hard to establish brand identities. A *brand* reflects a common thread that runs through a range of products, services, or concepts. At a minimum, that thread usually includes a shared corporate name and logo, but brands usually also extend beyond shared symbols to shared attributes, concepts, stories, philosophies, personalities, and goals.

One approach to conceptualizing the process of branding comes from S.M. Davis, who structured a Brand Picture, as shown in Table 7.2. Entertainment purchasers, according to this typology, base their purchasing decisions upon two crucial elements: the brand picture and the brand image.

Table 7.2 How Brands Impact Audience Decision making

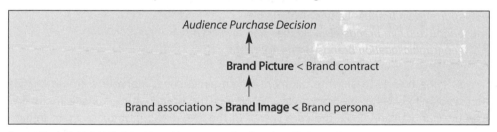

Source: Davis, S. M. (2002). *Brand Asset Management*. San Francisco CA: Jossey-Bass

The **brand picture** is composed of a *brand contract*, defined as a set of promises that the brand makes with the consumer, which are communicated via a number of media. For instance, Helen Reddy concert providers promise audiences that they will enjoy her music in a safe venue environment. The second component, **brand image**, has two parts, association and persona. The *brand associations* are the feelings, entities, or people that are associated or linked with the brand. Associations come to mind instantly once the brand is mentioned. The *brand persona* deals with the personality of the brand; i.e. if the brand were human, what human attributes would it have? Brand image is discussed more in depth in the next section.

Brand associations work on a three-level pyramid, which is shown in Figure 7.1. At the bottom level, the brand relies on its features and attributes (tangible assets the brand has), while, at the middle level, the consumer remembers the brand because of its benefits (what the consumer gets from the brand). It is at the top level where the core benefits of branding are obtained, and it is here that consumer feelings are revealed when the brand comes to mind; here the consumer believes in the brand, and it becomes a lifestyle rather than simply a product or service.

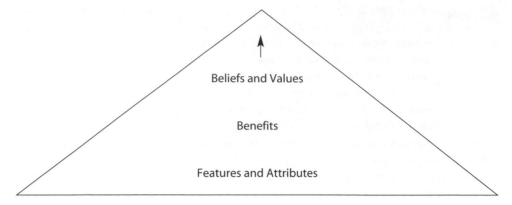

Figure 7.1   Brand Association Pyramid

Branding involves creating mental structures for a venue, place, or performer and helping audiences organize their knowledge about entertainment experiences in a way that clarifies their decision making and provides value to the producer. Among products, brand distinctions are related to specific attributes or features and to product benefits. With entertainment (although venues have specific features) the benefit of all experiences should be an enjoyable emotional association. Brand symbols make intangible or abstract experiences more concrete. Here are examples of entertainment brands:

* *venue brands*—Hilton Hotels, Disneyland, Staples Center Arena
* *people and organization brands*—Paris Hilton, Sony
* *sports team brands*—Lakers, Trojans
* *bands and film brands*—The Beatles and *Iron Man*
* *geographic location brands*—Paris, Montana

By tying brands to an entertainment-driven experience, marketers create brands as personalities rather than products to connect the brand with audience members. Experiential branding takes the core values of the brand and introduces them into an actual environment; good branding is the fusion of entertainment and marketing because together they make consumers happy about the brand.

Brand Extension   A brand extension is the application of a brand to another category or genre different from the original brand. When Apple extended its brand beyond computers into the music storage business, it entered another category of entertainment distribution. Recognizing the power of branding, Disney has also extended its brand to a variety of related enterprises including theme parks, hotels, merchandise, and cable stations—all of which strive to be consistent with the quality, wholesome family entertainment brand image.

In some cases, Disney simply extended its brand by expanding its operations into other industries, while in other cases it relied on strategic mergers, acquisitions, or partnerships. The idea is that people will choose Disney movies, merchandise, or vacations because they would rather stick with a brand they trust than take a risk on an unknown entertainment provider.

These branding strategies factor heavily into Disney's decision to pursue new projects. The fact that Disney produced movies titled *Angels in the Outfield* and *The Mighty Ducks* and purchased the professional sports franchises of the same names was no accident. Each new Disney film—*The Lion King, Toy Story, Monsters, Inc.*—becomes a sub-brand that is leveraged throughout Disney's network in merchandising, theme park attractions, TV spinoffs, and so on.

Every advance in communication technology, from print to broadcast radio and television, to cable, and finally to the Internet, has provided the entertainment industry with more opportunities for brand extension. Disney is one brand that has capitalized on these advances by expanding its brand into home videos, TV programming, and cable channels. At the other end of the spectrum, Playboy is another brand that took full advantage of these opportunities. Worldwide, Playboy is one of the most popular and widely recognized brands in adult entertainment. As technology advanced, the Playboy brand extended from the original magazine into Playboy videos, The Playboy Channel on cable, and Playboy novelty merchandise. With the advent of the Internet came the Playboy web site, providing original content and serving as a portal to all other Playboy-branded entertainment. Other popular print media organizations, however, did not take advantage of these opportunities. Instead, new brands emerged to fill these niches. Today, it is not *Sports Illustrated* or *Time* or *Newsweek* that we watch on cable—it is ESPN and CNN.

Licensing   A form of brand extension called licensing allows a brand to use its image and logo to change genres. Disney cartoon characters became recognizable through T-shirts and merchandise sold at theme parks. Licensing works when a unique property or character is developed and a license is negotiated with a manufacturer of clothing or accessories. The manufacturer pays the licensor a royalty based on sales. Entertainment media opportunities exist for characters building brand recognition in digital content, DVDs, or TV programming. SpongeBob SquarePants generated in excess of $4 billion in licensing revenues in 2008.

Brand Image

Branding should be focused on an image or a personality, not on a specific product or service. The brand's identity must be broad enough that it can be expanded in a variety of ways, yet specific enough that it will differentiate the brand from its competitors. Marketing programs create a brand's image by using strong creative messages that link favorable associations of the brand with a person's memory. Brand associations are created directly through experience, commercials, reviews, word of mouth, and indirectly through identification with a company, country, or event.

Brand imagery is often developed through associations with the type of person who uses the brand. The focus on image instead of specific products and services explains why many organizations try to associate themselves with famous personalities. Celebrity endorsements can enhance branding by tying the image of the celebrity to the image of the brand. Athletes are brand favorites because they can help tie images of strength and success to products. Certain celebrities have distinct personalities and images that have been partnered with different organizations to enhance certain images: Arnold Schwarzenegger is associated with fitness, Oprah Winfrey is viewed as the embodiment of open sincerity, and celebrities like Paris Hilton and Jessica Simpson convey sexy youthfulness.

Celebrity Branding   Celebrity endorsements can be very powerful, but they must be approached wisely. To be successful, personalities must be consistent with the brands they endorse. Some things do not fit; for example, although Paris Hilton is youthful, a high-profile partnership between Hilton and Disney might not be the best fit for Disney's family-oriented image. Even with the best fit, celebrity endorsements still involve a certain amount of risk. Consider the case of Martha Stewart. As a long-lauded icon for tasteful style, Stewart was a popular product endorser. However, her reputation—and, as a consequence, the reputations of the products she endorsed—were severely tested when she was indicted and later convicted on felony charges related to some of her financial dealings.

Untypical of celebrity endorsement deals that pay a single annual fee, new types of agreements are increasingly linking stars with companies that offer a bigger piece of the action. Ellen DeGeneres bought a 15 percent stake in Halo, a pet food company, which she endorses. Sales of Halo at Petco stores doubled in 2007, and DeGeneres's spots are geared toward pet owners like herself. The most successful endorsements occur where there is a real connection between the celebrity and the product—especially when the celebrity is also a part owner of the brand.

SPOTLIGHT ON CELEBRITY BRANDS   Tyra Banks

With a recognizable face and two successful TV shows, Tyra Banks is becoming a recognizable—and equitable—brand. Tyra (36 in 2010) began modeling at age 15, and considers modeling a "science" that can be engineered and managed to change the course of one's life.

Like her hero Martha Stewart, Banks wanted her name to suggest a distinct point of view. Her brand, like her trademark smile, is consistent with her shows: empathetic, empowering, and always aimed at women across all races. Her audiences for both *Top Model* and her talk show—young girls high school age to mid-30s—attract more than 13 million viewers weekly. Her glamour and drive seem to be compelling to young girls, especially if they feel disenfranchised or shut out by mainstream TV. Banks

believes she was put on earth to instill self-esteem in young girls. And as audiences become increasingly colorblind, younger viewers are especially prone to modeling themselves after African Americans.

Banks makes an estimated $18 million a year with a net worth of around $75 million. Between her two shows, she is always working. Her goal is to help girls become professional models, not just to become known for their appearance on *Top Model*. She defines the Tyra brand as "attainable fantasy," dedicating herself to making the dreams of others come true. Empowerment for young women is a goal she embraces in every aspect of her private and professional life.

"If Michael Jordan can sell tennis shoes and Tiger Woods can sell cars, I can sell cornflakes. I can and I will," said Banks in a *New York Times* interview.

Source: Hirschberg, Lynn (2008). Banksable: How Tyra Banks turned herself fiercely into a brand. *New York Times Magazine*, June 1

What do you think?

- *What qualities does the Tyra brand evoke in you?*
- *Is your thinking about her consistent with her branding goals?*

Entertainment genres are often communicated as brands. Messages about a brand must reach the audience at each point of contact—thinking about buying a ticket, locating a place to buy it, actually buying the ticket, and attending the event or performance. At each stage of promotion, a positive brand image must be communicated to the target audiences through promotional materials and media, and personal contacts with staff, and reviewers.

Brand Fans

Similar to alpha consumers profiled in Chapter 6, brand fans are vocal advocates of a product or service by combining branding with the digital communications landscape. The concept of brand fans is the way of organizing thinking around how to socialize a brand and encourage consumers to be part of it. At its most basic form, a brand fan will join a fan page on Facebook; at its most extreme, fans will contribute to the brand's marketing efforts.

Statistics have proved that social media brand loyalty is a more powerful version of brand loyalty. According to Anderson Analytics' May 2009 survey, 52 percent of social network users had become a fan or follower of a company or brand, while 46 percent had said something positive about a brand or company on a social networking website—double the percentage who had said something negative (23 percent). Basically, if a brand or company provides good products and services, people will talk about it online because what the company is doing means something to them.

To attract brand fans, marketing allows consumers to contribute to the brand's message. By inviting consumers to share their input, brands can generate interest compelling enough to have over 500,000 fans on Facebook. Rather than simply talking about a product, marketing engages consumers on topics that interest and affect them. One example is the Obama presidential campaign. He clearly set out a point of view on hope and change, then invited voters to become part of the effort—it was not about him but about them.

SPOTLIGHT ON BRANDING   Do People or Does Time Kill our Brands?

People

With the right managers and staff in place, there is no reason to adjust to marketplace fluctuations. Regardless of changes in technology, global economics, or consumer confidence, brands with savvy brand professionals at the helm can be flexible and survive transitioning business climates. Mismanagement kills brands, not time.

Time

Eventually, every brand becomes obsolete. As time passes, relationships change and brands simply can-not maintain strong relationships with consumers as evolutions in technology, values, and demographics influence the marketplace. Despite the best efforts of the most talented branding professionals, time not only ages all brand identities, but kills them too.

Source: www.brandchannel.com/forum.asp?bd_id=94

What do you think?

- *Which killer do you think is the most likely assassin: people or time?*

Facebook branding has been successful because of the sheer size of their fan base (over 300 million members as of September, 2009) and the extent of consumer interaction that is offered (six hours a month per person, according to Nielsen). Some big-name players—Coca-Cola, Best Buy, Starbucks, and Microsoft among them—are performing especially well on the social networking site. One example of success is Old Spice, a Proctor & Gamble brand, that ran an ad on Facebook the first week in October, 2009, hoping to increase its 55,000-strong fan base. In one week, Old Spice boasted nearly 175,000 fans.[1]

Sometimes brand fans take the lead ahead of company marketing efforts. Even though IKEA didn't create an online social hot spot, their fans did; they personalized their experiences and created their own spot online (IKEApedia). Another example is the online sneaker community created by one of Nike's brand fans.[2] Coke's huge Facebook brand page was created by two fans in August 2008, going on to become the top product page on the site. In support of the activity, Coke brought the two consumers to company headquarters and invited them to continue running the page with backing from the brand. As of fall 2009, Coke has 3.7 million fans and offers a promotion that solicits videos for a shot at appearing in a Coke commercial.[3]

The most active brand fans are tech savvy teenagers who are invited to use their grasp of the Internet to promote the brands they buy—and often get paid in the process. As part of a strategy by brands to create online communities, vodcasts, blogs, and social networks are used to enable the next generation of consumers to shape the direction of the brands they love. If the product is great, teens can let their friends know and receive cash payments for successful referrals from the manufacturer and be instrumental in the growth of that brand.[4]

The only problem with mounting a campaign on social media is its lack of measurement, as there is no standard framework for measuring the importance of a brand fan, although nearly everyone agrees it has value.

SPOTLIGHT ON BRAND DEALS   Branded Entertainment

A new deal-making process received attention during the biggest buying time of the 2008 TV season: branded entertainment. Conversations took precedence over large-volume prime-time bookings in **upfronts**—the time when networks negotiate deals for the upcoming season. To get that $16 billion in cable- and broadcast-TV upfront dollars on the table, the networks offered marketers the option to meld their brands' DNA into a story line that captured the audience's interest.

With ratings steadily declining, networks and marketers often fight a losing battle to keep viewers hooked during ad breaks. Branded entertainment is an increasingly attractive solution, giving marketers more engagement with products and allowing networks to charge more for exclusive relationships.

To allow time to secure long-term integrations with ad clients, NBC's co-president of entertainment took his network's 65-week program schedule to buyers a month ahead of time this year, dubbing his strategy an "infront." The strategy generated a deal with General Motors that integrated two of its new vehicles into the 2008 fall series *My Own Worst Enemy*, starring Christian Slater.

Another branded-entertainment deal on cable paired up Dodge and TNT for *Lucky Chance*, a branded microseries. The series of 20 two-minute installments follows an undercover Drug Enforcement Agency agent named Lucky Chance who uses his 2009 Dodge Challenger to transport $50 million in four days to a mob boss threatening to blackmail him for a crime he didn't commit. Turner Entertainment's exec VP-ad sales and marketing said the project was developed with directors, writers, producers, and ad clients all involved from day one. Consequently, AT&T also came onboard as an integrated sponsor for its global positioning system and will help Dodge cross-promote the series through on-air spots.

Source: Andrew Hampp, for *AdAge*, May 26, 2008; Uadage. com/madisonandvine/article?article_id=127312

Branded Entertainment

Using various mediated venues, brands are reaching consumers by associating viewer values with the program's values that are consistent with the brand's values. Branded content uses entertainment to generate consumer dialog and involvement off-air and on multiple platforms. Branded events, branded viral teasers, branded video games, branded concerts, branded mobile content, branded music CDs, and branded online content are all important elements of a core TV property.[5]

The branded entertainment sector has three major segments: event sponsorship and marketing; product placement; and advergaming and webisodes. Continued migration of advertising dollars to fast-growing marketing services segments like branded entertainment, public relations, and trade shows have had a profound effect on advertising spending.

In the 1970s, advertising accounted for 40 percent of total media budget. By the end of 2007, advertising spending decreased to 23 percent. The diminished effectiveness of traditional media has prompted marketers to aggressively pursue alternative channels for building brand image, targeting audiences effectively, and driving sales.[6]

According to a report from PQ Media, branded entertainment grew more than 14 percent in 2007 to reach $22.3 billion. Branded entertainment continued this growth rate in 2008, reaching more than $25.4 billion (a 13 percent increase). Content has breathed life into advertising where engaging, enriching, educational, informational, humorous, entertaining, and dynamic content is key.

From the *New York Times* to the *Orange County Register*, from NBC to KWYB in Bozeman, Montana, from XM Radio to your local college's radio station, content separates successful advertising platforms from the failures. Given the plethora of choices and power consumers have in today's media environment, it's no surprise that branded entertainment is experiencing rapid and explosive growth.

Since 2005, branded entertainment has nearly doubled its size as big brands capitalize on this ever-changing alternative advertising world. Advertising alternatives like the Internet and mobile space engage users far more effectively than traditional methods. According to Patrick Quinn, President and CEO of PQ Media, "this trend has led to increased investment in alternative marketing tactics."

 FLASH FACT

The growth of branded entertainment in 2007 shows these increases: event sponsorship—12 percent; product placement—33 percent; webisodes and advergaming—34 percent. Through 2012, branded entertainment overall is expected to show a 12 percent growth to reach more than $40 billion in revenue.

One example of branded entertainment is McDonald's *The Lost Ring* game that blends online and offline clues and relies on player collaboration to solve the puzzles.

Source: BizReport

Lifestyle and Social Advertising

Advertisers constantly look for new ways to connect with consumers. At a new web site from Nike (nike+.com), people log in on their own to connect with other sports enthusiasts who share their lifestyles. Users post running routes, log details of their runs, and connect with others worldwide to share their experiences. Nike is spending its advertising dollars on services for consumers, such as workout advice, online communities, and running clubs—a form of **lifestyle advertising**. Nike and other global brands are increasing their non-media spending by one-third or more, causing a radical shift in the way advertising is used and viewed.

Other companies favoring nontraditional media are Kraft's virtual ads on Second Life, Continental Airlines' logo on chopstick packets, Geico brand on turnstiles, and Disney characters on the paper used on doctors' examination tables. Hoping to generate buzz on- and offline, Procter & Gamble opened a temporary Charmin brand public bathroom in Manhattan. And Target suspended magician David Blaine in a gyroscope above Times Square for two days.

Digital signage connects people to brands through entertaining clips and powerful content, and stands at the epicenter of what drives the advertising industry's growth— digital media spending doubles every year at many big companies. Digital signage networks foster engaging conversations with consumers through content that speaks to people's lifestyles and leads them to measurable actions. Branded entertainment embraces innovations in traditional and emerging media platforms and mobile marketing, to continue the new wave of nontraditional advertising.[7]

Behavioral targeting (often used as tracking cookies) uses content to lure users and to sell adjacent ads. Companies like NebuAd and Adzilla pitch tools to Internet service providers that enable them to track users and show them relevant ads. But, eventually, consumers get barraged with ads and tune them out the same way they tuned out television commercials.

Social Networking   The online answer to managed ads is the world of **social networking**, which has taught people how to manage their own data about themselves. Social networking allows each user to determine who will get into his own garden. Travelers can intentionally allow preferred airline vendors to contact them; in turn, vendors pay a sponsorship fee to be the traveler's "friend." Users are much more likely to respond to vendors within a trusted site or for a specific offer than to an unsolicited message over the phone or in newspapers. Value is created in users' own walled gardens, which they will cultivate for themselves in real estate owned by social networks like Facebook and Doppir that know how to build and support online communities.

Event Sponsorship

Often the purview of public relations efforts, event sponsorship is an important marketing strategy for connecting brands with audience members. A fast-growing, high-profile industry, event sponsorship provides a promotional occasion that attracts and involves the brand's target. Billions of dollars pour into sponsorships of entertainment, sports, venues, and attractions annually.

Reasons accounting for sponsorship popularity are: breaking through advertising clutter by creating a corporate brand image associated with an event; and pairing financial responsibilities by partnering with non-profit organizations benefits a corporation's brand image.

SPOTLIGHT ON BRAND PARTNERSHIPS   Social Marketing

The music video for Radiohead's *All I Need* begins with slow, somber musical beats and a split screen revealing images of children. One side shows a child waking up, dressing for school, and eating breakfast. The other shows youngsters living in dingy conditions and toiling in a sweatshop. The last shot pairs the one boy back from school removing his kicks with a boy assembling the last pieces of a strikingly similar sneaker in a factory. The tagline: "Some things cost more than you realize."

All I Need, which debuted in 2008 on MTV properties worldwide, ends with an MTV logo. It was created for MTV Exit (End Exploitation and Trafficking), a multimedia initiative launched in Europe in 2004 by Viacom's MTV Europe Foundation, an independent charity based in London. The effort includes the distribution of anti-human trafficking information at Radiohead's concert tour in North America, Europe, and Asia. MTV Exit—which recently expanded into Asia—also plans to release an animated film on human trafficking, as well as to produce other live events.

The network's efforts illustrate the growing use of branded entertainment as a way to distribute corporate-responsibility campaigns, which are geared to creating deeper relationships with do-gooder consumers. Other brands using this tactic include Boost Mobile, the Microsoft Network, and Virgin Mobile USA.

According to the president of Magna Global Entertainment, content creates an emotional bond with the consumer by forging a connection between the brand message and the viewer in a way that a 30-second ad can't do. Microsoft's consumer marketing group uses social responsibility branded-entertainment marketing, considering it to be the next big wave of content and marketing investments.

A partnership between U.K.-based company What On Earth Is Going On and MSN focuses on socially relevant marketing initiatives. Users of the portal (WhatOnEarthIsGoingOn.msn.com) can connect to global brands based on their interests and passions.

One such project involves a partnership with Filmaka.com, a destination for filmmakers seeking to get their talent showcased for Hollywood decision makers. What On Earth works with brands to create topics for short films. The challenge is for brands to ensure that their approaches and messaging are seen as authentic.

A study on the effects of cause marketing on consumers conducted by *Self* magazine found that people support causes they see as a reflection of how they see themselves. The *Self* study found that sincerity remains a challenge for marketers, no matter the degree of their good intentions because respondents wanted corporations to show real commitment to a cause, not just create a onetime event. Always the challenge with branding is handling the creative so it gets the message across without sounding like a paid sponsorship.

Source: http://www.adweek.com/aw/content_display/news/media/

Question

- *What other social marketing brand associations can you name?*

NASCAR, the granddaddy of sponsorship opportunity, has soaring TV ratings, flowing corporate money, and exploding crowds—which is why entertainment companies are lining up to get logos placed on cars. With 84 TV cameras on a 2.5-mile track, no aspect of the 43-car, 400-mile race escapes viewers. Generating revenue from NASCAR partnerships comes from a variety of sources: TV and media, tickets (average price $88), merchandise licensing fees, food and beverage (8,000 gallons of soda per race), primary team sponsorship (mar-

Coors Light sponsorship of a Dodge for NASCAR

quee branding on driver and car), NASCAR sponsorship (logo on front quarter panels), and associate team sponsorship (small logos on driver and car locations). These and other types of overt sponsorship increase brand loyalty and create a high level of national awareness and visibility.

But not all brands lend themselves to event sponsorship—some logos receive more attention with more subtle forms of placement such as making them movie stars and giving them leading roles in TV programming. When logos and brands are part of the programming, we call the strategy "imbedded advertising."

Imbedded Advertising

Advertising's function has shifted from selling a product to associating enjoyment with a brand. By providing enjoyable and technologically enthralling commercials, advertisers now entertain rather than promote. The best spots revolve around a story or present a series of action vignettes that have little to do with the product and everything to do with how viewers feel about a brand. The GEICO gecko's English accent amuses us, and the Aflac duck make us smile.

However, as we become resistant to blatant brand builders, advertisers make the transition to a softer, gentler form of branding—imbedded. Three forms of imbedded advertising are product placement, advergaming, and webisodes, which are discussed in this section.

Product Placement   The most popular type of imbedded advertising is **product or brand placement**. Brands, imbedded in actual content, now appear in almost every form of TV programming. From the Coke cans of *Survivor* to plots built around product characters, prime time is loaded with logos. Practically a main character in *CSI: Miami*, GM's Hummer speeds up and down the coast carrying star David Caruso from crime scene to crime scene.

The grounding for product placement in sitcoms draws from three basic literary theories:[8]

- *Genre theory*, a type of classification method, enables sponsors to match plot and characters with products within a specific situation.
- *Feminist theory* looks at gender, specifically sex-based attitudes toward sponsors of particular products and placements in sitcoms.

- *Persona theory*, which looks at the personality of the speaking characters, here focuses on the sponsor. Sponsors can be visible within the plot where characters interact with them, or invisible outside the plot as a commercial sponsor of the show.

SPOTLIGHT ON PRODUCT PLACEMENT   *The Apprentice*

Donald Trump on Fifth Avenue

Mark Burnett, executive producer of *The Apprentice*, charged up to $25 million per company for a significant product placement on the Trump-hosted show. As a result of his efforts, the series became a test site for a range of different approaches of linking brands and series content. Below is a list of ways it is involved in branding.

- *Brand as protagonist*—Host Donald Trump casts himself and his corporate empire as protagonists. Viewers visit his companies, meet his staff, and learn about his business philosophy.
- *Brand as taskmaster*—Entire episodes were dedicated to specific brands in the second season, where contestants were asked to: test toys for Toys "R" Us and Mattel; create a new flavor for Ciao Bella ice cream; redesign a Pepsi product; sell a new M&M candy bar; and market new vanilla mint toothpaste for Procter & Gamble.
- *Branding process as entertainment*—To create buzz for a new Crest product, contestants showed ways to link brands and entertainment (circus acrobats and clowns).
- *Brand as helper*—In return for exposure on air, small companies acted as consultants to contestants.

- *Brand as prize*—Trump rewarded contestants with access to his "stuff," luxury meals, and services.
- *Brand as tie-in*—After the ice cream episode, viewers were able to sample the new flavors. Later, Mattel marketed the Mighty Morpher toy car designed by contestants.
- *Brand as community*—Fans revealed affiliations with specific contestants, allowing the producers to collect data about audience responses.
- *Brand as event*—Yahoo! Hot Jobs and Trump launched a $25,000 sweepstakes competition to encourage new initiatives. And NY City cabs with signage took losing contestants away.
- *Contestant as brand*—Females were showcased as "Women of the Apprentice" modeling lingerie in *Maxim* magazine.
- *Brand as judges*—Company executives helped Trump winnow down the finalists.

Brand tie-ins work for this show, not only because the show is well-developed but because the chosen brands are linked to the show's core mechanics. Audiences care about the brands because they shape their identifications with the characters. *The Apprentice*'s original and compelling format allowed successful brand showcasing and delivered sponsors with image and economic benefits.

Source: Jenkins, Henry (2006). *Convergence culture: Where old and new media collide*. New York: New York University Press, pp. 69–72

What do you think?

- *What other reality show placements use similar tactics for branding products within the story line of the series?*

Your last encounter with the movies probably included an interaction with products and brands. If you saw *Other People's Money*, you heard Danny DeVito say, "If I can't count on Dunkin' Donuts, who can I count on?" in front of the shop's logo. Voice and visual brand placements like these mean $60,000 annually for the film business.

Product placement is the process of creating and negotiating positive brand exposure by placing products, brand names, services, or brand locations into feature film programs whether drama, comedy, or lifestyle, pre-recorded or live. This type of imbedded advertising has been significant since 1982 when Reese's pieces increased their sales by 300 percent after appearing in the film *ET*. Soon Tom Cruise was drinking Coke and wearing RayBan sunglasses in *Top Gun*, and the placement rush was on. Companies were lining up to bid for appearances in major motion pictures.

By learning about audience attitudes toward the character and toward the brand, placements can be accurately directed. Researchers found that attitudes toward characters with permanent roles who use products are much stronger than with characters who play temporary roles in situation comedies, and attitude varies with gender. For instance, if a returning character is perceived to be overtly pushing a product, men often feel negatively toward that character. Whereas, characters perceived to be leaving the show or only appearing for one segment who embrace a product are not subject to ill feelings from audiences of either gender.

The reason for placement frenzy is simple. Films offer outlets for products otherwise banned or prohibited from traditional outlets, like cigarettes and alcohol. Promotions can be tailored to fit theater and home videos in several forms, including trailers, teasers, billboards, and video jackets. With television advertising getting the heave-ho from TiVo, brand managers are looking to other forms of visual impressions, and films are a natural. In fact, the practice is now accomplished with studio professionals negotiating with advertisers well in advance of their production.

SPOTLIGHT ON ADVERTISING   Recession Ideas

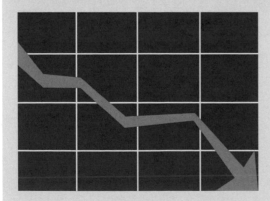

For recessionary times, marketers devised a list of top ten ideas to reach entertainment audiences with their corporate messages:

1. *Green marketing*—No longer a luxury, sustainability will become a necessary part of a company's persona.
2. *Technology for billboards*—Mini-Cooper tested RFID (Radio Frequency Identification) activated billboards, a customized approach that linked "old" (outdoor) with "new" (online), transforming an integrated media platform into a cult-building club.
3. *Game advertising*—Online and video games are pervasive, creating lots of opportunities for marketers to connect. The economics of creating and monetizing games now rivals that of traditional media businesses such as TV and film.

4. *Mobile marketing*—Delivers highly personalized and useful information when and where needed; mobile marketing may be the missing link in personalized communications.
5. *Social networks*—Wise marketers will capitalize on the growing appeal of social networks. Besides the giants MySpace and Facebook, social networks exist in niches from teens (Pizco and Tagged) to seniors (Eons).
6. *Widgets*—Quickly becoming a delivery mechanism of choice for marketers vying for hard-to-reach places like network pages, blogs, desktops, and mobile phones.
7. *Video*—An enormous opportunity to engage, educate, and entertain, which are the three new "Es" of successful marketing.

8. *Behavioral targeting*—Added to contextual "search" efforts for more effective marketing.
9. *Experiential marketing*—Marketers realize that interactive brand experiences can be far more effective than advertising and should be the starting point of a customer conversation.
10. *Marketing as service*—Taking relationship management to whole new levels, marketers should continually support their customers through the course of life, providing value in each communication.

Source: http://www.ebrandmarketing.com/2007/12/20/around-the-net-top-ten-marketing-ideas-for-2008-advertising-during-recession/#more-120

Not all product placements are smooth transactions. Some companies have landed in court over problems with their branding choices. Philip Morris, for instance, sued to have its name deleted from *Harley Davidson and the Marlboro Man* (1991). Orkin forced a change in the language of a pest control man wearing its uniform in *Pacific Heights* (1990). And when a Black & Decker placement was cut from an edited scene in *Die Hard II* (1990), the company settled out of court for $150,000.

Product placements usually take one of three formats:

- *visual or script placement* where the product is mentioned or talked about in a conversation
- *verbal or screen placement* that incorporates the brand into scenes or it is used or talked about on the set
- *plot placement* when the product takes a major role in the story line or building the persona of a character.

Such placements often combine verbal and visual aspects from a brand's mere mention with a brief appearance to sole identification with a single star. James Bond films' tie-in with BMW is an example of such a high-intensity placement.

Product placement in conjunction with pleasurable advertising renders the experience of seeing the brand as enjoyable. Brand placement on television and in film can be analyzed on four dimensions:

- *Personal relevance*: the degree to which the viewer connects himself or herself with the brand.
- *Experimental*: emotional identification of the audience with the brand; this is the most effective source for placement.
- *Informational*: relevant brands that become part of the story bring symbolic imagery to the experience. For instance, Humphrey Bogart's use of cigarettes associates smoking with masculinity, elegance, and sensuality. This affective process allows viewers to become directly involved in the brand's symbolic meaning.
- *Executional*: a good match must be made among the brand and its stars.

In successful placements, the viewer's own experience with the products or brands will reflect the experience portrayed in the film or video. Such placements have several implications for audiences and content production. First, scripts may be tailored around products rather than using products to add realism. Second, place-based ads may limit the diversity of film content as requirements from sponsors become increasingly strict. Third, concerns about artistic control have caused some alarm among film directors who feel compromised by advertisers' demands. In order to address those concerns, Hollywood executives have established a trade association to self-regulate the placement industry (Entertainment Resource Marketing Association) with a code of ethics that address client–agent relations.

SPOTLIGHT ON AN ETHICAL ISSUE   To Blog or Not to Blog

Matt, a college student, blogs to earn money. Advertisers—connected with bloggers through PayPerPost—pay him to write about products for a fee. His last assignment was for a liposuction company. Weighing 145 pounds with 14 percent body fat, the triathlon participant can hardly provide first-hand testimony for that product. But that was the assignment, so he complied, relying on hearsay for his testimony.

Advertisers dole out writing assignments based primarily on a blogger's Google Page Rank, a score that measures a site's influence. After making $146.88 extolling the virtues of a Hamilton Beach Eclectrics Stand Mixer, Matt complained that people used PayPerPost for offers from term paper writing to shady loans. And although he hateed this way to boost search engine rankings, such spam often connected him with work opportunities. For instance, he wrote 53 meaningless words to provide a paid link to a Colorado real estate site, and feigned a knee injury so he could plug Freeze it Gel.

PayPerPost, after complaints about the ethics of the site, changed its name to Izea to keep its place on paid links. Matt still writes product reviews and an occasional term paper, rationalizing that the authenticity of the blogosphere that disguises paid messages as candid blog posts is just another way to make a buck.

Source: Honan, Matthew (2008). Hawker media: Advertisers paid me to blog about them. Is that so wrong? *Wired*, Feb.

What do you think?

- *Is Matt justified in his thinking about blogging?*
- *Are such sites as Izea destroying the credibility of product blogs?*

Advergames When Internet games are paired with marketing content, we have a concept called **advergaming**, which is a strategy that encourages consumers to engage in a branded experience. Many game web sites include elements of mainstream advertising and interactive capabilities that include game show hosts and player massaging. Automobile companies use digital games to promote new car models, and diaper manufactures use parenting games to promote their brands.

Bennetts, one of the U.K.'s major players specializing in motorcycle insurance, has revved up bikers with a hot game to raise brand awareness. Super Jump, designed by marketing communications agency Dig For Fire, has been played over 20 million times by 400,000 people since it launched on March 22, 2008, on Motorcycle News and Bennetts' website (www.bennetts.co.uk).

Players of the game, which runs with the tagline "You can't beat a good jump," are encouraged to clear a line of buses and random people—including The Beatles on Abbey Road!—by the "Bennetts Babes," who pass saucy caustic comment and remove clothing as longer distances are jumped. The game is supported by real-time reporting and at its height was attracting 100 players a minute.

Webisodes   If you missed a program or can't wait till fall to get more original programming, you're in luck. Networks and cable channels offer up new and past episodes of their hit shows on the Internet. Called **webisodes**, these episodes appear online at network sites. And yes, you'll probably want to have broadband Internet to view these things, or else you'll be sitting there waiting for them to download all day.

Webisodes are also created by companies to teach consumers about how to use their products, such as showing them how to operate an iPhone or teach a few strategies for day-trading the stock market. Webisodes offer brands the opportunity to share their stories with the world; visuals and b-rolls that correspond with whatever expertise is being shared enhance the experience.

A more elaborate form of brand imaging is created through a process called theming, which is used to give distinction to restaurants, attractions, parks, and even cities. The next section reveals the importance of theming for branded entertainment venues and places.

Theming and Themed Spaces

Themed places involve a presentation of place as a conscious representation of something else. More precisely, a themed place has a *unified grammar* that controls the details of its decor and character, and a themed place consciously presents that grammar and character as different from the grammar and character of local everyday places, and as based on a unified meaning established elsewhere. What a theme is not:[9]

- A theme is not just a distinctive architectural character. Theming is easier than creating unique architectural character, because a theme provides a ready-made normative identity.
- A theme is not a decor. Decor and atmosphere by themselves do not create a theme, which involves the normative grammar of a place. Themes *use* decor.
- A theme is not a style. In an Irish bar the green color on the walls and the kind of beer and the painted shamrocks refer to a pre-established identity.
- A theme is not a deception. In a themed restaurant you are not being fooled into thinking that you are in 1920s New York. You are enjoying the complexity of being in a California restaurant and having the identity of 1920s New York playing about you.

Today, both metropolitan and suburban spaces feature themed environments that merge contemporary, commercialized popular culture with the entertainment media.[10] To embrace the spirit of merging, we define **themed environments** *as spaces that serve as containers for human interaction where the public can mingle, and where themed material forms are used as symbols to convey meaning to those who use them.* Staging themed environments to convey meaning has become big business. By staging experiences within themes, companies are able to *engage* consumers, not simply attract them. The basis for themed entertainment emanates from the notion of symbolic reality, which is explained next.

Symbolic Reality

Prior to the 1900s, thematic content was limited to symbols of ethnic enclaves, religious institutions, and business-oriented buildings. At the turn of the century, designating class status became a major social marker of a population. Since the 1960s, symbolic differentiation has been accomplished with material objects, facades, and interior space motifs. Symbols moved way beyond ethnic, religious, and class distinctions to an expanding repertoire of meanings. Derived from our popular culture, today's themes come to us directly from novels, TV, films, and music. By fusing commercialized popular culture with entertainment, we get themed environments.

Today, nothing escapes theming. Sports stars and logos pepper our competition venues; national parks are converted into idealized versions of mother nature; music characterizes cities (Nashville), immortalizes rock 'n' roll as a restaurant (Hard Rock Café), and promotes singers as theme parks (Dolly Parton). And to indulge our fantasies, the entire city of Las Vegas provides miniature cities and ancient motifs to amuse us. As cultures, cuisine, and countries become familiar to us through theming, we feel connected to what otherwise would be an alien experience.

Realms of Experience

Theming encourages different realms of experience and both active and passive levels of participation.[11] As audiences and consumers become bored with passive types of entertainment experiences, they actively seek the unusual and unique. Staging experiences within the context of specific themes enhances consumption activity and promotes commerce. Themed environments can be educational, escapist, or esthetic in purpose.

Educational experiences require absorption and active participation. Exploratoriums (science museums) like the one pictured are edutainment[12] venues where visitors learn while they play.

Themed
museum of
natural history

Escapist experience involves supreme immersion for the actively involved participant. Consumers escape into themed building like Ghost House, casinos, and virtual environments for an ultimate experience.

In an *esthetic experience*, consumers are passive about their immersion in a staged environment. Visitors to the Beach Café, although immersed in ocean artifacts, are usually more interested in eating than exploring the staged reality.

All three realms of staged, themed experiences characterize our lives whether we live in the central city or the suburbs. We eat lunch in the nostalgia of Ruby's Café, buy jeans at Diesel, and vacation in Las Vegas. Forms of symbol-ridden environment occupy all aspects of our daily lives. Themed spaces, defined by media culture motifs, characterize our cities, suburbs, shopping places, airports, and recreation spaces such as sports stadia, museums, restaurants, and amusement parks. Each environment is designed to entertain us within a commercial enterprise so we are amused while we spend our money.

Staging Reality

Themed environments strive to look "authentic," which is often taken to mean untouched by the marketplace. Here, we use the term *authentic* as something that is accurate and representative, but not necessarily real—hyperreal retail, perhaps. And some real is better than other real. As technology improves an architect's ability to reproduce and imitate, the copy is often a more enjoyable experience than the real. Visitors to New York, New York in Las Vegas claim to prefer the clean, safe, and abbreviated experience of the replica to visiting the actual city. An artificial place like this one can yield a very authentic experience for willing participants. Five principles for developing a themed environment are shown in Table 7.3.

Table 7.3 Five Principles for Developing a Themed Environment

1. An established sense of place that visitors recognize as different.
2. An altered sense of reality in space, time, and matter where size, past/future, and sensation are manipulated.
3. A cohesive, realistic whole where a completely new reality is created.
4. Multiple places within a single space that puts the visitor in motion in the experience.
5. A theme that reflects the character of the enterprise and gives visitors what they expect from the venue.

Semiotics, the science of signs and symbols, helps researchers to study and understand how theming affects our perceptions of reality. Many people understand popular culture through themed experiences. By incorporating recognizable symbols into everyday environments, theming provides a way for us to experience a historical era, a faraway place, or an exotic culture at will. According to researchers, the presence of symbols enhances our enjoyment of almost every activity in which we engage. We can understand the entertainment value of theming by comparing attendance at themed vs. non-themed environments—the former far surpasses the latter. Success manifests itself as theming because people enjoy the familiar and they respond positively to symbols of their own reality as provided by all forms of mass media.

What about creating a Naziworld park?

People certainly travel to Berlin looking for contact with the horrors of the past. They will find them indicated at the Jewish Museum, and at the Holocaust memorial. But what about a simulation? Imagine paying your money and riding through a presentation of Speer's extravagant plans for Berlin, or visiting replicas of Nazi science and industry—and their medical experiments and their slave workers. Imagine being ordered around by the park's SS soldiers, or forbidden to eat at the restaurants because of the color of your hair. Imagine never finding the Holocaust but having it hinted at constantly. There is nothing in the notion of a theme park that demands that the park be a pleasant experience.

Source: www.dkolb.org/sprawlingplaces

What do you think?

• *If we want to drive home the lesson of "never again!," could theming help? Or would it romanticize the horrors? Or is it too late?*

Themed Buying: Shoppertainment

A highly regulated, private commercial space designed to make money, the mall is a stark contrast to public, city shopping. Some malls, called Gallerias, are replicas of the Palazzo Vecchio in Florence, Italy, which was constructed in the Middle Ages with two levels and no roof. Galleria malls in America (Houston, New York, San Francisco) are enclosed spaces and may have more than two storys. Accounting for over half of all retailing sales in America, modern malls use thematic appeals in their design and advertising to attract business in a very competitive marketplace.

Malls are not only centers for shopping, they are highly organized social spaces for entertainment, interaction, and other types of consumer excitement.[13] Disenchantment with traditional shopping centers caused designers to create retail entertainment complexes that integrate entertainment and esthetic experiences with the shopping experience.[14] Most theorists view malls as the embodiment of the postmodern condition, stressing their theatrical and hyperreal character.[15]

The first mall conceived as a shopping destination is the Mall of America in Minnesota. The largest in the U.S., this 76-acre mega-mall has over 400 specialty shops, a 14-screen movie theater, nightclubs, bars, nine family entertainment areas (Camp Snoopy, Golf Mountain), 22 restaurants, and 23 fast food outlets. You'll also find a theme park with 23 amusement rides, a roller coaster, high tech virtual reality simulations (interactive virtual reality laser game Star-Base Omega), and Underwater World Aquarium.

A more manageable themed mall is located in Ontario, California. Ontario Mills Mall publicity claims that it offers "the art of shopping in an entertaining environment and shopping that is diverting, engaging, pulsating, dynamic and vibrant."[16] Patrons of the 38-football-field-sized mall may drive on a virtual car track or tee off on a virtual golf range at Dave & Buster's game place. The mall employs a director of tourism to maintain high levels of motor coach business. Tour buses bring shoppers from as far away as South Korea to the ten color-coordinated neighborhoods (retail zones) that cater to tastes from upscale adult to grungy adolescent. Overhead, 65 giant screens run an endless series of commercials produced by the mall's studio, Mills TV. OMM's destination shopping

U.A.E. Dubai's Mercato shopping center

provides everything to lure and entertain shoppers within one cutting-edge architectural space.

Department stores, while not overtly themed, often characterize themselves for specific audiences. Paris's two largest department stores, Le Bon Marché and Les Galéries Lafayette, use three domains of cultural manipulation to differentiate themselves: public space (the surrounding area), social (store windows), and personal (store itself).[17] Located in the Left Bank neighborhood within a modern building, Le Bon Marché fashions itself as an upscale shop for local and Parisian shoppers. Les Galéries Lafayette, on the other hand, caters to tourists and mass shoppers by providing a historical setting that is by itself an attraction in the fashionable area adjacent to L'Arc de Triomphe. For one store, the theme is local status, while the other store uses the historic tradition theme to attract consumers.

Malls were instrumental in developing social shopping, which allows a break from routine peppered with sensory stimulation, exercise, amusement, and fantasy. Formed on the uses and gratifications theory, shopping has become recreational and hedonic—simple barter has become browsing satisfaction and consumption pleasure. The act of buying—an appropriation of signs—becomes a means of self-realization; a shopper is both the audience and the performer of the show.

Shopping areas—*marketscapes*[18]—have become the dominant socializing space in our postmodern society. The primary dimension of sociality practiced in malls is observing and being observed. Participants become actively immersed in social communication, enjoying an escapist experience. Teenagers (also called Mall Rats), use the mall as a stage, while seniors see it as an exercise center. These social arenas possess characteristics of both leisure sites and public spaces, and are enjoyed by shoppers and browsers worldwide.

SPOTLIGHT ON THEMED AIRPORTS   Straighten Up and Fly Right!

Airport visitors, after enduring lines and searches, may welcome the diversions of airline terminals and airport architecture to get them back in a good mood for traveling. Many use theming to bring design and function to busy spaces.

Large metropolitan airports build themed interior spaces to amuse their annual 3.2 billion passengers[19] between flights, and to persuade travelers to select them for trip departures. No longer amused by the experience of air travel, passengers look to airports to define their journey's pleasure. Emulating the massive expanse and retailing atmosphere of malls, airports cater to passengers with time on their hands. The McCarran Airfield in Las Vegas has slot machines in every available place throughout the concourse

Terminal T4 in the Barajas airport, Madrid

area. There's a winery and tasting room at Dallas-Forth Worth International. Art exhibits and concourse exhibitions, such as the type presented in the O'Hare and San Francisco Airports' United terminal, are an attempt at non-paid entertainment. These spaces lure travelers to the places where they can buy replicas of what is currently being exhibited.

Innovations such as "guaranteed street pricing," Duty Free shops, banking services, health club facilities, fine dining restaurants, food courts, and family fun centers make sanitized airport environments excellent retailing opportunities. Chicago, Dallas, Denver, Pittsburgh, and Los Angeles are examples of airports that embrace the mall concept. Outdoing its American counterparts, Germany's Frankfurt airport is the ultimate stopover with an underground mall of its own. If you're traveling with children, layover at Amsterdam's Schiphol Airport offers a low-light nursery with cribs to keep baby safe while parents visit the nearby casino and art exhibitions.

What do you think?

- *How do themes enhance the travel experience for tourists? For seasoned travelers?*
- *What other amenities might airports include to enhance air travel?*

Themed Restaurants: Eatertainment

The way people eat has been significantly changed. No longer reserved for special occasions, eating out is a leisure activity enjoyed by millions of people on a regular basis. Faced with endless competition, restaurant owners choose the most popular strategy for differentiating themselves from the competition—theming. Their goal is to have diners absorbed by the restaurant's esthetic experience.

We can identify three common traits among themed restaurants:[20]

- Themes are drawn from popular culture genres such as film, sport, popular music, and ethnic cultures.
- Theme narrative is communicated through the use of props, artifacts, sound, menu, and merchandise.
- Eating is not the central focus of a visit.

An offshoot of the roadside diner or decorated shed, themed restaurants began as hamburger stands or freeway stops like Stuckeys. Specialty restaurants such as the Cannery in Newport Beach, California, have converted factories into eateries with artifacts as decor. Using photographs of the historic site, artifacts from the original building, and navigational equipment typical of the times, such cannery restaurants are crafted in the theme of a fish-processing factory.

Restaurants have used themes of nature, adventure, and celebrity to differentiate themselves. The Rainforest Café seats diners in safari animal-skin chairs under a faux sky that promises occasional storms complete with lightning and rain. Dive restaurants feature going underwater in a submarine for diners who don't get seasick or experience claustrophobia. Now defunct Planet Hollywood overwhelmed patrons with media memorabilia, perhaps to camouflage the mediocre food it served.

Hard Rock Café uses a 1950s rock music theme—this one is in New York City

Launched in England, the Hard Rock Café is the best-known fully themed restaurant. The motif comes from the rock music industry, including nostalgic elements from the 1950s when rock began. The restaurant's exterior is framed by large neon guitars, and the front end of a 1950s Cadillac convertible is embedded in one interior wall. Copies and original memorabilia of the rock industry—gold records, concert posters—serve as wall decor. Proving very successful, the rock music theme still attracts both diners and lookers. Marketing's role is evident by the fact that profits from Hard Rock's logo merchandise often surpass food revenues.

Restaurants with *ethnic* themes are common: Italian (Olive Garden), Mexican (El Torito), and Japanese (BeniHana) are among the most popular. Nostalgic diners have become themed. Ruby's Diner (soda shop theme) and Mel's Diner (deli theme) are franchised throughout California, offering burgers, fries, and sandwich fare. Reflexive theming,[21] commonly found in franchises, is used when the theme is a brand and the brand is the theme. Here, the brand becomes a symbol of the dining experience. McDonald's, Burger King, KFC are themes that are also brands.

Diners experiencing the esthetic of themed eateries acknowledge the venues as fakes, but are amused by the staged reality that contains gastronomic consumption. How many restaurants have you visited lately without a theme? The number should tell you something about the prevalence of esthetic experiences expected by those who eat out.

Branded Theming: Logotainment

Like reflectively themed restaurants, branded venues rely on the brand to produce the theme (Nike = sports, Sony = electronic games) and the theme to reinforce the brand. Typical of this concept is Metreon, a 350,000 square foot San Francisco entertainment complex where shoppers become immersed in this atmosphere's electronic esthetic. Every design element of the Sony **servicescape**[22] encourages impulsive behavior and invites instant gratification. Resembling a "spiritual gameplace" or a cathedral of consumption,[23] Metreon is a combination of amusement-centered themed environment and mega-boutique.

Metreon Servicescape   What happens in this place is more subliminal than active commercialism. Parents show their kids around in the same way as they might point out exhibits in a museum. The sales staff don't apply pressure; in fact they are more informative than persuasive. The educational and esthetic experiences enjoyed in this logo monument will, in theory, be transferred to the Nike brand. Visitors are encouraged to increase their "brandscape" through their engagement with this environment. Brandscapes are "material and symbolic environments that consumers build with marketplace products, images and messages."[24]

Located in the city's South of Market district, Metreon's Airtight Garage is an interactive adventure zone with electronic games created especially for Sony: Quaternia (team capture-the-flag game), Badlands (demolition derby), and HyperBowl (combines miniature golf, bowling, and a TV sports event) provide escapist experiences for all active participants.

Each floor provides shopping for Sony music, Sony electronics, and brand extensions of products from branded artist attractions. Products from sponsors Citibank, Pepsi, Levis, Intel, Mercury, and others are sprinkled among the shop offerings. Five themed restaurants feed visitors to Metreon and its theaters. The Sony brand is the hero of this venue. Rather than thinking about Sony as a product, we are expected to experience Sony as a pleasant diversion, as a brand that belongs in our lives.

Other brandscapes include Coke and M&M retail venues that present brand histories and brand memorabilia for nostalgic viewing and purchasing. The primary purpose of themed venues is to provide entertainment for potential consumers within the context of a brand that becomes synonymous with enjoyment, fun, and wonder. The innovative brand stores and retail entertainment complex link names and logos of major companies to exhibits and attractions to develop cross-marketing opportunities in which retailers and sponsors promote each other in and outside the mall.[25]

Flagship Stores   Flagship stores have become a way for fashion brands to enhance their image and display merchandise in a luxurious immersion experience for consumers. Armani, for instance, has a seven-story store in Hong Kong that features Armani brand furniture, apparel, flowers, accessories, shoes, and sportswear, all displayed in architectural spaces with limited merchandise and a multi-lingual sales staff.

Themed Neighborhoods: Archetainment

Regions where activities are conducted in centers that are functionally specialized and separated by travel time of 15 to 30 minutes are labeled as "postsuburban" areas.[26] Residents travel by car across city boundaries for work, socializing, and shopping. Postsuburbia consists of separate spaces for living (neighborhoods), shopping (malls), and working (industrial parks).

One such postsuburban space is Orange County, California, home of Disneyland, several major universities, large destination shopping malls, the Crystal Cathedral, and the Mighty Ducks hockey team. Orange County is dotted with neighborhood shopping centers, upscale malls, swap meets, and consumer warehouses (Cosco), each of which plays a different role in the postsuburban marketplace. Theming prevails in offices, health spas, universities, and religious buildings. In fact, some call Orange County a 786-square-mile theme park where the theme is "you can have anything you want."[27]

The town of Mission Viejo, known as a super-dormitory and home of the perfect high dive (boasting nine gold, two silver, and one bronze Olympic swimming and diving medals), is billed by its developer as "the California promise." Recognizable residential themes such as Greek Island, Capri Villa, and Uniquely American punctuate the "promise." Viejo "clones" have sprung up throughout the county with names like Alicia Viejo (straining over the hills for an ocean view), Ranch Santa Margarita ("where the West begins again"), Coto de Caza (outgrowth of a tennis and riding resort), and Monarch Beach (to revolve around a "world-class" golf course). And for 21,000 retired elderly, Leisure World, the largest retirement community in America, has sprouted business such as brokerage houses, banks, and money handlers in a supermarket of financial services.

Orange County's Knott's Berry Farm in Buena Park is designed as a city that imitates a city. Even as a toy city, it has a studied illusion of reality that takes over as you walk down the streets. It pretends to be real like wax museums that pretend to feature real people—real fake. The oldest themed amusement park in the world, Knott's celebrates the "wholesome aspects of an idealized and simpler America." The Farm is a stark contrast to the hyper-modern county that surrounds it. Knott's neighbor, Disneyland, makes it clear that within its magic enclosure is a *fantasy*, not a mere reproduction.

Emerging as an important economic region, Orange County has become an information-oriented, postsuburban society with shopping environments that serve as a metaphor for life in general. Thanks to the advanced credit system, which supports and drives consumption activities, Orange County—like its many counterparts across the country—will continue to support themed spaces for their social, commercial, and psychological needs.

Themed Cities: Faketainment

Hershey, Pennsylvania, is an eastern city all dressed up for visitors to the chocolate capital of America. Complete with its own chocolate river, Hersey is adorned with street lamps in the shape of kisses and retailers that expand the brand motif with brown decor and chocolate souvenirs. Such a brandscape relies on tourists with a sweet tooth who come to eat. According to a *New York Times* writer,[28] surrogate experience and synthetic settings have become the preferred American way of life.

Environment has become entertainment. A replica of New York City, built in Las Vegas as a skyscraper casino with Coney Island rides, is a "crowd-pleaser without the risk of a trip to the Big Apple."[29] If we were to rank fakes on a scale of one to ten, ten being the best, Las Vegas would get an 11. Here, imitation has become an art form. Vegas's outrageously real fake (as opposed to a fake fake) has developed its own style from the ground up to become an urban design frontier.

The famous Vegas Strip is itself a linear theater, evolving over the past 90 years in a uniquely American way. The opposite of a modern city with an identifiable center, Vegas is represented by its construction around the Strip on which theme hotels become way-stations to energize the consumer in motion. Now thought of as a family destination, Las Vegas offers casino hotels, amusement parks, and shopping malls, all themed and prefabricated and available as a packaged vacation. Plus, you get Wayne Newton and animatronic dinosaurs as well. Such extravaganzas—Caesar's Palace with its heroic Styrofoam statuary, Luxor's sphinx and mirror-glass pyramid, Bellagio's art masterpieces,

Las Vegas, the ultimate themed city, offers visitors a scaled-down New York City

Venice's canals, Paris's Eiffel Tower—are but a few of the city's monuments to simulation. Ironically the faux New York, a colorful Gotham hodgepodge of a casino hotel, was built in 1997 without the twin towers of the World Trade Center. After the terrorist attacks of September 2001, the Vegas replica suddenly became more accurate for its omission.

A farcical theater-of-the absurd character of contemporary life, Las Vegas is neither intended nor taken seriously by tourist consumers. Visitors receive an escapist experience, becoming immersed in fantasy. Banking on our desire to return to our childhood, Las Vegas lets us play the game of dress-up, pig out, and stay out all night. Our quarters feed the slots and our fantasies of winning the ultimate jackpot—freedom to keep on pretending that we don't have to grow up. Vegas is a play-pen for the middle class and middle aged; what makes it unique is simply the scale of the carnival.[30]

Themed Parks: Mousetainment

Born as Coney Island at the turn of the nineteenth century, the first theme park had a recipe for entertaining large crowds: play, escape, release, fantasy, thrills, and family outings. This forerunner of Disney made three important contributions to outdoor amusement in each of its three parks.

- The idea of structuring amusements around sea animals, water rides, and aquatic exhibitions began with Sea Lion Park, created in 1895. Today, every major amusement park contains some kind of water slide like Shoot the Rapids, Mill Chutes, or Log Flume.
- Steeplechase, a technology-driven fun center featuring Human Roulette Wheel, Earthquake Floor, Blow Hole, and Electric Seat, was developed in 1897. This pattern of mechanical rides, sideshows, midway, fun houses, audience participation, and voyeurism were to become the industry standard.
- In 1903, Luna Park was created with a concern for physical appearance, illusion, crowd control, live spectacular shows, and ambience. This amusement park blended foreign cultures, pleasant atmosphere, staged events, and illusion rides into a new, more successful version of commodified leisure.

After Luna was destroyed by fire, Disneyland appeared in 1958 looking new but actually just extending the Luna/Dreamland fantasy park that evolved and prospered during the first decade of the twentieth century. Disney was a master of displaying popular images like Medieval Castle and World of Tomorrow, which were inspired by the 1930 World's Fair. Disney's practice of parading employees in Mouse or Duck costumes was patterned after Luna Park's storybook characters Alice in Wonderland and the Mad Hatter who mingled with park visitors. Disneyland was designed to deviate from the vulgarity, clowning, and exuberance Coney Island was famous for. Ironically, former Disney employees are building a new park at Coney Island that conforms to its historic past.[31] Today, the Disney theme park form is the most popular attraction on earth.

Indiana Jones attraction in Disneyland, Paris

Fabrication Unlike Las Vegas, which is fake, Disneyland is a *fabricated* entity of its own. It's not a copy, it is an original concept duplicated in several geographic locations around the globe. Disneyland hides all things fake. In Disney terms, "imagineering" designates the creative process of "making the magic real," or translating fictions and fantasies to concrete themed architecture and attractions.[32] Disneyland is a master of planning, crowd control, and crowd movement. After standing in line and performing obediently to the prescribed traffic control, one critic warned: "What you and your 10 to 20 thousand cohorts are performing is a huge, choreographed, aesthetically quite arresting species of close-order drill."[33]

By blending common mass culture symbols and an appealing physical design, Disneyland has had a profound impact on the construction of themed environments across America. Visitors leave their usual modes of transportation and enter the park as pedestrian travelers. The main attraction of theme parks is its stark contrast to the everyday lives of the people who visit them. Traits of the park act as liberators from daily constraints.

- Theme parks are crime-free, unlike many cities and urban areas.
- Parks offer a contrast to routine at-home dining with a festival of food varieties.
- The experience encourages family interaction in a child-centered environment.
- Park entertainment is a live festival, not a mediated spectacle.
- Leisure and play clothing allow people to cast aside fashion rules for workplaces.
- Parks provide an illusion of escaping from the demands of personal economy. Once the admission price is paid, all rides are perceived as "free."
- Visitors encounter fantastic architectural structures that provide themed entertainment in themselves.

SPOTLIGHT ON CULTURE

Lessons for Hong Kong Disneyland

After only six months of operation, Hong Kong's Disneyland park had serious drops in attendance. Chinese travel-industry representative said that Disney didn't have a big enough presence in China—people knew the name but were not compelled to visit the park. So the Ogilvy & Mather Agency launched a new marketing campaign in June, 2006, with television advertising. One problem with past advertising was the concept of family. Commercials featured a nuclear group of mom, dad, and two kids on Disney rides—in a country where parents are encouraged to have only one child. The new campaign features mom, grandma, and granddaughter instead.

Seeming more confused than amused, past Chinese visitors didn't show up with the imbedded Disney infusion characteristic of Westerners. Changes to the park's interior were also made to make the experience more understandable to Chinese. Eating

habits had to be addressed first. Chinese guests took an average of ten minutes longer to eat than Americans, so 700 seats were added to dining areas. In addition, warnings were placed in front of "Space Mountain" that the attraction was a roller coaster—unsuspecting guests had reported illness from the ride.

Waiting-line protocol was addressed at the park's "Jungle Cruise" attraction where language narration directs visitors on the ride. With three languages (Mandarin, Cantonese, English), it was important to get visitors into the correct language line. While Disney always staggered lines so that no line was given the advantage of moving more quickly, this park needed labeled lines so visitors did not find themselves with a foreign-speaking narration they couldn't understand. Mandarin speakers were added to the park's staff as guides, along with reading materials and subtitles added to shows like "Festival for the Lion King" and "Golden Mickeys" because audiences were missing cues to laugh or applaud.

Complaining that the park was smaller than province-region theme parks, some visitors didn't feel Disneyland had anything special to offer Chinese visitors. So expansion is planned to accommodate ten million visitors by 2012. Phase 1 will have three new rides and "Cool Zone," a water-play area. "It's a Small World" boat ride was added to Fantasyland in Summer 2007. Travel agents, who are central to funneling visitors from the mainland to the park, say they're happy about the changes, and that Disney officials are finally listening to them about Chinese tourists' needs.

Source: Merissa Marr and Geoffrey Fowler for *The Wall Street Journal*, June 12, 2006, B1

What do you think?

- *How might Disney have avoided the cultural faux pas before opening the park?*
- *What other obvious cultural differences need to be addressed for Chinese visitors?*

Combining retail and park theming, Disney Village at EuroDisney presents authentic representations of four American nostalgia themes so that Europeans may experience the "old West," rock 'n' roll, 1950s sports, and famous American places of the past in a single location. Displaying bows and arrows, guns and Indian artifacts, Disney Village captures visitors' hearts with an accurate depiction of Buffalo Bill's Wild West show that was performed in England and France between 1883 and 1913. A red and blue motif is backdrop for vintage cars and Hollywood memorabilia reproduced to entertain park and Village visitors.

With parks in America, France, Japan, and Hong Kong, Disney has captured the mind and hearts of consumers with an age-old formula to provide carefully fabricated fantasy and social interaction for families across cultural and geographical boundaries. Visitors become immersed in an escapist experience that allows them to visit any place on earth—and in space.

So where do we go from the $78 a day entry fee to interact with a mouse? Disney-jaded tourists may want to make a pilgrimage to ancient Jerusalem in Orlando's new Holy Land Experience for only $17 a ticket.[34] Fulfilling the need for synthetic history that is tidier and sweeter-smelling than the real kind (camel hoof prints but no camel dung), this theme park's virtual history has engendered controversy. Christian leaders criticize the park for trivializing religion, and a Baptist minister was accused of intending to use the park to convert Jews to Christianity. When the park opened amid heavy security and a barrage of TV news crews, the fake seemed not very different from its Israel prototype.

FADE TO BLACK

As marketers of experiences explore innovative ways to advertise, consumers become more sophisticated branding experts. Delivering persuasive messages is challenging as well as expensive; agencies specialize in brand identification search for creative visuals to capture attention and foster loyalty. As we have seen, branding is the most important aspect of the promotional mix.

Advertising is both blatant and hidden, and all forms are used to bring awareness and attention to a brand. Audience members have more tolerance for imbedded brands because they do not interrupt the entertainment experience like commercials do.

Disney and other extensions of theme environments sell experiences to people who draw on their own cultural codes for engagement that is both enjoyable and meaningful. Toy stores, bridal salons, hair salons, grocery stores, and even wilderness attractions also rely on themes and staged esthetics to attract and retain consumers.

Familiar sign systems in themed environments enable users to satisfy their consumer desires. We are not "strangers in a strange land" inside a themed mall or park because we understand how to navigate and negotiate the space. We find comfort in the familiar and enjoyment in our skills at achieving consumption success.

We must not underestimate the importance of branding and themed motifs for marketing and entertainment. They provide experiences that come from our highly developed, image-driven and commodity-driven popular culture that is fostered by the merging of commercial retailing, advertising, and mass media. Themed and branded environments work because they offer consumers spatial and visual experiences that are both entertaining and fantasy driven. Because they work, and because they are profitable, themes will dictate the nature of all our branded interactions from now forward.

A CLOSER LOOK AT THEMING

Social Space or the Marketplace: The Demise of Local Pubs

This case study illustrates the impact of theming on local socialization. It involves the destruction of some of Ireland's best local pubs and the emergence of theming as a marketing factor that has changed their role in community socialization. How does theming connect to the balance of social forces and change the way we relate to history and memory?

According to one critic, *the creation of theme pubs is part of the agenda to replace real history with false history to generate revenue*.

The layout of the pub has traditionally reflected the class and gender division of the wider society; a public bar for the working class, the saloon bar for gentlemen and ladies, with sometimes a smaller club for a particular group such as women or the elderly. Now those divisions are largely gone, replaced by a more democratic consumerism, reflecting modern trends in marketing and consumption.

A pub's location has traditionally been the main factor in determining the class of its locals and a pub environment reflected the people who used this space, who they were, and what they used the space for. But increasingly nowadays a pub interior tells you only who is supposed to use the pub and what you are supposed to do there—the authority of the environment attempts to assert itself on customers' behavior. These choices have been made by the brewery marketing men and their designers.

In the past two decades, rapid image changes for pubs were common, and breweries intensified the capitalization of every aspect of pub life. Drinking space was carved up and allotted to specific social groups according to age and spending power; decor and design were invoked to attract the desired clientele as defined by the marketing men—all part of the streamlining of consumer targeting.

The creation of the Theme Pub has limited or destroyed any traces of autonomous social culture that previously existed in the pub environment. The Theme Pub represents a manufactured image of authenticity (Irish-ness) which is in reality its complete opposite. A Theme Pub's theatrical decor often makes visitors feel like a bit-part actor in someone else's play.

The Irish pub kept much of its historical, individual, and social character long after most other public spaces and areas of consumption were economically standardized. For centuries occupying a central place in the community, going to the pub was truly a visit to "the local." The pub name generally had some relation to either local or national history and the pub was often a geographical, and sometimes historical, landmark itself.

But the emergence of identical chains of pubs is changing this. Nag's Head pub became "O'Neill's"—part of a chain of Irish Theme Pubs. In response to unsuccessful protests by local residents a spokeswoman for the brewery which runs O'Neill's said "Pub names do change over the years, usually when investment is made. There are 80 O'Neill's bars around the country and the aim is to create bars so that the one around the corner will be the same as any other one around the country."

Theme Pubs like O'Neill's attract customers partly by appealing to their feelings of nostalgia fed by an increasing sense of dislocation, loss of identity, and need for escape in the modern world. Irish-ness, for instance, lends itself to stereotyped interpretation, which can also be seen in Irish beer advertisements as well as most other ads for Irish products.

Today for many people there is no longer anything very local about one's locality. And now pubs can be added to this list of Legoland amenities. The false history of the Theme Pub environment is superimposed over the real history of the place; changing names and interiors are examples of this. History that locates and situates us is replaced by an instant

Murphy's Pub, a themed Irish bar

mass-produced history, changing appearances and eras according to passing fashions and marketing strategies. Ironically, it is partly this de-historicizing of the daily environment that encourages nostalgia and an attraction to the Themed environment.

Themed locations are *pseudo-environments* in the sense that they are parodies or copies of other places that possess a real history of specific uses for their location—while the Themed space is mere transported appearance, taken out of its original context and given a different function for the purposes of commodity consumption. In the original *real* environment the appearance was largely determined by the use the place was put to—while in the *Theme* environment the appearance is intended to determine the use of the space. The Theming attempts to pre-determine what can happen in such spaces; the script is already written and a role already prescribed for you, which means various forms of consumption. But what is being consumed is not only the food,

drink, but also a kind of *framing* of the pub as consumption venue, framing the permitted limits of behavior.

Pubs have historically been the predominant and most long lived working-class public social space. Theming and gentrification give the illusion of movement, development, and innovation—and encourage us to identify with this enforced trendiness—but the unchanging basis of commodity relations and class society is the necessary foundation for these marketing trends and modifications of social space.

The surreal nature of Theming was taken to new heights by a lost soul in search of an identity when his local pub was turned into an Australian Theme Bar. Irish beers were replaced by Aussie lagers, a Kiwi manager, toilets marked Blokes and Sheilas, surfboards on the ceiling, food served in billy cans, and so forth. The customer decided to Theme himself, speaking in a pronounced Aussie accent, taking a Kiwi girlfriend and thinking of emigrating down under.

Source: www.endangeredphoenic.com

What do you think?

- *What role does the Guinness brand play in your image of Ireland?*
- *What features would you expect to find in a themed pub?*
- *How many Irish pubs can you name that are part of a chain?*

DISCUSSION AND REVIEW

1. Discuss the role of flagship stores for promoting products and for generating image. Which factor is more important, sales or brand equity? Why?
2. What sponsorships or brand associations can you identify that link a product with an activity? How does the product or brand become part of the entertainment experience?
3. How do we distinguish themes from related notions such as decor, atmosphere, ambience, and from allusions and references? When Paris presents itself to tourists, is it a themed place? Does Boston's Quincy Market have only decor and not a theme? Just what does it mean for a place to have a theme?

EXERCISES

1. Visit an ethnic themed restaurant and make a list of all the icons, artifacts, and symbols of the theme. Then ask ten friends what icons, artifacts, and symbols they would choose for that theme. Compare the two. What conclusions can you draw from this comparison?
2. Visit a themed mall and list all the experiential realms available at the mall. Which experiences are tied to brands? Which are linked to age demographics, like children? What role do the mall restaurants play in supporting the theme? What evidence can you see of reality engineering?
3. Develop a new theme for a mall or park. Describe the space, retail venues, and artifacts you would incorporate into this destination. What audience would you target for your venue? List factors from the chapter that helped in making your selection.
4. Make a list of all the branded entertainment types you have encountered in the past month. Now make a list of theme parks you know about. How do the items in your lists differ? How are they the same?

BOOKS AND BLOGS

Gottdiener, M. (1997). *The theming of America: Dreams, visions and commercial spaces.* Boulder CO: Westview Press.

Halter, M. (2000). *Shopping for identity: The marketing of ethnicity.* New York: Schocken Books.

Pine, B.J. and Gilmore, J.H. (1999). *The experience economy.* Boston MA: Harvard Business School Press.

Ritzer, G. (1998). *The McDonaldization thesis: Explorations and extensions.* London: Sage.

Schmidt, B. and Simonson, A. (1997). *Marketing aesthetics: The strategic management of brands, identity and image.* New York: Free Press.

Sherry, J.F. Jr. (ed.) (1998). *ServiceScapes: The concept of place in contemporary markets.* Chicago: NTC Business Books.

www.brandchannel.com—current news on all facets of branding.

www.veryfunnyads.com—a compendium of humorous commercials for viewing.

http://consumerlab.wordpress.com—Alcone Marketing Group's consumer activation site.

www.insidebrandedentertainment.com/bep/index.jsp—site concerned with entertainment brands and branding entertainment.

8 A QUESTION OF STANDARDS: LEGAL RIGHTS AND RESPONSIBILITIES

Laws alone cannot secure freedom of expression; in order that every man present his views without penalty there must be a spirit of tolerance in the entire population.

—Albert Einstein

In this chapter we will explore the intersection between law and entertainment. Like entertainment, policy and law both shape and reflect the society in which they are crafted. The formation and enforcement of policy and law involve a collective action of the whole society or its representatives, which entails extensive public discussion and the formation of public opinion on what to do. Different societies are guided by different rights and regulations. Although we will make some international comparisons, we will mostly limit our focus to policies and laws as they have been enacted and enforced in the United States.

Policy reflects government and public consideration of how to structure and regulate social or collective activities, such as those of the media and entertainment industries, so that they can contribute to the public good. Many groups, such as churches, private companies, industry trade groups, minority groups, and public-interest groups also monitor entertainment activities and lobby the industries and government to make changes. For example, lobbying by a number of groups led the Federal Communication Commission (FCC) to crack down on indecent content on television in 2004. In this chapter we will discuss laws, policies, and standards that have been applied to entertainment. **Laws** are binding rules passed by the legislatures, enforced by the executive branch and applied or adjudicated by the courts. Governments and private organizations craft **policies** that govern specific practices or activities. Government policies are often turned into laws in order to make them legally binding on people and companies. **Standards** or technical characteristics, such as the number of lines on the TV screen, must be agreed on for a technology or practice to be widely adopted.

Rather than waiting to be regulated by law or government policies, many enter-tainment industries formally regulate themselves. Thus, we will also examine industry self-regulation through industry codes and practices of self-monitoring and control, such as the rating system used by the film industry. Some issues cut across all of these factors. For example, concerns about sex and violence in the media have resulted in government laws and policies, such as FCC restrictions of language used on radio, and the 1996 Telecommunications Act requiring a V-chip screening system for television. In addition to standards established by the film rating system, concerns about violent and sexual content have led to further industry self-monitoring. A number of TV stations declined to air the film *Saving Private Ryan* in 2004, fearing its violent content might lead to audience protests and government scrutiny.

Entertainment laws and regulations are far too numerous and varied to cover them all in a single chapter. Instead we will isolate several key legal issues focusing on how they have impacted and been influenced by advances in entertainment including free speech, privacy, intellectual property, competition, compensation and government jurisdiction.

The First Amendment and the Freedom of Speech

The most central U.S. policy regarding the content and conduct within entertainment, particularly media entertainment, is the **First Amendment**. The first amendment guarantees citizens a right to free speech. This reflects an underlying agreement, dating back to the American Revolution in 1776, that **freedom of speech**, both in person and through media, is a basic requirement for the democratic political system and free society that the writers of the U.S. Constitution wished to create. Although many Americans today may take their freedom of speech for granted, the founders of the Constitution such as Thomas Jefferson, Benjamin Franklin, and Thomas Paine did not. In the early days of printing in Europe, both government and church authorities granted licenses to guilds or companies to print books, but they controlled what could be printed. Such licensing control came under increasingly severe criticism from writers and philosophers. In 1644, for example the writer and poet John Milton wrote a critique of this censorship called *Aeropagitica*, proclaiming the need for religious free speech.[1] Thus, founders of the constitution recognized how few places in the world at that time had free speech and how easily it could be limited. Their insistence that such a right be codified as the First Amendment to the U.S. Constitution illustrates how adamant they were that this freedom be protected. The First Amendment reads:

> Congress shall make no law respecting an establishment of religion, or prohibiting the free exercise thereof, or abridging the freedom of speech, or the right of the people peacefully to assemble, and to petition the Government for a redress of grievances.

Political Speech

John Stuart Mill, Edmund Burke, and other early advocates of democracy forwarded the idea of an active, informed citizenry. They pointed to the need for a free press to assist in the wide circulation of ideas.[2] If citizens were to make informed voting decisions, they needed unrestricted access to information about the issues involved. Along with economic ideas circulating at the time about the value of a marketplace competition for goods, the concept of a **marketplace of ideas** was developed in which different voices could compete for attention. In spite of this protection, over the course of our history, the government has allowed and enforced many limitations on speech.

Because of its perceived significance for the democratic process "political speech" has typically received greater protection than forms of expression deemed less essential such as the "commercial speech" made by companies trying to sell their goods. Therefore, when we think of "political" speech, we may not think of entertainment. Instead, we envision presidential speeches, political debates, or news commentary about current events. However, as we will see in Chapter 11, politics is actually a very common topic in entertainment. Musicians sing about it, comedians include it in their monologues, and TV and film dramas tell stories about it. In fact, it has been argued that all speech (including the comedy of radio talk show host Howard Stern) has political value to someone.[3]

Limits on the First Amendment

Generally, spoken entertainment receives the same protection afforded all other forms of speech. For example, in a recent case, a three-judge panel for the 8th U.S. Circuit Court of Appeal unanimously held that violent video games are entitled to as much protection as the Bible (*Entertainment Software Association v. Swanson*, 519 F.3d 768, D. Minn., 2006). Nonetheless, some kinds of speech are not protected by the First Amendment: defamation, obscenity, plagiarism, invasion of privacy, and inciting insurrection. Thus, as with any other form of expression, when entertainment is judged to fall into any of these areas, it is no longer protected.

Defamation

Defamatory statements (*libel*, if it is written or broadcast expression, or *slander*, if it is spoken) are false declarations about private citizens that might damage their reputation. Libel is generally defined as a false statement that holds a person up to public ridicule, contempt, or hatred or injures a person's business or occupation. Examples of potentially libelous statements include falsely accusing someone of professional dishonesty or incompetence (such as medical malpractice); falsely accusing a person of a crime (such as drug dealing); falsely charging a person with mental illness or unacceptable behavior (such as public drunkenness); or falsely accusing a person of associating with a disreputable organization or cause (such as the Mafia or a neo-Nazi military group).

The Supreme Court has ruled that private individuals have to prove three things to win a libel case:

- that the public statement about them was false
- that damages or actual injury occurred, such as the loss of a job, harm to reputation, public humiliation, or mental anguish
- that the publisher or broadcaster was negligent.

Entertainers have often brought defamation suits against journalists and news organizations for reporting information they claimed were untrue. For example, celebrities such as Kate Hudson and Cameron Diaz have sued the gossip magazine the *Enquirer* for making libelous claims about them. In many cases, entertainers have won these suits, but not all. U.S. policy balances libel concerns against the press's interest in maintaining its watchdog role in exposing corruption or incompetence by officials or public figures. If a court determines that a plaintiff is a public official or figure, that person has to prove falsehood, damages, negligence, and actual malice. The **actual malice** test means that whoever made or permitted the statement knew the statement was false, but printed or broadcast it anyway or acted with a reckless disregard for the truth. Although judges often have a hard time deciding who is a public figure, the courts are consistent in ruling that entertainment celebrities, including reality program participants, meet the public distinction. Thus, because actual malice is challenging to prove, it is often difficult for celebrities to win libel cases, even when the stories told about them may seem particularly offensive.

Entertainers, themselves, have also often been sued for defamation. Jerry Seinfeld was sued by children's writer Missy Chase Lapine. On David Letterman's show, Seinfeld joked about Lapine, including this jab: "If you read history, many people with three names do become assassins. Mark David Chapman, and you know, James Earl Ray. So that's my concern."[4] Lapine, who has three names, claimed that this implied comparison was slanderous. Seinfeld's lawyers argued that his comments were only made in the midst of being a funny comedian and thus, he was protected by the First Amendment. They argued that "[n]o reasonable viewer could have thought that Seinfeld really meant that Lapine— the author of children's books emphasizing the use of pureed vegetables—might become an assassin simply because she has three names."[5] As of the writing of this text, however, this case was still pending.

Generally speaking, libel applies only to misstatements of factual information rather than opinion, but the line between the two is often hazy. Thus, a common defense offered against libel is that the comments in question fall within the area of *opinion and fair comment*. Thus, libel laws protect satire, comedy, and opinions expressed in reviews of books, plays, movies, or restaurants.

One of the most famous tests of the fair comment defense occurred in the case of *Falwell v. Flynt*, 1988. The minister and activist Jerry Falwell sued *Hustler* magazine and its publisher Larry Flynt after a November 1983 issue parodied Falwell in a Campari aperitif ad. The parody described Falwell's first time drinking Campari as an incestuous encounter with his own mother and stated that he needed to be drunk

before he could preach. A disclaimer read: "Ad parody—not to be taken seriously." Falwell sued for libel, asking for $45 million in damages. The jury rejected the libel suit, but allowed that Flynt had intentionally caused Falwell emotional distress and awarded him $200,000. The verdict was unexpected and unprecedented, and the Supreme Court unanimously overturned it on appeal. Although the justices did not condone the spoof, they held firm that the magazine was entitled to constitutional protection. The decision suggested that, even though parodies and insults of public figures might indeed cause emotional pain, denying the right to publish them violated the spirit of the First Amendment.

The Fairness Doctrine

In some nations, people who have been criticized have a right to reply. Enforcing such a right has often meant that the medium in which the criticism was reported must afford the same coverage to the victims of the criticism should they choose to apply. In the U.S. this principle has rarely been applied to print media, because they are so numerous that it is assumed all sides have an opportunity to be heard. However, when radio emerged as a new media format, concern about limited access to the airwaves led to the passage of the Radio Act of 1927. The Act required equal opportunities:

> If any licensee shall permit anyone who is a legally qualified candidate for any public office to use a broadcasting station, he shall afford equal opportunities to all other candidates for that office in the use of such broadcasting station. (Sect. 315, Radio Act of 1927)

The FCC also developed a concept known as the **fairness doctrine**. Its central idea was that the public's right to be informed overrides the right of broadcasters to carry their "own particular views on any matter" (*Red Lion Broadcasting Co. v. FCC*, U.S. 367, 1969). This concept required stations to schedule time for controversial programming in issues and then to ensure the expression of opposing views. In practice, the FCC did not force stations to carry specific programming, so the rule focused on the right of reply to controversial points of view. By the 1980s, however, some broadcasters were arguing that the fairness doctrine was having a "chilling effect" in causing stations to avoid controversial programming entirely. In addition, the original argument that the scarcity of broadcast outlets meant that each one had a unique responsibility to be fair and balanced became less compelling as bandwidth and the number of broadcast outlets increased. In 1985, therefore the FCC stopped enforcing the doctrine and it was finally struck down by the Supreme Court in 2001.

Recently, however, there have been calls to reinstate the fairness doctrine, interestingly enough, in reaction to the growing popularity of radio talk shows. On political talk shows, a host will often introduce a topic and then invite discussion from one or more guest experts. Typically considered more entertainment than news, call-in shows where listeners are invited to share their opinions are a particularly popular format for these shows. Many political talkers are syndicated, but local shows are also popular. Typically conservative shows (with hosts such as Rush Limbaugh and Gordon Liddy) tend to fare better than more liberal-leaning programs. Not surprisingly, those who listen to such shows tend to be males who are older, more conservative, predominately white, and who are very interested in politics, are politically active, and hold anti-Washington attitudes. (See Chapter 13 for a more detailed discussion of talk shows and political speech in entertainment.)

FLASH FACT

An Annenberg national poll[6] found that 18 percent of adults listen to at least one call-in political talk show radio program a week. Nearly half of Americans (47 percent) believe that government should require all radio and TV stations to offer equal amounts of conservative and liberal political commentary.

The concern is that the lack of more liberal-leaning talk programs has created an imbalance that has stifled the marketplace of ideas. Some Democrats say conservative-dominated talk radio has enabled Republicans to mislead the public on important issues such as the Senate immigration reform bill. Not surprisingly, sentiments regarding whether to consider reviving the fairness doctrine to force stations to provide a better balance tend to divide by party lines. "These are public airwaves and the public should be entitled to a fair presentation," said Sen. Dianne Feinstein (D—Calif.), who is considering whether the fairness doctrine should be restored.[7] Republicans say that the policy would result in censorship and warn that it could return if Democrats have a majority in Congress. "This is a bad idea from a bygone era," Sen. Norm Coleman (R—Minn.) said at a news conference with five other Republicans announcing legislation to block reenactment of the policy.[8] See the *Spotlight on Fairness on Talk Radio* below to learn more about public perceptions on this issue.

SPOTLIGHT ON FAIRNESS AND TALK RADIO   And the Survey Says . . .[9]

According to a 2008 Rasmussen Reports national telephone poll, 55 percent of voters consider media bias a bigger problem than large campaign contributions. Nearly half of Americans (47 percent) believe the government should require all radio and television stations to offer equal amounts of conservative and liberal political commentary, but they draw the line at imposing that same requirement on the Internet. Thirty-nine percent say leave radio and TV alone, too. At the same time, 71 percent say it is already possible for just about any political view to be heard in today's media, according to a new survey. Twenty percent do not agree. Fifty-seven percent say the government should not require web sites and blog sites that offer political commentary to present opposing viewpoints. But 31 percent believe the Internet sites should be forced to balance their commentary.

Political Affiliation

Democrats are more supportive of government involvement in the airwaves than Republicans and unaffiliated voters. Fifty-four percent of Democrats favor it, and only 26 percent are opposed.

Republicans and unaffiliated voters are fairly evenly divided. Even Democrats, however, oppose government-mandated balance on the Internet by a 48 percent to 37 percent margin. Sixty-one percent of Republicans reject government involvement in Internet content along with 67 percent of unaffiliated voters.

Fairness Doctrine

Only 45 percent of Americans say they are following recent news stories about the fairness doctrine even somewhat closely, while 15 percent say they are not following the story at all. In the new survey, 42 percent say there are more conservative radio talk shows because they get better ratings, but 28 percent believe it is because station owners are biased. Seventeen percent attribute it to an unspecified other reason, and 13 percent are unsure. Most Republicans (61 percent) believe conservative talk radio has flourished because of the ratings, with only 11 percent saying it is due to bias. Democrats, on the other hand, see bias as the reason over ratings by a 42 percent to 28 percent margin. Among unaffiliateds, 42 percent say ratings and 27 percent say bias. Voters in all categories agree by sizable margins that it is possible for just about any political view to be heard in today's media.

In the 2008 election, 58 percent of likely Obama voters believed the government should make all radio and TV stations offer equal amounts of conservative and liberal commentary, as opposed to 40 percent of potential McCain voters who felt that way. But 63 percent of McCain voters and 53 percent of Obama voters rejected similar regulation of web sites and bloggers.

Source: Rasmussen Reports Survey 2008

What do you think?

- *You've heard what others think. What is your opinion on this issue?*

The Right to Privacy

Although most Americans assume that they have a right to privacy, this right is not directly enumerated in the U.S. Constitution. Some legal scholars argue that the first ten amendments focus on protecting people from invasions of their privacy by government. In 1965, Supreme Court Justice Harlan said that the right to privacy derives from the First, Third, Fourth, Fifth, Ninth, and Fourteenth Amendments, although it exceeds the sum of its parts (*Griswold v. Connecticut*, 1965).

This expansive view of privacy remains controversial, leading groups like the Electronic Privacy Information Center and the Electronic Freedom Forum to call for clearer, more specific laws to specify privacy rights.[10] The right to privacy for an individual assumes a generalized "right to be let alone" without his or her name, image, or daily activities becoming public "property." Whereas libel laws safeguard a person's character and reputation, the right to privacy protects an individual's peace of mind and personal feelings. Some of the most common invasions of privacy include one or more of the following:

- intrusion in which unauthorized tape recorders, wiretaps, microphones, or other surveillance equipment are used to secretly record a person's private affairs
- the publication of private matters, such as the unauthorized disclosure of private statements about an individual's health, sexual activities, or economic status
- the unauthorized appropriation of a person's name or image for advertising or other commercial benefit.

As we have noted, the courts have generally given the news media a lot of leeway under the First Amendment. The names and pictures of both private individuals and public figures can usually be used without their consent as part of news stories, and the courts have typically allowed the news media to record their quotes and use their images without the individual's permission. The argument is that the value of news coverage for the public good outweighs the individuals' right to privacy.

 **FLASH FACT**

People magazine reportedly paid $14 million for the first picture of Brad Pitt and Angelina Jolie's baby twins. The money went to the couple's charitable foundation.[11]

Public figures, including celebrities, have often accused the media of invading their privacy in the attempt to capture a revealing picture or get the inside "scoop" on a story. With increasing regularity, we hear about a Hollywood actor or sports figure punching a tabloid photographer or TV camera man who got too close. Actor Jennifer Aniston brought a privacy lawsuit against *Celebrity Skin* magazine in 2000 for printing photos of her sunbathing topless in her backyard. The suit claimed a photographer climbed her neighbor's fence to take the photos.

As with libel when applied to public figures, the standards for invasion of privacy are set higher. But the death of Princess Diana in 1997, followed by other high-profile cases, led to widespread calls for legislation in Europe and the U.S. to restrain the so-called "paparazzi" and protect celebrities and public figures from aggressive "stocking" by reporter and photographers.

In 1999, as a result of heavy lobbying by a coalition of celebrities, the Screen Actors Guild, and victims' rights groups, California enacted the first "anti-paparazzi" law in the U.S. which created tort liability for "physical" and "constructive" invasions of privacy through photographing, videotaping, or recording a person engaging in a "personal or familial activity." Since then, many other states have passed similar laws that have included the prohibition of trespassing or using electronic devices (such as zoom lenses on cameras) to capture audio or video images of a celebrity or crime victim during personal or family activity on private property or outside public forums. The verdict on the status of celebrity protection from invasion of privacy, however, is still out. The American Civil Liberties Union (ACLU) has challenged some of the new laws as an infringement of the First Amendment protection of free press.

Indecency and Obscenity

The First Amendment was originally framed to protect political speech, political criticism, and religious choice, but this tradition of free speech has gradually been extended to other areas such as the expression of sexuality. Not all such "expressions," however, are protected. For most of the nation's history, it has been argued that obscenity does not constitute a legitimate form of expression. The problem, however, is that little agreement has existed on how to define an obscene work. In the 1860s, a court could deem a book obscene if a single passage was believed capable of corrupting a person. In fact, throughout the 1800s, U.S. post office and customs officials and other authorities outside the courts also had the power to censor or destroy written material they deemed obscene.

James Joyce's novel *Ulysses* (1922) was held suspect because of the four-letter words contained in the novel, and in 1928 the U.S. Customs Office officially banned the novel as an obscene work. In 1933, a U.S. judge ruled that *Ulysses* was an important literary work and removed it from unprotected status. Other novels such as D.H. Lawrence's *Lady Chatterley's Lover* (1928) were widely subjected to censorship in the U.S. as recently as the 1950s. Since then books, magazines, radio, film, and TV have continued to be subject to content controls regarding sexuality and language.

Community Standards The courts have ruled that moral standards for print and other media cannot be decided on a national basis, because standards vary among communities. Communities are permitted to develop their own local standards for treatment of sexuality and obscenity. The U.S. Supreme Court defined **obscenity** in community-based terms: "whether to the average person, applying contemporary standards, the dominant theme of the material taken as a whole appeals to prurient interest" (*Roth v. United States*, 1957). Refining Roth, the current legal definition of obscenity derives from the 1973 *Miller v. California* case. The Supreme Court argued that an obscene work had to meet three criteria:

* The average person, applying contemporary community standards, would find that the material as a whole appeals to prurient interest.
* The material depicts or describes sexual conduct in a patently offensive way.
* The material as a whole lacks serious literary, artistic, political, or scientific value.

States can choose to prohibit the printing or sale of works that they have judged as meeting these criteria. For example, some communities define certain books, magazines, and videos as "obscene" and restrict their sales to adult bookstores or require their covers to be concealed when on public display. The courts have also restricted material deemed

Table 8.1   The Top 15 Most Frequently Challenged Books of 1990–2000

1. *Scary Stories* (Series) by Alvin Schwartz
2. *Daddy's Roommate* by Michael Willhoite
3. *I Know Why the Caged Bird Sings* by Maya Angelou
4. *The Chocolate War* by Robert Cormier
5. *The Adventures of Huckleberry Finn* by Mark Twain
6. *Of Mice and Men* by John Steinbeck
7. *Harry Potter* (Series) by J.K. Rowling
8. *Forever* by Judy Blume
9. *Bridge to Terabithia* by Katherine Paterson
10. *Alice* (Series) by Phyllis Reynolds Naylor
11. *Heather Has Two Mommies* by Leslea Newman
12. *My Brother Sam Is Dead* by James Lincoln Collier and Christopher Collier
13. *The Catcher in the Rye* by J.D. Salinger
14. *The Giver* by Lois Lowry
15. *It's Perfectly Normal* by Robie Harris

Out of 6,364 challenges reported to or recorded by the Office for intellectual Freedom, as compiled by the Office for intellectual Freedom, American Library Association

"indecent." **Indecent** material contains sexual or excretory material that does not rise to the level of obscenity. For this reason, the courts have held that indecent material is protected by the First Amendment and cannot be banned entirely. It may, however, be restricted in places such as school libraries or radio and TV broadcast during times of the day when there is a reasonable risk that children may be in the audience. See Table 8.1 for a listing of the books most commonly banned by children's libraries.

Limits on Broadcasting   In theory, communication law prevents the government from directly censoring broadcast content. The government may not interfere with programs or engage in prior restraint, although it may punish broadcasters for indecency or profanity after the fact. Concerns over indecent broadcast programming have been traced back as far as 1937. That year, NBC was reprimanded by the FCC after running a comedy sketch *Edgar* featuring actress Mae West and Edgar Bergen's famous wooden ventriloquist's dummy, Charlie McCarthy:

> WEST: That's all right, I like a man that takes his time. Why don't you come home with me? I'll let you play in my woodpile. You're all wood and a yard long . . .
> CHARLIE: Oh Mae, don't, don't . . . don't be so rough. To love me is peace and quiet.
> WEST: That ain't love—that's sleep.[12]

In the 1960s, topless radio featured deejays and callers discussing intimate sexual subjects in the middle of the afternoon. Although the discussion would likely seem tame compared to today's shock jock programming, in 1973 the chairman of the FCC denounced the broadcasts as "a new breed of air pollution . . . with the suggestive, coaxing, pear shaped tones of the smut-hustling host." Some stations were fined and a few even lost their licenses. That same year, the FCC disciplined the Pacifica radio station for broadcasting comedian George Carlin's monologue "The Seven Dirty Words You Can't say on Radio." The FCC defined indecency as "language that describes, in terms patently offensive as measured by contemporary community standards for the broadcast of the medium, sexual or excretory activities or organs," and its action was upheld by the Supreme Court (*FCC v. Pacifica Foundation*, 1978).

Obscenity and indecency have faced greater limitations on broadcasts because they come via airwaves straight into the home, presumably making them more accessible to children. Since the 1978 Pacifica decision, there has been a tendency to limit indecency on radio and television during the hours when children are likely to be listening and to create "safe havens" for absolutely free speech from midnight to 6 a.m. You may have noticed that cable channels often contain what might be considered indecent material at all hours, but, because cable does not use public airwaves, it has not faced the same FCC scrutiny.

During the 1990s, the FCC became gradually more permissive in allowing nudity and references to sexuality on cable TV, and to a lesser degree on broadcast as well. However, that began to change dramatically in 2004. That year, the FCC received major waves of complaints after Janet Jackson's breast was exposed during the Superbowl half-time show and then again after Monday Night Football featured an ad with a naked Nicolette Sheridan jumping into the arms of Eagles receiver Terrell Own to promote the show *Desperate Housewives*. More than 500,000 complaints over the Janet Jackson incident led the FCC to take a much harsher stance on indecency and there was a significant jump in the number of fines handed out to broadcasters.[13]

One highly publicized result of this shift was frequent FCC target Howard Stern's move to satellite radio. On his syndicated radio show, Stern prayed for cancer to kill public officials he did not like, joked about bodily functions, and has insulted virtually every societal group. The FCC had issued fines in excess of $1 million to stations that carry Stern's show, so Stern opted to move to satellite radio because it was not subject to the same indecency rules since ordering the service is voluntary. Some in Congress, however, have suggested applying broadcast rules to cable and satellite.

Indecency and the Internet   The Internet poses new challenges for the regulation of indecency, particularly regarding efforts to restrict access for children. There were several attempts to mandate filtering programs in schools and libraries that would screen and block sexual content. Civil liberties groups such as the American Library Association firmly opposed the use of filtering programs, arguing that they could unreasonably limit adult access to information. The Communications Decency Act (CDA) within the Telecommunications Act of 1996 tried to create a more inclusive definition of what might be deemed objectionable under the term "indecency," but its definition was problematic. It was unclear, for example, whether the word "breast" might be considered indecent in some contexts, like erotica, but not in others, like a discussion of cancer.

The CDA was challenged in court by the American Civil Liberties Union, the Electronic Frontier Foundation, and companies such as America Online who feared being held responsible for transmitting indecent material. In making their case, they argued that the Internet deserves the same broad First Amendment protection enjoyed by print, rather than the more limited protection granted broadcasting. They argued that the efforts to protect children were exacting too great a toll on the free speech rights of adults. The Supreme Court agreed, and overturned key aspects of the CDA. In hopes of passing First Amendment scrutiny, prohibitions of the 1998 Child On-line Protection Act were narrowed to cover only commercial sites, target only content harmful to children, and require age verification only on adult sites. Congress tried again to tighten controls on indecency via filtering software with the Children's Internet Protection Act of 2001. It required public schools and libraries to block access to material defined as indecent or risk losing federal funding. In 2003, the Supreme Court reversed its earlier stand and found the law constitutional. It has been enforced on all schools and libraries who receive federally funded assistance for Internet access under the FCC's e-Rule program.

Censorship and Incitement

People have often sought to place restrictions on expression that is considered inflammatory, inciting people to panic or riot. In many parts of the world, these fears have been used to justify heavy restrictions and even bans on media and individual expression. Although most common in totalitarian states, there are also many cases of such restrictions in democratic countries, particularly early in their development or during times of war or unrest. In 2008, the Iraqi government placed heavy restrictions on Al Jazeera and Al Arabiya, two of the most popular Arab networks, accusing them of inciting violence against members of the Governing Council and fanning animosities between Shiite and Sunni Muslims, the two main sects in Iraq.

In the United States, the Supreme Court ruled that expression that incites unlawful conduct is not protected under the First Amendment; however, subversive or inflammatory speech which falls short of such incitement has been afforded protection. In reversing the conviction of a Ku Klux Klan leader who gave a speech warning "that there might have to be some revengeance taken" for "continued suppression of the white, Caucasian race," the Court held that the First Amendment allows punishment only of subversive advocacy calculated to produce "imminent lawless action," which is likely to produce such action (*Brandenburg v. Ohio*, 1969). One, perhaps seemingly unlikely, form of entertainment that has been commonly accused of incitement is music.

Inflammatory Music   In early music, traveling musicians often carried news from one region to the next. There are old stories about Irish harpists having their hands cut for telling unapproved news. Totalitarian regimes in particular have censored music for the same reasons that they are prone to censoring literature, theatre, cinema, painting, and other art forms. Islamic fundamentalist governments, such as in Iran under the Ayatollahs and Afghanistan under the Taliban, have at times banned music completely, at least that of a secular nature. Similar laws were invoked in the seventeenth century in Britain under the Commonwealth of England. Though the Bolshevik Revolution in what would become the Soviet Union briefly inspired a new cultural renaissance, through most of its existence the Soviet Union censored all art forms, including music. Many of its prominent composers obviously felt restricted by this censorship, which often dictated that all pieces end in a major key and be uplifting.

In western democracies songs have been banned by the radio stations or the government from receiving radio airplay owing to their lyrical content. In the 1920s, some people viewed jazz as morally loose, whereas many white racists of the 1950s had unkind words for the early rock they associated with the "Negro" community. Others were angered by the war protest and drug-glorifying songs of the 1960s. Although the government rarely responds with direct efforts to censor music, the FCC has worked indirectly to keep some music off the market by pressuring radio stations to restrict the airplay of offensive songs.

This has often had a counter-productive effect, with the records concerned increasing sales as a result of the curiosity engendered by the ban: in 1977, year of Queen Elizabeth's silver jubilee, the Sex Pistols' single "God Save the Queen" reached number two in the U.K. Top 40 after being banned, largely for political reasons. In the U.S., religiously inspired outrage has also been known to lead to the public burning of music considered unholy: in 1966 recordings by The Beatles were destroyed by conservative Christians in the U.S. after John Lennon stated that the Beatles were bigger than Jesus.

FCC broadcasting regulations include a mandate that radio stations that are dedicated to serving the public interest should know the content of lyrics they play. The implication? Police the songs you play, or risk losing your broadcast license. The logic is that record labels, recognizing their dependence on airplay, become equally hesitant to produce offensive music.

In the 1980s, groups such as the Parents' Music Resource Center (PMRC) came out strongly against popular music lyrical themes focusing on sex, violence, Satanism, and drugs or alcohol use, claiming links between explicit lyrics and inciting social ills such as teen suicide, teen pregnancy, physical abuse, broken homes, and criminal activity. Some of the songs singled out for opposition included Prince's song "Sister," thought to glorify incest; Mötley Crüe's "Live Wire," for its fascination with strangulation; and Guns N' Roses songs, accused of expressing racism.

Music labels responded to the pressure exerted by these groups with voluntary labeling schemes, as mentioned above, to warn consumers about songs containing explicit lyrics. Although some groups lauded these efforts, many felt they did not go far enough. Some critics advocated censorship and age-restricted sales policies, arguing that voluntary labeling only increased the music's appeal to curious and rebellious young listeners. In the highly publicized case of Ice T's song "Cop Killer," Time Warner did eventually pull the music from the market.

SPOTLIGHT ON MUSIC CENSORSHIP   Time Warner "Cop Killer" Protest[14]

In 1992, Time Warner rap music recording artist Ice T (a.k.a. Tracey Marrow) and his new band, Body Count,

released their first album. Included on the album was a song called "Cop Killer," in which the lyrics openly advocated the killing of police officers as a form of social protest.

Police officers from across the nation, as well as many others, were outraged by the release of this song, accusing it of intentionally aiming to incite violence against law enforcement. Time Warner defended the album as a free speech issue protected by the Constitution.

Police associations called for citizens to boycott Time Warner and all of its subsidiaries, including its publications, cable companies, and amusement parks. One form of protest included taking subscription cards from Time Warner magazines and mailing them back with a written protest. Not only did Time Warner have to pay the postage for the returned cards, it had to pay their employees to sort through them. Literally thousands of these cards were mailed to Time Warner from across the country.

In July 1992 Time Warner's annual shareholders' meeting was held in Beverly Hills, California. CLEAT (Combined Law Enforcement Associations of Texas), along with major police associations from across the nation, planned a protest for the day of the shareholders' meeting. Hundreds of police officers flew to California for this protest, which attracted national media attention. Even Ice T showed up and indicated his opinion of the protestors with a well-recognized hand gesture.

Time Warner eventually pulled the album from the market, a move that Ice T attributed in a later interview to the pressure the police put on Time Warner during the entire controversy.

Source: Combined Law Enforcement Associations of Texas (CLEAT)

What do you think?

- *Could music possibly incite people to violence, and if it can, does the government have a responsibility to restrict or even ban it?*

The Power of Film When movies first came into existence in the 1890s, many people were concerned about the power of this vivid new medium to create an illusory dream world and influence audiences. These fears spurred the formation of censorship groups which believed that movies would threaten children, incite violence, and undermine morality. In 1907, the Chicago City Council created an ordinance that gave the police authority to issue permits for a movie's exhibition. After Jack Johnson won the heavyweight championship in 1908, boxing films became the target of the first federal law aimed at the motion-picture industry. As the first black heavyweight boxing champion, Johnson's stunning victory over the fighter Jim Jeffries (who had earlier refused to fight black boxers) in 1910 resulted in race riots across the country. In 1912, the government outlawed the transportation of boxing movies across state lines. It is argued, however, that this law had more to do with Johnson's race than with concerns regarding the inflammatory potential of violence in movies. As the first black heavyweight champion, Johnson was perceived as a threat to the white community.

In 1915, the Mutual Film Company of Detroit sued the state of Ohio, whose review board had censored a number of its films. On appeal, the Supreme Court ruled that film was not a form of speech, but a "business pure and simple" and, like the circus, merely a "spectacle" for entertainment with a "special capacity for 'evil'" (*Mutual v. Ohio*, 1915). By 1923, 22 states and more than 90 cities in the United States had some type of movie censorship board made up of vice squad officers, politicians, or citizen groups.

Industry Self-regulation In the hopes of avoiding increasing government-mandated content controls, entertainment industries have made many attempts at self-regulation. Facing a new round of challenges in the 1930s brought on by the deteriorating economic conditions of the Great Depression, and protests made by the influential Catholic Legion of Decency, the film industry tightened its efforts at self-regulation to keep public pressure at bay. In 1927, the Hays Office had developed a list of "Don'ts and Be Carefuls" to steer producers and directors away from questionable sexual, moral, and social themes. In the early 1930s, the Hays Office established a more formal Motion Picture Production Code.

Its first general principle read: "No picture shall be produced which will lower the moral standards of those who see it. Hence the sympathy of the audience shall never be thrown to the side of crime, wrong-doing, evil or sin."

The self-regulatory code dictated how producers and directors should handle "methods of crime," "repellent subjects," illegal drug traffic," and "sex hygiene." Under "scenes of passion," the code mandated that "excessive and lustful kissing, lustful embraces, suggestive postures and gestures are not to be shown," and it required that "passion should be treated in such a manner as not to stimulate the lower and baser emotions." It included a section on profanity outlawing a long list of phrases and topics, including "toilet gags" and "traveling salesmen and farmer's daughter jokes."

The producers of *Gone with the Wind* had to seek a special dispensation so that actor Clark Gable could say "damn." The section on religion reflected the influence of Jesuit priest Daniel Lord and Catholic publisher Martin Quigley, who helped write the code: "No film or episode may throw ridicule on any religious faith," and "ministers of religion . . . should not be used as comic characters or as villains." The code was adopted by 96 percent of the industry, influencing almost all films made between the mid-1930s and the early 1950s. With advent of TV, however, increased competition for audiences led many producers to begin pushing the envelope on many of these standards.

In 1952, a movie distributor sued the head of the New York Film Licensing Board for banning Roberto Rossellini's 1948 film *Il Miracolo* (The Miracle). The Italian film tells the story of an unmarried peasant girl who is impregnated by a scheming vagrant who convinces her that he is St. Joseph and she is having the baby Jesus. A few New York City religious and political leaders considered the film sacrilegious and pressured the film board for the ban. The film distributor argued that banning the film constituted illegal prior restraint, which would be illegal to impose on a print version of the story, and so should likewise not be imposed on film. The Supreme Court eventually agreed, declaring movies "a significant medium for the communication of ideas" (*Burstyn v. Wilson*, 1952). They granted films the same protection as those extended to print media and other forms of speech, rendering most activities of film review boards unconstitutional, since they had generally been enforced via prior restraint.

Nonetheless, the film industry still engages in significant self-monitoring. The most widely recognized of these efforts is the film rating system. Instituted in 1966 by the Motion Picture Association of America (MPAA), the ratings were designed to alert people to what they might encounter in a film so they could make a more informed choice in deciding whether or not they wanted to see it. After several modifications, the MPAA rating categories are as follows:

Rated **G**—General Audiences. All ages admitted. No sex or nudity, minimal violence.
Rated **PG**—Parental Guidance suggested. Some material may not be suitable for children; mild profanity, non-"excessive" violence, only a glimpse of nudity.
Rated **PG-13**—Parent strongly cautioned. Some material may be inappropriate for children under 13.
Rated **R**—Restricted. Those under 17 must be accompanied by a parent or guardian; may contain very rough violence, nudity, or sexual content.
Rated **NC-17**—No one under 17 admitted; formerly rated X; generally reserved for films that are openly pornographic, although some mainstream films receive this rating.

These ratings have been the source of much debate. Some people argue that, although it is not government-mandated, as a form of industry self-censorship, the rating

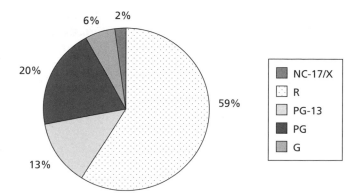

Figure 8.1 Ratings
Breakdowns 1968–2007

system still violates filmmakers' freedom of speech. This concern is amplified by charges of biases and inconsistencies in the ratings. For example, it is often charged that even mild nudity and sexual content leads to more restrictive ratings than strong violent content receives (see *A Closer Look* at the end of the chapter).

Others argue that, as with music lyric advisories, more restrictive ratings simply tempt the interest of young viewers. There are also complaints that audience restrictions for R and NC-17 rated films are not enforced by theaters who are reluctant to turn away the teens who are the main movie-goers. Furthermore, such enforcement is difficult because at multiplex theaters teens will buy tickets for a PR movie, then slip into an R-rated one. Last, those who might have hoped that such ratings would discourage filmmakers from producing films with sexually explicit and violent content have also been disappointed. According to the MPAA, R-rated films constituted 59 percent of films by rating from 1968 through 2007, and the percentage of R-rated films has been on the rise over the past five years.[15] However, many people, particularly parents of young children, have expressed appreciation for the ratings, which at least provide some information for guiding their viewing.

 **FLASH FACT**

The top grossing PG-13 rated film of all time, *Titanic* (1997), grossed $600,788,188, while the top grossing R-rated film, *The Passion of the Christ* (2004), grossed only $370,782,930 which raises the question of why so many R-rated films are being produced.

In 2003, the television industry proposed a similar set of standards for voluntary labeling of violent content, but critics felt that simple labeling was not enough. In response, Congress added a provision in the 1996 Telecommunications Act requiring a V-chip to permit TV viewers to block out programs rated as containing sex or violence. In an interesting combination of government and self-regulation, the industry was required to come up with a rating system. Although critics had hoped for a system with separate ratings for levels of sex, violence, and indecent language in each program, the industry settled on an age-based system modeled on film ratings.

Thus, the system represented a compromise between what industry, Congress, and critics wanted. The current TV rating system actually does make some content distinctions

(S for sexuality, V for violence, D for dialog). Ultimately, however, surveys of viewers with V-chip sets have shown that very few were using the screening option.[17] In turn, there have been efforts to establish rating systems for language, violence, and sexual content in music and music videos. There are many other examples of industry self-regulation such as the National Association of Broadcasters' standards for the amount of commercial time to be included in broadcasting hours. In the following chapter we will explore additional efforts at self-regulation in the entertainment industries in the form of established ethical standards and codes of conduct.

Intellectual Property and Copyright

Appropriating an author's or producer's work without consent or payment is not a protected form of expression. Published or unpublished writings, music and lyrics, TV programs and movies, still images, art and graphics are all considered **intellectual property**. Intellectual property is governed by patent, copyrights, and trademark law to insure that people receive the economic benefit from selling, leasing, renting, or licensing their work.

Patents give inventors the exclusive rights to their inventions for 17 years, during which time they can demand royalties from others who wish to use them. Patents are usually applied to new inventions, like RCA's patent pool to assemble all the new inventions required for broadcasting and receiving radio sounds. The goal is to encourage new technologies and industries through rewarding invention.

Copyright, identifying and granting own- The law takes copyright violations seriously
ership of a given piece of expression, is
similarly designed to promote the development of artist, scientific, and other expression by protecting the creator's financial interest in that expression. Article I, Section 8 of the U.S. Constitution authorized a national copyright system to "promote the Progress of Science and useful Arts, by securing for limited Times to Authors . . . the exclusive Right to their Writings." Many forms of entertainment such as the content of books, movies, video games, and music are considered intellectual property, and thus are subject to copyright protection. Producers now even copyright the format of reality TV programs, and then license the format to others. A British production company created the series *Wife Swap* and licensed it to ABC. When Fox created a similar series called *Trading Spouses*, the British company sued, claiming that the Fox series was a "blatant and wholesale copycat" of the British show.

Copyright laws have been subjected to extensive revision over the years. Current law says that you do not have to file any paperwork or make any claim in order to receive a copyright. Any creative work is automatically copyrighted when it is produced. A copyright means all rights reserved. No one can legally use or adapt the work without gaining explicit permission from the copyright holder. In 1998, the U.S. Congress passed the Copyright Term Extension Act (CTEA) which extended copyright protection for creators in all media to the span of their lives, plus 70 years. During this period, permission for the use of the material must be obtained from the copyright holder and, if requested, a fee or royalty must be paid and the original creators can sue people who imitate or adapt their works commercially without permission.

SPOTLIGHT ON STAR OWNERSHIP   The Legal Battle over Marilyn

More than 40 years after her death, Marilyn Monroe's photos are used to hawk everything from T-shirts to wine. The battle in 2006 over who controls the rights to her profitable image involved over $30 million in fees for the two litigants. Bringing suit are Anna Strasberg (wife of former acting coach) and her business partner (professional peddler of dead peoples' images), plus the families of four photographers who snapped her pictures but who have earned far less in licensing fees. Confusion over Marilyn's residency at her time of death is a central issue in the case.

Ms. Strasberg, majority owner of Monroe's rights of publicity—using images for commercial purposes—insists the star was a Californian. The photographers, who own copyrighted images of the star, have asked the courts to declare her a New Yorker. Unlike copyrights that are protected by federal law, publicity rights are creatures of state laws. Monroe was born and grew up in California and moved to New York to study acting, seven years before her death. In her will, the actress left much of her $800,000 estate to Ms. Strasberg and a smaller portion to her psychiatrist.

Ms. Strasberg launched her Monroe licensing business in 1982 and hired Los Angeles lawyer Roger Richman to harness publicity rights. Richman helped Strasberg to net over $7.5 million over 13 years.

In 1996, Strasberg dismissed Richman and hired Mark Roesler, owner of Indianapolis-based CMG Worldwide, to manage the Monroe publicity rights. Known as the "king of the dead celebrity business," Roesler also represents James Dean, the second most valuable dead-star brand.

The greatest threat to Strasberg's control of the Monroe image are the children of the deceased photographers who licensed her photos to makers of calendars, handbags, and a high-end winery. Strasberg is suing because she alleges some of the children's deals violated Monroe's publicity rights by excluding her from the licensing revenue. The photographers countersued, claiming Strasberg has no right to revenue because Monroe came from New York, where publicity rights expire at death. The photographers' children worry that the star's image is fading and manufacturers won't enter into licensing deals if they have to pay fees to two sets of rights holders.

Lawyers for the photographers' families attempted to prove that Ms. Monroe's Manhattan apartment where she lived with Arthur Miller until their 1961 divorce was her residence at the time of death. Strasberg's lawyers offer proof that Monroe's California residence has an inscription that reads, "Here my journey ends." At this writing, the trial had not begun.

Source: Nathan Koppel for *The Wall Street Journal*, April 10, 2006

What do you think?

- *Should publicity rights cease at a star's death?*
- *Should federal law supersede state law in this instance?*

In most cases, if you make money from someone else's creative work, that money belongs to the person who owns the copyright to the material unless you have obtained his or her prior approval. Once copyright expires, and, if the creator does not renew it, the material passes into the **public domain**, which means that it can be used without permission. Countries vary in the copyright protection they afford, however, so some works that are still copyrighted for years to come in the U.S. are not protected in other parts of the world. For instance, in the United States, the novel *Gone with the Wind*, written by Margaret Mitchell, will not enter the public domain until 2031, 95 years after its original publication. However, in Australia and elsewhere, the book was free of copyright restrictions in 1999, only 50 years after the author's death. Songs by 1950s and 1960s artists like Elvis Presley and The Beatles are nearing the end of copyright protection in some European countries, so the International Federation for the Phonographic Industry, a trade group for record companies, is urging the European Union to extend copyright protection for them.

Two specific qualifications of copyright law have been extended to recorded music and cable TV. Although most cable companies do create some of their own content, the crux of their profits come from collecting material from original sources (other production, broadcast, and syndication companies) and selling it to their subscribers. Owing to the sheer volume of material that cable companies import and deliver, obtaining permission from all the copyright holders would be very difficult. To solve the problem of compensating content creators, the Copyright Royalty Tribunal was created, to which cable companies paid a fee based primarily on the size of their operation. The money collected was then distributed to the appropriate producers, syndicators, and broadcasters; however, Congress abolished the Tribunal in 1993, and cable copyright issues were left to several different arbitration panels overseen by the Library of Congress.

Songwriters face an even greater challenge in collecting royalties from all those who use their music—not only film producers and radio and television stations but also bowling alleys, supermarkets, and restaurants. **Music licensing** companies were created to solve this dilemma. The two largest of these are the American Society of Composers, Authors and Publishers (ASCAP) and Broadcast Music, Inc. (BMI). These companies collect fees based on the users' gross receipts and distribute the money to songwriters and artists.

New Media Concerns   New media are at the heart of the heated battle over intellectual property rights. Some of the primary advantages of many forms of new media entertainment are that they allow for easy, high-quality duplication, manipulation, and circulation. Unfortunately, this advantage is what concerns many intellectual property owners. As we have seen, many authors, artists, and others who own this property argue that today's technology makes it too easy for others to copy their work without properly compensating them. In computer software, TV programs, and music, in particular, it is sometimes hard to prove that someone else has copied your idea.

From a software perspective, patents are superior to a mere copyright because they protect against **reverse engineering**—making a copy of an invention that performs the same basic functions as the inventor's but uses different underlying components or instructions. In contrast, copyright offers protection only against duplication of the underlying computer instructions and of the screen display and command sequences—the general "look and feel" of software, such as a spreadsheet program. Until 1990, computer software was considered unpatentable because it was argued that computers merely executed mathematical formulas that were the product of mental processes, rather than patentable devices. Today, however, software, and even the practices of Internet-based businesses, can be patented. Amazon.com holds a patent on the "one click" shopping methods that let consumers return to the site to place additional orders without re-entering their credit card information. Priceline.com holds a patent on its "reverse auction" method in which buyers set the price and sellers bid to meet it.

Although patent and copyright holders are happy with the added protection recent legislation has afforded, some critics argue that the balance has tipped too far in their favor. In addition to extending the life of copyright to life plus 70 years, in 1998 the CTEA also made Internet service providers (ISPs) liable if they knowingly carry sites that violate copyright rules. Companies such as Disney and Time Warner have become very aggressive in bringing legal action against sites that use images from copyright works they control. Since much of the content on many web sites is user-generated, however, ISPs have questioned their liability for user activity and pointed to the difficulties of policing and preventing copyright violations.

In January 2000, a California Superior Court ruled the posting of DVD decryption software to be illegal. The defendants argued that they did not violate copyright, but the court ruled against them because they posted "tools" on the web that would allow others to violate copyright. This decision led tech writer Gillmor to sarcastically comment, "Let's ban cars next. Were you aware that bank robbers use them for getaways?"[18] That same year, a New York court reaffirmed the ban on posting decryption software, adding that even posting links to sites that offer the software was a violation of copyright.

SPOTLIGHT ON DIGITAL RIGHTS Publishing Industry Tackles Copyrights

EReader, a leader in electronic books, uses a home-made licensing scheme for its downloadable books, with the encryption key for each book based on the credit card number used to purchase the book. The system pretty much eliminates public swapping of license keys, while giving broad rights to the purchasers.

Rights Expression Language (REL), a standard published by the International Standards Organization (ISO), is a good starting point that would give publishers a common framework for communicating their copy-protection intentions.

Although there's no Napster for books, creators of text and images still have to deal with a lot of the same digital rights management issues perplexing the movie and music industries. Publishing industry experts at the Seybold 2004 trade show in San Francisco considered a variety of digital rights management (DRM) challenges during panel discussions, beginning with the proliferation of schemes for securing digital wares.

Creative Commons, a nonprofit group promoting a "some rights reserved" approach to DRM, espouses similar goals but with different technology. Its approach would imbed each document with metadata that tell the consumers what level of protection the author seeks. The approach has several advantages, including the ability to present multiple views of the rights documentation —a wordy legal version, a machine-readable version, and a "regular humans" version minus the legalese.

While text publishers face some of the same DRM issues as entertainment studios—consumer acceptance, hackability versus ease of use—the industry also poses some unique challenges.

Educational publishers, for example, face the prospect of a whole product line being wiped out from a few file swaps. Carline Haga, director of the global rights group for textbook publisher Thomson Learning, said the publisher's biggest copy protection headaches come from illicit copies of the sample test questions teachers get as part of a textbook package.

According to Haga, one purloined test key can mean a book has to be junked, resulting in a potential loss of $20 million for a popular textbook. Teacher solution manuals are showing up on peer-to-peer networks, eBay, and other places. Once that happens, it can kill a textbook. "It means we're in a position where our biggest concern isn't protecting the things we sell, but the things we give away," she said.

Source: David Becker Staff Writer, CNET News.com, August 18, 2004

Napster, one of the first major music exchange sites on the Internet, ran afoul of provisions of the CTFA and Millennium Copyright Act. In its defense, Napster cited another part of the law that exempts ISPs, claiming that it had no way of knowing which music files were pirated. The company also cited the Audio Home Recording Act of 1991, which established the right of consumers to make copies of their own records and tapes for their own non-commercial use. The recording industry argued that most Napster users did not own the recordings they were "sharing" and that widespread swapping was undermining the market for copyrighted recordings. It added that the Home Recording Act only protected hardware devices (like tape recorders) that make copies, not software that makes copies, like Internet exchange programs or even digital personal video recorders. As the result of lawsuits alleging that it facilitated piracy, Napster was driven out of business, but other Internet sites and programs emerged to offer similar services. Napster, itself, re-emerged under new ownership as a pay-to-download music site in 2003 and music rental site in 2005.

 **FLASH FACT**

The Recording Industry Artists Association had taken over 4,000 music exchangers to court by 2005 to make the criminalization of digital music copying more visible and effective.[19]

I Want My MP3: Dubbing and Piracy   In the 1970s, instead of buying records and tapes, people began dubbing music from shared records or live concerts onto inexpensive blank tapes. Radio stations would often even announce when they would be playing uninterrupted albums so dubbers could tape off the radio. The Internet and organizations like Napster and MP3 revolutionized dubbing by enabling listeners to post, find, listen to, and download music from the web.

Of course, if people dub instead of buy their music, the recording industry and artists lose that potential revenue. Some people, however, claim that music sharing on the

Internet has actually led them to increase their legal music purchases by making them more aware of new and different music. Nonetheless, the Recording Industry of America estimates that the industry loses $1.5 billion a year—the equivalent of about one-fifth of its sales—as the result of illegal dubbing.

The industry has taken several steps to try to compensate for losses like these. First, in 1992, the U.S. Congress approved a "taping tax"—a 1 percent fee on blank tape sales that is passed along to songwriters, music publishers, and others who lose royalty income from home dubbing. The tax was later extended to blank CD purchases. As discussed above, the industry has also engaged in lengthy legal battles to shut down illegal dubbing operations, including Internet sites that facilitate online dubbing. The four major recording companies eventually began entering into licensing agreements with online music distributors such as

Hong Kong customs officials sort through 600,000 smuggled music and video compact discs

iTunes and others; however, the debate still rages on regarding the best way to guard against illegal music sharing and downloading.

Internationally, piracy poses an even greater problem. Information software and entertainment products are among America's main exports to the rest of the world. It is particularly difficult to ensure that no one copies these products in international markets without paying for their use. Some countries have permitted practices that the United States considers illegal. Pirating and nonpayment of royalties have been particularly sensitive issues between the U.S. and China.

Chinese entrepreneurs have duplicated cassettes, often distributing first-run films before they hit theaters in the U.S. The image above shows Hong Kong customs officials sorting through music and video compact discs after they seized 600,000 discs worth $1.3 million. The discs were being smuggled in 1998 from the nearby Portuguese enclave of Macau, which, with Hong Kong, saw an explosion of copyright piracy after a clamp-down in mainland China.

As many countries other than the United States, including China, have their own stake in protecting national revenues from intellectual property sales abroad, international negotiations have made much more progress in recent years. Both the World Trade Organization and more specialized organizations such as the World Intellectual Property Organization (WIPO) have worked on gaining endorsements for international standards and agreements. Two new WIPO agreements extend copyright protection into digital formats, particularly the Internet and digital storage of music and film. Some U.S. policy makers, however, are concerned that these two treaties are restrictive, endangering the fair use protections that are afforded by U.S. law.

Fair Use There are instances considered *fair uses* in which material can be used without permission or payment. Fair uses include (1) limited non-commercial use, such as photocopying a passage from a novel for classroom use; (2) use of limited portions of a work, such as excerpting a few lines or a paragraph or two from a book for use in a magazine article; (3) use that does not decrease the commercial value of the original, such as videotaping a daytime football game for private at-home evening view; and (4) use in the public interest, such as an author's use of line drawings of scenes from an important piece of film.

Until recently, parody was usually considered to be covered by the fair use exception, but the Supreme Court did not actually rule on this until 1994 (*Campbell v. Acuff-Rose Music*, 1994). In a unanimous decision, the Court ruled that the rap group 2 Live Crew did not violate U.S. copyright when it parodied Roy Orbison's 1964 uplifting anthem "Oh, Pretty Woman," in its own, more subversive and cynical, 1989 song "Pretty Woman." The rap group had originally sought permission to use the song's famous first line for its parody, but Acuff-Rose Music, who owned the copyright, rejected their request. When 2 Live Crew went ahead and used the line anyway, creating a hugely popular and profitable hit, Acuff-Rose sued for copyright infringement in the federal court. Ultimately, the Supreme Court sided with 2 Live Crew, agreeing that their parody fell within the fair use exception to copyright protection (see *Spotlight on Fair Use*). The extent of this exception, however, remains unclear. Claims of copyright infringement are decided on a case-by-case basis. Whether or not a parodist, or anyone else, is granted protection under copyright law is still subject to the general rules governing fair use. For instance, if a parody is likely to damage the market for the original work, then the creator may be able to collect damages from the parodist.

SPOTLIGHT ON FAIR USE   That's My Woman: The Case of 2 Live Crew

2 Live Crew wins "Pretty Woman"

When 2 Live Crew decided to use Roy Orbison's 1964 classic song "Oh, Pretty Woman" as inspiration for its own 1989 hit "Pretty Woman," it argued that its version was intended as a parody, a form of speech traditionally understood to be protected as fair use.

In a letter to Acruff-Rose, who held the copyright to "Oh, Pretty Woman," the group's purpose was "through comical lyrics, to satirize the original work."[20] Considered offensive and sexist by many, these lyrics transformed Orbison's pretty woman into a "big hairy woman," "a bald-headed woman," and a "two-timin' woman." Even though 2 Live Crew gave credit for "Oh, Pretty Woman" to Roy Orbison and his coauthor, William Dees, on its album *Clean as They Wanna Be*, Acuff-Rose argued that 2 Live Crew's song was nothing more than a commercial ripoff that made money for the rap group at the copyright owner's expense. Attorneys for the rappers countered that "Pretty Woman" was a legitimate parody and thus exempt from copyright claims.

A federal district court in Nashville decided in favor of 2 Live Crew, but a U.S. court of appeals later reversed the decision, creating concern among the creative community. The appellate court concluded that by "taking the heart of the original and making it the heart of a new work," the rappers had used too much of the original song. In addition, the court ruled that "Pretty Woman" could not be protected as fair use under copyright law because the band had recorded its version for "blatantly commercial purposes."

In a unanimous decision, however, the Supreme Court rejected the appellate court's ruling. Writing for the Court, Justice David Souter suggested that the rap version could be understood "as a comment on the naiveté of the original of an earlier day, as a rejection of its sentiment that ignores the ugliness of street life and the debasement it signifies." In stating that parody's "art lies in the tension between a known original and its parodic twin," the Court ruled that works that adapt or transform an original song "lie at the heart of the fair-use doctrine's guarantee of breathing space within the confines of copyright." Souter stated that 2 Live Crew's parody deserved credit for both "shedding light on an earlier work . . . and creating a new one."

At a time when sampling by musical artists and composite computer imaging and videos have become commonplace, the "Pretty Woman" case drew widespread interest and divided opinions among the entertainment community. Satirists ranging from *Mad Magazine* and political humorist Mark Russell filed friend-of-the-court briefs on behalf of 2 Live Crew, but many songwriters and composers filed briefs in support of the music community. For many artists, it's a difficult call to make. On the one hand, artists don't want someone else to be able to unfairly profit from their hard work; on the other hand, most artists also don't want limits placed on their ability to use existing work as inspiration for their own creative efforts.

Source: www.bc.edu.bc_org/avp.cas/comm/free_speech/campbell.html

What do you think?

- *What sort of fair use allowances and limits should be placed on using or sampling existing work?*
- *Can you think of specific tests or standards that might apply in making these distinctions?*

Policy makers must devise both legal and policy means to help protect intellectual property as technology and society change. Critics, however, also caution that copyright exists to encourage the flow of art, science, and expression, and it grants financial stake to creators, not to enrich those creators but to ensure that there is sufficient incentive to keep the content flowing. According to copyright expert Siva Vaidhyanathan, "It's always important to remember that copyright is a restriction on free speech. Therefore we have to be careful when we play with copyright, because it can have some serious effects on public discourse and creativity."[21]

Would-be authors and artists argue that rules governing intellectual property rights are becoming too strict, limiting artistic and creative freedom. In addition, as we have seen, many new forms of entertainment incorporate elements from entertainment that has come before them. Old stories are made new with updated characters and new twists. A new song might include melodies or lyrical references to older songs. The question becomes: When are such adaptations close enough to the original that individuals must get permission from and provide compensation for the owner of the original work? In addition to the difficulty in determining when permission is necessary, with the proliferation of content on the Internet, it can also be difficult to track down who created a work and ask them for permission.

The fear is that, if permission and compensation requirements are set too rigidly, it may stifle innovation and creativity, particularly among newcomers who lack the financial backing that large, established entertainment producers have for compensation and legal fees.

These concerns inspired a group of legal experts and industry executives to try to develop a system that would enable individuals to protect their rights to their creative work as well as their rights to allow others to legally share and build upon that work, if they so wished. A non-profit organization called Creative Commons (CC) was formed, which released several copyright licenses known as Creative Commons licenses.

These licenses, depending on the one chosen, restrict only certain rights (or none) of the work. The Creative Commons licenses enable copyright holders to grant some or all of their rights to the public while retaining others through a variety of licensing and contract schemes including dedication to the public domain or open content licensing terms. The intention is to avoid the problems current copyright laws create for the sharing of information. Creative Commons defines the spectrum of possibilities between full copyright © (*all rights reserved*) Creative Commons licenses (cc) (*some rights reserved*) and the public domain (pd) (*no rights reserved*) (see Figure 8.2).

When you see the (cc) symbol, you can look up the license type to find out what uses and restrictions the creator has placed on the work. A growing percentage of the entertainment that you can find on the Internet, such as music on MySpace.com and videos on YouTube.com, is covered by these licenses. Although such licensing does not completely resolve the intellectual property rights versus creative freedom debate, it does appear to offer some relief. This debate will likely continue to be an important concern for years to come.

Figure 8.2   Spectrum of Possibilities

Ownership Issues and Business Disputes

The laws and policies governing business practices, not only in the media industries but also in the wider range entertainment industries such as sports, gaming, and hospitality, are far too numerous and varied to address here. However, we can review some key points related to all industries as well as a few examples of how legal issues in specific cases have been negotiated.

Concentration of Ownership

In Chapter 6 we discussed economic and technological forces that have encouraged entertainment enterprises to merge and consolidate into oligopolies where ownership is concentrated in the hands of a few mega-corporations. Government agencies scrutinize all proposed mergers and takeovers, and companies must convince regulators that the advantages gained by such deals are not made at the expense of shareholder and consumer interests. We have reviewed the factors that have motivated companies to consolidate. Corporations gain greater control when operations are all internal rather than spread across different players, and risk is reduced because it is dispersed across a wider range of corporate holdings. Corporate executives argue that the volume and efficiency that such concentration permits enable them to keep costs low and pass on those savings to their shareholders and consumers.

However, we have also noted the government's concern that, if ownership becomes too concentrated, it may unduly limit competition, and thus corporate incentive to set fair market prices. This debate extends beyond entertainment to almost every conceivable industry from agriculture to automobiles. U.S. industries have faced waves of regulation and deregulation as opinions swing regarding whether consolidation or competition better serves societal interests. This battle has been waged particularly fiercely, however, among media industries. As we have seen, the democratic need for a free and diverse press had originally led to particularly stringent limits of concentrated media ownership. As technological advances enabled the capacity for a nearly limitless number of new media outlets, however, many of these restrictions were significantly loosened if not eliminated.

Regulation of Vertical and Horizontal Integration   As explained previously, concentrated ownership can be reflected in **vertical integration**, in which a company owns nearly all aspects of a single industry or **horizontal integration**, in which a company has many holdings of the same medium. The government has placed specific restrictions on both vertical and horizontal media ownership. For example, vertically, the Financial Interest and Syndication (Fin-Syn) Rules, imposed by the federal government, once prohibited the major networks from producing or owning most of their programming. The goal was to ensure that a number of production companies would compete with each other, thus increasing the diversity of content. The networks, however, complained that the Fin-Syn rules weakened them too much, particularly as competition from cable TV increased, and the rules were relaxed in 1991. As a result, however, the diversity of producers has diminished, as a large portion of programming is now produced in house by networks and studios owned by the same groups, forcing many independent production houses to close or merge.

Similarly to promote diverse, preferably local ownership and content, previous U.S. policy also restricted horizontal ownership, for example, first setting the maximum number of radio or TV stations that a single company could own at seven and then expanding it to 12. The 1996 Telecommunications Act eliminated that limit, raised the proportion of U.S. households that could be covered by a TV network's own stations from 25 percent to 35 percent, and set a cap of 30 percent of households that could be covered by a cable system owner. Media owners are even challenging that these limits interfere with their free speech. In 2001, the FCC lifted its ban on one company owning more than one broadcast TV network. There are no national limits on radio ownership, and local ownership limits increase with market size. In 2002, the FCC considered removing more of these limits, but public backlash in the form of millions of complaint letters about concentrated ownership led Congress to prohibit the FCC from increasing ownership limits beyond 39 percent of the national TV market.

The 1996 act also deregulated telephone ownership to permit new combinations of cable TV and phone services. In 2002, AT&T and Comcast took advantage of this deregulation and additional court challenges to ownership limits by merging and greatly expanding the market covered by a single cable operator. In 2004, the FCC lowered requirements for existing providers, such as telephone companies, to facilitate competitors' use of their infrastructure.

Traditionally, U.S. regulators also prohibited a single company from owning various kinds of media, such as radio, TV, newspaper, cable, and telephony systems, again fearing that too much control across platforms would limit the diversity of ideas. The 1996 Telecommunications Act, however, also removed many barriers to cross-ownership, and in 2002, federal courts threw out rules prohibiting cable and TV station cross-ownership rules. These actions permitted the integration of many entertainment platforms such as movie studios, broadcast networks, cable providers, and cable stations. As a result, a few major firms such as Disney/ABC, Fox, and Time Warner now dominate film and TV production, film distribution, network and cable TV distribution and syndication (see Chapter 6).

Similarly, horizontal integration has increased in telecommunication to the point where, in radio, for example, one company, Clear Channel, owns over 1,200 radio stations including most of the stations in many small and large local markets. The extent of this consolidation has led some critics to call for a reassessment of government policies. In addition, to the extent that deregulation and a lack of government oversight has been blamed for precipitating recent scandals and dangerous collapses in real estate, banking, and other industries, we may see another swing toward increased regulation in all industries, including media and entertainment.

Disputes and Negotiations

As we have seen no entertainment industry exists in isolation. They are just as dependent upon each other as they are on the governments, consumers, and communities that they serve. Media such as TV and radio rely on entertainment talent to create programs, music, and personalities that they air. Professional sports organizations rely on TV and radio to broadcast their games to worldwide audiences. These same sports organizations, as well as theme parks, casinos, and other tourist attractions rely on the airlines, hotels, and restaurants that transport, house, and feed their guests. Given these often complex relationships, it is not surprising that conflicts often arise. In this section we will explore some examples of legal disputes that have arisen within and between different entertainment industries and the deals that have been struck to resolve them.

Within Industries: Labor Disputes Many of the legal disputes that have emerged within various industries revolve around conflicts between management and employees or contracted workers. In many of these industries, workers have banded together and organized into **trade or labor unions** to achieve common goals in key areas such as wages, hours, and working conditions. These unions select leaders who bargain with the employer on behalf of union members and negotiate labor contracts with employers. This may include the negotiation of wages, work rules, complaint procedures, rules governing hiring, firing, and promotion of workers, benefits, workplace safety, and policies. The agreements negotiated by the union leaders are binding on the rank and file members and the employer and in some cases on other non-member workers. Trade unions have sometimes been traced back to the guilds of medieval Europe. Medieval guilds existed to protect and enhance their members' livelihoods through controlling the instruction and training of artisanship and the progression of members from apprentice to craftsman, journeyman, and eventually to master and grandmaster of their craft.[22] Modern-day unions, however, first gained traction during the rapid expansion of industrial society in the eighteenth century as women, children, rural workers, and immigrants were drawn to the workforce in larger numbers and in new roles.

Unions were illegal for many years in most countries owing to concerns that they fostered schemes by both employers and employees to fix wages or prices, thus limiting fair market competition. Today, however, the right to unionize is recognized in most democratic societies, and it is also advocated in Article 23, subsection 4 of the Universal Declaration of Human Rights (UDHR), which also states in Article 20, subsection 2, that "No one may be compelled to belong to an association." Prohibiting a person from joining or forming a union, as well as forcing a person to do the same (e.g. "closed shops" or "union shops," see below), whether by a government or by a business, is generally considered a human rights abuse. Attempts by an employer to prevent union membership among staff is known as union busting. Similar allegations can be leveled if an employer discriminates based on trade union membership. The **National Labor Union (NLU)** was the first national labor federation in the United States. Founded in 1866 and dissolved in 1872, it paved the way for other organizations, such as the Knights of Labor and the American Federation of Labor. Although U.S. workers are not required to form or join unions, the workforces in many entertainment industries are organized into, arguably, some of the most powerful trade unions in the nation.

Unions gain their bargaining power through their ability to enforce strikes and lockouts that can effectively shutdown industry production. Trade unions may also promote legislation favorable to the interests of their members or workers as a whole. To this end they may pursue campaigns, undertake lobbying, or financially support individual candidates or parties for public office. There are many recent examples of labor disputes in various entertainment industries that have led unions to strike or take other actions.

In professional sports, there have been several instances where players have gone on strike. Notably, there have been eight work stoppages over the course of baseball history, with the most recent in 1994 resulting in the cancellation of between 931 and 948 games overall, including the entire 1994 postseason and World Series. On September 16, 2004, the National Hockey League Players Association (NHLPA) failed to accept a salary agreement resulting in a lockout that led to the cancellation of what would have been the 88th season of the National Hockey League (NHL). It was the first time the Stanley Cup had not been awarded since 1919, and the first time a major professional sports league in North America had canceled a complete season because of a labor dispute.

SPOTLIGHT ON THE NATIONAL HOCKEY LEAGUE   The 88th UnSeason

In most labor disputes in professional sports, the primary issue is players' salaries. In the most recent ice hockey strike, the National Hockey League (NHL) led by Commissioner Gary Bettman, attempted to convince players to accept a salary structure linking player salaries to league revenues, guaranteeing the clubs what the league called **cost certainty**. According to an NHL-commissioned report prepared by former U.S. Securities and Exchange Commission chairman Arthur Levitt, prior to 2004–5, NHL clubs spent about 76 percent of their gross revenues on players' salaries—a figure far higher than those in other North American sports—and collectively lost $273 million dollars during the 2002–3 season. Although the NHL's numbers were disputed, there was no question that several franchises were losing money, as several had declared bankruptcy. Other franchises had held "fire sales" of franchise players, such as the Washington Capitals. The league does not have large TV revenues in the US, so the NHL is reliant on attendance revenues more than other leagues.[23]

To address these losses, the league presented the NHLPA with six concepts to achieve cost certainty. These concepts are believed to have ranged from a

hard, or inflexible, salary cap similar to the one used in the National Football League to a centralized salary negotiation system similar to that used in Major League Soccer. Most sports commentators saw Bettman's plan as reasonable, but some critics pointed out that a hard salary cap without any revenue sharing was an attempt to gain the support of the big market teams, such as Toronto, Detroit, the New York Rangers, Dallas, and Philadelphia—teams that did not support Bettman during an earlier 1994–5 lockout.

The NHLPA, under executive director Bob Goodenow, disputed the league's financial claims. According to the union, "cost certainty" was nothing more than a salary cap, which it had vowed never to accept. The NHLPA preferred to retain the present "marketplace" system where players individually negotiate contracts with teams, and teams have complete control of how much they want to spend on players. The players, however, lost this particular dispute, ultimately accepting a negotiated deal that did include salary caps. Analysts have suggested that players may have been forced to concede because the NHL put much more effort into the public relations war than did the NHLPA, leading to a large amount of one-sided public feeling on the issue. Also hurting the NHLPA was the fact that its players had very visible high salaries, which removed much sympathy from lower-to-middle-class fans. Other critics wonder whether both sides ended up losing more than they gained as the dispute and loss of an entire season threatened the support of an already relatively small hockey audience in the U.S.

Source: Podnieks, Andrew (2005). *Lost Season*. Bolton, Ontario: Fenn Publishing

What do you think?

- *How are disputes such as these perceived by sports fans?*

Salary disputes have also been quite common in the tourism and hospitality industry. As of the writing of this text, union workers at the Congress Hotel had been on strike for five years, since June 2003, after hotel owners cut wages and benefits—arguably, the longest strike in the country. The union charges that, during the course of the strike, the average wage of Chicago housekeepers had risen to $13.90 an hour, while the Congress Hotel still paid just $8.83 an hour. Although the strike has led some groups and conferences to move or cancel their events, the hotel has remained firm in its refusal to negotiate with union workers. In 2007, Las Vegas hotels managed to narrowly avert a strike by more than 10,000 food, beverage, and housekeeping workers.

Because the entertainment industries are so intertwined, the effects of a strike in one industry can reverberate through several others. For example, when professional athletes go on strike, the TV networks and radio stations that typically carry game broadcasts are affected. They must scramble and pay for programming to cover the open timeslots created by game cancellations, and they can also lose revenue from advertisers who would have paid a higher premium for game ad placements. Similarly, if hotel or transportation operations at travel destinations are shut down because of workers' strikes, the theme parks, casinos, restaurants, and other attractions that rely on traveling guests are also affected. In some cases, the effects of such strikes can extend far beyond just these industries.

In 1997 President Clinton invoked emergency powers granted under a rarely used 70-year-old law to block a strike called by American Airlines pilots. The pilots and the company were locked in intense negotiations over pay and conditions of work but it became clear that the two sides remained far apart and the pilots were posed to strike. White House sources said the President had been initially reluctant to intervene in the labor dispute but did so after Department of Transportation officials had briefed him on the damage a stoppage would inflict on the national economy. Informed that the strike would cost the American economy about $200 million a day and strand a fifth of American Airlines' 200,000 daily passengers, the President signed his executive order.[24]

We have seen how new technology has been a driving force behind many legal controversies, and labor disputes are no exception. In many cases, workers have become concerned that advances in automation will threaten their jobs. The recent dispute between the Writers Guilds of America East and West (WGAE and WGAW) and the Alliance of Motion Pictures and Television Producers (AMPTP), however, more directly echoes many of the themes that we have seen throughout this chapter.

Every three years, the Writers Guild negotiates a new basic contract with the AMPTP for its members. This contract is called the **Minimum Basic Agreement (MBA)**.

In 2007 negotiations reached an impasse. There were several key issues of

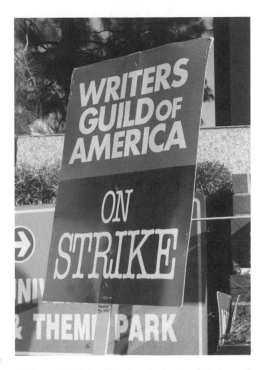

A Writers Guild strike sign in front of Universal Studios

contention including DVD residuals, union jurisdiction over animation and reality program writers, and compensation for "new media" (content written for or distributed through emerging digital technology such as the Internet).

In previous agreements regarding residuals, the Guild accepted a formula in which a writer would receive a small percentage (0.3 percent) of the first million of reportable gross (and 0.36 percent after) of each tape sold as a residual. As manufacturing costs for video tapes dropped dramatically and the home video market exploded, writers came to feel they had been shortchanged by this deal. The WGA requested a doubling of the residual rate for DVD sales, which would result in a residual of 0.6 percent per DVD sold.

Exactly if and how the WGA's MBA should apply to TV and film categories such as reality TV and animation had been inconsistent over the years and were areas of much dispute. Programs such as *Real People* and *That's Incredible!*, which were arguably "reality" shows of the 1980s, were covered by the MBA, whereas more recently produced reality shows such as *Survivor* and *America's Next Top Model* were not. Producers of reality programming would argue that since these shows are mostly, if not entirely, unscripted, there is no writer. The WGA counters that the process of creating interesting scenarios, culling raw material, and shaping it into a narrative with conflict, character, and story line constitutes writing and should fall under its contract. In the summer of 2006, the WGA West attempted to organize employees of *America's Next Top Model*. The employees voted to join the WGA, but then they were fired and production continued without them.[25]

Animated films and TV programs have also been an area of heavy contention. The majority of animated film and TV writing has not been covered by the WGA's MBA. Most animated feature films have been written under the jurisdiction of another union, the International Alliance of Theatrical Stage Employees, Local 839, also known as The Animation Guild. IATSE's jurisdiction stemmed from Walt Disney's tradition of creating an animated feature via storyboards written and drawn by storyboard artists. In recent years, most studios have begun hiring screenwriters to write script pages which are then storyboarded. According to the WGA, 100 percent of animated feature film screenplays in 2005 were written by at least one WGA member.[26] Recently, some animated features, such as *Beowulf*, were written under the WGA contract. The only animated TV programs affected by the strike were Fox's *The Simpsons*, *Family Guy*, *King of the Hill*, and *American Dad!*. The WGA and the IATSE have an ongoing disagreement as to which union should represent animation writers.

One of the most critical contract disputes was over residuals for "new media," or compensation for delivery channels such as Internet downloads, IPTV, streaming, smart phone programming, straight-to-Internet content, and other "on-demand" online distribution methods, along with video on demand on cable and satellite TV. Previous contracts included no arrangement with the companies regarding the use of content online, and thus writers received no residuals from Internet distribution. WGA was seeking compensation for two models of Internet distribution. The first is **electronic sell-through** (also known as "Internet sales" or "digital sell-through").

In electronic sell-through, the consumer purchases a copy of the program and downloads for subsequent viewing at their convenience. Examples include movies and TV shows purchased through the iTunes Store and Amazon Unbox. In the second model, streaming video, the consumer watches a program in real time as it is transmitted to their computer but is usually not saved. Current examples of this model include advertising-supported TV programs streamed free to the audience, such as those available at nbc.com, abc.com, fox.com, cbs.com, thedailyshow.com, and hulu.com. Internet distribution was widely seen by most WGA writers as the central issue for the strike based on the belief that new media will eventually supplant both DVD in the home video market and TV in the broadcasting market as the primary means for distribution.[27] The AMPTP, however, argued that new media were still an unproven and untested market and asked for additional time for study.

FLASH FACT

According to an NPR report, the 2007 Writers' Strike cost the economy of Los Angeles an estimated $1.5 billion. A report from the UCLA Anderson School of Management put the loss at $380 million, while economist Jack Kyser put the loss at $2 billion.[28]

The Writers' Strike, as it is commonly called, had significant repercussions throughout Hollywood's entertainment industries. Within the first week of the strike, AMPTP member companies fired writers' assistants, production assistants, and other lower-level staffers working on shut-down programs. All scripted Hollywood shows except *October Road* were expected to shut down by the week of December 19, 2007.[29] Hollywood journalist Nikki Finke reported, "CEOs are determined to write off not just the rest of this TV season (including the Back 9 of scripted series), but also pilot season and the 2008/2009 schedule as well. Indeed, network orders for reality TV shows are pouring into the agencies right now."[30] The "Big Four" networks—CBS, ABC, NBC, and Fox—faced severe ad shortfall as their prime-time ratings declined sharply. The WGA eventually settled on agreements with the AMPTP and various industry companies in early 2008. The new deals established a scale of royalty payments for DVDs and for writers whose work is sold over the Internet or streamed for free. The contract was ratified without resolution regarding the jurisdiction of reality and animation, which remained an issue that was under negotiation.

Between Industries: Rocky Marriages Given the interdependence of many entertainment industries, it is not surprising that disputes often emerge between these industries. Consider the relationships radio traditionally has had with advertisers and the recording industry. Radio depends on the recording industry for a continuous flow of new material to broadcast and on advertisers for its revenue, and the recording manufacturers and advertisers depend on radio for the exposure of their product to potential consumers. Despite their close affiliation through the years, these industries have often clashed over issues. Once again, new media lie at the heart of the emerging disputes, this time in the form of Internet radio.

There are two basic models for Internet radio: *radio simulcasts*, where over-the-air broadcasts are streamed simultaneously on the Internet, and *web-only radio*, which can be accessed only over the Internet. In 2001 there were about 5,000 traditional and 500 Internet-only broadcasters streaming news, sports, and some of the most eclectic music programming imaginable, according to BRS Media. By the end of 2001, however, traditional radio simulcast broadcasters had been virtually swept from the web. Many of the industry's largest broadcasters had ordered their stations to cease live streaming. Several factors contributed to this abandonment. First, an act advanced by the Recording Industry Association of America (RIAA), required stations to pay royalty fees to the artists for Internet streaming. Emerging court cases also threatened other fees. These costs were in addition to what radio stations across the nation already paid through licensing arrangements with the Society of European Stage Authors and Composers (SESAC), Broadcast Music, Inc. (BMI), and the American Society of Composers, Authors, and Publishers (ASCAP) for traditional radio broadcasts of the same music.

Beyond these costs, the American Federation of Television and Radio Artists (AFTRA) drew attention to a little-known provision of the Recorded Commercials Contract instituted in October 2000 that requires advertisers to pay union talent *300* percent of the normal session fee if a spot originally recorded for radio is used on the Internet. Thus, rather than welcoming the added bonus of reaching audiences via Internet streaming, advertisers began protesting and threatening to pass along the added costs to the radio stations. Broadcasters like Clear Channel Communications, Emmis, Radio One, ABC/Disney, and others started closing down station live streams nationwide because they were fearful that future court rulings might involve retroactive fees to be paid to AFTRA members.

By the early 2000s, stations began live streaming again as technology enabled them to block advertisements to the Internet feed and advertisers negotiated new contracts. However, soon Internet radio faced another legal battle, again regarding royalties, this time for the music itself rather than the advertising. Both terrestrial radio and Internet or digital radio broadcasters are responsible for royalties collected by performance rights organizations (ASCAP, BMI, SESAC) on behalf of the *composers* of recorded works. However, in 2007, the United States Copyright Royalty Board proposed a rate increase in the royalties payable to *performers* of recorded works broadcast on the Internet. There was concern that this decision, retroactive to 2006, could undermine the business models of many Internet radio stations.

According to a report issued in March 2007, under the newly proposed rates, annual fees for all station owners were projected to reach $2.3 billion by 2008. This figure is more than four times that for terrestrial radio broadcasters who, owing to terms set forth in the 1998 Digital Millennium Copyright Act, are exempt from the additional royalties imposed on digital broadcasting outlets.[31] Many performers of recorded works have voiced their opposition to the Copyright Royalty Board's rate increases, fearing that the rate increases could bankrupt the Internet broadcasters that have given them valuable exposure.

Between Governments: Regulating Indian Gaming   Disputes have also emerged regarding governmental jurisdiction over the operation and regulation of different entertainment industries. For example, we have seen how differing community standards led local governments to argue for and win the right to regulate indecency and obscenity, thus overriding the jurisdiction of state and federal authorities. In today's connected, global world, however, few forms of entertainment reside solely within well defined borders, and thus governments often clash regarding who should have the authority to oversee various industries. The gaming operations of Native American tribes have been the focus of one particularly heated dispute regarding government authority.

Gambling has long been an important part of American Indian culture and tradition. One ancient game called "stick game" among northwest tribes has variations among most tribes and is still played at tribal gatherings. Horse and foot races were an important focus of traditional gambling. Today, many popular gambling destinations such as the Pechanga Resort and Casino in California are owned and operated by Native American Tribes. Following the success of gaming operations in California and Nevada, gambling now provides tribes in many states with revenue for essential governmental services. Disputes arise, however, because, although recognized Native American tribes are considered to be independent nation states, many of the U.S. states in which they reside place major restrictions against most types of gambling and impose criminal penalties for violations.

Early on, states attempted to severely restrict or stop tribal gaming operations and did so on the grounds that tribal gaming violated state law prohibiting a particular type of gaming. However, it had been a longstanding rule of law that state law did not apply to

Morongo Casino near Cabizon, California. Gov. Schwarzenegger persuaded the legislature to allow expansion of Indian casino gambling in exchange for millions of dollars of revenue to the state. The controversial deal pitted labor groups against tribes over working protections and rights to organize into unions

Indian tribes or Indian people within their reservations absent express authorization by Congress. A law passed by Congress in 1953, commonly known as Public Law 280, authorized some states to extend their criminal laws to Indians on reservations and also authorized state courts to hear and decide cases arising on reservations where one or both of the parties were Indian.

In a case between the State of California and the Cabazon Band of Mission Indians, the court ruled that Public Law 280 did not grant states jurisdiction to regulate Indian activities on reservations, but it did grant the state power to regulate activities that fell under its criminal laws that were extended to reservations.[32] Thus, any activity that was totally prohibited by state criminal laws was applicable to Indian reservations under Public Law 280. On the other hand, any activity that was allowed but regulated under state law was deemed by the Court to be civil/regulatory and not within the scope of Public Law 280—even if violation of the regulations resulted in criminal sanctions. In the context of Indian gaming, this meant that, if a state generally prohibited gambling but allowed some form of gambling for charitable organizations, state lotteries, or otherwise, Indian tribes could engage in those forms of gaming. Only if the state totally prohibited gaming by all persons, organizations, and entities could state law be used to curtail Indian gaming. A final determination must be based upon what activities are allowed as a matter of the state's public policy.

This decision, and the expansion of Indian gaming that followed it, set the stage for the development of the Indian Gaming Regulatory Act (IGRA). The balance struck in IGRA did not please either states or tribes. Tribes preferred to operate within the scope of the Cabazon decision and viewed the state involvement in any form as extremely undesirable. States, on the other hand, felt state involvement was too limited and disagreed with their new exposure to lawsuits under the act. IGRA provides an entire statutory structure of Indian gaming.[33] By its terms it applies to "Indian Lands" which are defined as all lands within the limits of any Indian reservation. The National Indian Gaming Commission is established within the Department of the Interior and given the authority and responsibility of administering IGRA.

The act divides Indian gaming into three different categories. Class I gaming generally includes social and traditional games and is within the exclusive jurisdiction of Indian tribes. Class II includes bingo and games similar to bingo which can be operated by a tribe if it is located in a state that permits that type of gaming for any purpose by any person or entity and if it is authorized by tribal resolution or ordinance. Class III gaming includes all types of gaming that are neither class I nor class II and is arguably the most important type of gaming for tribal gaming enterprises. Class III gaming must also occur in a state that permits that particular type of gaming for any purpose by any person or entity and must also be authorized by tribal resolution or ordinance. In addition, there must be a compact negotiated between the tribe and state which defines how the class III gaming will be conducted.

A tribe seeking to engage in class III gaming is required to give notice to the state that it wishes to negotiate a compact. Originally, the act gave the United States District Courts jurisdiction over cases brought by an Indian tribe as a result of the state's refusal to enter into negotiations. The United States Supreme Court, however, has since held that the Eleventh Amendment to the Constitution of the United States prevents Congress from authorizing Indian tribes to sue states (*Seminole Tribe of Florida v. Florida*, 1996). As a result, the act has been interpreted as not imposing an obligation on states to enter into compacts with Indian tribes, only an obligation to negotiate in good faith. It does not require that states negotiate with tribes over gaming activities that are not allowed under state law.[34]

Unlike gaming activities operated by non-tribal entities, the revenues derived from gaming by Indian tribes can be used only for specified purposes, namely: to fund tribal government operations or programs; to provide for the general welfare of the tribe and its members; to promote tribal economic development; to donate to charitable organizations; or to help fund operations of local government agencies.

A statute as broad and complex as IGRA almost always results in lawsuits raising questions about its interpretation and application. IGRA is no exception. Case law that has evolved since the passage of the act has served to clarify and define several important aspects of IGRA.

Despite litigation over the interpretation and application of IGRA, tribal gaming has flourished and provided Indian tribes with a new, and important, economic base. This success has brought additional attention to Indian gaming. In 1996 Congress established the National Gambling Impact Study Commission to study and report on the economic and social impacts of all forms of legalized gambling. A separate subcommittee was established to study Indian gaming. The Commission's final report was released on June 18, 1999. The report recognizes tribal sovereignty in the context of gaming as well as the positive impacts tribal gaming have had on tribal economic well-being. Since that time, many state laws and regulations have been passed that further qualify tribal gaming rights and obligations. There have also been regular attempts to have Congress amend IGRA or enact laws that would further affect Indian gaming. A variety of bills have been introduced that would alter the current regulatory scheme under IGRA. Other measures would have the effect of reducing federal funds to tribes in proportion to the revenue they derive from business activities—primarily gaming—and others would impose taxes on tribal gaming revenues. While none of the proposed federal measures had passed as of the writing of this text, the prospect of amendments being made to the act remain a possibility.

FADE TO BLACK

This chapter has explored the way in which entertainment industries have shaped and been shaped by government laws and regulations. Because many of the most popular forms of entertainment are media-based, much of the legal considerations that have impacted entertainment surround the rights and regulations governing the media industries, particularly with regards to protections and limitations on free speech.

In some cases, the entertainment industries have resisted government regulations, viewing them as unfair, and even unconstitutional, limitations on their business practices. In other cases, these same industries have often demanded government intervention to help them protect their assets. We have seen how developments in new technology have played a particularly influential role in the evolution of the laws governing the entertainment industries.

We have discussed both government and worker attempts to place limits on the concentration of power within entertainment businesses in an effort to curb unfair market and labor practices. And, we have also reviewed how the interdependent nature of the entertainment enterprises can lead to legal disputes between sister industries and between governments. In all cases, the only thing that is certain is that the laws and regulations governing entertainment will continue to change and evolve both as a cause and effect of the changes and evolutions that occur within the industries themselves.

A CLOSER LOOK AT MPAA RATINGS   Female Sex and Male Violence: The Divide in Movie Ratings

(Warning: This essay is rated NC-17 for graphic discussion of sexual expression that would not be allowed in an R-rated movie.)

As some Hollywood wag has famously, and probably apocryphally, said, "You can slice a breast off onscreen, but you can't kiss it." Why? Because the Motion Picture Association of America, the organization that rates films for American release, says so.

Male versus Female Depictions

The movie *Let's Talk about Sex* initially received an NC-17 rating for a scene in which it is demonstrated, using a peach as a prop, how to perform oral sex on a woman. A similar scene using a banana as a stand-in for a man was not an impediment to an R rating. An erect penis on screen garners a film an automatic NC-17, but a film in which women are fully, graphically nude has no problem earning an R rating.

Eyes Wide Shut initially received an NC-17 rating for intentionally un-erotic missionary-position intercourse. (The rating was dropped to R when the glimpses of thrusting penises were covered up in some instances by—you guessed it—strategically placed nude women. An image of three naked women pleasuring one another for the benefit of male onlookers obviously was also not a barrier to an R rating.)

Only a year earlier, *8MM* got an R despite sexualized imagery of women being viciously murdered. The MPAA has subjectively decided that the depiction of male sexual pleasure is more important than that of women, that men deserve a measure of dignity when it comes to nudity that women do not merit, that watching a women being murdered is less objectionable than watching a woman have an orgasm.

Sex Versus Violence

The MPAA's subjectivity comes into play when it deems that the brutal violence of movies like the R-rated *Robocop*, *Terminator 2*, and *The Matrix*—to name but a few—may be witnessed by children as long as they are accompanied by an adult but that under no circumstances may these children watch two adults make love with the same level of anatomical detail with which we frequently witness limbs get blown off a human body.

S is For Sex, V is for Violence

The MPAA's ratings could be more pointed and more helpful while simultaneously becoming less subjective. The recent *Three Kings* is rated R for "graphic war violence, language and some sexuality"; *American Beauty* is rated R for "strong sexuality, language, violence and drug content." But you won't learn that from movie posters, TV advertisements, or newspaper ads for either of these movies. In fact, that information is not particularly easy to find, nor is it readily at hand when deciding what film to take the kids or oneself to.

The MPAA should take a cue from the new TV ratings system, which tells us right up front what potentially objectionable content a program contains: D for suggestive dialog, S for sexuality, V for violence, and so on. It's not a perfect system for television, and it wouldn't be a perfect system for films. But . . . it could . . . alert audiences to a film's content and turn the decision whether to watch that film back over to the people it belongs to: parents, and moviegoers in general.

Source: Mary Ann Johanson, Flickfilosopher.com[35]

What do you think?

- *Do you agree that male and female depictions and sex and violence are rated differently?*
- *Do you think that is a problem? Why or why not?*
- *What, if anything, might be done differently?*

DISCUSSION AND REVIEW

1. Review some of the limits that have been placed on free speech. What implications have these had for the entertainment industry?
2. In some cases, the entertainment industry has protested government regulations, and in others it has demanded it. Discuss some examples of each of these and see if you can identify common themes regarding when each of these stances have been taken. Also consider instances in which some people in entertainment have welcomed restrictions, while others have not.
3. Review the arguments for and against government restrictions on concentrated ownership in different entertainment industries.

EXERCISES

1. Laws and regulations are changing constantly. Look up some of the topics covered in this chapter for any recent legal developments or cases. Discuss the implications they may have for the industries involved.
2. Review the different types of disputes discussed in the chapter (within and between industries and governments). Can you come up with different examples for each type of dispute?
3. There are many areas of law that affect various entertainment industries that were not addressed here such as talent representation, zoning regulations, and international trade agreements. Select an entertainment industry or issue of your choice and research the various laws, regulations, and legal cases that have influenced both creative and business practices.

BOOKS AND BLOGS

Campbell, R., Martin, Christopher, R., and Fabos, Bettina (2006). *Media & culture 5: An Introduction to mass communication*. New York: Bedford/St. Martin's.

Straubhaar, Joseph and LaRose, Robert (2006). *Media now: Understanding media, culture and technology*. Belmont CA: Thompson.

http://reporter.blogs.com/thresq/free_speech/index.html—*The Hollywood Reporter Entertainment and Media Law* blog

9 ETHICS IN THE INFOTAINMENT AGE

The difference between unethical and ethical advertising is that unethical advertising uses falsehoods to deceive the public; ethical advertising uses truth to deceive the public.
—Vilhajalmur Stefanss

Once upon a time, journalists reported news, companies promoted products, and entertainers produced drama and diversions. Today, news, promotion, and entertainment are blended together in an endless array of offerings commonly touted as infotainment. People learn about current events from talk radio, magazine shows, and late-night comedy. Companies shop their goods through branded entertainment and product placement in documentary-style reality TV programs. Meanwhile, audiences are producing their own news, promotions, and entertainment shared in social networks, weblogs, and virtual worlds. As we saw in Chapter 8, efforts to deal with entertainment's changing landscape have resulted in the rise of many laws and regulations. However, it is not only impossible to create legislation that can anticipate and remedy every troublesome issue but also unconstitutional, as many of the controls that might curb some of the questionable practices in entertainment would violate implicit and implied rights such as free expression and privacy. Recognizing the need to try to develop some sense of standards, many industries have developed codes of conduct and ethics to govern their practices, that, while not obligatory, have served as a level of self-regulation.

Traditionally, journalism, commercial speech such as advertising, and entertainment media were fairly distinct in terms of style, content, and intended effects. As such, professionals in each discipline established different codes of ethics and standards. Entertainers enjoyed greater creative license in their storytelling, while journalists, marketers, and advertisers were expected to make clear distinctions between fact, fiction, and opinion. Standards for journalistic and commercial speech have often been guided by a sense of social responsibility not only to report the truth but also to report it thoughtfully and conscientiously. In addition to these moral obligations, the distinctions traditionally made in news stories and commercial messages were supported by legal and economic considerations. If journalists or advertisers were caught making false claims, their reputation would suffer and they would lose customers. In some cases, they might even be sued or fined. Contemporary infotainment, however, blurs the boundaries between fact and fiction almost by definition, creating an often conflicting mix of values, conventions, and audience expectations. This blending has made it increasingly difficult to determine when and how specific ethical standards might best be applied.

In addition to concerns regarding entertainment and "infotainment" content, a number of ethical issues exist regarding the production, promotion, and distribution of entertainment. In this chapter, we will address all of these issues by first exploring some basic ethical tenants, and then examining some of the specific ethical issues that plague contemporary entertainment.

Ethical Principles and Guidelines

Consider what you would do in the following situations:[1]

1. You are making a student video that you hope will land you a job in Hollywood. Violence isn't really integral to the plot, but a couple of your actor friends have some fake blood and suggest that it would be "more dramatic" to stage a fistfight. Do you take them up on the offer?
2. You are an aspiring young disk jockey. An independent consultant who works for a record company offers you tickets if you will listen to some new recordings from the company label—no strings attached! Do you accept?
3. Someone online gives you a link to download a movie that is not in the theaters yet. Do you use it or pay to see the movie?
4. You are planning a campus fundraiser event for a local charity. A friend of yours knows a popular, local comedian who is willing to come perform for free, helping you more than double the money you could raise. You have heard some of the comedian's material, however, and feel that many of his jokes can be very racist and sexist. What do you do?

Six Philosophical Perspectives

What factors or guidelines would influence your decisions in these scenarios? Ethical decisions can be influenced by a variety of factors including religious, philosophical, and cultural considerations. Although there are no clear-cut ethical formulas that can be applied to every ethical situation, philosophers have forwarded several principles and ideals that can be useful in evaluating ethical dilemmas such as those found in entertainment.

The Golden Rule   **The golden rule** philosophy has its roots in Judeo-Christian religions. It teaches people to "love your neighbors as yourself" and "do unto others as you would have them do unto you." Following this tradition, we should treat each other as we would like to be treated. We should be as humane as possible and try to protect others from harm inflicted by our actions. "Love," according to Christians, Rotzoll, and Fackler, "is personal, dutiful, but never purely legalistic."[2] Jay Mather, who won a 1979 Pulitzer Prize, wrote simply, "Human kindness has always been an effective and impartial editor."[3] The golden rule should not be interpreted to mean just giving others specific things that we would want. Just because we might enjoy loud rock music at one o'clock in the morning doesn't mean our neighbors do. Nor does the golden rule compel us to always give others everything they want. For example, a young child might want to stay up all night watching scary movies, but that does not mean it would be ethical to allow it. Loving your neighbors like you love yourself means giving other people's best interests the same respect and consideration that you give your own.

Rawls and the Veil of Ignorance   Similarly, in his book *A Theory of Justice*, the contemporary philosopher John Rawls urges decision makers to recognize and consider the values of all affected individuals, not just those who have the power to influence decisions.[4] Rawls recommends two particular techniques for an ethical decision making process:[5]

*   Rawls suggests that, before a decision is made, decision makers figuratively don a **veil of ignorance** that strips away their rank, power, and status. The veil of ignorance

strategy asks decision makers to examine the situation objectively from all points of view. In particular, it asks them to imagine lifting the veil of ignorance only to discover that they are now one of the affected individuals instead of the decision maker.

• Rawls suggests that, to redress social injustice, the most disadvantaged individuals in a situation should receive the most advantages—with the exception of freedom. Freedom, he says, is an advantage that must be shared equally. All other resources, however, should flow to those who have the least. Power should flow to the powerless, and wealth should flow to the poor.

Since the terrorist attack on the World Trade Center in 2001, Hollywood has been accused of increasingly typecasting Arabs as terrorists in TV programs and films. As an example of how you might apply Rawls's veil of ignorance, consider how you would feel about these depictions if you were a Hollywood producer, an actor of Arabic descent, or an Arab American in the audience. Then consider what resources each of the three has in this situation. All three can be said to have certain powers and freedoms.

Producers have the power to control what is depicted in their films and programs, and actors have the power to choose whether they want to accept the roles they are offered, and audiences have the power to pay for, ignore, or even actively boycott such depictions. Producers have the freedom to express their views, not only in the shows they create but in other forums such as interviews. Actors and audience members are also free to express their views to friends, family, and increasingly to larger audiences through Internet postings, blogs, and other channels. What do you think? Are power and freedom equally distributed in this situation or are there imbalances? Consider the distribution of any other resources you feel are important. As the decision makers, if producers were to follow Rawls's recommendations, what might they do?

Kant and the Categorical Imperative   The eighteenth-century German philosopher Immanuel Kant contributed the concept of the "categorical imperative" to the study of ethics. When you are considering a course of action, Kant advocates turning it into a universal maxim—a clear principle that would apply to all people in all situations. So for example, you might be faced with deciding whether or not to keep a promise that you made. Keeping your promise could be articulated into a universal law, "always keep your promises." Ethical crises often have many possible solutions. Thus, you would imagine that each possible course of action created a maxim that everyone in the world would follow. You would then reject any course of action that created a maxim that could lead to undesirable behavior if it was followed without exception. In *Fundamental principles of the metaphysics of morals*, Kant writes, "Act only on that maxim whereby thou canst at the same time will that it should become a universal law."[6] When you discover a course of action that could and probably should be a universal law, that is a **categorical imperative**, which Kant says is a course of action that you must follow.

Aristotle, Confucius, and the Golden Mean   The ancient Greek philosopher Aristotle believed that "moral virtue" exists as a balancing point between two extremes, a compromise he called the **golden mean**. For example, Aristotle would contend that it's unethical to never lie (one extreme) just as it's unethical to always lie (the other extreme). A century before the birth of Aristotle, the Chinese philosopher Confucius established a similar principle with his **doctrine of the mean**: "The superior man . . . stands erect in the middle, without inclining to either side."[7] The middle way does not involve a precisely mathematical average, but is an action that approximately fits that situation at the time.[8]

The Golden Mean

There have been many recent labor strikes in entertainment-related films including screenwriters, actors, and workers at hotels and resorts. In each case, what the employers are offering differs from what those employed want in terms of compensation, benefits, and working conditions. Although it might be tempting to say that the ethical solution would be to simply split the difference between the two views (for example, make salaries the average of what is offered versus what is being demanded), determining the golden mean is not that easy. As Christians et al. wrote, "The mean is not only the right quantity, but at the right time, toward the right people, for the right reason, and the right manner."[9] Depending upon the extremity of demands associated with each position, from a more objective vantage point, the exact midpoint might still unduly favor one side over the other. In some cases, a true "mean" maybe impractical or even impossible. Consider sensitive political issues such as the death penalty, abortion, or euthanasia. It is hard to come up with a pragmatic halfway point between life and death. Finding the golden mean is achieved not by trying to divide an issue down the middle but by seeking the fairest balance after giving each side equal, impartial consideration.

Mill and Utilitarianism   The philosophy of **utilitarianism** is largely credited to the nineteenth-century British philosopher John Stuart Mill. As one of the more popular philosophies applied to the impacts of media, such as television, film, and other popular forms of entertainment, it warrants particular attention. People commonly interpret Mill's recommendations for ethical decisions as doing the "greatest good for the greatest number." According to ethics scholar Deni Elliott, however, "they would be wrong."[10] The democratic process is often lauded as an example of the utilitarian principle at work. Citizens express their preferences, votes are tallied and decisions are based on majority rule. According to Elliott, however, utilitarianism, at least as espoused by Mill and his collaborator, Harriet Taylor Mill, does not teach us to add up the people potentially helped by an action and subtract from that number the people potentially harmed, with the presumably "ethical" choice of having the majority win. Indeed, most democratic societies are not "pure" democracies but instead recognize that moral governing requires a more complex system of checks and balances between different interests.

Elliott argues that Mill's utilitarianism requires determining which action is most likely to produce the *aggregate good*: the overall good for the community as a whole, or for *all* people identified as being affected by a particular action. Simply allowing the greatest *number* of people to benefit from an action implies that happiness of the majority is more important than the happiness of those harmed in the bargain. This approach can lead to the mistaken conclusion that having some happy and others not happy is good for the community. Mill's notion of aggregate good stresses the importance of valuing all people involved.

If causing harm is justified at all, it is justified on the basis that causing harm in those particular types of cases is good for the community, including the individual harmed.

Sometimes, it is better for individuals to be harmed, sometimes not. But the ability to distinguish between those instances involves more than mere computation. In contrast to the simplistic reasoning sometimes offered: it is okay if an individual is hurt by an action, for example someone getting injured performing a dangerous stunt or becoming a "copycat" victim of a crime shown on TV, as long as the producer can argue that many more citizens might benefit from having the knowledge or seeing the show. Mill requires a more thoughtful calculation of what is truly good for the whole community. Making such determinations is not easy. The decision maker must be truly impartial with regard to his or her own interests and the interests of all others involved. In order to do so, decision makers must work diligently to understand the views and implications regarding all parties and issues that are involved. The duty of every citizen, according to Mill, is to reason carefully about matters of governance and to continually test the validity of one's beliefs. He claimed that citizens have a duty "to form the truest opinions they can."[11]

Hedonism   **Hedonism** is another perspective that has particularly significant implications for the study of entertainment ethics. Hedonism comes from the Greek word for pleasure and is closely related to the philosophies of nihilism and narcissism. Aristippus, a student of Socrates, was the founder of the ethics of pleasure.[12] Aristippus believed that persons should "[a]ct to maximize pleasure now and not worry about the future."[13] Aristippus, however, referred to pleasures of the mind—intellectual pleasures. He believed that people should dedicate their lives to pleasure, but he also believed that they should use good judgment and exercise self-control. His famous phrase is: I possess, I am not possessed. Contemporary usage of the hedonism philosophy and the pleasure principle, however, has ignored his original intent. Phrases such as, "Eat, drink, and be merry, for tomorrow we die," "Live for today," and "Don't worry—Be happy" are present examples of the hedonism philosophy.

We mention this philosophy not to extol the virtues of modern-day hedonism as a framework for ethical decision making but because it is integral to the nature of entertainment. Entertainment is hedonistic by definition. As discussed in earlier chapters, the primary function of entertainment is to bring pleasure and serve as diversion from worries and problems. Entertainment is produced, consumed, and critiqued based on its hedonistic ability to maximize pleasure. It is this single-minded focus that gives rise to many of the ethical concerns that are discussed in this chapter. Using violence or controversial humor to attract audiences, offering bribes to get music played, illegal music downloads, in these and other issues we can see the dilemmas that can emerge from attempts to maximize pleasure entertainment can provide. Thus, if we are to accept hedonism as the driving force governing the production and consumption of entertainment, we might be best served if we also heed Aristippus' admonition to exercise self-control and good judgment and not allow our pursuit of pleasure to possess or consume us. As we explore the ethical issues in entertainment, consider how you might apply each of the six ethical perspectives we have discussed. A well-known framework for making ethical decisions is the Potter's Box, featured in the *Spotlight*.

SPOTLIGHT ON DECISION MAKING   Potter's Box

One framework for making ethical decisions is called Potter's Box. It is often used by communications professionals, but can be used in entertainment-based situations as well. Potter identified four universal dimensions of moral analysis to help determine answers to dilemmas in situations where facts, values, principles, and loyalties come into question. Using the Potter's Box involves four steps:

1. **Define the situation or dilemma**.
   Considering the *facts* of an issue is where an analysis begins before making any judgments. Look at the details, varying points of view, and any insights that might cause bias in decision making. Why is the information important? Why am I making this decision?

2. **Identify the values**.
   Values allow us to compare the merits of different views to understand the influences they have on decision making. We acknowledge different perspectives and judge them according to esthetics, professional relevance, logic, socio-cultural importance, and morality. Acknowledge the beliefs that define what you stand for. These act as standards of choice through which we seek consistency. Both instrumental (codes of conduct) and terminal (end result) values are considered.

3. **Identify the principles**.
   Principles are ethical philosophies or modes of reasoning used in a particular situation to better

equip the decision maker, such as those espoused by Aristotle, Confucius, Kant, Mill, and others. Use moral philosophies rather than dogmatic advice. What professional guidelines or organizational policies should I consider?

4. **Choose your loyalties**.
   Loyalties concern to whom the decision maker has loyalties. For example, in journalism, a reporter's first allegiance is to the public; others include employer, the industry, and co-workers. What stakeholders or individuals claim your loyalty? Analyze who benefits and who loses. You may have competing loyalties yourself. Identify them. What if the roles were reversed? What are the consequences of your actions?

Make the decision.

Be certain you can defend your decision. Can you justify your position and stand behind it?

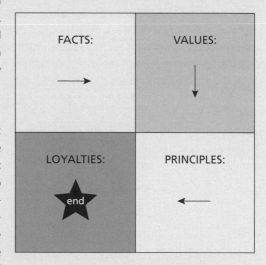

Figure 9.1 Ethical Decision Making

Consider the following example of how Potter's Box might be applied.[14]

Michael Jackson's Last Close-up

Situation. When Ben Evenstad, who co-founded the photo agency National Photo Group, and photographer Chris Weiss were snagging the "money shot" of pop legend Michael Jackson in the ambulance before his death on June 25, 2009, they said that Jackson's bodyguards were practically begging them to stop. They tried to block the camera and said, " 'C'mon man. Don't do this. This isn't cool,' but Evenstad said, 'When it's this big, we have to,' and I ran around to the other side, because at a certain point there's no delicacy. We gotta do what we gotta do." Did the photo agency act ethically?

Values. Michael Jackson and family: privacy, dignity, respect. Photo agency: public's right to know, freedom of expression, duty not to suppress information, professional and personal gain . . . The public: all values listed above.

Principles

- *Golden rule:* The reporters should treat Michael Jackson with the same respect/consideration they would want . . .
- *Veil of ignorance:* Jackson has power/privileges of

fame, but also less privacy/protection from media. Photo agency has "power of the press," but also is dependent on Jackson/other stars for the photos it sells . . .

- *Categorical imperatives:* Always . . . protect privacy, tell the truth, etc.
- *Golden mean:* Find a compromise. Take limited pictures such as only the outside of the ambulance . . .
- *Utilitarianism:* The community is best served . . . when the media provides all the information they can . . . when the media honor privacy/act with restraint in collecting information . . .
- *Hedonism:* Each party should freely pursue their own happiness . . .

Loyalties. Bodyguards loyal to Jackson, Jackson to his family/fans. Photo agency (as media watchdogs) to the journalistic code and public interest . . . Which should be supported?

Judgment. Which values should be most protected? Which principle is best applied? Which loyalties should be supported? What would the ethical thing to do be in this situation? Support your decision based on these judgments.

Fact and Fiction: The Ethics of Storytelling

Her name was Bree, a shy home-schooled teenager with a web camera. In the summer of 2006, she started posting video web logs (v-blogs) on YouTube.com, under the user name lonelygirl15. Her videos were a hit attracting thousands of viewers. The problem was none of it was real. In early September, it was revealed that lonelygirl15 was a 19-year-old actress hired to play the part of a 16-year-old.[15]

In 2007, Margaret B. Jones wrote *Love and consequences*, a critically acclaimed memoir about her life as a half-white, half-Native American girl growing up in South-Central Los Angeles as a foster child among gang-bangers, running drugs for the Bloods. Within a week of publication, her own sister came forward with the real story of Margaret Seltzer's (a.k.a. Ms. Jones) middle-class, suburban childhood in Sherman Oaks, California.[16] Just a week before Seltzer's memoir was exposed as a fake, author Misha Defonseca, whose real name is Monique De Wael, issued a statement admitting that the Holocaust memoir she published 11 years earlier was fiction.[17] De Wael's book, *Surviving with Wolves*, was recently turned into a film. That same year, James Frey was revealed to have duped readers, his patron Oprah Winfrey among them, with his fictionalized memoir *A Million Little Pieces*.[18]

In 2008, videos circulated on the Internet seemingly demonstrating that cellular phone radiation was so strong it could pop corn. In less than three weeks, the videos had been viewed more than four million times. Wired.com debunked the video as fake with the help of physicist Louis Bloomfield and speculated that a video-editing program or hidden heating pads caused the popcorn to pop. Bluetooth headset retailer Cardo Systems confessed that it had commissioned a marketing agency in Paris called LastFools to make the videos.[19]

Falsehoods and fabrications are not entirely new in storytelling. In the late eighteenth century, English poet Thomas Chatterton passed off his own work as the verse of medieval "secular priest" Thomas Rowley. In 1971, Clifford Irving was found guilty of forging the biography of reclusive millionaire Howard Hughes. Recent deceptions, however, are distinctive in their subtlety as well as their rapid increase in frequency, sophistication, and proliferation. Of even greater interest is the seeming lack of concern both storytellers and their audiences have shown in reaction to these ethical breaches. The next section reviews more specific philosophies that have governed the ethics of storytelling and expression in the United States and other Western democracies and explores how views may be changing.

Ethical Considerations

Two aspects of ethical considerations ground many of our decisions: libertarianism and social responsibility.

Libertarianism   A philosophy which champions free expression, libertarianism is based on the self-righting principle, expressed in 1644 by the author and poet John Milton in his book *Areopagitica*. He stated the principle in two points:

> The free flow or trade of ideas serves to ensure that public discourse will allow the truth to emerge.

> Truth will emerge from public discourse because people are inherently rational and good.

This argument has been traditionally invoked to protect political speech based on the belief that people cannot govern themselves in a democracy unless they have unfettered access and freedom to disseminate information. The principles, however, have often been invoked to protect all forms of expression including art and entertainment. As World War II spread across Europe at the end of the 1930s, the public's rationality and goodness and the assumption that truth would always triumph were called into question. In the United States, libertarians were hard pressed to explain how Nazi propaganda could succeed if this were the case. These concerns led to the development of a different approach to free expression called social responsibility theory which emerged as a cross between libertarian philosophy and practical admissions of the need for some form of control on the media.

Social Responsibility Theory   This is a normative theory—meaning that it proposes how the media should ideally operate—and it has served as the foundation of ethical standards for U.S. media. The social responsibility theory asserts that the media must remain free of government control, but in exchange media must serve the public. The core assumptions of this theory are:[20]

- Media should accept and fulfill certain obligations to society.
- Media can meet the obligations by setting high standards of professionalism, truth, accuracy, and objectivity.

- Media should be self-regulating within the framework of the law.
- Media should avoid disseminating material that might lead to crime, violence, or civil disorder or that might offend minority groups.
- The media as a whole should be pluralistic, reflect the diversity of the culture in which they operate, and give access to various points of view and rights of reply.
- The public has a right to expect high standards of performance, and official intervention can be justified to insure the public good.
- Media professionals should be accountable to society as well as to their employers and the market.

Professional Codes   To assist members in ethical decision making, various organizations of media professionals have adopted more concrete guidelines that reflect social responsibility assumptions. Such codes exist for professionals in all areas of media ranging from news to corporate communication to entertainment. Each code is uniquely tailored, anticipating specific situations that professionals in a given industry might face and offering guidance for how to deal with them. For example, the Society of Professional Journalists' Code says, "Test the accuracy of information from all sources and exercise care to avoid inadvertent error" and "Deliberate distortion is never permissible."[21] Similarly, the American Advertising Federation Code says "Advertising shall tell the truth, and shall reveal significant facts, the omission of which would mislead the public."[22] Even some of the more controversial industries in entertainment have developed ethical codes. The Free Speech Coalition, the trade association of the adult entertainment industry, has adopted a code of ethics advocating among other things that "members conduct business with integrity and professionalism" and "take appropriate steps to help parents control minor access to adult content."[23]

If you review these codes in their entirety you will note significant differences. Although the journalists' code of ethics emphasizes promoting a diversity of views and not imposing values, advertising and entertainment codes do not. Both journalists' and advertising codes stress the importance of honesty and not deceiving audiences, while most entertainment codes do not. This isn't to say that advertisers and entertainers are less concerned with upholding principles of integrity and fairness, but the expectations are different. Although it might be considered unethical for a hard new journalist to bias or fabricate a story, audiences are expected to understand that advertisements are biased—promotional messages—and that the stories in books, movies, and TV are fictional; untrue, by definition, and often even intentionally deceptive. When clear distinctions existed between news, commercial messages, and entertainment, the expectations for each "story" type were also relatively clear for both the storytellers and their audiences. However, as the lines between these media forms have begun to blur, so have the ethical principles that guide them.

Consequentialism: Is All Fair in Love and War Stories?

As the lonelygirl hoax and other deceptions detailed above indicated, many contemporary story "fabricators" do not appear to feel that they have done anything wrong, and they express little remorse for their actions. Monique De Wael continues to defend her fabricated Holocaust memoir work. "Ever since I can remember, I felt Jewish," she said in a statement issued by her lawyers. "There are times when I find it difficult to differentiate between reality and my inner world. The story in the book is mine. It is not the actual reality—it was my reality, my way of surviving."[24]

These fabrications are very calculated and premeditated and the storytellers appear to have little trouble enlisting the tacit and active support of others. The creators of the lonelygirl15 videos were Ramesh Flinders, a screenwriter and filmmaker from Marin County, California, and Miles Beckett, a doctor turned filmmaker. The project was developed much the same way as more traditional commercial films or television programs are produced, including casting, contracts, and film crew. They enlisted the services of Grant Steinfeld, a software engineer in

Jessica Lee Rose as Bree, a.k.a. lonelygirl15, a shy home-schooled teen on YouTube.com

San Francisco. "We were all under N.D.A.'s" Steinfeld said, referring to non-disclosure agreements that the cast—and their friends—were asked to sign to preserve the mystery of lonelygirl15. "They had a lawyer involved," he said.[25]

Amanda Solomon Goodfried, an assistant at Creative Artists Agency, the talent agency that was hired to represent the lonelygirl team, is believed to have helped Mr. Flinders and Mr. Beckett conceal their identities. Moreover, Ms. Goodfried's father-in-law, Kenneth Goodfried, a lawyer in Encino, filed the trademark "lonelygirl15."

Consistent with the artistic mindset traditionally reserved for fictional stories, these content creators appear to feel that these hoaxes and lies fall within the purview of fair creative license. This might be interpreted as a return to a more libertarian philosophical view that truth will ultimately emerge from the free flow of ideas. However, it is not clear that truth is as much of a concern as is the promotional value of the story. If these fabricators are guided by any moral or ethical sense, it would appear to be a consequentialistic, ends justifies the means philosophy. In some cases the intention is purely profit-driven to sell advertisers' products or the entertainment content itself. Other times, the intent may be more altruistically oriented to raise awareness of societal issues or concerns. In her gang memoir, Margaret Seltzer defended her decision to lie, saying that the story needed to be told and was based on accounts of real experiences. She said "I just felt that there was good that I could do and there was no other way that someone would listen to it."[26]

In the Netherlands, Patrick Lodiers offered a similar justification for the Dutch reality program he hosted called the *The Big Donor Show*. The show was designed as a hoax in which a terminally ill cancer patient pretended to select one of three patients to receive her kidney. Viewers watched testimonials from the three Dutch contestants, aged between 18 and 40, and could send in text message advice to the donor to help her decide who should receive the lifesaving operation. According to one blog account, in defending the show, Lodiers said that one of the aims of the program was to bring about a change in Dutch law surrounding transplants. At present, only family or friends of the recipient can donate organs—a fact that greatly reduces their availability in the Netherlands. "It is reality that is shocking," he said, "because so many people die each year in the Netherlands while waiting for a kidney, and the average waiting time is four years. But we are not giving away a kidney [on the show]. That would be going too far even for us."[27]

Even more interesting is how some industry professionals are not only defending but actually praising these deceptions. When software engineer Grant Steinfeld was approached to work on lonelygirl, he said "My first impression was like, wow, can this be legitimate? Is this ethical? I was very concerned about that in the beginning." But eventually, Steinfeld said he came to believe that something truly novel and progressive was at hand. "They were like the new Marshall McLuhan," he said, referring to a well-respected, iconic communication theorist.[28] According to the news web site, News. Scotsman.Com, the makers of *The Big Donor Show* were "widely praised when they revealed [the program] was a hoax aimed at raising awareness of the plight of patients waiting for organs."[29] In commenting on the hoax in his blog, marketing communication consultant Sam Smith lauded this ends-justified approach:

> There are two wonderful thing[s] about this little stunt. The first is that you could almost believe it. I mean, given the kinds of things that *do* happen in pursuit of a buck, you could imagine this kind of show happening. The second is that it was conceived as a way to attract attention to a worthwhile cause. . . . I like the idea here. It's over the top, to be sure, but if you're trying to call attention to a life/death situation, which is worse: this tasteless, offensive display (which, by the way, called the whole damned world's attention to your cause) or a tasteful, conventional, traditional campaign that gets a few hundred signatures on a petition while hundreds continue to die?[30]

In many cases, however, these hoaxes have been admired simply for their ingenuity and marketing savvy. Arguably, one of the first and most famous Internet hoaxes was the viral promotion of the horror film *The Blair Witch Project*. The movie was made for $22,000 and grossed $248 million at the box office by generating massive pre-opening "buzz" through video clips circulated on the Internet long before the public even knew the buzz was about a movie.[31] The rumor was that a camera was found with real footage taken by three college kids who were lost in the woods while investigating stories about a witch.

According to Internet marketing writer Charles Brown, "the hoax took on a life of its own . . . By the time the film was released, it had built up fever-level anticipation."[32]. In his review, Brown calls the hoax "remarkable" and "the stuff of legends." He does question whether such campaigns must be designed as hoaxes rather than as fictional stories in order to be successful, but he does not express any ethical concerns about the strategy. Instead, he appears more concerned about whether such stories can also work to promote many different products or services. The three men who created *Blair Witch* think they can, and so, apparently, do their clients. The creators of the film have formed a marketing company called Campfire. They are hired by advertising agencies to create viral marketing campaigns like the one they used to make their movie such a huge success. Reactions to other hoaxes such as the lonelygirl and the cellphone corn popping videos have been similar. Although, there are some audiences who initially express outrage about being duped, these hoaxes tend to generate more admiration than criticism for their deception. In their reviews, industry analysts, critics, and news reporters tend to quickly dismiss ethical concerns and focus more on analyzing the entertainment and marketing value of the stories.

Is Truth Boring? It has been argued earlier in the text that the competition for attention has fueled the blurring of media into infotainment. Whether you are writing a script, a news story, or an advertisement, your goal is to capture attention. In all cases, drama and intrigue offer a better guarantee of engaging audiences than do facts and thoughtful analysis. Thus, today's media face greater pressure to be entertaining than to be honest and accurate. Traditional economic theory maintained that brands were built for the long term, and that consumer trust was essential for brand loyalty. Accuracy and credibility were viewed as critical for consumer trust in news and commercial media. Today, however, many companies introduce brands anticipating a limited life expectancy, thereby

reducing market incentives to adhere to traditional standards.

It may be that audiences have become
so bored with predictable products and stories
that they may be willing to tolerate some
falsehoods or deceptions if it makes for a
more interesting or entertaining experience.
In addition to changing market forces, the
infotainment trend is exacerbated by user-
generated content contributed by individuals
with no grounding in or allegiance to ethical
conventions in any of the traditional media
disciplines. Furthermore, the hybrid nature
of new media makes it difficult to determine
what standards should be applied. The Internet
and other new media have certainly made it
easier to fabricate and disseminate these false
tales, and such advances also may also help
explain why so many industry professionals
and even audiences are embracing them.

Are we bored with truth?

Product Placement

As audiences become more adept at filtering out traditional advertising, efforts to infuse
corporate messages more directly into entertainment and news media content are
becoming increasingly important. Global paid product placement spending in TV, film, and
other media surged to $2.21 billion in 2005. As indicated earlier, companies also attempt
to secure editorial coverage of press releases and story pitches as a low cost, highly
credible alternative or complementary marketing messaging strategy to traditional
advertising.

Infusing organizational messaging more directly into editorial and entertainment
programming content not only lends third party credibility but also may provide companies
greater assurance that their messages are not filtered out. According to Jeff Greenfield,
vice president of 1st Approach, a strategic media marketing company, "since the
explosion of the Internet and new technology like TiVo, viewers are demanding fewer inter-
ruptions."[33] With over half a million households currently using the TiVo-style "personal
video recorders," a study revealed that users skip commercials 72.3 percent of the time—
a much higher rate than those watching live TV or those using videotape recorders.[34]
As a result, today we see cutting-edge companies, like clothing and accessory designer
Paul Frank, eschewing traditional advertising entirely in favor of media relations and other
non-traditional entertainment-infused strategies such as celebrity endorsements and
product placements in films, in TV programs, and at celebrity events and photo shoots. By
associating with entertainment commodities such as films and celebrities, even
companies selling more mundane products and services such as T-shirts (à la Paul Frank)
and parcel delivery (recall the film *Castaway* starring Tom Hanks) can become more glamorous. *A Closer Look* at the end of the chapter shows the lengths one Los Angeles boutique
went to in trying to "E-tize" its business.

Although product placement has become very common, entertainment and other
media professionals still need to think about whether such practices are ethical. As
discussed in several different chapters, product placement has moved far beyond simple

Prop placement of branded washing machine in television sitcom

"prop placements" in the background of scenes to become fully integrated into story lines. In some cases, product placement actually drives the story line. For example, the sitcom *Will & Grace* featured entire episodes about the character Jack, and his obsession with a doll replica of his favorite singer, Cher—an idea inspired by product placement requests made by the public relations firm that represented Mattel, the toy's manufacturer. Similarly, the writers for the sitcom *Friends* developed story lines specifically to feature placements for the furniture store Pottery Barn.

Although placements in content already framed as fictional entertainment may seem innocuous, there are concerns that audiences may be misled into believing that any claims made about products in a fictional show are actually authentic. Others argue that product placement can be perceived as a tacit endorsement by program producers and even by the actors involved. Placements in supposed "reality" programs pose even greater concern given the already ethically questionable effort that is made to portray events in the programs as spontaneous and authentic (see *Spotlight on Product Placement*).

SPOTLIGHT ON PRODUCT PLACEMENT   Reality TV Lets Marketers Write the Scripts

According to critics, the advertising industry is fighting back against TiVo and other ad-skip technology by altering pre-existing content in ways that could threaten the visual and editorial integrity of television programming.[35] They claim that brand integration is largely responsible for the reality TV genre as we know it and not vice versa.

The trend was pioneered with *Survivor*, which CBS greenlighted only after its executive producer explained that, instead of the network paying actors, advertisers would pay the network for a starring role. Envisioned as a commercial vehicle as much as a TV drama, *Survivor* is a pretext for contestants to interact with brands. According to *Advertising Age*, CBS thought it was one of the best bargains in TV history. Behind the program's long-term impact was the relentless promotion of the series by CBS's parent company, Viacom. To generate buzz, more than 100 affiliate radio stations ran segments, including dozens of drive-time interviews with Burnett, while 16 of CBS's TV stations and Viacom's MTV and VH1 covered *Survivor* as if its ins and outs were news.

Other series, such as NBC's *The Restaurant* and ABC's *Who Wants to be a Millionaire* were produced by Magna Global Entertainment Company, a branded

entertainment development wing of media giant Interpublic that is "dedicated to the creation of original television programming that is funded by and serves the needs of Interpublic's clients."[36]

By the time *American Idol* appeared, placing branded products gave way to placing branded wannabe pop stars themselves. Fox has reaped millions by making *Idol* contestants literally do backflips over corporate logos in mini-commercials disguised as music videos. The contestants who succeed are as much commodities as the product they hawk.

The argument against advertising-integrated program content is that the stronger the foothold, whether through ad buys or product placement, the more power advertisers have to define our collective values. Mike Darnell, Fox's reality guru, told *Entertainment Weekly* that his dream project would be a beauty pageant featuring female prisoners: "You give them a chance to get a make-over and it's a 40-share special." So will Miss San Quentin sashay her way into prime time? Only viewers have the power to say.

Real stars of *The Restaurant* were appliances and cookware

What do you think?

- *Is the reality-show platform a natural context for branded products, or are corporations designing reality content around their brands?*
- *Who should ultimately determine the amount and type of product placement appropriate for television audiences?*

E-tizing News   Companies are not the only ones having difficulty getting their messages seen and heard. Concerned over declining audiences for news programs and publications, many news organizations have turned to "infotainment" soft news strategies. Today's editorial decisions are often based on a story's ability as much to entertain audiences as to inform them. A report authored by Thomas Patterson (2001) found that soft news has increased dramatically in the twenty-first century. News stories lacking public policy content jumped from less than 35 percent of all stories in 1980 to roughly 50 percent of stories appearing by 2001. Stories with a moderate to high level of sensationalism rose from about 25 percent of news stories in the early 1980s to a a more recent tally of 40 percent. Stories that include a human interest element also figure heavily in contemporary reporting, accounting for less than 11 percent of news stories in the early 1980s, but more than 26 percent of reports today. The same holds true for stories with crime or disaster as a main subject, rising from 8 percent of stories in 1980 to close to 15 percent of stories today. These include tabloid syndicated programs like *Hard Copy*, and nightly network newscast features on personal finance, consumer affairs, and health. The regular features of network news magazines *Dateline* NBC, ABC *Primetime Live*, CBS *48 Hours*, and the made-for-soft-news spin-off ABC *20/20 Downtown*, are notorious for their soft news formats.[37]

Perhaps even more disturbing is the emergence of paid product placement in news publications and broadcasts. In July of 2008 the Fox affiliate in Las Vegas, KVVU, agreed to a six-month promotion for McDonald's where news anchors sit with cups of McDonald's iced coffee on their desks during the news-and-lifestyle portion of their morning show. Executives at the station said that the six-month promotion is meant to shore up advertising revenue and, as they told the news staff, will not influence content; however, the *New York Times* reported that the ad agency that arranged the promotion said the coffee cups would most likely be whisked away if KVVU chose to report a negative story about McDonald's.[38] "If there were a story going up, let's say, God forbid, about a McDonald's food illness outbreak or something negative about McDonald's, I would expect that the station would absolutely give us the opportunity to pull our product off set," said Brent Williams, account supervisor at Karsh/Hagan, the advertising agency that arranged the deal between McDonald's and KVVU."[39] If that did not happen, "it might lead to the termination of an agreement" to appear on the show, he said. KVVU, for its part, said it would continue to report truthfully and honestly about McDonald's. Mr. Bradshaw said the station would remove the cups, just as it would remove spot advertising from a newscast for any advertiser who is the subject of a negative report.

Corporate money may also be tainting more traditional public relations efforts to secure news coverage. Traditionally, media relations practices have been considered ethical in that reporters are expected to act as gatekeepers who fact check corporate information and adhere to "strict neutrality" in determining what corporate information is newsworthy. There is concern, however, that the integrity of this process is being undermined. Although it is difficult to document, off the record, many public relations practitioners and journalists have admitted to increased pressure to give more favorable news coverage to companies who also purchase advertising.

In sum, we are seeing a convergence of forces which make it increasingly difficult for both content creators and their audiences to distinguish between news, entertainment, and commercial speech.

 FLASH FACT

A 2004 online survey of 100,000 people asked participants about their opinions of popular entertainment. Results revealed that 83 percent believe much entertainment is an ethical failure; 13 percent believe some entertainment is ethically weak; 4 percent believe most entertainment is "decent enough."

Source: entertainmentethics.com

Reality Programming

Perhaps nowhere is the blurring between fact and fantasy more evident than in the rise of reality programming. One of the attractions of reality TV is the supposed "reality" of it—unscripted and unplanned situations and reactions. The ethical issue, however, is the fact that reality programming isn't nearly as "real" as it pretends to be. We have already discussed concerns regarding product placements in reality programs. Reality shows have been further accused and, in some cases found guilty, of manufacturing quotes; of constructing crushes and feuds, and planning whole episodes in multi-act "storyboards" before taping; and of stitching scenes together out of footage shot days apart. Of course, most TV programming is fictional. Certainly fabricating events and characters isn't inherently unethical in entertainment. The difference is

Blind Date gone comically wrong

that in dramatic shows one can expect the audience to understand that what they see on the screen doesn't necessarily reflect the reality of the actors' lives; the same, it is argued, cannot be said for heavily edited and contrived scenes one sees on reality shows.

Reality programs may not have line-for-line scripts (although reality writers have charged that Paris Hilton was fed lines on *The Simple Life*). But according to Jeff Bartsch, a freelance reality-show editor, there are many ways of using footage to shape a story.[40] Bartsch worked on *Blind Date*, a syndicated dating show that features hookups gone right—and horribly, comically wrong. If a date was dull or lukewarm, the editors would spice up the footage by running scenes out of order or out of context. To make it seem like a man was bored, they would cut from his date talking to a shot of him looking around being unresponsive—even though it was taken while she was in the restroom and he was alone. "You can really take something black and make it white," Bartsch says.[41]

On the ABC reality show *The Dating Experiment*, one of the female participants disliked one of her suitors, but the producers thought it would make a better story if she liked him. So they sat her down for an interview. "Who's your favorite celebrity?" they asked. She replied that she really loved Adam Sandler. Later, in the editing room, they spliced out Sandler's name and dropped in audio of her saying the male contestant's name. This trick, says Todd Sharp, who was a program consultant on the series, is called **Frankenbiting**, creating the "life" of the story by piecing different parts together—like Frankenstein.[42] Thus, the most obvious ethical question raised by reality programming, if it includes such blatant fabrications, is: should it be labeled as "reality" at all?

Conversely, producers are quick to emphasize that editorial devices can be used not just to deceive but also to tell a story more clearly, entertainingly, and quickly. News, producers, documentarians, and journalists all selectively edit raw material and get accused of cherry-picking facts and quotes. But on an entertainment show the pressure to deliver drama is high, and the standards of acceptable fudging are shadier. Reality producers say they often have to shuffle footage to tell a story concisely or make a babbling interviewee coherent. "We're using things said at different times, put together to imply a statement or observation that may not have been succinctly demonstrated," says J. Ryan Stradal, who was a story editor on *The Bachelorette*. "That's where Frankenbiting may come in."[43] Or producers may withhold information—such as downplaying a budding romance—to create suspense. Thus, a second ethical question is whether dramatic editing is wrong if it captures the essence of the moment.

A third ethical concern regarding reality programming has to do with the potential impacts these programs may have on those who participate in them. A primary premise of many reality shows is placing people in painful, embarrassing, and humiliating situations for the rest of us to watch—and, presumably, laugh at and be entertained by. In Chapter 4, you learned that such disparagement is a common form of humor. There is no question that disparagement is commonly used as a comic device in entertainment. The question is whether we need to see a real person suffer to accomplish this goal or whether it is better left in the realm of fictional entertainment and the albeit sharp, but not physically painful, verbal lashings of stand-up comedy.

Amateur Night   Given that individuals volunteer and must give their consent to participate in reality shows, some people may feel little sympathy for their suffering. Indeed, the participants themselves may think that they have little recourse, if they feel they have been wronged, since they usually sign a thick stack of waivers. Nonetheless, there have been lawsuits filed by people who have been injured and/or traumatized by the stunts these shows have staged. According to critic Annette Hill, it is important to keep in mind that most of the participants in reality programs are not actors but amateurs who may not always understand exactly what they are getting themselves into when they agree to be on the program. Hill has advocated the adoption of ethical standards for the treatment of non-professional actors in reality programs: "[f]irst, that non-professional actors be treated in a fair and responsible manner, and second, that program makers present the stories of ordinary people and their experiences in an ethical manner."[44]

Failing to take care in the treatment of non-professional actors fairly can have serious consequences, especially for psychologically unsuited participants. In 1997 the first contestant banished from *Expedition Robinson*—the Swedish inspiration for the program *Survivor*—threw himself under a train. Richard Levak, a consulting psychologist working for *Survivor*, has compared the producers of some reality shows to the psychologists who ran the Stanford Prison Experiment in the early 1970s. He believes that many reality TV shows would not be allowed to take place if they were overseen by the same human subjects committees that guard volunteers' rights in psychological experiments.[45]

There are producers who do claim to take the protection of participants seriously. One executive producer who was interviewed stated that an important part of his job was to prepare participants for what will happen to them, as well as to help them decompress if they are voted off the show. Furthermore, he claimed he makes it very clear to his employees that cast members should be accurately portrayed, in both taping and editing.[46]

Ad Action   As an extension of these concerns, some critics have also questioned the responsibility of companies who advertise on and in reality programs engaging in questionable ethical practices. It is argued that, if their funding makes such programming possible, they should also shoulder part of the blame. Blogger Austin Cline suggests that an ethical position would be to refuse to underwrite any programming, no matter how popular, if it is designed to deliberately cause others humiliation, embarrassment, or suffering. In his view "[it]'s immoral to do such things for fun (especially on a regular basis), so it's certainly immoral to do it for money or to pay to have it done."[47] Some advertisers, however, argue that holding them accountable for program content would set a dangerous precedent. They contend that not only would it be unfair to blame them for content they don't control but also that such a policy would only encourage advertisers to try to influence program content, a practice that has also been widely condemned as unethical. Reality programs offer many targets for ethical scrutiny, but no easy answers. Yet another criticism of this programming is discussed in the *Spotlight on Stereotyping in Reality Programming* on p. 264.

SPOTLIGHT ON SCANDAL   Vintage TV Quiz Shows

Popularized during the 1950s, quiz shows originated using questions that required substantial knowledge from contestants on a broad spectrum of topics. In 1954, the Supreme Court ruled that quiz shows were not a form of gambling, paving the way for their popularization on television. *The $64,000 Question* debuted in June, 1955, with a top prize equivalent to about $500,000 today.

Once producers discovered that influencing the game's outcome would increase the show's dramatic value, advertisers encouraged the practice to attract viewers. Contestant coaching and prop rigging were common. For instance, contestants placed in an "isolation booth" to prevent audience influence were denied ventilation after questions were asked to heighten drama. With hot stage lights and increasingly stifling temperatures, contestants would sweat, mop their brows, and look decidedly flustered.

Popular contestants were briefed or given easy questions, while less popular players had more difficult questions to remove them quickly. This practice

came to a head when Charles Van Doren deliberately refused to answer a question incorrectly and ratted on the show's producers. After two other contestants of *Dotto* and *Twenty-One* revealed similar scripting fixes, networks suffered a huge drop in audiences. During a grand jury investigation, contestants who had become celebrities from their show successes perjured themselves to avoid losing their prizes. Finally, Van Doren revealed his complicity in deception, claiming he was a victim because he was the show's "principal symbol."

Congress passed a law prohibiting quiz show fixing, and, although none of those who were prosecuted went to prison, all were victims of the exposé. Van Doren lost his job on NBC's *Today* show and was forced to resign his professorship at Columbia University. Without his permission, Robert Redford directed the movie *Quiz Show* in 1994 that portrayed the scandal. It wasn't until 2008 that Van Doren gave his account of the experience for a *New Yorker* memoir.

The outcome was a disappearance of quiz shows from prime time for decades, resurfacing as game shows that focused on puzzles until 1973 when *Pyramid* had a $10,000 prize. Forced to adapt winning limits to meet Standards and Practices guidelines, CBS imposed a winnings cap limit from $25,000 in 1972 to $125,000 in the 1990s. By 2006, caps were abolished altogether, but networks required show monitoring and contestants were kept away from audience members.

Source: en.wikipedia.org/wiki/Quiz_show_scandals

Media Effects

Two of the most harmful effects of media on viewers involve sex and violence and social stereotyping. Both are discussed here.

Sex and Violence

In the film *Grand Canyon* (1991), one of the main characters is a filmmaker who makes very violent movies. One day he is shot in a mugging attempt and he becomes remorseful, wondering if his films have contributed to the violence, of which he, himself, had become a victim. He recovers and, recognizing that violent films are his livelihood, ultimately sides on the need for free expression in art and entertainment—including the expression of violence in our culture. The film is satirical (see Chapter 13), but it addresses a significant issue that has plagued entertainment productions. Should producers be held accountable for the potential social effects of their creations?

Most entertainment professionals maintain that they are not responsible for the potential negative impacts of the films, programs, music, etc. that they create. However, there are many anecdotal examples of people who have imitated specific acts of violence or reckless behavior they have heard or seen in entertainment media. Even if such imitation is unusual, should a producer feel responsible? Many entertainment producers maintain that, if a fan of the *JackAss* films and programs gets hurt trying some of the stunts that were portrayed, that's the fan's problem, not the producer's.

Industry spokespeople often make two arguments supporting their immunity. The first claim is that individuals are not as vulnerable as commonly supposed. Indeed, as Chapters 5 and 12 discuss, even the researchers do not always agree on what effects permissive content such as sex and violence may have on audience members or society at large. However, as Chapter 13 will reveal, entertainment media have certainly been used to evoke positive social change such as getting people to engage in safer sex and using designated drivers when they drink. If media producers believe that entertainment can effect positive social change, it would seem difficult for them to deny that it might also cause social harm. Nonetheless, that does not necessarily mean that it is their responsibility to prevent such impacts.

A second argument that is often made is that individuals and families have a responsibility to make their own decisions about what to watch and what to make of it. However, some critics note some hypocrisy in this argument since many people in the industry also oppose a potentially effective new form of parental regulation.[48] Some companies now offer software that skips indecent scenes or words in DVDs, and real-time editing of TV shows and music CDs may soon be technically feasible. Generally speaking, it is hard to argue that audiences should not bear responsibility for their choices. Audiences always make choices about what to see. But, one concern is how well-equipped some audiences, particularly children, are to make the most responsible decisions. One recent response within schools is to teach *media literacy* and educate people regarding the nuances and potential impacts of entertainment and other media through courses such as the one for which you are likely using this text. A number of churches and other organizations offer similar programs. In this way people may gain the knowledge they need to make more informed decisions about their media choices.

Social Stereotypes

Even if you do not feel that the media should carry any responsibility for how audiences behave, do you believe they should be concerned about what audiences think? As discussed earlier in the chapter, it has been commonly held that journalists are obligated to take care in what they report because what is stated can influence what people think or feel about important issues. Do entertainers share a similar obligation? What if, as cultivation or dependency theory suggests, although a majority of people may not directly imitate anti-social behavior modeled in entertainment, they still come to view such depictions as normal or acceptable? Concerns about impacts on audience perceptions are often raised regarding the issue of stereotyping (see Chapter 11). Chapter 4 included a discussion of "stock characters" that are often used in drama and storytelling. These characters are easily identifiable by common characteristics that audiences can quickly recognize. This helps propel the story along without having to spend significant time on character development.

Many of these stock characters have been accused of promoting **social stereotypes**—such as African Americans as criminals or athletes, seniors as grumpy and senile, blondes as dumb, etc. Stock character stereotypes can even be found in reality programs (see *Spotlight* below). Of course, the argument some producers make here is that they are not creating these stereotypes but, instead, merely reflecting existing societal perceptions. Yet, not only do actual demographic statistics regularly refute these generalizations, research has shown that people watching a lot of TV programs and other media that include these stereotypes are more likely to embrace such views. And, so once again, the question becomes whether entertainment producers should be concerned about the impact they may have. Some critiques even go so

Social stereotype of African American as criminal

far as to suggest that producers should not only avoid reinforcing existing stereotypes but should also intentionally create characters that directly violate such typecasts in an effort to help dispel and correct them.

SPOTLIGHT ON STEREOTYPING IN REALITY PROGRAMMING   Whose Reality?

Some critics have voiced concerns that reality programs often perpetuate social stereotypes. Teresa Wiltz, a reporter for the *Washington Post*, singled out some of those stereotypes, noting in particular the similarity in many black female characters featured on several different programs.[49] According to Wiltz "[i]f you've ever seen a reality TV show, chances are you've seen her: perpetually perturbed, tooth-sucking, eye-rolling, finger-wagging harpy, creating confrontations in her wake and perceiving racial slights from the flimsiest of provocations . . . she's the sista with an attitude."[50]

As examples, Wiltz points to the sharp tongued Alicia Calaway on *Survivor: All-Stars*, Camille McDonald (a Howard University student) on *America's Next Top Model*, Internet message board favorite for comments on her "stank attitude" and the star of Donald

Trump's *The Apprentice*, Omarosa "I'm not here to make friends" Manigault-Stallworth. This character has become so pervasive that Africana.com has trademarked the expression The Evil Black Woman to describe her: brazen, aggressive, pointing fingers, and always lecturing others on how to behave.

Wiltz maintains that a pattern of "characters" has emerged in reality programming that isn't very far different from the stock characters found in fictional programming. In addition to the Black Woman/Man with Attitude, there's Small Town Girl/Guy, sweet and naïve, looking to make it big while still retaining hometown values. There's the "Bumbling Bigot" reminiscent of Archie Bunker, the Outrageous Party Girl/Guy, always looking for a good time and generating maximum shock value—and the list goes on.

Wiltz is not alone in noting the extent to which reality programming relies on these stereotypes. She quotes Todd Boyd, critical studies professor at the University of Southern California's School of Cinema-Television, as saying "We know all these shows are edited and manipulated to create images that look real and sort of exist in real time. But really what we have is a construction. . . . The whole enterprise of reality television relies on stereotypes. It relies on common stock, easily identifiable images."[51]

Why do these stock characters exist in "reality" television that is supposed to be unscripted and unplanned? "Because, well, that's entertainment," says Andy Dehnart, creator of realityblurred.com, a daily compendium of TV's top reality shows: "If you have footage of Alicia sitting around chatting about her favorite foods and if you have footage of her wagging her finger, screaming, it's much more interesting."[52]

In his commentary on "reality" stereotypes, About.com commentator Austin Cline adds that "drama is more readily propelled by the use of stock characters because the less you have to think about who a person really is, the more quickly the show can get to things like the plot (such as it may be). Sex and race are especially useful for stock characterizations because they can pull from a long and rich history of social stereotypes."[53]

Cline adds, however, that this is especially problematic when so few minorities appear in programming, whether reality or dramatic, because those few individuals end up being representatives of their entire group. "A single angry white man is just an angry white man, while an angry black man is an indication of how all black men 'really' are."

Similarly, Wiltz notes that "Indeed," the [Sista With an Attitude] feeds off preconceived notions of African American women. After all, she's an archetype as old as D.W. Griffith, first found in the earliest of movies where slave women were depicted as ornery and cantankerous, uppity Negresses who couldn't be trusted to remember their place. Think Hattie McDaniel in *Gone with the Wind*, bossing and fussing as she yanked and tugged on Miss Scarlett's corset strings. Or Sapphire Stevens on the much-pilloried

Amos N' Andy, serving up confrontation on a platter, extra-spicy, don't hold the sass. Or Florence, the mouthy maid on *The Jeffersons*.[54]

How do these stock characters appear in "unscripted" reality shows? Cline offers two reasons. First, he speculates that the people themselves contribute to the creation of these characters because they know, even if unconsciously, that certain behavior is more likely to get them air time. And, second, he maintains that the show's editors contribute to the creation of these characters by encouraging and highlighting controversy.

A commonly offered example of this distortion is Omarosa from the *The Apprentice*. While the program aired, she was called "the most hated woman on television" because of the behavior and attitude people see her with. But according to an e-mail by Manigault-Stallworth quoted by Wiltz, this on-screen persona was largely crafted by the show's editors:

> What you see on the show is a gross misrepresentation of who I am. For instance they never show me smiling, it's just not consistent with the negative portrayal of me that they want to present. Last week they portrayed me as lazy and pretending to be hurt to get out of working, when in fact I had a concussion due to my serious injury on the set and spent nearly . . . 10 hours in the emergency room. It's all in the editing![55]

Cline reminds us that reality TV shows are not documentaries. "People are not put into situations simply to see how they react—the situations are heavily contrived, they are altered in order to make things interesting, and large amounts of footage are heavily edited into what the show's producers think will result in the best entertainment value for viewers. Entertainment, of course, often comes from conflict—so conflict will be created where none exists. If the show cannot incite conflict during the filming, it can be created in how pieces of footage are stitched together. It's all in what they choose to reveal to you—or not reveal, as the case may be."[56]

Sources: Teresa Wiltz, *The Washington Post*, and Austin Cline, About.com

Industry Ethics: Promotion and Consumption

Entertainment industries face ethical issues not only about their content but also regarding the production, promotion, distribution, and consumption of that content. These issues raise similar concerns of social responsibility related to honesty, fairness, and consumer protection.

Business Transactions

Entertainment is often viewed as a group of rather free-wheeling, laissez-faire individuals and industries. As revealed, many entertainment trade and professional organizations and individual entertainment companies have developed ethical and conduct codes to outline recommendations for proper business conduct. Typically, specific elements of these codes are created in reaction to problems or scandals that have plagued a particular company or industry. Thus, statements in specific company codes regarding fair competition in business dealings have emerged in response to complaints of nepotism and insider deals in talent and production negotiations. Similarly, the factors driving key items in many industry codes are fairly self-evident such as the admonition to take proper precaution in preventing sexually transmitted diseases that is included in the adult entertainment industry's recommendations for "best practices."

Some issues relate to most all industries. For example, children are among the most active consumers of entertainment and they are also becoming increasingly involved in the production of entertainment as actors, musicians, and even producers. Because it is feared that children may not always make the most responsible choices, many industry codes include guidelines that specifically address dealings with them. See *Spotlight on Child Performers* for an example of a unique ethical issue related to children. Many, if not most, dilemmas that arise in entertainment are very unusual. The ethical issues that confront each entertainment sub-industry and profession are as varied as the industries themselves. We cannot possibly address them all here, but we can review some of the more common concerns that have emerged.

SPOTLIGHT ON CHILD PERFORMERS   What Price Fame for a Child Star?

Aspiring
child actor

Crafting child stars has become big business. Nine-year-olds trying to get movie roles take workshops, like Crying on Cue, that are part of the Child Actor Program at the Oakwood Toluca Hills complex near Burbank, California. The school residence for aspiring child actors, which charges $2,000 a month for a studio, prepares aspirants for the casting of 100-odd pilots from mid-January to May each year. Parents seem to believe that endless classes and coaching sessions will guarantee their children's success. Some even offer to pay to get their kid a part.

According to BizParents Foundation, a nonprofit group that provides information to families of acting kids, an increasing number of families uproot their lives to move to Los Angeles, reflecting today's societal pressures. Kids from all over the world pour into the International Models and Talent Association gatherings where agents are on hand to view the kids. Agents prefer families with no financial limits as well as the commitment of one parent to treat the child's career as a full-time job.

If a child's career begins gaining traction, it is ideal if the whole family can relocate to LA or maintain two homes to be near the child. An only child is preferred because the actor doesn't miss siblings and the mother isn't overstretched.

In addition to training, parents are encouraged to work to boost the child's visibility. One marketing ploy suggested by an agent has the child hand-delivering gift baskets—containing muffins, coffee, head shots, and résumé—to casting directors at the studios. They rely on the director's inability to resist a cute blonde, blue-eyed kid.

Parents have great incentive for supporting their child's efforts. Revenue derived from appearing in a nationally broadcast commercial can exceed $100,000, and a role on a pilot can yield between $5,000 and $50,000 depending on whether it's network or cable, and on the child's past credits. Parents rely on special attributes, like ethnicity or size, to help the child become noticed during auditions. Unfortunately, only about 4 percent of the kids who enroll actually become stars.

Source: Adrian Nicole LeBlanc for the *New York Times*, June 4, 2006, p. 44

What do you think?

- Do parents owe children the opportunity to pursue their dreams, even at the expense of the parents' own careers?
- Should agents use branding tactics to market child stars? Why/why not?
- Why is stardom so important to today's children?

Privacy and Intrusiveness

As with all corporations, the competition for attention has led entertainment companies to become increasingly sophisticated in the way that they identify and segment their consumers. Technological advances have facilitated their ability to compile massive individual files of consumer and media behavior and conduct "data mining" where they sift through these databases to come up with unique market segments such as sports video game users who like to discuss game play with their friends. These capabilities raise concerns about the misuse of personal information that is collected and stored. Many web sites require the disclosure of personal information including name, address, telephone listings, and credit card numbers. They can also track the media behavior of users while at their own web sites, collate that information with data obtained from other web sites and from consumers' own computers, merge it with their credit card information and sell the information to third parties.

Although companies in many different industries use these techniques, there are additional concerns associated with entertainment companies. When you go to a company's web site and perhaps buy something online or register to receive news alerts, you have knowingly acknowledged your interest in the company or products and provided them with your information. Recall, however, that entertainment has always been used as "bait" for corporate messages. but now entertainment content can be used not only to draw in audience attention for those messages but also to collect and share detailed information about those audiences. When you watch a TV program, you know that during commercial breaks companies will try to sell you their products. Thanks to ratings research, companies were able to get general information regarding the types of audiences they were reaching, but they couldn't specifically pinpoint you as a member of that audience. Today, however, you might join a social network or virtual world, add an icon of a steaming cup of coffee to your profile or declare your love of decaf mochas in a bulletin board posting, and next thing you know, you find yourself on MoJoJo's Coffee House's email list. Perhaps a slight exaggeration, but there is no doubt that such capabilities exist, and that, as has always been the case for traditional entertainment, most online entertainment such as social networks, games, and video sharing web sites exists for the sole purpose of luring in consumers for corporate advertisers.

The Federal Trade Commission has issued guidelines that require web sites to disclose their privacy policies, and privacy seal authorities have been established to monitor compliance. But some critics note that those disclosures often only offer the appearance of trustworthiness. When you actually read these disclosures you may find that instead of guaranteeing the protection of privacy they actually assure web site visitors that their privacy will be invaded and their information will be shared. Remember that people have dedicated significant time and resources to creating the elaborate entertainment content that you can often enjoy for free simply by logging on to their web site. It is certainly not unethical for them to want to receive compensation for their hard work. The ethical questions arise regarding how forthright they are in collecting and disclosing that compensation.

Consumer Ethics

One important change brought on by new media is that audiences or "users" can play a more active role in creating, distributing, and consuming entertainment content. As consumers begin to act more like entertainment producers, they also begin to face similar ethical scrutiny.

Internet Etiquette   The World Wide Web may sometimes seem more like the Wild, Wild West, untamed with no rules, but that really isn't the case. Most Internet providers have a code of ethics on their home page under "Acceptable Uses" or "User Policy." Separate from the company privacy policies discussed above, these are guidelines, not laws, and they address consumer or "user" behavior, not corporate behavior. These general rules usually focus more on "don'ts" than "dos," alerting users to activities that are not permitted on the web site. Although not criminally enforceable, the penalty for disobeying these rules can be an avid user's equivalent of death: termination of one's account. Listed below are some common rules, which whether explicitly stated on a web site or not, are recommended guidelines to follow for ethical online conduct:[57]

- *No harassment.* Don't use the Internet to harass other users such as by sending them abusive email, spam, or "mail bombs" of repetitive, unwanted messages. "Trolling"—making provocative statements in newsgroups to get people to visit your web site, for example—is also to be avoided. If your account is at a university, school authorites will take an especially dim view of sexual or racial harassment, and it may have legal or disciplinary consequences far beyond cancellation of your e-mail privileges.
- *No misrepresentation.* Middle-aged men posing as teenagers in hopes of luring young sex partners obviously violate this guideline. But it also precludes using someone else's name to sign up for services or listservs. Of course, if you are in a multiuser game or another Internet environment where everyone has a false identity and everyone knows and agrees on the rules, this "misrepresentation" is acceptable. However, "stealing" someone's identity online is a serious issue that could create real damage to the person you are pretending to be.

- *No hacking.* That means don't use the Internet to gain unauthorized access to other people's accounts or to computers run by organizations. Also, don't steal passwords or credit card numbers. And don't sabotage other people's computers or web pages or the Internet itself.
- *No lawbreaking.* If you use the Internet to commit an act that would be illegal in the "real world" you may make yourself liable to prosecution under laws that cover the real-world behavior. Thus, to make explicit what should go without saying, don't use the Internet to deal drugs, distribute child pornography, defraud others, violate copyright protection, or publish lies (libel) about others.

In addition to specific web site rules, your own Internet provider may have additional guidelines. For example, universities generally have a policy that forbids commercial use of the Internet. Using your web page to promote your rock band could get you into trouble, and using it to sell pirated, proprietary music almost certainly will.

Providers vary in how they may check for violations. Some companies only respond to complaints, while others take it upon themselves to seek out violators by monitoring activity. If your e-mail is an organizational account (such as a company or even a student account) you have *no right to privacy*. These organizations have the legal right to inspect your e-mail for violations of their policies. Recently, the FBI began working with a trade group, the Information Technology Association of America, to develop and disseminate ethical trade guidelines for young Internet users, schools, and parents. These rules are phrased as Kantian "categorical imperatives" or Biblical commandments such as: Thou shalt not vandalize web pages. Thou shalt not shut down web sites.

Piracy   As discussed in the previous chapter, the open culture of the Internet is posing serious challenges for the protection of intellectual property rights. The law is unequivocal; it is illegal to share copyrighted music and video files over the Internet or through other devices without permission from (and also payment to) the copyright owner. Although it is often called "sharing" or "downloading," it is in fact stealing, and, if the Recording Industry Association or Motion Picture Association of America targets you in a lawsuit, you will pay the penalty. Nonetheless, such violations are so rampant that prosecution of all violators is unlikely. As long as the likelihood of getting caught remains small, the decision regarding whether or not to file share comes down to personal ethics.

There are many arguments that people use to justify illegal file sharing. "Everyone else is doing it." "Just a few downloads isn't that big of deal." "Companies overcharge, so this just balances other things I've paid for." Whatever the justification you might try to offer, such file sharing is still stealing. Most people would agree that it is wrong for someone to walk into a store and take CDs or DVDs without paying for them. Obtaining pirated copies digitally with only a click of a button, may seem different, but it is not.

Some forms of copying are both ethical and legal. For their own use, consumers may make a videotape copy of a film that is being broadcast, but they may not sell or rent that copy to anyone else. In addition, a consumer may not copy one tape or DVD to another, not even as personal "back-up" copies. That is why all videotapes, CDs, and DVDs include FBI warnings against illegal copying. Again, however, because enforcement is difficult, the decision to copy or not to copy is a matter of ethics.

New technology continues to pose new ethical challenges, many of which consumers may not even think twice about. For example, do you use your DVR to skip obnoxious commercials? Many people follow the logic that if technology permits something, it must be OK. As we have seen, that isn't always the case. Although many technologies enable file downloads, that doesn't make them legal or right. Although there are no laws preventing viewers from skipping commercials, the TV networks that provide the programming consider it stealing. Recall that, on broadcast TV, programming is provided for free with the tacit understanding that audiences "pay" for it by watching the advertisements. Now that advertisers recognize that people can skip their ads, they do not want to pay as much for them, which means less revenue for the networks. Because there is no law against skipping, it is up to you and your own ethical standards to decide what to do. Keep in mind, however, that ultimately there will be a price to pay. We are already seeing these costs exacted as our favorite programs either sell out to intrusive product placements and/or move to pricey cable channels.

As we discussed in Chapter 8, consumers are not the only ones guilty of using and copying material without permission and exploiting new technology. Entertainment artists who have sampled and borrowed others' work and incorporated it into their own have frequently been sued for copyright infringement, and sometimes even libel or slander. At issue is whether the creator of a new work is directly profiting from the work of others or at their expense and, thus, either harming or depriving those individuals of profits that are rightly theirs. In many cases, however, it is difficult to determine when such activities cross the line from fair to illegal uses. Once again, the decisions regarding if and how to use another's work come down to ethical choices as much as they do to legal ones. See the *Spotlight on Lyrics Publishers* for an example of this issue.

SPOTLIGHT ON LYRICS PUBLISHERS   To Sue or Not to Sue

U.S. digital entertainment company Gracenote obtained licenses to distribute lyrics as music publishers mulled legal action against web sites that provide them without authorization. The service, to be initially available in North America, would be the first industry-backed move to provide lyrics legally. Until now, consumers' access to song lyrics has been largely through unauthorized sources, which usually provide inaccurate content.

Gracenote obtained the rights to the lyrics of more than one million songs from the North American catalogs of Bertelsmann AG's BMG Music Publishing, Vivendi's Universal Music Publishing Group, Sony/ATV Music Publishing, jointly owned by Sony and Michael Jackson, Peermusic, and other publishers. And it's talking with all of its partners, including Yahoo and Apple Computer's iTunes, about its plans to launch a service to offer legal and accurate lyrics for all digital media. "This license creates a new revenue stream which will guarantee that songwriters are paid for their work," said Nicholas Firth, chairman and chief executive officer of BMG Music Publishing.

Ralph Peer II at Peermusic said licensing lyrics should boost worldwide music publishing revenues, estimated at about $4 billion annually. Peer said he hopes the unauthorized sites would seek licenses.

Publishing industry officials cited web sites like www.lyrics.com and www.azlyrics.comc among those who provide their catalogs' lyrics without their authorization. There are copyright issues involving such unlicensed sites, which are making good income through advertising and other sources, while the composers are not getting their due.

Source: Reuters, July 14, 2006

What do you think?

- *Is illegal downloading a serious problem for this industry?*
- *Should unauthorized lyrics publishers be fined, sued, or ignored? Why?*

The Big Payola

Payola, a contraction of the words "pay" and "Victrola" (LP—long-playing—record player), refers to the practice where recording companies pay cash or gifts in exchange for airplay. Although payola schemes have probably existed from the advent of recorded music, such practices were not scrutinized or condemned until the late 1950s, when several independent labels recording rock began beating the majors—in par-

LP record player

ticular, Columbia, RCA, and Decca—in sales and airplay of popular records. This troubled not only the older labels but also the American Society of Composers, Authors, and Publishers (ASCAP). In the 1930s and 1940s, ASCAP had profited from the sales of sheet music, piano rolls, and recordings of Tin Pan Alley songs, but radio formats changed in the early 1940s when recorded music was introduced. Following a battle between radio stations and ASCAP over royalty payments, the stations decided to boycott recordings registered with ASCAP, and they began operating their own publishing corporation, Broadcast Music Incorporated (BMI). Because ASCAP tended to ignore music composed by Blacks and those they perceived to be hillbillies, BMI ended up with a virtual monopoly on songs in those fields. And as rock 'n' roll—at first the music of Blacks and hillbillies—emerged as a musical force, so did BMI.

As a result, it was hardly surprising when ASCAP, in 1959, urged a House Legislative Oversight subcommittee chaired by Representative Oren Harris to broaden its investigation of corrupt broadcasting practices, which had been centered on rigged TV quiz shows, to include the practice of payola in radio. When Representative Harris announced that his subcommittee would probe payola, *Variety* reported that ASCAP songsmiths took credit for switching the spotlight from TV quiz rigging to disk jockey payola. The assumption was that songs copyrighted with BMI would be revealed as having become hits fraudulently, thanks to payola.

These accusations were further fueled by critics who believed that rock 'n' roll was responsible for a breakdown of morals among youth, that it encouraged misogyny, that it was a subversive tool of "godless communism." It was commonly believed that teenagers were tricked into listening to this terrible music by greedy DJs who pocketed payola and then played a record so often it was imprinted on listeners' impressionable young minds.

In 1960, Congress, the FCC, and the Federal Trade Commission initiated an exhaustive probe of the entire music industry, from small publishing houses to major radio networks, covering 27 cities and digging for evidence of payola, including misuse of "freebies" (gifts), chart rigging, and kickbacks. In one of the first and most famous cases, the reputation and career of WINS New York disk jockey Alan Freed were destroyed when he was indicted on commercial bribery charges and accused of taking money to play records. Although rock 'n' roll may no longer be feared to be a communist plot and restrictions have eased considerably, the U.S. government continues to limit and investigate payola schemes under the auspices of ensuring fair business practices.

Even though it is illegal, many record company representatives and, more recently, independent promoters continue to dispense trips, contracts with artists, concert tickets, gifts, free music, and even sometimes drugs, sex, and bribes to get their records played on the air by DJs or placed into rotation by music directors. A similar practice, **plugola** implies providing consideration to get one's product mentioned or "plugged on the air." These practices are common enough that it presents a routine ethical choice to the DJs and music directors who are approached with such favors. Furthermore, in many cases, direct demands for radio play or plugs are not made but, instead, gifts are offered with a request just to give a listen to certain music or try a certain product with "no strings attached."

Such offers may not reach the level of illegal bribery, but they are still ethically questionable, and their subtlety makes it difficult to decide when the lines of propriety have been crossed. Record label representatives and music promoters are not the only ones to stretch ethical limits in securing the "play" they receive. In *A Closer Look* at the end of the chapter we learn about the questionable tactics used by one glitzy Los Angeles boutique to get play in celebrity magazines. Below, we explore ethical concerns regarding what tourist destinations and athletes are doing to improve their "play."

Beyond Media: Exploitation, Deception, and Doping

Ethical issues in entertainment are not limited to media; they can emerge in almost any recreational and leisure activity or industry. As examples, we have isolated issues regarding two popular activities, each supported by massive industries: tourism and sports.

Issues of Travel and Tourism Exploitation

Travel and tourism have been praised as a way to enhance cultural understanding, and thus ethical conduct, by encouraging people from around the world to treat each other fairly and with respect. However, tourist activity and the tourism industry have also been widely accused of behaving hedonistically, exploiting the local people and environments at tourist destinations to serve their own pleasures.

Tourism Concern, an independent charity based in the United Kingdom has outlined eight types of tourism exploitation: environmental damage, water abuse, displacement, cultural conflict, working conditions, the exploitation of women, child sex tourism, and foreign office travel advisories.[58]

Environmental Damage and Water Abuse   Environmental damage often results from rapid and uncontrolled development due to tourism. The lure of needed revenue often leads governments and private enterprises to prefer to maintain their tourist economies rather than their ecosystems. As a result, tourism developments—often built in the most beautiful landscapes and places in the world—threaten and destroy environments and exhaust limited natural resources, destroying these places for local peoples and future tourists. Waste created by the tourism industry is difficult to remove from fragile areas and means mountains of rubbish are appearing in the most beautiful landscapes on earth. Marine life is destroyed by irresponsible and unregulated tourism by diving, watersports, and coastal tourism. Skiing in northern Europe has led to mass

Bird feasting on tourist waste

tourism development which has felled forests and large numbers of tourists have been introduced into fragile and remote destinations. Golf tourism has created huge problems for local peoples using huge amounts of water and pesticides.

The presence of tourists naturally means a much higher demand for water. This places an extra burden on arid destinations facing water shortages. Showers, swimming pools, and watering of lawns can destroy water reserves, and often tourists are ignorant of the fact that the local populations lack water for their personal use and for irrigation. Local communities normally do not benefit, and in most cases are not allowed access to infrastructure built to ensure safe drinking water. The development of golf courses and hotel swimming pools is responsible for depleting and contaminating water sources for surrounding communities; this is especially true in Southeast Asia and the Middle East.

Although it might be tempting to condemn governments that prioritize profits over their environment, the issues are not that simple. Many of the most popular tourist regions are also some of the most economically distressed regions. Often the jobs and tax revenue generated by the tourism trade may seem to be the only way that local people can earn a living wage. It is difficult to argue that it would be more ethical for a government to risk further impoverishing its own people, in order to save the coral and trees. That is why many critics argue that the ethical obligation to insure ecological protections rests as much, if not more so, with the foreign investors and tourists who benefit from the development of these tourist destinations. As we will see, these same arguments can be applied to almost all issues of tourism exploitation.

Displacement and Cultural Conflict   Tourism development has caused many communities to be forcibly displaced—removed from their traditional lands—with indigenous groups being particularly vulnerable. Governments and private companies have forced many peoples off their land in the name of conservation to make way for eco-tourism, tourism resorts, and national parks. Families and communities are often evicted without warning, compensation, or alternative accommodation or homes. Mass tourism can seriously disrupt thriving local communities; small businesses are forced to compete with well-established multinational companies and local people are made to endure higher prices (from food to property) due to the presence of tourists.

As tourists, we are lucky enough to see and share experiences with different cultures, religions, dress, ideas. However, behind the scenes those very cultures that help to make our holidays so special are often violated. Indigenous people's cultures, beaches, sacred and religious sites, heritage, homes, and livelihoods have been wrecked in many instances by tourism. Once again, governments and citizens in tourist regions are faced with deciding whether or not to fight such displacement and try to preserve indigenous cultures. Following something akin to a utilitarian philosophy, it is decided that the benefit for the majority of the population outweighs the costs to minority indigenous groups. Others, however, might concur with Dr. Elliott that good for the greatest number does not always insure the greatest good for the community overall.

Working Conditions and the Exploitation of Women and Children   Cases of the exploitation of workers have been documented in almost every country, making it a global concern. Cruise ships, with no geographical boundaries, have been accused of contributing to the problem. One of the many reports of poor working conditions within the tourism industry is of trekking porters. Porters carry the supplies for tourists in trekking destinations such as Nepal, Tanzania, and Peru under similar appalling conditions—backbreaking loads, long hours, and sometimes even death.

Young boy making tourist goods in Delhi textile factory, India

There is an even greater chance for exploitation of vulnerable members of poor communities, including women and children. According to the International Labour Organization (ILO) women make up 70 percent of the labor force in the tourism industry and half are under 25 years of age. Women often are the most undervalued and underpaid workers and among the most exploited within the tourism industry. They are often left out of decision making and planning and the benefits of tourism. Women fish workers in Senegal have lived under the threat of displacement because public authorities prefer to defend the interests of the tourism sector—an experience shared by many women throughout the world. Worldwide, 13 to 19 million young people work in a profession tied to tourism. Children work as barmen, "fast food" employees, domestics, cooks' assistants, gardeners, laundry workers, informal tour guides, shellfish divers, roving beach vendors, and souvenir makers.

Women and children are also often victims of sexual exploitation. More than one million children are sexually abused by tourists every year within the global child sex tourism industry. Although there are a number of organizations working on this issue, the numbers involved in child sex tourism are increasing. In Vietnam, a child's services can be sold for as little as $10, with the trafficking of child sex workers becoming increasingly popular. Once again, while insuring humane working conditions and guarding against abuse should be a top priority of governments, it is also argued that tourists have some ethical obligations. No amount of government intervention can completely eliminate these problems as long as tourists continue to patronize questionable establishments, look the other way when they notice abuses, and indeed often even actively participate in such abuse.

Travel Advisories A final, perhaps unexpected criticism issued by Tourism Concern relates to travel advisories—notices issued by foreign governments advising their citizens as to the safety and suitability of a travel destination. The accusation is not that governments do not have a right, and possibly even a responsibility, to try to insure the safety of their citizens while traveling abroad. The concern is that, in their haste to be "safe rather than sorry," the warnings in travel advisories may be overstated, and in some cases unfounded. It is argued that travel warnings can have a devastating effect on many global tourism destinations. Tourism Concern produced a report highlighting the inconsistencies between travel advisories on destinations and the negative impacts they have had such as massive job loss, increased school dropout rates, and decreased government services—impacts which, they argue, are felt most by the poorest in the communities. As always, determining the correct moral course in these situations is not easy. Ethically, foreign governments should seek to insure their travel advisories are based on the most accurate information that is available, in fairness both to the travel destinations and to their citizens. Issues of safety are ultimately a judgment, however, and a case might be made that when in doubt, "safe rather than sorry" may appear to be the more ethical choice.

Tourism Industry Actions

In an effort to address many of the problems outlined above, tourism industry organizations have developed detailed codes of conduct and ethics. Most of these codes extend far beyond a simple listing of overarching principles. For example, the Global Code of Ethics for Tourism issued by the World Tourism Organization is broken down into ten articles each supported by several specific tenants. The tenants are quite specific. For example Article 1.4 reads:[59]

> It is the task of the public authorities to provide protection for tourists and visitors and their belongings; they must pay particular attention to the safety of foreign tourists owing to the particular vulnerability they may have; they should facilitate the introduction of specific means of information, prevention, security, insurance and assistance consistent with their needs; any attacks, assaults, kidnappings or threats against tourists or workers in the tourism industry, as well as the willful destruction of tourism facilities or of elements of cultural or natural heritage should be severely condemned and punished in accordance with their respective national laws.

In addition to the establishment of these codes, issues such as environmental protection, sustainable tourism, and labor exploitation are among the most widely discussed topics at tourism trade and professional meetings. Companies in the tourism industries are increasingly addressing these issues, not just because of ethical concerns but also out of economic expediency. Not only do they understand that protecting environments and preventing the exploitation of local people is necessary for preserving the desirability of tourist destinations, but they also recognize that tourists increasingly expect such efforts. The rise in popularity of eco-tourism (see Chapter 16) and philanthropic tourism, where tourists actually pay to assist with environmental preservation and clean-up and humanitarian aid projects, are viewed as clear indicators of increased consumer concern and support for sustainable tourism.

Sports Issues

Athletes and the sports industries have faced numerous ethical challenges ranging from bribery and deceit at colleges that woo student athletes with gifts and falsify grades to gambling scandals involving players and officials who try to "fix" competition results for bet payoffs to flat-out cheating by using ineligible players and illegal equipment. These ethical breaches commonly involve charges of deception and exploitation that result in certain competitors gaining an unfair advantage. Fair play is a central tenant of sporting activities, and as such there tends to be particular condemnation for any actions perceived to be "unfair." Many sports leagues and divisions have codified rules to guard against unfair practices, and violators may face fines, bans, or expulsions. Teams and athletes have been fined and banned from play for violating recruitment policies, eligibility requirements, and game play rules. However, regardless of the level at which you play—in organized leagues or neighborhood pick-up games—your decision to cheat or play by the rules is, at its heart, an issue of ethics.

Doping and Gaming Theory One questionable choice that athletes at all levels are increasingly facing is deciding whether or not to use performance-enhancing drugs. Given that doping is illegal in most organized sports, athletes tend to do it secretly, thus, ethically speaking, making it a form of deception, or more simply put, it's cheating. At the professional level, an increasing number of sports including baseball, football, track and field, and cycling are facing "doping" scandals where top athletes

How many cyclists enhance performance with drugs?

have been accused and often found guilty of using banned substances in an effort to boost their performance. According to the World Anti-Doping Agency,[60] the term "doping" is thought to have derived from the Afrikaans word "dop," a concoction made from grape leaves that Zulu warriors drank before going into battle. In sports, the term was first used to describe the illegal drugging of race horses at the beginning of the twentieth century.

Doping in sport now includes a range of practices, including "blood doping" (the practice of autologous or homologous hemoglobin transfusions) and the use of synthetic erythropoeitin (EPO) to increase the number of red blood cells; anabolic steroids and human growth hormone to grow skeletal muscle; stimulants to improve cognitive function and reduce fatigue; and nitrogen tents and "houses" to simulate the effects of sleeping at high altitude. The future holds the promise of more powerful and exotic interventions.[61]

Writer Michael Shermer has applied gaming theory to understand why athletes choose to dope.[62] Game theory is the study of how players in a game choose strategies that will maximize their return in anticipation of the strategies chosen by the other players. Originally designed by John von Neumann and Oskar Morgenstern to solve problems in economics, game theory relates economics to a game in which the players anticipate one another's moves. This theory goes beyond the classical theory of probability because it stresses the strategic aspects of game. The "games" for which the theory was first applied were not just gambling games such as poker or sporting contests in which tactical decisions play a major role; they also included deadly serious affairs in which people make economic choices, military decisions, and even national diplomatic strategies. What all those "games" have in common is that each player's "moves" are analyzed according to the range of options open to the other players.

The game of prisoner's dilemma provides a classic example. You and your partner are arrested for a crime, and you are held incommunicado in separate prison cells. Of course, neither of you wants to confess or rat on the other, but the D.A. gives each of you the following options:

- If you confess but the other prisoner does not, you go free and he gets 20 years in jail.

- If the other prisoner confesses and you do not, you get 20 years and he goes free.

- If you both confess, you each get five years.

- If you both remain silent, you each get a year.

Prisoner's dilemma

To analyze the prisoner's dilemma, we apply the "sure thing" principle. Although Person A can't be sure what Person B will do, he knows that he does best to confess when B confesses (he gets five years rather than twenty) and also when B remains silent (he serves no time longer than a year); B will reach the same conclusion. So the solution would seem to be that each prisoner does best to confess and go to jail for five years. Paradoxically, the two robbers would do better if they both adopted an "irrational" strategy of remaining silent, where each would serve only one year. The irony of the prisoner's dilemma is that when each of two parties acts selfishly and does not cooperate (confess), they do worse than when they act unselfishly and do cooperate (remain silent).

Athletes can be seen as facing a similar dilemma in deciding whether or not to dope. In sports, the contestants compete according to a set of rules. The rules of many sports clearly prohibit the use of performance-enhancing drugs. But because the drugs are so effective and many of them are so difficult (if not impossible) to detect, and because the payoffs for success are so great, the incentive to use banned substances is powerful. If some athletes choose to dope and others do not, it gives the "dopers" an advantage. The best option might be for all athletes not to dope, but, because there are no guarantees that everyone will abstain, the most rational choice is to choose to dope. Thus, once a few elite athletes "defect" from the rules (cheat) by doping to gain an advantage, their rule-abiding competitors must defect as well, leading to a cascade of defection through the ranks. Because of the penalties for breaking the rules, however, a code of silence prevents any open communication about how to reverse the trend and return to abiding by the rules.

The fact that doping might appear to be the most rational choice, however, does not make it the most ethical. The question of whether or not doping violates ethical principles has become a hotly debated topic.

Ethical Principles in Sports

Led by the international Olympic movement, most organized sports have taken the position that the use of performance-enhancing drugs is unethical and they have taken steps to prevent their use by banning them, establishing testing programs, and punishing athletes caught using prohibited substances. The basic anti-doping principles of sport which were laid down in 1967 by the International Olympic Committee are:

- protection of the athletes' health
- respect for medical and sports ethics
- insuring an equal chance for everyone during competition.

Arguments have been offered that doping is unethical because it violates each of these principles. Critics, however, have contested this position on several counts. They have debated whether or not doping violates each these principles, as well as questioned the principles themselves. Law professor Maxwell Mehlman has offered a comprehensive review of the various sides of this argument.[63]

Health   First, he acknowledges that it might seem hard to disagree with the first principle, "protection of athletes' health." Clearly some performance-enhancing drugs are dangerous. Steroids, for example, are associated with a range of side effects, including heart attacks and liver cancer. But he also notes that sports in general, and some sports in particular, are inherently dangerous. Athletes often injure themselves in training and in competition. For many people, it is the possibility of injury and even death that makes sports events fun to watch. Consider automobile or downhill ski racing, even football and hockey, not to mention boxing. So, the argument goes, if athletes are free to accept a certain degree of risk from dangerous sports, why shouldn't they be allowed to accept a comparable, or even greater, risk from enhancements? An obvious answer is that the fact that some sports are already dangerous does not justify making them more so by allowing the use of dangerous enhancements. But the question of how much risk is justifiable and whether the use of certain drugs might exceed this risk is not an easy question to answer.

An additional argument against the use of enhancements is that it is the athletic equivalent of the nuclear arms race. If everyone is using enhancements, then all advantage is eliminated. So instead of exposing everyone to unnecessary health risks, the better option is to ban enhancements. However, others counter that the effects of enhancements are not equal, and, like other adjustments in training such as diet, should be left to the athletes' discretion. Opponents, however, stick with their argument, that, left unchecked, athletes will have no choice but to use any and all enhancements that are available.

Assuming that protecting athletes' health is a legitimate concern, there is also a question regarding how much of threat enhancements really pose. Some enhancements, like nitrogen tents, do not appear to have any lasting negative effects, and some athletes use even potentially dangerous enhancements like steroids and EPO without seeming to suffer any significant or irreversible harm. This has led some proponents to suggest that if we are interested in preventing harm, we ought to invest the bulk of our anti-doping money in research to develop safer enhancements, rather than in preventing their use. Others, however, point to research and anecdotal cases where serious health problems have been tied to enhancement drugs. Still others contend that we just don't know. In debating the use of drugs in professional cycling, columnist Ryan Quinn notes:[64]

> Eight—the number of elite cyclists who have recently died suddenly from inexplicable heart failures. Cycling officials say these were freak tragedies. That's quite a coincidence. Especially since most of the drugs popular with endurance athletes do more than improve their endurance. The drugs also dangerously thicken the athlete's blood. Death is the highest price to pay when you're willing to win at any cost, but even the lesser side effects of blood boosters and steroids range from inconvenient to horrific. Sadly, because of the shameful, secretive nature of doping, many of the most serious risks are unknown.

Ultimately, most people will agree that it is clearly justifiable for sport to ban dangerous practices. If enhancements are unsafe or their safety uncertain and suspect, it is appropriate to discourage their use in order to protect athletes. Nor, most will agree, is it a contradiction for the rules to permit other dangerous practices. Although the nature of a sport, as defined by the rules, may create inherent dangers, it should still strive to be as safe as possible, and this justifies not allowing athletes to add to their risk with a new set of dangerous or potentially dangerous behaviors. The question, however, remains: if certain enhancement drugs meet that criteria, and even if they do, are bans a good idea, even if they can't be enforced?

Medical and Sports Ethics   It is also argued that the use of performance-enhancing drugs violates medical and sports ethics. The availability of performance enhancements creates ethical concerns for physicians who have athletes as patients. In general, the anti-doping rules of sport are aimed at athletes, teams, and, to a lesser extent, coaches and trainers, and not at physicians who may be the source of the banned substances. While the Anti-Doping Code of the World Anti-Doping Agency prohibits anyone from administering or attempting to administer a banned substance, or assisting, encouraging, aiding, abetting, covering up, or being complicit in a violation or attempted violation of an anti-doping rule, sports organizations rarely impose penalties on physicians, and then only on team doctors. For example, a Romanian team physician was asked to leave the Olympic Village at the 2000 Sydney Olympics after he gave a banned over-the-counter cold remedy to a gymnast.[65] Although penalties are rare, physicians still must decide whether they believe prescribing enhancements constitutes a breach of ethics. Since no drugs have been approved by the FDA to enhance sports performance, physicians who prescribe them to their athlete-patients are engaging in off-label prescribing. Such off-label use raises issues of medical ethics far beyond concerns about violating the rules of any given sports organization.

Regarding sports ethics, it is argued that performance enhancements must be banned because, according to those who make the rules of sport, using them is cheating. Clearly if a sport does not allow the use of performance enhancing drugs, then doping is, by definition, cheating. But, rules change all the time. Consider the evolution in the size of tennis racket heads, for example. In baseball, the pitcher's mound was lowered to make the curve and slider pitches more effective. Until the 1960s, the poles used for pole vaulting were made out of wood. Then someone began making poles out of fiberglass, which added an additional couple of feet to the maximum height athletes could attain. The rules could have prohibited the use of fiberglass poles, but they didn't, and everyone started using them. You had to in order to remain competitive.

In most cases, the argument for making the changes is that the new rules enhance the competitive experience for both the athletes and audiences. Thus, some might argue that performance-enhancing drugs that allow athletes to go faster, harder, and longer does indeed "enhance" the competitive experience. Others, however, disagree, saying that enhancement drugs detract from competition by making it less "authentic." Imagine if athletes could infuse a cocktail of enhancement genes and walk off with Olympic medals without going through the ordeals of practice and conditioning. The medal might seem unearned, the accomplishment unremarkable. In this sense, use of enhancements might be different from natural talents because athletes presumably must train and practice to make use of their talents, and we may be said to be rewarding the work involved rather than just the talent itself. But hard work is not the only thing we reward. We also reward unearned advantages, like talent or luck.

Equal Competition   This brings us to the third of the IOC's anti-doping principles, "insuring an equal chance for everyone during competition." As noted above, it may be the case that to remain competitive all athletes have to use enhancements if any do. But what if enhancements were not available to everyone? If they were too costly or the supply were too limited regardless of how much athletes were willing to pay, so that only some athletes were fortunate enough to obtain the performance advantages, the use of enhancements would seem unfair.

Yet, athletes are never equal at the moment of competition. They enjoy lots of unfair advantages. Some are born with greater natural abilities. Some have wealthy parents or the good luck not to become injured. Not every Olympic gymnast can be trained by Bela Karoly; not every figure skater is able to grow up practicing on her personal backyard ice rink, like Sara Hughes. Thus, some people find it difficult to understand why sport tolerates these advantages but would not permit the use of enhancements by those who could gain access to them. One answer is that it is fair to permit people to benefit from the distribution of natural abilities and good fortune because these factors lie outside of our control. But, we can control gaining undue advantages through doping. But proponents counter that control is exactly why performance-enhancement drugs should be allowed. They suggest that we could use enhancements to increase fairness, by allowing them to be used only by those who were disadvantaged by the natural lottery. For example, enhancements might enable athletes with disabilities to compete in the real rather than in "special" Olympics.

Disabled athlete in Ottawa marathon 2008, Canada

In Defense of Rules   Ultimately, however, Mehlman argues that it would be a mistake to dismiss the significance of rules. It is perfectly appropriate for a sport to make rules and to require competitors to stick to them, to say that you can use fiberglass poles or nitrogen tents, for example, but not steroids or EPO. Moreover, the rules can be completely arbitrary. Indeed, they often are, the reasons for them long forgotten. There is nothing inherently wrong with a sport saying that it must be played in a certain arbitrary way, like standing on your head, or without using enhancements.

Rules and the traditions they represent are important because they create a set of expectations among athletes, coaches, judges, and spectators. The playing field may not be level, but everyone understands that only certain bumps and dips are permitted. You don't expect to see someone slugged in the face with a cricket bat (although you might with a hockey stick). Moreover, athletes are expected to be role models for young people. The use of enhancements, particularly banned drugs, by professional athletes may be taken as a general endorsement of the use of those drugs and possibly other illicit drugs.

The consequences of disappointing these public expectations are not to be underestimated. Consider how upset baseball fans are at reports that home-run hitters use steroids. To preserve spectator loyalty, not to mention revenues, athletic organizations like the International Olympic Committee are perfectly within their rights to make their own rules and enforce them, even if the rules may not always seem defensible or fair. The question of whether athletes choose to violate those rules, however, remains a matter of personal ethics.

CONSIDER THIS

The 2008 Beijing Olympics gymnastic competition aroused a controversy that questioned the age of Chinese participants, suggesting they were years under the regulation minimum age of 16. In spite of their passports, three Chinese team members had ages listed on various documents that made them as young as 14 years. Similarly in 1991, a Korean girl was exposed as being much younger when her smile showed baby teeth still in place. But unlike doping, there isn't a test to determine someone's age.

What do you think?

· *Should age limits be abandoned for Olympic competition?*

FADE TO BLACK

In this chapter we have explored a wide range of ethical issues. We began with a review of major general ethical philosophies, as well as a discussion of specific theories that have been applied to media ethics. Much of entertainment is story-driven, so we then focused on the ethics of storytelling, revealing the ethical challenges that have emerged as the result of the rise of infotainment—the blurring of entertainment, news, and commercial media. We questioned the lack of distinction made between fact and fiction in biographies and documentaries, product placements, and reality programs. We also posed the question of whether entertainment producers should be held accountable for any negative effects of their productions, such as impacts of violent and sexual content and stereotypes.

We then moved from the ethics of storytelling to scrutinize other industry practices. We elaborated on the ethical challenges of protecting consumer privacy and corporate bribes in the form of "payola," and we considered several implications of new media technologies for ethical consumer behavior. Last, we discussed ethical issues beyond media entertainment, reviewing examples of ethical issues of exploitation and deception found in the tourism and sports industries. Repeatedly, we saw how laws and regulations and ethical guidelines cannot guarantee ethical behavior or replace individual obligations to make personal moral decisions.

A CLOSER LOOK AT E-TIZING PUBLICITY   When quid-pro-quo isn't

Kitson, a boutique selling celebrity, fashion, and gossip in Los Angeles, boycotted the use of advertising, and instead opted to take its chances, working at getting the brand name mentioned in magazines, via paparazzi pictures of Halle Berry leaving the store carrying an initialed handbag that created a run on

the bags, or coverage of a Nicole Richie book signing, or events promoting some celebrity's jewelry or perfume. Kitson's promotion system has become so ingrained that some retailers hire publicists to pitch their celebrity connections to publications. The magazines, in turn, satisfy readers' hunger for knowing how the stars shop, eat, and live; the paparazzi sell pictures; the celebrities get exposure, and Kitson attracts shoppers.

Such "back-scratching" tactics came under scrutiny in September 2006 when Kitson's owner, Frasier Ross, sued the publisher of *Us Weekly* for editing the store's brand out of its entertainment star coverage out of spite. A retailer suing to demand coverage in a magazine may seem like a publicity stunt, but Ross claimed the suit was about contractual obligation. After Kitson's hosting and underwriting a party for the magazine in exchange for two pages of coverage, *Us* never delivered (*Us* later paid for the party).

At the center of the dispute is the celebrity-fueled economy that capitalizes on the public's boundless need for minutiae about entertainment stars.

Retailers work hard to be mentioned as the source of celebrities' goods by alerting paparazzi and sending products to stars for free in hopes that they will be photographed using them. According to Martin Kaplaln, director of the Norman Lear Center in Los Angeles, which studies the impact of entertainment on society, the notion that ethical standards exist when the entertainment industry intersects with celebrity journalism is "an illusion." Standards vary from publication to publication, there are clear "no-nos," like asking for free products. Most fashion editors credit the designer and store with the name of the stylist at the bottom of a layout, but some magazines and retailers develop more incestuous relationships—like when Ross invested in Sunset Photo, a paparazzi agency whose owner was a former *Us* editor.

Although Ross claimed not to be in the fashion business, his retail store (with $24 million in annual sales) capitalized on a new James Bond film, *Casino Royale*, by selling $95 T-shirts and clothing tied to the movie in Kitson's window—"It's like having a billboard on Sunset," he boasted, proving that celebrity sells.

Source: Mireya Navarro for the *New York Times*, Sept. 21, 2006, E1

What do you think?

- *What's wrong with the unspoken arrangements between celebrity magazines and retailers?*
- *Can industry sanctions and lawsuits monitor and penalize offenders? Why/why not?*

DISCUSSION AND REVIEW

1. Not all ethical issues of entertainment can be resolved in the same manner. Review the six general ethical philosophies introduced in this chapter, and offer your opinion as to which ones are more or less useful for each of the different ethical issues that were discussed.
2. Explain the different ways that fact and fiction have been blurred in contemporary entertainment.
3. Some critics believe that entertainment producers should be held accountable for any negative impacts of their productions. Do you agree? Why or why not?
4. Compare and contrast the ethical challenges faced by entertainment companies and

professionals to those faced by entertainment consumers or "users." Can you find
common themes as well as unique concerns?

5. What are the two major ethical concerns discussed regarding industries other than
    entertainment media?

EXERCISES

1. Using Potter's Box, apply each of the six ethical theories discussed in the chapter to
    each of the four ethical dilemmas outlined at the beginning of the chapter.
2. Look through some of the more popular videos that have been posted on YouTube.
    Can you find examples of any of the ethical criticisms related to storytelling that are
    described in the chapter?
3. In this chapter game theory was used to explain doping behavior. See if you can apply
    this theory in helping explain other examples of questionable ethical behavior in
    entertainment.

BOOKS AND BLOGS

Boxhill, Jan (2003). *Sports ethics: An anthology*. Malden MA: Blackwell.

Fennell, David (2006). *Tourism ethics*. Clevedon, U.K.: Channel View Publications.

Valenti, Miguel (2000). *More than a movie: Ethical decision making in the entertainment
    industry*. Boulder CO: Westview Press.

www.mediaethicsmagazine.com/—has stories on media ethics.

www.networkworld.com/weblogs/gearblog/2005/009699.html—contains an article on ethics
    and entertainment.

www.twec.com/corpsite/corporate/code.cfm—contains the corporation code of ethics of Trans
    World Entertainment.

10 RELIGION AND SOCIALIZATION

For we are not fighting against flesh-and-blood enemies, but against evil rulers and authorities of the unseen world, against mighty powers in this dark world, and against evil spirits in the heavenly places

—Ephesians 6:12

Since the beginning of time, performance has had a symbiotic relationship with religion. That is to say, music and dance always accompanied religious ceremonies and worship and were integrally associated with both mystery and doctrine. The first great culture to infuse its entire society with the magic of music and dance was Ancient Egypt. Most of Egyptian religious life was marked by the performance of music and dance. Ceremonial palettes and stone vessels indicate the importance that music had even in the earliest of periods. Subsequently, all cultures and religions embraced song and dance, which were the earliest forms of entertainment,

In this chapter, we visit various aspects of entertainment as it relates to religious communication. Live performance—dance, drama, music, and theme parks—begin the discussion; mediated religion—movies, television, radio, comics, and the Internet—follows. The association between sports and religion is presented next. And because religion and communication are forms of socialization, we dedicate equal time to looking at how the way we interact and socialize impacts entertainment.

Religious Origins of Performance Arts

Hinduism is perhaps the oldest living religion. In fact, the origins of Hinduism can be traced back to at least 2500 BC and today there are close to a billion followers. Faith transformed into physical reality results in an almost infinite variety of religious expressions: architecture, music, dance, dietary laws, dress codes, and even belief systems. Religious architecture—for example, churches, mosques, synagogues, and temples—can be looked upon as the transformation or projection of faith into physical form. Each of these buildings have their particular architectural styles and they all arise from the collective faith of their worshippers. Similarly, in the realm of religious art, there are unlimited religious expressions beginning from the ancient rock paintings of early man in the caves of France or the outstanding Islamic designs found in the mosques of Saudi Arabia, or the ancient Greek and Roman sculpture found in the ruins of Athens and Rome. Music and dance are also expressions of religious faith. Taken together, each of the performance categories of religious expression—architecture, music, dance, dress—enhance the cumulative religious traditions of the world, which we call Hinduism, Judaism, Buddhism, Christianity, Islam, and so forth. Four live forms of religious expression are discussed here: dance, drama, music, and theme parks.

Religious Dance

Ancient Greeks believed that dancing was invented by the Gods and therefore associated it with their religious and worshipping ceremonies. They believed that the Gods offered this gift to some select mortals only, who in turn taught dancing to their fellow men. Eastern Oriental dance, centered on what we call "belly dancing," has traditional associations with both religious and erotic elements.

If we follow dance back to its roots, we see how the sensual dances which originated with Greek mystery rites and comedy dances traveled to Spain where it became what is today Flamenco, and that another form of this dance developed throughout the Middle and Near East as what we call belly dance. Both types of dance are also associated with the Gypsies, who came out of India, through Persia, and by the Middle Ages spread throughout Europe.

Dance, which began in temples, was eventually passed on to the secular in an erotic form, and evolved into a class of professional dancers. In pre-Christian time the belly dance was religious and also referred to sexuality. Thus dance has progressed from the religious sphere to the realm of dance as spectacle or entertainment. And, at the same time, various forms of eastern dance continue to be used in a religious sense in various trance dances found throughout the Middle East today.

During the Buddhist, Gupta, and medieval periods, dance played an important role in achieving the spiritual inspiration and identification of the people of that time. The existing temple sculptures, paintings and icons are compelling proof. Later, with the invasion of the Muslims, who considered it almost a scandal to use music and dance for divine worship, dance found its way into the courts and as a form of entertainment. The point is that culture, through its expressions in arts, art forms, literature, and language, shapes our very understanding of Christ and His Gospel.

SPOTLIGHT ON GOD ROCK   The Jesus Freak Movement

Christian Ixoye fish

The Christian embrace of hip youth scenes can be traced, like so much, to the cultural ferment of the 1960s. A generation of mystic hippies sparked the mass Jesus People movement, which injected a distinctly Christian feeling for love and apocalypse into a counterculture already up to its mala beads in love and apocalypse. By the early 1970s, a new Jesus had hit the American mind—communal, earthy, spontaneous, anti-establishment. And this Jesus and his "freaks" continued to transform American worship long after the patchouli wore off, inspiring a more informal and contemporary style of communion and celebration that, while holding true to core principles, unbuckled the Bible Belt from American Christian life.[1]

Along with the baggy hoodies or the four-fin surfboards, Jesus freaks adorn ixthus fish tattoos or T-shirts that say, "Jesus: Sweet Savior." Contemporary Christians believe that resistance is futile; Evangelist ministries and young believers have opted to enjoy pop culture's manic energy and style while splicing in inspiring messages and strict rules of moral conduct.

One of the earliest and most influential Jesus freaks was a guy with the fabulous name of Lonnie Frisbee. As told in David Di Sabatino's excellent 2006 documentary *Frisbee: The Life and Death of a Hippie Preacher*, Lonnie was a tripped-out young man who grew up in Orange County, California, saw God on LSD, and became a Christian in the Haight. Keeping his duds and long hair—not to mention his charismatic air of innocence and spiritual conviction—Frisbee hooked up with strait-laced pastor Chuck Smith. Together they began an enormously popular youth ministry at Smith's Calvary Chapel, a revival that almost single-handedly transformed the hippie Jesus vibe into a mass phenomenon. Jesus became a long-haired revolutionary of love, a real Superstar, and his followers used underground newspapers and beachside baptisms to turn others on to the convulsive power of the Holy Spirit.

They also used rock 'n' roll. Although we don't know how much our suburban mega-churches owe to the Jesus movement, there is no question that contemporary Christian music owes its billions to the freaks. The *Frisbee* documentary's soundtrack is a collection of Jesus freak folk-rock anthology that complements some of the fascinating reissues that have emerged over the last few years. The extraordinary urgency to All Saved Freak Band's combination of righteousness and rock anticipates straight-edge hardcore.

The *Frisbee* soundtrack includes some creepy mania recorded in the late 1970s during a time when the growing industry of contemporary Christian music (CCM) was making its saccharine pact with the pop devil. The music crackles with apocalyptic power and the desire to use the rock song as a vehicle of total transformation. Though it may be hard to reconcile the All Saved Freak Band with the slick suburban profile of CCM, they remain formative figures in the genre, with a messianic intensity that provides the essential rock 'n' roll element of *risk*.

Source: Davis, Erik (2007). I'd like to dedicate this next song to Jesus: The freaky origins of Christian rock, posted on slate.com

Religious Drama

Theater became an extension of church architecture after nearly eighteen centuries when the basilica was transformed into a radically new worship building, the auditorium church. This radical shift in evangelical Protestant architecture was linked to changes in worship style and religious mission. The auditorium style, featuring a prominent stage from which rows of pews radiated up a sloping floor, was derived directly from the theater, an unusual source for religious architecture but one with a similar goal—to gather large groups within range of a speaker's voice. Theatrical elements were prominent; many featured proscenium arches, marquee lighting, theater seats, and even opera boxes.

These worship spaces underscored performative and entertainment aspects of the service and in so doing transformed relationships between clergy and audiences. In auditorium churches, the congregants' personal and social power derived as much from consumerism as from piety, and clerical power lay in dramatic expertise rather than connections to social institutions. By erecting these buildings, middle-class religious audiences demonstrated the move toward a consumer-oriented model of religious participation that gave them unprecedented influence over the worship experience and church mission.[2]

Theater that reflects positive Christian themes started as early as the tenth century and flourished during the end of the fifteenth century in medieval Europe. There are two main kinds of Christian drama, Mystery or miracle plays, and the Morality play. Although the two are different in nature, they both aim to reinforce and teach Church doctrines and moral values.

Mystery Plays   Mystery plays began as representations of Biblical stories, from either the Old Testament or stories about Christ and the lives of saints. Churchmen or clergy performed in Mystery plays, with themes such as the Creation, the Murder of Abel, Adam and Eve's banishment from Eden, and The Last Judgment, which were presented in Latin on church premises. As Mystery plays gained popularity, non-clergy actors were included in the productions, and by the fourteenth century, these dramas were moved out of the church setting into the marketplace in native languages.

Morality Plays   Originating in the fifteenth century, mystery plays are allegorical in nature: the story revolves around a main character who meets personifications that have moral attributes and encourage the protagonist to live a life of virtue. Morality plays usually have protagonists who are representations of an entire social class, or humanity as a whole. The antagonists are not individuals, but are personifications of abstract virtues or vices. After being suppressed for wickedness in the sixteenth and seventeenth centuries, Christian drama flourished in evangelical churches that considered it an art form rather than blasphemy.

A modern version of the Morality play, *Jesus Christ Superstar*, was developed as a rock opera by Tim Rice and Andrew Lloyd Webber. The play highlights the political and interpersonal struggles of Judas Iscariot and Jesus, and the action follows the canonical gospels' accounts of the last weeks of Jesus' life, beginning with Jesus and his followers arriving in Jerusalem and ending with the Crucifixion. Twentieth-century attitude and sensibilities as well as contemporary slang pervade the lyrics, and ironic allusions to modern life are scattered throughout the political depiction of the events. Stage and film productions accordingly feature many intentional anachronisms.

Rock Opera   The rock opera was first heard as an album before being staged on Broadway and later in London's West End. The title song, "Superstar," and "I Don't Know How to Love Him" were both big hits. A cover of the latter song, recorded by singer Helen Reddy, reached the top 15 U.S. pop singles charts in early 1971.

Originally appearing as a record because producers were afraid to take a chance on such a daring production, *Jesus Christ Superstar* eventually premiered at the Mark

Jesus Christ Superstar on stage in London, 1972

Hellinger Theatre in New York on October 12, 1971. Despite opposition from certain religious groups, this production became a huge box office hit and ran for 720 performances. The 1973 film version featured Ted Neeley and Carl Anderson.

One year after *Superstar* premiered, *Godspell* the musical opened off Broadway and has played in various touring companies and revivals many times since. Several cast albums have been released over the years and one of its songs, "Day by Day" from the original cast album, reached number 13 on the *Billboard* pop singles chart in the summer of 1972. The structure of the musical is that of a series of parables, taken primarily from the Gospel of Matthew. These are then interspersed with a variety of modern music set primarily to lyrics from traditional hymns, with the passion of Christ treated briefly near the end of performance.

Godspell has remained an important part of the modern musical theater because of its versatility. The original production made the company a troupe of clowns who follow Jesus in an abandoned playground; subsequent productions have been set in museums, classrooms, on top of buildings, an apocalyptic world, or in an abandoned theater. The setting can be as advanced enough for the biggest Broadway producers, and small enough for any high school production. In one such production, the setting was simply three construction scaffolds. In another, it was done with a wall, some steps, and a treasure chest. The setting has even been in a McDonald's restaurant. In September 2007, an all new cast was chosen for a Revival U.K. Tour of *Godspell* that opened at the Peterborough Key Theatre. *Godspell* returned to Broadway in the summer of 2008 in a production that reunited the creative team of the 2006 production that played New Jersey's Paper Mill Playhouse.

Global Religious Theater   Around the globe, many forms of religious theater are popular today in Islam, Chile, Russia, the U.K., and the U.S. Recently, Islam theater—the transformation of pantomime to religious rituals—is performed as the Whirling Dervish dance. What had been originally an unconscious living art form became a conscious dramatization of life's illusion to celebrate a wide range of ceremonies that were symbolic intercessions of a divine nature that grants prosperity, health, peace, and so forth.

Andean peoples of Chile celebrate their spirituality with dramatic festivals that blend their indigenous beliefs with Catholicism to affirm their bicultural identity while honoring their town's patron saint. A new presentation of "Spectacles" festival explores this fusion of faiths and the degrees of accommodation and resistance to Catholicism.

The International Christian Theater Festival called *The Mystery* was held in Moscow in 2008. Created to revive church theater, more than 20 venues with stage productions went to Moscow from all parts of Russia and abroad. Billed as "interconfessional," the festival included theater from Orthodox, Catholic, Lutheran, Protestant, and other churches and was presented under the auspices of the government of Moscow, the Russian Union of Theater Professionals, and the Union of Christian Theater Professionals.

American Catholic Theater   Epiphany Studio Catholic Theater Productions of Minneapolis provides parishes, conferences, and conventions with evangelical entertainment tools and inspirational events for retreats and rallies to challenge contemporary culture with Catholic theater experiences. Billed as new evangelization, these dramas are performed to inspire and transform in the style of Rhapsodic Theater, which was founded in Nazi-occupied Poland in 1941. Rhapsodic Theater introduced a new genre of dramatic expression called "Theater of the Word" that combined dramatic theory with principles of art, esthetics, drama, poetry, philosophy, theology, all enriched and penetrated by the

Catholic faith. Reinvigorated by the Pope, plays and writings on the theater remain as a perpetual testimony to the profundity and beauty of the rhapsodic style.

Also in Minneapolis, audiences gathered in 2008 at the Hennepin Avenue United Methodist Church for a festival containing three dozen plays and films that explore spirituality and religion via a variety of theatrical styles and across the religious spectrum. Bible stories, traditional Hindu dance performances and a number of works that trace an individual's journey through darkness are included. Beginning as part of the Minnesota Fringe Festival, the event is now on its own. The program also included a number of dance performances, from Christian celebrations of faith, to Hula and Native American, to the Ragamala Music and Dance Theater, which presented a type of Hindu dance that traces its history back 2,000 years.

As evidenced, live theater espousing religious themes is a popular form of artistic creative expression around the globe today, and, if its popularity is any indication, will be continuing into the foreseeable future.

Religious Music

Music plays a vital role in shaping societies. The primary function of music in Egyptian and other early cultures was apparently religious, ranging from heightening the effect of magic to praising deities. In the West, music emerged around AD 500, when the Roman Empire was overrun by the Huns, Vandals, and Visigoths. The newly emerging Christian Church dominated Europe and generally dictated the destiny of music, art, and literature. During this time, Pope Gregory I is believed to have collected and codified the approved music of the Church, known as Gregorian chant. Since the Middle Ages, music has been linked with Jewish mysticism, as in the eastern European Hasidic movement, with its distinctive, strongly rhythmical men's songs sung to non-lexical syllables. The Hasidic style influenced east European synagogue music. In contemporary religions, such as Judaism and Christianity, people continue to use music as an integral part in the performance of their worship and religious celebrations.

In Japan, the first religious music was introduced with Buddhism, and largely consisted of chanting the Buddhist canon. Now, the historical Buddha himself seemed not to approve of music; other *sutras* have the historical Buddha spelling out strict rules for chanting prayers and *sutras*.

The history of Christmas music tells us that the word "carol" originally referred to a circle dance, "carola," performed without being sung. When words were added, they were used only as accompaniment to the dance movements. The first Christmas hymns were always aligned to Christian singing to the melodies of Jewish temple hymns and psalms. Hymns of the early church were about Christmas, used as part of a worship service. As the church struggled against the influences of pagan customs, carols were strictly prohibited from sacred services, but, outside the church, Nativity carols flourished.

Christian Music Often marketed as Inspirational, Praise, Worship, or Contemporary Christian (CCM), spiritually based music is written to express personal or communal belief about Christian life as an alternative to mainstream secular music. Christian music varies according to culture and social context, and is composed and performed for esthetic pleasure, religious or ceremonial purposes, or as an entertainment product for the marketplace. Common themes are praise, worship, and thanks to God. Music genres or styles include hymns, southern gospel, and urban contemporary gospel with subgenres of progressive southern gospel, Christian country music, Christian pop, Christian rock,

Christian metal, Christian punk, Christian alternative rock, Christian hip hop (including Christian rap), Jubilee quartet, and Mass choir music.

The younger generation of Christians is embracing music with a harder edge, according to a popular magazine for Christian teens that surveys readers' top music choices. For the past few years, singers from traditional pop or rock favorites claimed top positions in *Ignite Your Faith*'s annual readers' choice awards, dubbed the Golden Ear Awards. But in 2008, a majority of the 5,000 magazine readers who voted, aged 13 to 18, leaned in favor of hard rock bands, bumping down pop and soft rock groups.

SPOTLIGHT ON POP CULTURE   Teen Rallies as Christian Revival Concerts

Christian music concert

Acquire the Fire holds regional rallies across the country, and BattleCry is a group of larger rallies held in selected cities; both are products of the evangelical Christian organization Teen Mania. One part concert, one part Christian revival, the rallies seek to "stage a reverse revolution" against secular popular culture. They have the pull of headlining rock concerts that draw thousands of teen audiences and young adults.

From 2006 to 2007, a total of 127,830 people attended the 34 Acquire the Fire rallies, and 71,414 people attended the three BattleCry events held in San Francisco, California, Detroit, Michigan, and Bristow, Virginia, according to Teen Mania. "We don't have to be branded by the culture, we are branded by God," one participant said. "Be who God created you to be." But the glossy, glamorous appeal of popular culture too often obscures that path to God, Teen Mania followers say.

Ron Luce, the 46-year-old founder of the organization, has waged a modern-day crusade against "purveyors of popular culture," whom he has condemned as "the enemy." More than two decades old, Teen Mania estimates it has reached more than two million teens with its message "of living completely for Christ." The organization is sprawling. In addition to its live stadium rallies, there are BattleCry shirts and hats, mobile screen savers, books, and a TV program. There are international mission trips and even a Teen Mania internship, a one-year program called the Honor Academy, based in Lindale, Texas.

Source: www.cnn.com/2007/US/08/22/gw.teen.christians/index.html

Young people around the globe, particularly in Westernized societies, report music as one of their most preferred leisure activities. Music's popularity has been attributed to several factors. Research suggests that music produces pleasurable mood states and physiological arousal. Music can evoke a wide range of emotions, making us feel happy, sad, excited, even angry. Research has found that listening to favorite music can reduce unpleasant feelings of anxiety, lift the spirits, and pump people up.

Religious Theme Parks

By combining dance, drama, and music, entertainment providers have embraced a religious motif for their landscape. The Holy Land Experience in Orlando, Florida, brings the Bible to life through live shows and productions that range from historical recreations to theatrical and musical showcases. Performed both indoors and outdoors with original dialog, music, and lyrics, these presentations are a central part of the park's mission to communicate the gospel truth of God's Word. Featured exhibits, such as the Scriptorium center for Biblical Antiquities, The Wilderness Tabernacle, Jerusalem Model AD 66, and One Night With The King, provide firsthand, experiential learning environments through sight, sound, and touch.

A second religious park, however, is having trouble getting its construction approved. Developers of Bible Park USA, which planned to open by Easter 2010, have encountered objections to its concept. The $175–$200 million project was presented as an "edutainment" experience—a mixed offering of education and entertainment, which would allow visitors to visualize familiar Bible stories and a taste of life in ancient biblical times. Halting the process are fierce objections from opponents who claim the park will bring a host of unwanted problems to the community such as traffic congestion, noise, and unwanted commercialism.

The use of theming to recreate historical religious movements is a source of much criticism. For commercial success such parks must provide more than a recreation of history or significant religious events—rides and engaging activities are essential for entertainment-based success. Religious advocates, however, decry the use of elements that detract from or diminish the importance of the movements they embrace. And although religion uses music, dance, and mediated forms of entertainment to engage parishioners, entertainment venues are far less likely to enter the shaky territory of religious themes.

Religion of Performance: Scientology

A recent religion's contribution to entertainment comes in the form of persuasive production and communication. Scientology, often called the religion of the stars, was created by author L. Ron Hubbard from his self-help system (Dianetics). It attracts non-traditional religious followers who embrace its practices.

Scientology, which caters to artists, politicians, industry leaders, and sports figures, has attracted entertainers and Hollywood celebrities. With eight Celebrity Centers, Scientology has generated considerable publicity through entertainers such as John Travolta, Kirstie Alley, Lisa Marie Presley, Jason Lee, Isaac Hayes, Tom Cruise, and Katie Holmes. Scientology-related films, videos, and audiovisual materials produced within the Church of Scientology and its related organizations propagate the religion's philosophy. After briefly studying acting in Hollywood, Hubbard continued his interest in the ways in which actors assume their roles and what he termed the acquisition of a "synthetic" personality.

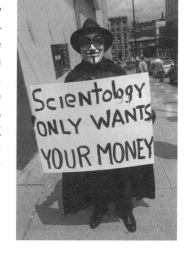

Church of Scientology protester, Vancouver, Canada, June, 2008

Hubbard studied European directing and worked with a number of luminaries within the Hollywood community using early Dianetics techniques. The early 1950s found him advising studios on story ideas and audience tastes, while his own story "Hoss Tamer" appeared on NBC's *Tales of Wells Fargo*. He set out in 1978 to form a cinemagraphic unit for the production of a new type of film—a dramatic training film *with* a story. A series of 24 basic texts were produced, including the fundamentals of lighting, set design, editing, costumes, and more. Annually producing hundreds of films and audiovisual works, Hubbard's Golden Era company features its own film lab, recording studios, and a film studio that incorporates all production lines and departments.

Scientology and the organizations that promote it have remained highly controversial since their inception, coming into conflict with the governments and police forces of several countries (including the U.S., the U.K., Canada, and Germany) numerous times over the years. Former members, journalists, courts, and the governing bodies of several countries have described the Church of Scientology as a cult and an unscrupulous commercial enterprise, accusing it of harassing its critics and abusing the trust of its members.

Active protests were initiated in February, 2008, by a group called Anonymous whose members have declared war on Scientology. Accusing it of trying to censor the Internet and conducting "campaigns of misinformation," the group's catalyst for attack was YouTube's decision to remove a video of Tom Cruise espousing the religion's virtues after the church asked that it be pulled.[3] Scientology officials argue that most of the negative press is motivated by interest groups and that most of the controversy is in the past. Nonetheless, artists and actors embrace the religion for its ability to inspire performance greatness.

Mediated Religious Entertainment

In the last 100 years, performance and the arts have been presented through a variety of media—comics, novels, radio, television, and the Internet. These media are used to disseminate religious doctrine, which has used entertainment to deliver messages of faith and belonging. This section presents some of the ways in which modern media have changed the nature of the way religious doctrine is spread. Pulpits that used to provide sermons to small congregations now use digital technology to reach millions of faith-based audiences with their messages. Print, broadcast, and the Internet are used to preach to the faithful and recruit the uncommitted. These are some of the vehicles in use today that are popular with religious followers.

Christian Comics and Novels

Various forms of printed materials have been used since the advent of Gutenberg's printing press to "spread the word" of religion and entertain readers in the process. Christian comics such as *The Beginning* tell of the dawn of humankind in detailed graphics. Comics are used by missionaries in countries where illiteracy prevails, and where visuals can be used effectively to tell their story.

Another valuable tool for reaching the masses, graphic novels help religious institutions communicate values and mores. In the novel *2048*, when scientists have created a hybrid called *bumans* (human-ape chimeras), a U.S. senator faces a tough re-election campaign against a pornographer. Deciding whether to alienate backers by supporting "buman rights," the senator is among others with tough decisions to make. Should a pastor baptize a buman? Will educators push mainstream bumans in schools? The story's outcome is deadly, bringing home the message of Christian brotherhood.

Worthy Tunes, a web site featuring religious cartoons and comics, offers an electronic version of graphic illustrations in their Kartoon Nuggets and comic strip characters, including Bishop Biglow, Reverend Fun, Altar Ego, and Church Mice, as found on www.worthytoons.com.

Graphics from a comic rendition of *Daniel in the Lion's Den*

Global Comic Projects Internationally, comics have delivered spiritual messages to all parts of the globe. Here are some examples of current comics-based projects.

- COMIX35, an international nonprofit ministry teaching the production and effective use of visually oriented literature, launched an African Christian Comics Project to be written and drawn by Christian comic creators from all over Africa for an audience of unbelieving African readers. The project provides encouragement and income for existing and up-coming comics creators in Africa. The "pilot" issue of the 24-page, black and white comic magazine arrived in late 2008; three more editions were planned.
- The Christian clown ministry in Brazil has launched a new comic, *O Mundo de Otávio*, created as an outreach to children, which will be sold by subscription and delivered free-of-charge to poor and hospitalized children. In addition, the comics are being sent to the U.S. for the large Brazilian community that does not have any similar literature in Portuguese.
- A *manga* bible series developed by NEXT has printed 590,000 English, 25,000 Japanese and 5,000 Indonesian editions of *Manga Messiah*. The first 40,000 copies were printed for distribution to school children in Uganda. Although the book was originally created by Japanese Christians who are *manga* professionals, it was printed first in English. Editions are being prepared for publication in Chinese, Russian, Tagalog, Spanish, and Portuguese.

Comics and novels have played a crucial role in bringing religious and moral teachings to children and adults worldwide, many of whom are partially illiterate.

Religious Films

Applying the power of visual narrative with religious passion produces inspirationally empowering films, as evidenced by Mel Gibson's *The Passion of the Christ*. The 2004 film was based primarily on biblical accounts of the arrest, trial, crucifixion, and resurrection of Jesus Christ, including strong scenes of violence, whipping, and suffering. Gibson departed from the usual film marketing formulation for a heavy promotion by church groups, both within their organizations and to the general public, often giving away free tickets.

After months of controversy that led to more pre-release sales than any film in history, the movie opened in the United States in 2004 on Ash Wednesday, the beginning of Lent. It earned $25 million per day in its first five days of release and became the highest-

Jonah: A VeggieTale Movie premiere

grossing R-rated film in North America. The *Christian Science Monitor* reported that *Passion* was also a great success in the Muslim world; it was the top-grossing movie for three consecutive weeks in Egypt, Lebanon, and Turkey, and also for two consecutive weeks in the United Arab Emirates. Visual Translation and the Jesus Film Project joined to craft a short film about Jesus Christ in Japanese *anime* style for use in Eastern Europe.

More often than not, comic characters make their way into videos, games, and films. One example is Big Idea, Inc., who released a VeggieTales' fifteenth anniversary commemorative DVD, *Where's God When I'm S-Scared?*, the first-ever VeggieTales animated video title, in partnership. With a mission dedicated to enhance the spiritual and moral fabric of society through creative media, VeggieTales is a series of animated videos, featuring stories and classic songs. Universal Pictures' latest animated VeggieTales movie—*The Pirates Who Don't Do Anything*—sailed into theaters in January 2008. Creators of the super-successful *Jonah* use the zany VeggieTales characters for another great adventure about learning to become a real hero. To complement the film are an all-new VeggieTales "God Made You Special" live tour, new books from Random House, *The Pirates Who Don't Do Anything* apparel from Crossroads Apparel, and a variety of other toys, puzzles, and ornaments from other licensees.[4]

Religious Video Games

Christian video games first appeared in the late 1980s for Nintendo (Wisdom Tree's *Bible Adventures*). Today, many other developers, who meet annually at the Christian Games Developers Conference, offer religious-based games. Crave Entertainment released the first game based on the Bible for Playstation 2, Xbox, and Game Boy Advance, *The Bible Game*. They have also released the first VeggieTales video games for the Playstation 2 and Game Boy Advance. Breakthrough Gaming is also one of the only Christian video game companies to release multiple games using original characters, such as *ZJ the Ball*, *Zippy the Circle*, *Forgiveness: The First Chapter*, and *Nik & Kit*.

From the demonic violence of *Doom* to the sinister *Resident Evil* series, many of today's most successful titles draw inspiration from dark places. But a growing band of Christian game developers are taking a stand. One such developer is Reverend Ralph Bagley, 41, who has filled the market's "gaping hole" with a more peaceful approach to religious gaming.

After creating the Christian Game Developers Foundation, Bagley took Christian games from obscurity to the mainstream. His company N'Lightning

Christian apocalypse video game *Left Behind* was criticized for excessive violence

Software has sold some 80,000 copies of *Catechumen* for the PC in the U.S., U.K., Australia, the Netherlands, Germany, Sweden, and Denmark. But for Rev. Bagley, and other Christian developers, the benchmark for success is breaking the console market. Where PC games can be brought out on a shoestring, several million dollars are needed to develop a console title, more to market it—plus the console makers' approval to run it.

"No blood, no guts, no gore," says Rev. Bagley. "What we want are emotionally full games that don't just rely on adrenaline." But how about games like *Left Behind* where players evangelize New Yorkers and kill the enemy with tanks, helicopters and rifles? At least the good guys need to pray throughout the game in order to function! According to a 12-year-old gamer, "I'm just running through converting everyone, and there's not much of a detailed plot." Whether or not this genre of Christian games will sell is questionable; replacing revenge with wholesome fun seems a bit off-target for games designed to excite its players.[5]

Global Religious Video Games   In India, a push for religious entertainment is partly driven by parents in search of cleaner programming. Six-year-olds are able to play the role of super-hero Hanuman on Sony's portable Playstation where the player makes choices between good and evil. This game teaches religious values to children and teenagers. An animated movie of the same name matches the quality of Hollywood films such as *Finding Nemo* and *Shrek*. The cute baby Hanuman also appears on kids' T-shirts.

In Japan, religious games are much more artful and stimulating than Christian games.[6] *Okami*, an action-adventure religious game for the Playstation 2 console that was released in late 2006, has a unique graphics engine that makes the game look like a 3D Japanese watercolor painting and a soundtrack that fuses Japanese traditional music with a Western orchestra. And, according to players, the game is incredibly fun. Unlike more subdued Christian games, Japan has produced a well-made game promoting the Shinto religion. This genre of media–religion interaction in Japan has either created new forms of religious practice or has affected existing ones. Ritual performance and consumption for new religions evolve in games modeled by media, which play a central role in creating, re-shaping, and innovating the identity of new religious movements. According to game developers, Japanese gaming and cartoon media are not just *informing* about religion, they are *making* religion.[7]

Faith in the Box: Religious TV[8]

With many Americans professing a belief in God and a majority asking for programming which reflects that belief, it seems expected that television would portray religion positively. Reality programming shows Americans demonstrating their faith in unscripted settings, but scripted drama and comedy programs often portray religion in a negative light. According to critics in the Parents TV Council (PTC), broadcast TV dramas and comedies depicted laity as hypocritical, clergy as depraved, and religious institutions as hopelessly corrupt.

 FLASH FACT

In a 2006 Parents TV Council study examining the treatment of religious content on television, an entire year of prime-time broadcast programming was analyzed. The PTC examined a total of 2,271 hours of programming containing 1,425 treatments of religion. The study found that network TV was basically anti-religious: Fox was the most anti-religious network where one in every two portrayals of religion was negative; NBC came in second with well over a third of such portrayals being negative; ABC registered 30 percent and CBS 29 percent negative portrayals; WB network featured the fewest negative depictions of religion (21 percent).

Religion-based Networks   In order to counteract the seemingly anti-religious tone of broadcast networks, two religion-based networks deliver spiritual and faith-based TV programs to believers. Two Christian TV networks (CBN and TBN), operating out of the U.S., reach global audiences with religious programming.

Founded in 1960, Pat Robertson's Christian Broadcasting Network (CBN) was the first; forty years later, it is one of the largest TV ministries in the world. CBN provides programming by cable, broadcast, and satellite to approximately 200 countries, with a 24-hour telephone prayer line. On the air continuously since 1966, "The 700 Club" has a news/magazine format that presents a mix of information, interviews, and inspiration to an average daily audience of one million viewers. CBN programs have aired in approximately 71 languages from Mandarin to Spanish and from Turkish to Welsh. *First Landing*, a CBN and Regent University produced movie, aired on ABC Family and various syndicated stations across the United States.

TBN, founded by Paul and Jan Crouch and Jim and Tammy Bakker in 1973, is the ninth largest broadcaster in the United States. The network has a larger U.S. viewership than its main competitor networks combined (followed by Daystar Television Network, Three Angels Broadcasting Network, World Harvest Television, The Hope Channel, GOD TV, and INSP—The Inspiration Network).

Carried on over 275 TV stations in the U.S., TBN claims five million viewer households per week. Programs are translated into 11 languages for cable systems in 75 countries around the globe, making it the world's largest Christian TV network. TBN has produced a number of major Christian movies, including *The Revolutionary* and *The Revolutionary II*, based on the life of Jesus; *The Emissary*, a film on the life of Paul the Apostle, *The Omega Code, Carman: The Champion, Megiddo, Time Changer, Six: The Mark Unleashed*, and *One Night with the King*.

TBN hosts gospel music concerts from Nashville, talk shows, health and nutrition programs with Christian family doctors, fitness programs, children's shows, and contemporary

This print ad encourages Christians to not drive SUVs. The ad campaign, including a TV commercial, uses a play on a popular Christian acronym "WWJD" which stands for "What Would Jesus Do?"

Christian music videos. On *Praise the Lord*, TBN's flagship production, performers share their faith in God. TBN venues contain 50-seat Virtual Reality Theaters to present visitors with an experience that combines high definition digital video technology and a 48-channel digital audio system. The theaters showcase four original productions from TBN Films. TBN programming is carried on 33 international satellite networks in Europe and the Middle East, Central Africa, Russia, Spain and Portugal, Australia, New Zealand, the South Pacific islands and Southeast Asia, Taiwan, India, and Indonesia, and broadcasts Portuguese language programs to Brazil, Latin America, and Spain.

In India, Ramayan has catapulted NDTV *Imagine* to the third position in prime time where religious entertainment has evolved into an industry of its own. In the process, traditional stories are being retold from different perspectives, or even being modernized.

Global TV has remained a constant for delivering content in the forms of drama, comedy, action, news, sports, and documentaries. Commercial TV networks and cable stations sponsor popular mainstream programming with advertising, while religious networks and public broadcast bring niche programming to viewers with donations and dedicated supporters.

Religious Television Audiences   Viewers of religious programming tend to be middle-aged women with low levels of education. A recent study of TBN viewers[9] reveals that watching religious television fills audiences' needs in five areas: spiritual, psychological, social, utilitarian, and media. The need most mentioned by viewers was media. Entertainment value was found to be TBN's strongest role for viewers who sing along to music and delight in the strong visual images. Mentioned next in importance were social needs, which TBN meets in a variety of ways. Families watch programs together. Viewers see the Crouches as charismatic and inspirational leaders, and some even form para-social relationships with program personalities. By bonding with TV actors, audience members may "make friends" and feel socially fulfilled through the mediated interaction.

Although TBN specializes in spiritual enlightenment, this network functions best as a barometer for how viewers perceive their place in the vast concepts of God, religion, world, and self. As with other forms of mediated entertainment, the appearance, agenda, and content of televised religion offer few clues about why audience members watch. The fact is, they watch in large numbers and they watch often. Religion has met the challenge of competing programming by providing entertainment that attracts and retains audiences.

Internet and Religion

The faith and spirituality market in the U.S. is strong and continues to grow. According to the Pew Internet Project, over 82 million Americans and 64 percent of all Internet users utilize the Web for faith-related matters. In addition, a division of Marketresearch.com put the demand for religious and spiritually oriented materials like books, DVDs, software, etc. at well beyond $8 billion.

To keep pace with the trend, Fox Entertainment Group (FEG) acquired Beliefnet, a web site that enables consumers to better understand their faith and build diverse spiritual communities through content and tools for a broad range of religions and spiritual approaches. Beliefnet, the largest online faith and spirituality destination, in 2008 became part of Fox Digital Media, which took on an expanded role to support FEG's vast cable, TV, and film brands online, and drive FEG's continued growth in the online market.

The acquisition provides Beliefnet with resources to further build and enhance its already popular brand. It also offers an online platform for FEG to distribute content from its extensive media library and for News Corp. to expand its faith-based businesses, including HarperCollins' Zondervan and HarperOne brands, and 20th Century Fox Home Entertainment's faith-based programming initiative.

Beliefnet provides spiritual programming to the company's various businesses, partnering closely with Fox Interactive Media to leverage the group's technology and "FIM Serve" targeted advertising delivery platform. Beliefnet provides devotional tools and a portfolio of web-based social networking tools. Social networks and their importance to socialization are discussed in a later section of this chapter.

Marketing to Faith-based Audiences[10]

For religious movies, word-of-mouth marketing may be as effective as traditional advertising. But many films, such as *Narnia* and other Disney movies, have benefited from faith-based marketing, and Christian production companies continue to find innovative ways to market to faith-based movie-goers.

Cloud Ten Pictures and Pure Flix preview films in churches before DVD releases to create a groundswell of grassroots marketing and buzz within the community. Pure Flix, along with Lionsgate, Fox Faith, and Disney, release their theatrical or direct-to-DVD titles through its church distribution system of up to 10,000 church screens nationwide. In exchange for a license fee of $99–$599, the church can screen a film as many times as it wants on the opening weekend. Cloud Ten also found success releasing *Left Behind: World at War* in 3,200 churches across North America in 2005 for an average license fee of $100 per church. Other companies coordinate advance ticket sales for church congregations to orchestrate strong opening weekends and hold special screenings for pastors, hoping they will promote the films in their sermons. For *The Great Debaters*, Denzel Washington taped a personalized greeting for 25 major African American churches. Rev. Robert Schuller interviewed Washington about his faith on the *Hour of Power*, and clips from the film were made available for pastors to use in sermons.

Buzzplant, a new-media marketing company, uses e-cards and other online viral marketing, as well as ad buys on faith-based web sites, to market movies to the Christian community online. Another recently launched web site, WingClips.com, allows clergy to download film clips to use in their sermons. Fox Faith offers church-related film resources through its web site while holding special screenings and grassroots outreach through Christian organizations.

Although Christians remain the largest and most fertile faith market, others have received occasional attention. *The Kite Runner* was a natural for the Muslim community, and Grace Hill held screenings at synagogues for *Evan Almighty*.

SPOTLIGHT ON THE GOOD BOOK   Celebrities Help Brand the Bible

Jane Fonda brings spiritual poetry to Atlanta, 2007

Familiar with branding themselves and endorsing products, a select group of celebrities have come together to brand the Bible. After Canongate's *Pocket Canons*—individual books of the Bible reprinted with introductions by cultural luminaries—sold more than 900,000 copies, *Revelations: Personal Responses to the Books of the Bible* presented a collection of the introductions written for the *Pocket Canons* that were star-studded.

According to the publisher, the best way to understand the layers of meaning in the Bible is to get writers to bring their own passion and insight

to the task. So his hand-picked contributors to *Revelations* brought insights—and sales—to the Bible. Testimony included rock star Bono's spiritual musings on Psalms, in which he claims that David performing music for King Saul was similar in spirit to the Spice Girls performing for Prince Charles. "David was the Elvis of the Bible," said Bono. The Dalai Lama compared Buddhist and Christian teachings about charity as they relate to the New Testament book of James, and Peter Ackroyd called Isaiah "the highest poetry." But even the stars' interpretations are not the same as faith.

Faith is the topic of Antonio Monda's book, *Do you believe? Conversations on God and religion* (2007), which is credited with bringing scriptural messages to the masses and directly addressing the notion of belief. Eighteen literary and cultural celebrities talked about their faith; Jane Fonda told Monda that her decision to convert to Christianity centered on the fact that Jesus was the first feminist. Her faith, she claims, is not about dogma but rather a spiritual experience. Author Saul Bellow's description of prayer is "an intimate checkup with the headquarters of the universe."

Other contributors to the book—Spike Lee and Martin Scorsese among them—present their views in a warm and fuzzy format not unlike the PBS show, *Inside the Actor's Studio*. By soliciting cultural-celebrity thoughts, these books used celebrities' personal feelings to teach the audience about the Bible.

Source: Rosen, Christine (2008). Heaven help us: Stars expound on scripture. *The Wall Street Journal*, May 13

What do you think?

- *Do stars have a corner on the market of spiritual insight?*

Religion and Sports

Many comparisons have been drawn between sports and religion. This is perhaps an obvious connection, considering that the original Olympic Games served as religious rituals in which the athletes were also representations of the gods. Although modern sports spectators live in a relatively secular age, today's fans are said to be as passionate about their sports and as devoted to their teams as religious followers are regarding their spiritual leaders and beliefs. In fact, it is suggested that contemporary sports fill the vacuum left by the decline of religion.

In the United States, football is often isolated for these comparisons. Media analysis scholar Arthur Asa Berger notes that "the passionate feelings people have about football (and their teams) and the intensity of our collective interest in the games leads me to think that football has a dimension far beyond that of simply being a sport."[11] He argues that, in today's secular societies, many religions have become increasingly more rational and continue to demythologize themselves, becoming more scientific and less ritualistic, while football has become superstitious with folklore and complex rituals that are compared to traditional religious theology. According to Berger, "People seem to have a need for myth, ritual, mystery and heroism, and football perhaps more than religion in contemporary societies, is helping people satisfy these needs."[12] Thus, it is suggested that sports functions for many people as an alternative to religion. Table 10.1 illustrates some interesting parallels between football and religion.

Religious connections to sports and media allow a variety of beliefs to be presented in more engaging, entertaining ways than ever before. Churches themselves have become mediated venues themselves. Visitors to a Presbyterian church in Menlo Park, California, for instance, sit among four giant flat panel monitors where performances are larger-than-

Table 10.1   Football as Religion

Professional football	Religion
Superstars	Saints
Sunday game	Sunday services
Ticket	Offering
Great merger (into a single league in 1920)	Ecumenical movement
Complex plays	Theology
Players on the way to the Super Bowl	Knights in search of the Holy Grail
Coaches	Clergy
Stadium	Church
Fans	Congregation

Source: Adapted from Berger, A. (1982). *Media analysis techniques.* Beverly Hills CA: Sage, p. 129

life. Usually based on the sermon's theme, screens feature coral singers, dancers, short skits, and natural wonders playing simultaneously or solo in conjunction with the pastor's pulpit lesson. Bottom line: those who pray together are more likely to play together with the help of entertainment tools.

Getting Together: Social Structures

Human beings are not solitary animals. From the beginning of time, people with some commonality have clustered together for protection, worship, hunting and gathering, and—most important for this discussion—companionship. As with religious activities— worshiping, celebrations, retreats, pilgrimages, and media—most people choose to experience leisure-time activities with friends; as such we are social animals. This section looks at understanding the process and effects of socialization for their contribution to and impact on the entertainment industry. We begin with social networks, then look to the social aspects that role models, superheroes, celebrities, and sports icons bring to our gregarious culture.

Social Network Theory

Networks are a fairly familiar concept in today's world. They can apply to everything from a collection of affiliated television stations to subscribers on a telephone system, office servers full of tangled blue leads, or even something that business people do over lunch. People have used the network metaphor to connote complex sets of relationships between members of social systems at all scales, from interpersonal to international.

Twenty-first-century technology has facilitated a process of analyzing socialization by using social networks, which form the basis of both personal and online communities. Social network analysis (SNA) is the mapping and measuring of relationships and flows between people, groups, organizations, computers, web sites, and other information or knowledge processing entities. The nodes in the network are the people and groups while the ties or links show relationships or flows between the nodes. There can be many kinds of links between the nodes. Links might represent shared values, friendships, exchanges, or other commonalities. These concepts are often displayed in a social network diagram, where nodes are the points and ties are the lines (see Figure 10.1). Research in a number of academic fields has shown that social networks operate on many levels, from families up to the level of nations, and play a critical role in determining the way problems are solved, organizations are run, and the degree to which individuals succeed in achieving their goals.

Looking at a social network (Figure 10.1), we see that entities are connected if they regularly talk to each other, or interact in some way. Andre regularly interacts with Carol,

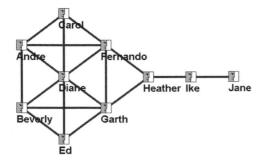

Figure 10.1   Social Networking

Source: orgnet.com

but not with Ike. Therefore Andre and Carol are connected, but there is no link drawn between Andre and Ike. Most online communities consist of three social rings—a densely connected core in the center, loosely connected fragments in the second ring, and an outer ring of disconnected nodes, commonly known as lurkers—that represent various levels of belonging. Specific organizations and web sites build online social networks. To understand networks and their participants, analysts evaluate the *location of actors in the network*, which provide insight into the various roles and groupings in a network. Analysis provides answers to questions such as:

- Who are the connectors, mavens, leaders, bridges, isolates?
- Where are the clusters and who is in them?
- Who is in the core of the network?
- Who is on the periphery?

Social Networking on the Internet

With the advent of Internet sites like Facebook and MySpace, people began connecting with others through self-promotional blogs and gossip-based conversations. Connections are key in online social networks—people are loyal to what they are connected to and what provides them with benefits. People stick with established ties they trust. Interacting with those we know and trust brings a sense of warmth and belonging to the virtual communities we visit via our computer screens. Everyone wants to be connected and included in vibrant communities that provide benefits to members.

Social networking has made explicit the connections between people, so that a thriving ecosystem of small programs can exploit this "social graph" to enable friends to interact via games, greetings, video clips, and so on. But according to Charlene Li at Forrester Research, future social networks "will be like air. They will be anywhere and everywhere we need and want them to be." No more logging on to Facebook just to see the "news feed" of updates from your friends; instead it will come straight to your e-mail inbox, RSS reader, or instant messenger. No need to upload photos to Facebook to show them to friends, since those with privacy permissions in your electronic address book can automatically get them.[13]

 FLASH FACT

Since 2004, social networking sites have rocketed from a niche activity into a phenomenon that engages tens of millions of Internet users. More than half (55 percent) of all online American youths ages 12–17 use online social networking sites, according to a national survey of teenagers conducted by the Pew Internet & American Life Project. The survey found that older teens, particularly girls, are more likely to use these sites. For girls, social networking sites are primarily places to reinforce pre-existing friendships; for boys, the networks also provide opportunities for flirting and making new friends. Recent research also indicates that having a strong social network may help elderly women stay mentally alert and prevent dementia. In a five-year study that followed 2,249 women 78 years old or older, fewer cases of dementia were found among ladies who socialized with family and friends. Eighteen percent of the women who scored low in their social network had developed dementia, compared to 10 percent who had strong social networks. Research focused on women because social isolation tends to occur more among females.

Source: in.reuters.com/article/lifestyleMolt/idINN05471978 20080606?pageNumber=2&virtualBrandChannel=0 and www.pewinternet.org/ppf/r/198/report_display.asp

Social capital offers benefits similar to those offered by economic capital and is thought to be essential to any democratic society. An increase in the size of any social network will increase social capital. The opening of social networks may now accelerate thanks to web-mail. As a technology, mail is old-fashioned. But Google, Yahoo!, Microsoft, and other firms are now discovering that they may already have the ideal infrastructure for social networking in the form of the address books, in-boxes, and calendars of their users. "E-mail in the wider sense is the most important social network," says David Ascher, who manages Thunderbird, an e-mail application.

Why? Because the extended in-box contains invaluable and dynamically updated information about human connections. On Facebook, a social graph notoriously deteriorates after the initial thrill of finding old friends from school wears off. By contrast, an e-mail account has access to the entire address book and can infer information from the frequency and intensity of contact as it occurs. Joe gets e-mails from Jack and Jane, but opens only Jane's; Joe has Jane in his calendar tomorrow, and is instant-messaging with her right now; Joe tagged Jack "work only" in his address book. Perhaps Joe's party photos should be visible to Jane, but not Jack. Facebook has an economic incentive to publish ever more data about its users, says Mr. Ascher, whereas Thunderbird, which is an open-source project, can let users minimize what they share. Social networking may end up being everywhere, and yet nowhere.

Gated Sites: For Members Only   As MySpace, LinkedIn, and Facebook have expanded to people of all ages, classes, and affiliations, there is a backlash against the open culture of social networking. Three **gated sites** are among those with tough membership requirements and, presumably, more elite social networking. In October 2008, British news giant Reuters launched a private online networking community for hedge fund managers, traders, and analysts. Dubbed Reuters Space (space.reuters.com), the industry-specific site leverages its own pool of proprietary data on thousands of companies to verify the employment status of applicants. Members each have a feeds page (where they collect news from Reuters and other sources tailored to their financial specialty) and a profile page—a personal blog where they post notes to colleagues and close industry contacts and set privacy controls to determine who has access to their contact information.

One of the other exclusive sites is INmobile.org, a network of more than 900 executives who work in or close to the wireless industry. To qualify, you have to be at least a director at a large company, a vice-president at a midsize company, or in the C-suite of a startup. The other is diamondlounge.com, an invitation-only social and business network that relies on a selection committee elected by all members on the site. The committee has already chosen 100 members out of more than 7,000 applications that came in before Diamond Lounge went live. Members, who pay a monthly $60 fee, can hail from any industry and have two identities: a social profile in "the Lounge" and a business profile in "the Boardroom." For the social profile, members set limits on who can view them based on such characteristics as age, physical build, and gender; for the boardroom they provide their income, industry, and job title. They can exchange gifts, much like Facebook, where members buy icons of cakes and teddy bears, for example—but Diamond Lounge gifts include real Gucci bags or tickets to business events.[14]

Social Network Advertising   One of the problems encountered by social network users of all classes is unwanted advertising. Although no business has figured out how to advertise successfully inside a social network, advertisers have penetrated them with unwanted messages. In 2008, more than four in five social networking site users

(83 percent) received unwanted (spam) messages, invitations, or postings. Unsolicited spam promoting products, phishing, or redirection to other sites has increased, says a June 2008 study by Cloudmark, a messaging security company. On average, users reported receiving 64 unwanted messages or postings daily. With nearly half of the online adult population claiming membership on at least one social networking web site account, spam has flourished.[15]

Facebook's membership doubles every six months, and MySpace has more than 110 million monthly active users worldwide. To broaden their membership base, many social networks use a viral approach to recruit new members and provide multiple ways for members to interact with one another, including e-mail, mobile text messages, chats, blog or profile postings, and message broadcasting. Unfortunately, the very qualities that make social networks successful—the wide variety of communication channels, the openness of the networks, and the size of the audience—are also powerful lures for spammers and hackers.

Social networks have even become platforms for reality programming. TruTV (formerly Court TV), for instance, is trying to drum up interest for a new reality show about oil drilling through a game on three popular social networking sites. In the game, which can be played on Facebook, MySpace, and Bebo, players drill for virtual oil. The more of their friends that players get to join their teams, the faster they drill. Every time drilling begins, the players are entered into a drawing to win a $50,000 cash prize.

Social Networking by Phone

Mobile telephones provide an increasingly important communication channel in facilitating social connections. With 250 million mobile subscribers in the U.S., more Americans own a mobile phone than have an Internet connection. Mobile phones are ubiquitous in many parts of the world today, with an estimated two billion subscribers worldwide. New services for mobile phones have been developed that purport to allow people to create, develop, and strengthen social ties. Much like social networking sites on the Internet, these services may help users to build valuable networks through which to share information and resources.

MySpace and Facebook have each made deals with wireless carriers to develop limited versions of their services on mobile phones. In addition, software for mobile phones has been explicitly designed to help people

Capturing friends on a mobile camera phone

network through location-centered interactions. As social networking sites migrate from the computer to the mobile phone, issues concerning privacy are of concern to site users.

Music and Socialization

As previously suggested, music is an important component of culture, particularly for teens. The content of popular music can act as an agent of *socialization*, providing young people with information about society, social and gender roles, and behavioral norms. Furthermore, adolescents learn to define themselves by their music, imitating the speech, dress, and even actions of their favorite artists. Music videos, with their powerful visual imagery, can be especially influential sources of information about social roles, consumerism, and culture.

Listening to music may help shape adolescents' *self-identity* and *group-identity*. Popular music creates shared meanings that may ease peer-group identification and facilitate social communication among peer subgroups. Teens' musical preferences both shape and reflect the friendships they develop, the clothes they wear, and other lifestyle choices they make. Shared musical preferences can bring young people from different social strata into the same cultural subgroup. Being part of a shared subculture can ease the transition away from parents and toward peers.

Music preferences established in young adulthood tend to predominate throughout a person's life. Given that music is integrally tied to our social identities, it is not surprising that individuals who share music preferences also tend to share other characteristics. For example, when fans of late 1980s punk rock music were compared with non-fans, several interesting differences were observed. Punk fans were significantly more likely to have engaged in vandalism and antiauthority behavior, owned weapons, committed a crime, and gone to jail. Research has found that hard rock and heavy metal fans tend to score high on traits such as machismo, tough-mindedness, excitement seeking, and drug use. Although there has been less research examining rap and pop music, findings suggest shared fan traits for these genres as well.

The Recording Industry   Apart from a brief stint in the 1950s, the recording industry has existed as a tight **oligopoly** dominated by a few large companies. In 2007, four large international conglomerates owned and controlled an estimated 81.87 percent of the U.S. music market[16] and 71.7 percent of global retail sales.[17] Figure 10.2 shows world market share breakdown comparisons for the big four and independents.

Critics argue that this concentrated ownership allows commercialism to undercut artists' musical freedom and creativity. Profit-driven record labels are said to favor familiar formulaic music from established artists rather than taking risks on new and different sounds from unproven newcomers. As far back as the 1950s there is evidence that the major labels would refuse to record music they felt violated existing norms and would insist that artists modify songs to make them more mainstream. Because of the integral

Super troupers
Market share, %

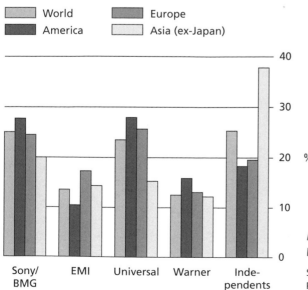

Figure 10.2   Music Industry Market Share

Source: International Federation of the Phonographic Industry

role that music is said to play in cultural development, sociologists and cultural historians worry that this mainstreaming creates *cultural homogenization*, resulting in bland sameness instead of rich cultural diversity. To them, killing artists' autonomy and authenticity is tantamount to killing their cultures.

Although industry-dictated commercialism and homogenization may continue to be a concern, they are perhaps less of a problem today than they were in previous decades. Record label executives may try to dictate everything from artists' music to their hairstyles and wardrobes, but many performers today will not just meekly accept such commands. Technology has made high-quality, low-cost recording and mixing equipment affordable for many start-up or garage bands. The number of home recording studios has risen to more than 10,000 while commercial studios have dwindled from 10,000 to 1,000 in less than 20 years. Thanks to the Internet and sites like YouTube, start-up bands are also rapidly gaining a high-quality, low-cost alternative for distribution. And some of these self-made musicians have made significant cultural impacts. Rap or hip hop and early Seattle grunge, two styles of music that have each significantly influenced distinct American subcultures, were homegrown. However, the high costs for marketing and publicity and industry control over traditional distribution and concert venues still make it difficult for independent bands to reach large audiences and make large profits.

Star-studded Society

Audiences love movie stars. Some of the best evidence we have that film has radically changed society's values lies in the growing phenomenon of the celebrity. Folklore characters (Paul Bunyon) and renowned individuals (scientists, artists, politicians, etc.) once served as our heroes and our role models. Actors were mostly anonymous, known only on stage in their character roles. However, after 1912, actors were liberated from anonymity by the appearance of fan magazines. Today, actors and their fictional characters have fused to become "stars," resulting in a unique relationship between stars and their publics. In contrast to celebrities who are well-known people appearing as themselves, **stars** are extraordinary psychological models of a type that never existed before.[18] Stars are created by a group of people for an admired quality they possess.

According to a *New Yorker* columnist,[19] *stardom* is the name for a discrete and recognizable episode in the life of a star. Stardom means you are what people want; stardom is the intersection of personality with history, a perfect congruence of the way the world happens to be and the way the star is. But every episode of stardom, he cautions, carries within it the seeds of its own negation, for it can last only three years.

Stardom can be a phenomenon of production (what filmmakers provide) or of consumption (what the audience wants). Fashion is a function of star production—a star serves to fix a type of beauty that defines norms of attractiveness. Because of the economic importance of stars, image-building and character-typing suggest the power of the forces of cinematic production. However, audiences and other consumption factors also play a dominant role in star-building. Four categories of star/audience relationship have emerged:[20]

- *Emotional affinity* where the audience feels a loose attachment to a star that extends from the personality of the audience member.
- *Self-identification* when the audience member becomes so involved with the star that s/he lives the part being played.

- *Imitation* occurs when the star acts as a role model for the viewer.
- *Projection* is an extreme form of imitation that develops into being "star-struck."

Stardom is also an image of the way stars live. They are a combination of the spectacular and the everyday, special and ordinary that articulate basic American or Western values. With the impact of consumerism on media, both film stars and TV celebrities adopt "personality" personae. This is to say, we judge them through their appearance and the significance of their lifestyle.[21] Star lifestyles are elements of the "fabulousness" of Hollywood. Large houses and limousines, parties, expensive clothing, svelte bodies, consumptive sphere, and glamorous leisure activities indicate star fashion.

Audience fascination with film stars continues to be fueled by paparazzi, entertainment TV, fashion magazines, and advertising commercials. Film tie-ins and trailers promote stars; stars also sell products, politics, and philanthropy. Michael Jordan became a shoe style for Nike. In fact, stars themselves have become brands by creating a strong identity between the star and a film style. Woody Allen films are a mere extension of the person himself—a Woody Allen-brand film.

One example of branding of a star's power—"hyper-personification"—is Vince Vaughn's dramatic performance in *Prime Gig*. Here, his role was the antithesis of the normal comic hysteria usually associated with Vaughn-ness. We expect films starring Vaughn to feature his comedy brand (as in *Break Up, Wedding Crashers*), and are disappointed if this image is not consistent with our expectations.

The role of celebrities in a global society also includes their ability to raise funds for philanthropic causes. Willy Nelson began the trend by presenting concerts for Farm Aid during the 1970s when farmers lost their land to foreclosure. Stars rally behind diseases such as Jerry Lewis's annual MS telethon. Bono's AIDS awareness campaigns and international efforts made by Brad Pitt, Mia Farrow, George Clooney, and other celebrities bring awareness to causes and global problems. Without their star power, many social and economic disasters may remain unknown and unfunded. Check out the top actors for 2007 in Table 10.2.

Table 10.2 Top ten actors for 2007

Selections are based on the search behavior of 42 million users of the IMDb.com movie database.		
1. Johnny Depp	6. Jessica Alba	
2. Brad Pitt	7. Zac Efron	
3. Hayden Panettiere	8. Lindsay Lohan	
4. Christian Bale	9. Matt Damon	
5. Angelina Jolie	10. Tom Cruise	

Source: STARmeter reports

Role Models

Entertainment also provides us with role models. Audiences pay close attention to the behavior of actors, musicians, and athletes whether they are in their roles as entertainers in films, music video, or a sports contest or out of their roles in their everyday lives. Chapter 3 discussed the para-social relationships that audiences develop with entertainers. Audiences become attached to their favorite actors, recording artists, and athletes, feeling a special bond to them. They often carefully follow their favorite entertainers' careers and personal lives from their performances and from the news and gossip media.

Social learning theory suggests that people may adopt or reject behaviors that they see modeled by entertainers based on whether those behaviors are rewarded or punished. Entertainers usually possess many desirable traits—they are talented, successful, good looking, and well liked. These qualities or the desire to possess these qualities provide even further incentive for people to view entertainers as role models for their own values and behavior. There is concern, of course, about what sort of roles these entertainers are modeling given the sexual scandals, drug use, deceit, or violent altercations they portray in movies, music videos, and even sports events, not to mention similar highly publicized activities in their personal lives.

Sports Heroes

The switch from movie hero to sports hero was a natural transition; players were physically fit, talented, and honorable. At least that's what the public was led to believe. In reality, sports heroes often had help from drugs, steroids, and enhancements. And they had scandals built around their off-season antics.

Criticisms of the violent behavior of modern-day athletes go hand in hand with criticisms of the athletes themselves. These critics argue that today's sports do not produce heroes like Joe DiMaggio, whose achievements include a 56-game hitting streak in 1941 that may never be surpassed. "It is hard to think of anyone today, in sports or out, who comes near [DiMaggio's] sustained dignity (hoopster Michael Jordan seems to have qualities of that gold, but this will take some years to validate). In the arena of public affairs, there's hardly a name that does not come with an asterisk."[22] Psychologist Frank Farley identified six character traits he believes define the essence of heroism (see Table 10.3).

It is not the athletic prowess of today's athletes that most critics question, for clearly we have many remarkable sports stars—impressive risk takers who possess courage and strength, skill and expertise. It is their moral fiber—their honesty, kindness, and generosity—that is considered questionable. According to one critic, contemporary athletes "merely reflect the heroic attributes of physical vitality and unconquerable spirit on the surface. Yet beneath these superficial characteristics, modern athletes lack the ethical uprightness necessary to qualify them as real heroes."[23]

Some might be surprised to learn that politicians rate first as the most commonly mentioned heroes. Neck and neck for second place are entertainers (Barbra Streisand is big among women, Clint Eastwood among men) and family members. Religious figures rank fourth, whereas most of the rest come from the military, science, sports, and the arts.[24] There are several possible reasons sports figures rank so low. One factor may be the sheer number of them. It was much easier for Joe DiMaggio to become a hero when baseball and football were the only sports of any popularity. Another consideration is that sports have become big business, with athletes seemingly motivated as much by financial gains as by athletic ones; for example, they often charge fans for autographs. Others argue that sportswriters and tabloid journalists are to blame. This line of reasoning suggests that

Table 10.3   What Does It Take to Be a Hero?

Six Important Character Traits Consider how today's top sports figures compare against this list.	
Courage and strength	Whatever a hero is, he isn't a coward or a quitter. Heroes maintain their composure—and even thrive—under adversity, whether it be the life threatening sort that war heroes face or the psychological and emotional strains that politicians and business leaders must endure.
Honesty	It's no coincidence that "Honest Abe" Lincoln and George "I cannot tell a lie" Washington are among our nation's most cherished figures. Deceit and deception violate our culture's conception of heroism.
Kind, loving, generous	Great people may fight fiercely for what they believe, but they are compassionate after the battle is over—toward friend and foe alike.
Skill, expertise, intelligence	A hero's success should stem from his or her talents and smarts, rather than from mere chance—although, for the sake of modesty, a hero might well attribute his or her hard-earned achievements to luck.
Risk taking	No matter what their calling, heroes are willing to place themselves in some sort of peril.
Objects of affection	We might be impressed on an intellectual level by somebody's deeds. But admiration is not enough—heroes must win our hearts as well as our minds.

Source: Adapted from How to be great! What does it take to be a hero? Start with six basic character traits. *Psychology Today*, 28: 6 (1995, November–December): 46(6)

today's sports figures, as well as others in the public eye, are no more or less noble than they have been in the past. It is simply that today's journalists spend more time focusing on human failings and frailties than on nobility and heroics.

Heroes are thought to have depth. "Depth," it is argued, "is that timeless, mythical, almost otherworldly quality that marks a hero. It's hard to articulate exactly what this is . . . but we all know it when we see it—it's what makes even physically diminutive heroes seem larger than life."[25] Thus some might argue that an overemphasis on athletic prowess at the expense of education and other pursuits has created a generation of one-dimensional sports stars. Psychologist Frank Farley wonders if public disillusionment with professional athletes means that most of tomorrow's sport heroes will be fictional characters like Rocky.

Heroes are said to be the window into the soul of a culture. If you look at a nation's top heroes, you'll get a pretty good idea of its citizens' values and the ideals they cherish. American heroes tend to be individualists and risk takers. But in China, heroes might be more likely to uphold tradition. These distinctions have important implications for everything from international business dealings to political and military negotiations.

In this context, a recent survey reporting that nearly half of American children have no heroes at all has ominous implications.[26] There is concern about how these kids will learn to transcend adversity—such as poverty or racism—without the example of the great men and women who came before them. "The great American story is the person starting from nothing and becoming something," Farley says. "We need more depictions of that."

According to Farley, "Being inspired by people who do great things is one of the oldest, most reliable forms of motivation."[27] In reviewing Farley's work, one author notes that "we sorely need heroes—to teach us, to captivate us through their words and deeds, to inspire us to greatness. . . . Above all, they spur us to raise our sights beyond the horizon of the mundane, to attempt the improbable or impossible."[28]

Contemporary Sports Icons

Although some may bemoan a lack of modern-day sports heroes, others suggest that today's heroes are bigger and better than ever. Clearly, one of the most notable current sport icons is Michael Jordan. If heroics were to be measured in dollar figures, his value would be unquestionable. It has been estimated that Michael Jordan had a $10 billion dollar effect on the United States' economy while he was playing in the National Basketball Association (NBA) from 1984 through 1998. The success of Gatorade's "Be Like Mike" campaign certainly supports Jordan's heroic status.

And even if late twentieth-century America were in short supply of heroes, some would argue that today's pool of potential heroes has never been greater. Following on Jordan's heels was the neck-and-neck home run record race between baseball's Sammy Sosa and Mark McGuire, and Tiger Woods's domination on the golf course. Women's sports have also produced inspiring athletes, such as soccer players Mia Hamm, basketball's Sheryl Swoops, and tennis stars Venus and Serena Williams. In addition to athletic prowess, in true heroic fashion, these athletes have been noted for their poise and sportsmanship.

Many critics and fans, however, remain cynical about whether or not today's athletes are suitable heroes or role models. Recently, alarms have been raised by professional athletes' use of steroids and other performance-enhancing drugs. Less than a week after the 2006 Tour de France it was revealed that winner Floyd Landis had tested positive for an elevated testosterone/epitestosterone ratio (with normal levels of testosterone and deficient levels of epitestosterone) after his stunning stage 17 victory. The 2006 book *Game of Shadows* alleges extensive use of several types of steroids and growth hormone by baseball superstar Barry Bonds, and also names several other athletes as drug cheats.[29] That same year, American Olympic and world 100-meter champion Justin Gatlin failed a drug test. Marion Jones, described as the fastest woman on Earth after winning five Olympic medals at the 2000 Olympic Games in Sydney, Australia, has also been

Sports icons Sammy Sosa, the Williams sisters, and Tiger Woods

plagued by rumors of performance-enhancing drug use although she has never failed a drug test.

An obvious concern is that amateur athletes, particularly young athletes, who look up to these sports heroes might be encouraged to use such drugs. An additional concern is that denial and deceit that have typically accompanied professional doping scandals also set a poor example for others to follow. Some research does suggest that the use of steroids and other doping agents is prevalent among high school athletes. In the United States there have been statistics that anywhere from 4 to 11 percent of high school football players have used performance-enhancing drugs.[30] It is difficult to say, however, if and how professional athletes' use of such substances has influenced this usage. Traditionally, professional sports associations have been responsible for self-policing and setting penalties for drug use and other regulation violations. However, growing concerns about the use of performance-enhancing drugs has led governments in several countries, including the United States, to begin drafting ant-doping legislation.

Effects of Social Media

Considering that young people make up a significant portion of media users, it is not surprising that negative effects speculations have centered on how new media may affect children. The Internet has no doubt resulted in many positive impacts, including increasing access to limitless information and entertainment as well as facilitating the production of new information and entertainment. While surfing the Internet or satellite TV channels, children and adults alike may be exposed to new ideas and information that may increase their knowledge and perhaps spark their own creativity and innovation. By playing on the Internet or with entertainment software, children can also improve their general technology and computer literacy. New media technologies have also been enlisted as helpful learning aids in most disciplines—math, language, sciences, arts—for almost any age based on the belief that the interactive nature of new media can help make learning more engaging and fun.

But in addition to these potentially positive impacts of new media, there are also some concerns. Many echo traditional worries about the impact of TV, films, music, and the like—that is, that new media entertainment may have negative impacts on children's psychological and physical health. The fear is that children will spend all of their time surfing the Internet or playing games online instead of getting exercise playing outside or learning how to socialize with other playmates. There have also been reports of children developing repetitive strain injuries from using computer keyboards and video game controls that affect muscles, nerves, tendons, joints, ligaments, cartilage, or spinal disks (such as tendonitis and carpal tunnel syndrome).[31]

FADE TO BLACK

We have seen how religious institutions are using entertainment to deliver spiritual messages using live performance and media like the Internet, games, movies, TV, and comics. Each medium has a special connection with its audience to communicate thoughts and images important to the doctrine of the religion. We suspect that entertainment will continue to permeate the services, festivals, and activities of faith-based teachings.

Belonging—whether to a congregation or to a social network—is an important social need among residents of all global communities. As social beings, we look to people of prominence to set examples and act as behavioral models. Such needs have created an enormous celebrity industry, both in the movies and sports, where stars are created and marketed for our consumption. We bond with media personalities, keeping their images with us in all aspects of our lives. Our lives are shaped by the portrayals of those we admire and respect—as well as those whose actions have been ethical or legal disasters. We take our collective cues from superheroes to sports heroes, rock stars to news commentators, and our lives are shaped by the people who make up our social cultures.

A CLOSER LOOK AT SOCIAL NETWORKS   Global Socialization

The dominant global social networks are shown by country in Figure 10.3. In the U.S., dominant social networks are MySpace and Facebook. But other services, such as hi5.com, Bebo, Orkut, and Friendster have established and maintained footholds outside the U.S. Unsurprisingly, social networks, which let people share news, photographs, and other content with their friends, benefit from network effects. A dominant local site, such as Orkut in Brazil, can hold off the competition because it's the default, and nobody wants to migrate to another site, however much more advanced, if their friends won't follow.

Globally, the dominant social networks in 2008 are discussed here:

- **Orkut** leads in the Indian subcontinent, as well as Brazil.

- **Facebook** is stronger, internationally, than **MySpace**, with surprising strongholds in the Middle East.

- **hi5.com** is the most international of all the social networks, leading in Peru, Colombia, Central America, and other, scattered countries such as Mongolia, Romania, and Tunisia.

- **Bebo** and **Skyblog** follow colonial patterns, the first strong in smaller English-speaking countries such as Ireland and New Zealand, and the latter in French-speaking countries.

- **Friendster**, the original social network, leads all across Southeast Asia.

- **Fotolog**, a photo service defeated in the U.S. by Friendster, has re-emerged as the dominant social network in Argentina and Chile.

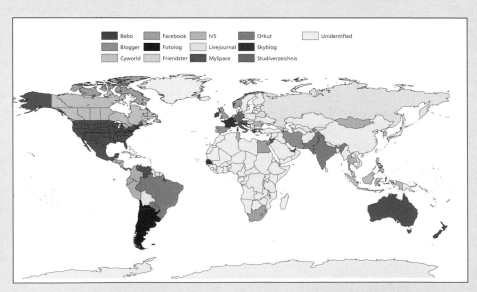

Figure 10.3   Global Social Networks

Table 10.4 Percentage of online consumers visiting social networking sites

United States	United Kingdom	France	Germany	Japan	South Korea
25	21	3	10	20	35

Figures include consumers who visit at least monthly.

Source: 2007 Technographics surveys. From Li, Charlene and Bernoff, Josh (2008). *Groundswell: Winning in a World Transformed by Social Technologies*. Copyright 2008 Forrestor Research, Inc.

A 2008 Groundswell survey reports that South Korea has 10 percent more social network users than any other country, as shown in Table 10.4.

Source: valleywag.com/tech/data-junkie/the-world-map-of-social-networks-273201.php and Josh Bernoff for blogs. forrester.com/charleneli/2008/06/data-chart-of-t.html

What do you think?

- *Does Korea have the highest participation because of Cyworld, or because Koreans love to connect?*
- *Why are Germany, and especially France, so low?*

DISCUSSION AND REVIEW

1. How do religious organizations connect with their parishioners and worshipers through the Internet?
2. Discuss ways in which sports and religion are similar and different.
3. Why are social networks so popular among young adult and teen audiences? Are they here to stay, or will there be a "next big thing" in social communication?
4. Why are we so fascinated with celebrities and stars? What examples can you give of stars supporting nonprofit causes that have caught your attention?

EXERCISES

1. Visit a bookstore like Borders and catalog the magazines dedicated to celebrity or star gossip. What does this proliferation tell you about our culture's interest in them?
2. Come up with a plot or scenario for a faith-based video game. How can you create interest without resorting to physical violence?
3. Write a short story about your own or a fictional experience with a social network. What key elements did you include? Why?
4. Attend a religious service of any denomination and observe all the ways in which media are used to enhance the experience. Can you suggest additional features or activities to improve the experience?

BOOKS AND BLOGS

Grewal, D.S. (2008). *Network power: The social dynamics of globalization*. New Haven CT: Yale University Press.

Nelson, M.Z. (2005). *The gospel according to Oprah*. Philadelphia PA: Westminster Press.

Redmond, S. (2007). *Stardom and celebrity: A reader*. Thousand Oaks CA: Sage Publications.

Robertson, C.K. (2002). *Religion as entertainment*. New York: Peter Lang Publishing.

www.godtube.com—watch videos and post your own on this social network.

www.rapzilla.com—online Christian hip-hop magazine.

www.skyangel.com—provides Christian videos and a variety of music.

www.filmbug.com—a movie star guide with thousands of pages about actors, directors, screenwriters, and other celebrities with bios, forums, images, etc.

www.celebrities.com—gossip and information about everyone famous.

11 ETHNICITY, CULTURE, AND GLOBALIZATION

All vestiges of truth—and thereby of intercultural understanding—give way before the onslaught of movieland's mythic creations.

—Ward Churchill

Entertainment is a worldwide phenomenon. Much of what we know about other people comes to us in some form of entertainment. We are exposed to people of other ethnicities and cultures through movies, television, and newspapers. What we understand about others is often a result of mediated communication, which may be from the point of view of the writer, producer, or director. The line between truth and fiction may be breached, causing false impressions for audiences. In this chapter, we look at portrayals of ethnic groups and global cultures as created by various forms of mediated entertainment.

Ethnicity and Culture

Every one of us is a member of an ethnic group, which is composed of people who share common genetic ancestry. Unfortunately, media treatment of some ethnic groups is less kind than treatment of others. **Ethnic identity** is group-based identity formed and developed by socialized processes and experiences, both personal and mediated. Media present societal expectations and views about members of a society—where each group stands in the social structure—and presents "societal attitudes" toward minority members.

Bombarded by a sea of images, many of us fail to see our own images reflected in the media. Or we see ourselves portrayed differently than we think we should be. Because media reflect trends of the society from which they originate, every nation's media have different ways of reporting on each of the various ethnic groups. Entertainment media say a lot to viewers about who counts in society. This section looks at the ways in which media portray, stereotype, and use entertainment to characterize individuals and groups of people who are members of a particular ethnic culture. We also look at the impact of American media on ethnic groups and cultures.

Media Portrayals

Visual messages are products of our sense of sight; they are highly emotional and have long-lasting staying power. Think of the power of TV! We learn from media portrayal associations, frequencies, and omissions. Cultural images you have seen in media—especially print, TV, film, and computers—are usually shortcut pictures based on culturalism, which is a belief that one cultural group is better than another cultural group.

In 1993, the American Screen Actors Guild (SAG) began collecting statistics on the number of ethnic and minority actors appearing in American TV and movies. The grim results caused advocacy groups to pressure the industry to produce shows and films that accurately reflect the racial and ethnic diversity of our nation. By 2000, SAG reported a 7 percent increase in industry jobs and roles for performers of color. And in 2008, another 8 percent increase showed progress.

Still, Asians and dark-skinned villains seem to prevail in video games. In 2006, a Canadian researcher studied four video games, *Kung Fu*, *Warcraft 3*, *Shadow Warrior*, and *Grand Theft Auto 3*, for their portrayals of evil gangster ethnicity. According to his study, non-white gangsters are ultimately blown away by white heroes. Such "below the radar" racism is not tolerated in other media such as television and film, but is very prevalent in video gaming. But with video games a $40 billion industry worldwide, negative portrayals have a significant impact on users. And although there is no academic consensus that racism in media affects real-world attitudes, the impact of racist images is hard to counteract.[1]

Canada, where 15 percent of the population are immigrants and minorities who comprise up to 51 percent of the larger urban centers, has become the most diverse country in the world. Yet media have not kept pace. For instance, major media stereotypes of First Nations, Inuit, and Native American peoples regularly occur in film, TV, and the news. Portrayals of Native characters are either primitive, violent, and deceptive, or passive and childlike. Because most city dwellers rarely come in contact with Native populations, these portrayals have all the more impact.

The recent climate of political correctness has countered some of the more overt forms of racism in films and TV, but subtle stereotyping still exists as romanticization, historical inaccuracies, omission, and simplistic characterizations. The romantic images of Indian Princess, Native Warrior, and Noble Savage have captured the imagination of global audiences. Inaccuracies occur because producers never let details get in the way of a good story. Artistic license is liberal when portraying dress, customs, livelihoods, and spiritual beliefs and ceremonies of Native people.[2]

Indians are the only population to be portrayed far more often in historical context than as contemporary people. Native Americans are rarely portrayed in TV dramas such as *CSI* as accident victims or police. It's almost as if television producers have cultural amnesia. But the most destructive to images of Indians is the lack of character and personality the media attribute to them. They are cardboard fixtures in a moving drama.

Chief Wahoo of the Cleveland Indians

Another controversial issue is the use of images of American Indians as mascots, symbols, caricatures, and namesakes for non-Indian sports teams, businesses, and other organizations. Damaging to self-identity, self-concept, and self-esteem, major league sports-based symbols still attract national attention. The Atlanta Braves, Cleveland Indians, and Edmonton Eskimos all show the tendency to objectify these cultures. Such symbols are part of a socially constructed reality supported by an unconscious assumption of superiority by the dominant culture.

With regard to other ethnic groups, a recent study suggests that minority audiences in the U.S. have a different pattern of media usage and response to media messages that is distinct from that of whites.[3] Minority members are more frequent media users, they are more likely to consider media content as real, and they are more critical audiences when evaluating how the media present in-group members.

Davis and Gandy[4] suggested that African Americans have developed and use protective strategies to deal with negative media images of Blacks. Negative media images may activate a Black audience's identity that, when activated, become "self-referencing." So, as suggested by **social identity theory**, Blacks' desires to hold positive views of their group may lead them to use coping responses to those images when they are perceived as threatening to their identity. Coping strategies may include (a) asserting stronger group identity, (b) engaging in competitive behavior, and (c) exhibiting defensive reactions. For example, Black responses to news coverage of African Americans are more critical than Hispanic and Asian responses are to coverage about their groups. Most often criticized is the unfair treatment of Blacks in televised crime news. By continually portraying African Americans as thieves and murderers, news and dramatic TV often seem to promote harmful stereotypes of that culture. So why stereotype? Read on.

SPOTLIGHT ON MEDIA IMAGES Indians in the Movies: *Comanche Moon*

In the three-part television series *Comanche Moon* (1997), all Indians are bad guys. They attack towns in acts of aggression rather than shooting soldiers in self-defense. It seems as if Indians want to kill just because whites won't let them steal horses in peace. Here, white men are innocent and Indians are guilty; the conflict is civilization vs. savagery.

Indians in this film are all evil:

- Blue Duck is an attempted assassin.
- Kicking Wolf and Three Birds are horse thieves.
- Ahumando is a torturer.
- An unnamed Comanche is a rapist.
- Buffalo Hump is a genocidal revenge seeker.

Other than speaking their native language, these Indians show no evidence of culture. Rather, they live to steal horses, capture women and kill white men. The only Indian given favorable attention is Famous Shoes, a Kickapoo scout for the Rangers. He is clever and well spoken, and talks of visiting his grandmother, so we know he's a good guy.

Following closely to the book by Larry McMurtry, this typical Western series portrays Indians as spiritualists who speak in methodical cadences and stroke feathers to the sound of wind instruments, or patricidal maniacs bent on racial vengeance. Eight years into the new millennium, American Indians are still portrayed on screen according to a narrow range of stereotypes.

Source: www.bluecorncomics.com/commoon.htm

What do you think?

- *What evidence have you seen that media portrayals of Indians are changing? Any evidence to the contrary?*

Stereotyping

The media are often accused of encouraging *stereotyping*, or the application of a standardized image or concept to members of a certain group. These portrayals are usually based on limited information. The media, particularly entertainment media, present only a slice of life, but that slice is not necessarily representative of real life. Mundane, normal, everyday people and events typically are just not all that interesting or entertaining. Instead, entertainment often focuses on unusual or exceptional individuals and situations. Content analyses conducted over the last 40 years have demonstrated that people of color are depicted as perpetrators of crime and aggression more often than is the case in the real world. And women and people of color are more likely to be depicted as victims of aggression than they are in the real world. Other portrayals also encourage stereotyping, such as the dumb blonde, the jolly fat guy, and feeble-minded old folks.

Many theories such as dependency theory, cultivation analysis, symbolic interaction, and social construction of reality predict that the repeated, regular exposure to media and entertainment containing distorted representations might lead to stereotyping people in the real world. The fear is that the media influences our perceptions and that these perceptions then influence our behavior toward stereotyped groups.

Should a lone female feel safer walking alone in Oklahoma City or New York City? Or in Rapid City, North Dakota, or Washington DC? Consider how you develop your stereotypes of the people who live in these places. Where did you get the images and ideas that form the basis for constructing your understanding of these places and the people who live there? What theories might explain how these stereotypes develop? Then consider the actual statistics. The FBI reports that in Oklahoma City, the incidence of forcible rape is 73.9 per 100,000 females, three times the levels of New York City and Washington DC, and the city with the highest rate of forcible rape in the United States is Rapid City.

Playing into the irony of ethnic stereotype self-deprecation, author Christian Lander used an accumulation of blog posts to write *Stuff white people like: The definitive guide to the unique taste of millions*. According to Lander, his book "investigates, explains and offers advice for finding social success with the Caucasian persuasion." The list of 105 things begins with #1: coffee and #2: religions their parents don't belong to. The list extends through #104: girls with bangs and #105: unpaid internships. Speaking to NPR, Lander said his book was a tongue-in-cheek approach to thinking about his race. Each item has an explanation, such as this commentary about the number one thing white people like, coffee.

> The first person at your school to drink coffee was a white person, I promise. White people all need Starbucks. They're also fond of saying "you do NOT want to see me before I get my morning coffee." They also call it anything but coffee, like rocket fuel, java, joe, black grind and so forth. White people REALLLY love fair trade coffee, because paying the extra $2 means they are making a difference.

The blog, www.stuffwhitepeoplelike.com, had 38,000 hits in its first six months of operation. Do this publication and blog promote stereotyping and being racist? Or is it simply a white guy making fun of other white guys (and girls)? Log on and judge for yourself.

Documenting Race

The intersection of media globalization, race, and religion fosters the production of documentaries by global TV networks such as Discovery that necessitates rethinking Eurocentric representations of iconic figures like Jesus. Religious imagery is being replaced by discourses of science and technology in order to appeal to international audiences.

For example, Discovery and BBC presented a scientific breakthrough, claiming that the historically accurate portrayal of Jesus defined him as a "swarthy, coarse, vacant-eyed, short-haired man." The documentary asked why Jesus' race was culturally significant. The potential of programs to reshape our ideological assumptions is a reality. Questioning Christ's portrayal as white when he was Middle Eastern according to reports is a global reality.[5] Yet many found offense in the documentary.

Likewise, film documentaries of Native American reservations that portray Indians as captives of the land, deprived of work and resources and ignored by the government, are hard to take. Yet they present an existing truth of our treatment of the people who occupied America first. And, as is true with all portrayals, the reports are seen from the perspective of the director and/or producer. One set of videotapes can be edited to reflect opposing points of view. What examples can you cite of a documentary that affected your feelings about a race of people?

Ethnic News

America has a very ethnically diverse population. Because we have so many different cultures living in the U.S., there are many foreign-language media outlets for news, including TV.

 **FLASH FACT**

In the year 2010, the breakdown of U.S. population is projected by the census bureau to be: White 68 percent, Hispanic 13.8 percent, Black 12.6 percent, Asian 4.8 percent, and Native American 0.08 percent.

The largest foreign-language station, Hablernos de Salud, sponsors call-ins to its TV program in its twelfth season in 2008. Jade World is a Hong Kong-based TV station out of New York, Los Angeles, and San Francisco aimed at Asian populations. MH2 is an independent, non-commercial TV channel delivering newscasts and programming from around the globe with diverse cultural perspectives for globally minded American audiences. It is produced out of Virginia and Washington DC.

A 2008 study comparing news related to immigration[6] produced by English and Hispanic language newspapers showed differing views on the ethnic coverage. The study found that Spanish-language news outlets generated a larger volume of immigration coverage than U.S. news outlets. While this is not surprising, the issue is this: What are the implications of these results for creating public opinion on the topic?

U.S. magazines published for Hispanic readers

We might use Pierre Bourdieu's Field Theory[7]—a concept of interconvertability of cultural and media capital—to examine the rise of regional and global centers of broadcasting that seek to compete with CNN and BBC in Latin America, Arabia, and Qatar. These centers now question the inevitability of following the Anglo-Saxon model of commercialization, depolitization, and trivialization of news. By divorcing themselves from international news sources, these countries seek to avoid ethnic bias and cultural stereotyping.

U.S., British, and French governments are trying to fend off the competition from Latin America and Arab media. But why? Isn't diversity and expansion of news healthy? We believe competition helps news-gathering and reporting worldwide against the rising trend of infotainment that is tainting serious news dissemination in America.

Targeting Kids

Children's animation TV and programming carry ideas about race, gender, age, class, and other social groupings and identity.[8] The definitions of childhood that circulate in the animation industry derive from and reinforce particular institutional practices and economic arrangements. In the forefront of channel transnationalization are Nickelodeon, Discovery Kids, Cartoon Network, and Disney. Animation has been globalized with new technologies of distribution but still has U.S.-centric shows. Programming taps into universal themes as a business strategy to sell films. Korean animation is coming to us with universal story lines.

Because kids love animation, many countries now animate children's programming. Technological developments in online flash animation have driven down animation production costs as the creation of web-based animation outlets compete with traditional TV for viewers. For instance, a "tween" targeted girls' series, *Princess Natasha*, is on AOL in five-minute episodes. The series was picked up by the Cartoon Network and put into merchandising deals for a book, DVD set, and branded merchandise like clothing, games, school supplies, and beach towels. Tendency toward subscription digital broadcasting services in many countries suggests that the primary audience for newer delivery platforms is kids in wealthy nations.

Advertisers also segment children's audience. The Minimax Hungarian kids channel crafts programming according to age preferences: kids under the age of two prefer formless animated characters with sound and music; kids aged two to five prefer simple story lines, recognizable characters, and non-violent educational programs. Ages five to twelve want more complex stories and less educational content. Hungarian television produces and airs programs consistent with the needs and uses of the age-based segments of child audiences. Some countries' shows, such as U.K. Cartoon Network, resist using escapism in educational programming. The problem is, if the show's not fun, kids won't watch. Perhaps that's why *Sesame Street*'s integration of fun and learning was so successful.

The developmental model of child psychology and routines of the advertising industry combine to create discussions about what unites kids beyond cultural differences. Analyses of age-based experiences are derived from Western nations. Ad executive Kate Eden[9] identified five enduring themes that reach across cultural and linguistic differences among European children: mastery, up-ageing (pretending to be older), belonging, bravery, and morality. These themes are fine for Western programming, but not appropriate for non-Western cultures where age differences are performed through formal rituals rather than through clothing and behavior that Westerners use as age indicators. In Canada, one can tell a girl's age by her style and outspoken preferences. In Iran, age is only obvious as a girl passes from one stage of religious understanding to the next.

Media Impacts

As American programming invades the global landscape, viewers are bombarded by the values and ideas projected by its shows and stars. Most Americans base their understanding of international events only from American news. We watch children starving in Africa and terrorists bombing civilians in Lebanon. We hear commentary from American news media broadcasting live from trouble spots, and we understand the world according to the network's perspectives. Next time you need a news fix, turn to BBC on radio or television and compare its perspective of news events to those of Network TV affiliates in your area. Note which stories receive the most emphasis, and which ones are omitted altogether.

News media images that shape our views of the world and stereotype peoples of the world

Think about the role television plays in your life and in your perceptions of the world. Can any other medium compare to the power of televised images for their influence on how we think about ourselves and our world? Although measurement may be difficult, the social impact of television may best be reflected through the attitudes we hold toward ourselves, our culture, and our society.

Prior to the Beijing Olympics in 2008, TV crews invaded China to make documentaries. Americans, curious about this "communist" country, were eager for programming that revealed aspects of this culture that had been hidden for so long. One program, *Wild China*, was aired on the Discovery Channel to introduce Western viewers to Chinese people and their progress. Do you think these glimpses of the country, its people, and their struggles will overcome American skepticism about inferior products made in China? Will the media's coverage modify or change U.S. views of a nation where media and personal freedom are controlled? Or will the perspectives of national news media focus our attention on natural disasters and environmental issues instead?

Ethnic Origins of Entertainment

In the United States, entertainment ranks ahead of clothing and health care as a percentage of household spending (entertainment 5.4 percent, clothes 5.2 percent, health care 5.2 percent). Each year Americans spend at least 120 billion hours and more than $150 billion on legal forms of entertainment. Because "entertainment" spans a diverse set of industries, it is difficult to place a dollar figure on the revenue entertainment generates. Some figures estimate that, in the United States, entertainment is a more than $480 billion industry, including domestic and international business. That figure does not include tourism or consumer electronics such as TV sets and VCRs, which, many would argue, are bought primarily for entertainment.[10]

The question, then, is: Why is the entertainment sector outpacing growth in other industries? The simplest answer is: because it can. Economies grow with supply and demand, and, in the case of entertainment, we've seen rapid growth on both ends. Technological advances have increased both the quantity and the quality of entertainment choices (the supply). Meanwhile, because other sectors of the economy were doing well, people had more money to spend on entertainment "extras" (the demand). However, even as world economies began to slow down at the beginning of the twenty-first century, entertainment industries remained relatively healthy.

One of the healthiest industries is music, which is an integral component of a region's culture. Music unifies and identifies cultures and subcultures in much the same way languages, dialects, clothing, foods, and other traditions do. The types of instruments used as well as the tone, tempo, melody, and lyrics convey the nature and values of a culture. Popular music and radio are thought to both shape and reflect popular culture. The conceptualization of music as culture can be seen through a comparison of two distinctly different styles of American-born music: country and rap or hip hop. Television and the movies also have origins in ethnic-based forms of entertainment. This section presents an overview of ethnic-originated media.

Pickin' 'n' Strummin': Country Music

Country music, said to have roots in the Southern Appalachians, has a slow, often melancholy sound that perhaps reflects the slower pace of rural life in the early Deep

South. It relies heavily on string instruments like fiddles, banjos, and guitars—instruments that were relatively inexpensive and easily portable for singers peddling their music across the Southland. As the name suggests, country songs speak of the hard work and hard luck, heartache, and homecomings of country life.

Some historical accounts[11] suggest that American country music was inspired by the ballads and songs of the British Isles, which were brought over by early British settlers. The British songs often focused on the supernatural, avenging spirits, love stories, and violent tales. Yet they tended to be very objective, often relating gruesome stories in a very matter-of-fact style. In America, the songs became more subjective and personal. They downplayed the supernatural, and songs about crime emphasized the evil acts while minimizing the gore. When the songs had to do with love gone wrong, the Americanized ballad usually removed the violence and vulgarity altogether. These changes may have been due to the rise of the Victorian Age, but they also seemed better suited to the philosophy of the Southern lifestyle.

American country ballads also tended to add moral statements at the ends of songs, reflecting the Puritan belief that art must be functional or else it is frivolous. Ballads throughout the centuries were often written to share news and happenings from around the world, but with the invention of the printing press this trend declined in many places in Europe. In the vast, rural American Southlands, however, these ballads continued to serve as a fairly accurate way for the more isolated townsfolk to get news of current events. To this day, the instruments, sounds, tempo, and lyrics of country music continue to reflect the stories, people, and culture of country life.

Country Goes Global   Country music has evolved and mixed with other genres, just as the cultures that shape them continue to evolve and mix—and travel. Just because we call it "country music" doesn't mean it's only about America. The 2007 Country Music Association (CMA) festival was attended by visitors from Chile, Japan, and Scandinavia, with a total of 21 nations on five continents present.[12] Music lovers came to hear songs that reflect the values of rural heritage and national pride. Germany identified three groups that gravitate to country music: people intrigued with the American cowboy icon, middle-aged fans who seek an alternative to rock music, and younger listeners drawn to the pop-influenced sound that underscores many country hits.

The word "country" is often stereotyped, so a new term—highway rock 'n' roll—was suggested by a Bavarian broadcasting personality. According to him, international country music should focus on a mainstream audience because there aren't enough pure country fans in Europe. Artists abroad can reach as many as 80 million people by visiting ten radio stations in Germany and France, and maybe another million fans in Australia where country is very popular.

Hoppin' 'n' Rappin'

The language of the world's new generation, hip hop is popular from the townships of South Africa, Masai villages in Tanzania, regions of Italy, concert halls of Amsterdam to New York clubs. Kids are rhyming about corruption, AIDS, and civil war, creating a powerful outlet for protest and global recognition. By localizing and vocalizing hip hop beats into French, Wolog, Arabic, Hebrew, Twi, Swahili, and Spanish, hip hop is a tour de force that inspires creativity and provides youth with alternatives spaces and venues to voice their opinions and educate and empower each other.

Rap and hip hop, according to rapper Kurtis Blow, were born in crime-ridden urban neighborhoods:

Gifted teenagers with plenty of imagination but little cash began to forge a new style from spare parts. Hip-hop, as it was then known, was a product of pure streetwise ingenuity; extracting rhythms and melodies from existing records and mixing them up with searing poetry chronicling life in the 'hood, hip-hop spilled out of the ghetto.[13]

Faster and often angrier than other types of music, hip hop reflects the culture of the young urban teens who created it. Early rap, often viewed as a subset of hip hop, frequently consisted of nothing more than talking in rhyme to a rhythmic beat—music that could be performed without expensive instruments. The term *hip hop* typically refers to the broader genre of music and culture. According to musical artist and social activist Afrika Bambaataa,

Hip Hop means the whole culture of the movement . . . when you talk about rap. . . . Rap is part of the hip-hop culture. . . . The emceeing[,] . . . [t]he djaying is part of the hip hop culture. The dressing[,] the languages are all part of the hip-hop culture. The break dancing[,] the b-boys, b-girls[,] . . . how you act, walk, look, talk are all part of hip-hop culture . . . and the music is colorless. . . . Hip-Hop music is made from Black, brown, yellow, red, white . . . whatever music that gives you the grunt . . . that funk . . . that groove or that beat. . . . It's all part of hip-hop.[14]

Hip hop has evolved to reflect not only different sounds but also different perspectives. Even the work of individual artists has changed and evolved over the years. For example, the early rap of Dr. Dre starting in the early 1980s reflected hardcore but cautionary tales of the criminal mind, but his records with Ice Cube in NWA (Niggaz With Attitude) in the late 1980s and early 1990s celebrated the hedonistic, amoralistic side of gang life. After he left NWA in 1992 and began producing on his own again for himself and others, his music progressed further into G-Funk, a slow-rolling variation that relied more on sound than on content.[15] In recognition of their role in the progression of hip-hop, Dr. Dre and Ice Cube received lifetime achievement awards at the *Source* Hip Hop Awards in 2000.

Hip hop, both as a mixed genre and as a pure form of music, has been recently identified by corporate brands as one of the most profitable music genres. Toyota's youth marketing efforts for the Scion unites musical artists with marketing by showcasing their talent and promoting their music. Scion covers all production and licensing costs and studio time, with all proceeds going back to the artists themselves. Slick Rick, from the skate and streetwear world, has his own Scion lifestyle show, and Ghostface Killah introduced the brand into the French electro mix.

Toyota's Scion boosted its popularity by promoting hip-hop musicians such as Slick Rick

The Business of Hip Hop   Evidence of a convergence between business and hip hop emerged in 2008. To encourage entrepreneurship, a hip-hop business summit was held in August to bring together music industry executives, business leaders and music celebrities. The summit's purpose was to provide transitions for athletes and entertainers to host charity events in global communities. Fueling a free six-city concert tour featuring hip-hop artist Lupe Fiasco, Coca-Cola sponsored a "Refresh Your Flow" tour in the summer designed to connect African American teens with something they love—Coke and hip hop. And a string of superstars performed at the Fashion Rocks event in New York where hip-hop clothing brands such as Dereon by Beyonce debuted new pieces during the music event broadcast on CBS TV.

SPOTLIGHT ON RAP   It's Not Easy Being White

Stealing and altering hip hop has resulted in some interesting hybrids, such as rap music performed by a white artist. Gifted musician Eminem began performing rap music as M&M in the basement of his friend's home when he was 14. Being white, he had to overcome some racial boundaries and the predominantly African American domination of the genre. Eminem's first recorded single was released in 1995, after which he developed an alter ego, Slim Shady, to express his hidden feelings. His exaggerated, nasal-voiced rapping style and white skin earned him the title of music's next "great white hope." With a platinum album in 1999, controversy about his lyrics came to a head. In 2000, he had the fastest selling rap album of all time, close to two million copies in its first week of release.

Fans loved the publicity created by his battle with pop star Christina Aguilera over lyrics about her sexual exploits and a lawsuit by his mother over defamation of character. Mainstream media, however, were not as enamored with his antics. Inflammatory lyrics in songs "Kill You" and "Kim" that advocated violent murder of his wife of the same name caused his divorce and a turn in his career. After filming *8 Mile*, which was loosely based on his life, Eminem had some hit singles and albums, a tour, and finally a stay in rehab for sleeping-pill dependency.

The singer's appeal reached across ethnicities, and he had success with African Americans, Latinos, and Asians in America and with Europeans, South Americans, and Asians abroad. His apparel line, Shady Clothing, Shady Records with seven gold and four platinum albums, and an official web site keep his name alive with teens and young adults.

It's What You See: Visually Communicated Ethnicity

The most noticeable ethnic communication is demonstrated in movies and on television. On television, for instance, white images of beauty have a negative impact on the self-images of African American women, but not on men.[16]

Many ethnic groups are offended by the use of stereotypes and racial slurs in film. This reaction is consistent with the social identity theory,[17] which says that we seek positive social identity through comparisons of our group with other groups. And that group feedback impacts our social identity, our self-perception, and our cultural status.

Table 11.1 Ethnicity and Offensive Film Themes

Group	Theme	Overall percentage
All	Anti-social, criminal, violent	26
All	Deficiencies in motivation, language, intellect	8
E	Racial superiority/bigotry/exploitation	5
	Ridicule of culture or behavior	7
AA, H	Passive, helpless, easily exploited	4
AA, A, NA	Historical or contemporary miscategorization	8
A, NA	Absent from or ethnically undifferentiated	4.5
	Vulgar language or behavior	5
E, H, A	Behavioral or occupational stereotyped	13
AA, E, H	Sexually promiscuous	9

Key: NA = Native American A = Asian E = European AA = African American H = Hispanic All includes Muslim

A study of 1,226 movie-goers,[18] ages 13 to 74, consisting primarily of European, African, Asian, and Hispanic Americans, rated offensive ethnic and racial incidents in film content. Thirty-six types of offenses were noted, but ten themes emerged as significant. Table 11.1 shows the relationship between ethnic group, theme, and overall percentage of respondents finding offense.

These findings show that Asians were especially frustrated with actors cast as one Asian group playing another. An example is the use of Chinese actor Chow Yun-Fat to portray Thailand royalty in *Anna and the King*. Asians also disliked stereotypes typical of Jackie Chan films. Hispanics cited portrayals of them as violent or criminals more than twice as often as other groups, such as in films *Up in Smoke* and *American Me*. African Americans were most offended by films that characterized them as intellectually deficient, such as *Boyz n' the Hood*.

Among Europeans and Americans, viewers of both Italian and Irish decent were offended by the types of films portraying them as members of the mafia or IRA. Certainly films such as *The Godfather*, *Goodfellas*, *Casino*, and TV's *Sopranos* advocate the mob stereotype. And Irish films like *Patriot Games*, *In the Name of the Father*, and *Some Mother's Son* foster the notion of religious violence among the Northern Ireland militants.

Study results clearly demonstrate the longstanding tendency for movies to use stereotypes or overgeneralizations about culture and personality. Commonly held prejudices toward minority groups correspond to respondents' reactions in this study. Over the course of film history, groups cycle in and out of unfair portrayals, and others continue to remain the objects of offensiveness. In what ways have you seen members of your ethnic origin characterized in films?

SPOTLIGHT ON ETHNICITY   Native Americans Tell Their Own Story

A coming of age story, *Four Sheets to the Wind* is a debut feature set in Tulsa that was written, directed, crewed, and acted by Indians. Producers Chad Burris and Ted Kroeber are backing the first film by novice Sterlin Harjo because typical Indian Old West films do not portray what's current on today's reservations. And they think there's a real story to be told.

Movies defined by ethnicity must skirt stereotypes and be careful not to dwell on the negative. Harjo's script, which went through the screening lab of the Sundance Institute, is neither negative nor self-consciously Indian. The intention was to tell a story about human beings who happen to be Native Americans.

But not all Indians are the same and neither do they agree on how their culture is translated into film. Debates about the creation of so-called Indian cinema are founded on the issue of whether or not film is a proper medium for telling stories that are based on oral traditions rather than definitive imagery. Some have voiced suspicion of any chroniclers of their culture. Others agree that the media are so influential that movies may be the best way to convey the Indian message.

The Indian film effort was begun in 1988 with *Smoke Signals*, which made a splash at Sundance Film Festival, which showcased Indian movies in its Native section. To reach a wider audience, the Festival discontinued the Native section and programed the films festival-wide.

Four Sheets is a unifying movie that shows the diversity of native peoples. With no star to put on promotional posters, Indian filmmakers feel they have a definite marketing disadvantage. But with a limited budged and unlimited pride, these novices trust their audience with the truth they need to tell.

Ethnic Miscommunication

Hollywood has recently been accused of "white-washing" ethnic roles in movies by casting Anglos in roles of true stories that involved other ethnic groups. For example, white actress Mena Suvarti played a young black woman named Brandi who hits a homeless man and leaves him to die in the 2008 film *Stuck*. And the real whiz kid and his partner in crime in the film *21* were Asian Americans; the filmmakers made all but one kid white and cast Jim Sturgess, a Brit, as the leader. According to the producer, the film is not a documentary, it's an artistic vision. As such, he can take liberties with the source material. In 2007, Angelina Jolie played Mariane Pearl, an Afro-Cuban and Dutch woman who grew up in France. According to producers, bankable stars are necessary to ensure a film's success at the box office. Apparently, they don't think ethnic stars have reached that point. It's about bankability, and there is only one Halle Berry, only one Will Smith, who are actors that can do whatever they want.[19]

Independent films, on the other hand, can cast non-white unknowns that audiences will pay to see in movies. Expecting to see authentic stories, audiences of independent films are more willing to take a chance on a film without a white superstar. Indie films embrace ethnic diversity and strive for realism rather than box office dollars. At least that's what they claim. The hope is that, in Hollywood, talent will supersede race; and studios, filmmakers, actors, and audiences will all play a part in demanding change from the longstanding, traditional approach to casting white stars.

SPOTLIGHT ON COMICS   New-age Ethnic Heroes

Historically the faces behind the masks of comic book heroes differed only in hair color, and green skin was much more common than any shade of brown. In 2006, however, diversity hit the $500 million comic book business when DC and Marvel Comics introduced heroes that are gay, Black, Asian, and Hispanic.

At Marvel Comics, Black Panther, king of a fictional African nation, married Storm, the weather-controlling mutant and X-Man. The teaming of an ex-cop and African King is termed a "buddy action movie." Luke Cage, a strong-as-steel Black street fighter, and his white girlfriend play key roles in *New Avengers*, the company's best-selling book.

The new heroes' ethnicity reflects American society and comic readers in much the same way that the multicultural casts of TV shows like ABC's *Lost* and *Grey's Anatomy* mirror their audiences. Many DC heroes are closely tied to *52*, a weekly series that forces the new heroes into bigger roles at the expense of established heroes Batman, Superman, and Wonder Woman. Mindful that readers can be especially resistant to new faces, the creators are carefully orchestrating introductions and linking unfamiliar characters to "legacy" heroes. According to writers for both comic companies, what used to look like a social agenda has become the world we live in. And although these heroes are developed for American market segments, global superheroes are also coming of age, as presented later in the chapter.

Some of the new heroes at DC Comics include Blue Beetle, a Mexican teenager powered by a mystical scarab; Batwoman, a lesbian socialite by night and a crime fighter by later in the night; and the Great Ten, a government-sponsored Chinese team. DC's *Outsiders* has a multi-ethnic cast that includes Grace, a rowdy Chinese American powerhouse, and Thunder, the daughter of Black Lightning. Green Arrow, mayor of Star City, even legalized gay marriage.

Source: George Gene Gustines for the *New York Times*, May 28, 2006, p. 25

Preferring adult readers, **alternative comics** are almost entirely written for and by men. The genre's roots are traced to books by Robert Crumb, the man whose "Zap Comix" defined underground comics in the 1960s. Recently successful alternative artist Daniel Clowes writes and draws *Eightball*, a series of comics aimed at adults. Influenced by everything from "Peanuts" to punk rock and magic realism, Clowes's memoir-like narratives have raised the medium to a new art form.[20] He is sponsored by the largest publisher of alternative comics, Fantagraphic Books, which features many of the country's best artists.

Global Entertainment

Entertainment is the fastest-growing sector of the global economy. According to PriceWaterhouseCoopers, the entertainment and media (E&M) industry will be a $2.2 trillion dollar business by 2012. Spurred by digital and mobile segments in Asia, growth is broken down by percentage of total revenue, as shown in Table 11.2. The use of critical technologies—broadband, mobile, digital cinema, and HDTV—will influence the pace and duration of entertainment and media growth in the five years following 2007. Because American consumers prefer free or discounted content and services, Asians will drive the new digital environment more forcefully.

Table 11.2 Entertainment and Media in 2012

Entertainment genre	Percentage of global revenue
Internet access	12.1
Video games	10.3
Television subscriptions	10.1
Casino gaming	6.5
Sports	6.5
Film	5.3
Theme parks	5.0

Entertainment Everything?

Entertainment has blurred beyond its traditional boundaries into other sectors. You can find entertainment in hotels, restaurants, and shopping malls, on news programs, on web sites, and in classrooms throughout the world. We are entering an age when entertainment touches every aspect of our lives. And, once again, the question is: Why? This chapter explores how economic, technological, and societal forces are shaping and are shaped by the evolution of global entertainment.

Converging technologies make it unlikely that there will be a complete reversal where entertainment conglomerates fragment all of their various holdings back into independent companies under separate ownership. In addition, changes to FCC regulations in 2003 further relaxed restrictions on the number and variety of media outlets that one corporation can own, changes that were strongly supported by conglomerates such as Disney, Viacom, AOL Time Warner, News Corp., and other corporations eager to increase their holdings.[21]

Today, the relationships between entertainment corporate entities are changing as quickly as those of the celebrities they create. In 2003, Vivendi merged with NBC, which was then bought out by General Electric. Also in 2003, Sony partnered with Bertelsmann on Sony BMG music, but then in 2006 Bertelsmann announced a proposed sale of its music holdings to Vivendi (owned by General Electric).[22] Thus, while it is likely that we will continue to see more splintering and downsizing, we may also see additional strategic mergers and holding shuffles as big media companies continually search for a balance between diversification and streamlining.

SPOTLIGHT ON GLOBAL EXPRESSION   **Graffiti Art**

Graffiti has been a global form of communication for centuries, but only recently has it been studied as an art form. Modern-day emergence in America began in the late 1960s in its most basic form—tagging. These heavily stylized signatures and symbols that comprise much of graffiti were a form of vandalism and protest, a declaration of person and cultural identity, and a way to reclaim neglected spaces.[23]

A form of expression, protest, and beautification, graffiti art is both loved and hated the world over. International cities are brimming with stencils, stickers, and wheat-pasted posters that counterbalance commercialized advertising and its assault on consumers. Globally, graffiti have caused regulatory problems and opposition from people who see them as urban gang expression. But the vibrant subculture that lies behind graffiti is a result of extreme creativity and dedication to the art form.

Jon Reiss's 2007 documentary *Bomb It* explores this controversial subculture through themes of public space, freedom of speech, corporate advertising, and social and political issues. The film visits London, Paris, Amsterdam, Barcelona, Cape Town, São Paulo, and Tokyo, as well as Los Angeles and New York City, to explore how writers have incorporated graffiti into their cultures.

The film brings both pro and con views from throughout the world to reveal the depths of graffiti culture. Issues such as who controls visual public space take the art form into societal and historical realms. In addition, the film asks poignant questions such as: Who owns public space? Why do advertisers have the right to control our visual landscape with vulgar or disturbing images? The film suggests that there is nothing natural, neutral, or normal about the relationship between money buying control and access of public space. Countering the notion that graffiti are ugly and gang-related, the film gives graffiti back their history and philosophical and social virility as an outsider art movement.

The film's international perspective reveals graffiti culture as something innately human, dating back to the early days in caves. Today, graffiti use art as a weapon to fight and express the alienation and ugliness of modern cities.[24] And unknown to most of us, many clothing lines we wear, technology we use, and advertising we see have roots in graffiti art. And as graffiti become a staple in popular culture, city walls will become alive with social drama that tells us about our own culture and the people we share it with.

What do you think?

- *How would you defend an artist's right to use public space for graffiti?*
- *How would you argue against defacing public property with graffiti?*
- *Which argument is most compelling?*

The Global Movie Industry

Today's entertainment is an international enterprise. The major Hollywood studios—almost all owned by the eight mega-conglomerates—make more than half of their money outside of the United States. Table 11.3 lists the highest grossing American movies of all time and the percentage of revenue derived from outside the U.S. As you can see, outside revenues account for more than half of the total profits generated (except those released in 2008, which had not yet maximized their global distribution at this writing).

Entertainment enterprises worldwide are growing, and many are also expanding their reach far beyond their own national borders. In the United Kingdom, the earnings of *Trainspotting* (film), Jamiroquai and the Spice Girls (musical artists), *Tomb Raider* (video game), *Teletubbies* and *Mr. Bean* (TV programs), and *Miss Saigon* (musical) have created a trade surplus greater than the British steel industry.[25] One of the largest recording companies is also British-owned, along with one Japanese/German partnership; one American and one French-based corporation round out the "big four" music groups.

Table 11.3 American Films and Global Percentage of Total Revenue

Rank	Title	Studio	Worldwide ($ m)	Overseas (%)	Year
1	Titanic	Paramount	1,842.9	67.4	1997
2	Lord of the Rings: Return of the King	NewLine	1,119.3	66.3	2003
3	Pirates of the Caribbean: Dead Man's Chest	Buena Vista	1,066.2	60.3	2006
4	Harry Potter and the Sorcerer's Stone	Warner Bros.	976.5	67.5	2001
5	Pirates of the Caribbean: At World's End	Buena Vista	961	67.7	2007
6	Harry Potter and the Order of the Phoenix	Warner Bros.	938.5	68.9	2007
7	Lord of the Rings: The Two Towers	NewLine	926.3	63.1	2002
8	Star Wars: Episode I— The Phantom Menace	Fox	924.3	53.4	1999
9	Shrek 2	Dream Works	919.8	52.0	2004
10	Jurassic Park	Universal	914.7	61.0	1993
Most recent films:					
27	Indiana Jones	Paramount	744.4	57.8	2008
53	The Dark Knight	Warner Bros.	597.4	33.9	2008
44	Iron Man	Paramount	567.4	44.4	2008
99	Hancock	Sony	395.8	45.4	2008

Source: boxofficemojo.com/alltime/world/

Change and Consolidation

Structural changes in communication and media markets within countries and globally reveal:

- a perceived threat of new media technologies
- relaxation of media concentration rules
- pursuit by communication and media industries of greater vertical and horizontal integration.

As shown in Table 11.4, media ownership is dominated by public and privately owned companies in four countries, U.S., U.K., Japan, and Germany

A 500-channel universe is just around the corner. Hollywood studios are losing their iron grip on film audiences, and the growth of the Internet may render media concentration obsolete. Vertical integration across supply and distribution of film and TV programs has three effects.[26] Vertical integration

- gives Hollywood studios secure access to more distribution outlets in satellite and cable channels. TV networks gain access to a steady source of film programs; 80 percent of new series are acquired in-house.
- locks up access to both resources—content and distribution—and helps media firms manage risky nature of the media business.

Table 11.4   Global Media Ownership 2007

Firm	Revenue ($ billion)	Owner	Nation
Time Warner	43.7	Diverse	USA
Disney	39.1	Diverse	USA
*Bertelsmann	28.9	Bertelsmann/Mohn	Germany
*News Corp.	25.3	Murdoch	USA
*Viacom	24.1	Redstone family	USA
*Comcast	22.7	Roberts family	USA
NBC/Universal	14.0	Diverse	USA
Pearson	7.5	Diverse	UK
Fuji TV	5.0	Diverse	Japan
ITV	3.9	Diverse	UK

*owner controlled companies

- holds over content and distribution, creates barriers for independents, and rivals and limits creativity and diversity of the marketplace for cultural commodities.

One consequence of growing consolidation is the ability of a handful of owners to exert influence over media content and people's view of the world. Resources are being diverted from news and production to meet the high cost of financing mergers and acquisitions. Media are enacting cuts in news bureaus, and settling for inexpensive reality TV and game shows. There is a trend toward integrated news operations that serve multiple channels, allow budget cuts, require smaller journalistic staffs, and have fewer foreign bureaus, and toward the replacement of drama programming with low-budget shows.

These trends, however, are bound by audience tastes and the complexity of media business. And although audiences have more channels than ever, source diversity is shrinking. We're getting the same stuff on every channel! Media professionals experience changes in quantity and quality of work available; bottom line pressures have had a huge impact on quality. The structure and feel of media are being altered as media organizations strive to maximize control over content. Control is exerted through litigation to expand copyright laws and implement digital rights management technologies. These new laws would increase audience surveillance and set limits around what people can and cannot do with new media. How happy would you be about that?

SPOTLIGHT ON ASIA   Media Revolution

According to Mike Walsh's report on how young people in Asia consume media, a global view dominates. Consuming media from mobile devices is standard practice. The eTech conference in March 2008 highlighted other ways in which Asians are using media:

- *For entertainment.* Because Chinese television has limited programming, most kids focus on the Internet for entertainment; only half use the net for e-mail.

- *For mobility.* More people use mobile devices than stationary computers. All devices—even car GPSs—have digital tuners.

- *For identity.* Personal identity is created on the Internet. Using multiple accounts for special purposes, kids assume a whole range of different identities.

- *For information.* Consumers are faced with much more information than their Western counterparts. Much like the signage in Times Square, Asians scan complex data pages in their entirety for information, where, in America, readers on average look at only the top two search results.
- *For fame.* Internet avatars and virtual characters land sponsorship deals for product endorsements as well as celebrities.
- *For right now.* With a focus on instant gratification, media consumption consists of large quantities of copyrighted material that circumvents region coding for immediate access.
- *Multi-tasking.* According to Synovate's third annual Young Asians survey, conducted in 11 markets across Asia Pacific, this groups forms a "digitally nimble" generation that puts Internet, mobile phones, and TV at the center of its lifestyle.

Here are some interesting data revealed by the survey:

- Koreans and Thais fit the most activities into one day—over 44 hours of media in tandem.
- Malaysians had the highest level of media activity in the region, spending 12.9 hours online, watching TV, DVDs, newspapers, magazines, and radio.
- Internet and mobile phones are the media 15–24-year-olds can't live without. Internet is their major source of information, entertainment, and enjoyment; its main use in Hong Kong (the largest at 66 percent) is for communication and watching videos (50 percent), while China reported the highest (63 percent) number listening to music and free downloading (64 percent). Singapore youth spend the most time playing online games (62 percent).

Source: www.oreillynet.com/conferences/blog/2008/03/futuretainment_the_asian_media.html and www.warc.com/LandingPages/FeaturedContent/youngasians/youngasians.pdf

Global Communication as Superhero Icon and Digital Internet

Feel-good characters have always appealed to a wide variety of audiences. The arrival of new technology has allowed heroes from every country to take the global stage. Using animation, our best-loved characters hop from pages of comic books to the big screen. This sections looks at comics for Japanese boys, regional superhero movie stars, religious superheroes, and America's Iron Man as examples of how nationalities express their values and culture through their heroes. Finally, we take a brief look at the Internet as a global communicator.

Comic Heroes and Global Animation

Adolescent boys are the prime audience for 350-page comic sagas called *manga*. These comics are illustrated sagas of male response to removal from infant paradise and assignment to a journey of adult conflicts and demands. From a Freudian perspective,[27] these comics present distinct themes of oral, anal, and Oedipal stages of male maturation. Oral themes are presented as constant eating and reference to food in plots of oral delights, oral monsters, oral aggressions, and oral eroticism. Anal aggressions are overly apparent in these comics in portrayals of mooning, farting, and defecation. Issues revolving around toilet training strike responsive notes in young readers of these comics. The Oedipal stage is evidenced by allusions to phallic sexuality and phallic tales in "locker-room" type humor. Male transition into adulthood is shown in stories about boys who excel in individual sports like boxing and wrestling in contrast to adult conformity with group desires. Because the transition from infancy to adulthood is a journey of ever-increasing social pressures filled with conflict for Japanese males, young men devour and idolize *manga* heroes who protest the transition and rebel against it.

The most well-known form of story animation was developed in Japan. Known as anime, it has a distinctive character and background esthetics that visually set it apart from other forms of animation. In Japan, the word *anime* is used to refer to all forms of animated film from around the world. While some anime is entirely hand-drawn, computer-assisted animation techniques are, in recent years, quite common. Story lines are typically fictional; examples of anime representing most major genres of fiction exist. Anime is often influenced by Japanese *manga* comics. Some anime story lines have been adapted into live action films. Anime features a wide variety of artistic styles, which vary from artist to artist, and is characterized by detailed backgrounds and stylized characters in a variety of different settings and story lines, aimed at a wide range of audiences.

Manga Boy

Anime has as many genres as traditional, live action cinema. Such genres include action, adventure, children's stories, comedy, drama, erotica (*hentai*), medieval fantasy, occult/horror, romance, and science fiction. Most anime includes content from several different genres, as well as a variety of thematic elements. While different titles and different artists have their own unique artistic styles, many stylistic elements have become common to the point that they are described as being definitive of anime in general, and have been given names of their own. A common style is the large eyes style drawn on many anime characters, to show emotions and expressions distinctly.

Superheroes Abroad

Locally nostalgic Indonesian superhero characters have been revitalized for global audiences. Developers used character studies of other superheroes to create figures that were universally successful. Jabbar the Powerful, alter-ego of a teenager, was the first of 99 superhero characters in an Islamic culture-based comic book series called *The 99*. The comic seeks to act as a metaphor for what's happening in the Islamic world. Each of the superheroes personifies one of the 99 attributes of God in Islam. Fatah the Opener, for instance, can create a portal dimension used to travel anywhere on earth. The struggles happen between characters representing the classic good–evil dichotomy. The characters work in threes and do not carry weapons. Representing Islam's spread around the world, characters always originate from two nations; for instance, Bari is from Sudan but grew up in France; Hadya is from Pakistan but grew up in the U.K. The series sells as well in Kuwait and the U.A.E. as Spiderman, said a comic seller. In 2007, the series was brought to America for Islamic audiences.[28]

In an effort to save the planet, superheroesneeded.org solicited children to create characters that could help save the environment and stop global warming. The 2008 project hopes to get kids ages 8–14 worldwide mobilized to develop social and environmental awareness so they become effective adult activists. The organization communicates using technology through interactive and relevant participation. They want to show how small changes can have a ripple effect globally with tracking devices that update membership and raise funds, and provide organization, tools, and templates for writing letters to legislators and the media.

Faith-based Superheroes

Middle Eastern superheroes are predominantly religious. Israel's superhero, Seraph, is a Jewish school teacher granted biblical powers that are not affected by natural forces. He has invulnerability, super-wisdom, teleportation, and power from a staff to split things in half. Two religious superheroes are female: Iman is a Muslim teenage girl-hero who uses faith as a source of her power. She always quotes the Quran to explain that Islam is a great religion that expects Muslims to be tolerant, kind, righteous, and non-judgmental. Janissary is a Turkish sorceress, heroine, and role model for Islamic women featured in that country's comics. Other global superheroes include:

- Archer of Arabia (Saudi Arabia)
- Ibis the Invincible (Egypt)
- Mohammed Ibn Bornu, war hero (North Africa)
- Sandstorm (Syria)
- Sirocco, ally of Superman, and Super-Shayk (Iran).

Mythical Superheroes

Hanuman, the animated monkey God who usually chatters in Hindi, now speaks German, Italian, and Spanish as well.[29] Adopting India's Bollywood *masala*, global audiences love this emotional mythical hero. Hoping to establish the brand as a global icon, the story was written for a world audience, including America and Europe. Anticipating a generic need among consumers for new wonder men, producers of Hanuman, Percept Pictures, are also taking animated versions of other Indian heroes to global children audiences. Already a top grosser in DVD sales, Hanuman soars into the skies for its third sequel.[30]

Hanuman of India

Internationalhero.co.uk covers lesser-known creations with international diversity, including heroes from Europe, Asia, Central America, the Pacific region, and South America. Nationality is not easy to define in most characters. And others are designed to appeal to and educate teens.

Teen Titans' fifth season was released on DVD in July 2008. In this series, Robin, Starfire, Speedy, Aqualad, Wonder Girlk, Beast Boy, Cyborg, and Raven face off against the Brotherhood of Evil, led by the Brain and Monsieur Mallah. The Titans go on a worldwide membership recruiting drive where they gain new allies. With titan foes like Control Freak, Mother Mae-Eye, and Billy Numerous, these teen cartoons, which originally aired in 2006, also includes *Titans East* with Mas y Menos who went from cartoon to his own comic book.

Iron Man as Global Superhero

One American superhero was created to reflect a world morality. Iron Man, who chose greatness rather than being born into it like Superman, is likened to the global superheroes of antiquity: Moses, Jesus, Ram, Muhammad, Robin Hood, and Gandhi who were moral responses to the injustice around. These were not superheroes but choices that make heroes of men and women. And while other superheroes are relegated to their locality, Iron Man is the product of injustice at a global level when he rescues an American held captive in Afghanistan. He resonates the birth of a new global super-hero who plays a greater role in the scheme of the fictional world he inhabits.[31] Does this mean we are on our way to making the fictional world a better place by fighting greater foes—like capitalism? Does Iron Man have the potential to save an increasingly intolerant and conflicting world? We may have to wait for the sequel to answer these questions.

According to Danny Fingeroth, author of *Superman on the couch*, there is a superhero consciousness that transcends religious and national boundaries that infect us with do-gooder inclinations. His book is a psychological journey through comic history that purports to explain what superheroes tell us about ourselves and society.

Digital-speak

Superheroes may tell us about our society, but language communicates the message. Language is one of the Internet's few boundaries, so icons often replace words. To over-come the language deficit, a group of Chinese/China-focused digerati (the elite of online communities) are bridging across the Chinese and English Internet. These "cyber elite" are the doers, thinkers, and writers who have tremendous influence on the emerging communication revolution. The digerati evangelize, connect people, and adapt quickly. They ask each other questions they ask themselves. One such person is Keso, who has subscribed to over 600 people's FriendFeed, an online community, that can be used to trace the intersections of Chinese and non-Chinese digerati.[32]

New Internet iconography lets people "read" one another even if they can't speak the same language. FriendFeed, for example, displays just three icons, one for the blog, one for a Twitter feed, one for gmail/gtalk. With 43 different services, each with its own icon—ranging from Digg, YouTube, and "blog" to more obscure things like Kisqus, Mister Wong, and identi.ca—FriendFeed visuals do away with knowing how to speak Chinese or French or English to be able to pick out the icon superheroes found on Keso's subscription feed, such as the one you may find at www.virtual-china.org/2008/07/26/friendfeed-superheroes-global-iconography/ developed by Jacky Zhao.

American Influences on the World

Although the majority of people from Africa, Asia, and the Middle East may never visit the U.S. or ever meet an American face to face, they inevitably encounter images of Los Angeles and New York in the movies, television programs, and popular songs exported everywhere by the American entertainment industry. Many of those images exert a more powerful influence on consumers abroad than they do on the American domestic audience.

The intense emphasis of American entertainment on violence, sexual adventurism, and every inventive variety of anti-social behavior provide a very narrow picture of the U.S. for global audiences. For that reason, Islamic people look upon America as a cruel, godless, and vulgar society. Five movie theaters in Pakistan showing U.S. films, for example, were burned to the ground in protest.

So we look to see how the national icons from Mickey Mouse to Madonna represent the power of our ideals of free expression and free markets. Are our images used as weapons for America-haters or embraced for their creativity and boldness? This discussion provides some examples of how our entertainment media are incorporated into or rejected by nations around the world.

Entertainment Provider

Western entertainment has proliferated throughout the world for a variety of reasons, including the ability to create programming and distribute it abroad. Even closed societies like China import our entertainment.

For example, millions of young people in China have embraced American entertainment for years. During the Tiananmen Square rebellion, pro-democratic reformers carried the Statue of Liberty as a symbol of their movement as they dressed in American fashion and played American music. In Singapore, most clubs and pubs are styled after American establishments. And the city has a Hard Rock Café and jazz clubs indicative of U.S. fare.

One country with a decidedly American flavor in its cultural landscape is Germany. The impact of our television and the sounds of our entertainers have influenced Germany's leisure time activities. They love coming to America to see the old West, especially the Indian villages. And from jazz to jeans and Coke to CNN, Germans experience aspects of America daily.

 **FLASH FACT**

More than 85 percent of the films playing in German theaters are Hollywood films. After Japan, Germany is the largest market for American movies abroad. Our television shows air on German channels either dubbed into German or as German remakes of American originals. About three-quarters of the music heard on German radio and played on MTV Europe is either American or English.[33]

In Australia, all the major news channels are American; all of the reality TV shows are knock-offs of American reality TV; most of the songs played on the radio are by American artists. And American products are imported. The truth is, most countries embrace Western style movies and music, but accusations of "cultural imperialism" still dominate Middle Eastern societies. Even after they immigrate to America, Muslim groups protest against entertainment's flagrant use of foul language and sex. In spite of the media objections, Middle Easterners are visiting (and moving to) America in droves.

Industry expert Michael Wolf suggests that there is a critical difference between how entertainment developed in the United States and Western Europe and how it is evolving in today's developing countries. In the West, entertainment was at first seen as a luxury. Televisions, VCRs, and computers were items reserved for those with discretionary income. Adoption of new forms of entertainment and entertainment technology happened at a slower pace, as the innovations trickled down from the upper to the middle and lower classes. In today's world—even in many developing countries—entertainment is seen not as a luxury but as a necessity. As entertainment offerings become a more integral part of our global society—tied closely to news, politics, and everyday life—to actively participate in this society, one must have access to these offerings. Thus, the pace of the "entertainmentization" of today's economies is accelerated, particularly in developing nations that are anxious to catch up with the rest of the world.

Global Proliferation   Recognizing this potential, leaders in the entertainment industry are investing heavily in opportunities in developing regions, predominantly in Asian countries such as China and India. Savvy leaders have learned, however, that you cannot always simply export Western entertainment products—you must adapt to your audiences. *Time*'s efforts to export its generic U.S. magazine were not well received, but Hearst's *Cosmopolitan* adapted to local audiences by using local editors who edited international content and added relevant local stories. These adaptations can be subtle. "With more than 36 editions of Cosmopolitan in more than a hundred countries," Wolf notes, "Hearst has found that women everywhere are interested in the same topics; sex, sex, and more sex—albeit in their own language."[34]

Occasionally, the entertainment industry uses its power and celebrity to make a political statement. One singer who used her global tour for this purpose was American singer Alicia Keys. On tour in Indonesia, she demanded the withdrawal of tobacco industry sponsorship of her July 2008 concert in Jakarta by Philip Morris's Indonesian subsidiary Sampoerna. She appeared on billboards advertising Mild Cigarettes' sponsorship, which she refused. "I don't want to influence teens in any country toward smoking," said Keys. The music industry also uses its stars to support international causes such as AIDS and poverty.

Fashion and the Middle East

American fashion magazines have extended their reach into Middle Eastern editions that balance fashion and tradition. On newsstands in Lebanon, Jordan, and Morocco, *Elle*'s edition mixes glossy photos of stylish clothes with fashion advice for readers who want loose-fitting *obayas* or *chandors* in public but want to look chic underneath and indoors. Women in most Muslim countries cover their heads and bodies in public in keeping with religious tradition. But underneath, a growing number of them are wearing elegant, fashionable, and often revealing attire. Accessories, from designer shoes to handbags, scarves, sunglasses, and jewelry, are permitted almost everywhere.

In Saudi Arabia and Kuwait, social calendars are filled with women-only parties where a globalized understanding of beauty prevails. But is it a gamble to launch a magazine in a region that doesn't always welcome Western culture? *Elle*'s strategy is to take the best of an international brand and localize it. Editorial content includes articles about protecting the skin from sun damage to Muslim women who are fighting for custody of their children. Profiles, such as that of a Lebanese designer who dresses celebrities, are also featured.

Advertisers in *Elle*, including Christian Dior, Cartier, and Giorgio Armani, are also adapting their messages to the market. Coty cosmetics shot a special ad campaign for its Jennifer Lopez perfume for the Middle East, showing only the singer's face instead of her curvy silhouette in the original ad. The magazine must tread carefully to avoid government censorship, which varies from country to country.[35]

Turn Toward Tabloids

Patterned after American tabloids, Russian tabloids like *Komsomolskaya Pravda* have taken the country by storm. Moscow staffers seek out and publish celebrity news and sensational drama. A recent story was about the intrigue-filled death of a supermodel from Kazakhstan who jumped from her Manhattan balcony. Another told a tear-jerking tale of a World War II veteran who had been robbed of his medals. Still others featured a hockey player hit with a cake and the closing of 50 street cafés in Krasnoyarsk.[36]

Such is the vibrant tabloid culture under Vladimir Putin: tabloids can be as raucous as they like as long as they don't threaten the Kremlin or its friends. The paper's investigative journalism tends toward exposés of incompetent police work, corrupt low-level officials, and dirty train stations. Once too poor to have a consumer culture, Russia's new consumer society is more interested in shopping than in politics.

That said, *Pravda* has pursued its own brand of muckraking by spotlighting problems of violence against immigrants from Central Asia and the Caucasus. It also exposes crime at railway stations and crime against the homeless. And, while revealing, the stories pose no threat to Putin or President Medvedev. Some readers from Russia's intelligentsia have criticized the paper for being too patriotic

Russians read the latest issue of a Moscow tabloid

and too obsessed with sex and scandal. Circulation numbers, however, support the paper's strategy with 750,000 daily readers and 3.1 million readers of the weekly edition. So, regardless of narrowing press freedom in Russia, the tabloids are thriving with bold headlines, revealing photos, and stories that keep readers amused.

American Music Goes Global

Once exported, American ethnic music takes on new forms that suit the country adopting it. For example, hip hop is changing the music business in Nigeria with untested artists turning traditional gospel into mainstream hip hop. One group called Rooftop MC's was formed at the University of Lagos. Its hit track, "Lagimo," is about not letting pride take over, and going back to God when you are about to derail. According to the group, "We sing hip-hop like Jay-Z, but without words like 'shaking the ass.' "[37] Non-violent and slang-free lyrics replace U.S.-style vocal, but the beat remains true to hip-hop origins.

Hip hop has also traveled to India. In 2008, Snoop Dogg gave the " 'what up' to all the ladies hanging out in Mumbai"[38] with a guest appearance on the title track of Bollywood movie, *Singh Is Kinng*. A fusion of hip hop and bhangra, the music is finding an enthusiastic audience among India's billion-plus population. Snoop Dogg wears a Sikh turban and an ornate long coat (*sherwani*) in a video of the title song, which is being distributed by Geffen Records.

And in China, rapper Wang Xiaolei looks to Jay-Z as a model and brings a taste of China to the hip-hop world. According to Wang, hip hop empowered him because he can identify with Blacks in America. "We don't have a good life, but we have to stay optimistic," said Wang. "Hip hop lets me be free." Wang raps about cold rooms and cold faces, about lies and people changing. He says he's dissatisfied with people, but not his government. After years absorbing Western hip-hop culture, Wang is focused on things Chinese, embracing who he is and where—China at a time of change.

In celebration of hip hop's influence on the world, a Global Underground Film and Music Fest was celebrated in an April 2008 event in New York City. From global hip-hop label Nomadic Wax and sponsor World Hip Hop Market, the Global Underground Film and Music event celebrated world culture and positive hip hop with film screenings drawn from the global diaspora. Examples of their offerings included: *Diamonds in the Rough* about how a group of young people from Uganda use hip hop to spread their revolutionary message and hope of change; *Estilo Hip Hop*, which portrays the use of hip hop in Latin America as a voice and agent of social change; and *African Underground: Democracy in Paris*, which shows the attitudes and concerns of France's immigrant and hip-hop communities during the elections of 2007.

In Park City, Utah, in January 2008, Palestinian hip-hop group DAM was featured at the Sundance Film Festival that focused on the emerging Middle East music scene. The group's documentary features rapper Mahmoud Shalabi, who offers an alternative form of resistance against "Israeli occupiers" of Palestine. DAM launched a record label to distribute Arab and Palestinian music in the U.S. According to Abeer, Palestine's first lady of R&B music, rap and hip hop are among the world's most popular forms of music—lyrics of the oppressed and marginalized—and are best for communicating the Palestinian message to a new generation.[39]

Effects of U.S. Entertainment

Although global audiences are still keen on American pop culture, Hollywood may want to temper its imports for Muslim countries. In a 2007 Pew Research study of global attitudes in 47 nations, about 60 percent have a positive view of U.S. movies, music, and TV. But favorable ratings declined in 26 of these 33 countries. The survey indicated that the percentage of countries that don't like American entertainment is growing.

Western European countries, of course, expressed the highest approval of American culture. Views in Africa and Eastern Europe were mixed. Predominantly Muslim countries gave U.S. pop culture the lowest marks, but Indians and Russians weren't that fond of American culture either. At the bottom, Pakistan's approval rating of U.S. entertainment was only 4 percent; Bangladesh had a 14 percent approval rating, Turkey 22 percent, India 23 percent, and the Palestinian territories were at 23 percent. Russia rated our culture with a 38 percent approval.

Our culture did well in the Ivory Coast with 86 percent approval, the highest surveyed. Sweden (77 percent), Canada (73 percent), Israel (72 percent), and Spain (72 percent) gave us thumbs up. Lebanon and Venezuela tied at 72 percent, edging out Japan at 70 percent. Japan, U.K., and Germany lead overseas box office results. Muslim audiences don't like American culture. More than two-thirds of Bangladeshis, Pakistanis, Turks, Palestinians, and Indians said they didn't like American entertainment offerings on film, TV, and in music.

Overall, the survey indicated increasing concern that "Americanization" is spreading unwelcome customs to other societies through bootlegged and imported media and entertainment.[40] So we ask the question, is it Americanization or globalization that is most pervasive? Here is one perspective.

Americanization or Globalization?

In spite of all the complaints about American imperialism from the Middle East, Europe, and Latin America, it may be important to recognize that American entertainment—movies, TV, and theme parks—is more cosmopolitan than imperialistic. According to author Richard Pells, discomfort with the global impact of American culture results from fear of losing cultural identity and fear of a trend toward cultural uniformity.

In fact, America is as much a consumer of foreign influences as it has been a shaper of the world's entertainment. As a nation of immigrants, the U.S. is more of a recipient than an exporter of global culture. We did not invent Disneyland—it was patterned after Copenhagen's Tivoli Gardens. And for the first two decades of the twentieth century, France and Italy—not the U.S.—were the largest exporters of movies around the world.

American culture has spread around the world because it has incorporated foreign styles and ideas, says Pells. And postmodernism's removal of boundaries between high and low culture has contributed to the growth of mass culture on a global basis. Modernism provided the foundations for a new culture that was transformed by Americans into a global phenomenon. This relationship between America and the rest of the world is evident in popular culture for a variety of reasons, some of which include:

- the ability of American-based media conglomerates to control the production and distribution of their products
- the effectiveness of English as a language of mass communication—simple structure and grammar, shorter sentences, less abstract words; it has permeated song lyrics, ad slogans, cartoon captions, newspaper headlines, and movie and TV dialog
- international complexity of American audiences which has forced media to experiment with messages, images, and story lines that have a broad multicultural appeal
- mixing musical cultural styles by musicians such as Leonard Bernstein; incorporation of folk melodies, religious hymns, blues and gospel songs, and jazz into symphonies, operas, and ballets.

For decades, Hollywood has functioned as an international community, built by immigrant entrepreneurs and drawing on the talents of actors, directors, and so forth from all over the world. For example, the influence of Moscow's Stanislavsky's Method Stage Acting technique was adopted by American movies, then conveyed to the rest of the world as a paradigm for both cinematic and social behavior. Also, the refusal by Hollywood and TV to browbeat an audience with a social message resulted in focusing on human relationships and private feelings. This is why global audiences flocked to see *Titanic*—not because it celebrated American values but because people could see some part of their own lives reflected in the stories of love and loss.

America's mass culture has transformed what it received from others into a culture everyone, everywhere can embrace. In the end, American mass culture has not transformed the world into a U.S. theme park; rather, American dependence on foreign cultures has made the U.S. a replica of the world.

FADE TO BLACK

This chapter has taken us from American media treatment of ethnic groups to ethnic media circulated and distributed in the U.S. We saw how stereotypes create attitudes that may lead to anti-social behavior and we looked at the ethnic origins of American country and hip-hop music genres. By going global, we saw the rise of superheroes that reflect national, cultural, and religious values. And we overviewed the way American media have influenced media worldwide. Finally, we presented an argument for positioning American media as delivering ethnic diversity rather than cultural imperialism. And we invite you to explore global media on your own through the Internet, film festivals, comics, and music using your own resources and the resources provided at the end of this chapter.

A CLOSER LOOK AT GLOBAL VALUES   Hofstede's Universal Cultural Dimensions

How does American culture differ from others around the world? Dutch social scientist Geert Hofstede[41] compared cultural values across 50 countries and identified five dimensions on which societies differ. These dimensions help us understand similarities and differences among entertainment audiences across the globe. To understand these dimensions, we ask that you answer the short quiz question for each of the five traits to see how it relates to the respective cultural dimension.

1. Individualism vs. Collectivism
Q: In America, most people will

a. *attend live performances that are nationally popular or that their friends want to see.*
b. *buy tickets for live performances they alone want to see.*

You probably checked answer b. because our society is individualistic rather than collective. This dimension concerns whether the well-being of the individual is considered more important than the well-being of the group. Collectivist cultures, such as those typical of South Korea, Mexico, China, and Indonesia as well as the South American countries of Guatemala, Panama, and Venezuela, have close ties between people, and they value group interest over self-interest: kind of a "we" vs. "me" approach to selecting amusement and activities.

2. Power Distance
Q: In America, most people will

a. *long for a chance to see a football game in exclusive box seats with important people.*
b. *willingly sit in the bleachers with other football fans who enjoy the game.*

In America, sports fans will most often opt to sit with people who share their sports passion. Power distance is the extent to which less powerful people accept the authority of more powerful ones, such as folks with lots of money or celebrity status. In cultures where large power distances occur, people with status are expected to have special considerations, which are accepted by others. Americans traditionally consider themselves psychologically equal to each other, even when other educational or monetary differences prevail. In countries with large power distances—such as the Arab world, India, Hong Kong, Brazil, France, Thailand, Mexico, China, and the Philippines—the family head would make the decision about where to sit or which game to attend, and the rest would defer to him. In America, Europe, Australia, and Canada where low power distance is the rule, the entire family participates in decision making.

3. Uncertainty Avoidance
Q: In America, most people will

a. *be the first to see a new film, even if it means standing in line for hours.*
b. *wait until the reviews are out before committing time and money to seeing the movie.*

Most Americans don't fear the uncertainty of seeing a movie on its first weekend. In fact, most of us will try new things without fearing the consequences. But countries where people need more certainty about the movie's quality or interest before going are uncomfortable with uncertainty and try to avoid it. Cultures with people who feel threatened by ambiguous situations include Greece, Portugal, Guatemala, Belgium, Japan, Spain, and France. Northern Europeans generally have lower tolerance for uncertainty than people in Mediterranean nations and Singapore, Jamaica, Denmark, Hong Kong, Sweden, and the U.K.

4. Masculinity vs. Femininity
Q: In America, most people will

a. *choose travel with adventure, thrills, excitement, and even danger.*
b. *pick a travel option where they can enjoy the serenity and other tourists.*

Americans are known for their adventuresome spirit, and as such the U.S. is classified as a masculine nation along with Japan, Austria, Venezuela, Switzerland, Italy, Spain, Mexico, and the U.K. In contrast, cultures that value harmony, peace of mind, caring for others and quality of life are known as feminine. Feminine countries include Sweden, Norway, Netherlands, Denmark, Thailand, and South Korea. Travel to museums, historical sights, and national forests dominates in feminine countries. Some masculine countries are more masculine that others, such as Mexico where being "macho" is important. For example, travel to a bullfight, a macho sport, is preferred by Mexican and Spanish cultures.

5. High Context vs. Low Context

Q: In America, most people will:

a. *come right out and say they hate rap and hip hop and refuse to listen to that kind of music.*

b. *tolerate whatever kind of music is being played or presented at a concert regardless of their feelings about it.*

Americans are very vocal about what they like and dislike, and make decisions quickly; we are a low-context culture. In high-context cultures, layers of meaning that are often hidden are taken into consideration. In this case, a person from a high-context culture—such as India and most Asian countries—considers the feelings of others, and understands that situational conditions help determine decision-making. If a Japanese person is asked whether or not s/he wanted to purchase tickets to a Police concert, the person would probably say "I want to think about it," rather than hurting the ticket seller by saying no. Here as in most Eastern nations, people are not as forthcoming with their opinions as are people in low-context cultures that include most Western nations.

What do you think?

- *How can marketers use Hofstede's dimensions to sell movies internationally?*

DISCUSSION AND REVIEW

1. Use the social construction of reality theory to explain how media shape the way we think and behave.
2. How are superheroes used to transmit cultural and religious beliefs and values?
3. What stereotypes can you describe that are not included in this chapter? How do you think they were developed as characterizations of a particular group?
4. Is cultural imperialism the new globalism (global compression and growing perception of the earth as an organic whole)? Or is it Americanism?

EXERCISES

1. Watch two dramatic TV shows and note the number of ethnic people on screen and the number of stereotypes associated with race. What conclusions can you come to about media portrayals of ethnicity?
2. Log on to www.veryfunnyads.com and watch a few video clips of commercials from different countries. Discuss the use of humor and visual imagery to reinforce views about groups of people.
3. Muslim groups have immigrated to America in great numbers since the Iraq war. Using the Internet as a resource, identify the media being circulated in the U.S. intended for Muslim audiences. In which cities or regions are they produced and delivered? What stereotypes have you seen in American media that perpetuate the notion of Muslims as religious zealots or terrorists?

BOOKS AND BLOGS

Bose, D. (2006). *Brand Bollywood: A new global entertainment order*. Thousand Oaks CA: Sage.
Cooper-Chen, A. (2005). *Global entertainment media*. Hillside NJ: Lawrence Erlbaum.
Thussu, D.K. (2008). *News as entertainment: The rise of global infotainment*. Thousand Oaks CA: Sage.
The Source, a U.S.-based monthly magazine covering hop-hop music, politics, and culture.
www.hiphopglobal.com—news, music, and shopping related to hip-hop culture.
www.global-culture.org/—a blog on global citizens and the quest for cosmopolitanism.
www.atimes.com/atime/South_Asia/IH30Df01.htm—*Asian Times* news online.
www.fair.org/—a site dedicated to fairness and accuracy in reporting around the world.
www.allafrica.com/—African news and information for a global audience.

12 SIN CITY: VIOLENCE, SEX, DRUGS, AND GAMBLING

It's not about if you won or lost—
But how you played the game.
—Grantland Rice

Entertainment has often been criticized for appealing to our baser instincts—sex, aggression, gambling, risk-taking. Indeed many of the most popular and profitable entertainment industries—music, TV and film, casinos—are fueled by these themes. Undoubtedly, the activities showcased in these diversions are not always ones that we would encourage people, particularly youngsters, to engage in as part of their regular daily activities, if at all. Thus, questions have been raised, on many fronts, regarding the potential impact these forms of entertainment may have on audiences and society at large. The understandable concern is that audiences will be inspired to imitate and overindulge or at least become more tolerant of immoral and unsafe behaviors that are depicted in many forms of entertainment. We have seen, for example, in Chapter 8 how concerns regarding gambling and violence, indecency and obscenity in films and on radio, television, and the Internet have led community leaders and activists to push for regulations, limitations, and in some cases outright bans on expression and activities that are considered questionable. Others, however, have fought such restrictions, arguing that entertaining diversions are just that, diversions: they serve not as a model for real life but as an escape, a release that may actually serve as a safer outlet for those "baser instincts" thereby reducing their manifestation in society.

The impact made by these diversions, gambling, violence, and pornography, may have some serious unintended consequences. Betting on sports, buying lottery tickets, gambling at casinos, and watching films with violent or sexual content are safe diversions—unless they become compulsive and habitual. This chapter looks at the outcomes of specific types of entertainment that can become addictive and harmful to players and audience members who indulge to the extreme. We begin with a discussion of media violence and its effects on society. We then examine concerns regarding how sex and drugs are depicted in entertainment, and then conclude with a discussion of the pros and cons of gambling both as a form of entertainment and as a growing business sector.

Violence as Entertainment

No entertainment effect has received more public, legislative, or industry attention than the impact of violence in entertainment (media entertainment, in particular) on societal aggression. Violent entertainment has been accused of increasing juvenile delinquency and violent crime rates (including instances of spousal abuse, rape, and murder) and of scaring people to the point that they are afraid to go outside their homes. Studies have analyzed the impact of violence in films, TV programs, live sporting events, music, and video games, yet research on the subject is far from conclusive. Although some studies have found a relationship between observed violence and aggressive behavior, others have not. And results each way are almost always questioned and criticized by other researchers. Thus, the question of whether or not media and entertainment violence can encourage violent behavior has not been clearly answered. Nonetheless, several theories suggest that such a relationship may exist.

Many theories suggest only short-term impacts. *Priming theory* suggests that observing violence may prime aggressive ideas or thoughts, which may lead people to react more aggressively for a period of time after viewing violent entertainment. Similarly, *excitation transfer theory*, discussed in Chapter 4, suggests that the excitement and adrenaline generated by witnessing violence, such as in an action film or at a sporting event, may keep people in an agitated state so that, for a brief time afterwards, they may react more intensely and aggressively than they would otherwise if provoked. *Catharsis theory*, however, suggests the exact opposite: that witnessing aggression in a film, game, or other form of entertainment allows us to vent our aggression vicariously along with the characters or players, thereby purging our hostility so that we may actually become less aggressive for a short time afterward.

The effects of media violence are unclear

Other theories suggest more lasting impacts. For example, *social cognitive theory* suggests that we might learn from violent forms of entertainment to behave aggressively if such behavior is rewarded. Conversely, however, we should learn to be *less* aggressive, if such behavior is punished. *Cultural and cumulative theories* suggest that the nature of the violence displayed (by whom, against whom) can have significant societal influences on the perpetuation of social stereotypes and the status and power of certain groups.

Thus, the exact relationship between media violence and real violence is still unclear. At one extreme is the view that media violence can actually decrease violent tendencies and reduce real aggression. At the other extreme is the view that media violence significantly increases real-life violence. Most researchers, however, tend to take a middle-ground perspective that certain depictions of violence under certain conditions may prompt violence in certain persons.

Sports and Violence

To many fans and critics, modern-day sports seem more violent than ever. Anecdotal evidence of violence, where athletes attack not only each other but also referees and fans, abounds even in non-contact sports such as baseball and basketball. Of even greater concern to many is the fact that athlete violence doesn't always end when the games end. The media delight in reporting the skirmishes athletes get into off the court or field. In fact, ESPN began including a daily crime report in its broadcasts. Nonetheless, others contend that today's sports and their athletes are relatively tame compared to the life-and-death gladiator matches of yesteryear.

It has always been difficult to separate sports from violence. Indeed, research suggests that many audiences, particularly male audiences, enjoy sports more if they contain high levels of violence and roughness. The logic is that aggression heightens the drama and suspense of sports and acts as a cue to observers that athletes are so highly motivated to win that they are willing to take life-threatening risks. Some argue, however, that it is not the actual degree of violence in a game but the viewers' perceptions of violence that influence their enjoyment of sports. Interestingly, research suggests that sports commentary is capable of altering viewers' perception of violence such that when commentators stress the roughness of the play, it appears even rougher.

Even more disputed than the perceived amount of violence in modern sports is the question of how this violence affects those who view it. The relationship between sports and societal violence has received significant attention in both popular and academic literature. As is true for other depictions of violence, however, theorists are split in their views.[1] According to one view, aggressive sports can have a cathartic effect on audiences, reducing their own aggressive urges and thus minimizing actual violence. Evidence for this effect, however, is rather weak. A more popular view maintains that viewing sports may promote spectator violence. Theories supporting this view were reviewed in Chapter 5.

Security guards at a rugby game

Incidents ranging from parent brawls at youth league games to full-scale riots at professional sporting events are pointed to as examples of sports-induced violence.[2] In Sarasota, Florida, a man was arrested and charged with battery after storming the field to punch the referee in his seven-year-old son's flag football game. In Salt Lake City, two women were charged with assault after allegedly attacking a mother, leaving her unconscious, following a youth baseball championship game. At a National Football League game in Cleveland, the referees literally had to run for their lives as angry fans hurled beer bottles and other debris at them for making a delayed call that dashed the Browns' playoff hopes.

And in New Orleans, the mother of a Duke University basketball player suffered a concussion after fans at the University of Maryland hurled water bottles and other debris because the Terps had lost the game. Perhaps most alarming is the case of a 44-year-old American man who killed a fellow parent while they were watching their sons take part in an ice hockey practice match in Cambridge, Massachusetts.

Backing up these examples of fan violence, empirical research suggests that sports violence can make spectators more aggressive. This research suggests, however, that audiences may react differently to televised sports than they do to live events. Sports commentary and other features of mass media may influence audiences more than the violence itself. If sportscasters speak favorably of the violence, as they often do, then observers may be more apt to learn and perhaps perform violent behaviors than if the sportscasters condemn the violence or if there is no commentary at all. So the aggressive effects of watching televised sports may be greater than the effects of watching live sports. Yet because television viewers are often more isolated from others, they do not face the same crowd situations that tend to provoke aggression at live events.[3] Nonetheless, the evidence found in these studies poses a significant dilemma for sportscasters. If they want to enhance the entertainment value of a sporting event, research suggests that they should emphasize violence and roughness. However, if they do so, they risk encouraging violent behavior in their audiences, an impact that many would argue runs counter to the journalistic creed to promote the public good.

Football **hooliganism** has no specific legal definition. The term was created by the media, the tabloid press in particular, in the mid-1960s and since then they have been extremely flexible and indeterminate in ascribing the "hooligan" label to different incidents. Hooliganism

Football fans at a match

in football (known as soccer in the U.S.) is seen by most to mean violence and/or disorder involving football (or soccer) fans. However there are two very specific "types" of disorder that have been labeled "hooliganism": (a) spontaneous and usually low-level disorder caused by away fans at or around football matches (the type that typically occurs at U.K. matches), and (b) deliberate and intentional violence involving organized gangs (or "firms") who attach themselves to football clubs and fight firms from other clubs, sometimes a long way in time and space from a match.

In the U.K., the first type of hooliganism is relatively rare considering the number of supporters attending matches. However, abroad, English fans have often been involved in disorders. Often the extent of this disorder is exaggerated by excessive media reporting, and in many cases English supporters are the victims of attacks by local fans or police rather than the aggressors. The press has typically claimed such disorder is the result of "hooligans" traveling with the intention of fighting and being able to draw drunken English fans into disorder. However, analysis of incidents from 1990 to 2007 in Stott and Pearson's *Football hooliganism: Policing the war on the English disease* criticized this view and suggested that external factors such as indiscriminate policing and the presence of aggressive local youths were usually the cause of rioting involving English fans abroad.

Second is the more serious disorder caused by hooligan "firms" in the U.K. Domestically this is still a huge problem, with most football clubs having groups of "risk supporters" who wish to fight rival firms. U.K. police have to deal with the problem of organized firms trying to confront each other on a regular basis, although the disorder is rarely reported (owing to the lack of coverage of incidents) and, as it usually takes place far from the field, "normal" fans do not tend to be directly affected by it. One example of high-profile disorder between firms (which was reported) was the clash between Everton and Manchester United "hooligans" in 2005. Footage of this can be found on YouTube under the search term "Everton Valley."

Football hooliganism has been called the "English disease" on many occasions. However, it is not limited to England, and many other countries have serious hooligan problems. In Italy, violent groups within the Ultra factions have recently been involved in a number of serious violent incidents including attacks on English fans (particularly in Rome) and in 2007 were implicated in the death of a police officer. This continued serious disorder between factions of Ultras has led to ground closures and also possibly Italy's failure to host the 2012 European Championships. It is probably fair to say that Eastern Europe, Belgium, and the Netherlands all have greater problems in terms of "hooliganism" than the U.K., where disorder in and around stadiums is very rare. However, perhaps the most serious football-crowd disorder takes place in sub-Saharan Africa and South America where serious crowd rioting, often inside stadiums, is much more commonplace than in the U.K.

Hands Up or I'll Shoot: Onscreen Violence

Driven by economic factors, media businesses strive to provide their audiences with what they want to see and hear. Two primary factors are credited as powerful draws for audience attention: violence and stardom. In the filming industry, for example, box office success is thought to be largely driven by the amount of violence (and other provocative activities) in the film and the popularity of actors who star in the films. Violent content, however, can affect the film's rating. Thus, a filmmaker often treads a fine line in trying to include enough violence to attract audiences, but not so much that the film receives a more restrictive R or NC-17 rating which could limit audiences. The film rating system, summarized in Figure 12.1 is detailed in Chapter 8.

Figure 12.1
Movie Rating
System

We don't need research to prove to us that violence is prevalent in Hollywood entertainment. Studies have confirmed this, documenting notable increases in violence in all types of film and television programming. For example, a study of Disney films produced between 1937 and 2000 found 464 violent incidents and 564 weapons used in these incidents. Moreover, this analysis found an increase in violence with each successive decade of Disney films.[4] For another interesting look at how violence has become more prevalent, see the *Spotlight on Violent Documentaries*.

Why are film and television audiences so attracted to violence as entertainment? Some critics contend that Sam Peckinpah's trend-setting piece *The Wild Bunch* makes us see the beauty of a massacre and other atrocities. "Audiences are alternately horrified by the butchery and exhilarated by the orgiastic energy his balletic spectacles stir up," said one critic of this film.[5] Editing and special effects also affect audiences' attraction to violence, as we saw in Hitchcock's shower scene in *Psycho*.

SPOTLIGHT ON VIOLENT DOCUMENTARIES   Caught on Tape

Early in the history of film, audiences were drawn to documentaries which promised to show the extremes of human experience—medical operations, attacks on animals and real life executions became popular even as mainstream cinema shied away from on-screen kisses. Ever since, such films have remained cult viewing, from the "Mondo" films of the 60s to recent "shockumentaries" like *Terrorists, Killers and Other Wackos*.[6]

A documentary often seems to have a special relationship with its viewers, affecting them in a more profound way than pure fiction does. When the material is especially violent or offensive, the questions become: Is the work intended to inform or to

titillate? Will audiences be educated or damaged by what they see?

Recently there has been a huge surge of interest in violent films and videos, which take their cue from the MTV series *Jackass* but go even further in pushing the boundaries of taste and of safety. In works that have clear appeal to young viewers, U.K. regulators have taken action when extremely dangerous acts are glamorized and imitation is encouraged with no indication of the potential dangers.

The U.K.'s *Dirty Sanchez* series had warning captions put on screen, for instance, where an aerosol spray and lighter are used in a makeshift flame-thrower which is then used on a man's buttocks. The U.K. required cuts to *Steve-O—Don't Try This at Home*, which features an intravenous vodka injection and potentially fatal stunts involving fireworks, which are easily accessible to the young. Still more complex are cases where the "harm" seems to be not in directly encouraging a particular type of behavior but rather in adversely affecting the general attitudes of viewers. This issue often crops up in relation to "compilation" documentaries.

The video *Terrorists, Killers and Other Wackos*, for example, features news and documentary clips including accidents, executions, and suicides, strung together without narrative. To many viewers these are intensely shocking and upsetting images. But in a world where fictional, palatable violence is commonplace, shouldn't we encourage works which show violence and its consequences for what they really are? Or should we be on guard against the dangers of "desensitisation," where viewers become inured to real violence and thereby more likely to be violent?

In *Terrorists*, the critical factor for the censors was that its portrayal of human suffering and cruelty seemed designed purely for entertainment, with an often comical soundtrack and "amusing" captions commenting on the—largely non-white—victims and aggressors that encourage callous and sadistic attitudes on the part of its viewers.

What do you think?

- *Greater concern might be raised regarding the impact of "docu" violence because it is "real." What you do you think is the appeal? Is the impact of this violence different than fictional aggression, and if so how?*

Audience Enjoyment   In Chapter 4, the appeal of violence was framed in terms of its ability to foster suspense and drive a story line. Action films, for example, keep us enthralled with the anticipation of violence—fears that the hero may be harmed, and the resolution of violence—satisfaction when the villains receive their just desserts. To put its appeal in perspective, however, we must remember that violent entertainment is not as popular as comedies and sitcoms among most audiences. Often it is not the violence per se but other forms of gratification that attract audiences. Violence may be a means to an enjoyable end, enjoyed not for what it is (aggression, blood, and gore) but for what it represents (adventure, risk, excitement). The thrill of fantasy and challenge stimulates players of violent video games, for example.

We know that images of violence are jolting and they provide fodder for discussion and social posturing. But because audience segments differ in their reasons for enjoying violent portrayals, no one theory addresses all our motivations for watching. Taken together, several theories provide an integrated approach to understanding the attractions of violence that are relevant to entertainment.

Child advocates proclaim that violence is harmful to children, yet we know that all children find most displays of excess exciting.[7] Boys like to watch violence more than girls, and adolescent boys like violent entertainment more than any other group,[8] as evidenced by their preference for toy guns and combative video games. Cartoon violence is more joyful for children than watching realistic physical violence as portrayed on the news.[9] Research shows that children who enjoy violent entertainment have high levels of aggression, but no evidence exists to suggest that violence produces aggressive behavior.[10]

Some researchers believe that we enjoy violence because of our notion of fair play and retribution. When someone has been wronged, we enjoy seeing the "eye for an eye" notion played out. Violence in the name of getting even is not only tolerated, it's justified and enjoyed. We all love to see the good guy win over the bad guy. The degree of predictability present in films containing violence may contribute to its level of entertainment value.

One of the most attractive features of violent entertainment media is its ability to take us into fantasyland. Suspension of disbelief may enhance a tolerance for violence for media consumers. But in order to maximize enjoyment, audiences must feel safe in their viewing environment. They must be able to detach from the book, film, or program far enough to feel the security of space existing between themselves and what is taking place in the narrative or images they experience.

The appeal of violence can be experienced in three distinct ways.[11] First, we may enjoy violent films for the violent images that evoke pleasure. Or we might have overall enjoyment for the movie but find the violent scenes unpleasant. Finally, we might enjoy a violent movie for the gratifications that are indirectly related to the images but are experienced after viewing them. A theory of sensation-seeking is one idea that says a combination of delight in the visuals and novelty of violence[12] explains its appeal.

According to a compendium of authors, violence is attractive when a variety of subject characteristics, appealing image characteristics, and context conditions are met.[13] And while those conditions are known, questions remain about the "why" and the cultural implications of those conditions. Regardless of their reasons for watching, audiences make the final determination of what are acceptable and unacceptable displays of violence. In other words, we can choose to watch or not to watch. Of course, as long as long lines form at theaters showing *Terminator* genre films, as long as we tune into video footage of police beatings, and as long as we buy Stephen King novels, violence will remain a prominent fixture of our media landscape.

Violent Impacts   Although critics have reservations about the potential impact of all screen violence, many express more concern about violence viewed on TV than in movie theaters. In this case, it isn't the nature of the violence they find most troubling but the context and frequency of viewing. First, TV raises more alarm simply owing to the amount of time that viewers spend watching it. People may go to the movies several times a month, but the time they spend in theaters is still just a fraction of what most will typically spend watching TV. Second, the viewing experience is markedly different. In theaters, viewers have clear choices regarding what they might see. If you choose to view an R-rated horror film you know what you are in for—a film that is probably very scary and violent, but you also know that it is all fantasy. Although audiences are free to make similar choices with TV viewing, they are often more distracted. They may be flipping through channels or multi-tasking while they watch, and, thus, may not be thinking as critically about what they are viewing. Because fictional programs on television are mixed in with news and documentaries, the concern is that audiences may not make as clear distinctions between fantasy and reality. It is feared that this distraction combined with the sheer volume of viewing may allow TV to have a more pervasive influence on audiences' thoughts and behaviors. As a result, the effects of violence on TV have received far more attention by researchers than have other effects or other entertainment media.

In keeping with the limited effects paradigm discussed in Chapter 5, during the 1960s the prevailing view was that *some* media violence affected *some* people, *some* ways, *some* of the time. Many scholars believed, however, that media violence did not greatly affect most "normal" viewers. However, the coinciding of the rise of TV and the turbulent events of the 1960s, increases in youth aggression, unrest and riots associated with the civil rights, women's rights, and anti-Vietnam War movements, and the assassinations of Robert F. Kennedy and Reverend Martin Luther King, Jr., led to the creation of the Surgeon General's Scientific Advisory Committee on Television and Social Behavior in 1969. The committee's members, who had to be approved by the TV networks, spent two years and $1 million on research,[14] which led Surgeon General Jesse L. Steinfield to conclude to the U.S. Senate that:

> While the . . . report is carefully phrased and qualified in language acceptable to social scientists, it is clear to me that the causal relationship between television violence and antisocial behavior is sufficient to warrant appropriate and immediate

remedial action. The data on social phenomena such as television and violence and/or aggressive behavior will never be clear enough for all social scientists to agree on the formulation of a succinct statement of causality. But there comes a time when the data are sufficient to justify action.[15]

Although this statement would appear unequivocal, disagreement persists regarding the relationship between media violence and social behavior. Most would agree that media violence *can* influence behavior, but the questions regarding when, how, why, and among whom remain points of contention.

The question of how and why media violence influences audiences has been addressed by many theories. *Cultivation theory* suggests that audiences may begin to adopt views that reflect what they see on TV, and thus, if TV depicts the world as a violent, scary place, where minorities are aggressors and women are helpless victims, then viewers may accept those views as reality. Similarly, *aggressive cues models* allow that TV portrayals can suggest that certain classes of people, for example women or foreigners, are acceptable targets for aggression, thereby increasing the likelihood that some people may act aggressively toward these groups. Perhaps the most compelling case that has been made is that media violence can *desensitize* viewers so that they become less bothered by and more accepting of violence in society. Other theories, however, such as *social learning/social cognitive theory* go further in positing a direct causal relationship between viewing televised violence and engaging in violent behavior.

Social learning has been a particularly popular theory to apply to TV violence because its concept of *vicarious reinforcement*—the idea that observing behavior that is reinforced can be as effective as actively engaging in and being rewarded for behavior. When applied to TV, this suggests that seeing a TV bad guy punished for violence should actually inhibit or discourage violent behavior. The problem, however, is that such punishment is typically doled out by an equally violent "good guy" who is seemingly rewarded for his or her behavior. Thus, most applications of social learning theory suggest that most televised violence is more likely to encourage rather than inhibit violent behavior. The notion of catharsis, however, proposes just the opposite, supporting the idea that watching media violence can reduce innate aggressive drives. Catharsis, however, has not been widely embraced as a reasonable explanation for the effects of violent TV. Critics not only point to a lack of empirical support, they also reason that, if we would not expect watching people eat to reduce hunger or watching people making love to reduce sexual drives, we should not expect watching TV violence to reduce aggressive behavior.

Vulnerable Viewers   The question of who is significantly influenced by TV violence has also been widely studied. It is clear that most people do not suddenly become aggressive after watching a violent TV program. Not surprisingly, research suggests that those predisposed to violence are more likely to be influenced by televised aggression. However, it also suggests that almost anyone could become "predisposed." For example, in experimental studies, frustrating or angering people before or after they view media violence can increase the likelihood of subsequent aggressive behavior. Similarly understandable are findings that those who watch more TV violence have been found to be more affected by it.

Survey studies have shown a relationship between violent behavior and heavy viewership of violent TV.[16] And, consistent with cultivation predictions, heavy viewers of violent programs are more likely to hold worldviews that match the TV portrayals they see.[17] If we see a lot of violence on TV, we are also more likely to expect violence in our own lives. These relationships, however, are relatively weak ones.[18] They may be either statistical artifacts or just indicative of inherent differences in the type of people who tend to be heavy versus light viewers.[19] Perhaps more convincing are longitudinal panels in which TV viewing and behavior are studied over time—days, months, or even years. Studies have suggested that TV viewing at an early age is related to violent behavior later in life,[20] and that these effects continue to mount even in later years.[21]

Effects on children have been a primary focus of study, given that they have even greater difficulty distinguishing between the real world and what they see on TV.[22] And TV is packed with violence. It is found in three-fifths of all prime-time shows, at a rate of 4.5 violent acts per program.[23] Some studies have found that children's programs have even more violence, glamorizing it just as much and trivializing it even more.[24] A common argument made is that, to a child's mind, if the coyote in the Saturday morning cartoon suffers no ill effects from a bash on the head with a frying pan, then the same should also be true for a little brother. Young children may be drawn to fast-paced car chase or shoot-out scenes, but, given their shortened attention spans, they may not stick around for, much less appreciate, the legal consequences that emerge in dull courtroom scenes at the end of a program. Children are among the heaviest TV viewers, often without super-vision, leaving their impressionable young minds particularly vulnerable to the medium's influence.

Hundreds of experimental studies, many similar to Bandura's Bobo doll study discussed in Chapter 5, have demonstrated that children can imitate violence they see. Some research suggests that televised violence can prompt children not only to copy specific acts of aggression but also to engage in novel forms of violent behavior. There is evidence that it can predispose them to select violent resolutions to conflicts in their daily lives and even prime them to engage in violent acts.[25] Children may also imitate violence even if it is not explicitly reinforced on TV.[26] It has been argued that the strength of these effects is comparable to those associated with proven public health threats such as lead poisoning and cigarette smoking.[27]

Given that most of this experimental research was conducted in controlled "labo-ratory" environments, some scholars reject these findings because they were observed under unrealistic conditions.[28] Field experiments in real-life settings have also demon-strated the effects of media violence,[29] but, when natural observations of violent behavior are used instead of relying on respondents' own questionable memories, the results are mixed.[30] One field experiment found evidence of a catharsis effect that reduces violent tendencies through exposure to fantasy violence,[31] but such findings are the exception, not the rule.

In spite of numerous findings supporting a relationship between exposure to TV violence and aggressive behavior, TV is clearly not the most important factor contributing to violence in society. Family and peer influence, socio-economic status, and substance abuse are more important.[32] So, the effects of TV violence remain controversial. Most experts would probably conclude that exposure to TV violence can have at least short-term effects in influencing perceptions of aggression and in promoting violent behavior; many would likely concede that there are probably some long-term effects as well. As suggested in other chapters, however, research also shows that many of these negative effects can be counteracted through parental oversight, media literacy programs, and proactive efforts by TV producers to take care in the way that violence and other behavior is portrayed, particularly in children's programming.

Virtual Violence   Video games have come a long way since the simplistic ping-pong and cascade games of the early 1970s, and the space-age *Asteroids*, *Space Invaders*, and *Pac-Man* that soon followed. Today, severed limbs, drive-by shootings, and decapitated bodies captivate a new generation of gamers, and gruesome scenes of violence and exploitation are the norm. In the award-winning *Grand Theft Auto* series, the principal game activity is carjacking. Once a car is stolen, the player can run over pedestrians. The player may also purchase guns to shoot at and kill rival gang members (or pedestrians) while completing missions for crime bosses. *Grand Theft Auto: Vice City* came under attack for allegedly implying racist hate crimes. The game, taking place in "Vice City" (a fictional Miami) in 1986, involves a gang war between Haitians and Cuban refugees, and the player often serves both gangs to plot against one another. Haitian and Cuban anti-defamation groups highly criticized the game and took particular offense to phrases that were used like

Blaze, a virtual killer who lives for tattoos and biking

"kill the Haitian dickheads." After the Haitian-American Coalition threatened to sue, Rockstar removed the word "Haitians" from this phrase in the game's subtitles. Games such as *25 to Life* are similarly controversial with story lines involving violent gangs taking hostages and killing cops. And even popular online, multi-player games such as *World of Warcraft* and *Doom* are obviously not designed for pacifists.

One of the first widely accepted controversial video games was *Death Race* (1976) in which players controlled cars that ran over pixilated representations of "gremlins." The game caused such protest that it was pulled from store shelves and profiled on *60 Minutes*. In the wake of this outcry, PTA president Ronnie Lamm pushed for legislation in the early 1980s to place restrictions on how close video game arcades could be to schools, asserting that they caused children to fight.[33] Portrayals of violence in video games became more realistic with time, alarming politicians such as U.S. Senator Joseph Lieberman, who conducted hearings during the 1990s to further investigate these games.[34] Concerns regarding video game content finally led to voluntary systems adopted by the gaming industry, such as the ESRB rating system in the United States and the PEGI rating system in Europe, which are aimed at informing parents about the types of games their children are asking to play (see Chapter 9).

Studies have found evidence that playing violent video games like *Doom*, *Wolfenstein 3D* or *Mortal Kombat* can increase a person's aggressive thoughts, feelings, and behavior both in laboratory settings and in actual life.[35] Furthermore, some researchers have argued that violent video games may be more harmful than violent TV and movies because they are interactive and very engrossing, and require the player to identify with the aggressor. Rather than the purely vicarious reinforcement that may occur from witnessing violence on TV or at the movies, video game players are more directly rewarded for their own violent actions in the game. According to researcher Dr. Craig Anderson, "Violent video games provide a forum for learning and practicing aggressive solutions to conflict situations. In the short run, playing a violent video game appears to affect aggression by priming aggressive thoughts. Longer-term effects are likely to be longer lasting as well, as the player learns and practices new aggression-related scripts that can become more and more accessible for use when real-life conflict situations arise."[36]

First-person shooter games, where players see through the eyes of the character have often been singled out for criticism because of how closely they simulate actual behavior. It was widely reported that the killers in the Columbine High School massacre were, like many teenagers, fans of first-person shooter games. The game *Doom* was mentioned in the shooters' suicide video, causing some activists and parents' groups to blame it (and other FPS games like it) for the school tragedy.[37] There is no proof, however, that game play in any way influenced the teens' behavior. A U.S. Secret Service study found that only 12 percent of those involved in school shootings were attracted to violent video games, while 24 percent read violent books and 27 percent were attracted to violent films.[38]

Indeed, no research has provided evidence that video game play can lead to major violent crime such as school shootings. Most research has focused on studying associations between video games and more limited aggressive behavior such as bullying.[39] Even in those cases, not all investigations have found a link between game play and aggressive tendencies. Meta-analyses that have examined large bodies of video game research have reached different conclusions: some ultimately supported a link between games and violence, but others did not.[40] In the wake of the Columbine incident, a 1999 study of the state of video game research by the U.S. government prompted Surgeon General David Satcher to say, "We clearly associate media violence to aggressive behavior. But the impact was very small compared to other things."[41]

Some criticisms from both game players and non-game players alike are directed at the game play in and of itself, which, some critics feel, may cause obsession or addiction. These criticisms have primarily focused on role playing in multi-player online and first-person shooter games. A prominent aspect of role-playing games is the immersion factor, or virtual reality of the gaming environments. Not only do critics contend that troubled individuals may increasingly turn to such games to escape reality, the games themselves have been accused of encouraging obsessive play. In most role-playing games, players can get stronger and move to the next level only by repetitive fighting of weaker enemies for a long time. In multi-player online games there is the added concern about "missing out" on the action if you leave while others continue to play. Few studies, however, have explored the potentially addictive nature of these games, making it a ripe area for future research.

The state of the science over any potential threat of violent video games remains uncertain. Even if a causal link was universally accepted, each one of the many attempts at state regulations of video games, at least in the United States, have been found to be unconstitutional by courts of law, as video games are protected speech, and some may rise to the level of core political speech (see Chapter 8).

Sex, Drugs, and (More) Violence

Critics have similar concerns about the impact of media portrayals of sex, drugs, and alcohol use. The primary accusation is that the media and other forms of entertainment glorify activities such as smoking, drinking, drug use, and sexual promiscuity, thus encouraging audiences to indulge in such behavior.

Onscreen Portrayals

Sex in the media erupted as an issue in the 1920s, in the aftermath of a wave of Hollywood scandals. As discussed in Chapter 8, Hollywood imposed strict self-censorship:

no cleavage, no navels, separate beds for married couples, no kisses longer than four seconds, cut to the clouds overhead if sex is imminent.[42] Elizabeth Taylor caused an uproar when she said the word "virgin" in a 1954 movie. Depictions of drug use go as far back as 1936 in the film *Reefer Madness*. The film was intended to be a scare tactic to warn people of the dangers of marijuana use, but it was criticized for having the opposite effect. Since then, movies such as *Easy Rider* (1969) often have been accused of glorifying the drug scene and contributing to illegal drug use among college students.

Increasingly, producers, and publishers push the limits of risqué content in depicting sexual and other taboo behavior such as drug use ostensibly in an effort to lure in audiences and make bigger profits. Thompson and Yokota analyzed movies from 1992 to 2003 and found that the total level of sex, violence, and profanity (SVP) has followed an upward trend.[43] According to a 2005 Kaiser study reviewed in the *Washington Post*, sexual content has also increased on television. In the slightly more than 1,000 shows scrutinized in the study, nearly 4,000 scenes had sexual content, compared with fewer than 2,000 in 1998, when the foundation started studying TV sex.[44] Under the watchful eye of the FCC, tobacco, alcohol, and drug use is less prevalent on broadcast TV, but very prevalent on cable, particularly on premium channels.

Research does suggest that such content "sells." For example, films that include sex have reaped higher box office sales to adults and students. And movies rated R and PG-13, in which sex and drugs are more prevalent, sell much better to international audiences, which helps explain why movie studios continue to produce many more of them than PG and G movies. Similarly, some critics have suggested that NBC, traditionally lauded for "cleaner" programming, ramped up the sexual content in its early 2008 program line-up as a desperate attempt to boost low ratings. See the *Spotlight on Tawdry TV* for a detailed critique.

SPOTLIGHT ON TAWDRY TV   NBC Joins the Sex Parade

(Warning: Includes graphic language, sex, and violence.)

Models Carol Alt, Jennie Finch, and Tiffany Fallon at the *Celebrity Apprentice* finale in Rockefeller Center, New York City, March 2008

Until recently, NBC was touted as the best (or perhaps a better designation would be "the least bad") in terms of inappropriate and offensive depictions of sex during prime time. Certainly NBC's new fall season did not feature the flood of tawdry, sex-obsessed sitcoms and boundary-pushing dramas that ABC, CBS, CW, and Fox did. Unfortunately, this is changing. Since the beginning of 2005, NBC is increasingly joining the other networks in pumping sexual situations into its programming.

This unwholesome new trend was first evidenced this year on the premiere episode of *Celebrity Apprentice*. One of the "celebrities" featured—and given the most prominence in this particular episode—was *Playboy* Playmate of the Year Tiffany Fallon, complete with a quick shot of her *Playboy* cover. In allowing her to take a place with the other accomplished celebrities and professionals, NBC implied that someone who takes her clothes off for a living is every bit as respectable and appropriate a role model for children as an Olympic gold medalist or a multi-platinum country singer. Also appearing in the episode was Jenna Jameson, demurely billed on camera as an "Adult Film Star" (i.e., "actress" in pornographic movies). The episode ended with Donald Trump firing Fallon, after berating her for failing to enlist Hugh Hefner's aid in her enterprise. Trump sneers, "I've known a lot of Playmates of the Year," and repeatedly boasts of his close friendship with the elderly exploiter of women. Nor was *Celebrity Apprentice* the only reality show to feature *Playboy* centerfolds; the January 11 episode of the game show *1 vs. 100*, airing at the Family Hour of 8:00 p.m. ET (7:00 p.m. CT/MT), featured former *Playboy* Playmates of the Month, triplets Nicole, Erica, and Jaclyn Dahm.

But promoting porn stars and centerfolds is merely the tip of NBC's tawdry iceberg. In keeping with the program's continual downward slide, the January 10 episode of *My Name Is Earl* showed Earl himself becoming a stripper. While patronizing the suggestively named Club Chubby strip joint, Earl shines a laser pointer at a stripper's chest, causing her to fall off her pole and become injured. To make up his debt to the injured stripper, Earl performs a striptease. He takes off his shirt to reveal tassels covering his nipples. As the crowd hoots, Earl spins the tassels. Later, Earl states that "some old Texan dude just offered to buy me a boob job." Naturally, this episode also aired during the Family Hour. And, as if one scene of breast-tassel twirling in a week were not sufficient, the very next night's episode of *Las Vegas* saw Danny, in an attempt to empathize with his pregnant wife, donning a female fat suit—complete with tassels covering his "breasts."

While the foregoing examples are distasteful, they are as nothing compared to the horrifically gory scene of sexual violence that greeted viewers of *Law and Order: Criminal Intent* on January 16. Within a

minute of the episode's opening, a camera focused on a pool of blood on the floor of a medical examination room. Panning along the floor, the camera revealed a dead man's body, his legs in stirrups used for gynecological exams, his pants around his ankles. The puddles of blood on the floor apparently emanate from the man's mutilated genital region, and the shot ends by showing a vaginal speculum jammed into the murdered man's mouth. This grotesquely graphic and gratuitous imagery is more appropriate (if that is the word) to an R-rated movie than prime-time broadcast television. The episode, which also featured a teenage boy bragging about manufacturing cocaine and calling a red-headed female police officer "firecrotch" as he swills vodka, aired at 9:00 p.m. ET—which is only 8:00 p.m. in the Central and Mountain time zones.

NBC's newfound fascination with the tawdry shows no sign of abating. Prominent in NBC's recent prime-time advertising has been a commercial for the network's forthcoming program *Lipstick Jungle*. The ad goes on to show a woman's dress being ripped off, and an apparently nude man asking a female character, "Do you want to take a picture?" But the commercial's biggest brag is the tagline, "by the creator of *Sex and the City*." If ever proof was needed of network television executives' desire to flood prime-time broadcast TV with the graphic and explicit content previously reserved to adult premium cable, that commercial provides it . . . with NBC as a willing collaborator.

Source: By Christopher Gildemeister. Reprinted with permission of the Parents Television Council, as posted on ParentsTV.org January 25, 2008, at http://www.parentstv.org/ptc/publications/tvtrends/2008/0125.asp

What do you think?

- *Are stations like NBC pushing the envelope with risqué content in order to boost ratings?*
- *If so, how do you feel about the use of this strategy?*
- *Do you think that today's TV is too "tawdry"?*

Hollywood isn't shy about portraying sex and drug use, but studies suggest that negative consequences such as unwanted pregnancy or addiction are rarely portrayed. One study of 87 box office hits released since 1983 found that none portrayed unwanted pregnancies or sexually transmitted disease.[45] Drug use received similarly mild treatment. Twenty-eight of the top films contained sex scenes, but only one even hinted at safe-sex practices—use of condoms. There were no depictions of important consequences of unprotected sex such as unwanted pregnancies, HIV, or other STDs.

Researchers found that 8 percent of the films depicted marijuana use, and 7 percent showed other non-injectable drug use. About half of the scenes showed marijuana use in a positive light, while the rest were neutral in tone. Sixty-eight percent of the films showed characters smoking, and 32 percent depicted people getting drunk. The concern is that failing to note the negative consequences of risky behavior may encourage people, particularly teens, to be more likely to engage in such behavior.

Impacts on Risky Behavior   As we have noted, social learning theory states that imitating behavior seen in television and films is largely determined by whether or not such behavior is rewarded or punished. If sex and drug use are depicted as fun and rewarding, then theory would suggest that audiences would be more tempted to try it. For example, glamorous depictions of cigarette smoking in movies have been shown to encourage young people to smoke.[46] Similarly, the film *Juno* received criticism when 17 students in one Massachusetts school turned up pregnant after the film was released. The film was about a high school girl who gets pregnant. This was labeled the "**Juno** Effect": by depicting the sunny, even redemptive side of Juno's plight, some experts have argued that Hollywood had perhaps made motherhood attractive for teens.[47] Although there is no empirical evidence that the film had influenced the pregnant teens, research has found that watching sexual content may influence sexual behavior.

Again, greater attention has been paid to the influence of sexual content on television, particularly among teens. The average American teenager watches three hours of TV a day. Typical teen fare contains heavy doses of sexual content, ranging from touching, kissing, jokes, and innuendo to conversations about sexual activity and portrayals of intercourse.[48] As in films, sex on TV is often presented as a casual activity without risk or consequences.

In one study, a total of 1,762 adolescents were asked about their sexual experiences and also their TV viewing habits and, one year later, were surveyed again.[49] The researchers measured levels of exposure to three kinds of sexual content on TV: (1) sexual

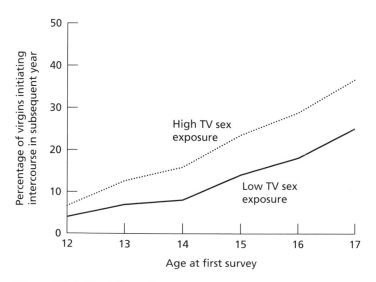

Figure 12.2   The Effect of TV Sex Exposure on Teens' Sexual Activity

behavior, such as kissing, intimate touching, and implied or depicted intercourse, (2) talk about sexual plans or desires or about sex that has occurred, and expert advice, and (3) talk about or behavior showing the risks of or the need for safety in regard to sexual activity: abstinence, waiting to have sex, portrayals mentioning or showing contraceptives, and portrayals related to consequences, such as AIDS, STDs, pregnancy, and abortion.

The results showed that heavy exposure to sexual content on TV related strongly to teens' initiation of intercourse or their progression to more advanced sexual activities (such as "making out" or oral sex) apart from intercourse in the following year. Youths who viewed the greatest amounts of sexual content were more likely than those who viewed the smallest amount to initiate sexual intercourse during the following year (see Figure 12.2) or to progress to more advanced levels of other sexual activity. In effect, youths who watched the most sexual content "acted older": a 12-year-old at the highest levels of exposure behaved like a 14- or 15-year-old at the lowest levels. The results also showed that talk about sex on TV had virtually the same effect on teen behavior as depictions of sexual activity. This finding runs counter to the widespread belief that portrayals of action have a more powerful impact than talk. The study, however, also identified other factors that increased the likelihood that teens would initiate intercourse, including being older, having older friends, getting lower grades, engaging in rule-breaking such as skipping class, and sensation-seeking.

If TV can encourage sexual activity and risky behaviors, then conversely, it can be reasoned that it might be similarly used to discourage such behaviors. Thus, these same researchers undertook a second study to examine TV's potential as a tool for educating teens about sexual risks and safe behavior.[50] Funded by the Kaiser Family Foundation, it examined the effect on teenage viewers of a particular episode of a popular sitcom (*Friends*) that dealt with condom efficacy. During the episode, one of the main characters (Rachel) reveals that she is pregnant, even though she and another character (Ross) used a condom during intercourse. The show gave specific information about condom-efficacy rates, noting that they are successful 95 percent of the time. At the time of the episode's first airing (2003), *Friends* was the most popular show on American TV. According to the Nielsen Corporation, 1.67 million adolescents between the ages of 12 and 17 saw this episode. The possibility of condom failure and the resulting consequence of pregnancy were thus vividly communicated to a very large adolescent audience, as was the message that condoms almost always work. Given the size of the audience, the episode was seen as having the potential to influence large numbers of teens.

To gage the episode's impact, RAND used information from its earlier study to identify adolescents who watch *Friends* regularly, and phoned them to ask about the *Friends* condom episode and assess its impact on their perceptions of condom use and failure. The results showed that:

- The majority of teens (65 percent) whose viewing of the episode could be confirmed recalled the show's specific information about condom-efficacy rates.
- The majority of teen viewers continued to perceive condoms as somewhat or very effective, as in the earlier survey, though the episode caused about equal amounts of positive and negative change in that perception.
- As a result of watching the episode, many teens (10 percent of viewers) talked with a parent or another adult about the effectiveness of condoms.
- Teens' reactions to the episode were changed by viewing or discussing the episode with an adult. These teens were more than twice as likely to recall information about condom efficacy.

The study did not find dramatic changes in teens' sexual knowledge or belief. However, it looked at only a single episode of TV, and one that included the somewhat complicated message that condoms almost always work, but sometimes fail, and with huge consequences. The researchers concluded that entertainment shows that include portrayals of sexual risks and consequences can potentially have two beneficial effects on teen sexual awareness: They can teach accurate messages about sexual risks, and they can stimulate a conversation with adults that can reinforce those messages.

Although less attention has been paid to Hollywood depictions of drug use, anecdotal evidence suggests that its use is not as glamorized as sex is, particularly on TV. A&E's show *Intervention* trades free treatment for addicts' stories to use in the series' content.[51] While filming drug and alcohol addicts at their weakest moments—while they shoot up heroin or down liters of liquor—has turned the show into a TV phenomenon, it has also made the cable channel the target of complaints that the show is exploitive. But addiction specialists writing on ABCNEWS.com said that offering addicts complimentary treatment in return for their stories could make a huge difference in their chances of recovery. *Intervention* makers record hours of footage of bingeing crack addicts and drunks spiraling out-of-control before eventually organizing a family-led intervention and a 90-day stay at a rehabilitation center—all for free.

In one *Intervention* episode, a camera catches "Ryan," a young drummer addicted to OxyContin, shoot up as many as 15 times a day. Other episodes depict a a former high school valedictorian spending her days betting at the racetrack to support her Vicodin habit; a former child preacher tells how being molested by a male friend caused him to turn to meth, and he now smokes meth in his bedroom while his mom sings religious songs downstairs; and a crack addict smokes up in the parking lot of the rehab facility he's about to enter. And although the show confronts the reality of drug abuse and addiction, it sheds no light on viewer effects from TV or movies that portray a more glamorous version of drug usage.

Studies have also examined whether these negative portrayals and consequences of drugs (e.g., TV programs such as *Intervention* and movies such as *Trainspotting* and *Boyz N' the Hood*) can decrease drug use and found mixed results. Nonetheless, to encourage the entertainment industry to depict alcohol and drug abuse accurately, NIDA, the Entertainment Industries Council Inc. (EIC), and the Robert Wood Johnson Foundation decided to reward the entertainment world with the PRISM awards. The movie studios and television networks submit entries to the EIC's nomination committee, which includes physicians, counselors, researchers, and policy makers. The committee members then cast a vote in each category, such as drama series, talk shows, and soap operas. For example, accurate depiction of tobacco addiction earned the show *Sex and the City* a PRISM award. Star Sarah Jessica Parker plays a nicotine-addicted woman who is trying to quit smoking. "My character Carrie's smoking has not been something that we have taken lightly on the show. We . . . felt that it was a rare opportunity to show a likable character with an unlikable habit," said Parker at the awards ceremony.[52] See another example of one proactive media effort to address the negative consequences of drug use in *Spotlight on Media Campaigns*.

SPOTLIGHT ON MEDIA CAMPAIGNS   The Montana Meth Project

"My friends and I share everything. Now we share Hepatitis and HIV." A slogan featured in the Montana Meth Project advertisements.

The same media that glorify drug usage also portray its dangers. Advocates of drug prevention have successfully used advertising to take their message to teen users. One such effort is the Montana Meth Project. Montana's largest advertiser, the campaign reached 70–90 percent of teens three times a week with saturation-level advertising. From September 2005 through September 2007, the Meth Project sustained a large-scale, statewide prevention campaign spanning TV, radio, billboards, newspapers, and the Internet. This campaign included: a web site, 45,000 TV ads, 35,000 radio ads, 10,000 print impressions, and 1,000 billboards.

The research-based messaging campaign—which graphically portrays the ravages of meth use through print, broadcast, and Internet ads—has gained nationwide attention for its uncompromising approach and demonstrated impact. The campaign's core message, "Not Even Once®," speaks directly to the highly addictive nature of meth.

The first campaign focused on the impact meth has on the individual—the user—by showing the collateral damage that occurs to users' family and friends. This concept was based directly on input from Montana teens. The second campaign showed the devastating impact meth has on the friends and family of meth users.

A documentary, featured in HBO's Addiction series, took a personal look at the physical and psychological damage caused by meth, whose effects range from tooth decay, skin lesions, and paranoia to brain damage, convulsions, and death. The filmmaker, Eames Yates, featured several Montana addicts and recovering addicts whose lives were crippled by this drug.

Research showed that—across all measures—the effectiveness of the Montana Meth Project campaign was significantly higher than the norm and at levels realized by only the world's most recognized brands. The Project's print advertising, featured in high school newspapers and on billboards across Montana, revealed the severe physical and psychological impacts associated with meth use. Recognized by the White House as one of the nation's most powerful and creative anti-drug programs, Montana Meth's recent statewide survey data demonstrated that attitudes and behaviors toward meth had changed substantially since the Meth Project initiated its prevention campaign. As of April 2008, Montana's teen meth use had declined by 45 percent.

Source: Montanameth.org

What do you think?

- *After viewing the campaign on the Project's web site (montanameth.org), comment on the message content and delivery for its effectiveness for drug prevention.*

Song Lyrics

Although music styles change over the years, research suggests that lyrical themes remain fairly constant. Love is, perhaps, the most common lyrical theme. In the 1940s and 1950s, lyrics centered on romantic love. During the 1960s, lyrics began to focus more on physical love and, reflective of the era, themes such as drug use and war protests also emerged. In the 1970s, romance and fun re-emerged in disco lyrics. Violence and occult themes began to appear in the lyrics of 1980s punk rock and heavy metal genres. Lyrics of the 1990s became increasingly more explicit with violent, sexual, and misogynistic themes reflected in rock music and newly emerging genres like gangsta rap.

 FLASH FACT

An analysis of song lyrics from the 1940s through the 1970s revealed that references to women's physical characteristics rose significantly each decade, with mentions in 6.4 percent of songs sampled in 1946, 11.7 percent of songs sampled in 1956, 13.6 percent in 1966, and 30.4 percent in 1976. From the 1960s to the 1970s, characterizations of women as "childlike" with terms such as *baby* or *girl* increased from about 25 percent to 50 percent of songs sampled; however, references to women as sex objects remained steady at about 20 percent.

Suggestive lyrics posted on the web by Lyfe Jennings were viewed 658,398 times in six months. The chorus to his song goes like this:

Girl it's just your
S.E.X.
Ain't no more secret
And Daddy gone go crazy when he finds out that his baby's found her
S.E.X.
Take a deep breath
And think before you let it go

According to a 2006 study reported by MSNBC, dirty song lyrics can prompt early teen sex. Teens whose iPods are full of music with raunchy, sexual lyrics start having sex sooner than those who prefer other songs, the study found.[53] Whether it's hip hop, rap, pop or rock, much of popular music aimed at teens contains sexual overtones. Its influence on their behavior appears to depend on how the sex is portrayed, researchers found.

Songs depicting men as "sex-driven studs," and women as sex objects, and with explicit references to sex acts are more likely to trigger early sexual behavior than those where sexual references are more veiled and relationships appear more committed, the study found.

Teens who said they listened to lots of music with degrading sexual messages were almost twice as likely to start having intercourse or other sexual activities within the following two years as were teens who listened to little or no sexually degrading music. Among heavy listeners, 51 percent started having sex within two years, versus 29 percent of those who said they listened to little or no sexually degrading music. Exposure to lots of sexually degrading music gives kids a specific message about sex, said a researcher for Rand Corp. in Pittsburgh. Boys learn they should be relentless in pursuit of women and girls learn to view themselves as sex objects.

Music Videos

The content of music videos, particularly violent and sexual content, has also faced strong public criticism, and it has been the subject of much research.[54] One analysis showed found sexual imagery in between 40 percent and 75 percent of music videos. Almost half of all women in music videos were found to be dressed provocatively compared to only 10 percent of the men. Women were much more likely than men to be treated as sex objects. One study reported that women were "put down" by or dominated by men in approximately three-quarters of the music videos that were sampled. Women and men tend to be portrayed at the polar ends of their stereotypes, with women portrayed as affectionate, nurturing, and fearful, whereas men are portrayed as adventuresome, aggressive, and domineering. Occupational roles depicted in videos also reflected sex-role stereotypes, with women frequently portrayed as waitresses, hairstylists, dancers, or fashion models, and men shown in roles of police officers, scientists, athletes, and business executives. In addition, in the videos studied, white characters tended to be older and of higher social status than non-whites.

Girls as sex objects?

Pushing the boundaries for artistic expression has always been a part of popular music. In the music industry today, however, it's often the drive for profits that is pushing the envelope of what is acceptable. Violent, racist, homophobic, or sexist lyrics in much of today's popular music could have an impact on impressionable young people who are just developing a sense of identity and self-worth. Numerous studies indicate that a preference for heavy metal music may be a significant marker for alienation, substance abuse, psychiatric disorders, suicide risk, sex-role stereotyping, or risk-taking behaviors during adolescence (source: American Academy of Pediatrics, 1999).

Other studies have found violent imagery in more than half of the music videos sampled. A similar percentage of videos has been found to contain anti-social content, including rebellious and socially unacceptable behavior. And drug, alcohol, and tobacco use have been noted in from 20 percent to 27 percent of videos.

Music video stars All Saints, a British girl band

A study that investigated the effects of hip-hop music videos with varying degrees of sexual imagery on viewers' acceptance of the objectification of women, sexual permissiveness, and gender attitudes found significant differences in male reactions. Male participants in the highly sexual condition indicated greater objectification of women, sexual permissiveness, and stereotypical gender attitudes than male participants in the low-sex condition. In addition, hip-hop fandom played a significant role in participants' objectification of women and sexual permissiveness.[55]

Perhaps the most obvious and uncontested effect of sexual themes is that audiences like them. Research finds that individuals report liking the music and the visuals better in sexy videos. However, studies have found that violent video content, particularly when combined with sexual content, may actually decrease the appeal of the visuals and the music.

Critics of lyric and video content, of course, are concerned that such content encourages immoral, anti-social, stereotypical, and criminal attitudes and behaviors, particularly among impressionable adolescents. Countering these accusations, some researchers argue that adolescents do not seem to perceive song lyrics in the same way that the critics do. Some studies have found that young listeners do not know or understand all of the words in popular songs and that, what they do comprehend, they may interpret differently. For example, Led Zeppelin's "Stairway to Heaven" song has been condemned for glorifying drug use or sexual experiences. When teenagers were asked what the song meant, however, they interpreted it quite literally, stating that the song was about climbing steps into the sky.[56]

There is a growing body of evidence that listeners can be affected by even brief exposures to popular music and music videos. These studies often find that the effects of rock music and videos reflect their thematic content.[57] Although many of the theories discussed in Chapter 5 might help explain the potential effects of music and music videos, much of the existing research tends to support a *priming model*. It is theorized that thematic content such as sex and violence "primes" viewers' cognitive schemas, which, in turn, influence subsequent impressions and social judgments in ways that reflect those themes. Take, for example, a rap music fan. Rap songs and videos are likely to trigger positive feelings for most fans (which is the reason they are fans). Many rap songs and videos, however, portray women as sex objects. Listening to these songs and watching these videos is thought to trigger fans' "women as sex object" schemas. And because the fans associate positive feelings with the music, they may also begin to associate positive feelings with these schemas. As a result, fans may begin to consider women as sex objects. In support of this theory, many studies have found that subjects are more likely to endorse violent, anti-social, and sexually permissive attitudes and behaviors after watching rock videos with those themes than after watching neutral videos. Research has also found greater endorsement of sex-role stereotyping after watching videos with stereotypical portrayals.[58] Practical constraints on research (see Chapter 5 for discussion) makes it difficult to know if such effects are only short-lived or if they have more lasting impacts, but it is reasoned that these attitudes may become more stable personality traits.

Excitation transfer theory suggests another possible explanation for the short-term impacts of music and music videos. Physiological arousal is thought to be an important component of music appreciation. As previously discussed, music, like many other forms of entertainment, makes us feel. The reactions inspired by music are thought to be particularly powerful. Music arouses us both physically (increasing our heart rate, blood pressure, and breathing) and emotionally. As explained in Chapter 4, research has found that arousal from one experience can unconsciously influence our reactions to subsequent arousing experiences. Thus, listening to arousing music or watching arousing music videos may influence how we react to other people or events we encounter while we are listening or watching, or immediately afterwards. Say, for example, you are listening to

Rihanna, Monster Jam

your favorite CD on the way to work. If someone suddenly cuts you off on the freeway or if your boss yells at you for being late, you might react differently than you normally would, perhaps responding more intensely without knowing it. Thus, according to this theory, listening to music or watching music videos may lead people to react in more stereo-typical, violent, or sexist ways simply because they are more aroused. If this theory is correct, then any form of arousing music might have the same effect, regardless of whether or not the songs or videos contain stereotypical, violent, or sexist content.

Clearly, there are many questions regarding the impact of music and music videos that have yet to be answered. Some experts speculate, however, that with the growing global popularity of contemporary rock music and other genres that some consider questionable, we may witness a similar growth and interest in research that addresses these questions.

Racy Reads and Video Games

Sex, drug use, and other risqué behavior are common themes in adult literature, but parents may be surprised to find that they are also increasingly prevalent in books, video games, and comic books popular with teen audiences. Interestingly, such content has become a driving force in books targeting young, "tween-age" girls. According to an MSNBC article, in the teen fiction section, the trend is now more *Sex and the City* than *Nancy Drew*.[59] In the teen novel *A-list*, author Zoey Dean writes about a 17-year-old who gets drunk and nearly has a tryst with a Princeton University student on her way to Hollywood; while another controversial teen read, *Teach Me* by R.A. Nelson, tells of a student–teacher affair. In *Claiming Georgia Tate*, a father has sex with his daughter, and, in *Rainbow Party*, teens make plans for an oral sex party.

These racy reads are publishing's fastest-growing segment and young girls are the biggest consumers. Most books for the 12-and-up age group sell fewer than 20,000 copies, but some of the edgier titles have sold close to a million.[60] Thirteen-year-olds are devouring the *Gossip Girl* series by author Cecily Von Siegesar, which depicts the "glamorous" lives of rich New York City teens doing drugs and having sex. "It's fun to read about people doing that stuff and having sex," said one 13-year-old. "Everyone wants to be 21 and 18 when they're really just 13," explained a second. "I don't think they would sell as well if they didn't have sex in them," said another.[61]

Some experts say books like these are gratuitous, even dangerous, and have called for restrictions or ratings similar to those used by other entertainment media. Author Russell Nelson, however, who wrote *Teach Me*, defends teen books with mature themes. "I feel like it fills an important niche in moving the readers to a higher level of maturity," he said.[62] Indeed, if that's what it takes to encourage teens to read, some parents and educators might be willing to accept it. To date, no published studies have researched the impacts that such literature may have on teen readers, but it is a likely target for future investigations.

Comic Books and Video Games   Sensing the popularity of comic strips, artist/authors began publishing "feature length" stories in book form. **Comic books**, once described as "movies on paper,"[63] impact the fantasy lives of children, giving them superpowers to defeat the monsters of their dreams. Soon, monsters became war-mongers armed with savage weapons. When comic violence became prevalent, the industry established self-censorship against violence and promoted domestic drama, gag strips, political satire, parody, and adult comics instead.

You many not have noticed, but Japanese comics have gripped the global imagination. *Manga* sales in the U.S. have tripled since 2004. Titles like *Naruto* and *Death Note* have become fixtures on American best-seller lists. But, unlike most American comics, *manga* isn't reserved for freaks, geeks, and pipsqueaks—everyone reads these comics. Some feature chaste affairs of yearning and unrealized passion; other depict sexual encounters graphic enough to make Larry Flynt blush! Young females are often sexualized with prominent breasts and narrow waists as in the image below. And of course, violence infuses many editions. Given that these comics often appeal to young audiences, this medium has also raised concerns regarding violent, sexual, and drug-related content.

For this same reason, video game content is beginning to face similar scrutiny. In Western video games, sexuality is not prevalent to the degree seen in movies, books, or even TV shows. Almost no American video games display full-frontal nudity. Sexual themes are more common in some Japanese PC games; however, console companies such as Nintendo and Sony do not license adult-only content games for their systems. Nonetheless, there are many video games readily available that feature sexuality quite prominently.

For example, in the game *The Witcher* there is full-frontal nudity present in the form of cards that you receive after completing "sexual conquests"; this nudity is also found in the depiction of the games dryad. In the *Grand Theft Auto* series a player is able to pick up a prostitute, have sex to replenish health, then kill her to take back the money spent. It should be noted, however, that any activity of this sort in the game is done completely by choice and players are punished for committing crimes by the police. Nonetheless, this game series has frequently been singled out

Character typical of those found in *manga* comics

because of concern regarding its content. In June 2005, code for an interactive sex mini-game was found buried within the main script of *Grand Theft Auto: San Andres*. Users found ways to activate this code (called playing in "Hot Coffee Mode"), which prompted lawsuits and a rating of the game to "Adults Only" on July 20, 2005. The game was pulled from many stores, and Rockstar Games posted a loss of $280.8 million that quarter.[64] Sexual overtones are prevalent even in more mainstream games such as *Grand Theft Auto* and *Xtreme Volleyball* which feature provocative, scantily clad, and typically female avatars.

Again, however, while sexual content in comic books and video games is becoming increasingly common, little research has examined how it may influence audiences Just as with violent content, the added concern for video games is that the interactive nature of these games may amplify the effect any questionable content may have.

Pornography In addition to the increased sexual content in mainstream Hollywood productions, video games, and print publications, the last decades have seen a dramatic increase in highly pornographic material through magazines, home video, and now the Internet. Experimental studies show that when males are exposed to explicit pornography they are more likely to express negative attitudes toward women, to think that relatively uncommon sexual practices (such as fellatio and anal intercourse) are widespread, and to be more lenient with rape offenders in hypothetical court cases.[65] In studies on the impact of pornographic violence, a common procedure is to have males deliver "electrical shocks" to females. (The shocks are simulated, so no one really gets hurt.) The males have been found to administer greater shocks after exposure to pornography; however, this only applies to effects of violent pornography,[66] where women are shown to be enjoying the abuse.[67]

In the real world, however, the availability of pornography does not appear to be related to rape in the same area.[68] Sex offenders do not have any more exposure to pornography than anyone else. They are, however, more likely to consume pornography before criminal sexual activities and are highly aroused by material that matches the nature of their activities.[69] Thus, it would seem that, although pornography does not promote sexual aggression in most men, among those who are at "high risk for aggression" pornography greatly adds to that risk.[70]

Compulsion or Addiction? Even non-violent pornography can present a problem for some audiences. In November 2004, a panel of experts testified before a Senate sub-committee that pornography was dangerously addictive. The effects of porn on the brain were called "toxic" and compared to cocaine, as an estimated 420 million adult web pages exist online. Porn consumption can get people in trouble—in the form of maxed-out credit cards, lost sleep, neglected responsibilities, or neglected loved ones. So is porn behavior compulsive or addictive?

The difference between describing the behavior as a compulsion or an addiction is subtle, but important. One of the key features of addiction is the development of a tolerance to the addictive substance. In the way that drug addicts need increasingly larger doses to get high, porn addicts need to see more and more extreme material to feel the same level of excitement they first experienced. There are three main reasons why people turn to pornography: to see their fantasies acted out, to avoid intimacy in a relationship, and simply to aid masturbation.

A researcher at the Kinsey Institute criticizes the use of the term *addiction* when talking about porn because he says it merely describes certain people's behavior as being addiction-like, but treating them as addicts may not help them. Many people may diagnose themselves as porn addicts after reading popular books on the subject, he says. But mental health professionals have no standard criteria to diagnose porn addiction. A psychologist at the University of Pennsylvania, and one of the witnesses at the Senate hearing on pornography addiction, said the same criteria used to diagnose problems like pathological gambling and substance abuse can be applied to problematic porn use. "The therapists who treat pornography addicts say they behave just like any other addicts," she told WebMD in a 2008 interview.[71]

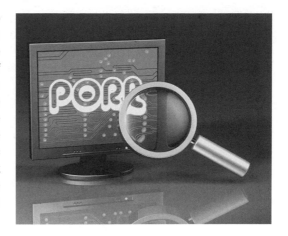

The Verdict is Still Out

Research of media effects on behavior such as aggression, sex, and drug use face the same methodological limitations as all effects research. From a classic scientific perspective, to accurately evaluate the impact of the media on behavior, you must have complete control over exposure to the media in question and valid, reliable measures of media content (violence, sex, drugs, etc.) and resulting behavior. As mentioned earlier in this chapter, this is extremely difficult to do. Researchers usually have only very limited control of people's media exposure. They may be able to control a single movie, sporting event, or concert they see, or even a series of films or events, but they cannot control all of the other media people are exposed to. Thus, it is difficult to establish a control comparison group that has not already been repeatedly exposed to media depictions of violence, drugs, and so on. And, any group that has managed to avoid exposure has probably done so intentionally because they do not want to see media violence or sex or drug use. As a result, even if they would be willing to participate in a study, they would probably not be representative of the type of people the researchers would want to study.

Researchers also have difficulties measuring impacts on aggressive and sexual behavior and drug use. Such behaviors are typically not ones that participants or research review boards are readily willing to let you observe. Most research review boards will not allow researchers to place participants in hostile, health-threatening, or legally questionable situations and, even if they would, if people knew they were being observed, they might behave differently than they would otherwise. As a result, researchers are often limited to pencil and paper, asking questions such as "What do you typically do . . .?" or "What would you do if . . .?" These measures ask people to self-report their behavior, which may not accurately reflect what they would actually do. Nonetheless, each additional study can potentially add to our understanding of the relationship between media and entertainment portrayals and audience behavior. And the significance of these issues encourages researchers to continue their efforts to understand these effects.

Gambling and Addiction

Gambling occurs when players bet something of value on the outcome of a game or uncertain event whose result may be determined by chance. They risk money in the hopes of winning. Gambling activities range in complexity from a coin toss to betting on cards in poker. Outcomes may be determined solely by chance (craps and roulette) or by a combination of strategy and chance (poker). Gamblers may participate while betting on the outcome in card games and craps, or they may be restricted from participation in the cases of lotteries and sport.

Concerned with the analysis of random phenomena, **probability theory** states that the outcome of a random event cannot be determined before it occurs, but it may be any one of several possible outcomes. The actual outcome is considered to be determined by chance. Outcomes of games of pure chance are equally probable, as in the lottery where every player has the same chance of winning as any other player. In such games, each instance is a completely independent one—each player has the same probability as each of the others of producing a given outcome. The distinctive feature of games of chance is that the outcome of a given trial cannot be predicted with certainty, although the collective results of a large number of trials display some regularity. Probability found in games of chance alone can be expressed as a formula: probability (p) equals the total number of favorable outcomes (f) divided by the total number of possibilities (t), or $p = f/t$.[72]

In gambling games, probability is expressed as "odds against winning," or the ratio of unfavorable possibilities to favorable ones. Players get into trouble when they falsely assume that each play is *not* independent of the other, and that outcomes of one sort should be balanced in the short run by the other possibilities. The lure of a "winning streak" is an example of why some gamblers keep throwing the dice rather than settling for a single win. Gamblers invent "systems" based on this "Monte Carlo fallacy"; in reality, most game advantages go to the dealer or some other participant.

Slot machines are one of the most popular forms of casino gambling. But no matter how you slice it, slots are a game of chance. Anyone claiming to have a bullet-proof formula or winning system is trying to sell you something that's a waste of both time and money. But while there are no sure things when it comes to slots, common sense combined with a positive attitude can improve your odds of claiming a large jackpot, maximize your smaller wins, and minimize those inevitable losses.

Gambling Phenomenon

Gambling, playing a game of chance for stakes, occurs in many forms: pari-mutuels (horse and dog tracks, off-track-betting parlors, Jai Alai), lotteries, casinos (slot machines, table games), bookmaking (sports books and horse books), card rooms, bingo, and the stock market.

In 2006, $82 billion in profit was generated from the total gaming industry of wagering, lotteries, bookmaking, and gaming. Gambling worldwide was projected to top $144 billion in revenues by 2011. According to PriceWaterhouseCoopers, the Asia/Pacific region is becoming the world's second-largest casino market, with revenue reaching $18.5 billion by 2009, up from $8.8 billion in 2004. The booming Chinese gaming enclave of Macau is expected to account for most of that growth.[73]

Gambling is also a tremendous growth vehicle on Wall Street as more state and local governments view gaming as a way to bolster sagging tax revenues. Table 12.1 shows the increasing revenue generation expected from the American gambling industry. An increased public acceptance of gambling is reflected both in opinion polls and in the willingness of Americans to allocate considerable time and money to gambling pursuits. Five key factors explain gambling's increased presence and commercial success.

- Voters support the "voluntary tax" collected from gaming sites.
- More people choose gaming as their leisure activity of choice.

Table 12.1 U.S. Gambling Revenue ($ billion)

	2006	2007	2008	2009
Nevada	12.8	13.8	14.8	15.8
Atlantic City	5.4	5.7	6.0	6.3
Tribal Casinos	21.8	23.3	24.7	26.0
Regional Casinos	14.5	15.0	15.5	16.0
Total:	54.5	57.8	61.0	64.1

Source: American Gaming Association, National Indian Gaming Association, Nevada Gaming Commission, New Jersey Casino Control Commission, PriceWaterhouseCoopers, Wilkofsky Gruen Associates

- Retired people, whose numbers increase annually, are the single largest segment of the casino market.
- Casino marketers are attracting a "low roller" segment not previously targeted by advertisers.
- There is an increasing diversity of locations from casinos to riverboats and Indian reservations, new technologies, and product innovations. Video lottery terminals, slot machines, racetrack-based gaming devices, and video poker machines are some of those innovations. Online gambling is also impacting the industry where chance dominates.

Rolling the dice is part of playing craps

Gambling Segments

Industry experts identify four broad gambling segments, each with a somewhat different profile. They are:

- *High rollers*, composed of sophisticated gamblers who tend to be wealthy, older, and male. They tend to play games of skill rather than chance.
- *Day trippers*, dominated by retirees who make several short trips to venues within easy driving distance who mostly play the slots.
- *Low-stakes or new adopters*, who have recently discovered gaming as leisure diversion. Most are aging boomers and their parents with time and money to enjoy, and young women seeking a new diversion.
- *Family vacationers*, who gamble as an offshoot of a family vacation to a theme park or other attraction.

An important sector of America's economy, gambling employs about half a million people nationwide. And $6 billion in gaming tax revenue is paid annually to states and communities where casinos operate, providing funding for programs benefiting schools and seniors. Noted for their philanthropy, casino companies give more than $10 million annually to United Way campaigns and donate more than $60 million to charities each year.[74] For every $1 million in revenues generated by the casino industry, 13 jobs are created.[75] In the early 2000s, Las Vegas was the fastest growing city in America.

Neon Castles: Casino Gambling[76]

Casinos are legalized establishments where commercial gambling operators make their profits by regularly occupying advantage positions against players. Concentrated in pockets around the world, casinos locate in areas with relaxed legal restrictions supposedly enacted to combat cheating. Actually, more laws have been oriented around efforts by governments to derive tax revenues from gambling than to control cheating. Casinos typically offer card games such as poker, baccarat, and blackjack. Many also have slot machines and roulette as well as wagering on sports events. Maintaining web sites as marketing devices and reservation systems, casino operators are not in the business of providing online gambling.

Winning at the slot machines

Casinos, riverboats, and Indian reservations are meccas for American gambling. In the race to develop entertaining themes, Las Vegas casinos invested in billion-dollar properties that load on huge shopping malls, theaters, spas, restaurants, and thousands of hotel rooms to lure guests. Atlantic City, a popular destination for local players, buses in middle- and low-income gamblers from nearby cities and states to gamble in boardwalk casinos.

Congress's revisions to laws governing casinos have transformed the once sleepy Indian gambling business into a $26 billion-a-year behemoth with 423 casinos across the country.[77] Connecticut is currently the nation's top tribal gambling market with the most profitable casino in the U.S. Foxwood Resort Casino, operated by the Mashantucket Pequot Tribal Nation, averages over 55,000 patrons each day and more than 20 million visitors each year. The nation's largest casino, Foxwood employs over 10,000 people. Elsewhere, tribes in California, New York, Florida, and Minnesota reap hundreds of millions each year from gaming operations.

FLASH FACT

John McCain, one of the greatest advocates of relaxing regulations on Indian casinos, received over $500,000 from the gambling industry for his presidential campaign in 2008: 67 percent from casinos, racetracks, and other gambling operations, 28 percent from tribal interests, and 5 percent from gambling supply manufacturers and consulting firms.

Source: Center for Responsive Politics

Realizing the benefits of gambling revenues, locations **worldwide** are fast incorporating gambling into their national economies. In developing countries such as Slovenia, casinos are positioned adjacent to Italian border towns and cater to Italian gamblers by using Italian-language dealers. International destinations such as Macau, Isla De

Margarita off the Venezuelan coast, and Bermuda tempt tourists to gambling tables from around the world. Casinos have the potential to lure travelers and bring tourism to areas devoid of natural wonders, historical monuments, or recreational resorts.

Macau, located in China, is the newest global gambling hotspot. Macau's clutch of casinos has outpaced the Las Vegas Strip in gambling revenue, taking in around $10 billion in 2007 compared to almost $7 billion on the strip. Macau became a special administrative zone when it was returned to China in 1999, making it the only place in China where casinos are legal. Wynn Resorts, MGM Mirage, and Australia's Crown companies were granted licenses by the Beijing-backed government of Macau. About 10.5 million mainland Chinese visited Macau in 2005, and nearly 15 million were expected in 2008, according to the Pacific Asia Travel Association.

This former Portuguese colony caters primarily to gambling and as such is not an equal counterpart to Las Vegas as an all-round tourism destination. More than 25 casinos offer a mix of gambling, hotel rooms, and restaurants. Live performances are limited; only the Grand Lisboa has two shows that include a can-can style dance act and performances by a troupe of Japanese dancers. Another draw, NBA games, appeared at the Venetian Arena, a 15,000-seat stadium at the Venetian Resort & Casino. The Police and Celine Dion have appeared there, and the Cirque du Soleil booked a permanent show in a larger theater constructed in 2009.[78]

Online Sports Betting

With Internet gambling surpassing $20 billion in 2008, and with illegal wagering accounting for $150 billion in the U.S., the temptation to influence game outcomes has never been greater.[79] Gambling scandals in sports have raised an uncomfortable question—Are the games we watch fixed? On indications that gamblers are profiting from inside information, major tennis governing bodies have recommended investigating 45 tennis matches played since 2003. Betfair, an online wagering site started in 2002, detected improprieties in match-fixing among its users in 80 countries. Described as an eBay for gamblers, Betfair offers real-time wagering, usually after matches have begun.

Betfair, offering 4,000 kinds of bets a week, has been the watchdog for sports gambling. More than one million customers wager against each other at betfair.com, setting their own odds and paying a fraction of what traditional bookmakers charge. Now a $6 billion industry, Internet gambling has yielded U.K.-based Betfair profits of $64 million by taking 2 percent to 5 percent commission on winning bets.

Tennis professionals are calling for a global anticorruption body for sport to combat insider trading. So how many other of the world's sporting events are fixed? Officials hesitate to guess. However, over 2 percent of Division 1 football and basketball players said they had been asked to influence the outcome of a game, and over 1 percent acknowledged actually affecting the outcome. American sports, on which more money is bet illegally and without regulation, have a greater potential for corruption than sports in other countries.

Online gambling is illegal in America

Dreams for Sale: Playing the Lottery

Millions of other Americans each day invest in the lottery, where they have the chance to win hundreds of millions of dollars without so much as breaking a sweat. State lottery games have exploded in popularity in the last two decades and are now legal in 40 U.S. states, plus the District of Columbia. States love the games because they raise funds for everything from education and natural resources management to prison construction and general use, while allowing politicians to say with straight faces that they aren't raising taxes.

And despite the overwhelming odds against winning, the public loves the games even more. Local newscasts often report about the huge numbers of ordinary folks lining up to buy tickets when multi-state jackpots reach into a stratospheric $300 million-plus. One such lottery, the Mega Millions, available in 12 states including California and New York, offers players a 1-in-135 million chance that their $1 bets will hit the big payoff. Unbeknownst to most ticket buyers, the house keeps half the sales.

The *house edge* is the percentage of total dollars bet that the states keep instead of returning the money to winners; the huge house edge for the lottery illustrates why it is such a bad investment. The easiest way to decide which gambling option is the best investment is to compare the house edges.

Casino games may seem riskier than lottery tickets, but they leave less for the house. Slot machines have house edges that vary from 0 percent to 20 percent, and the house edge for roulette is 5.28 percent. For three-card poker it's 2 percent. In blackjack, depending how a person plays, it's between 1 percent and less than zero (meaning the player actually stands a chance at eliminating the house edge). Even horse racing has a lower house edge, 15 percent to 17 percent.[80]

In contrast, the house edge for a typical lottery is more like 50 percent. So why do we play? Because the lottery sells dreams, the kind of dreams not offered by the other games. In other words, consumers are willing to forgo a huge chunk of payoff for the chance to win a life-altering jackpot. A Gallup survey found that 61 percent of us believe daydreams help us to cope with emotional stress.[81] When we're not stressing, we're looking for an easy way to make money. Lottery players buy the expected value of life, and short-term gratification predominates.

The merger of GTECH and Lottomatica created a company that now controls 63 percent of the worldwide online lottery business. The companies employ more than 6,300 people worldwide and earned in excess of $1.5 billion in 2005. GTECH maintains operations centers in Australia, Belgium, Poland, and Brazil. The most popular American lottery game is **Powerball**, which is operated by the Multi-State Lottery Association (MUSL), a consortium of lottery commissions in 29 states, the District of Columbia, and the U.S. Virgin Islands. Other states, like California, operate independently.

To convince people to play lottery games, 40 states now spend millions of dollars each year on advertising. Ads promise to give everyone a decent life— the rich and easy life. Ads feature ordinary people and their dreams, which of course are fulfilled by winning the lottery. Some ad campaign scenarios feature people who have achieved their

Lucky Penny lottery game

wildest fantasies; like telling your boss you've just bought the company, and he's fired. Or driving a taxi to amuse yourself in between trips to your private island and your Italian villa. If you spend a dollar, one state's advertising claims, you may earn a 2,600 percent return on your money. What these ads don't tell you is the odds are greater that you'll be struck by lightning than winning the lottery.

To keep advertisers' persuasive messages legitimate, The World Lottery Association executive committee has established and formally approved a marketing and communications guideline, which may be implemented as a globally recognized standard. Key elements from similar guidelines already in use by 11 major lotteries were instrumental in the development of this document. Marketing and communications specialist from these member lotteries formed a working group, which provided additional feedback. The resulting document is the culmination of their effort.

As long as people have dreams and a dollar to bet, lotteries will profit. And, as jackpots soar toward the $100 million mark, people will continue to line up for a chance at fame and fortune. Put into perspective, if you bought 100 one-dollar tickets a week your entire adult life (18–75 years of age), you'd spend $296,400 and still have only a 1 percent chance of winning the lottery. Who cares about odds and reality when dreams cost as little as one dollar?

SPOTLIGHT ON LEGALIZED GAMBLING
Lifesaver for a Depressed Town?

Casino gambling brought prosperity to Tunica, a dirt-poor town of black poverty in Mississippi. When Jesse Jackson visited the town in 1985, he called it "America's Ethopia." Then *60 Minutes* came in to film Sugar Ditch Alley, a neighborhood of crumbling shacks named for its open sewer.

Today, nine Vegas-style casinos have sprung up amid the cotton, soybean, and rice fields where the state legislature, in 1990, legalized dockside gambling. Boasting the fifth-largest gaming market in the U.S., Tunica has huge gaming parlors on enormous barges along the river. A 31-story hotel, Gold Strike, sits on dry land with a neon glow.

Thanks to gambling, Tunica has generated jobs for its 10,000 residents and 15,000 workers from three adjacent states. Gaming tables and slots generated over $1.2 billion in revenue in 2007, 4 percent of which has gone into senior homes, a rec center, and public school budgets.

But the future is not all roses for Tunica. Competition from emerging markets in China and India is threatening the city's growth. According to international strategic advisor Mark Minevich, "Casinos don't grow skills or nurture talent." So in spite of the infusion of cash into the local economy over the past few years, the high school is still underperforming, and quality housing is scarce. Even worse, the poor are still poor; over 25 percent of the residents live below the poverty line.

New homes near the National Golf and Tennis Center north of town are aimed at retired people and second-home owners, not working people. Casinos, however, have brought some upward mobility to Tunica, and they have also had another positive social impact—integration. Working side-by-side, black and white employees have bridged the traditional gap between landowners and laborers.

As communities around the world look to the gambling industry for economic cures, most will not be able to duplicate Tunica's success. Good fortune has resulted from a combination of location, luck, and timing. With a clientele averaging 58 years, the city caters to day-trippers and uses profits for high-end attractions. Not the best model for solving poverty problems.

The city has established itself as a tourist destination, but it still needs to diversify the economy. Trying to attract new industry is a struggle, and the gambling industry has reached a plateau. But big employers want affordable housing for employees and good schools to educate workers' kids, which Tunica has yet to produce.

So the question remains: Will Tunica meet the challenge of a global economy, or will it remain a casino company town for ever?

Source: Stephanie Mehta, *Fortune*, March 15, 2007

What do you think?

- *Will the city's casino business grow and prosper, or should Tunica look to other industries for future economic stability?*

Gambling's Impact

We all enjoy games that are played in a variety of forms, venues, and technologies. We play for enjoyment, we play to compete, and we play to realize our dreams. When considering the impact of game playing on our lives, it is important to focus on the **outcome of play**. Are we happier? Are we more astute? Are we winners or losers? What gratifications are derived from playing games? Outcomes are often studied as effects, and gaming outcomes are no exception. To illustrate the role of effects of gaming, we expose negative effects, and contrast similarities and differences in emotional, self-esteem, and pleasure outcomes of playing video games with those of gambling.

Studies of video games focus on possible **negative effects**, arguing that interactivity makes players personally responsible for the atrocious acts and implicates players in morally dubious actions. Games of action, which elicit strong arousal from violent images, aggressive player reactions, and point-of-view editing, are critics' most popular targets. Gambling addiction is also cited as a negative outcome of gaming. In the film *Spy Game*, Brad Pitt's character says, "It's not how you play the game, it's how the game plays you." To all pathological gamblers, the game takes hold of their lives and refuses to let go. Players who succumb to the idea of winning may become addicted to betting. The result is excessive gambling debt that often leads players into depression, withdrawal, and even theft to cope with the results of their addictive play. Society's focus on consumption and spectacle is identified by sociologists as a prime motivator for the growing numbers of gambling addicts.

Interactivity in video games and participation in gambling are often preconditions for eliciting strong **emotions** in players. Competition in both activities can provide stimulation that causes physical arousal. A general physiological process, arousal creates emotions.[82] Playing video games stimulates emotions that are close to real-life experiences. Gambling stimulates emotions of anticipation that transcend reality and become fantasy.

Interactivity and participation are directly related to levels of **self-esteem**. In games of skill, players are responsible for their wins and losses. Losing may cause loss of self-esteem because losing is linked to the player's assessment of his or her own performance. Because of the element of chance, gamblers may not feel personally responsible for winning or losing. Therefore, higher levels of

Sign for teen gambling awareness

self-esteem may be maintained by gamblers than by video game players, even as they face devastating financial loss.

Finally, the **pleasures** derived from immersion in virtual reality and immersion in gambling are passive pleasures. Interactive game players, however, may switch to an active control of their emotional states, while gamblers have little opportunity for control over a game's outcome.

Gambling Addiction

Problem gambling refers to any gambling that goes beyond "normal" bounds of gambling for fun, recreation, or entertainment. **Pathological gambling** is the inability, over an extended period of time, to resist the impulse to gamble. It is often characterized by increasing preoccupation with gambling and a general loss of control. Pathological gamblers often "chase" their losses, feel a need to bet more frequently and in larger amounts, and continue to gamble in spite of the serious negative consequences of their behavior.

The National Opinion Research Center study found that 1.5 percent of 16- and 17-year-olds could be considered problem or pathological gamblers, or about half the rate for adults. It is not yet known, however, to what extent adolescent gambling predicts problems in an adult. Pathological gambling is a progressive disease that devastates not only the gambler but everyone with whom he or she has a significant relationship. In 1980, the American Psychiatric Association accepted pathological gambling as a "disorder of

Addiction is destructive

impulse control." It is an illness that is chronic and progressive, but it can be diagnosed and treated.

Pathological gambling affects the gamblers, their families, their employers, and the community. As the gamblers go through the phases of their addiction (see below), they spend less time with their family and spend more of their family's money on gambling until their bank accounts are depleted. Then they may steal money from family members. At work, the pathological gambler misuses time in order to gamble, has difficulty concentrating and finishing projects, and may engage in embezzlement, employee theft, or other illegal activities. Illinois Institute for Addiction Recovery (IIAR) works with employers to offer a comprehensive program of evaluation, treatment, counseling, and support for employees and their families.

The IIAR considers slot machines and video poker to be the "crack cocaine" of gambling. It claims that it is their immediate gratification that makes video poker and slot machines so very addictive. Also, the Institute has found that gamblers progress much more quickly to the dangerous phases of gambling addiction when playing electronic machines.

Robert L. Custer, M.D., identified the progression **phases of gambling addiction** as including three phases: winning, losing, and desperation. During the *winning phase*, gamblers experience a big win—or a series of wins—that leaves them with unreasonable optimism that their winning will continue. This leads them to feel great excitement when gambling, and they begin increasing the amounts of their bets.

During the *losing phase*, the gamblers often begin bragging about wins they have had, start gambling alone, think more about gambling, and borrow money—legally or illegally. They start lying to family and friends and become more irritable, restless, and withdrawn. Their home life becomes more unhappy, and they are unable to pay off debts. The gamblers begin to "chase" their losses, believing they must return as soon as possible to win back their losses. During the *desperation phase*, there is a marked increase in the time spent gambling. This is accompanied by remorse, blaming others, and alienating family and friends. Eventually, the gamblers may engage in illegal acts to finance their gambling. They may experience hopelessness, suicidal thoughts and attempts, arrests, divorce, alcohol and/or other drug abuse, or an emotional breakdown.

Current estimates suggest that 3 percent of the adult population will experience a serious problem with gambling that will result in significant debt, family disruption, job losses, criminal activity, or suicide.

SPOTLIGHT ON CASINOS   Leaving Las Vegas: Finding Macau

Since the 1850s when the Portuguese government legalized gambling in Macau, this island off the China coast has become known worldwide as the "Monte Carlo of the Orient," and gambling has become a significant part of the city's economy.

Until Western-style casino games were introduced in the twentieth century, only Chinese games were

played, the most popular being Fan-Tan. Today, gambling in Macau can be divided into three different categories: casino games, horse racing, and greyhound racing. There are also sports betting and a number of lotteries. Baccarat is the most popular casino game, but yields less revenue than the more lucrative slot machines, which Asian players have virtually ignored for lack of interest.

The night scene of Casino Lisboa, Macau

To change that habit, gambling innovators are creating culturally specific slot machines and computerized games to lure Asian players away from well-worn seats at the baccarat tables to more profitable pursuits. In the face of rocketing labor costs and a need to diversify gaming revenue away from the traditional table game, casinos are hoping the new designs will recreate the success of slots in Las Vegas.

Asians are well versed in games with themes like Star Wars and Spiderman but they do not have an emotional or cultural attachment to the Western heroes. According to Tony Tong, chief executive officer of PacificNet, a gaming technology company, computerized games for Asians must use stars like martial arts actor Jackie Chan, and singers from the hit television series *Super Voice Girls*, the Chinese equivalent of *American Idol*, for users to better relate to the games.

While gaming revenues in Macau in 2006 overtook those of the Las Vegas Strip, government figures show up to 88 percent of it was spent on baccarat tables, where one dealer can serve only a maximum 12 players at any one time. Chinese gamblers tend to congregate around tables they feel are on a lucky streak, with tables nearby standing empty, cutting into casino profits. Government figures show that only 4.3 percent of the city's total revenues were from slot machines, compared to as much as 60 percent in Las Vegas.

Some industry observers doubt slot machines will ever take off in Asia, arguing that Asian players prefer communal games and try to predict the game results by looking at their dealers' facial expressions. Chinese customers are generally more technologically advanced than U.S.-based customers but they tend to be less comfortable with slot machines because they don't have much experience with them.

Meanwhile, the race is on to provide electronic tables that retain the element of live dealers and real cards while the wagering is done electronically, without the hassle of making changes or payout. New machines could deal with between 200 and 300 players at one time, cut the length of each deal from two minutes to 30 seconds and minimize dealer errors and fraud.

With roaring growth expected to continue, after surpassing the Las Vegas Strip, Macau is poised to overtake all of Nevada as the biggest gambling jurisdiction. Las Vegas Sands, which owns the Sands Macau and the newly opened Venetian Macau, took the lead because of its success in winning more wealthy gamblers. The Venetian, a resort casino, opened in 2007 on the Cotai Strip, Macau's answer to the Strip in Las Vegas. Wealthy gamblers from around the world are driving the sharp growth in the local gambling industry, along with booming property and stock markets in mainland China and Hong Kong. A number of new casinos and resorts were set to open in Macau by 2010.

Macau's gaming revenue grew 45.7 percent in 2007 and were expected to expand 29 per cent in 2008, according to Las Vegas-based gaming research firm Globalysis. Casinos' revenue from gambling in Nevada in 2007, however, was $12.8 billion, an increase of only 2.8 percent. Slow growth on the Vegas Strip is an indication of the power of Macau's new venues and hearty attention from global gamblers.

Source: www.asiaone.com/Travel/News/Story/A1Story2008
0610-69949.html

What do you think?

- *What cultural aspects must casino owners consider when designing games and slots for global players?*
- *Do you think the new gambling hotspot in Macau will curtail some of the Chinese migration to Las Vegas? Why?*

FADE TO BLACK

Sex, drugs, and violence are prominent in today's entertainment. Provocative content can be found in films, books, songs, video games, sports, and, of course, on television. Greater concern is raised regarding the effects of media violence, sex, and drug portrayals on children. Results regarding the impact of this content have been mixed; however, most scholars believe that at least some media can affect some audiences, some of the time.

Taking chances may be inherent in human nature, and games of all sorts give us an opportunity to challenge fate and enjoy the glory of winning. Formed to create a better understanding of gaming, the American Gaming Association (AGA) provides information to the public, elected officials, and the media through education and advocacy. Part of their mission is to address the problems of underage gambling. With more Americans going to casinos than visiting major league baseball parks or attending movies, Broadway shows, and concerts, the AGA has a growing role in publicizing the downside of gambling. And its evidence suggests that economic performance from gambling will continue to improve dramatically in the future.

A CLOSER LOOK AT CHANCE · Using Psychographics to Promote the Lottery[83]

Using a system developed and revised by Stanford Research Institute (SRI), advertisers are zeroing in on the values and lifestyles of potential lottery ticket purchasers that rely on more than just flair and humor. Research is key to targeting the right market segments. What follows is a sampling of how three state lotteries used research to drive successful advertising campaigns to peddle tickets.

• *Virginia* lottery research indicated that scratch ticket customers tend to play the lottery on impulse, are guided by what others will think, and watch TV in late morning and late evening.

Marketers classify game prospects as Belongers, Emulators or Achievers according to VALS II typology. To attract "high rollers" who prefer dice and card games, a Star Trek theme was designed to appeal to upscale enthusiasts. In the state's most popular campaign, "Lady Luck" engages in all sorts of clever promotional tricks. One ad featured the lady coming down the chimney to stuff Christmas stockings with instant scratch tickets. Another version showed a man and woman rejoicing at her knock in anticipation of becoming winners, only to have their hopes dashed when they realize no one purchased the ticket that week. Lady Luck reminds the losers that they missed out on $50,000 a year for every million dollars in the jackpot by not buying a ticket. Lady Luck was responsible for selling millions of tickets for Virginia.

• *Maryland* segmented Keno players into three sub-clusters: Fragile Egos, Entertainment Seekers, and Solitary Gamblers. They learned that Pick 3 Numbers players are superstitious and play numbers until they happen to dream a number or get a hunch. With this information, advertisers crafted a campaign to exploit superstitions, including fears of failing to play a lucky number every day. A spot called "Linguine" featured a diner customer who sees a number "6" in the waitress's hairdo, a "2" in his pasta bowl and a "0" in the water ring under his glass. When he fails to play the 6–2–0 combination that night, that sequence turns out to be the Pick 3 winner. "Your numbers," a voice-over says, "are out there." Another state study concluded that Maryland players care far more about total winnings than the likelihood of winning—a prescription for bigger jackpots and longer odds. When they learned from focus group participants that players preferred using lottery winnings to "do with my time anything I like" than to buy luxury items, the state's ad agency created a TV commercial for the million-dollar Big Game. It showed a winner lounging happily in his lawn chair while his neighbors trudged to work in lockstep to the tune of "Sixteen Tons."

Washington DC used a commercial for Powerball to suggest that a winner's lifestyle could be magically transformed by winning a "life-altering" multi-million dollar jackpot, omitting the 1 in 55 million odds against such a win. They identified the target for small-stakes Lucky Numbers as blue-collar, and big jackpot Powerball as better suited for middle-income folks. Using the market as creative directors, the ad agency asked players to submit strategies that would motivate people to play Lucky Numbers who might not ordinarily play the game.

Source: Babington, C. and Chinoy, I. (1998). Lotteries win with slick marketing. *Washington Post,* May 4

What do you think?

* *What are the lottery advertising themes in your state?*
* *What research might have been conducted to create these themes?*
* *At which psychographic segment are the commercials aimed?*

DISCUSSION AND REVIEW

1. Summarize the research findings discussed in this chapter on the effects of portrayals of violence, sex, and drugs in entertainment on audience perceptions and behavior. Based on what you have read, what advice would you offer parents regarding their children's exposure to these portrayals?
2. How does e-gambling fit into the scheme of gambling addiction? How can this addiction be curtailed?
3. What arguments would you use to convince an advertiser to switch its product placements from film to video games?
4. What role do shows like *Intervention* play in curtailing drug usage? What other medium might be used to influence potential users not to "get hooked?"

EXERCISES

1. Go to a local library or bookstore and look through some of the "young adult" books (if there isn't a separate section for these, look online for a list of young adult literature titles). Do an informal "content analysis" by making a tally of the topics of the books you look through. What topics seem to be the most popular? What percentage of the books, if any, would you consider to be "racy reads?"
2. Visit the sites listed in this chapter to play an online game of skill and a game of chance. What role do technology and new media play in gaming? How do you think technology will characterize gaming of the future?

3. Invoke the uses and gratifications theory to explain player fascination with action games. Use expectancy theory to explain human fascination with gambling. Are the two theories interchangeable? Why? Are games and gambling interchangeable? Why?

4. Buy a dollar lottery ticket at a convenience store during a time when the jackpot is high. Describe the other ticket buyers at this location in psychographic terms using the VALS II system (see the SRI web site below for more information on VALS), or create your own sub-categories. What kind of advertising campaign would you use to persuade these players to play more often?

BOOKS AND BLOGS

Bryant, J. (2001). *Television and the American family*. Mahwah NJ: Lawrence Erlbaum.

Bryant, J. and Vorderer, P. (2006). *Psychology of entertainment*. Mahwah NJ: Lawrence Erlbaum.

Gross, E. and Morse, E. (2007). *Governing fortune: Casino gambling in America*. Ann Arbor MI: University of Michigan Press.

Hoffer, R. (2007). *Jackpot nation: America's love affair with gambling*. New York: Harper Collins.

Kamalipour, Y.R. and Rampal, K.R. (2001). *Media, sex, violence, and drugs in the global village*. Lanham MD: Rowman & Littlefield.

Potter, J. (1999). *On media violence*. Thousand Oaks CA: Sage.

Scheri, Saverio (2005). *Casinos most valuable chip: How technology transformed the gaming industry*. Morgantown WV: Institute for the History of Technology.

www.trendspotting.com—videogame statistics and industry data.

www.digitaltrends.com—consumer electronics news, reviews, and insights.

www.gambling.com—world's largest gambling portal with 16,500 links to relevant sites.

www.world-lotteries.org/—world lottery association web site.

www.addictionrecov.org/aboutgam.htm—information on help with addiction.

www.sric-bi.com/VALS/—psychographic consumer marketing segmentation system.

PART 3

INNOVATIONS: CONTEMPORARY TRENDS AND PRACTICES

13 ADVOCACY IN ENTERTAINMENT: POLITICS, ACTIVISM, AND EDUCATION

There may be times when we are powerless to prevent injustice, but there must never be a time when we fail to protest.

—Elie Wiesel

By definition, the goal of entertainment is first, and foremost, to entertain, but, as you should be finding throughout this text, it can also serve a variety of other purposes. In this chapter we will explore how entertainment has been used for advocacy and education. **Advocacy** can be defined as the "the act of pleading or arguing in favor of something, such as a cause, idea, or policy; active support." Similarly, to **educate** can be defined as "to provide with knowledge or training in a particular area or for a particular purpose; to bring an understanding or acceptance."[1] Thus, both advocacy and education involve conveying ideas and information, with the intention of influencing people's thoughts and actions. Chapter 5 introduced ways that entertainment can both intentionally and unintentionally influence audiences' thoughts and actions. In this chapter we will explore some of the intentional uses of entertainment as a vehicle for political and social advocacy and education.

Politics and Entertainment

Politics and entertainment intersect in society in many interesting ways. Political issues and governments have long served as inspiration for drama, satire, music, and other forms of entertainment. In turn, entertainers and entertainment forums have been used to promote political and government agendas. Politics is certainly a predominant topic in news media, and, as fictional entertainment is often inspired by news and current events, politics is also a popular topic in Hollywood films and TV dramas. Traditionally, the difference between political news media and entertainment media has been more distinct, but the increased blurring of media that has been discussed in many other chapters has led to some creative political, infotainment hybrids.

 FLASH FACT

Saturday Night Live logged its best season premiere since 2001 on Sept. 13, 2008, with guest host Michael Phelps and Tina Fey doubling as Sarah Palin. It was the most-watched *SNL* for any dates since December 17, 2002, when Al Gore was the guest host and jam band Phish was the musical guest. According to Nielsen Media Research, the show averaged a 7.4 household rating and 18 share in the top 55 "metered" markets, proof of the popularity of political satire on TV.

Source: Reuters.com/entertainment news

Political "Talk" and Satire

Notably, in the case of politics, some of this blurring is not entirely new. One of the most common ways we see politics addressed in entertainment is through satire. Wherever organized government has existed, so has satire. **Satire** is a form of comedy in which human or individual vices, follies, abuses, or shortcomings are criticized through parodies and caricatures. **Political satire** specializes in gaining entertainment from politics, using politicians, government officials, and public affairs as fodder for jokes

Tina Fey parodied Sarah Palin on *Saturday Night Live* in its best season's premiere in seven years

and ridicule. It commonly aims simply to provide entertainment, but often it may carry an agenda and seek to influence the political process. It has also been used subversively as a method of advancing political arguments when political speech and dissent are forbidden by a regime. By framing criticism within a humorous, presumably "non-serious" context, critics found an outlet to voice their concerns in a manner that was less likely to provoke censor and retribution from governing leaders. As a form of disparagement humor (see Chapter 4) which attacks one's "enemies" and frustrations, satire rarely offers a constructive view in itself. Thus, when it is used as part of protest or dissent, it tends simply to establish the error of matters rather than to provide solutions.

One of the oldest documented examples of political satire is the work of poet and playwright Aristophanes, whose work in the 400 BCs satirized well-known citizens of Athens and their involvement in the Peloponnesian War.[2] Political satire is also found in literature ranging from the writings of Paul of Tarsus in the New Testament of the Bible[3] to classics such as George Orwell's *Nineteen Eighty-four* and political cartoons (see image below) in newspapers and magazine such as *Doonesbury* and *Boondocks*. During the twentieth century, politics moved from print media and theater to electronic media including radio and TV shows and audience-centered forums such as talk shows and blogs.

On political talk shows, a host will often introduce a topic and then invite discussion from one or more guest experts. On radio, call-in programs where listeners are invited to share their opinions are a particularly popular format for these shows. Many political talk shows are syndicated, but local shows are also popular. An Annenberg national poll found that 18 percent of adults listen to at least one call-in political talk radio program a week. Typically conservative shows (with hosts such as Rush Limbaugh and Gordon Liddy) tend to fare better than more liberal-leaning programs. Those who listen to such shows tend to be males who are older, more conservative, predominately white, and who are very interested in politics, are politically active, and hold anti-Washington attitudes.[4]

THURSDAY MORNING, JULY 7, 1949

HARDLY A CHOICE CORNER FOR PANHANDLING

A political cartoon from 1949 with U.S. looking at postwar Britain, broke and begging

A wide range of political talk and commentary shows can also be found on TV. Many political programs are packaged as hard news and public affairs programming. Political shows can be built around an expert panel (*Washington Week in Review*), a panel and news figure (*Meet the Press*), a magazine format for a single topic (*Nightline*), a magazine format that deals with multiple topics (*Sixty Minutes*), or a one-on-one host/guest interview (Bill Moyers's *World of Ideas*). Again, however, the line between political programs packaged as news and those featured as entertainment is not always clear. Programs such as *The O'Reilly Factor* and *The Colbert Report* are more editorial and satirical in format and content, and, yet, many people still identify them as one of their primary sources for political news. In addition, late-night and daytime variety talk-show hosts such as Jay Leno and Oprah Winfrey, as well as comedy sketch programs like *Saturday Night Live*, also focus frequently on political issues, campaigns, and elections.

A poll released in 2008 by the Pew Research Center for the People and the Press found that nearly one-in-ten Americans (9 percent) say they regularly learn something about the presidential campaign from late-night talk shows, such as those hosted by Jay Leno and David Letterman. Slightly fewer people (8 percent) say they regularly pick up election news from other comedy programs, like *Saturday Night Live* and *Politically Incorrect*, while 5 percent say the same about MTV. But far more young people than older Americans say they sometimes learn something about the campaign from these sources (see Table 13.1).[5] As far back as 2000, nearly half (47 percent) of those under 30 are

Table 13.1 Presidential Campaign Comedy

Prior to strike, learn about the campaign from comedy shows? (%)[1]	Total	Age 18–29	30–49	50+
Regularly	8	12	7	6
Sometimes	20	27	22	14
Hardly ever/Never	59	51	60	63
Don't watch	12	7	10	16
Don't know/Refused	1	3	1	1
	100	100	100	100
Prior to strike, learn about the campaign from late-night talk shows? (%)[2]				
Regularly	9	10	8	9
Sometimes	19	25	21	16
Hardly ever/Never	59	53	63	57
Don't watch	12	10	8	18
Don't know/Refused	1	2	–	–
	100	100	100	100
Missing information about campaign because comedy and talk shows not on? (%)[3]				
Missing out on information	28	37	28	21
Not missing out on information	70	62	71	75
Other/Don't know/Refused	2	1	2	4
	100	100	100	100

1 Comedy shows such as *Saturday Night Live* and *The Daily Show*
2 Late-night talk shows such as *David Letterman* and *Jay Leno*
3 Asked of those who regularly/sometimes learn from late-night or comedy shows

informed at least occasionally by late-night talk shows (13 percent regularly and 34 percent sometimes), with significant numbers saying the same of comedy shows (37 percent) and MTV (25 percent). Nearly one-in-four Blacks (22 percent) report being regularly informed about the upcoming elections from the late-night shows, compared to 8 percent of whites.[6]

Another Pew survey in 2007 found that the regular audiences of the comedy shows were as well informed as the audiences of elite news sources such as the web sites of major daily newspapers and the *News Hour with Jim Lehrer*. While many viewers of these shows undoubtedly learn while laughing, the Pew studies suggest that part of the reason for the high knowledge levels of those who faithfully watch these shows is that they tend to be heavy news consumers. Those who said they regularly learn from late-night shows are far more likely than others to also report regularly learning from sources such as cable TV news shows, the Internet, National Public Radio and talk radio, public TV, and C-SPAN. That may help account for the fact that only about a quarter (28 percent) of those who get at least some campaign news from comedy and late-night programs say they feel like they missed out on information about the campaign when those shows were not on. Among those under age 30, however, a larger minority (37 percent) says they feel like they missed out on campaign news in the absence of these programs.[7]

Recognizing the potential impact of this media, in 1992, Clinton blew his saxophone into campaign history on *The Arsenio Hall Show*, boosting his carefully calculated image as a fresh candidate who was better suited than incumbent George Bush to lead a new generation of voters in a post-Cold War world. Since then political candidates and government officials have made regular appearances on talk shows and even in comedy sketch programs. In 2000 Hillary Clinton actually used a *Letterman* appearance to announce her candidacy for the U.S. Senate. "I knew that if I were going to run for the Senate, I had to come and sit in 'this' chair, and talk to 'the' big guy," she said on the air.[8] Similarly, even daytime variety talk show host Oprah Winfrey has garnered exclusive interviews with political heavy hitters such as Arnold Schwarzenegger, elected in 2002 to govern California, and Condoleezza Rice, George W. Bush's National Security Advisor.

SPOTLIGHT ON HUMOR   *Politically Incorrect* with Bill Maher

Bill Maher

Bill Maher is an American stand-up comedian, TV host, political commentator, actor, and author. Maher is known for his political satire and sociopolitical commentary targeting a wide swath of topics, ranging from the right wing to the left wing, political correctness and the mass media, among others. Maher gained fame as the host of *Politically Incorrect*, which aired on ABC and the Comedy Central television network. ABC decided not to renew Maher's contract for *Politically Incorrect* in 2002 after he made a controversial on-air remark on September 17, 2001, in which he agreed with guest conservative political commentator Dinesh D'Souza that the 9/11 terrorists were not cowards. He then went on to say, "We have been the cowards lobbing cruise missiles from 2,000 miles away. That's cowardly. Staying in the airplane when it hits the building, say what you want about it, it's not cowardly."[9]

In the context of the sensitive aftermath of the attacks, such a remark was deemed too controversial for some financial supporters. Although some people, including conservative radio host Rush Limbaugh, supported Maher in pointing out the distinction between physical and moral cowardice, companies including FedEx and Sears Roebuck pulled their advertisements from the show, costing the show a significant portion of its revenue. Ari Fleischer, who was the White House Press Secretary at the time, responded to a reporter's question about Maher's comments by saying: "they're reminders to all Americans that they need to watch what they say, watch what they do. This is not a time for remarks like that."[10]

The show was subsequently cancelled on June 16, 2002, although the Baltimore-based Sinclair Broadcast group had dropped the show from its ABC-affiliated stations months before that. Six days after the cancellation of *Politically Incorrect*, Maher received the President's Award (for "championing free speech") from the Los Angeles Press Club, and he soon had a new cable TV show on HBO as host of *Real Time with Bill Maher*. On June 1, 2006, he also began hosting an Internet-exclusive talk show on Amazon.com called *Amazon Fishbowl*. Similar to Howard Stern's shift from broadcast to satellite radio, subscription-based media has been willing to air more controversial programming both because they are not as restricted by advertising dollars, FCC regulations, and concerns about offending larger broadcast audiences.

What do you think?

- *Should Maher's comments be tolerated as harmless political satire or could they have more serious implications?*

- *Should political satire be treated differently than other controversial programming?*

- *Review the chapters on law and ethics. Do you think Maher's political commentary deserves greater free speech protection or should broadcasters be able to or be obligated to censor such programs to the same degree that they censor violent or sexual entertainment content?*

Political Activism

Oprah Winfrey and other celebrities are becoming increasingly politically active, often directly endorsing politicians and acting as advocates for specific policies. Marty Kaplan, director of the University of Southern California-based Norman Lear Center for Entertainment, noted a marked increase in celebrity involvement in politics in the 2004 United States Presidential election. According to Kaplan, "[w]hen Drew Barrymore and Cameron Diaz appear on *The Oprah Winfrey Show* and in other forums to tell young people that voting is cool, when *The Sopranos* star Edie Falco is seen in TV spots as the spokeswoman for a group dubbed Mothers Opposed to Bush (aka MOB) and Bruce Springsteen and like-minded rockers are trooping through battleground states on the anti-Bush Vote for Change tour, it definitely marks a sea change for entertainers and their engagement in the electoral process."[11]

Ironically, just as political news is becoming more entertainment-focused, celebrity advocacy is making entertainment news more politically focused. One journalist noted that "the turf for magazine shows like *ET*, *Access Hollywood* and *The Insider*, usually more interested in Angelina Jolie or Lindsey Lohan, has expanded from red carpets to campaign rallies."[12] The new interest in politics by entertainment media was particularly evident in their coverage of the 2008 Presidential race. According to Bill Carroll, an expert in the syndication market for Katz Television, Oprah Winfrey's endorsement of Barack Obama was a key moment in turning the attention of these shows to politics: "Wherever the celebrities [like Winfrey] are, that's where the celebrity magazines are going to be," he said.[13]

FLASH FACT

Meet the Press is America's most-watched and No. 1 Sunday morning public affairs broadcast and is in its sixty-first season in 2008. The format provides three interview segments featuring guests and newsmakers of national and international importance. The longest-running program on network TV, *Meet the* *Press* made its debut in 1947 after two years on radio. Broadcast in digital high-definition, the program has featured every president since JFK. Tim Russert served as moderator for 14 years until his death on June 13, 2008.

Entertainment companies have also made concerted efforts to encourage young people to become politically involved. The music cable station MTV has been promoting its Rock the Vote Campaign, since 1990. It has aired TV spots featuring popular musicians discussing political issues and encouraging young people to vote, and the network has sponsored street teams and voter registration drives. More recently, the children's TV network Nickelodeon has also entered the political ring. Its 2008 fall season included extensive presidential and election-themed content in its regular programs and also added special news features including a *Kids Pick the President* Election Connection Team—who followed the campaign trail, providing kids with an insider point-of-view at the Democratic and Republican National Conventions. All of this led up to Nickelodeon's kids' vote which began on October 12. "This presidential election has ignited so many young people to become more involved," said Marva Smalls, Executive Vice President of Public Affairs for Nickelodeon/MTVN Kids and Family Group. "We want to connect our audiences to the process—the candidates and issues. Kids—although not legal voters—don't want to be on the sidelines."[14]

Drama, Comedy, and Documentaries   Government and political issues have always been popular topics for Hollywood films and TV programs. Like talk shows and stand-up comedy, these productions may be designed purely as entertainment, or they may use satire and dramatic devices to make intentional political statements. In a political satire of government propaganda and manipulation, the film *Wag the Dog* tells the story of a U.S. president who is caught in a sex scandal 14 days before an election, so his advisor and Hollywood manufacture a war that deceives the American people and he ultimately wins the election. The TV cartoon sitcom *Family Guy* has poked fun at a wide range of politicians including U.S. Presidents Bill Clinton and George Bush and mocked perceived government failings ranging from homeland security and immigration to electoral policy and public education.

A popular TV drama, *West Wing*, about a fictional president and his close advisors, was accused of forwarding a decidedly liberal political agenda by portraying the religious right as anti-Semitic buffoons, ranting against guns and generally glorifying liberal sentiment, while demonizing Republicans and conservative politics.[15] As media dependency and cultivation theory suggest (see Chapter 5), for those of us not directly involved in politics or affected by certain issues, our understanding and experience of political issues may depend almost entirely on what we see and hear in the media. And, given that most people spend more time consuming entertainment media than news media, often our thoughts and opinions may be shaped, albeit perhaps subtly, more by Hollywood films and TV programs than by *Time* magazine or CNN. See the *Spotlight on the State of War* for a deeper discussion of these concerns.

SPOTLIGHT ON THE STATE OF WAR   Excerpts from "Politics and War as Entertainment"

Randolph Bourne's observation "war is the health of the state" is familiar to most critics of militarism, but few have delved into why this is so. Statism is dependent upon mass thinking which, in turn, is essential to the creation of a collective, herd-oriented society. Such pack-like behavior is reflected in the intellectual and spiritual passivity of people whose mindsets are wrapped up more in *images* and *appearances* than in concrete *reality*.

Such a collapse of the mind produces a society dominated by *entertainment*—which places little burden on thinking—rather than critical inquiry, which helps to explain why there has long been a symbiotic relationship between the entertainment industry and political systems. Entertainment fosters a passive consciousness, a willingness to "suspend our disbelief." Its purpose is to generate *amusement*, a word that is synonymous with "diversion," meaning "to distract the attention of." The common reference to movies as a form of "escape" from reality, reflects this function. Government officials know what every magician knows, namely, that to carry out their illusions, they must divert the audience's attention from their hidden purposes.

The entertainment industry helps shape the content of our consciousness by generating institutionally desired moods, fears, and reactions, a role played throughout human history. Ancient Greek history is tied up in myths, fables, and other fictions, passed on by the entertainers of their day, the minstrels. We need to ask ourselves about the extent to which our understanding of American history and other human behavior has been fashioned by motion pictures, novels, and television drama. Through carefully scripted fictions and fantasies, *others* direct our experiences, channel our emotions, and shape our views of reality. The fantasies depicted are more often of *conflict*, not cooperation; of *violence*, not peace; of *death*, not the importance of life.

Nowhere is the interdependency of the political and entertainment worlds better demonstrated than in the *war system*, which speaks of "theaters" of operation, "acts" of war with battle "scenes," "staging" areas, and "dress rehearsals" for invasions. The pomp and circumstance of war is reflected in military uniforms that mimic stage costumes, all to the accompaniment of martial music that rivals grand opera. A Broadway play can become either a "bomb" or a "hit"; troops are "billeted" (a word derived from the French meaning of a "ticket"); while the premiere of a movie is often accompanied, like a World War II bombing raid, by searchlights that scan the skies. Even the Cold War was framed by an "iron curtain." Is it only coincidence, devoid of any symbolic meaning, that at the end of the American Civil War—one of the bloodiest wars in human history—its chief protagonist was shot while attending the theater, and that his killer was an actor who, upon completing his deed, descended to the stage and exited?

Entertainment is a part of what we call "recreation," which means to "re-create," in this case to give interpretations to events that are most favorable to one's national identity and critical of an opponent. In this connection, entertainers help to manipulate the "dark side" of our being which, once mobilized, can help to generate the most destructive and inhumane consequences. World War II movies portrayed Japanese kamikaze pilots who crashed their planes into Navy ships as "crazed zealots," while American pilots who did the same thing to Japanese ships or trains were represented as "heroes" willing to die to save their comrades. German and Japanese soldiers were presented as sneering sadists who delighted in the torture of the innocents, while the American soldiers only wanted to get the war over with so they could get back home to mom and her apple pie! How many of us, today, think of nineteenth-century U.S. cavalrymen—as portrayed by the likes of John Wayne and Randolph Scott—as brave soldiers, while Indian warriors were "savages" for having forcibly resisted their own annihilation?

All of this leads me to ask whether the *entertainment* industry is an extension of the *war* system, or whether *war* is simply an extension of our need for *entertainment*? What should be clear to us is that

entertainment is one of the principal means by which our thinking can be taken over and directed by others once we have chosen to make our minds *passive*, which we do when we are asked—whether by actors or politicians—to suspend our judgment about the reality of events we are witnessing. When we are content to be *amused* (i.e., to have our attention diverted from reality to fantasy), and to have our emotions exploited by those skilled in triggering unconscious forces, we set ourselves up to be manipulated by those producing the show.

Source: Butler Shaffer at lewrockwell.com[16]

What do you think?

- *How much impact does entertainment, such as Hollywood films, have on our perceptions of war?*
- *Do world leaders and elites use entertainment to distract citizens and influence political perceptions?*

More direct, political agendas can be found in documentary films. Although politics and policy issues have always been popular topics for documentary filmmakers, their films have traditionally been viewed as more educational than entertaining and distribution was typically limited to film festivals, independent theaters, libraries, and occasional special interest TV airings. It is only recently that such films have enjoyed wide theatrical releases similar to major Hollywood films. In 2004, Michael Moore's *Fahrenheit 9/11*—a film harshly attacking the Bush administration for its handling of the September 11 terrorist attacks—won the top prize at the Festival de Cannes. *Fahrenheit 9/11* went on to set a new record as the highest grossing feature documentary by raking in $119 million at the domestic box office.[17] It also sparked equally partisan responses from conservative-leaning filmmakers, including Lionel Chetwynd's *Celsius 41.11*, Dick Morris's *FahrenHYPE 9/11*, and Michael Wilson's *Michael Moore Hates America*. In 2006, *An Inconvenient Truth*, a documentary on global warming presented by former United States Vice President Al Gore, became the fourth top grossing documentary film to date, earning $49 million at the box office. The film won Academy Awards for Best Documentary Feature and for Best Original Song. A companion book by Gore, *An inconvenient truth: The planetary emergency of global warming and what we can do about it*, reached number one on the paperback nonfiction *New York Times* best-seller list that same year.[18]

Music as Political Expression   There is a rich history of the connection between music and politics, particularly political expression in music. This expression has most often centered on anti-establishment or protest themes, although pro-establishment ideas are also used, for example in national anthems. Folk music has a tradition of political discontent, with songs sung to commemorate popular uprisings and strikes, and to protest against injustice and social inequity.[19] Classical music has often been used to glorify political leaders, largely because the patronage of the rich or powerful was the main source of income for composers in previous centuries. In recent times this has become less prevalent; the Master of the Queen's Musick in the U.K., for example, is no longer required to compose hagiographies to Elizabeth II. Even in the past classical composers registered dissent: Beethoven removed a dedication to Napoleon from his Third Symphony to protest against Napoleon's crowning himself Emperor.

In the twentieth century, the union movement, the Great Depression, the civil rights movement, and the Vietnam War spawned protest songs, such as Bob Dylan's "The Times They Are A-Changin'" (1964) and Woody Guthrie's "This Land Is Your Land" (1940). A 1983 protest song that gained considerable attention worldwide is "99 Luftballons" by Nena. The common form for protest music during the 1960s often included acoustic guitar and harmonica: this was popularized by the work of Woody Guthrie and Pete Seeger early in the twentieth century and continued into the later part of the century by Phil Ochs, Joan Baez, and Bob Dylan. The movie *Bob Roberts* is an example of protest music parody, where the title character—played by American actor Tim Robbins—is a guitar-playing U.S. Senatorial candidate who writes and performs songs with a heavily reactionary tone. The Civil Rights movement of the 1950s and 1960s used African American spirituals as a source of protest, changing the religious lyrics to suit the political mood of the time. The use of religious music helped to emphasize the peaceful nature of the protest; it also proved easy to adapt, with many improvised call-and-response songs being created during marches and sit-ins. Some imprisoned protesters used their incarceration as an opportunity to write protest songs. These songs were carried across the country by Freedom Riders.[20]

Popular music since the middle of the twentieth century has increasingly featured politically inspired lyrics. It has often been used to express anti-war sentiments; Jimi Hendrix famously satirized the U.S. national anthem, "The Star-Spangled Banner," through the use of extreme distortion and feedback as a protest against the Vietnam War. The majority of political popular music has an anti-establishment or left-wing perspective. Conservative and libertarian lyrics are mainly found in country music. In Western popular culture, it is rare except in times of war for pro-establishment music to gain a foothold in the popular consciousness. The punk rock genre was overtly political: its genesis in the mid-1970s was as a reaction to the aloofness of the bands in the rock scene at that time, and its lyrics often espoused anarchy or revolution. This position was epitomized by artists such as Crass and the Dead Kennedys, who were inspired by anarcho-syndicalism.

Today, working-class and left-wing political themes, commentary, and beliefs are still common with many popular and underground modern-day street punk, hardcore punk and oi! bands, such as the Dropkick Murphys, Leftover Crack, Rancid, Oi Polloi, The Bruisers and The Business to name but a few. Music of Black origin has a long tradition of protest, from the blues performers of the early twentieth century, up to and including the rap and hip hop more recently popular. A *protest song* is a song to protest problems in society such as injustice, racial discrimination, war, globalization, inflation, social inequalities, incarceration, the Greenhouse effect, and global warming. Protest songs are generally associated with folk music, but in recent times they have come from all genres of music. Such songs become popular during times of social disruption and among social groups.

Neil Young continues the theme in the twenty-first century in his song, "Let's Impeach the President"—a stinging rebuke against President George W. Bush and the war in Iraq, as did Pink with her appeal to Bush in "Dear Mr. President." Not to forget the band Dispatch and the anti-war underground hit "The General." Utah Philips, the Riot-Folk! Collective, and David Rovics, among many other singers, have continued the folk tradition of protest. Punk music from the 1970s to today has featured anti-war, anti-state, and anti-capitalist themes.

SPOTLIGHT ON PROTEST MUSIC   Lyrics of Change

Protest songs did not originate with Bob Dylan, but he certainly has laid claim to the genre. Audiences who love his words confirm the power of song to move a nation. Never at home in a specific movement, Dylan's artful approach to political songwriting remains an inspiration for today's musicians.

Here are some more examples of protest songs that came about during the Bush Administration.

- The Dixie Chicks' lead singer criticized the president at the beginning of the Iraq war, which began a series of pop-punk assault on the war agenda.
- Green Day's album *American Idiot* topped the charts and won a Grammy in 2005 for post 9/11 discourse.
- Kanye West's CDs such as *Crack Music* have been sarcastically fierce about Hussein's weapons stash and Bush's treatment of Blacks after Hurricane Katrina.
- Topping Billboard's Modern Rock chart, Pearl Jam's single "World Wide Suicide" mourns a son killed in battle.

- Bruce Springsteen's tribute to protest songs by Pete Seeger was captured in his *We Shall Overcome* album.

In the tradition of Woody Guthrie's Dust Bowl-poet persona, Dylan has provided America with some of its most active lyrics, such as the two stanzas of the one featured here demonstrate.

Union Sundown

Well, my shoes, they come from Singapore,
My flashlight's from Taiwan,
My tablecloth's from Malaysia,
My belt buckle's from the Amazon.
You know, this shirt I wear comes from the
    Philippines
And the car I drive is a Chevrolet,
It was put together down in Argentina
By a guy makin' thirty cents a day.

Well, it's sundown on the union
And what's made in the U.S.A.
Sure was a good idea
'Til greed got in the way.

Source: "Songs of Protest" from *The Nation*, May 15, 2006

What do you think?

- *Can song lyrics inspire listeners to take political action?*
- *What songs can you name that have inspired you?*

Candidates for public office often have campaign theme songs which they play at appearances. These songs are usually contemporary popular songs without explicit political content, though they may have easily politicized or sloganized lyrics. In both the United States and the United Kingdom since the 1990s, all the major political parties have appropriated popular songs at election time, not always with the consent or approval of the recording artist. It has also often been the case that, while the song's chorus may be "on message," the lyrics to the verses may espouse a different viewpoint that shows the party in a less than complimentary light. During the 1800s, particularly in the United States, political campaigners composed songs praising their favorite candidate, or criticizing their candidate's opponent. This practice gradually died out during the twentieth century. Unions have a long tradition of rousing or mournful songs, usually consisting of popular and/or folk tunes with pro-union lyrics or lyrics commemorating union organizers or events. These were often sung at events or during marches and while on picket or strike lines.[21]

New Media[22]   The Internet is living up to its potential as a major source for news about the U.S. presidential campaign. In 2008, nearly a quarter of Americans (24 percent) said they regularly learned something about the campaign from the Internet, almost double the percentage from a comparable point in the 2004 campaign (13 percent).

Moreover, the Internet has now become a leading source of campaign news for young people. Approximately 42 percent of those age 18–29 say they regularly learn about the campaign from the Internet, the highest percentage for any news source. In January 2004, just 20 percent of young people said they routinely got campaign news from the Internet. While most people report getting their campaign information from three major news sources—MSNBC, CNN, and Yahoo News—younger people who get campaign news online cite a wider variety of sources, including both MySpace and YouTube and other social media and more entertainment-oriented web sites.

About two-thirds of Americans age 18–29 say they use social networking sites, and more than a quarter in this age group (27 percent) say that they have gotten information about candidates and the campaign from them—including 37 percent among those age 18–24. Nearly one-in-ten of people under age 30 (8 percent) say that they have signed up as a "friend" of one of the candidates on a site. And the numbers are even higher for each of these activities among young registered voters. The use of social networking sites for political activity is far less common among older voters, even those in their 30s. About one-in-five people age 30–39 (21 percent) use social networking sites, but just 4 percent in this age group say that they have gotten campaign information from those sites; 3 percent have "friended" a candidate.

Political candidates are making full use of these new tools. By April of the 2008 primary elections, the Obama campaign had uploaded 840 videos to the YouTube/YouChoose web site, and attracted 42,000 subscribers who get video by e-mail. For Hillary Clinton, the totals were 308 videos and 12,000 subscribers; for Republican John McCain, 175 videos and 3,700 subscribers.[23] Each candidate also maintained pages on MySpace and other social networks.

While the Internet is an increasingly important source of news generated by the presidential candidates and their campaigns, it also provides a way for citizens to provide their own input and communicate with each other about politics. About one-in-six Americans (16 percent) have sent or received e-mails with friends and family regarding candidates and the campaign, and 14 percent have received e-mail messages from political groups or organizations about the campaign (see Table 13.2). Fewer Americans have gone to the candidates' web sites themselves: just 8 percent say they have done so, the same number who report having visited news satire web sites such as the Onion or the Daily Show. Republicans were slightly more likely than Democrats or independents to report having traded e-mail messages with friends and family, but otherwise there were no significant partisan differences in these activities. And except for visits to social networking sites, where young people are more frequent visitors, there are few systematic differences by age in each of these activities. Younger voters, however, tended to gravitate toward the Democratic Party and the Obama campaign at greater rates than their elders. Online Democrats outpace Republicans in their consumption of online video (51 percent vs. 42 percent). Furthermore, Democrats were significantly ahead among social

Table 13.2   Online Campaign Activity by Party (%)

	Total	Rep	Dem	Ind
E-mails with family/friends	16	21	14	16
E-mails from groups/orgs	14	14	14	16
Visit candidate web sites	8	9	7	9
Visit news satire sites	8	6	9	10
Get info from social networks	7	7	8	7

networking site profile creators: 36 percent of online Democrats had such profiles, compared with 21 percent of Republicans and 28 percent of independents.

New media have made politics more interactive and thus more interesting, even entertaining for audiences. One web site, pollClash.com, allowed voters to directly compare and vote on video soundbites from the 2008 election campaign. Viewers could watch campaign videos of candidates and other key players in side-by-side windows, and then vote on which are more credible, which are more effective, and which make the better case about critical campaign issues like the economy and national security. For example, one comparison let voters pick between a Hillary Clinton video thanking her supporters and a Barack Obama video in which he thanked The Grateful Dead and the deadheads for getting out the vote. It asks which candidate seemed more at ease, and which one seemed to be talking directly to the viewer. Another match up compared an interview with former White House press secretary Scott McClellan and an interview with his arch-enemy Karl Rove, who said McClellan doesn't sound like himself—"he sounds like a left-wing blogger." The pollClash asked which was correct and which was more credible. Individual users create political web sites, blogs, e-mails, and videos that may be circulated and viewed by millions.

User-generated content has been credited with raising candidates up and taking them down. What might have otherwise been discreet political missteps and slips-of-the-tongue witnessed by only small, local audiences can become widely publicized blunders. For example, Howard Dean's 2004 bid for the presidency was sparked online by a record-breaking, grass-roots fund-raising campaign, but his campaign may be most remembered by the way it ended online with "Dean's scream"—remixed and satirized viral videos of his red-faced, teeth-clenched, hoarse-voiced concession speech at a post-caucus rally for his volunteers in West Des Moines, Iowa.

Social Activism

Advocacy in entertainment has extended beyond criticizing and championing specific politicians, government actions, and policy issues, endeavoring to serve as an agent of change on a broad range of societal issues. TV is the most important medium for social commentary.

Television and Social Commentary

On TV, sitcoms and other serial programs have often veered into social commentary. Examples of these are sitcoms created by Norman Lear (including *All in the Family* and *Maude* in the U.S.). In Britain, Johnny Speight's *Till Death Us Do Part* (on which *All in the*

Family was based) and Ray Galton and Alan Simpson's *Steptoe and Son* are good examples. These shows would address controversial issues of the day, in an effort to get audiences to think about them a little differently. When *All in the Family* made its debut, a warning screen stated: "The program you are about to see seeks to throw a humorous spotlight on our frailties, prejudices, and concerns. By making them a source of laughter, we hope to show—in a mature fashion—just how absurd they are." Infoplease.com ranked the program third among the top ten television shows of all time stating that "Offensive, yet somehow likeable, Archie Bunker kept us in stitches even as he reminded us of life's less pleasant realities. *All in the Family* brought a new social con-

All in the Family creator Normal Lear attempted "to throw a humorous spotlight on our frailities, prejudices, and concerns to show just how absurd they are"

sciousness to television, dealing with issues ranging from bigotry to breast cancer with both humor and compassion."[24]

Ironically, even as *All in the Family* was being lauded for its progressive ideology, it was being criticized for perpetuating the very prejudices it was seeking to overcome. Although many viewers understood the intended sarcasm and parody of Archie's closed-minded views, some audience members failed to pick up on these cues or chose to ignore them. Instead of condemning Archie, they sided with him. It was feared that, in identifying with Archie's character, some people were becoming even more firmly entrenched in their prejudiced views. Confirming one of the most basic tenets of communication, the show's producers learned that a sender's and receiver's perception of a message can sometimes be very different.

The global success of reality television programming may also be serving as an agent of social change, although often, perhaps, unintentionally. In some authoritarian countries, reality TV voting represents the first time many citizens have voted in any free and fair wide-scale elections. In addition, the frankness of the settings on some reality shows presents situations that were formerly taboo in certain orthodox cultures, like the pan-Arab version of *Big Brother*, which shows men and women living together. Although critics have accused such programs of encouraging cultural imperialism imposing Western cultural values worldwide (see Chapter 11), others see them as potentially powerful, positive advocates for more free and open societies.

Music and Social Change

Music has served as perhaps the most popular, and arguably the most successful, entertainment vehicle for aggressively advocating social change. Many musical artists have worked to raise awareness and money for a wide range of social causes ranging from curing deadly diseases to preventing animal cruelty. One of the most well-known awareness and fundraising projects was Band Aid. Band Aid was a British and Irish charity supergroup, founded in 1984 by Bob Geldof and Midge Ure in order to raise money for famine relief in Ethiopia by releasing the record "Do They Know It's Christmas?" for the Christmas market. Bob Geldof, after watching a BBC TV news report by Michael Buerk from famine-stricken Ethiopia, was so moved by the plight of starving children that he decided to try and raise money using his contacts in pop music. He brought together an impressive number of top musical artists who collaborated in recording the song. The single surpassed the hopes of the producers to become the number one ranked song that Christmas. Today, musical artists extend their charity efforts far beyond benefit concerts and messaging into song lyrics. For example, Bono of U2 was a co-founder of Project Red, a fundraising effort for AIDS medicine for African nations which includes partnerships with a wide range of well-known companies such as Apple, American Express, and Motorola who donate a portion of earmarked sales proceeds to the project.

Kevin Wall, Al Gore, Pharrell Williams, Maná, Cameron Diaz, and the MSN Network invoked music on an even grander scale to mobilize global concern for climate change and the environment. As part of their Save Our Selves (SOS)—The Campaign for a Climate in Crisis—more than 100 of the world's top musical acts participated in Live Earth, a 24-hour concert on July 7, 2007, across all seven continents. Live Earth reached an estimated global audience of two billion people through an unparalleled media architecture of more than 500 media partners covering TV, radio, Internet, and wireless channels in more than 130 countries. The concerts were broadcast across TV networks in more than 100 countries with more than 20 of the world's leading broadcasters, including NBC (U.S.), Shanghai Media Group and CTV (China), BBC (U.K.), Pro Sieben (Germany), TVGLobo (Brazil), Fuji TV and NHK (Japan), South Africa Broadcast Company (South Africa), and Foxtel (Australia), dedicating a combined total of more than 100 channels to Live Earth concert coverage.[25] It is unclear whether such a campaign can effect actual political and policy change. As the largest global entertainment event on record, however, the event did succeed in drawing massive media attention to the issue of climate change, engaging audiences on the topic and stimulating discussion in every corner of the globe.

Internet Activism

Today virtually all activist groups are using new media to promote their causes. **Internet activism** (also known as e-activism, electronic advocacy, cyberactivism, e-campaigning, and online organizing) is the use of communication technologies such as e-mail, web sites, and podcasts for various forms of activism to enable faster, more interactive communication by citizen movements and to deliver messages to larger audiences. These technologies and social media such as MySpace and YouTube are used for cause-related fundraising, lobbying, volunteering, community building, and organizing. Such efforts can be mobilized very quickly. In the U.S., even before hurricanes such as Gustav and Ike in 2008 hit, bloggers, tweeters, and web designers came together to share experiences, information, and ideas. That same year in China, the instant messaging-based service Twitter was credited with breaking the news about the Sichuan earthquake even before the official earthquake tracking agency. QQ, another instant messaging program in Asia, had aggregated video shot by its users from many of the affected areas, while amazing footage from cellphones quickly found its way onto Tudou, a popular video-sharing web site. And on the fundraising side, China Mobile set up an effective system which lets subscribers donate by sending an SMS, which was then charged to their phone bill, sparking similar cellphone-based communication.

For some time, organizations have used the Internet to rally support for action and fundraising. MoveOn, a web-based liberal advocacy organization, raises millions of dollars for the Democratic Party. The group belongs to various coalitions, such as Americans Against Escalation in Iraq and Win Without War. MoveOn claims to have 3.2 million e-mail addresses of political progressives in America, although only about 10 percent respond to any given e-mail alert.

Carol Darr, director of the Institute for Politics, Democracy, and the Internet, thinks it works best as an organizing tool for "charismatic, outspoken mavericks" with outside appeal in elections.[26] Darr said the Internet also made it easier for small donors to play a meaningful role in financing political campaigns. "[The] Internet is tailor made for a populist, insurgent movement," said Joe Trippi, Howard Dean's campaign manager. Political observers think the Internet has considerable potential to reach and engage opinion leaders who influence the thinking and behavior of others.

And, according to *Business Week*, corporations are increasingly using the web to mobilize support for their causes, launching sites to lobby legislators and win support for takeovers. For example, cable giant Cox Communications launched makethemplayfair.com, a site intended to pressure ESPN and Fox Sports to lower their programming charges. Brewers and beer distributors lobby for lower taxes through rollbackthebeertax.com, and Kmart bolstered morale during its bankruptcy with kmartforever.com.

Critics of Internet activism suggest that negative discussions increase acrimony and increase extremism. They also warn that the impersonal nature of computerized communication may undermine human contact that is crucial to social movements. However, sites such as Meetup.com are used by activists to overcome just such social isolation that results from our television society.

Sports and Change

Like actors and musicians, sports professionals have also stepped up to promote social causes and endorse politicians. One of the more notable advocacy efforts by sports pros is the "Live Strong" wristband, a yellow silicone gel bracelet launched in May of 2004 as a fundraising item for the Lance Armstrong Foundation. The foundation was established in 1997 by cyclist and cancer survivor Lance Armstrong. The wristband itself was developed by Nike and its ad agency Wieden+Kennedy to promote the foundation's "Wear Yellow Live Strong" educational program. The program is intended to raise money for cancer research, raise cancer awareness, and encourage people to live life to the fullest. The bands have been sold as part of an effort to raise $25 million for the foundation. This target was achieved within six months and within a year more than 55 million wristbands had been sold. Yellow was chosen for its importance in professional cycling, as it is the color of the yellow jersey worn by the leader of the Tour de France.

Other charities were inspired by the success of the Live Strong wristbands, and have developed their own wristbands for raising money and awareness. Another innovative effort was made by NBA basketball star Stephon Marbury. Although often viewed as a controversial player, Marbury was praised for spearheading the development of an affordable basketball shoe to draw attention to making opportunities such as sports participation accessible for everyone (see *A Closer Look* at the end of this chapter).

Athletes as Advocates

Sports professionals have also become increasingly politically active. Contributions from professional sports donors to presidential candidates have been rising steadily over the past few elections. In the United States, typically professional sports figures have favored

Republican political candidates over Democrats, but in the 2008 campaign that gap narrowed significantly. By the start of the 2008 presidential conventions, professional athletes and executives had given $445,334 to the two nominees—55.8 percent to McCain and 44.2 percent to Obama, according to ESPN analysis of figures from the Center for Responsive Politics, a nonpartisan research group. With almost two months of campaigning still remaining, professional sports figures had already given twice as much money to all presidential candidates combined during the 2008 election as they had to candidates in each of the past two races.[27]

Candidates' popularity might have been fueling part of the increase, especially among Obama supporters, many of whom were first-time donors. Some sports scholars said donors were more motivated by law makers' interest in steroids, spying, and cheating in sports. Other issues such as rule-making for stadium financing, broadcast rights, and union contracts may also have played a role. It has been speculated that pro athletes have typically favored Republicans, believing that they would be more inclined to leave professional sports empires alone, whereas Democrats are viewed as pushing for more regulations. Pro sports donors also have trusted conservative leaders to take fewer taxes out of their big paychecks, said sports scholars and donors themselves.

In the 2008 election, however, pro sports donors were more divided. Sports agent and attorney Leigh Steinberg believes that race played a role as many African American athletes were drawn into Obama's campaign. African Americans account for about 8.2 percent of MLB players, 67 percent of NFL players, and 76 percent of NBA players according to 2008 figures from the Institute for Diversity and Ethics in Sports at the University of Florida.

NBA staff topped Obama's list of pro sports donors at $24,360. Obama's ties to basketball were well known. He played for his high school team in Hawaii and still shoots hoops to stay in shape. A YouTube video of Obama making a three-pointer was viewed almost a quarter-million times. Oddly enough, Obama's second-largest pro sports donor was a Chicago-based table tennis company called Killerspin, whose owners and employees gave $13,800 to Obama's presidential campaign.

Barack Obama meets with supporters and former Pittsburgh Steelers

McCain, however, still led Obama in support from professional athletics. McCain's biggest fans were in football. Six of McCain's top ten pro sports donors were with NFL teams, led by the San Diego Chargers, Dallas Cowboys, and Houston Texans. Chargers CEO Dean Spanos and Cowboys owner Jerry Jones were are among McCain's top fundraisers, helping bring in between $50,000 and $250,000 in donations by hosting parties or events at which they collected money from friends and associates.

Using Sports to Promote Patriotism

Considering the parallels between sports and religion (see Chapter 10), it is perhaps not surprising that religious, political, and cultural leaders have exhibited somewhat fickle attitudes toward sports, alternately embracing and opposing sporting activities.

This flip-flopping has largely centered on the question of whether sports support or threaten morality and good citizenship. Historically, sports organizers "often incurred the wrath or moral concern of dominant political and religious forces who abhorred the wasteful and dissolute behavior—drunkenness, wagering, violence and sexual promiscuity—that often accompanied [sporting events]."[28]

In AD 394, the Christians forced the Roman emperor to end all pagan rituals, including the Olympic Games.[29] In 1365 King Edward III issued an order that "able bodied men" who were at "leisure" on feast days should engage only in militarily useful "sport" using bows, arrows, and other approved weapons. Those who engaged in "vain games of no value like stone throwing, handball and football did so under 'pain of imprisonment.' "[30] Commitments to work and restrained leisure similarly led to the banning of the ancient football game in Ashbourne, Derbyshire, in 1860.[31]

Many authorities, however, worked to promote sports and physical activity as a way to "discharge unhealthy urges among the citizenry."[32] This view held that keeping the working class occupied with sports was preferable to allowing them to remain idle, free to engage in other vices or to become too weak to work or defend the country. Sports were seen as a means of promoting discipline, cooperation, leadership, and purity. It was this line of thought that led to the re-emergence of the Olympic Games in the late 1800s.

Today, sports and politics remain difficult to separate. National, state, and local governments allocate funds for school sports programs and other sports organizations. Local governments fund recreation facilities for public and professional sports use. Governments also pass legislation banning discriminatory practices in sports and restricting sports-related advertising and sponsorship of alcohol and tobacco products. Scholar David Rowe suggests an interesting role for the relationship between sports and government:

> [National governments] have invested heavily in sports and sports television (through national, public broadcasters) because of the highly effective way in which sports contribute to nation building. In countries divided by class, gender, ethnic, regional and other means of identification, there are few opportunities for the citizens of a nation to develop a strong sense of "collective consciousness," of being "one people."[33]

It is argued that events such as the Olympics are used to build patriotism and loyalty. Ironically, although there is some thought that countries that excel at sports appear more powerful and better capable of waging war effectively, it is also thought that international sporting competitions enhance international understanding and make actual military combat less likely. Similarly, sports are a popular diversion used to try to "straighten out" wayward youths. Again, it is reasoned that, in addition to keeping kids occupied and away from crime and violence, sports teach discipline, responsibility, and teamwork.

Not everyone, however, shares this optimistic view of modern-day sports. Marxist and neo-Marxist critiques of sports include accusations of racism, commercialism, militarism, nationalism, and imperialism. This disdain is usually limited to sports as practiced in capitalistic societies; in contrast, they embrace sports in socialized societies (such as the former Soviet Union) as benevolent, community-building activities. Many neo-Marxists are even more skeptical than Marxists; they disapprove of all sports, reasoning that governments use sports to divert potentially revolutionary energies away from political action. The argument, in essence, is that sports distract audiences from political and social problems and keeps them occupied so they have no energy or interest to rise up against their government. Or, as one author puts it, "the protest against political and economic injustice is drowned out by the spectators' mindless screams of ecstasy and rage as they identify with the gridiron gladiators and the stock-car drivers."[34]

Impacts and Influences

Chapter 5 outlined many theoretical explanations for how entertainment might be used to influence audiences' thoughts and actions. Many of these theories suggest different mechanisms for ways that entertainment can shape our views of politics and social issues, and are covered next. The prosocial effects of entertainment, educational games and the impact of media on children are also considerations for discussion in this section.

Theoretical Considerations

Agenda-setting would hypothesize that, with repetition, political and social messages in entertainment might only affect how important these issues are to us, whereas attitude change, social learning, dependency, and cultivation theories might suggest that entertainment advocacy may help shape and perhaps even change our opinions on political or social issues.

For example, if many of our favorite entertainers are endorsing a certain political candidate it might lead us to favor that candidate or at least to become more interested in politics. Similarly, films such as *Dead Man Walking* or *The Green Mile* might influence our thoughts and opinions about the death penalty, whereas songs such as Ani DiFranco's "Lost Woman Song," Ben Fold Five's "Brick," or Everlast's "What It's Like" might influence our thoughts about social issues like abortion, homelessness, and drug use. Both social learning and diffusion of innovations suggest mechanisms for how such messages might even influence our behavior. If fictional characters and celebrities are portrayed as being rewarded for certain behaviors such as voting, recycling, or donating to a charity, then audiences may be inclined to imitate this behavior. Likewise, if these same celebrities and "alpha consumers" are seen wearing "Live Strong" wristbands, soon these novelties may become more commonplace as they "diffuse" through the rest of society.

Prosocial Effects of Entertainment

Although many critics warn of potential negative impacts of media and entertainment, as some of the examples above have illustrated, they can also have positive impacts. Television, movies, music, sports, and video games often convey messages about tolerance and diversity, about honesty, cooperation, and friendship, about healthy habits, responsibility, and consequences. Although sports such as football and hockey can be very aggressive, they also often demonstrate positive values, such as teamwork and perseverance. Similarly, although video games may prevent some children from getting exercise or interacting with their peers, they may also sharpen reasoning skills and reflexes.

Indeed, research has found that the media can influence people, particularly children, in very positive ways.[35] A sizable body of research demonstrates that people, especially children, can and will model the good or social behaviors they see in the media. Research also suggests that media portrayals can encourage cooperation and constructive problem solving. Children's programs (such as the classic *Sesame Street*, produced by Children's Television Workshop, and Nickelodeon's *Blue's Clues*) are designed to educate and socialize children as well as to entertain them. And research suggests that these programs can be very effective. Furthermore, although the media and entertainment may shape our world, they are also reflective of that world. The media teach us about our society, values, customs, and concerns. The media show us parts of our world we might never see—African wildlife preserves, the top of Mt. Everest, hurricanes, snowstorms, the birth of a child. Not all of the stories and images are good; many do reflect the bad and the ugly of our society, but sometimes these stories and images can help us better cope with some of these less pleasant realities.

Sesame Street (original cast in 1969) was one of the pioneer television programs created to both entertain and educate its young viewers

Edutainment Combining entertainment with education is not new. In countries with rich oral histories, entertaining folktales with mores and larger-than-life heroes have been part of a child's informal education for thousands of years. Music, drama, dance, and other folk traditions have also been used for centuries in many countries for recreation, devotion, reformation, and instructional purposes. One of the most significant effects of the invention of books was the spread of education and literacy. The great increase in available reading matter after about 1650 promoted the spread of education to the middle classes, especially to women. The middle classes became readers of the prose novel in the eighteenth century while the less affluent bought almanacs and chapbooks containing stories or ballads. Non-fiction sells well today in the form of biography and scientific inquisition, bringing information to global readers. Today, educational institutions are a huge market for publishers of textbooks. Growth in the book trade led naturally to growth in libraries. Commercial lending libraries and free public libraries provide access to citizens from all walks of life. To the surprise of many booksellers who feared that free access would curb their sales, libraries have promoted rather than diminished the sales of books, and they are a market in themselves.

Although the educational impacts of entertainment media are not new, the concept of entertainment-education or "edutainment" in contemporary entertainment (such as radio, TV, comic books, and rock music) is relatively recent, emerging only in the last 25 years in forms of entertainment that have existed at least twice as long or longer. In radio, the first well-known example of edutainment began in 1951 when the British Broadcasting Corporation (BBC) began broadcasting *The Archers*, a radio soap opera that conveyed educational messages about agricultural development. In the late 1950s, a writer-producer trained at the BBC began experimenting with edutainment in Jamaican radio serials to promote family planning and other development issues. Edutainment for television was discovered almost by accident in Peru in 1969 through a television soap opera called *Simplemente María*. The program featured a single mother who worked and took adult literacy courses at night. As the program increased in popularity, the number of young women enrolling in adult literacy courses began to rise. Similar results were found when the program was broadcast in other Latin American countries. Among poor, working-class women, María became a role model for upward social mobility.

Inspired by this success, Miguel Sabido, a TV writer-producer in Mexico, developed a methodology for entertainment-education soap operas. Between 1952 and 1982, Sabido produced seven entertainment-education soap operas for social change that encouraged enrollment in adult literacy classes, consideration of family planning strategies, and acceptance of gender equality and other concepts. These shows were strong commercial hits, demonstrating that educational messages do not have to detract from the entertainment value of the programs. Since that time, this strategy has spread to many other countries, including India, Kenya, and Tanzania, promoting the same social messages and others, such as HIV/AIDS education.

The edutainment strategy has been used in a variety of ways, not only in TV and radio but also in films, print, and the theater. In India, Bangladesh, and Zimbabwe, films have been produced that contain social messages. Dr. Seuss in the United States and others around the world have produced books, comics, and cartoons to educate children and adults about social issues. Groups in India and other countries have used street theater and pantomime to promote educational messages. Edutainment has also been infused into rock music for promoting sexual responsibility among adolescents in Latin America and the Philippines, for promoting responsible parenthood in Nigeria, and in more than 60 other projects in more than 30 countries.

SPOTLIGHT ON EDUCATION   Using Edutainment for Social Change[36]

The designated driver concept was written into the story lines of the *Cosby Show* and other NBC programs

Writers and producers often incorporate specific messages or views into entertainment fare. In a book, film, or song, an artist might include a story line that makes a subtle or not-so-subtle statement about sexual harassment in the workplace or spousal abuse,

hoping that, in addition to entertaining audiences, the story might influence peoples' attitudes or behaviors about these societal issues. However, the entertainment industries have also embarked upon large-scale, collective efforts to change attitudes and behaviors about serious, social issues.

U.S. TV and Designated Drivers
In 1988, Harvard professor Jay Winsten launched a campaign to get the TV networks to push his novel "designated driver" concept. Today, most people are familiar with the term; a "designated driver" is the person in a group who abstains from drinking alcohol during an occasion and serves as the sober driver for everyone else in the group. Neither the concept nor the term existed until Professor Winsten, with the help of CBS executive Frank Stanton, contacted the chairman of NBC, Grant Tinker, and pitched his plan to use television programming to develop a new social norm. Tinker was intrigued by Winsten's

plan and helped him enlist the cooperation of the heads of the 13 companies that did most of the production for the major TV networks.

As a result, designated drivers were part of the story lines of 160 different prime-time shows in the following four network TV seasons. Winsten's designated driver message was viewed by hundreds of millions of viewers, and research suggests that these efforts did make a difference. Within one year of the introduction of the designated driver concept, 67 percent of adults said that they were aware of the concept. By 1991, 52 percent of adults under 30 years of age said that they had served as designated drivers. From the first year of the campaign in 1988 until 1997, the number of drunk driving fatalities dropped by 32 percent in the United States. Professor Winsten recognized that embedding such messages in prime-time TV wasn't a "magic bullet" that single-handedly injected the designated driver concept into viewers' thoughts and actions. But his work suggests that such messages can work as part of a larger strategy to make real cultural differences.

EDUCATIONAL GAMES   Games are also becoming popular edutainment tools. Board and flash card games have been used as a fun way to help people learn a variety of subjects like the game *Take-Off*, which was designed to help children and adults learn geography. The goal is to get your fleet of planes (two to four in all) across the map of the world—from Hawaii to Hawaii—before your opponents, by rolling dice, getting lucky, and answering questions about the nations of the world correctly from the deck of country profile cards. Video games have also been harnessed to create increasingly sophisticated entertaining learning platforms. One example of these is *DimensionM*, an immersive video game world that engages students in the instruction and learning of mathematics. Pre-algebra and algebra objectives are covered through a series of missions in a virtual game world similar to other recreational video games that kids enjoy. Some research even suggests that video games designed purely for entertainment may also have educational value. Research has not advocated the use of arcade style "shoot-'em up" games for educational purposes. A study in the U.K., however, concluded that simulation and adventure games—such as *Sim City* and *Roller Coaster Tycoon*, where players create societies or build theme parks —developed children's strategic thinking and planning skills. Parents and teachers also thought their children's mathematics, reading, and spelling improved.[37]

The military has used video games as a training tool since the 1980s. Now the practice is catching on with companies, too, ranging from Cisco Systems Inc. to Canon Inc. Corporate trainers are betting that games' interactivity and fun will hook young, media-savvy employees and help them grasp and retain sales, technical, and management skills. According to Digitalmill Inc., a game consultancy firm, video games teach resource management, collaboration, critical thinking, and tolerance for failure.[38]

The market for corporate training games is small but it is growing fast—these games make up 15 percent of the "serious," or non-entertainment market, which also includes educational and medical training products.

Playing an immersive video game that engages students in instruction and learning of mathematics

By 2010, the serious-games market is expected to double to $100 million, with trainers accounting for nearly a third of that. Companies like video games because they are cost effective. Why pay for someone to fly to a central training campus when you can just plunk them down in front of a computer? Even better, employees often play the games at home on their own time. Besides, by industry standards, training games are cheap to make. A typical military game costs up to $10 million, while sophisticated entertainment games can cost twice that. Since the corporate variety do not require dramatic, warlike explosions or complex 3D graphics, they cost a lot less. BreakAway Games Ltd., which designs simulation games for the military, is finishing its first corporate product, *V-bank*, to train bank auditors. Its budget? Just $500,000. Games are especially well-suited to training technicians. In one used by Canon, repairmen must drag and drop parts into the right spot on a copier. As in the board game *Operation*, a light flashes and a buzzer sounds if the repairman gets it wrong. Workers who played the game showed a 5 percent to 8 percent improvement in their training scores compared with older training techniques such as manuals. Games are obtained three ways: purchased outright for under $50,000, licensed by companies that pay a monthly fee to sponsor the game, or built for upward of $400,000.[39]

SPOTLIGHT ON ACTIVISM IN VIDEO GAMES   Saving the World with Games

Video games have long entertained users by immersing them in fantasy worlds full of dragons or spaceships. But a game called *Peacemaker* is part of a new generation: games that immerse people in the real world, full of real-time political crises. When used as a medium of change, "serious" video games are a movement with some serious brain power behind it. Advocates and nonprofit groups are partnering in the search for new ways to reach young people and maximize their educational potential.

Food Force, a game that helps people understand the difficulties of dispensing aid to war zones, was released by the United Nations in 2006. Serbian resistance leader Ivan Marovic produced a game that teaches the principles of nonviolent strategy. In *A Force More Powerful*, players must make dozens of decisions as they try to foment democratic uprisings, but each action brings unexpected consequences—a demonstration may get your leaders arrested by police, for instance.

Believing that young people raised on gaming are ready for a more mature medium, developers believe games can serve a variety of functions and become a good tool of communication. *Food Force* has been downloaded by four million players for free, and an online game called *Darfur Is Dying* had 700,000 people playing in its first month. By entering a political action area of the game, players can send e-mail messages to politicians and demand action on Darfur.

In all these games, players can teach themselves by trying things out. The major premise is that games are uniquely good at teaching people how complex

Food Force players must decide who should receive sacks of grain and other supplies

The game *Darfur Is Dying* attempts to make players more empathetic to the crisis in this region

systems work. Under development is a redistricting game in which players try to gerrymander different states, intended to show players how easy it is to rig the system. "A first grade class can fix Texas!" claims its developer who is a professor at Annenberg School for Communications.

Serious advocates say video games possess a persuasive element that is missing from books or movies: they let the player become a different person and see the world from new perspectives. *Peacemaker*, for instance, allows players to switch positions to see why the other side acted as they did. The game inspires an unusual kind of debate: an argument about how rule changes can affect society.

After the U.S. invaded Iraq in 2003, a professor and game developer in Copenhagen created *September 12*, which presents a gang of terrorists wandering through a packed Arab market in cartoon style. The player tries to bomb them but every explosion accidentally kills innocent bystanders. Relatives are driven by grief and anger to become terrorists themselves. The more you bomb, the more terrorists you create, until the screen is overrun with them. The game's argument: Bombing is not the way to win a war on terror. The impetus for serious game development is simple—if you're going to play games, why not learn something important in the process?

Source: Clive Thompson, *New York Times*, July 23, 2006

New Media Impacts on Children

Opinions about the impact of new media, particularly the growing popularity of youth-oriented virtual worlds (see Chapter 17), on the social and intellectual development of young children, have been mixed. Virtual worlds for children are very similar to those for adults. On web sites such as Club Penguin, children can create avatars, socialize, go on adventures, and play games. On the plus side, virtual worlds are argued to be a more "powerful and engaging" alternative to more passive entertainment such as watching TV. Some research further suggests that virtual worlds can be valuable places where children can rehearse what they will face in real life. In a study sponsored by the BBC, Professor David Gauntlett and Lizzie Jackson of the University of Westminster surveyed and interviewed children who were the first to test the virtual world Adventure Rock.[40] The online world is a themed island built for the BBC's CBBC channel by Belgian game maker Larian.

The research looked at the ways the children used the world and sought feedback from them on its good and bad aspects. Professor Gauntlett said the research revealed that children assumed one of eight roles when exploring a virtual world and using the tools they put at their disposal (see Table 13.3). At times children were explorers and at others they were social climbers keen to connect with other players. Some were power users looking for more information about the workings of the virtual space.

Professor Gauntlett said online worlds were very useful rehearsal spaces where children could try all kinds of things largely free of the consequences that would follow if they tried them in the real world. For instance, he said, children trying out Adventure Rock learned many useful social skills and played around with their identity in ways that would be much more difficult in real life. What children seemed to like about virtual worlds was

Table 13.3 Roles Adopted During Play

Explorer-investigator—focused on the game "quest" and solving the mystery
Self-stampers—focused on creating and personalizng their avatars
Social climbers—competitive, concerned with raising and posting their ranking
Fighters—frustrated that physical combat in the game was limited to beating the crocodiles
Collector consumers—collected pages and coins, wanted shops and gift-giving
Power users—played for 3+ hours, interested in how the game works
Nurturers—wanted to meet and play with others, wanted pets and a place to sleep
Life system builders—frustrated that they couldn't create new lands and add new elements

the chance to create content such as music, cartoons, and video and the tools that measured their standing in the world compared to others.

Many parents also defended these virtual worlds.[41] In contrast to adults who are often accused of using virtual worlds to escape real life and develop a separate identity, these parents view their children's virtual experiences as being extensions of their real-world relationships. Rather than meet new, possibly scary, strangers online, the kids were generally using the virtual worlds as a way to communicate with their friends from school. Then, they talk about it later (or concurrently) on the phone, or at school the next day. Some parents also argue that kids learn very real lessons regarding the relative costs of creating a "home." Kids may spend hours exploring, collecting, and buying the pieces necessary to build their worlds. For example, the Webkinz virtual world enables kids to create an online life for Webkinz stuffed animals they have purchased. Online marketer Todd Copilevitz argues for the value of these sites:

> My daughter is now scheming ways to afford her next Webkinz, #17 if I'm not mis-taken. Each has an online counterpart, that has friends, a home, a mortgage and rich world of imagination. Suddenly her world of imagination is being juiced by the online experience. That's something the PowerRangers never managed to deliver.[42]

Critics, however, do voice some concerns about these virtual worlds. Common Sense Media, which reviews many of these virtual worlds, says that problems can emerge in worlds such as Club Penguin when young kids try to be friends with other penguins who reject them. One reviewer explains that, "instead of using words to negotiate friendships, it's very easy in this virtual world to get a mean face icon in response to 'Wanna be friends?' Then the mean penguin is gone and the hurt, friendless penguin is left alone wondering what he did wrong. You can also throw snowballs at random penguins for no apparent reason."[43] Some parents have acknowledged that such experiences can be very upsetting for their children. Another criticism is that the sites promote materialism, rewarding game playing with money to buy "stuff" for your avatars. And you can get better "stuff" if you pay for a membership. Reviewers have also been concerned that playing in these worlds can become addictive. Although much research is still needed to explore both the potential benefits and harms that might be associated with children's online play, most experts recommend that parents spend time observing their children's virtual experiences, set limits, and balance time spent online with other activities.

The Value of "Old-fashioned" Play New media aren't the only element of contemporary play that has sparked concerns about children's educational and social development. According to Howard Chudacoff, a cultural historian at Brown University, radical changes in children's play can be traced to the TV debut of the Mickey Mouse club on October 3, 1955.[44] The show quickly became a cultural icon, a phenomenon that helped define an era, but the show itself is not Chudacoff's concern. What is less remembered but, he argues, more important, is that this is the day that the Mattel toy company began advertising a play gun called the "Thunder Burp." The reason the advertisement is significant is because it marked the first time that any toy company had attempted to peddle merchandise on TV outside of the Christmas season. According to Chudacoff, almost overnight, children's play became focused, as never before, on *things*—the toys themselves.

"It's interesting to me that when we talk about play today, the first thing that comes to mind are toys," said Chudacoff. "Whereas when I would think of play in the 19th century, I would think of *activity* rather than an object."[45] Chudacoff's recently published history of child's play argues that traditionally what children did when they played was roam in packs large or small, more or less unsupervised, and engage in freewheeling imaginative play. They were pirates and princesses, aristocrats and action heroes. Basically, Chudacoff contends, they spent most of their time doing what looked like nothing much at all. They improvised, made up their own rules and regulated their play. But during the second half of the twentieth century, play changed radically. Instead of spending their time in autonomous shifting make-believe, children were supplied with ever more specific toys for play and predetermined scripts. For example, instead of playing pirate with a tree branch they might play Star Wars with a toy light saber. Chudacoff calls this "the commercialization and co-optation of child's play"[46]—a trend which begins to shrink the size of children's imaginative space.

But commercialization isn't the only reason imagination may be threatened. In the second half of the twentieth century, Chudacoff says, parents became increasingly concerned about safety, and were driven to create play environments that were secure and could not be penetrated by threats of the outside world. Karate classes, gymnastics, summer camps—these create safe environments for children. And they also do something more: for middle-class parents increasingly worried about achievement, they offer to enrich a child's mind. The do so, however, in a much more formal, structured way than did traditional and spontaneous imaginative play.

Creative play

Change in Play, Change in Kids   Clearly the way that children spend their time has changed, and a growing number of psychologists believe that these changes in what children do has also changed kids' cognitive and emotional development. Playing make-believe is thought to actually help children develop a critical cognitive skill called executive function. Executive function has a number of different elements, but a central one is the ability to self-regulate. Kids with good self-regulation are able to control their emotions and behavior, resist impulses, and exert self-control and discipline.

Studies, however suggest that children's capacity for self-regulation has diminished.[47] A recent study replicated a study of self-regulation first done in the late 1940s, in which psychological researchers asked kids ages three, five, and seven to do a number of exercises. One of those exercises included standing perfectly still without moving. The 1940s three-year-olds couldn't stand still at all, the five-year-olds could do it for about three minutes, and the seven-year-olds could stand pretty much as long as the researchers asked. In 2001, researchers repeated this experiment. But, psychologist Elena Bodrova at Mid-Continent Research for Education and Learning says, the results were very different.

"Today's five-year-olds were acting at the level of three-year-olds 60 years ago, and today's seven-year-olds were barely approaching the level of a five-year-old 60 years ago," Bodrova explains. "So the results were very sad."[48] Self-regulation is believed to be incredibly important. Poor executive function is associated with high dropout rates, drug use, and crime. In fact, good executive function is a better predictor of success in school than a child's IQ. Children who are able to manage their feelings and pay attention are better able to learn. The reason make-believe is such a powerful tool for building self-discipline is because, during make-believe, children engage in what's called private speech: they talk to themselves about what they are going to do and how they are going to do it. And this type of self-regulating language has been shown in many studies to be predictive of executive functions.

Unfortunately, the more structured the play, the more children's private speech declines. Essentially, because children's play is so focused on lessons and leagues, and because kids' toys increasingly inhibit imaginative play, kids aren't getting a chance to practice policing themselves. According to researcher, Laura Berk, when they have that opportunity, the results are clear: Self-regulation improves.[49] Despite the evidence of the benefits of imaginative play, however, even in preschool young children's play is in decline. In some cases, teachers and school administrators may not see the value. The heavy emphasis on testing has led teachers to begin drilling students on their basic fundamentals earlier and earlier. Play may be viewed as unnecessary and a waste of time. As a result, teachers now often use what used to be free play time for structured activities to develop cognitive skills. It seems that in the rush to give children every advantage—to protect them, to stimulate them, to enrich them—our culture may have unwittingly compromised one of the activities that helped children most. All that wasted time was not such a waste after all.

FADE TO BLACK

Entertainment is an integral part of our lives. It can differently serve as a reflection of our world and as a projection of how it could be. As such, it cannot help but touch upon important societal issues such as governments, politics, health, education, and the environment, to name a few. In this chapter we have explored many ways that entertainment can serve as an advocate and an educator shaping what we know, think, and feel about issues and influencing our behavior as political and social citizens. It has documented the long history of the relationship between politics and entertainment as expressed through political satire, music, and sports. It has revealed how the blurring of news and entertainment in both traditional and new media and greater celebrity engagement has increased the role that entertainment is playing in politics. It has highlighted how both traditional entertainment and new media have been harnessed, both for political and social advocacy and for education. And, it has reviewed both praise and concerns for the ways in which different types of entertainment may impact our knowledge, opinions, and social and educational development.

A CLOSER LOOK AT ATHLETES AND ADVOCACY

Sneakers for Social Justice

Starbury One basketball sneaker

Stephon Marbury, the wildly talented and widely criticized point guard for the New York Knicks, usually carries a Q rating commensurate with Kim Jong Il. Making max dollars and being the face of the NBA's most dysfunctional franchise will do that. But Marbury has been drawing high-profile praise in recent days for promoting a new basketball sneaker described as "revolutionary."

What's "revolutionary" about the new Starbury One—a reference to Marbury's on-court moniker—is that it doesn't cost as much as a plane ticket to Maui. The Starbury Ones were listed at $14.98. That's $14.98. Not $149.80. As William Rhoden recently wrote in the *New York Times*, "This is an industry in which star athletes encourage children to buy shoes for anywhere from $75 to $200."

The shoe is not cardboard and canvas but serious and solid enough that Marbury pledged to wear them in NBA games. He says his motivation was rooted in discussions he had with Knicks GM Isaiah Thomas about the civil rights movement and Marbury's eventual legacy.

"[Thomas] was explaining to me how my generation never went through anything," Marbury told Rhoden. "There was a generation that went through things that we never even envisioned. For me to be able to talk with him, get insight on how things were back in the day, I got a picture of what he created for me to see. It made me feel like I want to put my mark on history as far as letting people know that I'm a part of something that I'm moving with. All this is brand new, this is revolutionary, the thing that we're doing right now." In tune with the idea of a sneaker for social justice, Marbury's web site urges visitors to "join the movement," and the chic insignia, familiar to those with a fascination for Che Guevara, is a stylized red star.

Marbury isn't all talk. He has a history of putting his money where his heart is. He pledged about $500,000 to help victims of Hurricane Katrina and then wept at a press conference. "It's not even about money," he said. "Now, it's more about everybody coming together and just trying to live as one. . . . I keep looking at my kids. You don't think about anything else, you just hold them so tight. They don't even know why you're looking at them like that. You want to cry in front of them, but they don't understand."

The Starbury One sneaker is being produced and retailed by Steve and Barry's University Sportswear—and they are flying out of the stores as quickly as they are being made. As Howard Schacter from Steve and Barry's told me, "The vision we shared with Stephon was to eliminate the incredible pressure kids and parents feel to pay top dollar for the latest and coolest sneakers and clothes. What we're saying is, You can pay a lot less for these things. . . . That message has definitely sparked a movement in this country, as consumers' eyes have been opened to the fact that it simply doesn't cost that much to make high-quality sneakers and clothes."

But the Starbury One—because of both its price and the fact that it is being marketed as footwear for social justice—has also invited scrutiny. The athletic shoe industry is notorious for some of the most appalling of sweatshop conditions. Are the Starbury Ones, made in China, produced in such a manner?

Schacter says no. "We are a member of the Fair Labor Association," he says. "More importantly, firmly embedded in our history and culture is a deep commitment to legal compliance and ethical business practices. This commitment is a fundamental part of the philosophy upon which we were founded."

Schacter says that costs are kept low because their business model "eliminates the middleman" by producing their own product and selling them in Steve and Barry's stores. They also rely on word-of-mouth instead of national advertising campaigns.

But some leading antisweatshop activists doubt this claim precisely because the shoe is manufactured in China. Jim Keady is a former professional soccer player and coach at St. John's University who is now co-director of the antisweatshop organization Educating for Justice. He is also a member of the City Council in Asbury Park, New Jersey. "One of the key ways to define a sweatshop is whether workers have the right to develop an independent, democratic voice in the workplace either by creating a worker-owned cooperative or an independent trade union,"

he said to me. "In China both cooperatives and independent trade unions are illegal, and therefore I would bet my professional reputation that these shoes are produced in sweatshop conditions. That said, Asbury Park has a poverty rate of 30 percent. I see kids buying sneakers I know they can't afford, so it is a good thing an affordable sneaker is available."

Scott Nova, from the Worker Rights Consortium, an antisweatshop monitoring group, also disagreed with Schacter's confidence in Steve and Barry's labor practices. "We have found serious human rights violations in factories producing for Steve and Barry's," he told me. "The company's response has been a mixed bag. In one case, the company did take action and progress was achieved. In another, we reported serious violations, including sexual abuse of women workers by managers. Steve and Barry's response was slow and ineffective.

"It is laudable that Steve and Barry's is offering affordable sneakers," Nova continued. "But there is another side to the moral equation: the workers who make the shoes. What are they paid? And what are their conditions of work? Ignoring worker rights could transform a worthy endeavor into another case of sweatshop exploitation. If the low price of these shoes means sweatshop conditions and sub-poverty wages for the workers who make them, then the positive purpose of the enterprise is severely undermined. Stephon Marbury is obviously trying to do something positive and deserves to be applauded for it. Addressing the worker rights issues will enhance his effort."

Marbury was not interviewed for this piece, but it's difficult to imagine him being unsympathetic to the plight of workers overseas. He has spoken out about selling sodas on the beaches of Coney Island as a young boy, trudging on the sand and trying to scrape a dollar or two from the tourists visiting the famed amusement park. It was a childhood that would be familiar to many children in the "market-Stalinism" world of China, where kids rush tourists offering cheap goods, attempting to get a crumb or two off the table.

As Jim Keady said, "The real slam-dunk would be if Stephon Marbury came forward and said, 'Not only do I want poor kids to be able to afford my sneakers.

I want their moms and dads to have good-paying factory jobs—in Coney Island, Bed-Stuy or Asbury Park for that matter.'" "Imagine that: a sneaker made for the players in Brooklyn by the people in Brooklyn," he said. "Would they be able to sell them for $14.98? Maybe not, but that would be a tremendous model that other athletes and other entrepreneurs could follow."

Source: Dave Zirin, *The Nation*[50]

What do you think?

- *Would Marbury's desire to promote social justice be better served by cheaper shoes or better working conditions?*

DISCUSSION AND REVIEW

1. What is the role of TV talk show hosts for presenting an unbiased view of political issues? Do you think that Oprah's endorsement of Barack Obama turned off her Republican viewers?
2. Explain how TV comedy uses agenda setting to make a political statement.
3. How would you use sports-based opinion leaders to advocate for a cause that did not revolve around sports? How would you make the connection between sports and the cause?
4. Review examples of the way entertainment has been harnessed for advocacy and education, as well as the praise and concerns that have been raised regarding unintended effects of entertainment on children's development.

EXERCISES

1. Go to an activist web site such as moveon.com and read its statement of purpose. How does its Internet presence impact visitors seeking information on the Democratic Party? Would the site appeal to independents as well? Why?
2. Using the editorial page of a large metropolitan newspaper, contrast the views in the political cartoons with the headlines that day. What is the relationship between the two? Do the cartoons show satire or bias?
3. Compare reading Shakespeare in its original form with viewing one of his plays as a film, such as *Midsummer Night's Dream*. Is watching the film version or using *Cliff Notes* the same as reading the original text? Does this make a case for or against entertainment as education?
4. Spend some time watching and/or interviewing several young children (between three and seven years old). Find out what they like to do for fun and have them tell you about their favorite toys and games. Take note of the extent to which they engage in activities that involve "imagination" and "free play." Do you see any patterns in temperament, personality, or maturity among children who spend more or less time engaged in imaginative/free play?

BOOKS AND BLOGS

Baylis, J., Smith, S. and Owens, P. (2008). *The globalization of world politics*. 8th ed. Oxford: Oxford University Press.

Cagle, D. and Fairrington, B. (2007). *The best political cartoons of the year*, 2008 edition. Toronto CA: Que Publishing.

Gibbons, A. (2007). *The Matrix ate my baby* (Educational Futures: Rethinking Theory and Practice). Boston MA: Sense Publishers.

Hauss, C. (2008). *Comparative politics: Domestic responses to global challenges*. Florence KY: Wadsworth.

Singhal, A., Cody, M.J., Rogers, E.M., and Sabido, M. (2003). *Entertainment-education and social change: History, research, and practice*. Mahwah NJ: Lawrence Erlbaum Associates.

www.crooksandliars.com—provides transcripts of *Meet the Press* interviews.

www.world-o-crap.com/blog—offers a daily diatribe about current events.

www.rolllingstone.com/rockdaily/index.php—lists the best protest songs.

www.politics-line.com—commentary from the political community of America's writers.

www.motherjones.com—an investigative news source for politics, commentary, and analysis.

14 MEDIA ENTERTAINMENT

The medium is the message.
—Marshall McLuhan

For about 100 years, media have brought news and entertainment into our homes. Today, media also come with us as we travel and go about our business. This chapter covers what's new and what's coming in our mediated world. Our coverage includes books, newspapers, magazines, radio, film, and TV, with an eye on trends in each medium.

Books and Publishing

The publishing industry produces a variety of publications, including magazines, books, newspapers, and directories. It also produces greeting cards, data bases, calendars, and other published material, excluding software. Although mostly producing printed materials, the publishing industry is increasingly producing its material in other formats, such as audio, CD-ROM, or other electronic media. These media are covered in this chapter for their contribution to the world of entertainment. Because publishing's origins have determined its progress, we cover it briefly to begin.

Early Beginnings

The history of publishing is characterized by the interplay of technical innovation and social change, each promoting the other. Publishing as it is known today depends on a series of three major inventions—writing, paper, and printing—and one crucial social development—the spread of literacy. Before the invention of writing, information could be spread only by word of mouth. Writing was originally regarded as a way to fix religious formulations or to record codes of law. Scripts of various kinds came to be used throughout most of the ancient world for proclamations, correspondence, transactions, and records; but book production was confined largely to religious centers.

Publishing in the modern sense—i.e., a copying industry serving a public readership—began with manuscripts in non-religious societies such as Greece, Rome, and China. The power of the printed word, as the saying goes, cannot be underestimated, even when challenged by electronic forms of content delivery.

Print has a long history, but many see the printing press as the origin of mass media. The oldest form of transferring ink to paper was accomplished using wooden printing presses as well as movable clay type and blocks. A surviving text from AD 594 indicates that printing originated in sixth-century China, and was probably stimulated by a need to examine Buddhist texts. Chinese innovations fed the technological push toward expanding the written word's range of influence. Wang Jie's *Diamond Sutra*, printed in 868, is the world's oldest known printed book. Between 932 and 953, 130 volumes of the Confucian classics were printed using a very labor-intensive arrangement of movable type to present an alphabet that uses thousands of visually specific ideograms.

Metal plates were used for printing by the eleventh century; movable metal type appeared in 1040. Learning block printing from the Egyptians, Europeans began using the process in 1375. In the early 1450s, rapid cultural change in Europe fueled a growing need for the rapid and cheap production of written documents. Gutenberg, a business-man from Mainz, Germany, developed a technology to address the economic bottleneck. His first printing job was the Bible. In 1476, England's first press printed Chaucer's *Canterbury Tales*, which was distributed by William Caxton. His contributions as an editor and printer won him a good portion of credit for standardizing the English language.

The church, the state, universities, reformers, and radicals were all quick to use the press. Not surprisingly, every kind of attempt was made to control and regulate such a "dangerous" new mode of communication. Freedom of the press was pursued and attacked for the next three centuries; but by the end of the eighteenth century a large measure of freedom had been won in Western Europe and North America, and a wide range of printed matter was in circulation. The mechanization of printing in the nineteenth century and its further development in the twentieth, which went hand in hand with increasing literacy and rising standards of education, finally brought the printed word to its powerful position as a means of influencing minds and, hence, societies.

Today in the U.S., much reading correlates with geography: consumers in the Northeast spend the most on reading materials; spending is lowest in the South. However, the ratio of customers to bookstores is highest in Nevada, Texas, and Mississippi. Perhaps this fact suggests bookstores are used for other purposes than buying books!

Publishing Issues

Publishing is a complex commercial activity during which words and illustrations are selected, edited, and designed. Publishers sell information in the forms of books, news-papers, directories, and periodicals that are copyrighted. Stimulated by the growth of professional authors, the spread of literacy, modernization of retailing, and the use of computers, publishing is the business of mass marketing printed forms of entertainment. Most publishing houses have their origins in printing or bookselling or both. Although mergers and acquisitions have created huge publishing conglomerates, electronic pub-lishing houses continue to emerge. With electronic publishing, data are communicated online to a customer's computer or transferred to a portable medium such as a disk or CD-ROM.

Unlike their electronic counterparts, printed documents are portable and user-friendly, and present content in a variety of ways. My recent experience with Tom Wolf's novel, *I am Charlotte Simmons* is an example of how print messages can be delivered and received. Excerpts of the book first appeared in a magazine where it came to my attention. Then I read a review of the novel in the newspaper, listened to an abridged form on audio tape and finally read the story in its entirety in a hard-bound volume. After completing the book, I heard the author read a chapter on radio and saw him interviewed on television. Then I attended a book signing for his autograph, and am looking forward to the movie version when it appears on screen. I gave the paperback edition to a friend for airplane reading.

Reading rendezvous

The versatility of mediated fiction and non-fiction allows content to be presented in forms that are convenient and affordable. Books go to the beach, magazines are available in flight, and newspapers keep us company as we commute to work. Nothing stimulates theater of the mind quite like the descriptions we read about faraway places, fascinating people, and suspenseful situations. Key to its endurance is print's ability to integrate content into our busy lives, keeping us informed, challenged, and entertained. Some of the disadvantages of print are due to its required focused attention and time consumption. Print's lack of sensory input may even serve as a welcome diversion from media overload.

Some of the issues that dominate the industry today involve piracy, multiple delivery methods, and technological innovation. After reading this chapter on the forms and content of print, you may be able to answer the question posed in the *Los Angeles Times Book Review*—"Is publishing dead?"

Portable Print: Soft and Hardbound Books

Book publishing is also dominated by a few very large companies, primarily based in New York City. However, some mid-size and small publishers across the country are thriving, particularly those that specialize in certain subjects. Textbooks and technical, scientific, and professional books provide nearly half of the revenues of the book publishing industry. The other half consists of adult trade—which is what is typically found in a bookstore—and juvenile, religious, paperback, mail-order, book club, and reference books.

Pessimists say books are anachronisms, things of the past, dying a slow death from competition such as web-based novels and books-on-tape. Our observation of the book publishing industry, however, shows healthy growth in specific genres like mystery novels and table-top compendiums that continue to be popular in spite of technology. In case you think all books are just airport reading material, consider the other major categories available for public consumption today:

- *Trade* books include adult, juvenile, fiction and nonfiction, hardbound and paperback. The largest market share in dollars and units is held by this category. Cooking and craft books occupy 11 percent of all adult books purchased. The best source of trade book titles is the *New York Times Book Review*.
- *Religious* titles are classified as nonfiction and are available in both hard and paper covers. Bibles and testaments make up the largest segment; religious biographies, histories, and inspirational works continue to be a growing market.
- *Professional* books in business, law, science, technology, and medical nonfiction are printed in both hardbound and paperback versions. English-language books sold globally are a growing market for publishers.
- *University press and college texts* continue to sell, although paperback editions are preferred by economy-minded students. This segment shows a growing electronic market.
- *ELHI* (Elementary/High School) consist of school textbooks of all genres and formats. A big business for publishers, ELHI accounts for 14 percent of national dollar sales. The market for electronic products is also growing in this category.

SPOTLIGHT ON DIGITAL RIGHTS

Publishing Industry Tackles Copyrights

Although there's no Napster for books, creators of text and images still have to deal with a lot of the same digital rights management issues perplexing the movie and music industries. Publishing industry experts at the Seybold 2004 trade show in San Francisco considered a variety of digital rights management (DRM) challenges during panel discussions, beginning with the proliferation of schemes for securing digital wares.

EReader, a leader in electronic books, uses a home-made licensing scheme for its downloadable books, with the encryption key for each book based on the credit card number used to purchase the book. The system pretty much eliminates public swapping of license keys, while giving broad rights to the purchasers. Rights Expression Language (REL), a standard published by the International Standards Organization (ISO), is a good starting point that would give publishers a common framework for communicating their copy-protection intentions.

Creative Commons, a nonprofit group promoting a "some rights reserved" approach to DRM, espouses similar goals but with different technology. Its approach would imbed each document with meta-data that tell the consumers what level of protection the author seeks. The approach has several advantages, including the ability to present multiple views of the rights documentation—a wordy legal version, a machine-readable version, and a "regular humans" version minus the legalese. See Chapter 8, for more discussion of Creative Commons.

While text publishers face some of the same DRM issues as entertainment studios—consumer acceptance, hackability versus ease of use—the industry also poses some unique challenges.

Source: David Becker, Staff Writer, CNET News.com, August 18, 2004

Book Marketing   Just writing or publishing a book doesn't mean anyone will buy it. To be successful, books of all types must be promoted. To that end, books are marketed in the following ways:

- *as mass market paperbacks* sold in airports, discount stores, warehouse clubs, food/drug stores, and supermarkets accounting for 20 percent of all units sold for a 6.7 percent market share
- *by book clubs*, which are a growing source of sales of fiction and nonfiction in both hard and paper formats and account for 18 percent of sales
- *in chain bookstores* such as Borders (26 percent of adult books bought here) and in small independent shops usually specializing in out-of-print, used (4 percent), or niche market books (20 percent)
- *by mail order*, which is declining in popularity (down to 5 percent) as a way to acquire titles
- *over the Internet* on sites such as amazon.com and barnes&noble.com, a growing market with no limits in sight.

And in the case of textbooks, through publishing representatives who sell directly to professors. More than half the books sold are distributed by non-bookstore retailers. Campus bookstores, libraries, schools, and wholesalers also distribute books to consumers. New titles, called *frontlist*, are the mainstay of most bookstores. *Backlist* titles, such as dictionaries and the Bible, remain in print and continue to sell long after publication.

The trick to getting books to readers is niche marketing, the identification and location of a book's audience. Aggressive news coverage and advertising campaigns account for the industry's increasing sales. Books written following a hit movie, for instance, benefit from the title's exposure. Titles become brands and are marketed as such by increasing awareness of a title's availability to its genre readers. Results of good marketing are best-sellers, which have trends of their own.

Book Trailers   The most visual form of book marketing has always been the cover design of a book's jacket. From its beginnings as a protective dust jacket to critical marketing component, the front cover and inside flaps did the most to capture a potential buyer's eye. Recently, a new marketing tool makes the book jacket obsolete—it's called a book trailer. This two- to three-minute video features the author and visuals that illustrate the book's content.

Essential for the book marketing mix, the trailer has become a popular way for publishers to promote new titles in an overcrowded market. Trailers on the Internet or on DVDs provide a new force of engagement for a media-savvy generation of readers, most of whom are connected to the Internet with broadband. Plus, they are less expensive than some other forms of book marketing. With production costs ranging from $2,000 to $5,000, trailers serve a variety of functions that include: securing media coverage, complementing virtual book tours, web ads, retail sales videos, presales material for book buyers, in-store video loops, and as book club promotions. Serving as both entertainment and advertising, book trailers even show up on YouTube. Production houses focusing on book trailers are Bookstream, Circle of Seven Productions, and Expanded Books. With the trailers come trailer awards, such as the Book Standard's Book Video Awards. And, like book covers of the past, trailers will develop into an art form that serves as a commercial message with its own set of rules and artistic devices.

SPOTLIGHT ON PR FOR BOOKS   Generating Word of Mouth

Each year, at least 50,000 authors are published in the United States. Tens of thousands of authors

publish electronic books. Most fail to get noticed. Very few achieve any of their goals as authors—to build up readership.

One way to get the word out and polish off a book before it hits the stores: sampling. Major corporations utilize focus groups, pollsters, and other marketing experts to build up their brand name. This is similar to planting seeds to get a garden or orchard to grow. The more seeds you plant, the better your chances to grow vegetables or apple trees. As an author, one can use sampling or "seeding," to build up book brand awareness.

Although most authors secretly fear peer reviews, here's reviewing with a twist. Instead of waiting until the book is published to read the reviews, post the book on a web site to accept all criticism in advance. Publishers of *Investing in the great uranium bull market: A practical investor's guide to uranium stocks* used a public peer review process.

Before posting the first eight chapters of the electronic version of this book, they notified subscribers to their stock-based web site that the book would be available on June 18 at 11:59 p.m. for Open Review. In the e-mail notification, they included a reminder to "tell a friend" about the book's pre-publication.

By the time this book was ready to be electronically published, the number of subscribers had jumped by nearly 10 percent! This marketing opportunity provided greater readership, and offered a broader range of opinions to improve the book. Previous tests, similar to this, have also drawn experts from the industry written about—in this case, the stock market. This adds more texture to the research, and ultimately creates a better product for readers.

Source: www.publishingcentral.com/articles/20060624-17-1d2e.html

Best-sellers

Trends are best characterized through the best-seller charts for fiction and nonfiction offerings. What follows is an overview of the fiction and nonfiction books that caught the imagination of the consumer during the first decade of the twenty-first century with sales that landed them on an annual top-ten list according to *Publishers Weekly*.[1] Calculations for the annual best-seller lists are based on shipped and billed figures supplied by publishers for domestic sales of new books.

Popular fiction accounts for half of the books purchased in the U.S. As a result of the Oprah Book Club, recommended books benefit from soaring sales following her adoption. A beneficiary of an Oprah promotion that began in November, 1996, when she launched her on-air book club was Robert Morgan. Pre-Oprah, Morgan had sold less than 12,000 copies; post-Oprah, about 638,000.

In 2006, one best-seller became a movie (*Da Vinci Code*), and the other resulted from a film (*The Devil Wears Prada*). The symbiotic relationship between film and fiction continues to grow, although some people who read the book version first say the film version never lives up to their expectations!

A big change for the industry began during the 1990s as a result of publishers' newly acquired skill of publication scheduling and the development of one-day *laydown* tactics, which feature massive distribution nationwide. Laydown distribution enables retailers to begin selling a book simultaneously using strong point-of-purchase displays and aggressive print and broadcast advertising campaigns.

Think about the books you take to the beach or the mountains, take on vacation, read on an airplane, or before you go to sleep. What kinds of pleasures do books provide you as reader that are not available from other forms of entertainment? How well does your imagination transform words into images? Is our electronic society keeping too many of us from enjoying a "theater of the mind"?

In addition to mental movies, reading provides us with in-depth information we cannot obtain from other sources in the form of **nonfiction** books. Nonfiction's popularity shifts and changes more often than fiction titles because politics, economics, and social issues have a more immediate impact on this group of best-sellers. What's hot and what's not depends on which entertainment and sports personalities are in the news. And which Hollywood star has written his or her memoirs. Unlike veteran best-selling novelists, the

FLASH FACT

The best works of American fiction of the last 25 years includes Toni Morrison's *Beloved*, which was chosen as the best American fiction written during that time by the *New York Times Book Review*. Runners-up were Philip Roth (*American Pastoral*), Cormac McCarthy (*Blood Meridian*), John Updike (*Rabbit Run*), and Don DeLillo (*Underworld*).

Author Toni Morrison was the 1998 Nobel Laureate

public taste in this arena is more fickle, and the 15 minutes of fame usually goes to new names.

How we dream and how we learn are often dependent upon our exposure to fiction and nonfiction books as we grow up. Depriving children of interaction with the printed word often stifles creativity and postpones their understanding of the world in which we live. By keeping popular print culture alive and well, we facilitate curiosity and develop an informed generation of citizens. Books are an inexpensive source of user-friendly entertainment—portable, poignant, and pleasing. Compare your best-seller experiences with those of a friend. What role do they play in your leisure time?

SPOTLIGHT ON BOOKS — All-time Best-sellers

Jaws sold over ten million copies

The top ten best-selling books of all time (fiction and nonfiction) are:

1. **The Bible**
   A recent survey, for the years up to 1992, put sales at six billion in more than two thousand languages and dialects.
2. **Quotations from Chairman Mao Tse-tung (Little Red Book)**
   Between the years 1966 and 1971 it was compulsory for every Chinese adult to own a copy.
3. **American Spelling Book by Noah Webster**

First published in 1783, this reference book by the American man of letters Noah Webster (1758–1843) remained a best-seller in the U.S. throughout the nineteenth century.

4. **The Guinness Book of Records**
   First published in 1955, *The Guinness Book of Records* stands out as the greatest contemporary publishing achievement.
5. **The McGuffey Readers by William Holmes McGuffey**
   Published in numerous editions from 1853, some authorities have put the total sales of these educational textbooks as high as 122,000,000.
6. **A Message to Garcia by Elbert Hubbard**
   Hubbard's polemic on the subject of labor relations was published in 1899 and within a few years had achieved phenomenal sales, largely because many American employers purchased bulk supplies to distribute to their employees.

7. **The Common Sense Book of Baby and Child Care by Dr. Benjamin Spock**

Dr. Spock's 1946 manual became the bible of infant care for subsequent generations of parents.

8. **World Almanac**

Having been published annually since 1868, this wide-ranging reference book has remained a constant best-seller ever since.

9. **The Valley of the Dolls by Jacqueline Susann**

This tale of sex, violence, and drugs by Jacqueline Susann (1921–74), first published in 1966, is perhaps surprisingly the world's best-selling novel. Margaret Mitchell's *Gone with the Wind*, which has achieved sales approaching 28 million is its closest rival.

10. **In His Steps: "What Would Jesus Do?" by Rev. Charles Monroe Sheldon**

American clergyman Charles Sheldon (1857–1946) achieved fame and fortune with this 1896 instructive religious treatise on moral dilemmas.

World's Best-selling Fiction

All the titles in this list have sold in excess of ten million copies in hardbound and paperback worldwide.

- Bach, Richard, *Jonathan Livingstone Seagull*
- Benchley, Peter, *Jaws*
- Blatty, William, *The Exorcist*
- Caldwell, Erskine, *God's Little Acre*
- Heller, Joseph, *Catch-22*
- Lee, Harper, *To Kill a Mockingbird*
- McCullough, Colleen, *The Thorn Birds*
- Metalious, Grace, *Peyton Place*
- Mitchell, Margaret, *Gone with the Wind*
- Orwell, George, *Nineteen Eighty-Four, Animal Farm*
- Puzo, Mario, *The Godfather*
- Robbins, Harold, *The Carpetbaggers*
- Salinger, J.D., *Catcher in the Rye*

The Guinness World Records' entry for *Best-selling Fiction Author* finds **Agatha Christie** at the top, with an estimated two billion copies of her works sold.

Publishers Weekly compiles lists every year of the best-selling hardbound fiction, hardbound non-fiction, trade paperback, and mass market paperback books of the past year. You can check for these on its web site or through the Information Please Almanac's section on Books, if you like.

Source: © The Regents of the University of Michigan

Who Done It? Mystery Novels

As evidenced by the sales of Clancy and Grisham, detective fiction is the most popular genre selling today. It all began with Edgar Allan Poe's *Murder in the Rue Morgue* (1841), considered the first true detective story. Detective fiction is usually divided into two schools: the classical school which features the intellectual detective (Sherlock Holmes and Poirot), and the American hard-boiled school, best represented by the writings of Dashiell Hammett. The genre also includes such sub-genres as the spy story (James Bond), the enforcer story (*Day of the Jackal*), the anti-thriller (Le Carré novels), and the police procedural (McBain novels).

Phillip Marlowe, the first world-weary detective who chased slinky femmes fatales, was created by Raymond Chandler in a 1940s mystery, *The Big Sleep.* Borrowing from Greek tragedy, Donna Tartt's *The Secret History* (1992) introduced the reverse mystery where the reader knew "whodunit" from the beginning. Alfred Hitchcock embraced this format for his suspense thriller films.

Charming, old-fashioned puzzle mysteries like Agatha Christie's *And Then There Were None* have been around for years. But in 1977 when Marcia Muller wrote *Edwin of the Iron Shows*, the first tough female private eye (Sharon McCone) began solving crimes. Female dicks? Yes. Gutsy female detectives contribute a sense of adventure and companionship for women travelers who thrive on these mass-marketed, portable novels. Women detectives, as the antithesis of their smoking, drinking, and womanizing male counterparts, bring humanity to mysteries.

SPOTLIGHT ON MYSTERIES Mystery Series Featuring Female Detectives

Female detectives with a series of mysteries to their credit are:

Detective: Lindsay Boxer. A San Francisco homicide inspector, Lindsay solves homicides with the aid of her friends. Claire is a medical examiner, Jill is an assistant district attorney, and Cindy is a crime reporter for the *San Francisco Chronicle.* Together, they call themselves the Women's Murder Club. Pooling their talents, this unlikely alliance proves to be unstoppable when it comes to finding a killer. Series by James Patterson.

Detective: Carlotta Carlyle. Six-foot-one red head Carlyle is a former Boston cop and sometimes cabbie.

She sets herself up as an independent private investigator ready to deal with anything from lost pets to grand larceny. Series by Nevada Barr.

Detective: Jane Marple. Miss Marple is a world-famous sleuth who is shrewdly inquisitive. Her knowledge of human nature gives her the insight necessary to solve crimes. Series by Agatha Christie.

Detective: Stephanie Plum. Bounty hunter Stephanie Plum tracks down bail jumpers in Trenton, New Jersey. Her bounty hunter pal Ranger often steps in to advise her and vice-cop Joe Morelli also joins in her cases. Series by Janet Evanovich.

Detective: Precious Ramotswe. Precious sets herself up as Botswana's first female detective. She spends the money she got from selling her late father's cattle to set up a Ladies' Detective Agency. Once the clients start showing up on her doorstep, Precious enjoys a pleasingly successful series of cases. Series by Alexander McCall Smith.

Detective: Jane Whitefield. Whitefield is a Native American guide who leads people out of the wilderness, not the tree filled variety, but the kind created by enemies who want you dead. She is in the one-woman business of helping the desperate disappear. Thanks to her membership in the Wolf Clan of the Seneca tribe, she can fool any pursuer, cover any trail, and then provide her clients with new identities. Series by Thomas Perry.

Readers of both sexes enjoy following their heroes and heroines as they solve intricate crimes. "Who done it" books continue to be popular as travel companions and late-night diversions among people who like suspense enriched with their own visions of action adventure that isn't available on a neighborhood movie screen.

Out for Show: Coffee Table Books

A philosopher once said that "we are what we read." But some books are not meant to be read. Skimming appreciably is a more suitable term for perusing stylishly photographed volumes of oversized images. Gift books with price tags that show you care enough to send the very best cover subjects from art to cooking. One handsome object popular with the haute **Hollywood** crowd is *Vanity Fair's Hollywood*, which provides a glimpse into an alternate universe. This book is basically a huge fan magazine as devoid of critical or historical sensibility as a bound volume of *Modern Screen* magazine.[2] Here, stars are presented in their purely glamorous essences. Featuring photographs by Annie Leibovitz, *Vanity Fair*'s book includes Madonna with child, Harrison Ford shaving in his underwear, and Kristin Scott Thomas without her shirt. As readers, we become voyeurs of the rich and famous, peeking into their private spaces and wondering how the photographer persuaded them to strike such poses.

You might also peek at *Hollywood candid*, 150 of photographer Murray Garrett's favorite black and white images of the 1950s when stars welcomed "at-home" photo shoots. Humorous, often revealing shots include Joan Crawford without makeup, Ava Gardner laughing with the kind of naturalness she never showed on screen, and Marlon Brando at home with his cat. This *Time*, *Life*, and *Look* photographer shows stars at their most compelling—when they are most candid.

A day in the life series features photos taken during a single day in a specific state, and makes for great perusing. Or you can stylize your surroundings with books on **fashion**. *Giorgio Armani* is a lavish volume that features Richard Gere and countless supermodels in the designer's minimalist creations. And *China chic* is a crimson-themed style guide that engagingly melds the history of cutting-edge Eastern culture with designer Vivienne Tam's own life journey. **Travel** journeys are also popular as books. *Jungles* brings you close-ups of rubbery, fluorescent orange frogs frozen in air to stunning vistas of a sun-splashed lake at dawn in such places as Hawaii, Madagascar, and Costa Rica. *Brazil incarnate* presents a hedonistic essence in each scene in the land of coffee, *carnivale*, and catwalkers. In black and white shots of everyone from cruising teens to primping cross-dressers, the Argentinian-born photographer Anthony Suan illuminates this locale.

Take a **historical journey** through *The postcard century: 2000 cards and their messages*, a book featuring every imaginable image from Lindbergh's *Spirit of St. Louis* (1927) to brightly thonged beach-goers (1990). Or get in touch with the 1960s through *Linda McCartney's sixties*, which provides photographs and commentary on the beginnings of rock 'n' roll and the music of the times. With 221 duo-tone and 32 color illustrations, the book's most interesting aspect is its inside-look at the Beatles, and particularly the author's husband, Paul.

Big sellers for publishers, books for display and giving often become sale items within a few years of publication. Price reductions do not diminish their popularity or their place in the living rooms of America. These books act as reflections of both the giver and the receiver, and often rate prominent places atop tables and podiums. People may define themselves through their collection of table tableaus. In an era of visualization, elegantly photographed compilations serve as illustrated histories and treasuries of all that is desirable. Next time you visit a friend's home, check out the coffee table books on display. What do these books say about their owner?

Comic Books

Sensing the popularity of comic strips that appeared in newspapers, artist/authors began publishing "feature-length" stories in book form. Comic books became popular during World War II among soldiers away from home who needed relaxation. But their reach and gratification goes way beyond relaxation for displaced Americans. Once described as "movies on paper,"[3] comics impact the fantasy lives of children, giving them superpowers to defeat the monsters of their dreams. Soon, monsters became warmongers armed with savage weapons. When comic violence became prevalent, the industry established self-censorship against violence and promoted domestic drama, gag strips, political satire, parody, and adult comics instead.

Superman, a gentle savior, is the purest example of the American superhero.[4] Motivated by an abstract concern for justice and fair play, Superman transcends nationalistic and religious boundaries. He hides his powers in the guise of journalist Clark Kent; both sides of Superman view the world objectively from the perspective of an outsider. Fighting for "truth, justice and the American way," Superman was the embodiment of all the values that Americans cherished in the 1930s when he was conceived to shore up the sagging spirits of a county that had lost its innocence in the Great Depression. His mission was not to punish the wicked but to save the innocent. He helped victims in the Tennessee flood valleys and the Oklahoma dust bowl, and rebuilt slums for the poor.

The presence of Superman dictated a change in the concept from hero to superhero, transcending reality into magnificence. Superheroes had few personal relationships and no sexual contact with mortals, no distractions from saving the world, and a sense of objectivity. Serialization enabled the superhero to move from adventure to adventure without restrictions, the basic plot pattern for comic heroes. Superheroes continue to exist to the present day, mostly because of the intervention of the editor of Marvel Comics, Stan Lee. Lee made superheroes flexible by giving them more human personalities.

SPOTLIGHT ON WRITERS   Stan Lee

One of the most prolific **cartoonists**, Stan Lee, aged 87 in 2009, is still producing out of his Encino (California) based offices. Creator of Spider-Man, the Incredible Hulk, the Thing, and the X Men, Lee created superheroes for kids in the 1960s and 1970s that are now appearing on the Internet. What makes Lee different is that his heroes are more absorbing than invincible, defined as much by their weaknesses as their strengths. Lee characters face real-life dilemmas and mundane problems—like family fights—similar to what readers experience themselves.

Spider-Man, for instance, is neurotically obsessed with status and worldly success, and hates to fight. The members of the Fantastic Four, a nontraditional family unit, spend almost as much time fighting among themselves as they do confronting bad guys. The Incredible Hulk was really Bruce Banner, a meek nuclear scientist transformed into a brutal behemoth by a gamma ray bomb.

All of his characters are the kind of heroes America seems to need and identify with. Spider-Man's motto is "With great power comes great responsibility." Lee's superheroes have influenced artists, writers, and filmmakers who prefer action to violence. Lee says he doesn't like too much violence, choosing instead action-packed stories that parents want their children to read.[5] Lee writes in the present tense, and his superheroes posses an immediacy that allows them to live on in popular imagination.

Although superheroes are still part of our popular culture, they have been updated for film, TV, and video games. Clark Kent, although still a wimp, is now a TV anchorman instead of a newspaper reporter. The

Fantastic Four still fly off from their apartment to fight Dr. Doom, even though they are distracted by mundane tasks like tenant meetings. Our superheroes sew themselves into new costumes (Spider-Man), pin traveler's checks inside their pants' waistband (Hulk's Bruce Banner), and get new parents (Superman) to make the fantasies more palatable to today's sophisticated audiences. Distinctions between right and wrong are not as clear cut for our more trendy versions of superheroes, but the bad guy usually still gets punched out in the end. Readers no longer rely on all-purpose superheroes, preferring instead multiple characters that possess both vulnerable and heroic qualities.

What do you think?

- *What does this shift from superhero to more humanistic "every-person" say about today's popular culture?*

Alternative Comic Books   Preferring adult readers, alternative comics are almost entirely written for and by men. The genre's roots are traced to books by Robert Crumb, the man whose *Zap Comix* defined underground comics in the 1960s. Recently successful alternative artist Daniel Clowes writes and draws *Eightball*, a series of comics aimed at adults. Influenced by everything from "Peanuts" to punk rock and magic realism, Clowes's memoir-like narratives have raised the medium to a new art form.[6] He is sponsored by the largest publisher of alternative comics, Fantagraphic Books, which features many of the country's best artists.

Clowes's stories are dreamlike and disturbing, set in Hopperesque bars and motels where lonely men are haunted by nightmares, rumors of the Apocalypse, and sexual drives. What distinguishes him is his gem-cutter's touch with language. His best known work is *Ghost World*, a 1998 graphic novel about Enid and Becky, two disaffected high school graduates who mock everyone as "pseudo-Bohemian" losers. This affecting portrayal of adolescence was made into a film of the same name. He also sells frames of his comics as pieces of art.

Today, the cross-pollination between cartoonists and artists produces work that appears in galleries and coffee table publications. Cartoonist Chuck Jones' galleries exhibit individual frames of his cartoon characters that are sold for thousands of dollars. In works such as these where art and words are conceived and fused into a single medium, comics become the mutant sister of fiction that does everything fiction can, and often more.

Social Print

Have you ever taken a date or met a friend at a bookstore for coffee or a book signing? If not, you're in the minority. Providing coffee cafes, reading areas, listening areas, and even discussion venues, bookstores have made reading a fashion statement. San Francisco's Borders, located in a multi-story venue just off Union Square, attracts hundreds of browsers and buyers who spend their evenings with print.

With multiple outlets in metropolitan areas, Borders and Barnes & Noble have put "occasion" back into book browsing. They have become quasi-libraries, complete with comfortable chairs, tables for doing research, and no "hands-off" policy for reading anything on shelves regardless of your intention to buy. More traditional booksellers such as Rizzolis that restrict their offerings to more high-end titles may have started the trend, but bigger has become better.

Discovering specialty bookshops like City Lights in San Francisco, and rare book emporiums is certainly more interesting, but their spaces often lack the social opportunities available at the larger retailers. Mega-bookstores offer popular events to stimulate traffic and host authors, critics, musicians, and scholars for intimate gatherings that conclude with opportunities to purchase. The phenomenon of collective book browsing provides a counter-activity to individual web browsing, and seems to be gathering momentum if our experience with Borders is any indication of its popularity. And by integrating popular brand coffee houses into their venues, bookstores have combined an ideal purchase environment for reading and socializing.

Publishing Outlook

Over the period 2004–14, wage and salary employment in publishing, except software, is projected to grow 7 percent, compared to 14 percent growth for all industries combined. As the need for news and information continues to grow, the publishing industry will be in the forefront. Books, newspapers, and magazines, produced in a variety of media, will be needed to keep people informed. However, efficiencies in production and a trend toward using more freelance writers will dampen employment growth.

Periodical and book publishing, along with miscellaneous publishing, will likely grow more slowly than in the past. Although mergers are becoming less frequent within the book publishing business, they are expected to continue in magazine publishing, leading to more efficiencies, thus slowing growth in employment.

However, several types of publishing should see increased growth. The segment of the industry producing textbooks is expected to benefit from a growing number of high school and college students over the next decade and the need to implement new learning standards in classrooms. Since 2002, undergraduate enrollment levels have been rising fastest in four-year colleges and for full-time rather than part-time students. Textbooks now account for over 40 percent of industry-wide sales, up from only 25 percent in the early 1990s.

Technical and scientific books and journals also will be needed to relay new discoveries to the public. Custom publishing, in which a specialized firm, magazine publisher, or newspaper publisher produces customized newsletters and magazines for clients, also is expected to grow, as more businesses and organizations use this format to directly market new products to clients and retain customer loyalty.

Once threatened by the challenge of electronic media, publishers worldwide now recognize the continuing need for print. Content is now available to us in multiple languages and physical forms. We can get books on tape and CD, and even download books on our computers and palm devices. The fact that most newspapers and magazines provide web sites where much of their editorial is available online indicates publishers' acceptance of complementary—not competitive—modes of presentation. Books and films are often released to promote the other format; films stimulate the paperback version and hardbound often initiates movie renditions.

The point is that, in spite of rumors to the contrary, **publishing is alive and well**. In fact, it's enjoying a very prolific and prosperous decade. If you have any doubts, log on to www.amazon.com and browse the plethora of reading matter. Or visit your local mega-bookstore to check out the endless aisles of global newspapers, magazines, fiction, and nonfiction offerings. With its new infusion of product, publishing is undoubtedly thriving in your neighborhood. And in your college bookstore!

Impact of Books on Society

The most significant effect of books was the **spread of education and literacy**. The great increase in available reading matter after about 1650 promoted the spread of education to the middle classes, especially to women. The middle classes became readers of the prose novel in the eighteenth century while the less affluent bought almanacs and chapbooks containing stories or ballads. Nonfiction sells well today in the form of biography and scientific inquisition, bringing information to global readers. Today, educational institutions are a huge market for publishers of textbooks.

Growth in the book trade led naturally to **growth in libraries**. Commercial lending libraries and free public libraries provide access to citizens from all walks of life. To the surprise of many booksellers who feared that free access would curb their sales, libraries have promoted rather than diminished the sales of books, and they are a market in themselves.

Censorship declined in Europe and was abolished completely by the mid-nineteenth century. In the United States, censorship has always been exercised through the courts under the law of libel. Efforts to suppress printed matter have centered on questions of libel, obscenity, or national security. Many countries still censor their citizens' reading options.

Piracy, often the result of copyright infringement, allows books to be printed and distributed without paying royalties to the author and the publisher. Commonplace in China and the Middle East, book piracy is less prevalent since the advent of CD versions.

Black and White and Read All Over: Newspapers

Weighing a fraction as much as coffee table books, newspapers carry reams of information in a portable format. A British author once said that "a community needs news for the same reason that a man needs eyes. It has to see where it is going."[7] For William Randolph Hearst, one of America's most important newspaper publishers, news was "what someone wants to stop you printing: all the rest is ads."[8] Both motives have contributed to the development of modern newspapers, which continue to attract millions of regular readers throughout the world despite stern competition from radio and TV.

Newspapers can be published daily or weekly, in the morning or in the afternoon; they may be published for the few hundred residents of a small town, for a whole country, or even for an international market. Newspapers differ from other types of publication because of their **immediacy**, characteristic **headlines**, and **coverage** of a miscellany of topical issues and events. Newspapers shape opinions in the "global village" where international concerns and issues are reported and debated.

Newspapers employ the largest number of workers in the publishing industry. With a staff of reporters and correspondents, newspapers report on events taking place locally and around the world. Despite the local nature of most newspaper reporting, the newspaper industry is dominated by several large corporations that own most of the newspapers in the country. It also is becoming common for companies to buy several newspapers in a single region, called "clustering." In this way, newspapers can be produced more efficiently. For example, advertising sales agents can now sell advertising space for multiple newspapers, which also share the same printing plant.[9]

Newspapers account for more than $45 billion in activity each year in the U.S. More than 60 million newspaper copies are purchased every day, and 55 million copies of paid and free circulation weekly newspaper circulate each week.[10] Of the 10,000 newspapers published in the United States, fewer than 15 percent are dailies. The ramification of this statistic on the industry is profound. To understand how the popularity of daily papers has diminished, we must look at the other ways news reaches us.

Nine general categories characterize newspapers. They are:

- international and national daily—*USA Today, Wall St. Journal*
- metropolitan and/or regional daily—*Boston Globe*
- local daily—*Orange County Register*
- non-daily general audience—*San Francisco Bay Guardian*
- minority—*American Arab Message*
- secondary language—*Chinese Times*
- religious—*Christian Science Monitor*
- military—*Hawaii Navy News*
- specialty—*Women's Wear Daily, Law Bulletin*

Newspaper Readership

According to the Newspaper Association of America, newspaper readership continues to be strong in the top 50 U.S. cities or regions, although BetaNews reported in September 2008 that readership was down among younger adults. But online TV viewing is on the rise, with news the most popular content category. Twenty percent of today's consumers are getting their news online rather than from newspapers and traditional broadcast TV, according to some industry surveys.[11]

Online newspaper users are younger than non-users, with 40 percent of users falling in the 18–34 age group. Non-users in this category represent 36 percent of the total.[12] If print readers and newspaper web site users are combined, newspapers are reaching significantly more adults in the market, particularly for younger demographics. The total number of non-readers uncovered by a spring 2008 survey by the Readership Institute was 36 percent. Yet readers spend an average of 27 minutes per weekday reading daily newspapers and 57 minutes on Sunday.

Newspaper Functions

Newspapers have served as our source of news since the invention of the printing press. After breaking ties with politicians and unions, today's serious newspapers have moved toward providing in-depth detail, analysis, and opinion on many current events. The quality of newspaper coverage of business affairs, the arts, and social issues is increasingly important as publishers deal with more sophisticated readers.

In addition to the latest local and global happenings, newspapers provide us with commentary and opinion. The Editorial page provides views on issues of economic and political importance, but what we enjoy most are the humorous takes on daily routines that run the gamut from mundane to the profound. Columnists often give us reports on what's happening socially—a kind of gossip column. A handful of star columnists are responsible for entertaining readers with humor and parody, serving to draw subscribers and Sunday readers. Commentary also comes to us as political cartoons. These satiric caricatures of notables and dignitaries poke fun at government and military figures so that readers may see the whimsical side of newsworthy events.

And although newspapers may not be the most entertaining medium, they are the gateway to entertainment news. Calendar sections provide readers with current events, reviews, and trends in the arts and film industries. When it's time to go to the movies, we turn to the newspaper for listings and locations. Reading about the stars and perusing the attraction ads are preliminary to most forays into entertainment activities. For those of us who enjoy breakfast with the morning news, or prefer a folding device for convenient travel to work, no other medium rivals the newspaper for currency and convenience.

Funny Pages

Visual narratives appear in all print genre. Cartoons bring to mind one-panel illustrations that you might cut out and tape to your refrigerator or office door. Comics are a series of drawings that read as narrative and are usually found arranged horizontally in newspapers, magazines, or books. Comic strips are multiple panels in a gag-delivery system, and comic books are stories about superheroes. Graphic novels often imply violence, while comics are more viewer-friendly.

The first **cartoon** appeared in 1734 but they were not prevalent until the mid-1800s when the first issues of *Punch Magazine* in London and *Puck Magazine* in America were printed featuring cartoon covers. Early in 1900, comic strips ("Buster Brown," "Mutt and Jeff") appeared in New York and San Francisco newspapers. By 1920, "Captain and the Kids," the "Katzenjammer Kids," and "Felix the Cat" appeared as strips and "Buck Rogers" was presented in the *Amazing Stories* comic book August issue.

By the end of the decade "Tarzan" and "Popeye" were born, and the 1930s gave us "Blondie," "Mickey Mouse," "Dick Tracy," "Alley Oop," "Lil Abner," "Flash Gordon," and "Secret Agent X-9." By 1936, comic syndicates were established and detective and action comics (*Superman*) made their debut. Marvel comics, "Batman," and "Donald Duck" emerged two years later. By the 1940s we had "Wonder Woman," "Pogo," and western comics to choose from. "Dennis the Menace," "Miss Peach," and "Andy Capp" hit newspapers; Jules Feiffer began his syndicate in the 1950s. The first comic book convention was held in New York in 1963, and in 1966 the first museum of cartoon art was established in Omiya, Japan. By the 1970s we had "Wizard of Id," Marvel superheroes, "Hagar the Horrible," "Scooby-Doo," "Flintstones," "Yogi Bear," and "Bullwinkle and Rocky."

"Peanuts" was Charles Schultz's popular newspaper comic strip

Comic Strips   Comic strips are so are popular among newspaper readers that some get the paper just to read the funnies. Comic strips fall into ten main categories:[13]

- *Gag strip*—depends upon an anecdote that ends with a bang in the fourth panel; continuity comes from the cast of characters ("Peanuts").
- *Single protagonist strip*—includes minor characters and a story line with changing scenes ("Orphan Annie").
- *Fixed cast strip*—story line and guest characters who live out long or short episodes (villains in "Dick Tracy").
- *Cartoon situation*—no story line ("Blondie").
- *Passage-of-time strip*—characters grow up and age realistically ("Gasoline Alley").
- *Special-milieu strip*—one theme ("Joe Palooka" and boxing, "Steve Canyon" and flying).
- *Adventure strip*—heroic-adversity nature ("Superman").
- *Fantasy strip*—usually based on mock-human animals ("Donald Duck").
- *Chain-of-subjects strip*—uses a variety of settings and topics and settings (fun of golf, joys of childhood).

- *Serious strip*—continuous story of the past ("Prince Valiant") or an uplift chronicle ("Mary Worth").

Newspaper Trends

The rising costs of paper and delivery have caused metropolitan dailies such as the *Los Angeles Times* to provide readers with diminishing editorial in exchange for pervasive advertising. Operated from advertising sales, newspapers receive 52 percent of their revenues from *retail* advertising and 36 percent from *classified* ads; *national* ads account for only 12 percent of advertising receipts. Advertising rates are based on circulation and readership, which are declining steadily. As a result, most metropolitan cities can support only one daily newspaper. In their continuing struggle to retain readers, metropolitan dailies have added sections on lifestyle, international business, health, and local news.

The financial strategies of the last two decades brought gains, but in retrospect may also have deferred long-term problems. Chasing demographics rather than readership was a lucrative strategy. But the industry invested comparatively little in things like training, research, and development, or in long-term projects to attract lost or emerging audience groups. If you were making a lot of money, what was the marginal advantage of investing heavily in more newsgathering to chase less affluent readers?

Trends indicate that, although daily circulation is down, Sunday editions and community weeklies are growing in popularity. As more people turn to magazines for national news and TV for local news, newspapers concentrate on features about local personalities, school team sports, and community events. They include calendar sections to provide entertainment reviews, information on performing arts, and movie listings. And they attract shoppers with classified ads and coupons.

Business Day[14] reported on a growing trend among large newspapers to accept some circulation declines because of the high expense of attracting and keeping new subscribers. Yet now the industry faces an important question. Given their history and their relative strengths, do newspapers believe that if they invest in creating new content and even new kinds of newspapers they can attract new readers? Or is this a mature and declining industry where investing in those things would be throwing money away?

Newspapers from around the globe

Magazine Mania

Most media have trends, fads, and new innovations. With magazines, all three can be summed up in a single word: *more*. More magazines, more advertising, more pages, more topics, and more readers.

Magazines are created to circulate relevant *editorial* content to subscribers who read product *advertising* that's related to the content. Published primarily in New York, Pennsylvania, Illinois, and California, national and regional magazines are owned by conglomerates. Publishers of the most titles are Condé Nast, Hearst, Meredith, Fillipachbi and Time Warner.

What distinguishes magazines from other printed material are their defined audience and the fact that they can be **issued in any frequency**. Unlike newspapers, magazines cater to **niche audiences** who read them for specific editorial and advertising information. Also, they can be self-supporting from circulation revenues. *Consumer Reports* is one such magazine that does not accept advertising. Rates for advertising are determined by subscribers, which are calculated either by paid subscription or by the numbers distributed free of charge. Many community magazines, such as *Coast* in Laguna Beach, California, are mailed to subscribers without charge and are supported by local retail and restaurant advertising.

Most magazines have web sites and hefty subscriber lists, which is why you see so many pages dedicated to advertising. Graphics and paper quality seem to be the most significant visual differentiation. Editorial content, of course, ranges in sophistication from simple single-sentence description to lengthy academic and professional discussion. We found most magazines entertaining in some form, especially those with unique photography and unusual advertising. Taken as a whole, the page proliferation staggers the mind, and makes one wonder what more can possibly be written. Each month's issues must struggle with that dilemma. If Borders' racks are any indication of what's to read, none of us should ever be without more and more pages to turn.

News Magazines[15]

A recognizable trend is the infusion of entertainment-oriented magazines and a slow and painful demise of new magazines. Apparently audiences would rather read about stars than suffering, which is apparent in the falling sales of America's top news magazines. Three trends in **news magazine** circulation and readership give us clues to the immanent threat they face.

- *No growth*. Readership surveys indicate that the audience for news magazines is holding steady, while the audience for pop culture, entertainment, and lifestyle magazines is growing. This fits with the trends in ad pages and revenues, and suggests one of two things either the market for news magazines is more or less at its capacity or the genre needs to be reinvented.
- *Aging audience base*. Despite changes in content designed to grab younger readers, the audience for news magazines is aging—more than for most other magazine genres. News magazine readers are also more affluent than magazine readers overall, but that is not a big consolation financially. Advertisers are often looking for youth more than money, particularly in general interest magazines like the news weeklies.
- *Competition mandates a new approach*. While the big three news magazines are finding it hard to increase their circulation, a few smaller circulation magazines that focus on news and public affairs have found steady growth over the past 15 years. This may suggest that the genre is ripe for change and indeed that the news magazine audience, or at least part of it, is looking for a new approach.

News Magazine Readers   Other key trends in news magazine readership, according to the Mediamark data, are affluence and age. News magazines are a graying habit. Despite the occasional hiccup in the data, the age gap is quite noticeable. And with few or no new titles entering the news genre, the hopes of significantly lowering the average age will probably go unmet.

Why does age matter? Advertising. Over the long term the aging of the news audience suggests fewer dollars will likely be flowing to news magazines, which have a higher average age than pop culture magazines. Advertisers, who seem ever interested in younger demographics, will likely be more interested in spending their money on entertainment and pop titles that reach those target age groups.

Offsetting the "age problem" is that along with age often comes wealth. News magazine readers have much higher income then the U.S. adult population overall and have had for some time. In 1995 news magazine readers were 28 percent more affluent than the U.S. adult population, and in 2003 that gap was about the same, 29 percent.

The advantage has allowed magazines like *Time* and *Newsweek* to charge more for the ads they run. Given that these magazines have had smaller increases in the number of ad pages they run than other magazine categories, this is some consolation.

Among the big three news magazines, readership tends to be male. *Time* and *Newsweek* each have about two million more male readers than female, and *U.S. News* has three million more men than women thumbing through its pages.

Time, the oldest magazine of the three, has the youngest readership, an average age of 43.1. *Newsweek* is a bit older with an average age of 44.4. And *U.S. News* is the highest, with an average reader age of 45.6

Newsweek's readers are slightly more affluent than *Time*'s. *U.S. News* readers, while still above the industry average as a whole, have a slightly lower average income. This finding is surprising because it is generally true that older readers have higher incomes. *U.S. News* seems to be an exception in this regard.

Move beyond the traditional three news magazines, however, and one can see more differences. Of all those listed in the news magazine

Many magazine readers are mature adults

category, *Jet*, a magazine with a predominantly Black audience, has by far the youngest readership. In the past decade the average reader age never got above 38.7 years old and some years its average age was in the early 30s. Its readership was also always more female than male. in 2003 it had two million more female readers than males. Among the news magazines examined, *Jet* readers also had the lowest median income.

The New Yorker and *The Atlantic* have the oldest readerships of any of the news magazines examined—45.4 years and 50.0 years respectively. But they also had the readers with the highest incomes, by a large margin. In terms of gender, *The Atlantic*'s readership tends to be more male than female—774,000 versus 615,000 in 2003. The opposite is true of *The New Yorker*, which has a few more women readers—2.1 million females compared to 1.9 million males.

Implications for News Magazines   The circulation numbers for the magazine industry make one thing clear: the news genre may not be dead, but growth and energy are outside the traditional big three news magazines. Whether that is a permanent condition, or a reflection of their current hybrid format, is a question that cannot be answered here.

But the attempts by these magazines to become younger by becoming lighter do not, according to the numbers, seem to be working. Magazines that have a little of everything but specialize in little are not where the growth in readership seems to be. Magazines that are more serious, like *The New Yorker*, or more strictly entertainment-oriented, like

In Style, are hotter. And magazines of ideas—and of opposition—seem to endure in having a place at the table. One question is whether bloggers, those influential writers of opinion on the Internet, will chew away at magazine audiences.

News magazines occupy a valued place in the life of most of their readers. They are a mass medium. But they are rarely the primary source for information about the events that shape the world, according to surveys by the Pew Research Center. TV, radio, newspapers, and the Internet are more likely to be the places where individuals learn about the news. News magazines have always been a more analytical forum, a synthesis of news, analysis, and opinion. Their readers tend to be a more select group of people who are interested in news. Readers' opinions, then, may matter more to these magazines than to other media. Since they are not the primary source of news and they revolve around analysis, they are also arguably more easily dropped by readers who feel they don't need them. Among the survey findings:

- Only a small numbers of readers say they are turning to magazines more often for news.
- Magazines increasingly are seen as less valuable when news breaks.

Without question, the number of news sources has multiplied in the past decade. And the rise of the Internet combined with the proliferation of 24-hour cable TV networks has changed the way people get news. Not only is instant information available, but so are instant analysis and instant opinion as well. Magazines have borne some of the toughest hits in this information revolution, according to a survey by the Pew Research Center.

Magazines and Celebrity

The fastest growing print media are those devoted to stars and celebrities. Publishers of celebrity magazines are experiencing surges in subscription and ad sales—*U.S. Weekly*'s ad pages were up 25 percent in 2005; *Star Magazine* ads increased 17 percent over the previous year; *In Touch Weekly* ads rose nearly 22 percent in the same time period. Why? Star and celebrity focused magazines and tabloids are advertising-friendly environments because readers cover them from front to back. As advertisers become increasingly interested in reaching women, they select celebrity magazines where the bulk of readers are women.

News magazines, as well as celebrity magazines, feature movie stars

Research conducted by *TV Guide* Publishing Group revealed that many readers buy two or three celebrity magazines because of the tremendous appetite for celebrity coverage. A sampling of readers on the street in New York City indicated that the attraction with celebrities has to do with escapism and a need to stay in the know on the latest gossip.[16]

Radio: Pop Goes the Music

The term *pop music* is commonly used to refer to a specific subset of music commonly played on "Top 40" radio stations. Pop music typically includes a danceable beat, simple melodies, and repetitive structure that is easy for audiences to follow and join in. Song themes are typically lighthearted, focusing on love, sex, dancing, and partying. Today's pop music often includes elements of rock, hip hop, reggae, dance, R&B, funk, and sometimes even folk. The pop music genre is associated with mass marketing and production by major record companies, efforts which are often criticized by other musicians.

In the 1990s, top 40 pop music flourished with a parade of boy bands and teen queens—led by the Backstreet Boys, 'N Sync, and Britney Spears. Music from Latin stars such as Marc Antony, Ricky Martin, Jennifer Lopez, and Christina Aguilera also enjoyed pop success at this time. Boy bands and teen artists, often referred to as bubblegum pop, continued to dominate pop charts for album and concert sales in the early 2000s. Radio play for teen pop, however,

Britney Spears managed to maintain high music sales and visibility in spite of receiving a decreasing amount of radio airplay

began to decrease. For example, Britney Spears's song "Stronger" was one of the best-selling singles in the United States for several weeks and reached the top spot in January 2001. But on *Billboard Magazine*'s airplay chart only two weeks later, it was not found among the 100 top songs playing on pop radio.

Analysts found this trend puzzling. Sky Daniels, general manager of *Radio & Records*, an industry trade publication, says,

It's as if there's a sense by a lot of radio programmers that now is the time that they're supposed to end the cycle. . . . [Programmers are saying,] "At any moment this is going to go, and I want to be the first one to proclaim it." They want to be trend-setting. They don't want to be the last one to pull out. . . . Sometimes the cycles change because there is a backlash from the fans, but you have to ask yourself: Do you see any backlash from the fans right now toward Britney Spears? The answer is no.[17]

Some analysts, however, question whether teen pop even needs top 40 radio now that live music venues, TV, film, the Internet, and other advances have multiplied the outlets for artist and music exposure. Although her songs were receiving a decreasing amount of airplay, in 2000 Britney Spears was the most-searched-for music star on the Internet, and in 2001 she was on the cover of *Time* magazine and began work on the film *Crossroads*. Spears, 'N Sync, and the Backstreet Boys were still staples on youth-embracing Disney Radio and Nickelodeon, and all three acts had a global stage as part of Super Bowl XXXV.

Bubblegum pop appeared to be declining at the turn of the early millennium, and hip hop was anticipated to emerge as the new pop music leader. But youth-oriented music gained renewed momentum, again not from radio play but thanks to the *American Idol* reality show and Disney TV and film productions. When *American Idol* debuted in 2002, audiences voted in their own new pop stars such as Kelly Clarkson and Clay Aiken. Network executives at Disney similarly created pop princesses such as by first casting them in films or Disney Channel TV movies or series that often showcased their music. In spite of these efforts, bubblegum pop was still viewed as a genre in decline until the success of the Disney Channel original movie *High School Musical* in 2006. The sound-track to the movie was the number one selling CD in the United States in 2006 with heaviest support among pre-teen girls.[18]

The teen market has also driven the popularity of other sub-genres of pop music such as pop-punk—in essence a hardcore punk sound softened for the benefit of the teenage crowd. Acts such as New Found Glory, Blink 182, and Hawthorne Heights became heart throbs to teenage girls. Some urban music also started to have a bubblegum pop feel to it. In late 2004, 2005, and some parts of 2006, artists such as Frankie J, Chris Brown, and Omarion started to become increasingly popular, matching even the popularity of the "Disney" artists who were prominent at that time.

New technology including the Internet and digital music players have also influenced the music charts. In addition to providing an alternative to radio play as a way to learn about new music, these technologies are making it increasingly difficult to determine which music is most popular. Traditionally music charts were determined by album sales and radio play. Terry McBride, CEO of Nettwerk Productions, one of Canada's largest independent labels, questions this system. He asks "In an age when music fans have so many options for checking out new music—from iTunes to MySpace, YouTube, eMusic, ringtones and still-rampant illegal file-sharing—how can you measure who's *really* #1 at any given time?" According to McBride, "The metrics of measurement are so messed up now because you have SoundScan, BigChampagne, iTunes, eMusic, streams from Yahoo! and AOL, and there's no chart that combines all that together to get a clear view of who is most popular right now. . . . Digital distribution has shattered the old monopoly on how music is distributed."

The Rise of Techno

Popular music has included many new genres over the years. Disc jockey (DJ) Allen Freed coined the term *rock and roll* to describe a new wild sound, emerging in the late 1940s, that mixed country western music, gospel, blues, rockabilly, and rhythm and blues. As technology continued to evolve, the melody and rhythms of electronic guitars, basses, and synthesizers accompanied by drum percussion became the mainstay of the rock and roll sound—a sound that dominated popular music in the Western world for the remainder of the twentieth century.

Writer Michael Dunaway argues, however, that, in the 1990s, the creative, cutting-edge, great music came not from rock and roll but from two upstarts: techno and hip hop. He identified bands such as Public Enemy (hip hop), Prodigy (techno), and Beck (hip hop—especially when you look at the underlying structure of his music) as those that were setting a new direction for music. It is difficult to trace the evolution of techno. Some sources claim it emerged from Chicago's mid-1980s house music explosion, caught the ear of London club DJs, and infused Europe's dance scene. Columnist Edna Gundersen characterized techno as "an aggressive, electronic revival of disco, concocted by synthesizer-savvy computer freaks with a do-it-yourself punk attitude and shoestring budgets."[19] Rapidly evolving into an icy, hyperkinetic (up to 140 beats per minute) sound seasoned with elements of psychedelia, punk, hard-core thrash, world beat, reggae, and funk, techno returned to the United States as a hot import.

Fueled by techno's popularity at underground dance clubs, in 1992 "James Brown Is Dead" by Belgium's L.A. Style became the first techno single to hit the *Billboard* chart. According to Dunaway, while most of the fans "in the clubs cared only that the beat was good and that the lyric had a suitably vague, detached, cynical feel, those words [James Brown Is Dead] stood as a kind of manifesto for many on the vanguard of the burgeoning techno scene—namely, that rock and roll has had its day, but now we're taking over. Techno is the wave of the future; rock and roll is a museum piece. James Brown is dead."[20] Major labels began signing techno acts, and the fan base grew. Hip hop—another new, influential genre—is discussed in the next section.

Radio Programming

Early radio was divided into independent and network-affiliated stations, and most programs aired in 15-minute blocks. Unlike today's focused, niche programming, a typical station's programming in 1932 averaged 62.9 percent music, 21.3 percent educational, 11.8 percent literature, 2.5 percent religion, and 1.5 percent "novelties" or special programming.[21] Radio also broadcast dramatic programs or stories such as mysteries, action adventures, and comedy sketches with sound effects and "actors" who would read different parts. By 1933, however, radio was starting to fear competition for dramatic programming from yet another new medium: TV.

In the 1950s, radio formats began to look more like they do today, under the direction of programmers like Todd Storz, who is credited with inventing the top 40 format, and Gordon McLendon. In 1955, programmers Chuck Dunaway and Kent Burkhart initiated what is believed to be the very first radio station playlist at KXOL Fort Worth, Texas. These pioneering programmers and others who followed began to coax radio stations to shift away from a "something for everyone" philosophy (playing a wide variety of music, often based on the personal preferences of the disc jockeys themselves), and toward today's tightly programmed, niche formats and carefully researched playlists targeted at specific demographics. Not everyone, however, supports this shift toward more tightly controlled programming. Some groups, including many of the DJs themselves, argue that radio play should be viewed more as an art than a science, thus allowing DJs greater freedom in music selection (see *Spotlight on Radio*).

SPOTLIGHT ON RADIO   DJ Jim Ladd

As popular music has grown into a billion-dollar industry, the competition between radio stations for listener attention has become fierce. Today's corporate-owned and corporate-controlled radio stations tend to view radio play as a science. They employ marketing consultants who use formal research methods such as surveys and focus groups to determine audience preferences and to strategically develop formatted playlists of music for disc jockeys to follow. Such an approach, however, is still relatively new. Traditionally, disc jockeys viewed their craft as an art, relying on their own artistic expertise and inspiration from listener suggestions to determine musical selections.

No one is more aware of the tension between creativity and commercialism in radio than Los Angeles disc jockey Jim Ladd. Since the mid-1960s, Ladd has been a popular member of the LA radio scene. More recently, he has become an outspoken advocate of what he refers to as *free-form radio*. Ladd refuses to work within the confines of formats and playlists; instead, he insists on controlling the music played on his show himself. "In my definition, free-form radio means that the person on the air gets to play whatever they want," he says, although he does regularly take listener requests as well. In this way, he maintains the unique listener–disc jockey relationship that once characterized rock radio.

Ladd regards music as a creative medium that can be used as a tool for social impact. His show commonly features music with a message, celebrating such ideals as peace, human kindness, and brotherhood. Often, he weaves songs together into thematic sets that segue neatly from one song to the next. "I try to use whole songs as [a rock musician] would use a note or a chord," he says, describing an approach for selecting songs that is clearly artistic.

Ladd refers to marketing consultants as "the suits," and he argues that their approach to meeting audience preferences results in little more than an endless repetition of selected songs. Ladd's refusal to bow to corporate pressure has, at times, kept him out of work. But he has a strong following, and currently his fans form a powerful audience.

Station revenues, of course, are dependent upon being able to deliver a large number of listeners for their advertisers. Marketing consultants argue that the problem with viewing radio play as an art is that not everyone appreciates the same "art." Thus, stations view free-form radio as a high-stakes gamble, and they are hesitant to rely on the creative hunches of individual disc jockeys regarding what listeners will like.

The consultants maintain that formalized research and structured playlists simply serve as a more efficient means of ensuring that radio stations are satisfying their audiences. Indeed, both the consultants and the disc jockeys pay close attention to listeners' opinions when choosing the music to be aired. But disc jockeys like Ladd argue that the consultant-controlled model prevents them from being able to interact meaningfully with listeners. They maintain that free-form radio allows them to introduce their audiences to new music and to new ways of looking at the music they love.

Ultimately, whether free form or "suit-motivated," radio programming is based on listeners' preferences. In the end, it is the listener who votes by turning the dial.

What do you think?

- *Should radio play be approached more as an art or a science? Consider your answer from several perspectives—that of a radio listener, a station manager, a disc jockey, and an advertiser— and see if your answer begins to change or if it remains the same.*

Radio's *niche formats* both reflect and shape changing music trends. By 1975, the once-popular nostalgia format was being quickly replaced with disco, reflecting the music played at a growing number of discotheques around the country. Country, MOR (middle of the road), and progressive rock stations, which first emerged during the 1960s, had also become prominent by the late 1970s. In 1982, Black-oriented stations across the United States developed an urban contemporary format that blended Black music with rock and pop. Although the format was popular, some programmers of Black stations felt that it diluted Black music to make it more acceptable for non-blacks. During the 1980s radio became big business as stations began trading for unprecedented dollar figures. Top programmers and talent began earning equally unprecedented sums, full-time satellite programming networks emerged, and radio took on a much more professional, corporate style. The growing radio industry has established a proven growth rate over the last two decades, remaining financially healthy even when other industries were struggling to remain competitive. Today, there are almost 12,000 radio stations in the United States, representing approximately 80 distinct formats.

Internet and satellite radio, however, are reducing the amount of time listeners are spending with terrestrial radio, according to a recent study by Bridge Ratings. Fifty-five percent of Internet radio listeners are tuning in to terrestrial radio less frequently. Other non-radio formats tend to complement radio listenership. Forty-three percent of those polled who download MP3s responded that they spend more time listening to terrestrial radio, and 58 percent of podcast listeners also said terrestrial radio was a complement to the format. In the 4,000-person poll the most popular radio formats were urban music and contemporary hits, with MP3 players being the most listened-to format. The poll was conducted among listeners ages 15 to 64.[22]

Digital and satellite technologies are transforming the entire music entertainment industry. With the potential of wireless Internet and high-speed digital connectivity, the music industry could be in a position for the first time to break free of its alliance with radio as its primary source of introducing new music to consumers. The music industry has not openly admitted to waging battle with radio. Critics, however, suggest that additional licensing and performance fees and higher fees for advertising talent and commercial content have been levied against radio stations to make room for the major record labels to get into the Internet game. By developing their own Internet radio sites and utilizing music downloading technology, recording companies might be able to bypass the retail industry and the radio industry, and instead promote and sell their music directly to consumers.

Under such a plan, the role of traditional radio would be reduced. The day could come when labels no longer send stations free music to promote but instead charge a subscription fee to them if they want to get the music first and fresh. To regain leverage before it is too late, some radio broadcasters have considered several strategies, ranging from simple blackouts of traditional advertisements from their Internet feeds to more radical changes, such as charging a promotion fee for airtime dedicated to specific songs or artists. The future of the music entertainment industry is uncertain. Nonetheless, the market for music will likely remain strong, regardless of who delivers the product.

Digital Radio   Several digital technologies now exist for the broadcast of traditional terrestrial radio stations, but stations were hesitant to make the conversion from analog because a standard had not been set by the FCC. However, as of the beginning of 2002, iBiquity Digital was the sole developer and licenser of digital AM and FM broadcast technology in the United States. The company's investors include 14 of the nation's top radio broadcasters, including ABC, Clear Channel, and Viacom; technology companies Harris, Lucent, Texas Instruments, and Visteon; and leading financial institutions such as J.P. Morgan Partners, Pequot Capital, and J&W Seligman. IBiquity's in-brand-on channel (IBOC) technology was also endorsed by the Geneva-based International Telecommunication Union (ITU). IBOC technology relies on digital compression to shrink digital and analog signals, allowing stations to broadcast both digital and analog formats simultaneously on a single channel without requiring additional spectrum.

Satellite Radio   Another outgrowth of digital technology is satellite radio. Satellite radio providers boast better signal and sound quality and more stations with more diverse offerings. The first two U.S. coast-to-coast satellite radio providers, Sirius and XM, each launched with the promise of 100 stations. Satellite radio delivers some commercial radio broadcasts, but most stations developed by the satellite providers and their partners offer commercial-free music and news talk and/or information, narrowly focused to suit specific style and interest niches. The tradeoff, however, is that listeners must pay for these satellite radio services (much like premium cable and satellite television services) whereas traditional, broadcast radio remains free. Thus, the question becomes whether audiences will find satellite offerings and sound quality worth the price.

As of mid-2007, the future of satellite radio was still uncertain. Both companies experienced rapid subscription growth. Sirius had gone from 30,000 subscriptions in 2002 to 4.7 million as of July, 2006, while XM has grown from 360,000 to seven million in the same frame. However, the competition for subscribers created high-priced bidding wars for radio content and talent. Sirius ponied up $500 million for Stern and $220 million for the NFL. XM has paid $650 million for Major League Baseball and $55 million for Oprah Winfrey. NASCAR, which XM paid about $15 million for in a five-year deal, then switched to Sirius. The two also lined up Eminem, 50 Cent, Martha Stewart, the NBA, and the NHL, to name a few. Such expenses led to massive losses, as of 2005—$667 million at XM and $863 million at Sirius. Stock prices of both companies began to sink rapidly. In 2009, Sirius and XM merged into a single entity that combines both stations' offerings.

Digital Music Players and Podcasting According to a new Ipsos research study, 20 percent of Americans over the age of 12 own portable MP3 players and one in 20 own more than one. Media player ownership increased 5 percent from one year ago. According to the Consumer Electronics Association, sales of headphone MP3 players reached 4.23 billion in 2005 and accounted for 85 percent of all factory-produced portable audio systems. The survey also found that younger Americans are driving recent growth, with over half of teens now owning a portable MP3 player (54 percent), and one third of 18–34 year olds (30 percent). The poll noted that nearly half (44 percent) of the content stored on MP3 players is ripped from the owner's personal CD collection, and another 6 percent is ripped from others' CD collections. Fee-based downloads (25 percent) and files obtained from file sharing services (19 percent) are also common sources of content.[23]

Digital music players can now also function similarly to radio, through podcasting. A *podcast* is a digital media file, or a series of such files, that is distributed over the Internet using syndication feeds for playback on portable media players and personal computers. The host or author of a podcast is often called a *podcaster*. The term "podcast" is derived from adding the acronym of "Playable on Demand" (POD) to the term broadcast[24] but is often mistakenly thought to be a reference to Apple's portable music player, the iPod, added to broadcast. Many independent and syndicated radio shows can be downloaded from station web sites as podcasts. Although web sites may also offer direct download or streaming of their content in other digital formats, a podcast is unique in its ability to be downloaded automatically, using software capable of reading feed formats such as RSS or Atom. Thus, individuals can "subscribe" to set podcasts that can then be downloaded automatically as new "shows" are released. These shows can then be played "on demand" on a personal computer or digital audio player.

Figure 14.1 shows the rapid growth of podcast listeners. In a July 2005 study of the U.S. market performed by the U.S. market research institute The Diffusion Group, it was determined that growth in the penetration of podcasting technology can be directly tied to the expanding use of portable digital audio players. Based on those figures, the institute projected that the number of podcast listeners is expected grow from 15 to 75 percent of portable digital audio player users between 2004 and 2010. Backing this into numbers, the institute further projected that the number of podcast listeners in the U.S. alone will increase to around 57 million within the next few years.[25] Technology has now advanced so that recorded video can also be podcasted, however, so it will be interesting to see what impact that may have on audio-only podcast downloads.

Film Animation[26]

Full-length feature films now dominate the animation genre. From the first animated character-star of 1902, Felix the Cat, to the first feature-length animated film, *The Adventures of Prince Achmed* from Germany, animation has entertained thousands. In 1928, Disney Studios developed Mickey Mouse. Fox's TerryToons began producing films with food item names, such as *Caviar*, *Pretzels*, and *Hot Turkey* in 1930. That same year, Looney Toones was released by Warner Brothers. By 1938, Popeye became a hero in the first series of animated shorts. Later, two feature-length animations were developed by Fleischer Studios: *Gulliver's Travels* (1939) and *Mr. Bug Goes to Town* (1941).

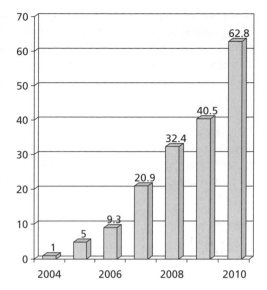

Figure 14.1 U.S. Listeners Who Have Ever Downloaded a Podcast 2004–10 (millions)

Source: Bridge Ratings 2005

For some 20 years, Chuck Jones produced over 300 animated cartoons, but only one feature-length film, *The Phantom Tollbooth* (1970). His most famous piece was a compilation of shorts into *The Bugs Bunny/Road Runner Movie* (1979). But the first full-length animated film was Disney's classic *Snow White and the Seven Dwarfs* (1937). Disney released more animated features in the 1950s than any other studio, including the three top-grossing films of that decade.

Animations with more mature subject matter began in the late 1970s and early 1980s with *Watership Down* (1978) and *The Plague Dogs* (1982), dark films with a nihilistic, pro-animal rights theme. Stop-motion animation technique *go-motion* was used to deliver *Return of the Jedi* (1983), *Indiana Jones and the Temple of Doom* (1984), and *Jurassic Park* (1993), among others. Rock-oriented animation favorites included *Star Wars* (1977), *Alien* (1979), and *Ghostbusters* (1984).

In the 1990s, the talking animal hit *Babe* (1995) and *Animal Farm* (1999) took Jim Henson's characters to the screen. Disney returned to animation with more mature themes such as *Beauty and the Beast* (1991) and *Aladdin* (1992). Disney's biggest hit, *The Lion King* (1994), set a box office record as the most commercially successful animated film of the times, winning two Academy awards from its four music-related nominations.

Pixar's *Toy Story* (1998) united the studio with Disney, and, in 2001, DreamWorks and PDI produced *Shrek* (2001). *Finding Nemo* (2003) was the highest-grossing computer-animated film ever (to date), the fifth collaboration of Pixar and Disney. Their combined efforts yielded *Cars* (2006), *Ratatouille* (2007), and *Wall-E* (2008). Shot as a live-action film before 30 artists who graphically "painted" the characters via computer (with a process called "interpolated rotoscoping") to create the illusion of a cartoon in motion was *A Scanner Darkly* (2005).

Motion capture technology produced *The Polar Express* (2004) with "performance capture," an advanced motion capture system where an actor's live performances were digitally captured by computerized cameras and used as a blueprint for creating virtual, all-digital characters. DreamWorks' sci-fi spoof of 1950s monster movie *Monster vs. Aliens* (2009) was the first computer animated feature shot directly in stereoscopic 3-D.

Making the transition from children to adult audiences, animators are fusing mature themes with real-life drawings to attract an older movie-going segment. In a cartoon first, Disney's *Bugs' Life* featured dozens of product tie-ins to snuggle up with the film's adorable candy-colored bugs. Part of Disney's overall merchandising efforts uses film to sell products. By cross-marketing toys and movies, Disney is able to convince parents that movies are not harmful for their kids while persuading kids to ask for spin-off items and toys.[27] Today, all types of joint promotions, tie-ins, and merchandising efforts accompany animated films.

SPOTLIGHT ON ANIMATED FILMS   Favorites of 2008

The Pirates Who Don't Do Anything:
A VeggieTales Movie

VeggieTales mania continues with this Universal Pictures production about a pirate-themed restaurant that leaves the vegetables skipping work and heading back to the seventeenth century to fight in a real pirate adventure.

Horton Hears a Who

This Dr. Seuss story plays out in a computer animated version with Horton the elephant who discovers the city of Whoville. Horton does his very best to protect the Whos from danger, and keeps his commitment to being a loyal and valuable friend.

Kung Fu Panda

This tells the story of Po the panda who learns martial

arts after he realizes his home is under threat by enemies of the Valley of Peace. It's set in ancient China. Jack Black plays the voice of Po in this 3D movie.

WALL-E

WALL-E is a robot from the year 2070 who has been appointed the job of cleaning up Earth as best he can. When he falls in love with a robot from a probe, he realizes he has to pursue his real passion in life.

Igor

This computer animated comedy features a hunchbacked lab assistant to a mad scientist, who plans to win the Evil Science Fair on his own. Star voices include Christian Slater, John Cleese, Molly Shannon, and Steve Buscemi.

The Smurfs

The Smurfs return from a long hiatus from the screen in this 3D computer animated version. It will be the first of a trilogy, to be released in 2011. The entire team of blue guys—and Smurfette—will share some insights on life in this full-length feature from Paramount Pictures.

Madagascar 2: The Crate Escape

All of your favorite characters from *Madagascar* are back in action as they explore Africa and learn the real meaning of home. Ben Stiller, Andy Richter, Jada Pinkett Smith, and Sacha Baron Cohen are just a few of the star voices for this sequel from DreamWorks Animation.

Walt Disney's *Bolt Movie* 3D
This family-friendly animated movie from Disney studios presents a dog who's achieved success in the show business as a dog with superpowers, but suddenly gets abandoned in the Nevada desert. When he meets up with a couple of animal friends, he soon realizes that he doesn't really have super-

powers and is just a "normal" dog. John Travolta, Woody Harrelson, and Bernie Mac are a few of the star voices in this one.

Sources: Sabah Karimi for Associated Content, www.associatedcontent.com/article/474227/top_animated_movie_releases_for_2008.html

What do you think?

- *Do stars' voices increase interest in animated films? Why?*
- *What is the advantage of using life-like animation in place of real stars?*

In China, *Panda* was an immediate box office hit. If you're wondering how Western filmmakers could have used Chinese themes to create such a brilliant animated move, you're not alone. In a commentary featured in *China Daily*, Lu Chuan, a Chinese movie director, wondered when China would produce a movie of that caliber. The film's protagonist is a national treasure and all the elements borrowed a number of sequences from classic kung fu movies in China, grasping the essence of Chinese culture.

In a way, the film is only the latest illustration of a centuries-old tradition whereby Western artists have used China and other Asian countries to produce enduring works of art. For instance, Gilbert and Sullivan's *Mikado* or Puccini's *Turandot* or the animated feature *Mulan* of a few years ago recall the strength of this tradition. The West's use of China as an artistic setting is unmatched by any Chinese use of Europe or America as backdrops for its own cultural productions.

Animation Trends

Movie audiences once wore red and green cardboard 3D glasses to view animated films. In 2005 with *Chicken Little*, the trend began again. Only today's glasses are very hi-tech, lightweight 3D specs that look like sunglasses. Dreamworks, the studio behind animation, claims that most of its movies will now be in 3D, such as 2008's *Kung Fu Panda*.

Director Jeffery Katzenberg said 3D filmmaking "is the greatest innovation to occur in the movie business in 70 years."[28] And according to MG Siegler, writer on techno media for *Venture Beat*, 3D enables us to live the experience. Similar to the IMAX treatment, 3D is a bit more expensive to produce, but the industry is banking on technology to get people back into the movie theater to see what they cannot get on the Internet or TV.

Viewing competition is fierce. Using Vudu, Roku, Apple TV, and Xbox 360, consumers are watching movies using sites like Netflix where they can download films to their computers. Experts claim that DVD and Blu-ray will give way to digital distribution that mimics music downloads on iTunes. To combat this trend, theater chains AMC Entertainment, Regal Entertainment Group, and Cinemark USA have already started bringing digital equipment to their combined 14,000 screens. The theory is that as 35mm film disappears, pictures will become sharper with digital projectors that produce images that simulate depth. They believe that this technology will return audiences to the big screen, the only place where digital depth takes us into new realms of mediated experience.

Lost in the Shuffle Bimini, the International Festival of Animation Films, and the Oscar nominees for animated short films, don't create much excitement among judges or voters. But in 2008, only one nomination could be seen by the general public: *The Little Matchgirl*, a watercolor-style Disney version of Hans Christian Andersen's classic tale that was offered for viewing on YouTube, for sale on iTunes, or on the *Little Mermaid* platinum edition DVD. The others . . . well, you have to seek out clips and hope they gain some recognition before the Oscars are announced.

Consuming TV Images

Driven by economic factors, media businesses strive to provide their audiences with what they want to see and hear. Two factors important for understanding why we watch television and film are presented here. *Violence*—said to foster our societal ills—and *stardom*—said to be the focus of our aspirations—deserve our attention as well as further investigation by you, the readers of this text.

A Search for Plots

Reality shows have flourished because they are cheap to produce, satisfy a voyeuristic urge, and have a frisson of authenticity. But that's not the only reason networks jumped on the reality bandwagon. It's because TV is experiencing a deep crisis in narrative.[29] Most plot structures originated in folktales and haven't changed much over time. Stories are structured like this: During some historical period, a protagonist takes action in a particular physical setting. One day he confronts the antagonist who is a source of conflict. In the end, the protagonist resolves the conflict and the story ends. All stories are a variation on that theme.

The *prime-time genre* lineup for 2008 suggested that the new shows were less about discovering "who did it" than figuring out what happened in the first place. Plots turned around kidnappings, hostage takings, art theft, fugitives, genetic mutations, and nuclear holocaust. Because of the hit *Lost*, shows spawned a generation of cinematic dramas that begin in the middle of the narrative and zigzag—often with time-lapse photography—from beginning to the middle and back to an episode-clinching cliffhanger.[30] NBC's *Knight Rider* and CBS's *Mentalist* tap into the supernatural. Two dangerous job series, *Shark Taggers* (NBC) and *Do Not Disturb* (Fox) revolve around precarious positions. A good example of prime time's tense mood is created in Fox's new *Fringe* and ABC's *Life on Mars* series.

As they continue to become a medium in search of a plot, TV programs are emerging as *humorous satire* (Comedy Central's *The Daily Show* and HBO's *Real Time with Bill Maher*), *surrealism* (USA's *4400*), and *totally improvised dialog* (HBO's *Curb Your Enthusiasm*). New scenarios will also provide *hybrid formats*, allowing audiences to play along using the web. Groundbreaker series like Showtime's *Weeds*, *Californication*, and *Dexter* compete with HBO's new hopefuls *Summer Heights High* and *No. 1 Ladies Detective Agency*.

Reality Television

After ten years of watching reality TV, we have stopped wondering when the fad will end. We're thinking never. Why? Because writers keep coming up with new ways to convert the "everyday" into a program concept. They use TV to staff Broadway shows, bring

The Season 2 finale of *America's Best Dance Crew* on MTV

street dance to the masses, and steal ideas from other countries. Here are three series presented in 2008 that expand upon those concepts.

Based on the 2007 series that selected a star for the Broadway musical *Grease*, *The Search for Elle Woods* is a competition held to choose the lead for Broadway's *Legally Blonde*. Bell Bundy, current lead, would be replaced by the winner sometime after the TV show's eighth and final episode. The gulf between the 27-year-old Ms. Bundy and the ten fresh-faces—average age 22—was purposeful, as young contestants could get women their own age to watch the show.

Dance anyone? It seems as if every channel worth its programming salt, from broadcast networks to TLC, Lifetime, and Bravo, has trotted out a dance-based reality show. As an unexpected side effect, street dance is now being popularized through television and on the shows' web sites, and newer moves are being documented and codified in a way not seen before.

Street dance has grown so popular that almost every dance reality show features it in some way. Not surprisingly, MTV has helped drive the interest with *America's Best Dance Crew*, which began its second season in June 2008. Brainchild of Randy Jackson of *American Idol* fame, the show pits dance crews from across the country against one another and enlists a panel of judges to offer technical opinions. Viewers vote to decide who continues in the competition.

Looking like a ballet class, except for the sideways caps and T-shirts, the dancers follow dance-master Jazzy J's every step, repeating the movements first on one side of the body and then on the other. Dance techniques like popping and locking were included in response to a wave of TV shows that have caught the interest of a new generation of students. "What it's really doing is educating people about hip hop," said Jackson. "When someone says break dancing, we correct them and say it's b-boying, which refers to toprocking, downrocking, freezes and power moves."

A significant trend of reality programming is the growing reliance on series concepts from abroad. Among the newcomers whose roots can be traced overseas are *The Ex List*

(CBS) from Israel; *Kath and Kim* (NBC) from Australia; and from Britain *Secret Millionaire* (Fox), *Worst Week* and *Eleventh Hour* (CBS), and *Life on Mars* (ABC). Among the series with an overseas genesis that are already on broadcast networks are hits like *American Idol, Dancing with the Stars, Deal or No Deal*, and *Survivor*.

The trend is popular because it's less expensive to acquire and adapt program rights than to develop something from scratch. And when revenue growth is threatened, cutting costs is accomplished by borrowing. Ben Silverman developed American versions of *Ugly Betty* for ABC and *The Office* for NBC. CBS added a Los Angeles setting for another *NCIS* series in 2009, duplicating the original show's format, as was the case with *CSI:* and its offshoots in Miami and New York.

Stars of *Kath and Kim*, a popular program from Australia

Gender Games: Men Working, Women Winning

Series of three shows by Thom Beers presents men working as Verminators (Discovery Channel) where bug control experts examine people's homes; Black Gold (TruTV) Texas drillers for oil, and AxMen (History Channel) featuring loggers. Guy stuff for certain, but with some gal types watching to catch a glimpse of the next celebrity bugger, driller, or logger. But that's OK, 2008 was a season of firsts for women in reality TV as well.

Ali Vincent became the first female winner in the five-season run of NBC's *The Biggest Loser*, then Kristy Yamaguchi became the first lady to seize the *Dancing with the Stars* crown since Kelly Monaco won six seasons ago. And two women took top honors in *Top Chef: Chicago* on Bravo. That year's burst of girl power was a departure from reality competitions in the past.

The Apprentice has produced only two female victors in seven seasons, and a mere one-third of the *Big Brother* winners have been women in its nine-season run. The female–male winner ratio on CBS's *Survivor* and Fox's *American Idol* is approximately 50/50.[31]

Perhaps the best gender-equal reality programming in 2008 was the contest waged in TV debates and appearances between Hillary Clinton and Barack Obama. From *Larry King* to *Saturday Night Live*, the two hopefuls provided both genders with firsts: first ever female presidential candidate and first ever candidate of mixed races. Supporters turned out in droves, donated money, blogged, and fought on to the finale after the last vote was cast. And although the speeches were scripted, the outcome was up for grabs until the end, maintaining interest and suspense for Democratic men and women in an *American Idol* format.

Vanishing Nuclear Families

Children Now,[32] the national child advocacy organization that examines media messages to children, says only about 11 percent of recurring prime-time characters on networks are parents of any kind—and only 61 percent of them are still married. HBO, for instance, presented a single mom selling pot to provide for her two sons, and *Big Love* featured a Utah man with three families. Single parents and odd familial configurations are present, but the absence of any family pervades many network series.

Why has the family faded from the spotlight? Perhaps shows reflect demographic and cultural shifts. Or perhaps, since families rarely watch shows together, it's no longer necessary to satisfy everyone with the same show. And as the definition of family changes, advertisers have been forced to adjust as well. The Family Friendly Programming Forum, a group of ad executives, presented an improvement plan for improving television scripts for "family" shows. They suggested acceptable "widowed" dads and moms to replace divorced parents. Well, maybe that will work. But for now, we'll continue to be entertained by gratuitous sex and foul language that characterize our televised family counterparts that include a mix-and-match of combinations that are supposed to reflect real life.

SPOTLIGHT ON INTERNET MUSIC   Vintage-inspired Rap

Claiming to be into emulation, not imitation, the Cool Kids are part of a small but newly influential hip-hop subculture meta-rap—created by artists raised entirely within the hip-hop culture. The Kids make music that is a commentary on what came before and turning it into something new and diverse.

Hardly acknowledged by radio or television, groups such as Kidz in the Hall, Duck Down, and Knux are extremely popular on the Internet. Fueled by old-school loyalists and genre outsiders committed to the style, these young artists have created a hip-hop generation gap.

Their music is mostly funny or deconstructive, and often finds it way into TV. For example, Knux had a song played on an episode of the HBO series *Entourage* in 2008, and Cool Kids have been featured in a national television ad for Microsoft's online music service, Rhapsody.

Except for Kidz in the Hall and Plastic Little, none of the meta-rap groups has released a major-label album, but their success has nothing to do with traditional sales. Instead, blog hype helps them perfect their style and capitalize on it before it's copied. Cool Kids have toured and claim they want to record everything to tape like it's 1991 and seeing how it sounds.

Source: Caramanica, Jon (2008). The mining of hip-hop's Golden Age, *New York Times*, September 14, p. 24

Online Video

According to CNN,[33] the future of TV is changing as media scramble for established turf in the landscape of Internet video. People are moving from their televisions to their computers to watch studio-quality movies, music videos, and TV shows. "Historically, the winners are the ones who embrace change," said Jason Kilar, CEO of Hulu.com, which was launched March 12, 2007, by the owners of Fox and NBC Universal. The site offers more than 3,000 full-length TV episodes and 100 movies—all available free.

Warner Bros recently joined Television Group, which just announced plans for two ad-supported web sites. One, TheWB.com, will feature shows such as *Friends*, *The O.C.*, and *Gilmore Girls*, and had a Beta launch in May 2008. A second WB site for kids will present animated programming from Looney Tunes, Hanna-Barbera, and DC Comics.

This activity is in response to viewers who are watching video online in increasing numbers. Is online video becoming a threat to the culture and technology of old fashioned TV? Perhaps. Viewers like alternatives, and today's kids are turning to YouTube and other sources for programming unavailable on American TV, such as Japanese action anime. Viewers fed up with commercials can watch their favorite programs online with fewer ads, and can see up-to-the minute news videos on CNN.com.

FLASH FACT

According to comScore, 72.8 percent of the U.S. Internet audiences are watching online video, especially men ages 18–34 who account for 40 percent of total viewers.

Seventy percent of Internet users who watch TV online say it's because they missed the episode on regular TV, according to Horowitz Associates.

"Yes, TV is changing," said Kilar, "but I don't think TV is dying, because the television experience in the living room is a very good one—and it's not going away." As for the TV culture in a post-Internet age, Massachusetts Institute of Technology web media researcher Geoffrey Long believes multiple video-delivery devices will fracture the traditional shared entertainment experience fostered by TV.

Marketing experts say consumers want free service supported by limited advertising. Hulu's commercials briefly greet viewers at the beginning of each TV episode and take up about two minutes for every 22 minutes of programming, about 25 percent of the standard TV commercial content. Apple and others have developed devices that aim to combine Internet and TV, but the perfect integrated TV–web invention appears to be a long way off.

FADE TO BLACK

This chapter has featured aspects of media that are particularly relevant for today's readers, viewers, and users. Paperback books seem to have a place among travelers, although wireless reading devices are being continually improved. As book titles grow in numbers, readers meet more often at bookstores to socialize. There are magazines for every hobby and interest; newspapers are most popular on Sunday. Electronic media improve with technology, affording listeners with digital music, commercial-free listening, and HD programming. As TV viewers cross over to Internet webisodes, advertisers take to computers in an effort to sell us more of what we don't need. We rely on media for both news and entertainment in all of its forms, and depend upon those who create new programming and cover late-breaking events.

A CLOSER LOOK AT THE MOVIES

Back to the Future of *Star Wars* with George Lucas

In the summer of 2008, Warner Brothers released an animated version of *Star Wars: The Clone Wars* that seemed to many fans as "one too many" attempts at continuing the saga that originated in 1977. But no one ever accused George Lucas of taking anyone's advice. *Star Wars*, he said, "is a sandbox I love to play in." Vowing to continue Star Wars projects, Lucas, 64, has also squeezed out another Indiana Jones movie (the *Kingdom of the Crystal Skull*) with aging Harrison Ford, who was said to have as much fun making the latest version as he did with the earlier films.

Most of Lucas's decisions are made in one of the two "temples" of homage to his movies, Skywalker Ranch in Marin County and the Letterman Digital Arts Center in San Francisco's Presidio. Characters from his six-film saga—including a life-size Darth Vader and Boba Fett, a Yoda fountain, and a carbonate block encasing Jar Jar Binks—adorn the Presidio facility.

Lucas began LucasFilm Animation in 2005 with a pair of studios at Big Rock Ranch in California and in Singapore. Then he hired a team of young *Star Wars*-obsessed artists, including Dave Filoni who directed *Cone Wars* movie and show. Formerly a director of the Nickelodeon action cartoon *Avatar: The Last Airbender*, Filoni is responsible for the anime-inspired look of *The Clone Wars*, both the film and the TV series. *Clone Wars* began as a series of shorts for the Cartoon Network, and was aired there as a full series in fall 2008.

Unfortunately, the 22-episode TV season was not enthusiastically received by the networks in 2007 because it wasn't compatible with a prime-time network schedule. When Warner Brothers became interested, Lucas decided to produce the film. In the works is a new live-action *Star Wars* TV series for one of Warner's cable channels (TBS, TNT, or HBO).

So the question was, just because a new *Star Wars* can be made, should it? Many fans are only ambivalent about further expanding the property that has yielded comic books, video games, and novels as well as movies and TV shows. "I'll do it because I can. And because I enjoy doing so," said Lucas. According to former colleagues of Lucas, the *Star Wars* projects have provided technological boons for the entire film business, including a special effects company and digital film-editing hardware.

Lucas financed the television series himself, charging Time Warner a licensing fee to distribute and film and broadcast the show. "It's much easier for me to do what I want with the show and then say, 'Do you want it or not?' No notes, comments. They either put it on the air or they don't," said Lucas, who is already working on the second and third seasons of *The Clone Wars* and forging ahead on his live-action *Star Wars* TV show. Next, Lucas will seek other films and television series for his animation studio and continue to develop *Red Tails*, a feature film about the Tuskegee Airmen that has been in the works for a long while.

From his first film, *THX 1138*, a science fiction released in 1971 to today's mega-blockbuster series, Lucas has taken chances and been financially very successful. "Even if I lose everything on these new films, I'll have fun doing it," he said.

Director Dave Filoni and Creator/Exec. Producer George Lucas at U.S. premiere of Warner Bros. *Star Wars: The Clone Wars* on August 10, 2008, at the Egyptian Theatre in Hollywood

Source: Itzdoff, Dave (2008). Free to follow his heart back to "Star Wars." *New York Times*, June 29.

DISCUSSION AND REVIEW

1.   As the competition for advertisers increases, what may be the outcome of the growing proliferation of magazine titles? Why?
2.   Are novels and nonfiction books likely to disappear with the expansion of Internet information and downloading capabilities? Why or why not?
3.   What social commentary can be derived from the growing prominence of celebrity publications? How likely are such publications to influence the level and type of reading and reader behavior?
4.   How has newspapers' role in society changed? What is the relationship between metropolitan and community newspapers? Which one plays the more important role in your life? Why?

EXERCISES

1.   Keep a media diary for a week to log your interaction with printed materials and audio books from novels. What does this tell you about the need for and future of the publishing industry?
2.   Visit a Barnes & Noble or Borders bookstore. Pick up a copy of their event calendar and check out what's coming for the month. Check out the authors selected to talk on the Internet and determine their potential draw for audiences of that particular genre. Which genres are most prominent? Which are absent? What can you determine about genre popularity from the calendar of events?
3.   Take an inventory of a magazine stand and count the number of different groups available to readers (sports, news, etc.). From your tally, which audience is targeted most? Least? What does your research tell us about advertising potential or drawbacks for magazines?
4.   Read an issue of the *New York Times*. Then go online and go over the same issue. Which experience was most entertaining? Why? What does your experience say about the future of newspapers in print?

BOOKS AND BLOGS

Breakenridge, D. (2008). *PR 2.0: New media, new tools, new audiences*. Upper Saddle River NJ: FT Press.

Hui Kyong Chun, W. and Keenan, T.W. (2005). *New media, old media: A history and theory reader*. London and New York: Routledge.

Hansen, M.B. and Lenoir, T. (2006). *New philosophy for new media*. Cambridge MA: MIT Press.

Harrigan, P. and Wardrip-Fruin, N. (2006). *First person: New media as story, performance and game*. Cambridge MA: MIT Press.

Jones, S. (2008). *The meaning of video games: Gaming and textual strategies*. London and New York: Routledge.

www.fanfiction.net—an anthology of stories where readers can contribute their own versions of favorite books and comics.

www.salon.com—a reader's guide to 225 contemporary authors with illustrations and author profiles, reviews and bibliographies.

www.gamespot.com—gaming site containing game reviews and online sales.

www.dmoz.org/Games/Video_Games/—offers an annual quantitative survey that describes gamers hardware, software, and connectivity set-ups.

www.rottentomatoes.com—has movie reviews and fan opinions.

15 LIVE ON OUR STAGE: THE PERFORMING ARTS

Magic is the ability to take people out of their boring, problematic day and leave them in a moment of astonishment.

—David Blaine

Before media transmitted action electronically, all entertainment was performed live. Today, the performing arts must struggle to maintain a slice of the entertainment pie. Founded on ancient traditions that established the basis for dramatic theory, the performing arts are important because they directly reflect our Western heritage. Although many different arts are classified under the rubric of performance, we will discuss those that are most important to twenty-first-century leisure.

Live performances are special events, and as such are different from other kinds of entertainment. Here, the audience is crucial for the event's successes. Active audiences become part of group and lived experiences. As part of a group, individuals increase their power to achieve reinforcement and pleasure. Not only do audiences contribute to the shows' financial successes, they also make personal connections to them. Audiences have esthetic experiences that involve attending to, perceiving, and appreciating performance for itself. The experience of being in the presence of performers is what drives audiences to attend live performances.

If you've ever been to a live performance, you understand the extent to which the show's success is dependent upon audience response. Laughter becomes infectious in a crowd while, if experienced alone, humor might leave you unmoved. Performance succeeds to the degree that the audience is excited. Audiences want to be thrilled, amused, or moved, and they want to know that other people are sharing their experience. When a performance succeeds, audience members subordinate their separate identities to the group. If the house is not full, the performance not only loses money, it loses force.

Live performance has demonstrated an unexpected tenacity in the face of competition from film, television, video, and other popular entertainment. Not simply media spectators, audiences become performers themselves in a live event. If the performance is to succeed, the audience must be active, must share with the performer and assist with the act of creation. Every audience member helps to make or break the performance. Because it can achieve a sense of occasion impossible for mediated events, live performance has retained its lure by providing a true sense of occasion. Buying the tickets, planning the event, socializing with a group, and enjoying post-event activities produce a more enjoyable experience than is usually achieved from viewing a film and watching a television show.

Audiences have levels of expectations for performance, and continue to attend depending upon how well the performers live up to expectations in the true sense of expectancy and uses and gratifications theories. Moreover, the socialization that takes place prior to and following performances lends itself to social theory. And, since each audience member takes away his or her own interpretation of the performance, the reception and reader response theories are also applicable here.

As the object of marketing and sales tactics, live audiences have been the subject of countless studies to determine how performing companies can best deliver exceptional entertainment to subscribers and supporters of the arts. Studies show that audiences want a spectacle in which they can participate. They want to share an experience as well as view a form of entertainment. Designing spectacles has become a paramount challenge for producers of live performance who must continue to compete with mediated entertainment for their share of audiences.

First we look at consuming experiences of attending performing arts. Next, we divide the performing arts into two groups. One we call *classical performance* because of its popularity with traditional audiences who often attend events for their social and lifestyle gratification. The other, *popular performance*, refers to events that are more accessible to mass audiences of varied socio-economic levels and interests. Capitalizing on niche or narrow markets, popular arts performances draw audiences from geographic and demographic segments that are often more interested in the performance itself rather than in the spectacle surrounding it. As interactive performance increases in popularity, distinctions between the two sections become blurred. Live theater that incorporates video or animation into its performance is just one example of genre mixing that is gaining popularity among audiences of both classical and popular events.

Formal Attire Requested: Classical Performance[1]

From the days of Greek theater, performing art has traditionally been categorized by events that appeal to either *elite* or *mass* audiences. Contemporary critics characterize elites (upper class) as people who dress up in expensive clothing, pay high ticket prices, and attend only socially acceptable performances with their socially acceptable friends. For many elites, the spectacle is more important than the quality of the performance. Appearance at these events rein-forces social status and proclaims

Listening to opera in the park

identity as a member of the elite group. With the passing on of the generation that embraced the elite tradition, however, this attitude is disappearing.

As attendance at expensive performance venues declines, arts marketers are devising creative ways to package the theater, ballet, and opera for younger audiences. The trend is away from stuffy, dark performance venues to open-air, well-lighted presentations. Pre-concert discussions, out-of-venue performances, and star power are being used to reduce the audience intimidation factor and to compete with mediated and other forms of entertainment. Short performances are being presented in shopping malls, elementary and junior high schools, and in public parks free of charge. Opera arias are sung in urban parks, and the Santa Fe Chamber Orchestra performs in a Neiman Marcus department store. Each of these events helps to bring performance to a wider audience and build attendance at performance venues.

Sociologists study classical performance audiences and their lifestyles for attendance motivations. Based on the premise that identity is derived from association, audiences frequent events that fit their desired social status. Ticket prices and expected attire have

Cats the musical performed in Moscow

promoted self-selection by audiences who are attracted to status-driven entertainment. With the encroachment of popular culture into even the highest-brow performances however, audiences are becoming homogenized.

This section presents an overview of performances traditionally presented to audiences who appreciate classical arts: theater, musicals, opera, dance, ballet, and symphony. Arts venue managers solicit corporate sponsors and individual donations to support these programs; only a few receive government assistance from the National Endowment for the Arts. Each event has its own tradition and following, and all are important for the roles they play in shaping our social and cultural identity.

Curtain Rising: Drama, Opera, Musicals, and Orchestral Concerts

Although we don't know exactly how the theater came into being, we do accept the traditions born in ancient Athens as dominant in Western theater. Basically, theater can be described at its most fundamental as the presence of an actor in front of an audience. The art of the theater is essentially one of make-believe, or *mimesis*.

FLASH FACT

The League of American Theaters and Producers reported that 12.3 million tickets had been sold during the 2006–7 season, up 2.6 percent from the previous record level. Grosses hit $939 million, up 8.9 percent, and Times Square box office sales were expected to break the billion-dollar barrier in 2008.

The bad news is that shows of the 1990s recouped their costs after 30 weeks, but it now takes over two years to turn a profit. This means that four out of five shows will never earn back their investments.

Source: *The Los Angeles Times*, June 10, 2007/entertainment

Drama   We can trace the origins of drama to simple storytelling. The storyteller would disguise his voice or create characters through movement and costume. Modern dramatic theater is still concerned with live performances that use action to create a coherent and significant sense of drama. Aristotle suggested that drama, tragedy in particular, would affect everybody by eliciting the emotions of pity and fear that would bring about a purging of these emotions. Such a notion is called "catharsis doctrine," which is the cornerstone of drama theory.[2]

In order for us to become involved in the plot, drama requires a degree of *plausibility*. The actors' ability to make the audience "believe in" their speech, movement, thoughts, and feelings determines believability. The connection established between the actors' impressions and the director's intentions contributes to this process. Make-believe is a factor of the distance that exists between actor and audience. To be successful, drama must contain realism and the characters must seem plausible to reduce the distance and engage members of the audience in the action.

Opera   Opera is drama set to music. The story is presented in a series of vocal pieces with orchestral accompaniment, overtures, and interludes. With origins in drama of the Middle Ages, opera developed along national lines during the nineteenth century. Italy, Germany, and France were most active in producing operatic performances. Italian composer Giuseppi Verdi's famous *Rigoletto*, *Il trovatore*, *La traviata*, and *Aida* are perhaps the best known works presented to American audiences today. Germany's Richard Wagner's musical dramas revolutionized opera with *The Ring*; French and Spanish operas are presented less frequently in the U.S. Because it is so recent, American-language opera has yet to be perceived as more than musical theater by opera aficionados.

Foreign-language operas once intimidated audiences, but, with the advent of digitized text translations, Americans are becoming more willing to approach operatic performance. And the emergence of opera "stars" has popularized its music. Public Broadcasting's televised presentation of the "Three Tenors" (Pavarotti, Domingo, and Carreras) attracted younger and more eclectic audiences to opera music. A performance by the Three Tenors brought 200,000 people to New York's Central Park in 1999, contributing to the integration of opera into our popular culture.

Opera is still being performed in the ancient coliseum in Verona, Italy

Originally intended as musical drama for the masses, opera was often performed outdoors for families who sang along while they ate and drank homemade bread and wine. In Verona, Italy, you can still partake in such a spectacle during the summer season when operas are performed in an ancient coliseum to thousands of enthusiasts. Operatic arias are often performed at no charge for the public in San Francisco's Golden Gate Park, continuing the Italian open-air tradition in an abbreviated format.

Musical Theater Generally speaking, Americans prefer their opera "light." One of the most entertaining outgrowths of opera, the musical theater receives the highest numbers of attendance, awards, and recognition. The universal appeal of song and dance has rendered musical theater the most popular show type. America is credited with pioneering modern classic musicals such *as Oklahoma*, *West Side Story*, *My Fair Lady*, and *A Chorus Line*. The most recent musical versions to hit Broadway feature media stars and popular music, setting to music story lines from a variety of popular genres.

Operettas, vaudeville, and burlesque (also called revues) were forerunners of modern musicals: operettas alternate speech and song; vaudeville is a series of variety acts; and burlesque satirizes other theatrical forms. Dance forms associated with the musical, such as tap, jazz, ballroom, and disco, were popularized by

Palace Theater in New York City

dancers and choreographers such as Fred Astaire and Gene Kelly who took musical dance to the status of a genuine art form. In the past two decades, however, musical theater has become more fragmented, and is slowly being replaced by conceptual musicals such as *Fantistiks*, the world's longest-running musical. Other musicals, such as *Mama Mia*, are based on music from performing groups, in this case Sweden's Abba. Or musicals such as *Spamalot*, which was adapted from the Monty Python television series.

Orchestral Concerts Some audiences prefer listening to music for its own sake. And because music has such a profound effect on our emotions, orchestral concerts featuring world-class symphonies are still popular forms of entertainment. And rumors of the demise of classical music are greatly exaggerated. In fact, in May, 2006, the *New York Times* declared this the "golden age of classical music."[3] Accounting for 12 percent of sales for iTunes tracks, classical music download revenues in 2006 have increased for both Sony BMG and Universal. In its first six weeks on iTunes, the New York Philharmonic's download-only Mozart concert sold 2,000 complete copies and 1,000 individual tracks. Small by pop standards, but much better than sales for classical CDs; the trend indicates a new market for more serious music. In addition, new symphony halls have opened in Miami, Nashville, Orange County, California, and Toronto. Why? Revivals, contemporary composers, and vigorous reconsiderations of Bach, Mozart, Beethoven, and Mahler, are bringing audiences back to performance venues.

Music directors are integrating popular vocalists and star performers into their concerts as well. And they are mixing media with live performance. A recent Los Angeles concert combined a symphonic orchestra with classic film cartoons projected on a large screen as background for the accompanying music. Classical concert subscription sales are enhanced with pre-concert lectures and events for single adults to create a social happening that competes for audiences with other more active forms of entertainment.

On Your Toes: Dancing the Night Away

Performing to live or recorded music, ballet and dance entertain us with swirling and twirling, leaping and jumping, and elaborate costuming. Shedding their tutus for more modern attire, dancers perform interpretations of love stories, wars, and comedy. Let's look more closely at each approach to performance.

Ballet Ballet is a vehicle of drama where dancers became characters in a story. When romantic ballet emerged, the ballerina became an ideal stage figure. With diversity and measured grace, the effortless movement of ballet's aristocratic ancestor still distinguishes it from other forms of dance. Just in case you think ballet is still an activity for women wearing tutus, tune into one of the PBS broadcasts to preview the wonderful physical expression that has displaced typical toe dance routines. Modern dance brings new dimension to ballet dramas set to rock and big band music as well as classical pieces. Keeping to the tradition of dramatic performance, ballets tell a story where conflict is danced into resolution.

Modern and Postmodern Dance Based in ballet yet related to the improvisatory forms of popular social dance, modern dance is defined by the choreography developed and performed by professional companies worldwide. As modern dance changes in the concepts and practices of new generations of choreographers, the meaning of the term *dance* grows more and more ambiguous. The separation of dancer and audience in theater dance has tremendous influence on the style of the dance itself and on its reception as an art form. The professionalism of dancer and choreographer, the presentation of movement, and the use of visual effects reach their most sophisticated levels in modern dance performances.

During the 1960s and 1970s a new generation of American choreographers, generally referred to as postmodernists, replaced conventional dance steps with simple movements such as rolling, walking, skipping, and running. A prime influence on the development of *postmodern dance*, the late Merce Cunningham began performing in nontheater spaces. He incorporated repetition, improvisation, minimalism, speech or singing, and mixed-media effects into his company's dance routines.

Most postmodern dance concerts are performed in outside spaces rather than in

Today, ballet companies incorporate modern dance in their repertoire

Pina Bausch performance

theaters as is typical with modern dance performances. In the spirit of Cunningham, postmodernists move in street clothes, use little or no set and lighting, and many performances take place in lofts, galleries, or out of doors. Such avant-garde modern dance companies are small and occupy a position on the fringe of the dance world, attracting only small and specialist audiences. Although "mainstream" modern dance now attracts large audiences in both Europe and North America, it too was for many decades a minority art form, often playing to only a handful of spectators.

Recently, new energy has invigorated theatrical dance. A look at any week's *New York Times* Sunday entertainment sections will evidence the innovations in modern dance performance. One example is Pilobolus, a company started by a Dartmouth College student in the early 1970s, which combines acrobatics, athletics, and gymnastics with dance as a signature choreographic style.

Characterized as being acrobatic mimes,[4] Pilobolus dance group performs worldwide to musical scores by Paul Sullivan that bring a unique postmodern element to performance dance. Another example is a fusion of ballet where hip hop, performed by Big Boi of the hip-hop duo OutKast, joined the Atlanta Ballet dancers in a performance of *Big*.

Using the Big Bucks: Corporate Sponsorship

Important to the continuing health of all forms of classical performance is corporate sponsorship. Used as a public relations tool for troubled industries, arts philanthropy helps bolster the corporate image of companies suffering from poor associations. The benefits are not always mutual. As with their media counterparts, live concerts must incorporate brands into publicity and promotion for their financial survival. Corporations are attracted to performance sponsorships because of the image they reflect. By underwriting a ballet, for instance, an oil company may enhance its otherwise unfavorable image by associating with an upscale, classical event. Next time you attend a live performance, check the program to see who is sponsoring the event and what that sponsorship is intended to provide for the donor. One danger posed by sponsorship affiliation is the loss of creative freedom for arts organizations. There is a tendency among some corporations to "possess" their sponsorship partners; however, as long as audiences are not forced to suffer commercial breaks, no one seems to mind the marriage.

FLASH FACT

Over one-half (56 percent) of those with an interest in the arts say they would "almost always" or "frequently" buy a product sponsoring arts or cultural events over one that does not. In contrast, only about one-third (36 percent) of NFL fans, one-third (34 percent) of America's Cup yachting enthusiasts and less than one-fifth (17 percent) of the Olympic Games audience chose products based on their sponsorships. Almost one-half (48 percent) of Americans with an interest in art events indicated that they hold a "higher trust" in companies that sponsor these events compared to those who do not, while only 16 percent of Olympic Games enthusiasts claim a "higher trust" in their sponsors.

Source: performanceresearch.com/arts-spnsorship

Come as You Are: Popular Performance[5]

Popular performance can be any dance, music, theater, or other art form intended to be received and appreciated by ordinary people in a literate, technologically advanced urban society. Popular art in general tends to reinforce mainstream beliefs and sentiments and to create identity in a social group. It is distinguished by rapid changes of style, by its revivals of earlier art periods, and by its constant borrowings from elite art, folk art, foreign cultures, and modern technology for its song tunes and lyrics, dances, trends, and fads.

The term *popular theater* denotes performances in the tradition of the music hall, vaudeville, burlesque, follies, revue, circus, and musical comedy, as distinguished from legitimate, high, or artistic theater. The singers, dancers, comedians, clowns, puppeteers, jugglers, acrobats, and ventriloquists of popular theater make up much of what is known as "show business." We present seven forms of recent trends in popular theater that both extend tradition and resist it, including: live art, rock concerts, comedy, magic, circus, rodeo, and dog shows. Although each genre has its own following and style, popular performances of all types have one thing in common: the support of passionate followers. As *fans* of popular culture, audiences integrate its fashion and idiosyncratic jargon into their lifestyles. Most fans actively support live performances and often participate in related activities such as Internet chat rooms, fan clubs, and reunions. The trends that continue to provide pop culture fans with innovative and unique forms of popular entertainment are presented in this next section.

Makeup artist with actress backstage

Live and Performance Art

Performance art and live art come in a variety of forms, including monolog, personal ritual, dance theater, and artists' cabaret. Live art is differentiated from classical performance in five ways. Live art:

- is relevant to current events
- has a spontaneous level of creativity
- involves small groups
- costs little to produce
- has a brief duration.

The history of performance throughout the twentieth century shows performance to be an experimental laboratory for some of the most original and radical art forms. Performance provides incomparable material for examining contemporary viewpoints on issues like the body, gender, or multi-culturalism.

The term *performance art* implies a state of perpetual animation. We can see performance in works of artistic creation in Jackson Pollock's *action paintings* that are developed to musical interludes during which he literally flings paint onto canvas. Ed Harris depicts Pollock's performance style, which is paramount for understanding and appreciating his art, in a film named for the artist. "Earth artist Christo," whose works are also considered to be performance art, wraps landscapes and buildings in various materials. Christo has wrapped forms and space such as the Surrounded Islands in Biscayne Bay near Miami, Florida, in 1983, and the Reichstag in Berlin, Germany, in 1995. His performances include planning, constructing, and dismantling the massive projects, which are photographed and preserved in books about each installation.

Bicyclist passing Christo's artwork *The Gates,* displayed in 2005 in Central Park

Festivals

An increasingly popular live music format is the multi-act concert festival. One such festival was The Vans Warped Tour, which showcased Green Day and the Mighty Mighty Bosstones. These types of festivals can be traced as far back as the three-day Woodstock festival held in 1969, which featured an impressive collection of artists, including Janis Joplin, Jimi Hendrix, the Grateful Dead, and numerous others. Since then, music festivals have become increasingly popular, likely owing in large part to their efficiency. Audiences can see several bands in a compact period of time, usually for less money than if they saw each one separately. And, in addition to music, these concerts, which may last for days, typically draw a range of venders peddling food, drink, clothing, and novelties to round out the festival experience.

Austin Texas's South by Southwest Festival became the place to be for bands looking for a musical platform in 2008. More than 1,700 bands performed day and night at Austin's clubs, halls, meeting rooms, parking lots, and street corners in what is called America's most important music convention, especially for rising bands. Gathering a critical mass of musicians, supporters, and exploiters from across the globe, the twenty-second annual festival had corporate sponsors who latched onto music as a dream and a symbol of cool. Citigroup, Dell, wineries, social networking sites, and chef Rachael Ray were among the sponsors of the event where subsidized bands came from Australia, Norway, Spain, and Britain. As major labels have shrunk, the festival has nearly doubled in size—up to 12,500 people registered for the 2008 convention—acting as a way to route musical careers around what's left of the major recording companies.

Burning Man is also a popular annual event, held in the Nevada desert where kids of all ages meet to break free from commercialism and declare themselves part of a pure and spiritual festival honoring nature. The festival features song and dance that culminates in the burning of a huge wooden figure. Participants—who are often nude—commune in song and ceremony for five days of creative expression.

Festivals of celebration also draw thousands on an annual basis. "Mardi Gras" (French for Fat Tuesday) is the day before Ash Wednesday, the final day of Carnival's three-day period. Cities most famous for their Mardi Gras celebrations

Annual Burning Man festival in the Black Rock Desert near Gerlach, Nevada

include New Orleans, Louisiana, and Sydney, Australia. New Orleans's Mardi Gras has resumed its partying with gusto since Hurricane Katrina, bringing costumes, food, and music to the streets of this jazz city. *Carnaval*, as spelled in Portuguese, is held in a variety of South American locations. Attracting thousands of people from all corners of the world, *Carnaval*'s wild four-day celebration is held in towns and villages throughout Brazil and other Catholic countries, but Rio de Janeiro has long been regarded as the Carnival Capital of the World. Foreign visitors to it alone number around 500,000 every year. The European Carnivale, held in Venice, Italy, features decorative masks and costumes to hide identity and promote a good time.

Costumes are part of the *Carnaval* parade at the Sambodromo in Rio de Janeiro

Band Bashes

The audience for popular music (as distinct from the music of the concert hall) grew tremendously in the first half of the twentieth century, partly because of technological developments. In 1954, electronic instruments accompanied Elvis Presley's nondenominational music that incorporated everything from hillbilly rave-ups and blues wails to pop-crooner ballads. Teen audiences became the prime target for **concerts** presenting most new forms of popular music.

| SPOTLIGHT ON ROCK | Band Partnerships for a Business in Flux |

When Duff McKagan, former bass player for hard rock band Guns N' Roses, was in the limelight, he never thought about keeping track of his cash. But with today's fluctuating music industry, McKagan tightly monitors the finances of his current band, Velvet Revolver.

Like other middle-aged rockers, he is also experimenting with new partnerships to increase the band's brand awareness and to generate additional revenue. Amid plunging record sales and Internet file sharing, rockers are eagerly plastering their names everywhere. Their "brands" are now found in TV commercials, tour sponsorships and merchandise as diverse as cars, private-label wines, and celebrity cruises. His new band has licensed its music to a Victoria's Secret commercial and movie soundtracks, formed partnerships with entities like video simulation game Guitar Hero, and appeared in ads for designer John Varvatos.

Merchandising and partnerships for rock bands take advantage of the appeal music has as a marketing vehicle. Rock band Kiss is among the most prolific merchandisers, selling products ranging from condoms to "Kiss Kasket," a limited-edition coffin! The band's latest offerings include musical toothbrushes, pool cues, window blinds, and baby bootees. Paul McCartney made a deal with iTunes and Starbucks to distribute his music. Even rock icon Mick Jagger toots the corporate horn. The Rolling Stones have teemed up with Sprint and Budweiser for concert tours and the band hawks everything from bras and panties to leather bomber jackets.

Band branding has expanded its boundaries—the Black Crowes market rolling papers, Bon Jovi offers $1,000 signed canvas art prints, and Mötley Crüe peddles Mötley Brüe, a carbonated drink. Special-edition wines from Celebration Cellars winery feature band logos of Bon Jovi, Kiss, Madonna, and the Rolling Stones and sell for $100 a bottle.

But not all associations work. Bon Jovi's manager Jack Rovner believes that commercial partners should complement musicians' vibe, lifestyle, and message. The right commercials, TV shows, and movie soundtracks can make or break a band. A Sting song, "Desert Rose," was doing nothing until Jaguar used it as background music for its commercial. Sting,

an environmentalist, was not the right person to endorse a gas-guzzler, but the commercial helped to sell three million records and got him a Grammy. But when Wilco did a Volkswagen commercial, their fans shredded them on Internet message boards and their brand suffered.

Some "purists" like Bruce Springsteen, Tool, and Nine Inch Nails refuse to form corporate partnerships. Putting music and art first, the performers even refuse to license their music for cellphone ringtones. But for those who are partnering up, record labels want their share of the promotional and merchandising income as a condition of getting record contracts. Other artists are quitting big labels and working directly with experts in merchandise, touring, and digital downloading.

Artists coming of age in the Internet era understand this new corporate alliance and all its nuances to their advantage. Following in the footsteps of hip-hop artists who always understood branding, new bands start clothing lines and jump into commercials. Like the artists, corporations see both sides of associations. Because so much money is being raked in through partnerships and merchandising, corporations tread lightly when signing up with musicians. According to one manager, rock is no longer just about the music.

Source: Morrissey, Janet (2007). If it's retail, is it still rock? *New York Times*, Oct. 28

What do you think?

- *What are the drawback with marrying rock stars with products?*
- *Is there any added value for consumers who purchase branded merchandise with band brands?*

Madonna Confessions Wine

Another aggressive form of music, punk rock, coalesced into an international movement between 1975 and 1980. Full of vital energy beneath a sarcastic and hostile facade, punk became an archetype of teen rebellion and alienation. An American rock band that played improvisational psychedelic music, the Grateful Dead was one of the most successful **touring bands** in rock history. The Grateful Dead combined jug bands with musicians in the San Francisco Bay area in the early 1960s. Remarkably eclectic, the Dead provided a key part of the free live music filling San Francisco during 1967's Summer of Love, when the city became a magnet for hippie baby boomers. The Dead created a new form of American performance follower: the groupie. Deadheads, as their fans were known, epitomized the counterculture. Draped in flowing scarves and granny dresses, they danced for hours to the jamming band on stage. The Dead pooled eclectic talents to pioneer an energizing blend of rock instrumentation and jazzy improvisation.

Meanwhile, **psychedelic bands** were drawing their share of enthusiasts. The 13th Floor Elevators from Austin, Texas, reflected the darker, more psychotic frenzy of acid rock. Acid was characterized by overdriven guitars, amplified feedback, and droning guitar motifs that were influenced by Eastern music. Pink Floyd was the leading group of the British scene, which revolved around venues such as London's UFO club and Middle Earth. Events like the 14-Hour Technicolor Dream drew counterculture celebrities such as John Lennon, Yoko Ono, and Andy Warhol. While few psychedelic bands lasted, the impact of the genre was huge, revolutionizing fashion, poster art, and live performance.

In the 1990s, Jimmy Buffett's audience flocked to his concerts in Hawaiian shirts to celebrate tropical fantasy in much the same manner as the Deadheads embraced their band decades before. The emer-gence of hip hop, straight edge and rap drew equally frenzied fans as the rock concert era continued to evolve into today's version of a high-energy musical event. Enhanced with giant video screens, light shows, and Dolby sound systems, musical concerts draw audiences by the thousands to large arenas and outdoor venues. Audience involvement in live band concerts makes them a popular form of live entertainment.

Jimmy Buffett's Las Vegas Margaritaville venue

Yucks-"R"-Us: Comedy

Comedy has always been a form of popular expression performers used to deliver political and social messages to live audiences. Parodies, satires, off-color jokes, and slapstick have amused audiences for decades in nightclubs, county fairs, and amateur nights. Joke-telling and comedy have grown to be acceptable performance formats for expressing opinions and critiquing society.

Comedy also consists of humor used to ridicule people we dislike. Why do we get pleasure from the misfortune of others? By making fun of other people's predicaments, we can forget our own. Mood management theory suggests that frustrated men and angry women tend to pick comedy more than people of other temperaments. Through comedy, anger dissipates. For many of us, humor appears to hold promise as a mood repairer by offering up light-hearted solutions to adverse conditions.

In times of stress, many people seek out laughter and relief. One place they can find a heavy concentration of humor in the form of jokes is a club specializing in comedy. **Comedy clubs** specifically dedicated to humor and improvisation have been around since 1960 and were very active until the 1980s when the proliferation of second-tier come-dians who were neither funny nor affordable diminished audiences. The best known venue for comedy was Chicago's Second City, where Bill Murray, John Belushi, and Chris Farley began their careers. In a theater that seats 300, Second City performers still combine scripted sketches with improvised bits from audience ideas in shows performed every night of the week.

The Ice House, a San Gabriel Valley (California) folk music club, started featuring comedy in the 1970s when Lily Tomlin and the Smothers Brothers recorded albums there.

The club recently added an annex to present weekend Comedy Clinics. San Francisco's Improv hosted comics like Robin Williams who still appears there on occasion to try out new routines. Veterans of stand-up comedy, talk show hosts David Letterman and Jay Leno use comedy to recast current events in nightly televised monologs to live audiences. *Saturday Night Live*, which began with an improvisational format, also features former club comics in their sketch-parodies.

Many "open mikes" are available in bars and malls where aspiring comedians can perform before live audiences. Men and women aiming for television auditions often begin their careers with original material at open mikes, graduate to comedy clubs, and eventually get an agent to promote them. A newsgroup dedicated to communication between agents, writers, and comics, www.alt.comedy.standup provides professionals with opportunities to interact and connect with one another. All in an attempt to amuse audiences with humor.

Jamie Foxx performing live comedy

If it's funny, we laugh. But why? One researcher who recorded 1,200 laugh episodes concluded that most laughter is produced by speakers, not listeners.[6] So we laugh more when our entertainer laughs. Also, a gender disparity in laugh rates was discovered, with women surpassing men. Ideally then, performers should gravitate to female audiences for the most active laughter available.

For whatever reason, comedy has had an important place in entertaining live audiences since jesters and clowns became professionals. Requiring a quick wit, the ability to write, and nerve enough to perform before live audiences, today's stand-up comics are tomorrow's TV and film stars. Their take on society, well crafted into funny anecdotes and characterizations, provides insight into perceptions of ourselves and others that may be no laughing matter.

Now You See It, Now You Don't: Magic[7]

A magician is an actor who pretends to do something impossible. The fire-eater, for instance, uses a loosely woven rope specially treated with chemicals to catch fire when it's removed from his throat. Onlookers see the rope's glow as it is swallowed and believe in the illusion. Using the psychology of deception and timing, magicians have mystified audiences for centuries. As mystifying illusionists, magicians have passed the secrets of their trade from generation to generation.

Illusionist David Copperfield performed tricks at the age of 12 to enthralled audiences. Best known for his ability for making large objects disappear (he made an airplane disappear from an airport runway), Copperfield staged an escape from Alcatraz prison in 1987. Copperfield, who performs over 500 shows per year throughout the world, said in August 2006 that he has found the "Fountain of Youth" in the southern Bahamas, amid a cluster of four tiny islands he had purchased on July 14 of that year. He claims that the

Magician David Blaine in water bubble, Lincoln Center

water brings dead leaves back to life, and brings near dead insects back to life. He said he has hired biologists and geologists to examine its potential effect on humans. Is this claim a precursor used to predict what his next illusion will be?

Taking up a trick never completed by Houdini who died first of a ruptured appendix, magician David Blaine is best known for his spectacle of entombment. He spent 72 hours inside a block of ice in front of the ABC building in New York, for instance. Most of his illusions are performed for individuals rather than before large audiences. To engage a kid on the street, Blaine will remove his baseball cap, reach inside, and pull out a large snake. And he doesn't charge admission! The antithesis of showman Copperfield, Blaine's style is low-key—no stage, no lights, no smoke, no curtains. It's just himself and a random audience.[8]

One of the most famous venues for illusion is the Magic Castle, a 1908 Victorian mansion located in the hills above Hollywood. The Castle is a clubhouse for the Academy of Magical Arts, an organization established to encourage and promote public interest in the ancient art of magic. A dress code is enforced at the Castle for audiences who come to watch performers create illusions that have the appearance of reality.[9] Magic continues to captivate live audiences composed of people who have become numb from the visual deceptions of mass media.

The Greatest Show on Earth: Circus

Circus entertainment combines the suspense of acrobatics, comedy of clowns, and curiosity about wild animals into a unique blend of enjoyment. Most Americans have heard about or have attended a Ringling Brothers or Barnum & Bailey Circus. These traveling shows were the highlight of pre-TV entertainment, causing young children to dream of "joining the circus" when they were old enough to leave home. The 130-year-old "greatest show on earth" still performs at Madison Square Garden and other venues around

America. Although attendance at circuses remains steady, such large venues are hard to fill.[10]

Responding to a demand for technologically innovative entertainment, the circus's struggle to retain its popularity as a local attraction has yielded new "hybrid" forms of ringside entertainment. The most recent innovation, nouveau cirque, is circus without animals, clowns, or fire-eaters. Started in 1984 in France, the Cirque Plume pioneered the idea of blending theater, music, dance, magic, acrobatics, and comedy and calling it circus, as featured in the following *Spotlight*.

SPOTLIGHT ON PERFORMANCE   Cirque du Soleil

Described as the modern circus, Cirque du Soleil focuses upon a story line with amazing performances using both resident and touring troupes. Emphasizing the use of humans as performers, Cirque du Soleil combines elements of street performances, circus, opera, ballet, and rock music. Acts include contortionists, jugglers, feats of strength, clowning, and trapeze artists. Cirque shows feature live music Cirquish, an imaginary language invented by the company.

Shows include both "house" and "guest" acts. House acts are performed by the full-time cast members, some of whom may be involved in several routines. Guest acts (typically clowns) rotate in and out over the run of the show, and performances can vary somewhat with shows tending to evolve over time. Cirque du Soleil recruits acts from Chinese and Russian circuses, blending them into the troupe's own style.

Regarded as one of the world's best circuses, Cirque performers receive higher than normal pay scales and benefits. The troupe features touring shows that appear regionally in specially erected tents, and shows in permanent residences in major hotels.

One of the touring shows, *Quidam*, is imagined by a young girl named Zoe who is alienated and ignored by her parents. She dreams up the whimsical world of Quidam in an attempt to escape her sadness. The title refers to the headless feature character, best described as a giant Headless Horseman sans horse, carrying an umbrella and a bowler hat. Quidam is said

Varekai opened in Berlin, Germany, in June, 2008

to be the embodiment of both everyone and no one at the same time, a solitary figure who cries out, sings, and dreams within us all.

KÀ, performed at the MGM Grand Las Vegas, was the first Cirque du Soleil production to deviate from the company's usual format, making the story presentation more straight forward and easier to understand than the abstract visuals presented by other productions.

Lacking a traditional "stage," *KÀ* relies on floating platforms that rotate and move with the performers on top. This floating stage twists from horizontal to vertical, sprouting poles for performers to climb, and being covered with sand where actors hide. *KÀ* features an off-stage orchestra, on-stage acrobatics, and singing. Musicians often perform directly on the stage dressed in costumes. *KÀ* combines complex hydraulics, automation, pyrotechnics, puppetries, and multimedia projections that allow the audience to immerse themselves in the story.

O has a permanent residence at the Bellagio in Las Vegas. The troupe's first aquatic show integrates underwater acts with above-ground performance where every member of the cast is SCUBA-certified. The costumes have a lifespan of 20 shows, with multiple costumes per performer. In order for the platform stage to rise and fall without a wake, the surface of the stage has thousands of tiny holes.

If you get the chance, don't miss the next performance appearing in your city. You won't forget the experience.

Source: www.cirquedusoleil.com

The down side of circuses is animal abuse, which is reported to occur regularly at Ringling Brothers. One organization, People for the Ethical Treatment of Animals (PETA), has worked to bring awareness to animal cruelty among circus providers. So far, the group has:

- driven away Ringling's national sponsors. Major corporations—including Denny's, MasterCard, Visa, Liz Claiborne and Sears, Roebuck & Co.—have distanced themselves from the trail of dead animals that follows the circus.
- uncovered evidence prompting the U.S. Department of Agriculture to open six investigations into Ringling's possible violations of the Animal Welfare Act.
- gotten several former Ringling employees to come forward and tell the public about the systematic cruelty that they witnessed. This has given the Ringling circus a black eye—and it's convincing compassionate families to spend their money elsewhere.

Ringling Brothers Circus arrives in Cleveland, Ohio, with Indian baseball banners on the performing elephants

Buckin' Broncos: Rodeo

By combining the thrill of circus acts with the primitive conflict of a sporting event, Westerners developed the rodeo. This series of contests and exhibitions in riding, roping, and other cowboy skills was developed between 1867 and 1887. Audiences cheered for bull riders, steer wrestlers, saddle and bareback bronc-riders, and steer or calf ropers. Cheyenne, Wyoming, claims to be the birthplace of the rodeo and has presented Frontier Days every year since 1897. For the past 25 years, the number of rodeos, attendance, and purse money have increased, and women now compete in their own rodeos with barrel racing as the main event.

Ennis hosts Montana's biggest local rodeo

Horses and steers play key roles in rodeos as adversaries to chapped and hatted riders and wrestlers. Once released from chutes, calves must be roped with three hooves tied together in under 15 seconds to be competitive. Champion wrestlers throw steer in record 10-second times. During riding events, contestants must stay on the horse for eight seconds, holding on with one hand while being judged on a point system for their performance.

Rodeo audiences relive the excitement of the Old West, watching as man is pitted against beast in the ultimate competition to tame or be tamed. They cheer their favorite performers and partake in festivities that are reminiscent of frontier times. The lure of the authentic is a primary motivation for rodeo participants. A truly American form of entertainment, the rodeo has an established place in popular culture history and is still enjoyed by enthusiasts throughout the western United States.

Fido Folly: Dog Shows

Animal competitions have always been popular with American audiences, but the dog show craze has swept the nation. Parodied in the film *Best in Show*, canine competitions pair dogs and owners or trainers against judges who rate them for structure, coat, and movement. Dog shows—attended by prospective buyers as well as owners—consist of barking noises, prancing movement, petting gestures, grooming rituals, and fancy trophies. Each breed is shown at a certain time in a special ring, and dogs are judged for their conformity to the breed standard. Dog fanciers attend shows every weekend, meeting friends and competing through their dogs. For participants, dog showing is much more than a hobby, it's a lifestyle. For audiences, dog watching is pure spectacle.

Breed rings present different levels of competition and dogs that are not champions compete at the class level by sex. Each class—puppy, novice, American bred, bred by exhibitor, and open—has four placement awards. The next level of competition yields "Best" awards: best of breed, best of sex, and winner. Best of Breed dogs are eligible to show in the *group*, the place where the real competition begins. Breeds are divided into seven groups: Sporting, Hound, Working, Terrier, Toy, Non-Sporting, and Herding. The winning dog in each group then competes for the grand prize, Best In Show. With the multiple judging stages needed to win, competitors must devote significant time and energy to the showing process.

Dog ratings are compiled by dog publications or breed clubs and only convey prestige to the top dogs in the country. With 70 percent of Americans owning dogs these days, dog shows are popular events where people and pets meet and mingle amidst the flurry of regimented fanfare. A walk through the grooming

Burmese mountain dog with its handler at a dog show

area provides a look at the best ambassadors of their respective breeds—perfect specimens. Everyone agrees: there is no substitute for the live action dog show extravaganza.

One explanation for our K-9 fascination is provided by identification theory. Owners derive a sense of esteem through their pet's accomplishments. The pride of ownership that accompanies a blue ribbon has less to do with the animal's championship lines than it does with a human desire for recognition. A positive relationship is found to exist between the corresponding levels of recognition from winning and enjoyment of participation. In other words, winners have more fun. Spectators who compare owner to pet may notice an uncanny similarity between the two, which reinforces the notion of shared identity.

Bullfighting

Spain loves bullfighting. As a result, matadors and fans gather in large stadiums to pit animal against man. But, as aficionados will tell you, bullfighting is not a sport. It's never featured on the sports pages in Spanish newspapers because sport implies a fair fight between willing opponents. Except in rare cases when his life is spared for bravery, bulls always die. This torero tradition has become an art; every combination of bull and bullfighter elicits a different, unpredictable, improvised performance. Admirers believe the true goal of torero is bringing out the innate bravery and nobility and distinct character of each bull. A newcomer with an open mind who goes to a bullfight can come away feeling that it is both artful and repulsive, a paradox that seems to represent the Spanish attitude.

Spanish matador Fernando Garcia Roble has a standoff with the bull

Once a people's pastime, torero has become akin to fine wine—the domain of the consumer elite. Torero is embraced because it's not manipulated or foisted on people by government, church, or state; and, even if it's a luxury item, it still has a popular aspect. There are more than 1,000 bullfights annually in the old style of performance, where matadors plant their feet and get bulls to make close, choreographed passes.

But today, Giorgio Armani has used the style—and the matadors—as models for his clothing. In the wake of hundreds of advertisements, every Spanish town wants a *corrida* (arena) with a star matador for its main attraction.

With so many forms of entertainment from which to choose, Spanish fans still attend bullfights because there's nothing else that offers so much reality. Bullfighting survives its own social anachronism not just because of its machismo mythology but also because of an irrational, purely visceral response that fans and bullfighters share. Being irrational, it remains exotic even in Spain. According to one fan, bullfighting will persist as the last heroic act, the last myth after astronauts and mountain climbers are no longer myths.[11]

Watching Sports

Today's sports organizations embrace their role as entertainment providers whole-heartedly. Reporter Keith Epstein of the *Washington Post* explains that professional sports events have become blowout entertainment extravaganzas. "Chants will blare from loud-speakers: 'Who let the dogs out? Woof-woof-woof-woof.' Crowd-rousers will lead dances and cheers. And before kickoff, fireworks will explode from the two end zones. . . . It's pageant. It's spectacle. It's theater. It's ear-pounding."[12]

A Word from Our Sponsor

Sports is big business these days—a business of endorsements, sponsorships, broadcast rights, and licensing agreements. Professional athletes like Michael Jordan, Shacquille O'Neal, and Tiger Woods endorse products ranging from burgers to briefs. Sponsorship spending by North American companies rose 12.6 percent in 2008 to $16.78 billion, according to IEG Sponsorship Report, the world's leading authority on sponsorship. That increase marked the sixth consecutive year that the growth rate was higher than the year before. However, an IEG survey found that 50 percent of companies cut their sponsorship

Companies such as Staples gain name recognition and add excitement to mundane products through association with sports and entertainment venues

spending in 2009 because of the economic downturn. The survey found that 36 percent of companies polled would keep spending at 2008 levels. Corporations are putting their names on stadiums and convention centers, from Philadelphia's First Union Center (home of the NHL Flyers and the NBA 76ers) to Landover, Maryland's FedEx Field (home of the NFL Redskins) to the Staples Center in Los Angeles (home of the NBA Lakers and Clippers and NHL Kings).

Although FedEx and Staples enjoy high name recognition, purchasing stadium rights can give even lesser-known entities much-desired advertising. Donna Ramer, managing director at the public-relations firm Makovsky & Co., cites 3Com Corp., the computer company that purchased the naming rights to then-Candlestick Park, host of the NFL's San Francisco 49ers. "Nobody really knew who 3Com was when they bought the rights. But it enabled them to get vital name placement and awareness. Companies want consumers to associate their product with a city," Ramer said.[13] In just the first six months, that $500,000 investment netted 3Com an estimated $48 million in national publicity at a time when 3Com's networking company was trying to establish itself as a nationwide leader in its field.[14]

The economic downturn that began with the new millennium forced some companies to consider making cutbacks in their sponsorship deals. In 1999, PSINet Inc. signed a deal to pay $105 million to put its corporate logo on the Baltimore Ravens' new football stadium. Less than three years into its 20-year contract, the Ashburn, Virginia-based company admitted that it soon might run out of cash and be forced into a bankruptcy filing, and it ended the original sponsorship deal. Meanwhile, Miami's Pro Player Stadium began looking for a new sponsor in the spring of 2000 when Pro Player's parent company, Fruit of the Loom, filed for bankruptcy.[15] And 3Com opted not to renew its contract with Candlestick Park.

When these deals fall through, the negative publicity sports franchises suffer for being associated with this failure can be as painful as the financial losses. It seems likely that sports sponsorships will remain a critical component of professional and amateur sports alike; however, both sponsors and sports programs are also likely to become more sophisticated and cautious in their dealings.

Venue Varieties

Ballpark food used to consist of frozen pizzas, sodden hot dogs on sullen buns, and bad fast-food chains. But in order to keep fans coming to events, sports venues have become culinary delights. As aging stadiums are either renovated or replaced, the ballparks have stepped up their game, and not just for the corporate skybox crowd. New stadiums have been laid out so that nosebleed sections have decent views, the concourses aren't dark passageways, and the food and beer offered are no longer an afterthought to the game.[16]

Hot dogs and peanuts still rule the food court, but concessionaires also

Baseball fans watch the Los Angeles Dodgers while eating traditional and Asian food, but the menu ranges from barbecued rack of ribs to lavender meringue

serve humanely raised meat, and fans drink beer from biodegradable cups made of corn, and a few might even have filled their cars with biodiesel made from the park's used fryer oil after the game. And dishes from other baseball-loving cultures have made inroads, like tonkatsu, Japanese fried pork cutlets; sweet-fried plantains from Latin America; and pressed Cuban sandwiches. *The* leading example of upscale food might be AT&T Park in San Francisco. Opened in 2000, the stadium has a classic, arched-coliseum look, but with modern amenities like wide concourses with great sightlines to the field. If you hear the crack of a bat and the crowd beginning to roar, you can pivot around in the beer line and follow the ball as it flies over the outfield wall. And instead of ferrying your food back to your seat, or eating over a trash can in some cinderblock tunnel, the airy concourse is dotted with counter-height tables that look out over the field.

FADE TO BLACK

What you learned from this chapter is that when you turn off the TV and log off the Internet to participate in live performances, you are in for a treat. The performance arts entertain us in ways that mediated forms cannot. As an audience member, you get to participate in what's happening, sing along, clap, stamp your feet, and cheer. And you get to do it with 10,000 of your closest friends! Performance has entertainment value, economic value, and social value. We can escape from routine for just a few dollars, or even for free. We can laugh, cry, and lose ourselves in the experience of the moment. Most audiences agree that no other form of entertainment is as fulfilling as live performance.

We hope that live performance is not a dying art because it brings to us an element of the real that no other type of entertainment can. We get to feel, see, taste, touch, smell, and hear everything in person. As audiences, we can actively participate in performance success. Think about it. Real people performing real music, art, and theater in real time. What a concept! By supporting these events, we can maintain our connection with the esthetic, with the beautiful, and with our cultural past. As the ancestors of mass media, the performing arts reflect centuries of talent and spirit. These arts are our heritage and our future; they also serve well as ambassadors to our global community.

A CLOSER LOOK AT CONCERTS	Aging Acts and the Demise of Performance Revenue

You can't steal a concert. You can't download the band—or the sweaty fans in the front row—to your laptop to take with you. If you want to share the concert-going experience, you and your friends all have to buy tickets. For this reason, many in the ailing music industry see concerts as the next great hope to revive their business.

As layoff's sweep the major labels, many industry veterans turn their attention to the concert business, pinning their hopes on live performances as a way to bolster their bottom line. But concerts might be a short-term fix. As one national concert promoter says, "The road is where the money is." But in the long run, the music business can't depend on concert tours for a simple reason: the huge tour profits that have been generated in the last few decades have come from performers who are in their 40s, 50s, and 60s. As these artists get older, they're unlikely to be replaced, because the industry isn't investing in new talent development.

Parts of the music industry are hurting. Labels must act more like management companies, and tap into the broadest collection of revenue streams and licensing as much as possible. The $3 billion-plus touring business is already competitive and not very profitable. Even so, belief in the touring business was so strong in 2007 that Madonna signed over her next ten years to touring company Live Nation—the folks who put on megatours for The Rolling Stones, The Police, and other big headliners—in a deal reportedly worth more than $120 million. Artists like these who are offered megamillions for a piece of their brand already have built it through years of album releases, heavy touring, and careful fan-base development.

According to Michael Rapino of Live Nation, a concert-tour company's margin is about 4 percent, while the take on income from concessions, T-shirts, and other merchandise sold at shows can be much higher. The business had a record-setting year in 2006, which saw The Rolling Stones, Madonna, U2, Barbra Streisand, and other popular, high-priced tours on the road. But in 2007, North American gross concert dollars dropped more than 10 percent to $2.6 billion, according to Billboard statistics. Concert attendance fell by more than 19 percent to 51 million. Fewer people in the stands mean less merchandise sold and less concession-stand food eaten.

If you pour tens of millions of dollars into a deal, you will need the act to tour for a long time to recoup your investment. Three decades ago, no one would have predicted that Billy Joel or Rod Stewart would still be touring today, yet the industry has come to depend on artists such as these, known as "heritage acts." The top-grossing tours of 2006 and 2007 included veterans such as The Rolling Stones, Rod Stewart, Barbra Streisand, and Roger Waters, as shown in Figure 15.1.

Younger stars, the ones who are prone to taking "media shortcuts," such as appearing on MTV, may have less chance of developing real staying power. With the instant-gratification mode of music discovery, buying an album or going to a concert becomes a big commitment, especially for young people who are unwilling to pay hundreds of dollars for a ticket. Instead, they'll opt to go out a few nights a week and see an emerging band play a club for a $15 cover charge.

Most major promoters don't know how to capture young people's interest and translate it into ticket sales. Most advertising dollars are spent on media that don't even focus on young demographics. Conversely, the readers and listeners of traditional media are perfect for high-grossing heritage tours. As long as tickets sell for those events, promoters won't have to change their approach.

These days, with the lack of record sales, it's the bands that do tour and have that fan base that are the ones that are going to last as artists. Live Nation and competitor, AEG Live, have recognized potential in the market for more intimate concerts. In recent

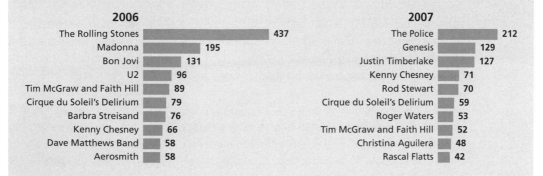

Figure 15.1   Top Ten Grossing Tours ($ million)

years both have snapped up small and middle-sized halls to go along with their huge arenas. Live Nation has the House of Blues and Fillmore chains nationwide, while AEG owns the 700-seat El Rey Theater in Los Angeles and recently opened the 2,000-seat Nokia Theater in Times Square, among other venues. Even as they tout the health of the megatour market, these companies are hedging their bets that the live-music arena of the future won't be a 20,000-seat venue, but rather a collection of 2,000–5,000-seat clubs and theater-sized houses.

The music industry still has hope that talent will win out, and that the public will buy what it has to sell. Industry leaders know that, ultimately, it's not about the package a song comes in—whether it's vinyl, magnetic tape, plastic disc, data on a hard drive, or experienced live from the tenth row—it's about the emotions a song invokes, and the communion it creates between a listener, the artist, and other fans. They just haven't figured out how to sustain profits from that communion as the packaging continues to change.

Historically, the era of the megatour is an anomaly. Baby boomers have come to expect that their rock heroes will put on massive concert events, yet, ten or twenty years from now, few heritage acts may have the stamina to stay on the road. According to Billboard statistics, only one of the top ten box-office draws in the last decade is an act that hit it big after the 1970s. The Dave Matthews Band grossed more than $500 million in its career and may have the consistent fan base necessary for long-term touring success. But even if the band tours regularly for the next two decades, it won't be able to sustain the megatour cycle on its own, and the Justin Timberlakes and Christina Aguileras of the pop world have yet to establish their long-term appeal.[17]

Source: Cohan, J. (2008). The show must go on. www.american.com

DISCUSSION AND REVIEW

1. Do "hi-brow" and "lo-brow" distinctions exist today with regard to audiences? To entertainment types? How can you tell?
2. What role do humor and jokes play in sports casting? In politics?
3. Discuss the marketing potential for televising and promoting dog shows to non-dog-owners. What is the role for product endorsement and sponsorship opportunities?
4. Respond to the notion that bullfighting is an art rather than a sport. What are the ethics involved in this activity?

EXERCISES

1. Using the calendar or entertainment section of your city's Sunday newspaper as a source, count the number of live performances offered this week. How does the number compare with the competing sports, film, and other entertainment offerings? Do your findings substantiate the chapter's notion of reduced offerings of performing arts?
2. Visit a web site dedicated to magic or comedy and consult the links as well as the content. If you were interested in attending a live performance, would the site help you locate a local venue? Does the site recommend places you can learn more about these two aspects of performance? Would you classify these events as suitable for elite or mass audiences? Why?
3. Recall a live performance that you have attended within the past few months, or attend one. Do you define it as classical or popular art? Was your attendance

motivation social or are you interested in a particular performance genre? What role did the audience play in your enjoyment of the performance? Do you agree with the chapter's assertion that live performance depends upon audience reaction? Why?

BOOKS AND BLOGS

Anderson, J. (1999). *Art without boundaries: The world of modern dance*. Iowa City: University of Iowa Press.

Christopher, M. (1996). *The illustrated history of magic*. Portsmouth NH: Heinemann.

Cunningham, M. (1999). *The rock concert industry in the nineties*. London: Sanctuary.

Kaye, E. and Barnes, C. (1999). *American Ballet Theater: 25-year retrospective*. Riverside NJ: Andrews McMeel.

Wagner, R. and Ellis, W.A. (1995). *Actors and singers*. Lincoln: University of Nebraska Press.

www.sfx.com—enter your zip code and find out about music, theater, and comedy shows and other live entertainment performing nearby.

www.geocities.com—find out what is happening in cities all over the U.S.

www.theaterhistory.com—collections of articles and links on the origins of theater and theater history in various countries, cultures, and time periods.

www.magicexhibit.org—provides the history of magic and illusion.

16 TRAVEL, ATTRACTIONS, AND RECREATION

The tourist is the other fellow.
—Evelyn Waugh

With so many entertainment options, appropriating our leisure time can be a daunting chore. Both individuals and companies are recognizing the importance of personal relaxation and rejuvenation. Nominated as the nation's best company to work for in 2007, Google provides employees with the opportunity and facilities to recreate and travel as part of their work-week. Technology has allowed us to work out of the office and often to incorporate travel and recreation into our job routines.

Unlike other entertainment options where we act as audience members and members of social communities, travel and recreation involve us as individual active participants. This chapter takes us through the various aspects of travel and tourism and the amusements we encounter in new places. We also present ways in which people use leisure time to engage in recreational activities and extreme sports.

Travel and Tourism

Tourism is the largest employer in the world. The industry provides services such as lodging, food, souvenirs, entertainment, and transportation to people who travel. **Travel** includes a journey to some destination and the services that facilitate that journey. **Tourism** is an industry that interacts with every aspect of the travel process where people leave home, travel to a destination, act as guests to hosts who serve them, collect souvenirs, and return home. The important elements of the tourism process are presented in Table 16.1. In this chapter, we approach tourism historically and structurally, then we discuss the guest, the host, and the destination. After identifying some problematic issues related to tourism, we look at the role of travel for the entertainment industry, the theories that drive it, and tourism's impact on global culture.

Route 66, which runs from Chicago to Los Angeles, was for decades the way West for travelers in America

Table 16.1 Elements of the Tourism Process

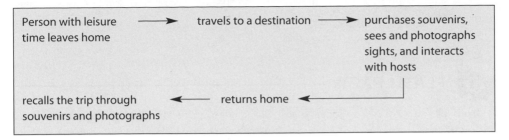

Around the World in Eight: Modern Tourism

We attribute the founding of modern tourism to British entrepreneur Thomas Cook who began packaging tours in the mid-nineteenth century. Cook created new markets for tourism, changing the nature of the relationship between travelers and their hosts for ever. Travel agencies were developed to mediate tourism and to create demand where it had not previously existed. In Europe and the U.S., railroads and steamship lines provided access to places previously inaccessible to the average traveler. Early hotels and resorts that catered to tourists were managed by railroad companies, and the American West became a favorite destination for city dwellers. Steamship companies replaced their cargo with passengers and were transformed into the first cruise lines dedicated to ocean experiences. European and American resorts, started as retreats for church groups, provided transformative experiences at beach and mountain resorts, where visitors learned how to "worship" the sun.

Contemporary tourism has social and economic implications, spreading modernity to rural parts of the world. By organizing mass travel and providing new rationalizations for traveling, founders of the modern tourist industry used nationalism and cultural pride to transport citizens around the countryside. During the 1950s, people were urged to discover America and to "see the USA in our Chevrolet." An imagery of recreational tourism that focused on spiritual and physical well-being glossed over the risks and discomforts long associated with travel.

The travel explosion of the last decade that reported expenditures of over $10 trillion on tourism worldwide can be attributed to several factors, including:

- global economic prosperity and increases in disposable income
- increase in retiring baby boomers
- advances in travel technology
- increase in leisure time
- access to credit and charge cards
- professional packaging of tours, cruises, and vacations
- awareness of distant lands provided by travel channels and nature-oriented programming.

The trip has become a commodity, the tourist a consumer, the world a supermarket of travel opportunities. Whether vacationing for an inversion of everyday life, consuming travel as imaginative pleasure-seeking, or delighting in the in-authenticity of the normal tourist experience, twenty-first-century travelers are embracing tourism. The motives of tourists are deeply rooted in their pattern of expectations, goals, and values. The promised experience must materialize if tourists are to successfully escape relief from their routines and problems. Existing marketplace goals and values serve to motivate and gratify tourists, suggesting that a compliance with the theory of uses and gratifications is alive and well in the tourism industry.

FLASH FACT

Among adults planning to take a home-based vacation during the last six months of 2008, fully one out of five (22 percent, or 5.1 million adults) expects to stay in a local hotel, motel, or resort at least one night on their "staycation." The *travelhorizons*™ survey also revealed that 83 percent of U.S. adults would travel more for leisure if they had more money; 63 percent believe that leisure travel brings family members together; and 58 percent feel that leisure travel is very important to their well-being.

Source: tia.org/pressmedia

Tourism Types   Tourism is an activity serviced by a variety of industries. Although we will focus our discussion on only a few types, we can identify the following as capturing a viable segment of the tourist industry:

- *Business tourism.* Travel conducted in work time rather than leisure time, business travel includes travel to meetings, training, conferences, fairs, exhibitions, and incentive travel (reward for performance).[1] Often a business traveler will extend the trip for pleasure or share the trip with an accompanying family member.
- *Cause tourism.* Here, tourists work for nothing on projects such as conservation, building, or teaching local populations.
- *Day trips.* Travel short distances to theme parks, zoos, museums, outlet malls, beaches, and so forth. May involve an overnight stay.
- *Educational tourism.* Traveling to learn a new language, study history, art, or drama on location, or take a class. School and university trips and specialty camps are also educational travel.
- *Hedonic tourism.* Experience is based on pleasurable activities including shopping and social interaction.
- *Health tourism.* Spas and therapeutic resorts that provide programs to improve one's health or appearance.
- *Pilgrimage tourism.* Travel to religious sites or to sporting events in groups of worshipers or spectators. Trips to visit relatives or to class reunions are included here.
- *Virtual tourism.* Travel via the Internet without leaving home.
- *Wilderness tourism.* Journeys to ecologically sensitive locations, backpacking or camping, cycling, sailing, and travel where outdoor activities prevail.

For all but three of the above tourism types, packages are available to travelers. **Packaged holidays** for all types of travel are remedies for stress. Many travelers never question why they leave a comfortable home to visit some unknown place in potential discomfort. They just know they can get a "deal" on an exotic location, a place to spend time and money away from home. Some vacationers never even leave the confines of their hotels. Instead, they search the new space for familiarities.

For whatever reasons, tourists sign up in record numbers for tours and packaged trips. There are three recent innovations that facilitate the package travel market. **Inclusive holidays** allow more distant destinations to become accessible to a mass

Volunteers from an eco project help cut a road through the Amazon

market. Professionals plan sightseeing, accommodations, and transportation so all travelers need to do is pack. The **Internet** and electronic devices enable more independent travelers to obtain their own tickets, hotels, and rental cars to personalize packaging without assistance. **Consortia** organize smaller hotels so they are competitive with large chains. Marketing consortia provide access to regional groupings or specific market segments with bulk purchasing. Airlines, hotels, and credit cards package trips to take advantage of consortia relationships. Regardless of what kind of traveler you are or what kind of package you choose, the process of becoming a tourist can be understood in terms of flow and regions.

Flow and Go   The flow of tourism has three route options. Access to the destination is most often a direct route by plane or other means of rapid transportation. The route home may be more circuitous, taking side trips or stopping off along the way. Another option is to view travel to or from the destination as a recreational and integral part of the trip itself.[2] This flow to and from destinations has three regions. The **generating region** is where our trip begins. Marketing activities, booking transportation, and making hotel reservations are essential for planning the trip. Upon leaving our point of origin, we enter the **transit region**. The time between departure and arrival is spent checking into and traveling on a particular mode of transportation and arriving at our **destination region**. Tourist attractions of all types are located where tourists arrive to be entertained.

Once a person leaves home to travel on a mode of transit to a tourist attraction, s/he becomes a tourist in search of locals, souvenirs, and memories. Essential to all types of tourism is this tourist, this person who goes off to experience a new place and who returns home enriched from the experience. The next section will help you understand basic tourist needs and motivations in the context of our entertainment culture.

Have Camera, Will Tour   Today, anyone traveling for pleasure or leisure can be called a tourist or guest in places other people call home. Although the term "traveler" is often used to refer to a tourist, we differentiate between the two terms from an activity perspective: the traveler actively engages in a purposeful journey, whereas a tourist takes a more passive and consumptive approach to travel. For our purposes, tourists use travel and leisure for entertainment, and our interest is in what entertains tourists and why. By understanding tourist motivations, the entertainment industry can maximize the travel experience.

Tourists develop a particular "gaze" directed to features of landscape and townscape which separate them from their everyday lives.[3] While gazing, tourists capture these "scapes" through photographs, postcards, camcorders, and so forth. Tourists set out in search of something new and different, whether authentic or simulated, to amuse themselves. Tourists gaze upon the objects of their travel in various ways. They may gaze romantically at one another, they may act as spectators or sightseers of street activity, or they may act socially as a collective. Gazes can also be directed at nature or at cultural antiquities.

Tourists are named according to their particular gazing characteristics. We call tourists on packaged tours who gaze as collective "groupies"; people who travel for adventure on their own gaze as "explorers"; "wanderers" with no planned activities gaze randomly.[4] Where explorers and wanderers prefer more casual and spontaneous accommodations, groupies usually stay in predetermined locations. They sometimes act as children, following tour guides, going where they are told to go and doing what they are told to do. In such cases, tourists seemed to be playing child-like games that involve breaking traditional adult rules. Excess, for example, is one taboo tourists break—they eat too much, spend too much, stay up too late, and wear outrageous clothes. Some seem to enjoy "playing tourist" by preferring simulation to experiential reality.

Such tourists prefer fakery and contrived experiences over "genuine" travel experiences.[5] If modern tourism is shaped by McDisneyization, is it any wonder that tourists seek travel experiences that reflect superficiality?[6] On the other hand, tourists may seek to escape the inauthentic associations of their everyday existence.[7] The quality of this escape experience depends in part on how entertaining it becomes for the tourist.

Regardless of what we call them or what they seek, tourists are people at leisure and tourism is the activities they engage in while at play.[8] A *touristic process* begins with the desire to leave home, travel to other places, and encounter people from different cultures. During this process, tourists engage in a series of transactions with people who serve them, such as travel agents, hotel managers, shop keepers, and others who work in the tourist industry. In order to facilitate the touristic process, tourist travel is generated through the marketing efforts of this industry. At the other end of the tourism process is the host society that is dependent upon tourist-generating areas to send visitors. Understanding the social relations between guests and their hosts is essential to marketing and delivering a successful tourist experience.

Many cities have yet to make travel easy for the disabled

Hosts and Hosting   People who live in tourist areas and districts are called

hosts. The relationship that is developed between host and guests is dependent upon several conditions, including:[9]

- the number of tourists visiting a place in relationship to the size of the host population. Small towns with large numbers of tourists are more encumbered than large cities.
- the type of observation that takes place. Tourists are welcome to observe objects, but hosts are uncomfortable with observations of them personally.
- the organization of the industry that develops to service tourists (commercial, ecological, local crafts, etc.).
- economic and social differences between hosts and guests. Wealthy tourists invading developing countries have a profound impact on inhabitants.
- effects of tourism on host economy and lifestyle. Tourism often changes the nature and quality of life for residents of tourist destinations.
- extent to which tourists can be identified and blamed for undesirable economic and social developments. Overcrowding and negative outcomes are easily attributed to visiting guests.

Examples of these conditions are presented later in an actual case study of tourism and its effects on a small seaside community.

Local residents become a tourist resource, providing entertainment and curious pleasure for outsiders. Here, a tension develops between locals and guests who are at odds in their preferences for the context of leisure time. In other words, guests seek beauty and exoticism, whereas locals may long for escape, progress, or economic growth. Locals sometimes feel that their space has been invaded by tourists who come to gaze on them. They accuse visitors of depleting the town's natural and commercial resources.

Residents living in tourist destinations usually approach tourism in one of two ways: active encouragement or passive acceptance. Acceptance or resignation separates locals from guests both spatially and socially. These locals patronize places tourists do not frequent, or they leave town to avoid them. Such an attitude may deter tourism but rarely ends it. A more desirable approach is active encouragement, which fosters local enterprise, arts, and entertainment through marketing and promotion. Once tourism becomes a location's primary source of revenue, services appear and grow to meet demand, which increases tourism, which increases demand. As the cycle expands, the destination has no longer any choice but to grow with it.

A local helps a tourist find his way around Barcelona

In Transit and at Destinations   One leisure hypothesis says that people seek the opposite kinds of stimulation in their leisure environment to what they have at work. Another hypothesis suggests that tourists seek the same kind of stimulation and enjoyment their work provides for them.[10] Whichever is the case, the main element of tourist space is that of "perceived space," which is the place in their minds—their expectations. Travel fulfills those expectations.

We usually travel to specific **destinations**. Three types of journeys provide clues for understanding travel and its relationship to the destination region:[11]

- *Departure is the destination.* Flight is the key here. Travelers simply want to get away from home. In this case the trip rarely yields deep or lasting effects for the traveler.
- *Arrival is the destination.* This is travel as amusement and acquisition where travelers prefer going somewhere without having to move. These travelers prefer the replacement of firsthand experience with simulation. Often photographs used to document the destination are the sole purpose of the trip. Las Vegas, theme parks, and packaged experiences prevail.
- *The destination is undetermined.* These travelers prefer exploratory or experiential trips that are spontaneous or impulsive rather than planned or packaged. Even getting lost can be fun for these folks.

For our purposes, arrival destinations are most important for their role as entertainment. People arrive to sightsee; sightseeing has become a regular tourist ritual. Destinations serve as temporary residences or overnight stays as well as "day trips." Identified as "sun, sand, and sea" locations, destinations are capital-intensive tourist attractions.[12] Destination attractions are specific geographic districts, retail or commercial establishments, and ethnic or cultural groups.

Tourist attractions are the relationships developed between a tourist, a sight, and a marker or piece of information about the sight.[13] One distinguishing characteristic of an attraction is the presence of markers or souvenirs. Urban areas of tourism have specific **tourist districts**. New York's Soho, Paris's Latin Quarter, and San Francisco's Haight Ashbury are examples of such districts. Once a district has gained tourist status, it tends to replicate the expected in new architecture and commerce, calling into question what is real and what authentic. Sante Fe, New Mexico, is an example of a city that tore down its original adobe structures and replaced them with new adobe structures that currently serve as shopping plazas. In spite of physical alterations, the town still serves its residents in much the same fashion as it did before it became a centre for tourism.

Roadside Attractions Hip postmodern tourists look for virtual reality through the roadside popular culture. Called roadside attractions, the Snake Pit, Animal Safari, and small theme parks like Flintstones Village pepper our highways. Antique shops and swap meets also serve as popular stops for travelers. Some places of interest are located on city streets. A pseudo-museum for the eccentric, the Museum of Jurassic Technology in Los Angeles parodies real museums with its pseudo-scientific exhibits about people and phenomena no one ever knew they wanted to know.

By making use of information that lies on the edges of our cultural literacy—things we've heard of but don't know much about—the museum seduces us with exhibits on bat radar, ultraviolet rays, and aspects of kitsch culture. A few other museums that are worth stopping for include: the Cockroach Hall of Fame in Plano, Texas, the Museum of Bathroom Tissue in Madison, Wisconsin, and the UFO Museum in Roswell, New Mexico. These and other populist museums deserve attention for their homemade artifacts not usually perceived as important as tourist attractions.

Travelers also like to visit places that were made famous by the media. **Themed tours**, based on books, TV shows, and movies, are on the rise to meet demands from travelers bored with passive vacations. Tours in the Caribbean based on the movie, *Pirates of the Caribbean* take travelers touring old pirate hideaways in Jamaica, reading seventeenth-century transcripts of trials of pirates, and listening to lectures from costumed experts on what it was like to be a pirate. Harry Potter tours in the U.K. consist of visiting castles and riding the train used in the movies as the Hogwarts Express. New Zealand is host to *Lord of the Rings* tours; France provides a scavenger-hunt-style trip based on *The Da Vinci Code*.

Created as a result of the popular HBO television series *The Sopranos*, tourism in Kearny, New Jersey, created quite a cash cow for commercial providers. Tour high spots include an auto body shop, a pork store, and a sleazy dance joint that serve as locations for Soprano hangouts Big Pussy's, Satriales, and the Bada Bing! nightclub where one

On-location tours to places like New York City where Will Smith and Alice Braga filmed *I Am Legend*

can buy T-shirts and Sopranos trivia. Tourists happily pay $30 to see some of the least attractive sites in New Jersey just because they are the places where the fictitious Tony and his gang conducted their business.[14]

Scenes of infamous crimes also lure tourists: murdered celebrity wife Nicole Simpson's condominium in Los Angeles, the Lorraine Motel in Memphis where Martin Luther King was assassinated, and the clinic where a Pensacola abortion doctor was murdered are among them. These and other places that house roadside popular culture attractions provide amusement for people traveling between here and there. Equally amusing as travel itself are finding and purchasing location souvenirs.

Kodachrome and Kandy   An important component of tourist destinations are **souvenirs** or **markers**. Collecting artifacts, an essential part of the tourist ritual, provides travelers with tangible symbols of their experience. The symbolic significance of artifacts is important for understanding the total tourist experience. Souvenir artifacts can be thought of as:[15]

- *pictorial images* (e.g., postcards, snapshots, books, etc.)
- *pieces-of-the-rock* (i.e., things saved from the natural, gathered, hunted, or taken from a built environment)
- *symbolic shorthand* (e.g., manufactured miniatures or over-sized objects)
- *markers* (i.e., souvenirs that in themselves have no reference to a particular place or event, but are inscribed with words that locate them in place and time)

Russian nesting dolls are common souvenirs marking a visit to Moscow

- *local products* (e.g., indigenous food, food paraphernalia, liquor, local clothing, and local craft).

A relationship exists between the degree of travel experience and the type of authenticity people need from souvenirs. Souvenirs with obvious or public meanings have **conspicuous authenticity**, whereas **idiosyncratic authenticity** comes from private meanings that tend to focus on the symbolic, intangible elements of souvenirs.[16]

Global revenues from conspicuous souvenir sales topped $100 billion in 2000 and are expected to continue rising as tourism expands. Sales of Hard Rock Café T-shirts, for instance, surpass food revenues in all its international locations; here visitors willingly pay for a marker that advertises their patronage. Wisconsin cheese, California wine, and Minnesota wild rice are a few American products packaged for tourists to commemorate their visits to a destination. Miniature Eiffel Towers, stuffed Florida alligators, polished and painted seashells, and visually stimulating postcards are examples of conspicuous souvenirs less experienced tourists purchase to commemorate place.

More seasoned travelers prefer locally produced or naturally gathered artifacts that signify the experience rather than the place. The production of arts and crafts for tourist consumption is often associated with a destination's rural population. Craft industries may grow and prosper with tourism because they retain what is perceived to be an "authentic" rather than mass-produced quality. Local artists may also benefit by associating their art with a regional ecology, such as California's Wyland, who is known for his "whaling wall" murals and porpoise statues. This artist's sea creatures are widely collected by international tourists who display Wyland marine art to symbolize both their excursions and their philosophical allegiance. In Wyland's case, "native art" has grown into an international multi-million dollar industry, bringing about the true form of what is best described as *tourist art*.[17]

Tourist attractions must be complemented by a variety of tourist services if revenue from tourism is to flourish. Services established for tourists often benefit locals who are

A "whaling wall" depicts ocean creatures that act as photographic tourist souvenirs

able to enjoy retailing and restaurants that cater to visitors. During the off season, tourist services often depend upon residents to sustain them through the lean months until tourists return.

Tourism and Hospitality Industries

When destinations foster tourism, services become part of the landscape. **Service** can be thought of as *mediation* because of its role in facilitating tourism. The mediation of tourism by individuals and institutions stands apart from the host/guest relationship. Service providers may not even live in or near the places where tourism occurs. Mediators are people who service tourists and include but are not limited to: planners, promoters, agents, artists, guides, investors, hotel managers, pilots, lifeguards, taxi drivers, clerks, restaurants, and on and on. Everyone who travels or encounters travelers can be considered contributors to the travel industry.

The business of tourism as developed by pioneers such as Fred Harvey is twofold. One task is telling potential tourists what they want and how to get it. The other is to produce places that conform to the expectations and desires the industry has helped create.[18] Both components turn to elements of entertainment for their success.

Chambers of commerce, convention and visitors bureaus, and travel consortia employ marketers to produce brochures, films and videos, and promotions to encourage people to travel. AmEx Corporation integrates elements of transportation and lodging to entice travelers on a budget. Advertising agencies create amusing commercials to inform potential travelers about destinations and transportation options. Vacation time-shares are created to facilitate distance travel, and pageants are performed to lure visitors. Travel writers, public relations agents, and video producers entice citizens to leave home for adventure and excitement.

Once people are persuaded to travel, they must be satisfied with their choices of transportation and destination. Industries serving the method of travel as well as the accommodations and experience are competitive and prosperous. Airlines promise on-time arrivals, trains extol the virtues of scenic transport, and ships lure us with gourmet dining. Hotels provide free movies and workout facilities, parks present 12 different types of water activities, and cities offer up gambling, games, and gifts.

Leisure, a crucial component of entertainment, is itself an industry. Cartoon characters attract and amuse visitors, surreal jungles make dining more fun, and giant roller coasters thrill us. To make travel from home to our destinations palatable, airlines entertain us with in-flight films, and ships provide live performance. Our hotel gives us games and places we visit offer venue-specific gifts. Without entertainment, travelers may become bored and seek other methods of amusement. To prevent boredom, the industry embraces entertainment to ensure pleasant and lucrative travel experiences.

Tourist Spaces   Tourist spaces are specific locations where people congregate to experience the unfamiliar. Entertainment providers must consider the issue of authenticity and how it determines the nature and quality of tourist space.

Tourists' curiosity for what is perceived to be "real" causes them to purposefully seek out "behind the scenes" places in tourist locations. Wandering into residential neighborhoods, peeking into private spaces, or probing hosts for answers to intimate questions are some examples of this phenomenon. Visitors are often heard asking directions to "places where the locals go." Tourists sometimes hide their cameras and try to look like they belong by shedding stereotypical identities. By establishing the perception of authenticity, tourism capitalizes on the quest for what is real.

The tremendous expansion of tourism has diminished much of what we consider to be authentic. To compensate, the tourism industry manufactures what is called "staged authenticity" and "pseudo events."[19] The success of Las Vegas replicated cityscapes (New York, Venice, Paris) attests to tourists' preference for visiting the "fake" place because it exists without the hassles and discomforts—traffic, poverty, dirt—they are certain to encounter in the "real" place.

Mediated experiences also facilitate reality through replication. Visitors to the Grand Canyon may visit the I-max version of a helicopter tour located on the south rim and return home feeling just as gratified as if they had actually hiked its Bright Angel trail. If tourists prefer well-produced visual exploits over authentic adventures, imagine the possibilities open to mass media for providing virtual tourism!

Four types of tourist spaces have been identified, as shown in Table 16.2.[20] Experienced tourists seem to know they are playing the tourist game in the obvious absence of what is truly authentic (type D). And they don't care! Visitors to Gettysburg understand that they are not time travelers, nor are they savages on Hawaii's tropical beaches, nor can they be invisible observers in foreign lands. They know that colorful brochures don't portray long lines of people waiting to enter amusement parks, nor do they discuss the confusion of exchanging local currency. Today's tourists may even revel in the confusion and disorientation that typify prefabricated destinations. The more elaborately staged the experience, the happier the tourist. At least that's what packagers of leisure travel depend upon to lure and retain vacation consumers.

Table 16.2 Types of Tourist Space

Tourist impression	Real	Staged
Nature of scene		
Real	**A.** Authentic and recognized as such	**C.** Suspicion of staging, authentically questioned
Staged	**B.** Failure to recognize contrived tourist space	**D.** Recognized as contrived tourist space

Source: Cohen, E. (1979). Rethinking the sociology of tourism. *Annals of Tourism*, 6: 18–35

New and Emerging Tourism Markets

Tourism worldwide is undergoing great change in terms of the demand for new product, popularity of older established forms of tourism, changes in the way product is purchased, and growth of outbound tourism countries not previously generating travel. Trends and new markets are highlighted here.[21]

Packaging Paradise   In the early days of tourism, packaged tours were the norm. The "if it's Saturday it must be Belgium" approach to travel provided tourists with security, no-hassle accommodations, and a pleasant introduction to a foreign country. Since 1960 we have seen a resurgence of all-inclusive tourism with travelers with specific expenditure or duration requirements as well as the luxury end of the market. Club Med is an example of a high-end vacation package geared around a single destination.

Cruises are a form of this concept that often provides passengers with theme-oriented activities while on board. Education cruises, including computer and language instruction, as well as dance cruises which feature "brain food" as well as sightseeing are offered to attract vacationers. In addition, the incentive travel business is instrumental in packaging and promoting destinations as rewards for company executives and high achievers.

SPOTLIGHT ON ALL-INCLUSIVE VACATIONS   Resuscitating Club Med

Massage center on the beach

Started as a nonprofit, idealistic village of canvas army tents in a secluded Spanish beach town, Club Mediterranée espoused egalitarian principles that would give everyone equal standing rather than the elitism of other resorts. After 56 years, the Paris-based company is moving upmarket after recently confronting a series of calamities from Asian cyclones and tsunamis to wars and vacations imitators that destroyed five of their most profitable resorts.

So instead of bunks and beach bashes of past Club Med villages, visitors to the new walled compound at their La Palmeraie resort will have suites sprinkled with fresh rose petals and a jasmine-scented pool and bubbling papaya baths. This Moroccan village was created to compete for leisure euros and dollars chasing the demanding tribe of free-spending tourists in a global industry that is worth an annual $2.8 trillion.

Distinguishing guests (GMs) from staff (GOs) by their initials, past villages encouraged interaction between the two by having shared meals and activities. But this culture of fraternization is undergoing refinement as part of the upmarket shift which was costing Club Med $128 million annually through 2008 to upgrade its villages. Seventy villages have been renovated from Mexico to Turkey and

20 new villages like the Riad in Marrakesh are already completed. More than 50 sites have been closed, and the company is selling properties to reinvest in remodeling.

Luxurious villages like Riad cater to privileged guests, nicknamed "pashas," or pampered tourist royalty who pay all-inclusive, individual rates up to $3,127 a week. The price includes expanded suites with living rooms, private gardens, room service, Internet connections, and daily tea. The cultural makeover also includes more than 27,000 employees on five continents who are being groomed with lessons in fostering ambiance.

Club Med's shift from high-volume approach to a "value strategy" was inspired by a steady loss of guests since 9/11. Because wealthy travelers are more resilient than budget travelers, resorts can rely on travel spending from the luxury segment even during economic and political crisis. So the company is out to lure these guests, and even provide a new business class with computer rooms and conference space within walking distance of the pools. But no need for bottled water—everyone at Riad drinks champagne!

Source: Doreen Carvajal for the *New York Times*, Sept. 5, 2006, C6

Children's Holidays   The summer camp, and school or group trip movement designates children as tourism consumers on their own right. As influencers, children will continue to play a larger role in determining which products their parents should buy.

The International Wedding Market   Honeymoon travel, big business in the U.S., is also flourishing in Japan and the U.K., where Las Vegas, New England, Caribbean islands, and Cyprus are popular destinations. A honeymoon package includes ceremony, video, flowers, music, food, and drink at a destination. Exotic wedding companies promote underwater, parachute, bungee jump, and ice cave ceremonies. The status of distance honeymoons has this business jumping.

FLASH FACT

U.S. destination wedding spending grows at an annual rate of 14 percent. Resorts in top destinations offer venues and services for larger weddings. Thirty-one percent of Hispanic couples say they are planning a destination wedding to incorporate Hispanic elements into their ceremonies. The most popular domestic wedding destinations are Hawaii, California, Florida, and Las Vegas; most popular international wedding destinations are the Caribbean, Mexico, Asia/Pacific, and Europe.

Source: *Destination Wedding Magazine* 2008 reader survey

Pop Culture Travel   An outgrowth of location filming, visiting places where TV dramas or films were shot is popular with tourists. The film *Sleepless in Seattle*, the book *A Year in Provence*, and both forms of *Angela's Ashes* (Limerick, Ireland) are examples of locations popularized by media. Backstage tours take tourists behind the scenes at places like Radio City Music Hall where Rockettes chat and pose for pictures.

No-frills Travel   Mediterranean and Gulf of Mexico cruises are available for travelers on a budget. Airline tickets and cruises are priced competitively and often offered online for the traveler's asking price. Discount travel services, online travel sites, donated trips (generousadventure.com), and frugal travel guide books have increased popularity of do-it-yourself or bargain vacations.

Couples-only Market   High disposable incomes and childless couples have launched romantic tours and bed and breakfast destinations to attract travelers to adult-only venues for weekend to week-long get-aways. Resorts such as Sandals cater to intimate get-aways in beach and mountain locations.

Travel for Health   One of the oldest trip motivators, health travel includes a variety of products such as holistic "health farms," resort-based fitness vacations, natural mud and mineral water treatments, and weight-loss spas. For example, Coastal Trek offers personalized health, hiking, and fitness programs in natural settings with gourmet cuisine on Vancouver Island, British Columbia. Many Americans are travelling abroad for transplant operations or plastic surgery, and flying to Mexico for cheaper dental or cancer treatments not FDA sanctioned. Popular in Europe for some time, medical travel is becoming very popular with U.S. consumers seeking alternative or more cost-effective health care.

Eco-tourism   With people motivated to travel to see wildlife and experience natural wonders, eco-tourism feeds on the growing concern for rainforests and endangered species. Wildlife and travelogue programs have increased awareness of habitat adventure. Belize in Central America is noted as a major site of eco-tourism development for its forest reserves, Mayan archeological sites, and the second-largest barrier reef in the world. Sustainable development is achieved in part through attention to preserving wildlife habitats.

Religious Retreats   Worshippers and travelers searching for spiritual experiences are traveling to retreats such as Mount Athos in Greece, and to cults and sects in Asia. Meditation and harmony are the products of these destinations that continue to grow in popularity. India, for example, specializes in spiritual vacations among lush jungle surroundings for worshippers of all religions or philosophical beliefs.

Adventure Travel   A plethora of new adventures are available to those with time on their hands and challenge in their hearts. Wilderness Travel, a 22-year-old company out of Berkeley, California, is just one of many companies providing travel to remote destinations with comfortable lodging or camping and good food "without sacrificing the spirit of adventure." For those with the resources and a sense of adventure, hundreds of new companies have sprung up to meet those needs. Space Adventures is taking deposits toward sub-orbital rides into space for about $100,000. Or one can take a two-week dog sled trip with Northwest Passage for $25,000, or climb Mount Everest for $65,000 with Alpine Ascents. Other adventure options include skiing cross-country at the South Pole ($45,000 for two months), taking a 25-day trek into Bhutan for $6,000, helicopter skiing in Canada in the Caribou range for $105,000, or riding the rapids of the Zambezi River for $3,000 excluding airfare.

Business Travel   Municipal tourism is fostered by convention operations that actively promote their cities as destinations for trade shows, meetings, and conventions. Effective marketing strategies in cities such as Boston, San Antonio, and San Francisco have created a lucrative business by involving private sector businesses in promoting the city with cooperative advertising and a dynamic convention and visitors' bureau.

Niche Cruises   Travelers who seek a cruise experience but want to avoid conventional cruise vacations can select ships operated by niche lines that offer smaller and more intimate experiences. Steamboat adventures, river barge trips, freighter tours, and clipper ships are among the options available for water travelers.

SPOTLIGHT ON SMALL-TOWN TOURISM   Hollywood Goes to Marfa

In isolated West Texas near the Mexican border, Marfa is a drought-plagued ranching town that has seen better days. So why would anyone want to visit Marfa? Because *Giant* was filmed there. Three hours from a commercial airport or shopping mall, the town experienced the production of two Hollywood productions in 2006. Joel and Ethan Coen (writer-directors of *Fargo*, *Big Lebowski*, and *O Brother,*

James Dean in Marfa

Where Art Thou?) came to Marfa to film *No Country for Old Men*. Starring Javier Bardem, Tommy Lee Jones, and Josh Brolin, the film's real hero is its border-town landscape.

South of town, director Paul Thomas Anderson (*Magnolia, Punch-Drunk Love*) also came to film *There Will Be Blood,* an epic starring Daniel Day-Lewis as a power-mad prospector. Anderson's film, however, actually takes place in Bakersfield, California. Because no ranches in Bakersfield had views without fast food restaurants in the distance, the director chose Marfa for its landscape and its personality. The desolate desert highway west of town is peppered with cactus and jackrabbits, which was ideal for

filming a scene where a volunteer townsman turned actor was shot in the head with a cattle stun gun.

Marfan residents are used to celebrity—their town of 2,400 is home to both the Chinaati foundation, an outdoor art space, and the Lannan Foundation's writers residency program. The eccentric place has become a haven for artists and art tourists, bringing new galleries, boutique hotels, and print coverage to Marfa. And because Marfa's economy is based on tourism, the presence of hundreds of crew members was somewhat inconvenient for businesses that cater to regular guests rather than sporadic influxes of movie people. According to one proud local resident, "It's tough when your town's a star."

Source: Whitney Joiner for the *New York Times*, Aug. 27, 2006, Arts 13

Wilderness: The New Luxury Tourism   According to data released by ILTM, the top 3 percent of tourists spend 20 percent of total tourism expenditure.[22] However, this 3 percent is a very significant segment of the tourist market, particularly considering its upward trend. Luxury travelers seek qualitative experiences and demand personal and confidential service. Today's luxury traveler is not only sharp, experienced, informed, well-traveled, and adventurous but also has an eye for value-for-money.

Luxury tourists are wiling to pay expensively for their holidays. For this they demand satisfaction, exclusivity, high quality, and impeccable service. An increasing number of people leading very hectic, urban lives put a premium on tranquility, wide open spaces, abundant nature, and privacy from other people. For them **wilderness** is the new luxury. At the extreme end Ted Turner is recreating the open American prairie with buffalo herds at his ranch. Celebrities such as Jade Jagger are just as likely to be found in remote retreats as larging it up in Monaco.

Tourists seeking to experience some of the world's last wilderness areas are prepared to pay for the privilege of eco-chic lodges and resorts—but wilderness conservation also comes at a price. Some wilderness areas are kept pristine only because local people use them wisely and sustainably. For example in developing countries parks and wilderness areas often have the best firewood, grazing, and water—by not denuding parks of these resources local people pay what is called an "opportunity cost." If they are not rewarded for this—beyond the knowledge that they are conserving their natural heritage—then very poor communities face no alternative but to support their families in any way that they can, often to the detriment of the wilderness. So while luxury travelers are nourishing their souls at wilderness retreats, we hope they make sure a holiday is also nourishing conservation and local people.[23]

Lodge huts cost visitors upward of $2,000 a day

Theoretical Approaches to Tourism

The "build it and they will come" theory of travel no longer ensures financial success in the tourism industry. Careful planning and execution have replaced the haphazard approach. Proven theories, marketing principles, and esthetics are invoked to successfully persuade people to travel, to tell them what they want while they're away, and to convince them to return. Highlights of those theories and principles are provided here.

Marketing Principles   The **4Ps principle** (see Chapter 7) is invoked to market all components of tourism. The **P**roduct (venue or transport) must be well conceived and tested for its desirability; the **P**rice must be competitively determined for mass or niche appeal; the **P**lace (location of the venue or transport) must be easily accessible; and **P**romotion (PR, advertising, direct sales, sales promotion) must be executed with skill. Because most tourists are experienced consumers, they have high expectations for each aspect of this marketing mix.

   Branding is an essential component of tourism. All modes of travel, places of accommodation, and tourist locations are brands. Disney has created and maintained one of the most successful examples of international brand identity ever developed. After all, doesn't everyone recognize and embrace Mickey? Recognition is only one aspect of brand success. Effective brand management is necessary to build lasting relationships between the traveler and the tourist industry brands.

   To make us to feel good about their brands, marketers use esthetics. **Marketing esthetics** refers to the marketing of sensory experiences in corporate or brand output that contributes to the brand's identity.[24] Here, we emphasize the esthetic value of the product or venue. Attractiveness of the venue is one aspect of esthetics. Another more important aspect of that concept is the esthetic that tourism provides by functioning as a symbol for pleasure and gratification. Gratification can be provided by the inherent qualities and structural features of a brand or by the meanings communicated through the brand. If we feel good about the Marriott—by being satisfied with the visual appearance of the hotel and the memories we attach to staying there—we are gratified by the Marriott brand.

Theory of Uses and Gratifications[25]   This theory suggests that as consumers we expect certain levels of gratification, and if we are not satisfied, we discontinue our use. Because tourists are said to be "fantasists or escapists"[26] in their flight from routine and problems, marketers promise a relief from that routine through tourism. To be successful, each component of the tourism industry must meet the tourists' expectations of that fantasy or escape.

Marketing esthetics, like uses and gratifications theory, draws from communications research by attending to peripheral messages (giving us information through entertainment). It also draws from product design (form and function) and spatial design (structure and symbolism). Arguing for esthetics as a provider of tangible value for a brand, marketers suggest that attention to message and design creates loyalty, allows for premium pricing, cuts through information clutter, and protects against competitive attacks. *The Design Management Journal* is dedicated to providing information on how to use marketing esthetics that have specific applications for the tourism industry.

Tourism Segments   Tourist-specific methods of target segmentation have been developed for promoting travel and tourism.[27] They are:

- purpose of travel (why are they taking the trip?)
- traveler needs (what basic requirement do they have for the trip?)
- motivations and benefits sought (what do they expect to receive during the trip?)
- traveler characteristics (what are their economic, geographic, psychographic, and demographic traits?)
- price (what do they plan to spend on the trip?).

Many tourism businesses have to deal with multiple travel segments. By directing their messages toward one or several segments, marketers are able to address the specific desires of tourism consumers and entertain them appropriately.

Tourism Effects

Tourism does not operate in a vacuum. Immigration and migration patterns and numbers affect destinations at all levels, socially, economically, politically, and environmentally. An overview of these effects may help you understand the complicated process of making policies that insure a sustainable global environment.

Social Effects of Tourism   Visitors to a region or country create social relationships that typically differ from those within the indigenous population. Tourist–host relationships affect individuals, families, and societies involved in the tourism process. Individuals may experience different degrees of cultural contact that are both rewarding and educational. Travel experiences have profound effects on travelers because their experiences often are among the most outstanding memories of their lives. Families experience memorable adventures when they travel together.

But tourists can also become victims of crimes perpetrated on them by locals. In Italy, boys on motor scooters grab purses from unsuspecting women while they shop on city streets. In Spain, tourists in cars are stopped along the road and robbed of their possessions. Such incidents create bad feelings about the host country and the people who live there.

Tourism's effects on societies may be equally disconcerting. The presence of tourists changes the living patterns of locals in both positive and negative ways. It may enhance their economic status, yet deprive them of the privacy they desire. In developing countries, tourists may influence locals' ways of dressing, consumption patterns, desire for the products they use, sexual freedoms, and a different world outlook. Tourism development may even affect the natives' entire way of life, fostering prostitution, gambling, drunkenness, and other excesses.

Negatives acknowledged, travel and tourism are primary ways in which members of different cultures may get to know one another. Interactions with local people can dispel the stereotypes formed from media portrayals or historical profiling. And immersion in a foreign nation can provide a new perspective of your homeland. Students who take a year to travel after finishing college return with a different perception of democracy and America than they had before they left home. Tourism is our best hope for fostering peaceful coexistence.

Environmental Effects of Tourism   Effects on the physical and natural environment of a tourist location are the most devastating to host countries. *Carrying capacity* is a key concept in analysis of the potential environmental impacts of tourism. The concept has three elements.[28]

- *Physical capacity* is the limit of actual numbers of tourists that can be accommodated in a region. Yosemite National Park is frequently jammed with bumper-to-bumper traffic during peak tourist seasons.
- *Environmental capacity* is the limit of users that an area can endure before visitors notice a decline in the area's desirability. The beaches of Miami, Florida, have become overcrowded and littered during winter months, reducing its attractiveness to sun worshippers.
- *Ecological capacity* is the maximum level of users that an area can accommodate before ecological damage is incurred. Hikers in the tens of thousands that swarm to the Waterton-Glacier Peace Park on the Canadian–U.S. border have all but destroyed the alpine flora plant life of that location.

Carrying capacities are determined by:

- the number of visitors
- the amount of use by the average visitor (day visit vs. extended stay RV camping)
- the quality of resource management and facility design
- the number of area residents and their quality-of-life needs.

With careful planning and management, governments can control and monitor carrying capacities for the mutual benefit of both hosts and guests. Controlling environmental damage begins with policy development.

SPOTLIGHT ON TRAVEL EFFECTS   The Price of Fame

Jiaju, China, is an area of Tibetan-speaking hamlets perched on an 8,000 foot-high mountainside that looms over the town of Danba. For decades a way station on a circuit through the country's southwest, the village is home to some of the Sichuan Province's most exotic travel destinations.

In 1998, three sisters helped start a tourist business in this once-remote village where hillsides now buzz with felling of trees to build Tibetan-style houses that become guest lodges. The sisters began by turning their home into a hostel for travelers, which proved to be both profitable and attractive to vacationers

looking for a remote and beautiful destination. Soon, the rest of the town followed their lead, and a tourist town was born. Arriving daily by bus, visitors pile into the once-pristine village to glimpse the exquisite vistas.

Along with the boom, however came problems often associated with development. Home-building has left the mountain nearly stripped of tall pines and cedars; ensuing erosion washes out the roads and brings dangerous landslides with each ran. With no public services, travelers and residents dump trash on the hillsides.

When the quest for the new and exotic drives hoards of tourists to the next "hot" place, destinations eventually lose their exoticism and charm. In 2003, the whole county received 10,000 tourists; three years later it had 50,000 in a single week. Travel writers, who called the village one of China's most beautiful places, helped to cause the traffic jams that now plague the town.

The three sisters who started the tourism boom are now calling for growth management and sustainable development. In the meantime, residents are still expanding their homes to receive more visitors.

Source: Howard French for the *New York Times,* Sept. 6, 2006, A6

Tourism Policy Development

The world is shrinking. As a result, countries are working to keep geography from destruction. Global policies are being developed and global tourism organizations work together to insure safe and sustainable travel.

Sustainable Tourism   Sustainable tourism is a concept being developed at a global level, where governments work together to preserve natural terrain and resources. Sustainability pertains to the ability of a destination to maintain the quality of its physical, social, cultural, and environmental resources. Policies that limit growth and access to sensitive areas, immigration policies, policies on wages and welfare, foreign investment regulations, zoning laws, currency exchange rates, and the legal system policies affect the appeal, attractiveness, competitiveness, and sustainability of a tourism destination. To help with this effort, destination management organizations work at the country level as the National Tourism Organization (NTO), at the state level as the State Tourism Office, and at the municipal level as a Convention and Visitor Bureau.

Tourism policy consists of a philosophy and the formation of a long-term vision for the destination. The vision guides objectives development, which in turn provide a basis for formulating long-term development strategies for the region. There are four major components of the policy formation process.[29]

- During the *definition phase*, the development of explicit statements that define the tourism system is formulated. Planners determine tourism development policies and objectives and survey and inventory the existing situation.
- The *analytical phase* is composed of internal reviews and audits and analysis of survey information. An external macro-level review of current and future demand and promotion policies is evaluated.
- Identification of strategies, implications, and policy recommendations are accomplished during the *operational phase*. Here, policy makers determine the scope of tourism development needed to achieve objectives and make recommendations for specific projects in specific locations.
- Finally, these recommendations and programs are executed during the *implementation phase* where responsibilities are allocated, funding support is identified, and a time line is put into place. Plans are monitored to determine if objectives are being achieved, and modifications of the plan are made as objectives change. Research methods are used to examine, plan, and evaluate policies during all four stages of development and implementation.

When regulation and management of resources fall short, the ecology of physical landscape will suffer. Residents of desert communities complain as ATV vehicles destroy natural habitat, and forest rangers worry about fire danger from careless campers. In developing countries, tourist litter can also be a problem. Prior to 1990, Budapest, Hungary, had no trash receptacles because citizens carried their own grocery sacks and containers for prepared food. After McDonald's opened, the city was inundated with Styrofoam containers and food wrappers flung in the street. The presence of fast food retailers poses problems for countries that opened their cities after the Communists left.

No-no Policies   As in the case of Cuba, some policies cause difficulties for travelers. The U.S. policy on travel to Cuba forces visitors to fly through Mexico and Canada to reach the island. Welcoming the revenue from tourism, Cuba is not policing American citizens who visit. However, the U.S. is levying fines on travelers if and when they are caught coming back into the country. Another example is Egypt, a heavily traveled country, where extremists have attacked women tourists who do not wear traditional dress. In an effort to preserve tourism, the Egyptian government has dedicated police to protect women as they tour Cairo and attractions along the Nile.

Old Havana downtown

Natural and Constructed Attractions

Each region of the world offers different places of interest and types of recreation. By looking at the things to do in a country or city you can see if that spot offers romance, family fun, sightseeing, or adventure. Attractions are visited for their inherent of exhibited cultural value, historical significance, natural or built beauty, or amusement opportunities. Some examples include monuments, zoos, museums and art galleries, botanical gardens, buildings and structures (e.g., castles, libraries, former prisons, skyscrapers, bridges), national parks and forests. Many tourist attractions are also landmarks. This section presents examples of attractions that include museums and national parks.

National Parks

A national park is a reserve of land, usually owned by a national government, protected from most human development and pollution. Travel to natural wonders lures ground transported visitors and campers to areas policed and controlled by rangers and park officials. The U.S. park system employs over 36,000 people to serve over 270 million visitors each year. Parks receive their revenues from appropriations and concessionaires.

Eiffel Tower in Paris, a popular tourist attraction visited by seven million visitors every year

The largest national park in the world is the Northeast Greenland National Park, which was established in 1974. The first effort by any government to set aside such protected lands was in the United States, in 1832, when President Andrew Jackson signed legislation to set aside four sections of land around what is now Hot Springs, Arkansas, to protect the natural, thermal springs and adjoining mountainsides for the future disposal of the U.S. government. The next American effort to set aside such protected lands was in 1864 when President Abraham Lincoln signed an Act of Congress ceding the Yosemite Valley and the Mariposa Grove of Giant Sequoias to the state of California.

In 1872, Yellowstone National Park was established as the world's first truly national park. Even with the creation of Yellowstone, Yosemite, and nearly 37 other national parks and monuments, another 44 years passed before an agency was created in the United States to administer these units in a comprehensive way—the U.S. National Park Service (NPS). The number of areas now managed by the National Park Service in the United States consists of 391 different sites, of which only 58 carry the designation of National Park.

Following the idea established in Yellowstone there soon followed parks in other nations. In Australia, the Royal National Park was established just south of Sydney in 1879. In Canada, Banff National Park became its first national park in 1885. New Zealand had its first national park in 1887. In Europe the first national parks were in Sweden in 1909. Europe today has 370 national parks. In 1926, the government of South Africa designated Kruger National Park as the nation's first national park.

After World War II, national parks were founded all over the world. The Vanoise National Park in the Alps was the first French national park, created in 1963 after public mobilization against a touristic project.

SPOTLIGHT ON NATIONAL PARKS   Glacier Park, Montana

Glacier National Park, located in Montana, bordering the Canadian provinces of Alberta and British Columbia, contains two mountain ranges with over 130 named lakes, more than a thousand different species of plants and hundreds of species of animals. Centerpiece of what has been referred to as the "Crown of the Continent Ecosystem" is a region of protected land encompassing 16,000 square miles. The famed Going-to-the-Sun Road traverses through the heart of the park and crosses the Continental Divide, allowing visitors breathtaking views of the rugged Lewis and Livingston mountain ranges, as well as dense forests, alpine tundra, waterfalls, and two large lakes. Five historic hotels and chalets are listed as National Historic Landmarks, and a total of 350 locations are on the National Register of Historic Places.

Some 730 miles of maintained trails crisscross the park, all running through country that's spine-tinglingly wild—just knowing that grizzlies are out there makes rounding each bend that much more interesting. It isn't often you find yourself encouraging your kids to be noisier on the trail, but that's what you need to do when you are, frankly, lower on the food chain and don't want to surprise anyone outranking you. An estimated 400 grizzly bears live in the northern Continental Divide ecosystem, which includes Glacier. A threatened species, the grizzlies coexist with about 800 black bears that are less aggressive than the grizzly.

A total of 63 species of mammals, six species of bats, and 260 species of birds have been recorded. Raptors such as the bald eagle, peregrine falcon, osprey, and hawks reside year-round. Because of the colder climate, reptiles are all but absent, and only six species of amphibians are documented, but 23 species of fish reside in park waters, and most have a "catch and release" caveat attached to them for fishermen.

Visitors may mix a steady diet of hikes and other outdoor activities with some requisite drives, which are so spectacular that even kids will stay awake. Rafting the Flathead River has a handful of Class III rapids, and visitors can go horseback riding and mountain biking along the banks of the Middle Fork on deserted trails. One of the best features is the drive along the Going-to-the-Sun Road in one of the park's fleet of restored 1936 "Jammer" buses with the canvas top rolled back.

What do you think?

- *What national parks have you visited?*
- *What problems did you encounter during your visit?*

National parks are a global phenomenon. Most countries of the world have set aside protected regions for visitors. One such park is Goreme National Park, which has the most interesting and beautiful land formations in Turkey. Erosion from wind and rain over centuries formed the countless fairy chimneys, caves, and beautiful rock formations, and the colors that used to be red, pink, and brown were transformed in time into gray, yellow, and green.

Some environmental problems facing the American national parks occur in seven main areas: overuse, insufficient funds for park operation, threats to wildlife, the concession

The Cappadocia region of Turkey contains formations used in the film *Star Wars*

systems, energy and mineral development, atmospheric pollution, and activities on adjacent lands. The popularity of National Parks, especially the crown jewel parks like Yellowstone and Yosemite, has overwhelmed them with visitors; parks see an increase of 10 percent each year. This massive increase in pedestrian and vehicle traffic has caused trails to become eroded from overuse, vegetation surrounding trails around popular attraction to be trampled by visitors, and litter, noise, water pollution, and smog have all impeded the enjoyability of national parks. This increase in visitors and the need for the few rangers employed by the park to meet the needs of more and more visitors have created a safety issue. Rangers can't monitor the entire park for criminal activity, and this impacts the safety of national parks.[30]

Museums

Most urban visitors include visits to museums during their travels. With rotating exhibits, social functions, and extraordinary architecture, modern museums are must-see attractions that provide memorable experiences. Often called **secular cathedrals**, museums have become storehouses of collective values and diverse histories—places where we seem to want to spend our free time. They are our new theaters of conscience, memorials to suffering, choreographed places of ritual genuflection, offering packaged units of morality that are guiltlessly entertaining.

Vacillating between being a university and a Disneyland, museums are places to show things people didn't know they wanted to see. And as such they are entertaining places.[31] What is becoming state of the art with museums is the integration of art, artifact, and replica to the extent that the distinction between them is often indistinguishable. Michelangelo's statue *David*, housed in Florence, Italy, is often mistaken for a copy, and the replica located in a public space is perceived to be the authentic statue. Does it matter to visitors whether they see the original or a copy? Should it matter?

Museums have to do with curiosity that serves the pleasure of the spirit. One of the last places one is supposed to be able to experience something "authentic" is in a museum. Museums display objects that exemplify originality and authenticity and truth, providing an experience that a reproduction cannot. Museums use two approaches to the display of objects: object as culture and object as art. Objects important as part of a larger whole, or as representative of a culture, are often displayed in ethnographic museums where the object is assimilated into its total environment. Reconstructed villages and mannequins provide realistic displays that serve primarily as backdrops for the objects themselves. They assist viewers in understanding the object's social role. A Brussels museum dedicated to artifacts of the former Belgian Congo integrates drums and masks into realistic settings that feature native dwellings and animals typical of the region.

Replica Shopping   Museum shops, located in both museums and shopping malls, sell reproductions of art antiquities that serve owners as *objets d'art*. You can buy a plaster cast of the nose of the *David* for $30 from the British Museum, or an Incan bathrobe from the Smithsonian Institution for $150. People buy these things to commemorate their visit, to show they have "done" the museum. Things and lifestyles, the past and present, are collapsed together into an appealing package, which can be purchased by the consumer who wants to be considered as "worldly" by others. We are all able to become time travelers, experiencing the past without ever leaving the comfort of the present—a truly postmodern activity.

Nonsense Museums?   Museums that reflect the **obsession with fantasy** are the essence of Las Vegas, where visitors can find a gambling museum, a neon museum, and two museums devoted to performers who came to personify the city: Liberace and Elvis. Inside the Tropicana Hotel's towering neon sign is a panel that invites revelers to visit "the world's largest gambling museum," which is more about Las Vegas than about gambling. And because the only other cultural icon of this city is neon, a dedicated museum presents examples of the only indigenous visual culture on the North American continent.[32] The neon museum is really just eight pieces of neon signage on display along a pedestrian mall—outdoors and on view 24 hours a day. It serves as a graveyard of signs that have been discarded and rescued for posterity. The Liberace museum, like its namesake, focuses on lavish excess and becomes a parody of itself. Visitors can see the musician's pearl-and-rhinestone cloaks, mirror-paneled cars, and jewelry dripping with diamonds. Somewhat more professional in presentation, the Elvis-a-Rama museum is devoted to artifacts belonging to the city's secular saint. Not to be outdone, casinos such as the Bellagio in Las Vegas have incorporated exhibition halls for the display of art master-pieces. The Venetian now presents works from Guggenheim and Hermitage collections: its first exhibit was "The Art of the Motorcycle."

Some critics are fearful that art museums are being reduced to the level of social historians and commodity showrooms. They worry that curators put sponsors, attendance figures, and historical narratives ahead of art.[33] One art critic believes that museums displaying artifacts such as guitars (Boston), motorcycles (New York), and *Star Wars* memorabilia (Houston) are "swindling the public" by using the prestige of art to collect money for exhibits that have only superficial appeal.[34] Opposing that view, the head of the American Association of Museums claims that "Museums today are taking the tack that they need to broaden the perspective of what is valued in culture, instead of saying only certain kinds of art should be shown."[35]

Accused of betraying art and artists, museums that succumb to material culture or inferior artwork are said to become rental exhibition halls rather than custodians of esthetic master works. Should museums commemorate the past? Should they glamorize the present? What is a museum's responsibility to its public sponsors?

Visitors to Madame Tussaud's wax museum can marry George Clooney (l) or share a glass of champagne with Hugh Hefner (r)

Some museums feature **historical journeys** through a profession or trade, or **parody** scientific achievement; they make no claims to being art custodians. Entertainment venues such as Madame Tussaud's Wax Museum in Times Square and Las Vegas provide replicas and memorabilia of famous people. Here you can see Larry King gossiping with a colleague, Woody Allen alone in a corner, and Barbra Streisand sitting on a fountain. Certainly reality here is in the eye of the beholder.[36] Museums that cater to the unusual include the American Sanitary Plumbing Museum in Worcester, Massachusetts; National Museum of Dentistry in Baltimore, the Museum of Jurassic Technology in Los Angeles, and the Hays Antique Truck Museum in Woodland, California.

Special Venues   Noteworthy for their entertainment value, some museums offer special environments to visitors. The Frick (New York) is housed in one of Fifth Avenue's only remaining mansions. The architecture of San Francisco's Museum of Modern Art takes visitors through a cat walk that is like being in a giant eye, and its cafés feature trendy food fares. Renovated in 1997, the Denver Art Museum is a model of comfortable, user-friendly venues with its discovery libraries, a great collection of American Indian art, and interesting shopping. The Menil, in Houston, Texas, often referred to as the country's most sophisticated museum, combines modern with ancient and tribal art in an urban neigh-borhood of art sites. In spite of its rating as seventh best overall, a favorite museum will always be the Metropolitan in New York City; visitors are always entertained by wandering through its vast collections, tomb rooms, or the shop's fascinating array of gifts. The Met introduces visitors to the art world in such a way that they become swallowed up in a marvelous menagerie of the immortalized art and sculpture, indulging their fantasies and outdoing expectations of what it means to visit a museum.

As old-guard curators and directors retire, we can expect exhibitions that illuminate something about objects on view regardless of whether they are paintings by Monet or a Nike swoosh. As audience-driven and ritual entertainment, museums are responding to their publics with sophisticated marketing programs that rival those of their entertainment competitors. The controversial role of museums as keepers of art will continue, we sus-pect, for at least a few more decades. Until then, we shall see the lines blurring between high art and popular culture in a true postmodern fashion.

Urban Attractions

Ethnic districts of cities always attract tourists. Tom Robbins describes just such a district in his book *Half Asleep in Frog Pajamas*:

> In Chinatown, neon is not just so much electrified signage, it is theme music, a visual soundtrack to the neighborhood. Tourists are yanked into Chinatown by shivering tentacles of unnatural color, to be swallowed up by a radiant carp maw infected with exotica. Neon gas courses through images of dragons and pagodas, hues of hibiscus and ginseng, silkworm and firecracker. Neon pushes its embroidery needle in and out of the sky above Chinatown, decorating the canopy that will both protect and advertise it, setting it apart from other parts of town.

Chinatown in Los Angeles

Functioning Establishments   One functioning establishment that acts as a tourist attraction is Fisherman's Wharf in San Francisco, which began as a working pier and has gradually changed to accommodate tourists at the expense of the fishing industry. An example of a complete establishment transformation is the train terminal in Paris that was recently converted into the Musée d'Orsay, a modern museum housed within the arched transportation center. Unlike districts that retain their original purpose, establishments are most often transformed from what they were into tourist attraction. One exception is the Empire State Building, where offices and tourist tower function in harmony.

And then there's Hollywood, which has recently undergone a substantial renovation to keep tourists coming. Betting on Hollywood Boulevard, Disney renovated the El Capitan Theater and purchased a next-door address for its live-action spectacles. Nine million dollars was spent renovating the Pantages Theater for the extended run of blockbuster musical *The Lion King*. A consortium of studio power-brokers raised $14 million to restore the Egyptian Theater, transforming the waterlogged venue into a majestic showcase for film preservation. And a real estate developer is spending $567 million on a facility that includes a luxury hotel, restaurants and shops, a broadcast studio, and a deluxe theater to serve as the permanent home of the Academy Awards. Attempting to return Hollywood to its former glory, Mann's Chinese Theater attracts visitors who can't resist comparing hand and footprints with those of 150 screen legends.

People as Attractions   Even **groups of people** can become tourist attractions: a Hare Krishna community is one example where group members are objects of sightseeing. Occupants of Chinatown lure tourists, as do Native American pueblo dwellers. People become attractions for their cultural or ethnic differences from those who visit them. Perceived as oddities, groups of human beings have lured tourists since the days when "circus freaks" were promoted to attract audiences. Some attractions are found or occur during a journey to or from a destination.

India offers tourists tours into its urban slums. Visitors to the Indian capital can take a tour of the living conditions endured by the 2,000 or so street children who live in and around Delhi's main railway stations. For two hours, tour guides, themselves former street children, show visitors what life is like for the city's most deprived inhabitants.

Tourists to the New Delhi slums see a widow begging in the streets with her child

The money raised (200 rupees a ticket—$5.00) goes to a well-respected local charity, which tries to rehabilitate these children. The trip is designed as an awareness-raising venture and organizers deny that this is the latest manifestation of "poorism"—voyeuristic tourism, where rich foreigners come and gape at the lives of impoverished inhabitants of developing countries. Bus tours of the shanty towns of Soweto or guided walks through the slums of Rio have attracted curious tourists for many years; the visit to Delhi's railway underworld has proved popular with Western and Indian visitors.

Recreation as Play

When many of us think about leisure time, we think of getting outside to ski, skate, bike, play tennis, hike, or go boating. Participation in outdoor activities and sports is one of the most long-standing traditions of civilization.

Sports undertaken for **recreation** include hiking or backpacking, and camping. Student travel often involves all three forms, especially when budgeting is a consideration. Youth hostels cater to hikers, providing shelter and a place to meet other travelers. Off- and on-road biking offers riders a chance to see the countryside more intimately than with other forms of transportation. Of course, huge industries have been developed around products designed for recreation and are continually improving current products and designing new ones.

In addition to the outdoor recreational activities discussed as attractions, people of leisure love to recreate indoors as well, especially in the form of **shopping**. From hitting the mall with your friends on a Saturday afternoon, to holiday spending on gifts, shopping is often called one of the world's favorite pastimes.

Global private consumption expenditures approached $32 trillion in 2007; personal consumption became a global phenomenon this decade as easy credit fueled a housing boom in the United States, Europe, Asia, and the Middle East. The ability to pull equity out

Many shoppers in Singapore seek local designer brands

of increasingly valuable homes helped spur spending on autos, second homes, exotic vacations, and high-end consumer goods.

Although India's consumer spending is forecast to quadruple by 2025, other developing countries are suffering from the large drop in funds flowing to them because of the global economic downturn. Net capital flows to emerging markets are estimated to fall from $466 billion in 2008 to $165 billion in 2009, according to the Institute of International Finance (IIF).[37]

As tourist attractions, shopping centers are often destinations for international consumers. Britons have been flocking to New York for bargains; Asians look to California for designer brands, and China attracts Americans looking for replica or fake brands.

For most people, shopping is finding a unique piece of jewelry, discovering an antique treasure, or purchasing to reward ourselves for working hard. But for others, shopping can become excessive or out of control. Called "shopaholics," compulsive shoppers have difficulty controlling their purchase impulses. The stereotypical shopaholic, darting from store to store to pick up anything and everything while racking up a hefty credit-card bill, is anything but stereotypical. They come in all shapes and sizes. New research reveals that, while some super-shoppers spend to boost self-esteem and band-aid other perceived internal shortcomings, others' motives are driven by plain old materialism. Whatever the motivation, however, researchers mostly agree that buying behaviors can range from frivolous fun to serious addiction.

Playing Sports

When we're not shopping, millions of people are participating in a variety of competitive physical activities. Research suggests the following three basic reasons why individuals participate in sports:

- *Personal improvement.* Release of tension/relaxation, sense of accomplishment, skill mastery, improved health and fitness, other people's respect for one's athletic skill, release of aggression, enjoyment of risk taking, personal growth, development of positive values, sense of personal pride.
- *Sports appreciation.* Enjoyment of the game, sport competition, thrill of victory.

- *Social facilitation.* Time spent with close friends or family, sense of being part of a group.

Although this list suggests that many individuals participate in sports for reasons other than entertainment, most people who play sports do so because they enjoy it. Certainly sports-related games such as miniature golf or even sports video games are designed for little more.

We begin our lives playing Little League baseball, Pop Warner football, and soccer. Team sports like rugby, lacrosse, ice hockey, tennis, basketball, become important in high school and college. Some of us prefer more solitary sports, like swimming, surfing, skiing, figure skating, fishing, biking, and horseback riding. Other sports are undertaken for business or social reasons, such as golf and boating. Some of us participate to compete, others of us simply enjoy the camaraderie and exercise. Then there are people who take up sports that challenge their physical and mental endurance.

Extreme Danger **Extreme** (or X-treme) **sports** represent another recent trend. If something is dangerous, it is interesting. Many extreme sports originate as new, daring twists on more traditional pastimes such as the off-road spin-off on traditional skate boarding. The extreme sports movement, however, has changed a lot since it began more than a decade ago with isolated collections of athletes using bikes, boards, and blades in unique ways. Consider the steadily increasing popularity of snowboarding, one of the original extreme sports. Snowboarders earned a

Skydivers building a star formation

reputation as rebellious troublemakers and were initially despised by traditional skiers because of their grungy attire and unorthodox maneuvers. Today, ski resorts welcome snowboarders as young and old alike convert from skis to boards.

The trend is toward riskier and more dangerous endeavors. Take epic accomplishments like the climbing of Mount Everest; climber George Mallory froze to death and Edmund Hillary and Tenzing Norgay nearly died. Now every corporate executive from around the world seems to be planning to attack Everest. But that's not enough. To up the ante, getting to the top of the highest peak in the world now means doing it without oxygen or racing up in record time or staying at the top longer than anyone else.

Extreme athletes are getting braver, bolder, and crazier. Those who want to push the limits are now pursuing activities such as *free flying* (a speedier, less disciplined form of skydiving) or *free soloing* (scaling mountains and icy ledges with no harnesses or ropes). Today, *extreme* is what was once considered *insane*. And the athletes themselves will tell you why they enjoy extreme sports. "I'm totally addicted to adrenaline," explains Travis Tripp, who competes professionally, hurtling downhill at 72 miles per hour on an 8-foot-long board called a street luge.[38] Although extreme sports are largely youth-dominated, one line of thought suggests that these sports simply reflect a larger, recent societal obsession with danger. These athletes do something larger than themselves by meeting a challenge that other people aren't up to. Critics find it difficult to justify the gamble these athletes take with their lives. Some say that these people are crazy.[39]

The athletes themselves are not the only ones crazy about extreme sports, as proved by the increasing numbers of extreme sports fans. Extreme sporting events such as the X Games draw sellout crowds. Following the new sportainment trend, these events are often large-scale celebrations with headlining bands, celebrity appearances, and rows of vendor booths. Extreme athletes are signing lucrative sponsorship and endorsement deals, and extreme sports films and bootleg videos also do well. Although many diehard extreme sports fans resent this commercialization, the appeal of extreme sports is not surprising. The more danger there is, the more suspense and excitement there is, the more entertaining it is. Sports participants demonstrate similar risk and excess that has characterized the business world of dot.com ventures and stock market gambles.[40]

Some people believe that extreme athletes just like the attention, but psychologist Jennifer Taylor disagrees. "They're not doing it for popularity or publicity, they do it to challenge themselves physically and mentally to see if they can withstand the pressure and . . . get in touch with who they are." She adds that athletes who risk their lives are masters of their crafts, with exceptional mental and physical brawn. They push the limits to test their skill. According to Taylor, these sports even provide some with a spiritual sensation or an inner peace: "The X Games . . . have spoken for the entire culture of the West: From loud, fast music to guerrilla filmmaking and outrageous ad campaigns, pushing the envelope is the mark of the era."[41]

Another extreme sport gathering momentum is big wave surfing. In California, the Mavericks Surf Contest®, held annually since 2003, brings 24 of the world's best surfers together to test themselves against the incredible challenges of 50-foot waves. Invitees have 24 hours' notice before they're expected to compete in cold water, strong currents, huge waves, and unpredictable conditions. Telecast simultaneously in San Francisco's AT&T Park and Fuel TV, the contest attracts thousands to the cliffs near Half Moon Bay.

According to one participant, "Mavericks is the biggest, baddest paddle-in spot in the world. When Waimea Bay (Hawaii) closes out, Mavericks is still ripping. When it comes to who's paddling into the biggest waves on this planet, the guys that surf here are the best." Mavericks returns at full force every winter, when perfect conditions—a menacing swell originating in the Gulf of Alaska that brings with it waves up to 50 feet tall—strike again.

A big wave surfer avoids a contestant who wiped out during the Mavericks Contest in February, 2008

FADE TO BLACK

This chapter has presented distinct methods and models for conceptualizing tourism and its main components: tourists, hosts, and destinations. We have suggested that the tourist industry is integrally related to leisure and entertainment activities. Studies on the sociology and psychology of tourism provide useful insights for understanding tourist motivations. Market segments and the marketing mix can be used to approach tourism from a consumption perspective. By conceptualizing a tourist destination as a brand, we understand the role of promotion and consumer satisfaction for successful tourism experiences.

Industries related to tourism exist to stimulate desire for travel, to take travelers safely to their destinations, and to accommodate guests at the destination site. Packagers and promoters are hired to reflect consumer fantasies in their advertising and incentive promotions designed to generate travel. Air, rail, bus, and rental car businesses incorporate entertainment into the transit experience. Hotels, sport venues, theme parks, malls, zoos, museums, and so forth require operations personnel and hire workers for every time of occupation conceivable to function as an integral part of the destination experience.

Sports, attractions, and recreation play important roles in leisure-time experiences related to travel. Whether undertaken in free time at home or during a vacation, cerebral activities like visiting museums or physical activities such as biking can enhance both personal and social lifestyles. With increasing amounts of time for us to devote to such pursuits, opportunities abound for entrepreneurs willing to come up with the next new activity, piece of equipment, or travel innovation.

A CLOSER LOOK AT DESTINATION TRAVEL   Laguna Beach Tourism

If we look closely at a resort town and its problems, we see how theories and models are used to analyze the situation and make recommendations to solve those problems. After reaching maximum saturation from tourist traffic during the summer of 2007, Laguna Beach, California, sought solutions to problematic issues concerning access to its attractions and residents' attitude toward hosting tourists.

Laguna's Main Beach life guard station

Location

Tourism is the primary industry of Laguna Beach, a Pacific Coast town of 45,000 people, where "beach, sun, and sand" and a Pageant of the Masters

performance attracts "inlanders" who come from a 50-mile radius to visit the city on day trips, and tourists who come for stays of between four and ten days. Each year, over 200,000 people attend the Pageant, which is a recreation of famous artworks depicted on stage by volunteer actors. Held in conjunction with a Festival of Arts since 1942, the Pageant is a world-renowned event staged to attract visitors and tourist to the city.

More than 500 registered artists live in Laguna Beach, exhibiting arts and crafts at three separate venues from Memorial to Labor Day. In addition, incredible vistas, quaint shops and galleries, and world-class hotels attract millions of tourists annually. The city can be accessed from north and south along Pacific Coast Highway or from inland via the Canyon Road. Traffic congestion and parking problems plague the city during summer months when tourists arrive by bus and coach to take advantage of the arts offerings and natural environment.

According to a survey conducted by the Visitors' Bureau to guests at 13 local hotels, the average stay in Laguna Beach is four nights and the primary reason for visiting the city is to attend the Pageant

(46 percent). The top four activities in the city are using the beach (77 percent), attending performance art venues (59 percent), shopping (39 percent), and visiting art galleries (36 percent). Eighty-four percent of survey respondents plan to return. Those who won't return cite parking and crowds as primary reasons for their dissatisfaction with the overall experience.

Hosts and Guests

By applying the host/guest relationship criteria presented in this chapter, we identified several destination problems:

- *The number of tourists visiting a place in relationship to the size of the host population.* During summer months and year-long weekends, tourists outnumber residents two to one.
- *The type of gazing that takes place.* Tourists park on residential streets for beach visits, preventing hosts from accessing their homes and invading their privacy.
- *The organization of the industry that develops to service tourists.* City tourist bureaus and the chambers of commerce work together to develop tourist-related facilities. Pageant and festival activities are determined by a board of directors.
- *Economic and social differences between hosts and guests.* Hosts locate in this community for its upscale lifestyle. Most tourists are of lesser socio-economic status and come to Laguna to experience "the good life."
- *Effects of tourism on host economy and lifestyle.* Residents may resent visitors because of limited parking, traffic gridlock, and because visitors litter beaches and destroy tide pools.
- *Extent to which tourists can be identified and blamed for undesirable social developments.* Congestion and crowding are visible results of visits by day trippers, weekend visitors, and seasonal travelers, preventing residents from maintaining their lifestyles.

Tourist Regions and Segments

Laguna's destination region is totally impacted by the transit region that services it. If transportation (cars and buses) cannot reach the city, destination activity declines with revenues. Laguna caters to two tourist segments, day trippers and hedonic tourists who come to attend the festival, shop for art, and enjoy the beach.

We can describe Laguna as a sun and sea destination for amusement and acquisition, providing tourists with a plethora of souvenirs of all types. Pictorial festival posters cost $10; seashells are "pieces of the rock" collected for free; symbolic shorthand is available as a miniature Hotel Laguna; Laguna Beach T-shirts are visitation markers; and local crafts provide some authentic artifacts for tourists seeking more meaningful souvenirs.

Marketing

Laguna Beach's brand is synonymous with the Festival of the Arts. A review of the marketing mix identifies some problems with Laguna's brand image today. Although the Festival is popular and well produced, the city as a product has some weaknesses in terms of the deteriorating image of its user-friendliness. Ingress and egress (place) issues as well as local discontent with outsider invasions are having a negative effect on the visitors' perception of gratification. Costs to dine, park, and attend art venues (price) are high and discouraging to travelers on a budget. Because of a limited budget, promotion efforts are limited to a web site, gallery location brochures, visitors' bureau collateral materials, and listings in local newspapers' event calendars. Given the competition from adjacent beach locations and the threat of losing the Pageant, Laguna Beach would be well advised to re-think its transit and destination spaces.

Recommendations

Planning and policy making must occur to set objectives for all three tourist regions, to set objectives and strategies for reaching those objectives, and to monitor their implementation. Specific objectives, strategies, and tactics of the planning process are stated below.

Generating region

- *Objective:* To stimulate tourism from regions outside of Orange County.
- *Strategy:* Promote price discounts and benefits of group travel.
- *Tactics:* Tourist center brochures. Internet site information. Coop promotions. Hotel discounts

to encourage seasonal patronage from visitors outside the 50-mile radius of the city. Hotel shuttles to provide ease of access from airports and bus depots to final accommodation destinations.

Transit region

- *Objective:* Control traffic into the city by car to provide stress-free beach and event access to sustain current visitations from day trippers.
- *Strategy:* Improve visitor transportation facilities.
- *Tactics:* More shuttles running between existing parking lots and town. Five-minute lapses between trips to improve the service.

Destination region

- *Objectives:* Control parking and traffic flow in commercial and residential areas.
- *Strategies:* Offer controlled parking options for

both hosts and guests. Distinguish between out-of-towners and locals for city-sponsored activities (such as Sunday free concerts at Bluebird Park) to simultaneously retain attendance numbers and sustain local support.

- *Tactics:* Additional parking structures to accommodate day trippers. Stickers for parking in residential areas. Short-term access to local shopping for residents. Proof of residence to gain access into city-sponsored events intended for hosts.

What do you think?

- *How might city officials evaluate the success of these programs?*
- *Should input be gathered from just tourists or both tourists and locals? Why?*

DISCUSSION AND REVIEW

1. How do the three types of destination regions contribute to understanding the impact of tourism on a local or national economy?
2. What threats exist for development in national parks and game reserves and how can they be managed?
3. What role does sustainable tourism play in developing tour packages that are marketed as "eco-tours"?

EXERCISES

1. Visit a local travel agency and collect brochures for three different locations or cruise lines. Compare these materials for similarities in visuals and rhetoric. Are differences significant enough to help you make a selection? What factors affected your selection decision?
2. Log on to the web sites of Lonely Planet (www.lonelyplanet.com) and Rough Guides (www.travel.roughguides.com) to research what tourists might find when they visit Paris. Compare each site's approach to recommending accommodations and places to visit in the city. What did you learn about Paris from these sites?
3. Rent a travel video of a place you have visited. After viewing, compare what you saw during your visit and what is presented on tape. What aspects of the place are omitted in the videotape? What does this comparison tell you about place marketing?

BOOKS AND BLOGS

Chambers, E. (2000). *Native tours: An anthropology of travel and tourism*. Prospect Heights IL: Waveland Press.

Cooper, C., Fletcher, J., Gilbert, D., Wanhill, S., and Harlon, R. (1998). *Tourism: Principles and practices*. New York: Longman.

Lippard, L. (1999). *On the beaten track: Tourism, art and place*. New York: The New Press.

MacCannell, D. (1999). *The tourist: A new theory of the leisure class*, 2nd edition. Berkeley: University of California Press.

www.travelbypicture.com—provides the Travel Industry World Yearbook statistics and travel trends.

www.highwayproject.com—a collection of photographs that document the disappearing culture of the American roadside.

www.recreation.gov—integrated site to search any recreational opportunities on federal public lands. One-stop shopping informational service.

www.maverickssurf.com—videos of the surf contest with statistics and contest news

17 NEW MEDIA AND FUTURETAINMENT

I don't know what entertainment will be like in 100 years' time. But it would be nice to have a piece of hardware that you could scrunch up like a cloth, chuck in your bag, then unscrunch so that it would deliver entertainment to you any time and anywhere.

—British celebrity Carol Vorderman[1]

What does the future hold for entertainment? Will "going to the movies" or "programming the VCR" seem as old-fashioned to tomorrow's children as the notion of "sounding like a broken record"[2] and taking "an E-ticket ride"[3] might seem to children today? Many of the chapters in this text have discussed trends in different forms of entertainment and speculated about what the future may hold for them. Often, these speculations have involved evolving new media technologies. This chapter reviews and continues this discussion, with a primary focus on new media and their implications for more general entertainment trends, to see if we can catch a preview of coming attractions.

Disney's classic E-ticket is used to describe new, exciting forms of entertainment

New Media

Beginning with print and continuing with radio, film, and TV, advances in mediated communication have opened new avenues for entertainment. Virtually all communication media have the potential for use as entertainment. It is perhaps not surprising, therefore, that today the term *futuretainment* is often used in reference to predictions involving the use of the Internet and other new media as vehicles for entertainment.

What Are New Media?

The term **new media** is difficult to define. Listed here are several definitions that have been offered by various researchers and organizations:

- a range of interactive digital products and services that offer new ways to trade, market, educate, and entertain, delivered through the Internet, CD-ROM, DVD, interactive TV, and intranets[4]
- the convergence of traditional media, such as films, music multimedia, games, and entertainment[5]
- interactive applications that combine moving pictures or sound (or both) with graphics or text[6]
- information and communication technologies relative to the convergence of computer technology and telecommunications, such as e-mail, the World Wide Web,

electronic publishing, video conferencing, computer-supported communications services, and personal communication services. In relation to the Internet, new media
include hypertext literature, web pages, and all virtual reality systems used for work
and leisure.[7]

Many people equate new media with advances in media technology. Indeed, many
of the definitions just mentioned allude to technological advances such as the Internet,
CD-ROM, and the like. According to these definitions, however, the most central feature
of new media is not the technology itself but the convergence or combination of media
technologies. Thus, in simple terms, the term *new media* (sometimes called *multimedia*)
refers to products or services that incorporate a variety of media. More often than not,
these technologies are combined in a way that permits interactive use.

Types of New Media

A new media product or service combines elements of computing technology, telecommunications, and content. Web sites on the Internet are good examples of new media
because they are accessed through telecommunications technology and they invariably
incorporate a variety of media, including text, audio, and animation. Virtual reality devices,
handheld computers, cellphones, and electronic book readers similarly fall within the new
media category in that they are combinations of several forms of media. Virtual reality
devices often combine visual, audio, and other technology. Handheld computers and
cellphones can be used for multiple media purposes—sending and receiving information,
recording information, game playing, and so on, and electronic book readers combine
traditional print with electronic technology.

 **FLASH FACT**

According to Fairfield Research, the number of people who regularly download an electronic book or
e-book to an e-book reader is expected to reach 16
million adults by 2010. Of those surveyed, 17 percent
of book buyers have purchased an e-book in some
digital format. E-book reader providers, including
Amazon's Kindle digital reading device and Sony's
Reader Digital Book, have policies that restrict
licensing agreements limiting reader transfer of
purchased books to another reader. E-book
ownership and rights issues have publishers and
authors worried about the future security of book
publishing.[8]

Consistent with the new media concept of convergence, emerging forms of new
media are rapidly becoming interdependent, and many of them connect back to the
Internet. Handheld computers and cellphones can be networked with traditional
computers, and many have wireless Internet access. E-books can be downloaded from
the Internet. And, of course, all of these types of new media can be, and often are, used
for entertainment. Today, traditional forms of entertainment—such as books, films, music,
sports, and games—can all be accessed in some manner through new media and the
Internet. Thus, the evolution of the Internet and other new media technology is influencing
almost all forms of entertainment.

As with so many other advances in communications technology (such as in print and radio), the Internet was not originally designed as a vehicle for entertainment or for commerce of any sort. The Internet is really nothing more than a network of computers developed by the Department of Defense to be used in case of a nuclear attack. Government officials wanted to be sure they would have access to their information if one computer or network was down. Universities and professors then began using the Internet to spread and gather information.

In 1989, software engineer Tim Berners-Lee created a system of codes and protocols he called the World Wide Web to serve as a system to allow physicists from around the world to be able to access each other's computer networks, data, and documents. The Web served as the basic platform that opened up the Internet for a larger number of users. A product called Internet in a Box, introduced in the United States in 1994, further opened up the Internet for general use by enabling people to connect with the web from their home computers. Although the Internet was initially designed for government intelligence and research, after general web access was established, entertainment and other commercial uses soon emerged. In fact, entertainment appears to be rapidly becoming the most popular use of the Internet (see *Spotlight on Internet-tainment*).

SPOTLIGHT ON INTERNET-TAINMENT   The Net Is Not Just for Information Anymore[9]

According to a poll conducted by Greenfield Online, more people log on to the Internet to play and be entertained than to gather information. In the company's biannual Netstyles survey, it was reported that more than 80 percent of the approximately 3,000 people surveyed viewed the Internet as a source of entertainment rather than as a source for news and information.

The study revealed several popular entertainment uses. Of those surveyed, 80 percent played games on their computers, both online and offline, and 66 percent of the respondents with multimedia capabilities used the Internet to download music. More respondents subscribed to sites that provided joke or game updates (52 percent) than to sites that provided daily news updates (43 percent), e-mail newsgroups (31 percent), business updates (30 percent), or stock market updates (22 percent).

Interestingly, the report also indicated that almost half of those interviewed claimed to be watching less TV since the time when they established Internet access at home. Nearly 75 percent of those polled log on to the Internet after work, displaying similar habits to those who "crash" in front of the TV after work.

New Media Users

Researchers find that new media users in the United States tend to be younger, more affluent, and better educated than the U.S. population as a whole. A study of Internet users in 2007[10] found that 80 percent of individuals ages 49 or younger were on the Internet compared to 65 percent or less of those age 50 or over. More than 93 percent of individuals with household incomes of $75,000 or more used the Internet, compared to 55 percent of the those with incomes of $30,000 or less. Ninety-one percent of individuals who had completed college used the Internet, with percentages decreasing down to less than 40 percent of those who had not completed high school. None of these trends should be particularly surprising. Younger individuals, as well as those who are affluent and well educated, are likely to have more exposure and better access to the Internet than others might typically have. Research does, however, indicate little gender or racial disparity for new media use in the United States, at least among English speakers. An almost identical number of adult males (71 percent) and females (70 percent) use the Internet, and 73 percent of white, non-Hispanics, 72 percent of English-speaking Hispanics, 62 percent of Black, non-Hispanics are Internet users.

Internationally, Internet use is also growing. In 2008, China reported that the number of Internet users in the country reached about 253 million, helping China overtake the United States as the world's biggest Internet market.[11] Table 17.1 and Figure 17.1 show that Oceania and Australia have the greatest percentage of Internet penetration, but that Asia has the largest percentage of Internet users worldwide.

The Internet provides access to entertainment in two primary ways: through *web site portals*, which provide access to entertainment products or services that can be purchased for delivery or downloaded, or through *web site services*, which provide direct entertainment experiences. Portals include sites such as Amazon.com, Sony.com, and

Table 17.1   World Internet Usage and Population Statistics

Region	Population (est. 2009)	Internet users as of 6/2009	% Population penetration	% World usage
Africa	991,002,342	65,903,900	6.7	3.9
Asia	3,808,070,503	704,213,930	18.5	42.2
Europe	803,850,858	402,380,474	50.1	24.2
Middle East	202,687,005	47,964,146	23.7	2.9
North Amer.	340,831,831	251,735,500	73.9	15.1
Latin Amer.	586,662,468	175,834,439	30.0	10.5
Oceania/Australia	34,700,201	20,838,019	60.1	1.2
TOTAL	6,767,805,208	1,668,870,408	24.7	100

Source: www.internetworldstats.com/stats.htm. Copyright © 2009, Miniwatts Marketing Group

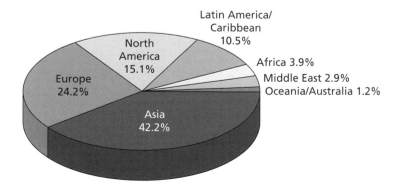

Figure 17.1   World Internet Users By World Regions, June, 2009

Source: Internet World Stats—www.internetworldstats.com/stats.htm. Copyright © 2009, Miniwatts Marketing Group

Ticketmaster.com where individuals can buy books, videos, video games, music, or tickets. In this case, the Internet is used more as a directory or gateway for entertainment than for entertainment itself, although many people may enjoy simply browsing a web site's offerings as a form of entertainment. Other web sites, however, provide direct entertainment experiences. Yahoo.com, Games.com, and numerous other sites allow users to play a range of video games, and sites such as Sony's EverQuest.com and Ultima Online (uo.com), which host complex, interactive, multiplayer role-playing games, are becoming increasingly popular. In addition to playing games on the Internet, you can listen to music, create music, watch videos, dress up Barbie, build cities, meet people in chat rooms—the range of Internet entertainment experiences is almost limitless. Many sites, such as Sony.com and Disney.com, function both as portals and as direct services, where individuals can purchase or download entertainment or enjoy entertainment offerings directly on the sites.

New Media Entertainment

According to futurist Mike Walsh, innovations in entertainment devices typically focus on increasing quality, with a focus on being better rather than different.[12] For example, the picture quality of color TV is better than black and white, and HDTV is clearer than analog. CDs and DVDs offer better quality than tapes. Yet, content delivered via the web or portable devices is rarely better than more traditional media. In fact, with low resolution, compression, and smaller screens, it is generally worse. However, what new media do provide is greater flexibility—enabling entertainment content to be distributed across multiple platforms, added to, remixed, and exchanged between audience members themselves. Walsh maintains, therefore, that new media entertainment is fundamentally different from traditional show business, and, to understand these differences, we should look not to the technology but rather to the people who are using it. "We can no longer assume that audiences will be content to be passive couch potatoes holding people meters. Through the web, social networks, and mobile phones—they are more intercon-nected than ever. And what's more—their desire to personalize, remix, and share media experiences will reshape the business of show business."[13]

Traditionally, entertainment was produced based on a factory model similar to other consumer goods. Entertainment products were "built" by entertainment "manufacturers" in bulk and distributed to mass audiences. Editors and broadcasters made decisions on what people wanted to consume, journalists and producers created it, marketers convinced people they actually did want what executives predicted they would, and audiences largely took what they were given. Walsh argues that today's entertainment world now resembles more of a network than a factory. A group of college students might record a song in their garage and post it on their web site. Someone else comes across the song and uses it for the soundtrack to a video they post on another web site. People who view the video then download the song and some of them might sample or remix it, creating new songs which they post on their own web profiles, where their friends hear them and pass them along to more friends, and so on. Today individuals can not only receive entertainment content from a network of sources but also create and modify content that they, in turn, can distribute through this same network.

In a sense, consumer-generated content is nothing new. People have always enjoyed producing their own content—whether it be photos, diaries, or home movies. What has changed in recent times is that it is much easier to share that material with a greatly expanded audience, and even use it to connect with other like-minded people. "Content is created by consumers within a network of connections and exchanged seamlessly. Even traditional entertainment products like movies and music are annotated with user reviews, remixed or simply exchanged across peer to peer networks . . . media companies are learning that in an online world the real distribution networks of the future are in fact the links between members of their audience."[14] Music downloading services are a perfect case in point. After protracted battles, music companies finally stopped fighting the concept of file sharing and embraced downloading as a revenue stream. According to IFPI's Digital Music Report for 2006, digital downloads worldwide generated $1.1 billion for record companies in 2005, triple the revenue recorded in 2004. This accounted for about 6 percent of their revenues, 40 percent alone of which was cellphone downloads.

Social Media and Networking Web Sites

A social networking site (SNS) is an online place where a user can create a profile and build a personal network that connects him or her to other users he or she designates as "friends." On these web sites, individuals can post profiles including personal information, graphics, pictures, and videos. Most significantly, based on the networking principles outlined in Chapter 10, individuals can expand their networks by searching for and contacting others who share mutual friends and interests. Most networking web sites have displays that document each user's "network." Some sites, such as Flickr, even include actual network diagrams (see the image below) that map out relationships between users. In the past few years, such sites have rocketed from a niche activity into a phenomenon that engages tens of millions of Internet users. Friendster.com, MySpace.com, and Facebook.com are all examples of fairly broad social networking web sites. Many specialty sites are designed for more specific interests. Some sites are more focused on media sharing (where users can post and download files) such as Flickr for digital photographs and YouTube.com for videos, while others serve more like classified advertisements, where you can shop for anything from a new sofa (eBay.com, Craigslist.com) to a new soulmate (Match.com, EHarmony.com). Still other web sites serve as advice forums such as Jobseekersadvice.com or 10w30 for autocare.

There are many web sites where you can find videos to download, sofas to buy, and autocare advice, but what differentiates social networking web sites is that the content and offerings on the web site are generated by the users rather than the organization or individual who hosts the site. In traditional media the content is provided by the "host," so magazines hired staff who wrote stories and radio and TV stations created or acquired programming for listeners. Even on most web sites the videos, sofas, advice, and other content are provided by professionals and commercial producers. Networking web sites, however,

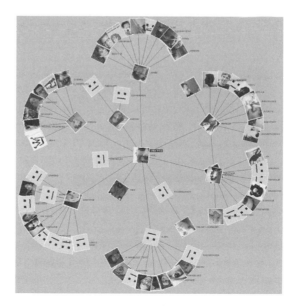

Flickr, a photosharing web site, includes a graphing function that maps out networks of friends on the site

merely provide the infrastructure for posting and searching for information, so the users are the ones who fill in the text, audio, and video content. A key metaphor in social media sites like Flickr (photos), YouTube (videos), and MySpace (teen lifestyle/music) is the ability to subscribe to someone. It's a bit like subscribing to a magazine or a Pay TV channel, except what you are really doing is tracking content created by a real person, who may in turn subscribe to you. In doing so, the clear lines between creator and consumer are blurred. It's just a network.

Increasingly, people are using social media not only for "socializing" but also for business networking and marketing. And, although young people still tend to be more active, spending more time on the site and maintaining more detailed profiles, social networks are aging fast. At the start of 2009, the average number of Facebook users over the age of 35 doubled in just 60 days. By the end of March 2009, people ages 26–44 made up 41 percent of the Facebook audience, and women over 55 became the fastest growing demographic, hitting 1.5 million. Facebook started catering more to families as all ages began signing up. Analysts speculated, however, that the influx of "moms" on Facebook might deter younger users from participating as actively on the network.[15]

Social networking isn't popular only in the United States. The U.S.-based site Bebo has found a strong international following, particularly in the U.K. Non-U.S. sites have also been very successful. With over 40 million users, Hi5 is the prominent SNS brand in India. Indeed, as India is a tech center, this brand reaches far beyond the Subcontinent—the site is increasingly popular in the EU, as users keep in touch with extended families. With over 20 million daily users, Cyworld, a South Korean social network, is emerging as a strong model for the future of social networks. According to press citations linked from Wikipedia, over 25 percent of the South Korean population has a Cyworld account, with up to 90 percent of South Koreans in their 20s having an account. Cyworld has been cutting edge; participants in this game-like social network can micropay for clothes, furniture, and accessories.

SPOTLIGHT ON SOCIAL NETWORKS   Becoming an Advertising Medium

Advertising media buyers are now adding the Internet to their media plans. YouTube, Facebook,

and MySpace, among others, have changed the way we think about and use media. Such sites attract 20 to 50 million unique visitors per month.[16] By facilitating consumer-to-consumer dialog on the Internet about a brand, advertisers expand their reach and take advantage of promotion by circulating paid-for stories. Media planners are now using web pages on social networks to enhance the media schedule. Such pages can help introduce a product, create buzz about a service, or simply provide a platform for branded discussions. The social aspect of the Internet via Usenet newsgroups, e-mail, and blogs gives consumers a way to interact and form communities. By creating a community around the brand in a portal-like fashion, marketers draw consumers to a brand site with content and features that include lifestyle and entertainment information.

The combination of community-orientation and selling features provide marketers with a distinctive way to reach a target audience. Second Life, a virtual landscape, is also a venue for media planners, establishing retail outlets and placing advertising in virtual locations where visitors use Linden dollars to purchase products for their virtual houses. Sony Corp. has signage on Second Life where tech-savvy avatars buy virtual gadgets. The purpose of using social networks is to engage consumers in brand messages. And in 2008, Intertainment Media announced its Itibiti voice-powered social network platform for college age men and women that provides advertisers with the ability to build brand loyalty with this hard-to-reach audience.

Blogging   Many web sites allow users to create text or video weblogs or blogs. Internet users can also create blogs for their own personal websites. People can use blogs to post public "diaries" and commentary. Although some people turn to blogs for information (product reviews, technical advice, political commentary), many people enjoy reading and viewing blogs purely for entertainment. There are blogs for all entertainment tastes from Hollywood Gossip blogs (Defamer.com, Celebritysmackblog.com, Celebspin.com) to sports blogs (Sbnation.com, Thebiglead.com) to startrek blogs (Soulofstartrek.blogspot.com). One that came to international attention was the video blog discussed in Chapter 9 that was posted by lonelygirl15 on YouTube (see the image below). The blog was purportedly a video diary of a 16-year-old girl named Bree who was home-schooled by strict, religious parents. Lonelygirl15 was eventually outed by suspicious viewers as a fictional hoax orchestrated by a team of filmmakers and the American-New Zealand actress Jessica Rose who played Bree. Even after the fictitious nature of the blog was revealed, the creators continued to post new video segments watched by a legion of loyal fans. The lonelygirl15 blog won the biggest web hit award on the music television station, VH1's Big in '06 Awards.

More recently, a new, shorter version of blogging has emerged, often referred to as **micro-blogging** where users write brief text updates (usually 140 characters) and publish them, either to be viewed by anyone or by a restricted group which can be chosen by the

Jessica Lee Rose as Bree a.k.a. lonelygirl15 from one of her YouTube weblogs

user. These messages can be submitted by a variety of means, including text messaging, instant messaging (IM-ing), e-mail, MP3, or the web.

As of the writing of this text, the most popular service in the U.S. was Twitter, which was launched in July 2006. Another popular micro-blog platform has been Jaiku. Recently, however, many new services, with the same feature of micro-blogging, are emerging, including a service called Pownce, which integrates micro-blogging with file sharing and event invitations. The popular social networking websites Facebook, MySpace, and LinkedIn also have a micro-blogging feature, called "status update." In May 2007, an article counted a total of 111 Twitter-like sites internationally.[17] and several new micro-blog type services were under development.

Micro-blogging is also popular in China. One service provider, QQ, accounts for about 78 percent market share among a total of 390 million active IM accounts in China. MSN Live Messenger has about 19 million active users, accounting for 4.9 percent market share, followed by Sina UC (4.1 percent) and Fetion (3.7 percent). QQ has been very agile in using its dominance to introduce a wide variety of other integrated products. But well funded competitors are now in close pursuit, including China Mobile's Fetion service which facilitates free texting between PCs and mobiles, and Baidu's Hi platform. Two weeks after launch Baidu already claimed that over one million people had tried its new IM service.[18]

Virtual Worlds   A **virtual world** is a computer-based simulated environment typically intended for its users to inhabit and interact via graphic representations of themselves, called avatars. This habitation usually is represented in the form of two or three-dimensional graphical representations similar to video game worlds, which in some cases look very similar to real-world environments (cities, countryside, homes, and buildings), while other virtual worlds can be more fantasy-based, imaginary environments. Some, but not all, virtual worlds allow for multiple users. This type of environment is most common in massive multiplayer role-playing games such as EverQuest and World of Warcraft.

The earliest virtual worlds, however, were not games. The first virtual worlds such as Habitat, created in 1987, were either communities or chat rooms where the avatars simply served to simulate face-to-face interaction or basic simulations of real-world environments or where individuals were encouraged to create buildings, art, and struc-tures, often without any avatars. Today, virtual communities such as Second Life and Entropia Universe are becoming increasingly popular. In these worlds, residents' avatars can explore, meet other residents, socialize, participate in individual and group activities, and create and trade or buy items, services, and property from one another. Communication has, until recently, been in the form of text, but now real-time voice communication is emerging using VOIP (Voice Over Internet Protocol). As with social networking web sites, the creators of the world simply provide the basic, bare landscape

An avatar on Second Life

and building tools, but the users are the ones who actually "build" the world. As of June 2007, the virtual world Second Life boasted a population of more than seven million total residents, who had developed close to 500 million square meters of land.

While the media have been abuzz about Second Life and adult virtual worlds, a bevy of virtual worlds for kids have been even more popular than their adult counterparts.

These sites, with names like Club Penguin (Canada), Cyworld (South Korea), Habbo Hotel (Finland), Webkinz (Canada), Piczo (Britain), WeeWorld (Britain), and Stardoll (Sweden), run the gamut from simple games and chat to virtual worlds where children can visit fantasy lands. When Evan Bailyn, chief executive of Cartoon Doll Emporium, created his site, he said, "I thought it would be a fun, whimsical thing." Cartoon Doll draws three million visitors a month. "But it's turned into such a competitive thing," he said. "People think they are going to make a killing."[19]

Indeed, some of the largest entertainment players have made significant investments in these web sites. In 2007, at a cost of $350 million, Disney acquired tween world Club Penguin which boasted more than four million visitors per month.[20] Club Penguin pro-jected $35 million in earnings that year alone, before interest and tax from subscriptions, according to Sharon Wienbar, managing director of venture capitalist Scale Venture Partners. While that's only an accounting figure and not necessarily a real indication of profitability, it's certainly indicative of potential.[21] Similarly, Nickelodeon's virtual world Nicktropolis launched in January 2007 and by the end of the year it had about 5.5 million registered users who on average spent 55 minutes on the site per visit, according to Jason Root, senior vice president of digital at Nick.com.[22]

The market is still relatively young, too, giving upstarts a chance to rival brands like Disney and Nickelodeon. Companies like Webkinz have proved that it's possible. In 2005, the company started selling Webkinz—special-edition plush toys with names like Googles, Cheeky Monkey, and Love Puppy—for $10 to $12.50 apiece. Each comes with a tag featuring a "secret code" that gets its owner into the Webkinz World web site. There the toys come to life on the screen, ready to be adopted. The kids give each toy a gender and a name and can spend "kinz cash" to buy food, clothes, and furniture. They're also invited to play games, enter trivia contests, chat with other pet owners, and even take jobs—such as flipping virtual burgers—to earn more spending money. In May 2007, it had 4.1 million visitors, up 1,300 percent from the previous year. Within two years, Webzinz had made $20 million in retail sales.[23]

For that reason, more newbies are piling in. Fashion doll-makers Barbie and Bratz both opened new virtual worlds, in an attempt to catch up with market-unknown Stardoll.com, a Sweden-based virtual paper-doll site. In less than three years, Stardoll has attracted 6.4 million worldwide members, according to the company.[24] Aardman Animations, creator of the cartoon *Wallace and Gromit*, also recently opened a kids' game site.

The reason the industry is booming is that the value of the youth market hasn't yet been tallied, but a 2005 report by Packaged Facts counted 29 million U.S. kids ages 8–14, with a combined annual purchasing power of $40 billion. Nearly 90 percent of these children are now online, which means there's a lot of money to be made by web sites that can capture the kids' attention and their impressionable eyeballs.[25]

 **FLASH FACT**

Increasingly kids are flocking to imaginative, character-driven environments. An expected 53 percent of children on the web will belong to a virtual world within four years, more than doubling the 2007 member population of 8.2 million members, according to a recent report from eMarketer.[26]

One venture capitalist summed up why the market is so hot by saying that kids' virtual worlds are the only ones that are successful so far. "In the children's market, that's where virtual worlds are really mainstream," Wienbar said at an industry conference. She was referring to sites like Webkinz and Club Penguin, which have millions of active members, as opposed to adult worlds like There.com and Second Life, which may have millions of registered users but only between tens of thousands and hundreds of thousands of active users.[27]

SPOTLIGHT ON FAME   Virtual Celebrities

Although most people desire celebrity status, the opposite extreme is true of a young man called Lazydork who performed on YouTube for hundreds of site visitors, complaining that no one knew who he was. Lazydork gained a fan base who followed him because he was a "regular person," not a celebrity.

Where traditional celebrities are elevated above their audiences and invested with exalted qualities, the new-model celebrities are expected to be no better than their fans. No one expects Tom Cruise to read his fan mail, but everyone expects lonelygirl to answer her e-mail. YouTube stars have all the benefits of anonymity plus a small paycheck. On the street they are in peace; online they are famous to their various micro-cults.

Lonelygirl created a narrative about herself through a video diary—without a movie studio or television show. Viewers embraced it in spite of, or perhaps even because of, the fact that it was lacking in talent and brilliance. According to a Northwestern professor, we are moving from a representation culture where stars represent us to a presentation culture where we can present ourselves. Momentary fame is available to all of us over the Internet—we don't have to be dead to be famous like old movie stars. In our presentation culture, if we create a story we can create a star—and we are all becoming great storytellers!

Source: John Leland for the *New York Times*, Sept. 24, 2006, WK4

What do you think?

- *In an era when anyone can have a celebrity following, Lazydork's popularity raises questions about the meaning of fame: If someone is celebrated for not being a celebrity, does celebrity itself still have any value?*
- *Has the concept of fame that meant something lasting for generations become as fleeting as today's celebrities?*

Traditional Entertainment Goes Virtual

At first those in the traditional entertainment businesses of TV, film, and music seemed hesitant to embrace new media; however, soon the popularity of these media could no longer be ignored. As futurist Mike Walsh explains, by the year 2006, show business had discovered the web.

> Whether it be Disney selling episodes of *Desperate Housewives* on iPods, Fox screening prime time TV shows on the Web, Hollywood Studios selling full versions of their movies online, or Mark Cuban blowing up sequence windows with his movie *Bubble*— this year [was] a major turning point for the titans of Tinseltown.[28]

As discussed in Chapter 9, well-established entertainment companies like Disney, NBC, and Sony are not only making their conventional entertainment (TV, film, and music) available via new media, they are also creating content unique to new media. Almost every film, TV show, actor, and musical artist maintain official web sites which include background, news, blogs, and even new music, videos, and other content that fans can access. Many fans also create their own web sites and blogs for their favorite entertainment. At first many companies and celebrities were wary of unauthorized web sites; however, now such sites are often actively encouraged.

Many sports and entertainment brands such as Nike, Sony BMG, and Comcast have a presence in Second Life and other virtual worlds (see the image below), and some are even creating their own. In 2006, MTV launched Virtual Laguna Beach, an online service that promoted the show through an avatar-based virtual world. The site is a blend of social networking and video games. "You can not only watch TV, but now you can actually live it," said Van Toffler, president of the MTV Networks Music, Film and Logo Group, regarding the game's interactivity.[29] In these worlds fans could "be" show characters and interact with others in settings taken from the program. Brands including Cingular, Pepsi-Cola, and Secret agreed to participate. The world quickly expanded to

VMTV (Virtual MTV) incorporating other MTV programs such as Pimp My Ride. Musical artists such as Korn and Linkin Park have given interviews and made "appearances" in the world, providing an opportunity for virtual interaction with fans. Dr. Henry Jenkins, a professor at MIT and author of *Convergence culture*, said that such virtual communities were a natural step for mainstream media companies seeking a deeper connection to fans.

Global brands have a virtual presence on Second Life

Driving Forces in New Media

For many forms of entertainment, particularly media entertainment, the audience is passive. Audience members are simply observers who have no impact or influence on the entertainment they experience. Stories, for example, whether in books or movies, usually follow a predetermined progression of events that play out oblivious to audience reactions. Other forms of entertainment, however, allow audiences to actively participate, interact, and influence the events as they unfold. Technically, any form of entertainment in which audiences participate rather than merely observe could be classified as interactive entertainment. Activities such as sports, games, and dancing can serve as both passive entertainment for audiences and interactive entertainment for participants.

Interactivity

The concept of interactivity is often used in reference to those forms of entertainment in which audiences can interact and influence events while remaining spectators rather than participants. To create this interactivity, audiences must have some way of communicating their wishes to the "entertainers." For example, musical performances in which audience members shout out requests can be considered interactivity, as can radio shows where individuals call in to make requests or to participate in talk show discussions. Such interactivity is not new. In fact, interactive entertainment might be traced back to the days of gladiators and court jesters where audiences were often empowered to decide the fate (to live or die) of entertainers following their performances.

Until recently, however, most interactive entertainment was limited to live events where audiences could directly communicate their wishes to the entertainers. Mediated entertainment—including most print, TV, and film—was considered passive because the audience could only submissively observe predetermined content. Over the years, however, some authors have dabbled with interactive "choose your own adventure" books that allow readers to make choices as events unfold (should Billy go through the door or turn back?). And now, new technology has enabled most media to be interactive. So much so, in fact, that today "interactivity" is most commonly used in reference to forms of "new" media. In this field, *interactivity* has been defined as "the extent to which users can participate in modifying the form and content of a mediated environment in real time."[30] Such forms of entertainment allow audiences to make choices and shape their own entertainment experiences as they are happening. The interactivity of many emerging forms of entertainment gives audiences additional control over their entertainment experiences. In role-playing online video games, individuals may have control over everything from the planet they play on to their character's favorite flavor of ice cream. Individuals can participate in chat rooms with people halfway around the globe. Providing ultimate control, new media also allow individuals to create their own entertainment software and hardware slide shows with sound tracks, digital videos, cartoons, music, even their own video games and virtual cities.

Audiences also have the choice *not* to interact but, instead, effortlessly sit back and let others entertain them. Audiences enjoy all these forms of control, and they are often willing to pay premium prices for them. Thus, products and services that increase audience autonomy will likely continue to figure prominently in futuretainment.

SPOTLIGHT ON INTERACTIVITY   Showtime Goes Interactive[31]

Showtime took an aggressive approach to interactive television utilizing the Internet on the TV set. Since 2001, each month people log on to Stargate SG-1.com to become part of an online version of the hit Showtime series. Players assemble themselves into 16 teams and play for points that advance their rank and allow them access to classified areas of the site. They are expected to "report for duty" regularly but, while on the site, they can also chat, catch up on the show's episodes, get information, and download photos. An elaborate fantasy filled with information about the universe as it's depicted in the series, StargateSG-1. com started out as a web site created by a fan. "It was getting a lot of activity, so we checked it out and liked it so much we hired the guy who'd created it," explains Mark Greenberg, Showtime executive vice president of corporate strategy and communications.

On the TV set, there's Showtime Interactive 24/7, which allows subscribers with access to Wink technology to check network schedules and pick up information about a movie, series, or event. The enhanced material for each show or movie also includes a Spotlight section that offers original, behind-the-scenes branded content about the program. Interactive 24/7 content is displayed along the bottom of the screen, so viewers can continue watching a show while delving deeper into related information.

Greenberg remembers the day when Showtime executives first realized that their viewers were keenly interested in interactive programming. Showtime Event Television was airing a heavyweight boxing match between Mike Tyson and Frank Bruno and, as an added attraction, the network offered live online scoring. "We were overwhelmed by the number of people participating online," he recalls. "We realized that if you give people a reason to interact, they will."[32]

Since then, Showtime has conducted periodic studies of the phenomenon of viewers watching and being online simultaneously. "On any given night, 25 percent of the people watching TV are also logged on," Greenberg says. Young people, in particular, are apt to "co-use" the TV and PC. Showtime research last year found that 48 percent of teens are simultaneous users, whereas about 30 percent of adults ages 18–49 are.

Those young viewers grew up with cable and are accustomed to paying for their TV, Greenberg says, but they also expect more from their premium services. Hence, options like StargateSG-1.com, which allow fans to delve deeper into the Showtime offerings they like most. "We don't expect every subscriber to watch everything we air," Greenberg says, "but for a service like ours, it's important that we create a culture and a community."[33]

Levels of Interactivity   Researchers have developed five criteria to evaluate levels of interactivity in electronic media.[34] First, the *degree of selectivity* ranges from low selectivity, where selection is limited to deciding when exposure starts and ends, to selecting between simultaneously presented offerings, to selecting different dimensions. Examples of highly interactive offerings according to this criterion are video games, which often allow the user to select the level of difficulty, the characters involved, and the environment (such as city, countryside, or space-age landscape). Second, the *degree of modification* is low when possibilities exist only to store or delete information and is high when it is possible to add more information along with the user's intention and interest. A web site like Yahoo.com, which allows users to add and delete pages as well as modify page color, content, and layout, reflects a high degree of modification. The third criterion, the *quantity of different content* that can be modified or selected, evaluates the sheer number of options (Can you choose from two doors or five? Do you only have one opportunity to choose or several?). Fourth, the *linearity* dimension evaluates whether or not the user has to accept the order of the presentation (as in movies) or may skip around or alternate sequences (as with hypertext functions on web sites). The fifth criterion considers the *number of different senses* (sight, touch, sound, and so on) that are activated. Simulator rides and games such as *Star Wars Pod Racer* allow users to see, hear, and feel their entertainment experience. Although these dimensions do not offer any guidance regarding how to effectively incorporate interactivity into entertainment, they do provide an idea of the range of opportunities.

SPOTLIGHT ON FUN

Interactive Entertainment News

E3, the 2008 annual game industry conference, gathered industry experts in Los Angeles to discuss the state of the gaming business. Because the level of creative talent in games is at an all-time high, the business is surging both financially and in cultural relevance. Eight new games were announced:

- *Dead Space* (Electronic Arts)—science fiction survival-horror genre with wild action and design. For PCs, Xbox 360, and PlayStation 3.
- *LittleBigPlanet* (Sony)—whimsical game of explo-

ration, jumping, climbing, and building with bean bag creatures. For PS3.

- *Fable II* (Microsoft)—rich yet simple fantasy role-playing adventure. For 360.
- *Guitar Hero: World Tour* (Activision)—user-friendly suite of electronic music-creation tools. For 360, PS3, PlayStation 2, and Wii.
- *Free Realms* (Sony)—multiplayer game with thousands of simultaneous players aimed at the junior high school set. For PCs.
- *Spore* (Electronic Arts)—evolution simulator. For PC and Mac.
- *Left 4 Dead* (Electronic Arts, Valve)—lots of Zombies where players must stick together to help one another survive. For PC and 360.
- *Fallout3* (Bethesda Softworks)—role-playing, tongue-in-cheek postapocalyptic series. For PC, 360, and PS3.

Source: Schiesel, Seth (2008). Video games. *New York Times*, July 23.

Interactivity in Practice   Some of the first forms of electronic interactive entertainment were video games. Even the earliest video games possessed enough interactivity that individuals considered themselves to be participants rather than spectators. Today's video games are so interactive that in many cases individuals are not only game players but also game creators, building characters, scenes, rules, and challenges. The Internet has played a large part in the proliferation of interactivity through web sites where individuals can shape their own entertainment in the form of pictures, stories, games, and music. Actors, musicians, film studios, hotels, theme parks, and so on all have web sites that provide interactive opportunities.

The technology also exists for films and videos that allow individuals to make choices in the same manner as in the "choose your own adventure" books; however, to date, this technology has been used more for educational tools rather than purely for entertainment. Still, it appears that almost any form of entertainment can be infused with interactivity, even music videos. Digital Hip Hop produced a video for the rapper Ja Rule in which viewers can choose several options throughout the video—for instance, whether the rapper vanquishes demons with swords or a chain saw. Viewers are prompted to make their choices from a series of icons that pop up at the edge of the video moments before the interactive portions appear on screen.

TV and film productions have also experimented with interactivity. Writers and directors have tried to encourage audience interaction for decades, but, because viewers cannot directly communicate their wishes through the screen, they must find other ways to interact with their audiences. Talent competition shows such as *American Idol* now commonly rely on viewer call-in polls that are posted during broadcasts, and on talk shows viewers can call in and have their comments aired live. Using Internet technology, programs are even allowing viewers to determine the fate of specific characters on regular television series.

Each of the three major networks has turned to the Internet as a way to get soap opera viewers more involved. On *All My Children*, online responses picked out a character's wedding dress, and another campaign asked viewers if a young character should tell her mother (Susan Lucci's Erica Kane) she was gay. *Passions* bumped off a main character chosen by web votes, and *Days of Our Lives* fans went online to decide the paternity of Hope's baby. Showtime Networks Inc. and FanLib took it a step further. They launched the first network-sanctioned, collaborative fan event featuring a writer from a TV series guiding fans in the development of a script using the characters of Showtime's hit series *The L Word*. The scripts were reviewed by a team of judges from *The L Word* staff, and finalists were placed on the web site for fans to vote on. The winning script was to be filmed and incorporated into an actual show episode.

Similarly, the creators of the movie *Snakes on Planes* posted a fan web site while the film was still in production and encouraged fan input. Ideas and dialog suggested by fans were actually incorporated into the film.

The sitcom *Just Shoot Me* allowed the audience to choose between three possible endings for one episode. The three endings, involving David Spade's character Finch, were called "Finch sleeps with Nina's sister," "Finch gets dumped by Nina's sister," and "Things get weird." What made this vote unique was that it happened in real time. Rather than conducting the vote weeks before, viewers voted on the web site during the first half of the broadcast, and the broadcasters were able to tally the vote and cue up the selected ending by the end of the show. Emerging technologies are also enabling TV to become more directly interactive. Although viewers cannot yet directly influence and change events in program content, they can control features such as freezing or forwarding programming as well as obtaining program listings and background information (see *Showtime Goes Interactive* earlier in this chapter).

Fan and contributor of scripts for network shows

Do Audiences Want Interactivity?   There is much debate about how much audiences enjoy interactivity. Much like "reality" drama, interactivity allows for spontaneity that might enhance suspense and thus, ultimately, be more entertaining. It is also argued that, by giving audiences a say in how events unfold, they may begin to feel responsible for those events, making them care and feel more deeply about what happens, which should also further enhance suspense and entertainment. By definition, however, interaction requires audiences to be active. They must pay attention and make choices, and, thus, some critics argue that interactivity may begin to seem more like work than play. They suggest that audiences might often simply prefer to passively sit back and be entertained.

As with most issues related to entertainment, it seems likely that audience enjoyment of interactivity may be influenced by a number of factors. Some audiences may generally enjoy interactivity more than others do. And some individuals may enjoy certain forms of interactivity but not others, or interactivity at certain times but not others. The degree of selectivity certainly seems to play a role in audience enjoyment. If audiences are allowed too few choices, they might become bored or frustrated, yet if they are given too many choices, they may become overwhelmed and equally frustrated. For game developers, dot.coms, and others eager to capitalize on interactive entertainment, the exploration of these issues is critical. Yet researchers are only now just beginning to explore how audiences engage with and react to interactivity.

Driving Industries

It is probably safe to say that new trends and advances in Internet entertainment, indeed all futuretainment, will continue to push the limits of what technology and the law will allow. Innovators looking for ways to create, reproduce, and blend different forms of entertainment will experiment with every new gadget or software application. Some ideas will succeed; others will fail. Some projects will flop owing to lack of interest, others because the developers cannot find a way to legally make money from them. If you want to try to predict the next entertainment hit, you need to identify who the successful innovators are and pay attention to what they are doing.

The Power of Porn   Interestingly, some of the most profitable and innovative web sites are adult entertainment sites. In fact, many experts argue that adult entertainment—what some might call pornography—is one of the most powerful technological forces driving new media. Technology is driven by demand. Cutting-edge firms develop products they think will sell fast. According to the experts, some of the strongest demand comes from porn "manufacturers" because they are looking for technological advances that will help them get over the one big problem their industry faces—the shame factor.[36]

Malcolm Hutty, general director of the Campaign Against Censorship of the Internet in Britain, explains that although demand for porn is high, it doesn't travel well: "People want porn, but they want it in the comfort of their own home, not in seedy backstreet cinemas or sex shops, and they don't want anyone else to know about it. Technology helps bring it straight to you. Each advance seems, at least, to bring you closer to the fantasy, and guarantee more privacy. The more private it becomes, the more comfortable consumers feel, particularly women. They enjoy it more, so they buy it more."[37]

 FLASH FACT

According to the Internet Filter Review, every second:[35]

- $3,075.64 is being spent on pornography
- 28,258 Internet users are viewing pornography
- 372 Internet users are typing adult search terms into search engines.

Every 39 minutes a new pornographic video is being created in the U.S. In 2006, pornography revenues were highest in China (28 percent), South Korea (27 percent), Japan (21 percent), and the U.S. (14 percent). In the U.S., porn revenues exceed the combined revenues of ABC, CBS, and NBC. In 2006, there were 4.2 million pornographic web sites (12 percent of all).

Porn producer Adam Glasser at the Erotica LA Convention

Adult entertainment is credited with driving many advances in new media, including better privacy and security guarantees for financial transactions online as well as better video streaming technology. Adult entertainment web sites were the first to introduce start/stop video streaming, thereby allowing customers 24- to 48-hour windows to view purchased online videos, and adult sites also pioneered technology for downloading still and moving images on handheld computers and mobile phones. Adult entertainment providers have become so good at developing technology and making money online that mainstream e-businesses—including not only entertainment but also commerce from banks to supermarkets—are now asking the leading practitioners for advice.[38] Thus, emerging trends in adult entertainment may serve as a useful gauge for all forms of entertainment.

Shall We Play a Game?   Another innovator to watch is the gaming industry. Video games have evolved at a rapid pace and they are growing increasingly popular. In 1997, video game sales began outperforming domestic box office movie sales.[39] As discussed in Chapter 11, not only do video games generate more gross revenue than motion pictures, they cost significantly less to produce, creating the potential for a significantly more favorable profit margin.

One of the more impressive aspects of the gaming industry is the multitude of platforms that exist for game play. There are handheld devices, TV, computer, and Internet platforms as well as large-scale, self-contained game units. Large-scale game units include those featured in arcade venues, which range from the small portable video game machines found in pizza parlors and gambling machines in casinos to the large-scale gaming theaters found in multiplex gaming centers like Dave and Buster's and GameWorks. Although video games have traditionally been considered children's entertainment, multiplex gaming centers cater to all ages.

Evolving from a joystick to drumsticks

Playing to Win

Every aspect of life has a pervasive sense of play attached to it. To argue that play is a part of the long journey of human civilization is not far from the universal truth, since evidence of play can be found directly in all our daily lives. Studies in cultural sociology and anthropology show that play possesses cultural dimensions and exerts symbolic meaning in our society.

The cultural function of play revolves around a notion that the great archetypal activities in human society are all permeated with play. As we learned in Chapter 1, games have been classified according to their degree of structure into four types of play. Games of competition, chance, simulation, and vertigo are placed along the dimensions of freedom from paideia (very free) to ludus (very structured). Because many are rule-based, the games we play have been studied to develop strategies for winning in other aspects of our lives. Much of play research focuses on game theory.

Video Games

Revenue from video games is now larger than profits generated by the film industry. Video game industry energy is expressed by its name, the "Prometheus Engine," which was inspired by a god in Greek mythology who is believed to have given humans power.[40] Similar to other forms of entertainment, video game players are influenced by the dramatic worldview (see Chapter 1) because they identify with the dramatic structure of plots, conflict building, and resolutions that lead to particular outcomes. And video games supply players with an array of dramatic consumption that serves their schematic reality.

In video games, digital computers are combined with primitive games for a new breed of finite play. The last three decades witnessed the fast-growing development in Silicon Valley that fosters the changing nature of video game playing.[41] Video games allow high degrees of computer control, isolate players from other people, and move closer to a hyperrealistic territory. Because video games are simulated or virtual reality, we call them "hyper real." Games we played 100 years ago are still being played today, but in an electronic format—sport, board games, and fighting are all part of video game play.

Video games[42] trace their original parents to arcade games and digital computers. A form of interactive media, video games allow players to engage in a reciprocating exchange of three-dimensional visual communication messages. As modes of popular culture, video games are novelties mass-produced by entrepreneurs for the gratification of a paying audience. Games are created for public consumption, exerting strong emotional impacts to players through various psychological mechanisms. We define video games as: interactive communication that players engage in while controlling a mediated video content, and games played on a dedicated console or computer screen.

Video games conform to one or a hybrid of the following genres:[43]

- role-playing games with a plot, based on history or literature stories, such as the *Final Fantasy* series
- real-time strategies involving two groups that fight with each other such as *Starcraft* and *Missile Command*
- first-person shooters who fight with an enemy such as *Doom*, *Time Crisis*, and *Alien vs. Predators*
- shoot-'em-up/shooting games such as *Space Invaders*, *Defenders*, *Robotron*, *Galaxian*, and *Battlezone*
- beat-'em-up/fighting games such as *The Street Fighter* series, *Mortal Combat*, *Ready 2 Rumble Boxing*, and *Pro Wrestling*
- racing games such as *The Grand Turismo* series and *Project Gotham*
- sport games like *ISS Pro Evolution*, *Tony Hawk's Pro Skater*, and *Madden NFL 2001*
- platform games/exploration games with a series of levels such as *Donkey Kong*, *Sonic the Hedgehog*, *Super Mario Brothers*, *The Castlevania* series, *Tomb Raiders* series, *The Mega Man* series, *Myst*, and *Raven*
- puzzle games like *Tetris*
- god games such as *Sin City*, *Sin Theme Parks*, *Populous*, *Civilization*, and *Flight Simulator*.

Like other media, video games have specific narratives or story lines. In all games, the player must be able to violate something, otherwise it's not a game, it's a movie. The use of interactive elements changes how story narratives are communicated.

Table 17.2 Print and Electronic Narratives

Print narratives (books)	Interactive electronic narratives (video games)
Author tells, reader listens	Player is part of story
Author is creative for reader	Designer is creative for player
Hot medium (low participation)	Cold medium (high participation)
Words based	Visual images and sound based
Imagination	Immersion
Strong characterization	Weak characterization
Endings strong	Endings weak or problematic
Reader external to events	Player internal to events
Participation by identification	Actual participation
Characters have freedom	Characters select from available choices
Illustrations simple	Graphics, music, and sound powerful
Story construction hidden	Story construction discovered
Many kinds of structure	Mazes and tangled rhizomes

Unlike more developed media like cinema, video game developers still struggle to define what it is exactly that makes an entertaining game. Denis Dyack of Silicon Knights, for instance, uses *engagement theory*, spinning games out of a combination of art, audio, technology, gameplay, and story. American McGee, on the other hand, prefers to start with characters and art, and simply let the gameplay come out later. Table 17.2 shows the differences between print and interactive electronic narratives.[44]

The gaming media have invoked graphic enhancements and microprocessors for a lifelike gaming experience. One company that revolutionized gaming graphics is 3DFX, which introduced a graphics card for PCs that is able to generate extreme display pixel enhancements. The Voodoo product line relies on an FX engine chip and a Texture engine that provide an infrastructure for expansion. The latest card in the Verto series currently sets the standard in generating lifelike pixel depth. Not to be undone, Intel's new Pentium 4 Processor has a chip structure that delivers the highest performance in video graphics and multimedia that is changing the way we view 3D graphics.

Gaming as a Cultural Playground

Video games exert the same cultural function as any kinds of play in human society, and they contain the same theoretical characteristics as play described above. Assuming that all forms of leisure activities are voluntary and have a symbolic message that conveys the meaning of freedom, players are not forced to play video games—they play because they want to play. Playing video games is experiential consumption of entertainment. Video game consumption is not real—it's played for amusement. Once the box is activated, video games take players to another world for a fixed period of time and, when the experience ends, players are transported back to their ordinary world.

Video games have **common rules** to which players must adhere. In adventure and sports games, rules appear to be as similar as the real sports in order to make a playing experience as realistic as possible. In fact, different genres of video games have different sets of specific rules that players have to learn for stimulating their complete playing experiences.

FLASH FACT

The Microsoft/Sperling survey revealed that the average age of a video gamer is 30, and 19 percent of gamers are older than 50. Men currently dominate the industry; however, the gap is closing. Forty-three percent of players are now women. The top five gaming cities in the U.S. are Seattle, Minneapolis, Atlanta, Detroit, and Phoenix.

Gaming Communities Gaming communities form to establish competition and to develop new games. A type of play that expresses a significant cultural function like other forms of play, video game consumption is a form of **modern hedonism** because it relates to the multi-sensory, fantasy, and emotional aspects of our experience with products.[45] As our society becomes more hedonistic—focusing on immediate gratification—we exchange our nationality for an identity of consumption for pleasure. As a contemporary phenomenon, consumption is an important cultural movement and entertainment is a vital part of its foundation. Hedonism, then, is the fun that a consumer derives from a product—the pleasure that the product evokes—and an appreciation of the product for its own sake.[46]

What role does **gender** play in gaming? Men and women have very different survival mechanisms and survival behaviors, the most prominent of which is hunting. An entire range of hand–eye coordination characteristics and skills are needed to hunt. When men use these skills, they are rewarded with the sensation of pleasure. Women, however, do not experience the same chemical sensations.[47] The chemical release experienced from action and sports games have become a common way for men to exercise their instinct for hunting. Designed by and intended for men, aggression-based computer games provide stimulation that is easily adaptable to a peaceful society.

Whether they act as fantasy, thrill, intellectual and emotional challenges, psychological control, creative art, or enjoyment, video games are a perfect venue for providing a dramatic construction through catharsis and tension release. Game players subconsciously identify with the dramatic structure of plots (good vs. evil, heroes vs. villains, gods vs. monster, etc.) and conflict building and resolutions (*agon*) that lead to particular outcomes in video games. Games also provide an array of dramatic consumption that serves players' schematic reality.

Video games, like other forms of play, come to provide what is missing from a person's need to communicate, self-definition, and self-identity that cannot be found in a bureaucratic workplace. At work, we encounter stress and tension; at home, video game playing in the virtual world gives players emotional arousal, sense of power, and release from the stress of real-world problems. Players call video gaming one of the purest forms of communication-pleasure!

SPOTLIGHT ON ETHICS   The Real Cost of Free Games

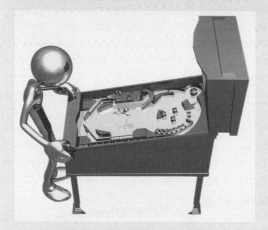

With such success come the dreaded marketing types, and with them come ads. What's downright obnoxious is the way ads are presented to gamers. Take a look at Pogo, the casual game site created by the world's largest video game maker, Electronic Arts. Here, you can play games for free. But you'll also have to pay for them: with your time because there's no way to opt out of looking at ads. One of the great free games on Pogo is *The Sims Pinball*, based on the best-selling simulation franchise created by Will Wright. Just as with any real-life pinball game, you get three balls on a table that pops up after you register on the site.

If you like casual games, you're not alone. For some of the world's biggest companies, there's gold in the casual niche, which was to become a $1 billion a year business by 2008, according to Jupiter Research. Right now, the people who make and promote these games are pulling in $350 million a year.

With *The Sims*, the game's often about getting experience for your character. In *The Sims Pinball*, you have the choice of a few career paths, everything from doctor to slacker. Each character has six experience levels, and it's hard to complete your experience with three balls—even with the exciting additions of multiball mode and an extra ball or two.

But here's the rub. This game is sponsored by Sharpie, the logo of which covers the middle of the playfield. If you rack up a certain amount of points, you're entered into a Sharpie contest. Since it's natural for a human to want to score better and better, you want to play again . . . and again. That's where Electronic Arts gets you. Every three or four games, your game stops, and you have to watch a pop-up ad. which stays up for 30 seconds. It's kind of like watching a TV commercial, except these ads don't have video.

When you go to Pogo, you'll find a game you like a lot. And because you like the free game, you won't be bothered by the ads which appear in the game. The salient thing about casual games and ads is this: because these online sites are still in their infancy, they probably will listen to you. If you don't like the ads, gripe in an e-mail. They probably won't lose the ads, but they may make them just a little more palatable. They definitely don't want to lose one thing: you.

Source: Harold Goldberg for the *Village Voice*, Aug. 30, 2006

For more on video games, visit www.villagevoice.com and www.pogo.com.

What do you think?

- *Should advertisers be allowed to function as part of free video games?*
- *Would you rather pay for a game without advertising, or get a free game with ads? Why?*

Gaming Trends

The video game market is expected to expand from $32.6 billion in 2005 to $65.9 billion in 2011. Why? According to a study from ABI Research, because of the fast-growing online and mobile gaming segments. The market's largest segments today—console, PC, and handheld hardware and software—will see much lower growth rates than the emerging segments.

As the new generation of consoles arrives with advanced networking and online gaming capabilities, the ability to download game demos and access advanced content, including HD video, will result in "online" becoming the key technology component of gaming for this and subsequent console generations. Mobile gaming is set to see significant growth through 2011, as the flood of interest from game publishers and mobile operators results in both imported and original game titles for download by mobile subscribers. Recent efforts by mobile gaming giants to develop an open gaming architecture in order to reduce development fragmentation will open the doors to more content for consumers and overall higher revenues for game downloads.

With 40 million monthly visitors, DigitalTrends.com is the first stop for mainstream readers and gadget enthusiasts looking to make sense of how consumer electronics, video games, home theater components, and other tech-related products fit into their everyday lives. Since debuting in 2001, the site's become an indispensable resource for those looking to shop for groundbreaking new gadgets and technological innovations. One of the site's reviewers thinks Wii from Nintendo is a wave of the future.

Nintendo's Wii system, an easy-to-use, inexpensive diversion for families, sold more than 25 million units in 2007, besting competition from Sony and Microsoft. *Wii Fit*, an exercise innovation, makes doing yoga in front of a TV as much fun as shooting in a traditional game. Japan's most successful cultural export, video games have made Nintendo's chairman the richest man in Japan with a net worth of $8 billion.[48]

Under the direction of inventor Shigeru Miyamoto, the Wii has evolved from a reliance on invented characters and outlandish settings to games like *Nintendogs*, *Wii Sports*, *Wii Fit*, and—in development—*Wii Music*. According to Miyamoto, Nintendo wants to create an experience where people are very simply able to get the feeling that they're creating music. By gravitating to everyday hobbies, Miyamoto has moved from the abstract into realism, providing games for the rest of us.

Analysis of the time spent on the top ten games over the years shows a substantial shift in the duration for which video games are played. A good majority now plays best-sellers for relatively shorter duration—10–20 hours—in contrast to 2005, where the majority used to play games for more than 100 hours. For a long time, the gaming industry primarily focused on hardcore gamers—a relatively small segment accounting for disproportionate share of revenue. Since 2006, gaming has become a mass-market entertainment industry on a par with TV, movies, and music. Segments such as

Virtual boxing with the Nintendo Wii

video game advertising, set to become a market worth close to $3 billion by 2011, will result in the further maturing of this industry. The ability to play music and media from powerful consoles and handhelds will drive overall industry growth as consumers begin to view gaming devices as one-stop-shop entertainment platforms.

The Future of Video Gaming

These days it seems almost everyone has a theory about the future of video games. Many software developers see themselves on a collision course with the film industry, with games having their own version of the Oscars. Others expect games to undergo a series of graphic reinterpretations. Actually, gaming seems to be following the evolution of the vehicle where games appear most—TV. Sales for TV-based game consoles are expected to increase variably among manufacturers, as shown in Figure 17.2.

Just as reality-based fare is among the most successful television of the last decade, it's possible that the new massive, multiplayer online games will follow a similar course. As more 18–34-year-olds check out of network TV and check into gaming, marketers will go after that valuable consumer demographic. Product placement and in-game ads may become so abundant that NASCAR will look like NPR in comparison. Play a driving game and you'll see familiar landmarks: the Shell gas station on the corner, the McDonald's on Main Street, the Budweiser billboards near highway exits. As the music industry looks for new ways to recapture its youthful audience, record labels will find even greater ways to cross-promote, such as putting popular music in games.

Gaming's permeation into just about all of society is creating fresh ways for marketers to connect. Millions of non-golfers are swinging virtual clubs with Nintendo's Wii; senior citizen centers use Wiis to entertain guests and connect with grandkids. MTV invested $500 million in online games, on top of the millions it spent for Addicting Games. Even business-to-business marketers are giving gaming a fresh look to incorporate blending in messaging, training, or recruiting.

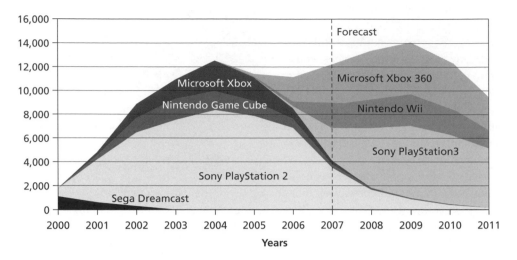

Figure 17.2   Software Sales for Games Consoles ($ million)

Source: Ed Barton—screendigest

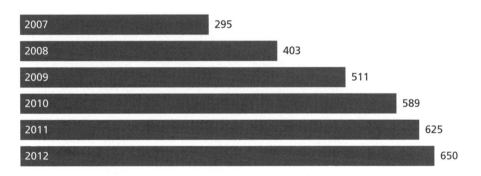

Figure 17.3   Spending Forecast for In-game Advertising, 2007–12 ($ million)

Note: includes static ads, dynamic ads, product placements, game portal display ads, and sponsored sessions in console-based, PC-based, and web-based games; excludes advergames and advertising on mobile games

Source: eMarketer, February 2008

Predictions from eMarketer indicate that U.S. video game advertising spending will reach $1 billion in 2012, up from $502 million in 2007. Of this total, in-game advertising spending will grow to $650 million in 2012, from $295 million in 2007.

Big-name brands will continue to embrace the game wave for their products: Toyota is featuring commercials exclusively on Xbox, and other brands are experimenting in this space (Nike, Adidas, Reebok, Coke, Pepsi, Mountain Dew, Gatorade, Ford, BMW, Samsung, McDonald's, KFC, Burger King, and Axe). However research reports skepticism around advertising to young people who don't seem to like game advertising very much. A survey by research company Bunnyfoot that sampled 120 players ages 18 and over found low recognition of ads in sports titles.

Video game advertising continues to be a trend marketers find appealing, given the game industry's explosive growth. In-game advertising can be static or dynamic. Static advertising is hard-coding a product or brand message into a game, which needs to be finalized months in advance of the game's release. Dynamic advertising integrates

2-D and 3-D objects into an online game environment in real time via predetermined locations.

Research shows that in-game ads have to be more than product placements, so marketers must improve their learning curve. They recognize that consumers have a hard time making sense of ads for current car models in a video game that takes place in the distant future, and that gamers are unlikely to seek out a cereal brand in a video game where the player is not required to eat to replenish energy levels. In lieu of this information, game publishers and advertising companies are working to address these problems and create more relevant video game integrations.

The future of gaming will not be all that different than the future of any other form of entertainment. As the masses of players determine what they want to get out of gaming, large corporations will throw their money and workforce into providing it.

The average age of the gamer is rapidly approaching 30. As people in their 30s and 40s continue to play video games into their senior years, the genres of games will expand to accommodate those audiences and their discretionary income.[49] And when gaming isn't enough, the same demographic often forays into a more dangerous form of gaming—gambling.

Internet gambling can be one of the easiest forms of gambling to hide from friends and family. Gamblers can shut the door and erase their Internet files to hide any evidence that they have been gambling online. Help Guide studied 389 gambling addicts who sought care at a health clinic. The study indicated that, while Internet gambling was the least common type of gambling noted, those who gambled on the Internet were more likely to develop problematic gambling habits.

As discussed in previous chapters, gamers are a fickle lot. They thrive on novelty. Thus, the gaming industry also has extra incentive not to become stagnant but to remain innovative. The gaming industry has led the way, with many advances in areas such as animation technology and software programming that, in turn, are often adopted by other entertainment industries. Ironically, then, it would seem that futuretainment is being guided by two of the most unlikely partners—adult entertainment on one end of the spectrum and, on the other end, gaming, which (apart from gambling) has functioned predominantly as a youth-oriented form of entertainment.

A New Media Model[50]

As discussed at the beginning of the chapter, in his new book *Futuretainment*, futurist Mike Walsh outlines a new media model that reflects the mutual influences of societal factors and entertainment advances reflected throughout this text.

Production

Walsh begins by reviewing the factory model of media that has been in place since the Gutenburg's invention of the printing press. If you ever have the opportunity to visit a newspaper printing plant—do so. It's an excellent metaphor of the way media used to be. Vast, loud, and mechanical. Across printing webs, conveyor belts, and hoppers—media are literally assembled right before your eyes, according to Walsh "like the product of some arcane Willy Wonka factory."[51]

The factory model was predictable. With good management and a rising population, you could be sure print circulation and profits would increase with time. TV and radio stations had a captive population, safeguarded by regulation which kept new entrants out.

Not everyone may have loved what was on all of the time, but they liked it well enough most of the time to watch or read anyway. But then, it changed. As previous chapters have demonstrated, today's entertainment world now resembles more of a network than a factory. Content is created by consumers within a network of connections and exchanged seamlessly

Programming

Walsh maintains that if production is one side of the two-headed coin of media, programming is the other. Many of us would remember a time when all of our entertainment choices were mapped out for us in TV Guides, Sunday Night Movies, Cinema Listings, Commercial Ad Breaks, and orderly release windows. Not for much longer.

Although early new media may have largely served simply as an extension of traditional media to "warehouse" and redisribute existing prepackaged programming, that is changing fast. The old factory model worked on intelligent guesswork. Editors choose the stories they think will best sell papers, programmers choose their prime-time line up to best secure ratings, and Pay TV networks aggregate a selection of content channels which they think will draw the most paying subscribers.

Walsh argues that the new networked audience model makes programming obsolete. He predicts that there will be an entire generation of consumers being born who will live in a world without programmed media. We can already see a rapid proliferation of user-generated new media "programming." On video posting sites like YouTube, people are creating their own continuing story series, such as the lonelygirl blogs discussed earlier. Fans of popular fantasy and science fiction such as *Star Trek*, *Buffy the Vampire Slayer*, and *Harry Potter* write their own stories or program "episodes" for the shows' characters on "fan fiction" web sites such as Fanfiction.net, Harrypotterfanfiction. com, Trekfanfiction. net, and Talesoftheslayer.com.

Distribution and Marketing

The easy access that media allows is also changing the way entertainment is marketed. When every piece of entertainment is available online to anyone who wants it—the consumption trigger is your ability to convince someone to click on a link. Under those circumstances, traditional marketing is actually not as powerful as buzz in new media —as revealed through blog posts on MySpace, popularity on download charts, conversation on web forums, and the results of Google searches on popular keywords. Walsh explains:

> Other people's opinions are literally the DNA of most web consumption decisions today. Amazon's book recommendation service is based on the consumption patterns of other like minded book buyers, Google's page rank algorithm works off the density of other people's webpages linking to a particular piece of content, bands on MySpace survive by the number of friends that they manage to signup and recruit to their webpage.[52]

We are accelerating to a point at which everything will be available to everyone at anytime. In that place, media becomes a signal bouncing around a network of users, rather than a series of satellites or transmission towers.

Early media scholar Marshall McLuhan coined the phrase "The medium is the message" meaning that the form of a medium imbeds itself in the message, creating a symbiotic relationship by which the medium influences how the message is perceived, creating subtle change over time. The phrase was introduced in his most widely known book, *Understanding media: The extensions of man*, published in 1964. McLuhan proposed that media themselves, not the content they carry, should be the focus of study; he said that a medium affects the society in which it plays a role not only by the content delivered over the medium but by the characteristics of the medium itself. Throughout this text we have reviewed the mutual influences between different entertainment media and the societies that both create and consume them. Even Marshall McLuhan, however, would have been impressed, and perhaps even surprised, at the impact of today's media. New media's networked audience is not just the medium. It is also writing the message.

Nonetheless, as long as a critical mass of people still enjoy being couch potatoes, at least some of the time, linear entertainment content is not going anywhere. However, the context in which major entertainment franchises are delivered will change. In the same way that, now, major motion picture releases are structured to take full advantage of merchandising and marketing opportunities, future entertainment blockbusters will more closely resemble platforms than products (see *A Closer Look* at the end of this chapter).

Signs of the Times

New entertainment trends will also continue to shape and reflect the economic, political, and social environments from which they are born. Just as today's stories, songs, games, and pastimes reflect today's people and issues, tomorrow's entertainment will similarly reflect the people and issues of the day. Chapter 2 explored how today's entertainment reflects the converging, postmodern era we live in. Postmodernism suggests a breakdown and recombination of traditional structures, and our entertainment reflects this with genre and era mixing in drama, music, art, and even dining, where restaurants feature *food fusion* (combinations of different flavors and ethnic dishes). New media, with their endless possibilities for breaking down, converging, and re-creating entertainment, are almost postmodern by definition.

Nonetheless, invariably, the pendulum will swing. Today's "anything goes" philosophy may eventually be replaced by new lines of thinking. Thus, the final, perhaps bold, prediction we will make for futuretainment is a *return to basics*. Following an era of funny horror films and dark comedies, popular alternative music and Peking Duck pizza, some individuals may begin to yearn for firmer boundaries, where horror movies are truly scary and comedies are truly funny, alternative music is truly alternative and pizza comes with pepperoni.

Some people will welcome these boundaries, while others will continue to shun them. As long as emerging entertainment continues to promote audience autonomy, however, both camps should have plenty of entertainment options to suit their respective tastes.

FADE TO BLACK—Cut and Wrap

This chapter has focused predominantly on how new media are shaping the future of entertainment. New media entertainment is defined as entertainment that incorporates a variety of media, and it is suggested that new trends in entertainment might be identified by paying attention to innovators in new media technology. Predictions for futuretainment include continued focus on integrated products and services that maximize audience control over the entertainment experience as well as a possible return to more traditional entertainment offerings.

New media, of course, are not the only significant force shaping the future of entertainment. Throughout this book, we have traced numerous ways that developments in entertainment have been shaped not only by technological advances but by the political, cultural, economic, religious, and legal realities that existed at the time. And, in turn, we have also explored how entertainment can exert a significant influence on the creation and perception of those realities. Future entertainment will likely be no different in this regard. The evolution of entertainment is forever intertwined with the evolution of the societies in which it resides.

A CLOSER LOOK AT NEW MEDIA

New Media Branding and Marketing: The Brand Dilemma

As the evidence mounts up that young people are spending more of their precious media consumption time on the web or playing games, advertisers are being forced to reconsider their marketing strategies. Unlike more traditional media advertising options, coming up with a predictable model for engaging with social media is not easy.

After all, how do you serve ads in an chaotic user-generated content environment where people are just as likely to attack your brand as rave about it? What kind of brands are best suited for placement in an online video game whose main premise is robbing, looting, and pimping in an urban ghetto?

When reality TV took over from drama as the dominant prime-time programming formula in the late 1990s, advertisers shifted their engagement model to product placement rather than formulaic commercials. The next evolutionary step is likely to be brand platforms—loosely structured environments in which users can engage with brand values and icons without strict controls or supervision.[53]

One recent example of the emerging brand platform model is Joga—an invitation-only social networking site for football (soccer) fans created by Nike and Google. "Joga Bonito" means "Play Beautiful" in Portuguese. Joga is based on Orkut, a social network very popular in Brazil.

Merging of media, branding, and sports in Trafalgar Square in London, England

The network allows members to create their own web sites and upload pictures, blog posts, and video clips as well as access Nike content relating to its sponsored athletes. In a sense Joga is a parallel brand universe, which allows its users to create content about their passions and lives, while at the same time orbiting the advertisers' core brand values.

Nike used Erik Cantona, a legendary footballer, as a spokesperson to deliver the message of "Play Beautiful" to promote "creative and attractive football by playing from the heart and eliminating unfair and unsportsmanlike play." Joga also simulates more traditional media with Joga Bonito Network Radio (JBNR) podcasts and Joga TV streaming video. Hosted by Cantona, Joga TV is portrayed as an underground broadcast channel "filmed live from the heart of Germany" and displays the greater side of football the skills, the flair, and the creativity—whilst lambasting negative play.[54]

In tandem with the launch of this new media branding campaign, Nike sponsored Joga3, an international indoor football tournament. Joga3 was hosted in 39 different nations, with each nation having multiple cities or towns that hosted it. There was a National Finals for every country, and the winners earned a place at the World Finals in Brazil.

Although it was originally targeted toward Brazil and other Latin American countries, to add local excitement for the 2006 FIFA World Cup competition hosted in Germany that year, Nike and Google also leveraged their "Joga Bonito" campaign in other areas such as Hong Kong. Nike's advertising agency in Hong Kong explained the reasoning behind its use of Joga Bonita: "we strongly believed it was a strong concept to capitalize on in Hong Kong and differentiate ourselves from competition during the period when everyone was talking about Football. To deliver an integrated marketing campaign was crucial to our success all through World Football 2006."[55]

In Hong Kong, the Joga Bonito message was led from local commercial radio to the JBNR through the usage of a local Hong Kong DJ, pop singer, and actor Jan Lamb. Joga Bonito was sung out by a group of pop singers in Hong Kong through the partnership with MOOV (a newly launched music channel on NOW.com.hk). A concept album was prepared and users could listen to this album on JBNR. According to the agency, "the objective and role of this digital media was to echo on the core communication message 'Joga Bonito' but more importantly, injecting local meanings to it and triggering responses—lead users to take a stand and ultimately play beautifully on football court!"[56] Joga users could win a chance to attend the Joga3 finale event by participating online in Joga's "Beautiful Movement" an interactive experience promoting Joga's principles of heart, honour, joy, skill, and team. These are concepts that resonated well with the traditional Chinese values and culture of the people of Hong Kong. At the finale event, fans saw Joga Bonito in action—the final game of Nike Joga3, a concert with singers who expressed Joga Bonito through music and an Interactive Installation to let users play beautiful.

Nike's Joga Bonito exemplifies many of the facets of contemporary entertainment that have been highlighted in this book—the rise of new media platforms, integrated info-advertainment, the dominance of interactivity and user-generated content, and the increasing globalization and cultural adaptation of all of these strategies. Yet, it also demonstrates that in spite of these advances, at the core of Joga Bonito and other new entertainment platforms you will still find traditional pastimes that audiences have enjoyed for centuries—sports, games, music, drama, travel, and recreation.

Consider other examples of how contemporary entertainment can simultaneously reflect both society's advancement and its heritage.

DISCUSSION AND REVIEW

1. Review how the text describes new media. Based on this description, come up with your own definition. Compare similarities and differences between qualities of the Internet and other forms of new media entertainment and traditional media. Give examples to illustrate your points.
2. What industries are leading the way for futuretainment and why? Can you think of other industries—both entertainment and nonentertainment—that may play a large role in shaping futuretainment? Explain.
3. What is the difference between a factory and networking model of entertainment production? Describe ways that new media have facilitated a networking model.
4. Discuss the characteristics of futuretainment reviewed in the chapter. Do you agree

with each of these? Use examples to make your case. Try to come up with other characteristics or trends that you think are emerging or will emerge for future-tainment.

EXERCISES

1. Look up terms like "futuretainment," "the future of entertainment," or "new technology and entertainment" on an Internet search engine and in a news database like ProQuest or Lexis Nexis. Report what you find. Select one or two articles that you find particularly interesting and discuss them.
2. Have a friend write down at least 20 things people do for entertainment. Review the list and see how many currently involve new media. For every item on the list, speculate ways that new media might be used to enhance, imitate, or modify these forms of entertainment.
3. Try several forms of new media entertainment. Prepare a written critique of each the way a critic might review a film, toy, or restaurant. Describe your experience. Did it meet your expectations? Review pluses and minuses and make suggestions for improvement.

BOOKS AND BLOGS

Darly, A. (2002). *Visual digital culture: Surface play and spectacle in new media genres* (Sussex Studies in Culture and Communication series). New York: Routledge.

Manovich, L. (2001). *The language of new media*. Cambridge MA: MIT Press.

Pavlik, J.V. (1997). *New media technology: Cultural and commercial perspectives* (Allyn & Bacon Series in Mass Communication). Boston MA: Allyn & Bacon.

Sayre, S. (2008). *Entertainment marketing & communication: Selling branded performance, people and places*. Upper Saddle River NJ: Prentice Hall.

Weibel, P. and Druckrey, T. (2001). *Net_condition: Art and global media (Electronic culture: History, theory, and practice)*. Cambridge MA: MIT Press.

www.internet-filter-review.toptenreviews.com—for what's happening in adult entertainment.

www.madison&vine.com—provides the latest news on convergent technology.

www.redherring.com—news on the business of technology.

www.insidebrandedentertainment.com—updates you on what's happening in the branded entertainment arena.

www.organicentertainment.net—interactive news.

NOTES

Chapter 1

1 See Rifkin, J. (2000). *The age of access*. New York: Penguin Putnam.

2 Huizinga, J. (1950). *Homo ludens*. Boston: Beacon Press.

3 From Stephenson, W. (1988). *The play theory of mass communication*. New Brunswick NJ: Transaction Books.

4 From McLellan, D. (2000). Circus atmosphere: First woman big-top publicist tells tales of three rings. *The Los Angeles Times*, August 13, B8.

5 From A brief history of puppetry. www.sunnieunniezz.com/puppetry/puphisto.htm, Oct. 13, 2000.

6 Mergen, B. (1984). *Cultural dimensions of play, games and sport*. Champaign IL: Human Kinetics Publishers Inc.

7 Plunket Research Inc., 2008, from plunkettresearch.com/Industries/EntertainmentMedia/ EntertainmentMediaTrends/tabid/228/Default.aspx.

8 See Wolf, M.J. (1999). *The entertainment economy*. New York: Times Books.

9 Ibid., p. 4.

10 Donaton, Scott (2004). *Madison & Vine: Why the entertainment and advertising industries must converge to survive*. New York: McGraw-Hill.

Chapter 2

1 From ciadvertising.org.

2 Jenkins, Henry (2006). *Convergence culture*. New York: NYU Press.

3 Bolton, J.R. and Grushin, V.V., *International Technology*, p. 224, as found on www.cyberartsweb.org/ cpace/infotecch/lectures/media/convergence.html.

4 From www.convergenceculture.org/aboutc3/convergence.php.

5 Book review located at http://home.grandecom.net/~maher/writing/convergence.html.

6 Review by Erica Barnett found on www.watercoolergames.org/archives/000590.shtml.

7 See www.timharrower.com/PDFs/convergence.pdf.

8 Budick, A. (1999). Exhibiting a little pizzazz. *Future.Newsday.Com*, para 1. Accessed Dec. 18, 2002, at http://future.newsday.com/8/ftop0801.htm#museum.

9 Advertisement for Ken Davis's video, *Is it Just Me?* Accessed Dec. 18, 2002, at https://www.kendavis. com/video/vt013.cfm.

10 The slogan of the Christian Comedy Index. Accessed Dec. 17, 2002, at http://christiancomedy.tripod. com.

11 From www.globalization101.org.

12 Excerpted from essays posted on www.thehumanist.org/humanist/articles/essay3mayjune04.pdf.

13 See Baudrillard, J. (1983). *Simulations*. New York: Semiotext(e).

14 From Denzin, N.K. (1991). *Images of postmodern society*. London: Sage, p. vii.

15 From Featherstone, M. (1991). *Consumer culture and postmodernism*. London: Sage, pp. 7–8.

16 Baudrillard, *Simulations*, p. 10.

17 http://www.spiritual-self.com/postmodern-definition.html.

18 From Cumming, R.D. (1965). *The philosophy of Jean Paul Sartre*. New York: Random House.

19 From Ewen, S. and Ewen, E. (1982). *Channels of desire*. New York: McGraw-Hill, pp. 249–51.

20 Quoted by Downey, R. (1999). Experience this! *New York Times*, Feb. 19.

21 Quoted by Verhovek, S.H. (2000). He's turning Seattle into his kind of town. *New York Times*, May 17.

22 See Jameson, F. (1991). *Postmodernism*. Durham NC: Duke University Press, ch. 4.

23 Quoted in Goldberger, P. (2002). High-tech emporiums. *The New Yorker*, March 25.

24 Excerpted from Root, D. (1996). *Cannibal culture: Art, appropriation & the commodification of difference*. Boulder CO: Westview Press.

25 Beaudrillard, *Simulations*, p. 130.

26 From a review by Pauline Kael, *The New Yorker*, Sept. 22, 1986.

27 From a piece by John Simon, *National Review*, Nov. 7, 1986.

Chapter 3

1 Gurvitch, G. (1955). The sociology of the theater. Reprinted in E. Burns and T. Burns (eds) (1973). *Sociology of Literature and Drama*. Harmondsworth: Penguin.

2 McQuail, D. (1994). *Mass communication theory: An introduction*. London: Sage.

3 Carey, J. (1975). A cultural approach to communication. *Communication*, 2: 1–22.

4 Based on a typology by Abercrombie, N. and Longhurst, B. (1998). *Audiences*. London: Sage, which uses the terms "simple, mass and diffused" audiences.

5 Example from Peterson, R., and Simkus, A. (1992). How musical tastes mark occupational status groups. In Michele, L. and Fournier, M. (eds). *Cultivating differences: Symbolic boundaries and the making of inequality*. Chicago: University of Chicago Press.

6 Crawford, D., Jackson, E., and Godbey, G. (1991). A hierarchial model of leisure constraints. *Leisure Sciences*, 13: 309–20.

7 See Tokarski, W. (1985). Some social psychological notes on the meaning of work and leisure. *Leisure Studies*, 4: 227–31.

8 Holt, D. (1995). How do consumers consume: A typology of consumption practices. *Journal of Consumer Research*, 22: 1–16.

9 From Mason, R. (1993). Cross cultural influences in the demand for status goods. *European Advances in Consumer Research*, 1: 46–51.

10 Perrin, D. (2000). *American fan: Sports mania and the culture that feeds it*. New York: Avon Books.

11 From McKinley, J.C. Jr. (2000). It isn't just a game: Clues to avid rooting. *New York Times*, Aug. 11, *Sports*, C1.

12 McQuail, D. (1997). *Audience analysis*. Thousand Oaks CA: Sage, p. 7.

13 Peters, K. (1998). Disney's magic works on Angels. *Houston Chronicle*, Sept. 13, 12.

14 Peters, K. (1998). Disney's wonderful world: First-place Angels aren't the only attraction at the ballpark. *State Journal Register* [M1, M2 Edition], Springfield IL, , Sept. 11, 24.

15 Cited in Shaikin, B. (2000). Angels rally round a monkey—and win; Sports: A moment of whimsy at Edison Field sparks a fan craze—and a big morale boost. *The Los Angeles Times* [Orange County Edition], July 8, 1.

16 Ibid.

17 Cited in Saxon, L.N. (2000). Angels fans are going bananas. *The Press—Enterprise*, Riverside CA, Aug. 13, C02.

18 From Lindlof, T. (1988). Media audiences as interpretive communities. In Anderson, J. (ed.), *Communication Yearbook II*. Newbury Park CA: Sage, pp. 81–107.

19 McQuail, *Mass communication theory*, ch. 3.

20 Chaney, D. (1995). *Fictions of collective life*. London: Routledge.

21 Abercrombie and Longhurst, *Audiences*, ch. 6.

22 A notion of Debord, G. (1994). *The society of the spectacle*. New York: Zone Books, p. 9.

23 From the ideas presented in Lasch, C. (1980). *The culture of narcissism*. London: Sphere.

24 See Sennett, R. (1997). *The fall of public man*. New York: Knopf.

25 From Narcissus and necessity: Why are we creating virtual realities? www.transparencynow.com/virtual.htm, Aug. 13, 2000.

26 A phrase coined by Umberto Eco.

27 See Rubin, A.M., Perse, E.M., and Powell, E. (1989). Loneliness, parasocial interaction and local TV news viewing. *Communication Research*, 14: 246–68.

28 Abercrombie and Longhurst, *Audiences*, p. 131.

29 From Elliott, P. (1974). Uses and gratifications research: A critique and a sociological alternative. In Blumler, J.G. and Katz, E. (eds), *The uses of mass communications*. Beverly Hills CA: Sage, pp. 249–68.

30 Newcomb, Kevin, clickz.com, Sept. 9, 2005.

31 For a close look at research techniques appropriate for entertainment, see Sayre, S. (2001). *Using qualitative methods for marketplace research*. Thousand Oaks CA: Sage.

32 For more information on the ethnography of media consumption, see Moores, S. (1993). *Interpreting audiences*. London: Sage.

33 See Lull, J. (1990). *Inside family viewing: Ethnographic research on television's audiences*. London: Routledge.

34 See chapter bibliography for works by David Morley (1992) and Ann Gray (1992).

35 See chapter bibliography for works by John Fiske (1987) and Ien Ang (1985).

36 From Stevenson, N. (1995). *Understanding media cultures*. London: Sage, p. 183.

37 McQuail, *Audience analysis*, p. 41.

38 From Blumler, J.G. (1985). The social character of media gratifications. In Rosengren, K.E., Palmgreen, P., and Wenner, L. (eds), *Media gratifications research: Current perspectives*. Beverly Hills CA: Sage, pp. 41–59.

39 McQuail, *Audience analysis*, p. 131.

40 Creswell, J. (2008). Nothing sells like celebrity. *New York Times*, June 22.

41 www.dbireport.com.

42 Based on a process described in Schultz, D.E. and Barners, B.E. (1999). *Strategic brand communications campaigns*. Lincolnwood IL: NTC Business Books, p. 99.

43 From en.wikipedia.org/wiki/Prosumer.

44 From www.futurematters.org.uk.

45 McQuail, *Audience analysis*, p. 150. Edited from a list presented in table 9.1.

Chapter 4

1 Cited in Simpson, J.B., comp. (1988). *Simpson's Contemporary Quotations*. Boston: Houghton Mifflin. Accessed Jan. 22, 2002, at www.bartleby.com/63/.

2 Freud, S. (1925). Formulations regarding the two principles in mental functioning. In *Collected papers*, vol. IV, ch. 1. London: Hogarth Press. As cited in Stephenson, W. (1998). *The play theory of mass communication*. New Brunswick NJ: Transaction, Inc., p. 52.

3 *Merriam-Webster's collegiate dictionary (10th ed.)*. (2001). Springfield MA: Merriam-Webster, Inc. Accessed Jan. 22, 2002, at www.m-w.com/cgi-bin/netdict?drama.

4 Zillmann, D. (1996). The psychology of suspense in dramatic exposition. In Vorderer, P., Wulff, H.J., and Friedrichsen, M. (eds), *Suspense: Conceptualizations, theoretical analyses, and empirical explorations*. Mahwah NJ: Lawrence Erlbaum Associates, pp. 199–244.

5 Ibid.

6 Phillips, M. and Huntley, C. (2004). *Dramatica: A new theory of story*. Glendale CA: Write Brothers.

7 Phillips, M. and Huntley, C. Posted on Dramatica.com. Retrieved on Sept. 25, 2008 at http://www.dramatica.com/theory/what_is_dramatica/index.html, para. 4–5.

8 See for review, Zillmann, D. (1980). *The entertainment functions of television*. Hillsdale NJ: Lawrence Erlbaum.

9 Vorderer, P. and Knobloch, S. (2000). Conflict and suspense in drama. In Zillmann, D. and Vorderer, P. (eds), *Media entertainment: The psychology of its appeal*. Mahwah NJ: Lawrence Erlbaum Associates, pp. 57–72.

10 Festinger, L. (1954). A theory of social comparison processes. *Human Relations*, 7: 2: 117–40.

11 Freud, S. (1958). *Der Witz und seine Beziehung zum Unbewussten* [Jokes and their relation to the unconscious]. Frankfurt: Fischer Bücherei. (Original work published 1905.)

12 Zillmann, D. (2000). Humor and comedy. In Zillmann and Vorderer (eds), *Media entertainment*, pp. 37–57.

13 See for review, King, C. (2003). Humor and mirth. In Bryant, J., Cantor, J., and Roskos-Ewoldsen, D. (eds), *Communication and emotion: Essays in honor of Dolf Zillmann*. Hillsdale NJ: Lawrence Erlbaum Associates.

14 Zillmann, D. and Bryant, J. (1980). Misattribution theory of tendentious humor. *Journal of Experimental Social Psychology*, 16: 146–60.

15 Adapted from http://en.wikipedia.org/wiki/Situation_comedy. Accessed Dec. 31, 2006.

16 Statistics found at http://dipaolo.wordpress.com/tag/interesting/. Accessed Dec. 31, 2006.

17 McArthur, T. (1992). *The Oxford companion to the English language*. Oxford: Oxford University Press.

18 Lucas, F.L. (1958). *Tragedy: Serious drama in relation to Aristotle's poetics*. New York: Macmillan, p. 175.

19 Ibid.

20 Deans, J. (2000). New media: Gagging to get on the net: TV comedy producers are investing in new entertainment ideas designed to make the City take them seriously. *Guardian*, May 22.

21 Ibid.

22 Ibid., para. 9.

23 Zillmann, D. (1991). Suspense and mystery. In Bryant, J. and Zillmann, D. (eds), *Responding to the screen: Reception and reaction processes*. Mahwah NJ: Lawrence Erlbaum Associates, pp. 281–304.

24 Goldsmith, W. (1975). Beloved monsters: A psychodynamic appraisal of horror. *Journal of Contemporary Psychotherapy*, 7: 17–22.

25 Zillmann, D., Weaver, J., Mundorf, N., and Aust, C. (1986). Effects of an opposite-gender companion's affect to horror on distress, delight, and attraction. *Journal of Personality and Social Psychology*, 51: 586–94.

26 See, for review, Tamborini, R. (1991). Responding to horror: Determinants of exposure and appeal. In Bryant, J. and Zillmann, D. (eds). *Responding to the screen: Reception and reaction processes*. Hillsdale NJ: Lawrence Erlbaum, pp. 305–27.

27 Johnston, D. (1995). Adolescents' motivations for viewing graphic horror. *Human Communication Research*, 21: 4 522–52.

28 Rosenbaum, R. (1979). Gooseflesh. *Harper's Magazine*, September, 86–92.

29 Lowry, B. (2001). Smile, you're in "assisted reality." *The Los Angeles Times*, May 2, F1.

30 Stephenson, W. (1988). *The play theory of mass communication*. New Brunswick NJ: Transaction Books, p. 45.
31 Ibid., p. 46.
32 Carter, B. (2001). TV this fall means taste has changed, analysts say. *The Sunday Patriot*, Harrisburg PA, July 22, E01.
33 Cited in ibid., E01.
34 Cited in ibid.
35 Cited in ibid.
36 Homes, S. (2004). But this time you choose! Approaching the "interactive" audience in reality TV. *International Journal of Cultural Studies*, 7: 2: 213–31.
37 Sardar, S. (2000). Consumed by voyeurism. *Australian Financial Review*, Nov. 10.
38 From Nancy Franklin's piece on television, Fright nights, *The New Yorker*, July 23, 2001, 84.
39 Rhonda Rundle for the Advertising column of the *Wall Street Journal*, Sept. 12, 2006.
40 Burton, R. and Howard, D. (2000). Recovery strategies for sports marketers: The marketing of sports involves unscripted moments delivered by unpredictable individuals and uncontrollable events. *Marketing Management*, 9: 1: 43.
41 Ganz, W., Wang, Z., Paul, B. and Potter, R. (2006). Sports versus all comers: Comparing TV sports fans with fans of other programming genres. *Journal of Broadcasting & Electronic Media*, March.
42 This title change was initially prompted by a lawsuit initiated by the World Wildlife Fund regarding rights to the WWF trademark.
43 Farhi, P. (2002). Lateral drop: Pro wrestling may be down, but don't count it out. *Record*, Bergen County NJ, Aug. 8, F06 (via Washington Post News Service).
44 Lelan, J. (2000). Why America's hooked on wrestling. *Newsweek*, Feb. 7, 46.
45 Mazer, S. (1998). *Professional wrestling: Sport and spectacle*. Jackson MS: University Press of Mississippi.

Chapter 5

1   Kuhn, T. (1970). *The structure of scientific revolutions* (2nd ed.). Chicago: University of Chicago Press.
2   Lippmann, Walter (1922/1934). *Public opinion*. New York: Macmillan.
3   Lowery, S.A. and DeFleur, M.L. (1995). *Milestones in mass communication research*. White Plains NY: Longman.
4   Lazarsfeld, P.F. (1941). Remarks on administrative and critical communications research. *Studies in Philosophy and Social Science*, 9: 2–16.
5   Katz, E. and Lazarsfeld, P.F. (1955). *Personal influence: The part played by people in the flow of communications*. New York: Free Press.
6   The bobo doll studies are detailed in Bandura, A. (1977). *Social learning theory*. Englewood Cliffs NJ: Prentice-Hall.
7   Hovland, C.I., Lumsdaine, A.A., and Scheffield, F.D. (1949). *Experiments on mass communication*. Princeton NJ: Princeton University Press.
8   Cooper, J. and Worchel, S. (1970). Role of undesired consequences in arousing cognitive dissonance. *Journal of Personality and Social Psychology*, 16: 1–13.
9   Travis, C. and Aronson, E. (2007). *Mistakes were made (But not by me)*. New York: Harcourt, Inc.
10 Klapper, J.T. (1960). *The effects of mass communication*. New York: Free Press.
11 Iyengar, S. and Kinder, D.R. (1987). *News that matters: Television and American opinion*. Chicago: University of Chicago Press. Also, McCombs, M.E. and Shaw, D.L. (1972). The agenda-setting function of the mass media. *Public Opinion Quarterly*, 36: 176–87.
12 Cohen, B. (1963). *The press and foreign policy*. Princeton NJ: Princeton University Press.
13 Bandura, A. (2002). Social cognitive theory of mass communication. In Bryant, J. and Zillmann, D. (eds), *Media effects: Advances in theory and research* (2nd ed.). Hillsdale NJ: Lawrence Erlbaum Associates, pp. 121–54.
14 See Roskos-Ewoldsen, D.R., Roskos-Ewoldsen, B., and Carpentier, F.R. (2002). Media priming: A synthesis. In Bryant and Zillmann (eds), *Media effects*, pp. 97–120. Also, Jo, E. and Berkowitz, L. (1994). A priming effect analysis of media influences: An update. In Bryant and Zillmann ((eds), *Media effects*, pp. 43–60.
15 See for review, King, Humor and mirth. Also, Zillmann, D. (2000). Humor and comedy. In Zillmann and Vorderer (eds), *Media entertainment*, pp. 59–72.
16 DeFleur, M.L. and Ball-Rokeach, S. (1975). Theories of mass communication (3rd ed.). New York: David McKay.
17 Rogers, Everett M. and Shoemaker, F. Floyd (1971). *Communication of innovations: A cross-cultural approach* (2nd ed.). New York: The Free Press.
18 Faules, D.F. and Alexander, D.C. (1978). *Communication and social behavior: A symbolic interaction perspective*. Reading MA: Addison-Wesley, p. 23.

19 Berger, P.L. and Luckmann, T. (1966). *The social construction of reality: A treatise in the sociology of knowledge*. Garden City NY: Doubleday.

20 Kong, L. and Goh, E. (1995) *Folktales and reality: The social construction of race in Chinese tales*. Singapore: National University of Singapore and Port of Singapore Authority.

21 Rohrich, L. (1991) *Folktales and reality*, translated by Peter Tokofsky. Bloomington and Indianapolis: Indiana University Press.

22 Gerbner, G., Gross, L., Morgan, M., and Signorielli, N. (1986). Living with television: The dynamics of the cultivation process. In Bryant, J. and Zillmann, D. (eds), *Perspectives on media effects*. Hillsdale NJ: Lawrence Erlbaum Associates, pp. 17–40.

23 Adapted from Baran, S. (2001). *Introduction to mass communication: Media literacy and culture*. Mountain View CA: Mayfield Publishing Company, pp. 334–5.

24 Calvo, D. and Abramowitz, R. (2001). Uncle Sam wants Hollywood, but Hollywood has qualms. *The Los Angeles Times*, Nov. 19. Available at http://pqasb.pqarchiver.com/latimes.

Chapter 6

1   Wolf, M.J. (1999). *The entertainment economy: How mega-media forces are transforming our lives*. New York: Random House, Times Books, p. 4.

2   Ibid.

3   Global entertainment & media industry will grow to $1.8 trillion in 2010. Posted on Sept. 19, 2006, at www.metrics2.com. Retrieved on Aug. 24, 2008, from www.metrics2.com/blog/2006/09/19/global_entertainment_media_industry_will_grow_to_1.html.

4   Noam, E. (1995). Visions of the media age: Taming the information monster. Paper presented to the Third Annual Colloquium, Alfred Herrhausen Society of International Dialogue, Frankfurt, Germany.

5   Goldhaber, M.H. (1997). The attention economy and the net. *First Monday*, April 7, 2 : 4. Online journal accessed Dec. 9, 2002, at www.firstmonday.dk/issues/issue2_4/goldhaber/index.html.

6   Cited in Petrecca, Laura (2006). Product placement: You can't escape it. *USA Today*, Oct. 10. Retrieved on Aug. 31, 2008, at http://www.usatoday.com/money/advertising/2006-10-10-ad-nauseum-usat_x.htm.

7   Whitney, Daisy (2008). Problems emerge measuring web video ads. *TV News*, Aug. 31.

8   Liodice, B. (2008). Essentials for integrated marketing. *Advertising Age*, June, 79: 23: 26.

9   Excerpted from McAllister, Matthew (2008). Integrated marketing culture? Paper presented at the annual meeting of the Association for Education in Journalism and Mass Communication, Chicago IL.

10 Ibid., p. 3.

11 Petrecca, Product placement.

12 McChesney, R.W. (1999). The new global media: It's a small world of big conglomerates. *The Nation*, Nov. 29. Retrieved on March 24, 2002, from www.thenation.com/doc.mhtml?i=19991129&s=mcchesney.

13 Wolf, *The entertainment economy*.

14 Ahrens, Frank (2002). These giants hope to dump angels and more; media conglomerates say non-core assets must go. *The Washington Post*, Oct. 24, E01.

15 Ibid.

16 Mulkern, A.C. (2002). Feds may propel media mergers Views differ on impact of relaxing rules. *Denver Post*, Denver CO, Nov. 24, K01.

17 Bertelsmann receives €1.63 billion from sale of BMG Music Publishing. Press release posted on Dec. 5, 2006, at http://www.bertelsmann.com//bertelsmann_corp/wms41/bm/index.php?ci=29.

18 And then there were eight: 25 years of media mergers from GE-NBC to Google-YouTube (March/April 2007). MotherJones.Com. Retrieved on Aug. 24, 2008, at http://www.motherjones.com/news/feature/2007/03/and_then_there_were_eight.pdf.

19 Columbus, Louis (2005). Lessons learned in Las Vegas: Loyalty programs pay. *CRM Buyer*, July 29. Retrieved on Aug. 31, 2008, at http://www.crmbuyer.com/story/45033.html.

20 Delta Air Lines, Northwest Airlines combining to create America's premier global airline. News Release posted April 16, 2008, at http://news.delta.com/article_display.cfm?article_id=11034.

21 Statistics and sources cited from Gliniewicz, L. Big summer concerts mean big prices. Accessed Dec. 5, 2002, at www.bankrate.com/brm/news/advice/20000509b.asp.

22 *Rock & Roll Daily*, www.rollingstone.com/rockdaily/index.php/2008/05/14/high-ticket-prices-could-hurt-concert-business/.

23 Larrea, Maria L. (2007). Is Ticketmaster a monopoly? *The Cypress Chronicle*, Dec. 5. Retrieved on Aug. 28, 2008 at http://media.www.cychron.com/media/storage/paper910/news/2007/12/05/Entertainment/Is.Ticketmaster.A.Monopoly-3123361.shtml.

24 Milicia, Joe (2008). Ticketmaster's near monopoly challenged as technology changes. *USA Today*, Jan. 19. Retrieved on Aug. 31, 2008 at http://www.usatoday.com/sports/2008-01-18-48774553_x.htm.

25 Ibid., para. 12.

26 Ibid., para. 6.

27 Cited in ibid.

28 Quoted in ibid.

29 See ibid.

30 From Litman, B.R. (2000). Windows of exhibition. In Greco, A.N. (ed.), *The media and entertainment industries*. Boston: Allyn & Bacon.

31 Pollack, Peter (2006, March 30). Theater chain head discusses DVD release windows. Arstechnica.com. Retrieved on Aug. 29, 2008, at http://arstechnica.com/news.ars/post/20060330-6497.html.

32 Cited in ibid., para. 11.

33 www.hollywoodreporter.com/hr/content_display/news/e3i5dab627a6e5e9f674598128170626f30.

34 Excerpted from Leeds, Jeff (2007). Not many big bands—Madonna, Pussy Cat Dolls, Paramore. *New York Times*, Nov. 11. Retrieved on Aug. 29, 2008, at http://www.nytimes.com/2007/11/11/arts/music/11leed.html?pagewanted=1&_r=1.

35 Hirschman, Celia (2007). The new deal: Band as brand: 360's aka blind ambition. *On the beat for KCRW*, Nov. 14. KCRW.com. Retrieved on Aug. 29, 2008, at http://www.kcrw.com/etc/programs/ob/ob071114360s_aka_blind_ambit.

36 Cited in Leeds, Not many big bands, para. 8.

37 Ibid., para. 21.

38 Cited in ibid., para. 15.

39 Berry, M. (2000). Keynote address. Proceedings from Entertainment Day, event hosted by the California State University, Fullerton.

40 Nintendo GAMECUBE and Game Boy advance to reinvent video gameplay for 21st century. Canada Newswire, Ottawa, May 16, 2001.

41 Statistics obtained from VGChartz.com. Retrieved on October 15, 2009 at http://www.vgchartz.com and http://www.vgchartz.com/chartsindex.php.

42 Despite competitors' gains, Sony to lead game consoles through 2010. Press release posted on March 20, 2006, at http://www.instat.com/press.asp?ID=1614&sku=IN0602145ME.

43 Snow, S. (1993) Pop/Rock: The morning report. *The Los Angeles Times*, Aug. 7, 2.

44 Quoted in Barron, K. (1999). Theme players. *Forbes*, March 2, 163: 6: 53.

45 Cited in Brownfield, P. (1999). It's not easy leaving "Home": series swan song saddens Tim Allen. Special from the *Los Angeles Times Record*, Bergen County NJ, May 16, y03.

46 Goldhaber, M.H. (1997). The attention economy and the net. *First Monday*, April 7, 2: 4. Online journal accessed Dec. 9, 2002, at www.firstmonday.dk/issues/issue2_4/goldhaber/index.

47 Johnson, Roy S. (1998). The Jordan effect. *Fortune*, June 22, 124–32.

48 Ibid.

49 Ibid.

50 DiCarlo, Lisa (2004). Six degrees of Tiger Woods. *Forbes.com*, March 18. Retrieved on Sept. 12, 2007, at http://www.forbes.com/2004/03/18/cx_ld_0318nike.html.

51 Goldsmith, Belinda (2008). Michael Phelps, the major advertising vehicle. *International Herald Tribune*, Aug. 18.

52 Adler, R.P. (1997). *The future of advertising: New approaches to the attention economy*. Washington DC: The Aspen Institute.

53 Statistics obtained from the Travel Industry Association of America via its web site at: www.tia.org/. Accessed Nov. 11, 2002.

54 Wolf, *The entertainment economy*.

55 Ednalino, P. (2001). Public finds an escape in books, film; Denverites flock to venues in days after terrorist attacks. *Denver Post, Rockies Edition*, Sept. 19, F.09.

56 Entertainment (Company Town; IN BRIEF): Video rentals soar for second week. *The Los Angeles Times*, Sept. 28, 2001, C5.

57 Rock 'n' Roll's holy war. *Time*, June 20, 1994, 48–9.

58 American Antitrust Institute Activities web site. Accessed Dec. 8, 2002, at http://www.antitrustinstitute.org/recent/21.cfm.

Chapter 7

1 Morrissey, Brian (2008). Brands seek fans on facebook. *Adweek*, Oct. 12.

2 www.viralblog.com/community-marketing/ikea-fans-the-real-brand-fans/.

3 www.mediaweek.com/mw/content_display/news/digital-downloads/broadband/e3ie50bfe67ab19c20ec175bce7f8853710.

4 www.retailtechnologyreview.com/absolutenm/templates/retail_general_news.aspx?articleid=641&zoneid=3.

5 From http://www.fbcmedia.com/en/be_whatis.asp.

6 From http://www.pqmedia.com/branded-entertainment-marketing-2008.

7 From http://dsinsights.blogspot.com/2008/03/branded-entertainment-future-of.

8 Stern, B. (2000). From art to science: Literary theory in the laboratory. Paper presented to the annual conference of the Association for Consumer Research, Salt Lake City.

9 www.dkolb.org/sprawlingplaces.

10 From Gottdiener, M. (1997). *Themed environments*. Boulder CO: Westview Press, p. 3.

11 From Pine, B.J. and Gilmore, J.H. (1999). *The experience economy*. Boston MA: Harvard Business School Press.

12 Philip Kotler, author and marketing professor, is credited with the idea of combining education with entertainment.

13 Firat, A.F. and Venkatesh, A. (1993). Postmodernity: The age of marketing. *International Journal of Research in Marketing*, 10: 3: 227–49.

14 Csaba, F.F. and Askegaard, S. (1999). Malls and the orchestration of the shopping experience in a historical perspective. In Arnould, A. and Scott, L. (eds). *Advances in Consumer Research*, 26: 34–40.

15 See Brown, S. (1995). *Postmodern marketing*. London: Routledge.

16 Reese, W. (2000). Shoppertainment: The Ontario Mills Mall. Unpublished paper, California State University, Fullerton.

17 Hetzel, P.L. (2000). Authenticity in public settings: A socio-semiotic analysis of two Parisian department stores. Paper presented to the annual meeting of the Association for Consumer Research, Salt Lake City.

18 From Sherry, J.F. Jr. (ed.) (1998), *ServiceScapes: The concept of place in contemporary markets*. Chicago: NTC Business Books.

19 From an article on Business Travel by Joe Sharkey, *New York Times*, May 30, 2001.

20 From Beardsworth, A. and Bryman, A. (1999). Late modernity and the dynamics of quasification: The case of the themed restaurant. *Sociological Review*, 47: 2: 228–57.

21 Ibid. p. 243.

22 Name applied to retailers in Sherry, J. (2000). The soul of the companystore: Nike Town Chicago and the emplaced brandscape. In Sherry (ed.), *ServiceScapes*.

23 O'Guinn, T. and Belk, R. (1989). Heaven on earth: Consumption at Heritage Village. *Journal of Consumer Research*, 16: 1: 147–57.

24 Sherry, J. (1985). Cereal monogamy: Brand loyalty as secular ritual in consumer culture. Paper presented to the 17th annual conference of the Association for Consumer Research, Toronto, Ontario, Canada.

25 See Csaba, F.F. and Askegaard, S. (1999). Malls and the orchestration of the shopping experience in a historical perspective. In Arnould, A., and Scott, L. (eds). *Advances in Consumer Research*, 26, 34–40.

26 From Kling, R., Olin, S., and Poster, M. (eds) (1991). *Postsuburban California*. Berkeley: University of California Press, p. ix.

27 From Loja, E.W. (2007). Inside exopolis: Scenes from Orange County. In Sorkin, Michael (ed.), *Variations on a Theme Park*. New York: Macmillan.

28 From Huxtable, A.L. (1997). Living with the fake, and liking it. *New York Times*, March 30, Arts & Leisure, 1.

29 Ibid.

30 From Belk, R. (1998). Las Vegas as farce, consumption as play. *Advances in Consumer Research*, 25: 8.

31 See Weinstein, R. (1992). Disneyland, Coney Island and cultural innovation. *Journal of Popular Culture*, Summer.

32 From The Imagineers (1996). *Imagineering. A behind the dreams look at making the magic real*. New York: Hyperion.

33 Carson, T. (1992). To Disneyland. *Los Angeles Weekly*, March 27, 27, 16–28.

34 From Goodheart, Adam (2001). Theme park on a hill. *New York Times Magazine*, Feb. 25, 13–14.

Chapter 8

1 Milton, John (1882). *Aeropagitica*, text transcribed in 1997 by Judy Boss for Renascence Editions: An Online Repository of Works Printed in English Between the Years 1477 and 1799 by Judy Boss, accessed Aug. 3, 2009, at https://scholarsbank.uoregon.edu/xmlui/bitstream/handle/1794/739/areopagitica.pdf?sequence=1.

2 Altschull, H. (1995). *Agents of power* (2nd ed). New York: Longman.

3 Lipschultz. J. (2000). *Free expression in the age of the Internet: Social and legal boundaries*. Boulder CO: Westview Press.

4 Quoted in Gardner, Eriq (2008). What's the deal with Jerry Seinfeld? Is he funny or is he Slanderous. Posted on The Hollywood Reporter Media and Law blog, June 23. Retrieved on Sept. 21, 2008, at http://reporter.blogs.com/thresq/defamation/index.html, para. 2.

5 Ibid., para. 1.

6 Annenberg Study, Call-in political talk radio background, content, audiences, portrayal in mainstream media. August, 1996, University of Pennsylvania.

7 Quoted in Puzzanghera, Jim (2007). Broadcasting—Democrats speak out for Fairness Doctrine—The

influence wielded by conservative talk show hosts draws calls to reinstate the policy. *The Los Angeles Times*, July 23, C-1.

8   Ibid.

9   *47% favor government mandated political balance on radio, TV* (2008, August 14). Rasmussen Reports Survey. Retrieved on Sept. 21, 2008, at http://www.rasmussenreports.com/public_content/politics/general_politics/47_favor_government_mandated_political_balance_on_radio_tv.

10 Straubhaar, Joseph and LaRose, Robert (2006). *Media now: Understanding media, culture and technology*. Belmont, CA: Thompson, p. 446.

11 Jolie-Pitt baby pics fetch $14 million. MSNBC.com, Aug. 1, 2008. Retrieved Sept. 23, 2008, at http://www.msnbc.msn.com/id/25967334/.

12 See Dummy and dame arouse the nation. *Broadcasting-Telecasting*, Oct. 15, 1956, p. 258.

13 Straubhaar and LaRose, *Media now*.

14 Reprinted with permission from the Combined Law Enforcement Associations of Texas. Accessed Dec. 5, 2002; full text available at www.cleat.org/remember/TimeWarner/.

15 *Entertainment Industry Marketing Statistics (2007)*. Report issued by the Motion Picture Association of America. Available online at: http://www.mpaa.org/USEntertainmentIndustryMarketStats.pdf.

17 Straubhaar and LaRose, *Media now*.

18 Gilmor, D. (2000). Digital Copyright Act comes back to haunt consumers. *San Jose Mercury News*, Aug. 18, 6C.

19 Campbell, R., Martin, C.R., and Fabos, B. (2006). *Media & culture 5: An introduction to mass communication*. New York: Bedford/St. Martin's.

20 Cited in Campbell, Martin, and Fabos, *Media & culture 5*, p. 550.

21 Cited in Anderson, M.K. (2000). When copyright goes wrong. *Extra!*, May/June, 25.

22 Webb, Sidney and Webb, Beatrice (1920). *History of Trade Unionism*. London: Longman and Co.

23 Podnieks, Andrew (2005). *Lost Season*. Bolton, Ontario: Fenn Publishing Company Ltd.

24 Carlin, John (1997). Midnight intervention by Clinton halts pilots' strike. *The Independent*, Feb. 16. Retrieved on Sept. 25, 2008, at http://findarticles.com/p/articles/mi_qn4158/is_/ai_n14093997.

25 Picket line, not catwalk, at "Top Model." *USA Today,* Aug. 10, 2006. Retrieved on Jan. 1, 2008, at http://www.usatoday.com/life/television/news/2006-08-10-reality-tv-strike_x.htm.

26 *WGA Contract 2007 Proposals*, Writers Guild of America. Retrieved on Sept. 25, 2008, at http://www.wga.org/contract_07/proposalsfull2.pdf.

27 Leopold, Tony (2007). Changing media landscape takes center stage in strike, CNN.com, Nov. 8. Retrieved on Sept. 25, 2008, at http://edition.cnn.com/2007/SHOWBIZ/TV/11/08/strike.impact/index.html.

28 Cieply, Michael (2008). Writers vote to end strike. *New York Times*, Feb. 12. Retrieved on Sept. 25, 2008, at http://www.nytimes.com/2008/02/12/business/media/12cnd-strike.html?_r=1&oref=slogin. White, Michael and Fixmer, Andy (2008). Hollywood writers return to work after ending strike. Bloomberg.com, Feb. 13. Retrieved on Sept. 25, 2008, at http://www.bloomberg.com/apps/news?pid=20601103&sid=aKdwR9oC54WM.

29 WGA strike shuts down most scripted shows (2007). United Press International.com, Dec. 14. Retrieved on Sept. 25, 2008, at http://www.upi.com/NewsTrack/Entertainment/2007/12/14/wga_strike_shuts_down_most_scripted_shows/8516.

30 Finke, Nikki (2007). Attempt fails to restart WGA-AMPTP talks; outlook very grim. *Deadline Hollywood Daily, LA Weekly*, Dec. 24. Retrieved on Sept. 25, 2008, at http://www.deadlinehollywooddaily.com/exclusive-attempt-fails-to-restart-wga-amptp-talks-outlook-very-grim/, para. 1.

31 Proposed net royalties to exceed $2.3 billion by 2008. Posted on clubnetradio.com, March 10, 2007. Accessed May 11, 2007, at http://www.clubnetradio.com/news/Proposed_Net_Radio_Royalties_to_Exceed_2_3_Billion_by_2008/general/271.html.

32 As summarized by Nash, Douglas Roger (1999). Indian gaming. Findlaw.com, Jan. Retrieved on Sept. 25, 2008, at http://library.findlaw.com/1999/Jan/1/241489.html.

33 Ibid.

34 Koller, Jethro (1999). *A practical guide to the Constitution*. Berkeley/Los Angeles: University of California Press.

35 Excerpted with permission from: Johanson, Mary Ann (1999) Anti-MPAA: Female sex and male violence: The divide in movie ratings. Posted Nov. on http://www.flickfilosopher.com/flickfilos/articles/mpaa.shtml. Accessed on Aug. 3, 2009.

Chapter 9

1   Scenarios 1–3 adapted from Straubhaar and LaRose, *Media now*, p. 446.

2   Christians, C., Rotzoll, K., and Fackler, M. (1983). *Media ethics*. New York: Longman, p. 16.

3   Cited in Sherer, M. (1986). Bibliography of grief. *News Photographer*, Aug., 26.

4   Rawls, John (1971). *A theory of justice*. Cambridge MA: Harvard University Press.

5 Cited in Guth, David and Marsh, Charles (2009). *Public relations: A values-driven approach*. Boston MA: Allyn and Bacon, p. 184.

6 Kant, Immanuel (1910). *Fundamental principles of the metaphysics of morals*. Harvard Classics, vol. 32. New York: P.F. Collier and Son, p. 352.

7 Confucius, *The doctrine of the mean*, translated at Classics.Mit.edu, para. 18. Retrieved on Sept. 18, 2008, at http://classics.mit.edu/Confucius/doctmean.html.

8 Lester, Paul M. (1999). *Photojournalism: An ethical approach*. Digital version of *Photojournalism: An ethical approach* (1991). Hillsdale NJ: Lawrence Erlbaum Associates. Retrieved on Sept. 19, 2008, at http://commfaculty.fullerton.edu/lester/writings/chapter3.html.

9 Christians, Rotzoll, and Fackler, *Media ethics*. pp. 9–10.

10 Elliott, Deni (in press). Getting Mill right. *Journal of Mass Media Ethics*, 22: 2&3: para. 1.

11 Mill, J.S. (1859). *On liberty and other essays*. New York: Oxford University Press, p. 23.

12 Lester, Photojournalism.

13 Edwards, R. (1979). *A theory of qualitative hedonism*. Ithaca NY: Cornell University Press, p. 24.

14 Cited in Gross, Michael Joseph (2009, July 2). Michael Jackson's last close-up, para. 15. Accessed on August 1, 2009, at http://www.vanityfair.com/culture/features/2009/07/michael-jackson-photo 200907?currentPage=1.

15 Heffernan, Virgina and Zeller, Tom Jr. (2006). The lonely girl that really wasn't. *New York Times*, Sept. 13. http://www.nytimes.com/2006/09/13/technology/13lonely.html?_r=1&ref=business&oref=slogin. Retrieved on Aug. 22, 2008.

16 Rich, Motoko (2008). Gang memoir, Turning Page, is pure fiction. *New York Times*, March 4. http://www.nytimes.com/2008/03/04/books/04fake.html?_r=1&pagewanted=1&oref=slogin. Retrieved on Aug. 22, 2008.

17 Van Gelder, Lawrence (2008). Holocaust memoir turns out to be fiction. *New York Times*, March 3. http://www.nytimes.com/2008/03/03/books/03arts-HOLOCAUSTMEM_BRF.html?ref=arts. Retrieved on Aug. 22, 2008.

18 Gang memoir the latest among literary fakes. http://www.findingdulcinea.com/news/entertainment/March-April-08/Gang-Memoir-the-Latest-Among-Literary-Fakes.html. Retrieved on Aug. 22, 2008.

19 Wortham, Jenna (2008). Company fesses up to corn popping cellphone clips. http://blog.wired.com/underwire/ 2008/06/bluetooth-compa.html. Retrieved on Aug. 22, 2008.

20 McQuail, *Mass communication theory*.

21 Society of Professional Journalists' Code of Ethics. Posted at www.spj.org, para. 3. Retrieved on Sept. 14, 2008, at http://www.spj.org/ethicscode.asp.

22 American Advertising Federation, Advertising Ethics and Principles, posted at AAf.org, para. 1. Retrieved on Sept. 14, 2008, at http://www.aaf.org/default.asp?id=37.

23 Free Speech Coalition, Ethics and Best Practices. Posted at www.freespeechcoalition.com. Retrieved on Sept. 14, 2008, at http://www.freespeechcoalition.com/FSCview.asp?coid=595&keywords=ethics+code.

24 Quoted in Waterfield, Bruno (2008). Wolf-woman invents Holocaust survival tale ("Surviving with Wolves" author admits fabrication), para. 4. *Daily Telegraph* (U.K), Feb. 29. http://www.freerepublic.com/ focus/f-news/1978327/posts. Retrieved on Aug. 22, 2008.

25 Quoted in Heffernan and Zeller, The lonely girl that really wasn't, para. 8.

26 Quoted in Rich, Gang memoir, Turning Page, is pure fiction, para. 5.

27 Quoted in Smith, Sam (June 3, 2007), para 3. http://blackdogstrategic.com/2007/06/03/reality-tv-hoax-raises-interesting-marketing-question/. Retrieved on June 8, 2008.

28 Quoted in Heffernan and Zeller, The lonely girl that really wasn't, paras 8–9.

29 Quoted in McNern, Ethan (2007). Dutch organ donor numbers soar after "Win a kidney" show hoax. News.scotman.com, July 17, para 3. http://news.scotsman.com/latestnews/Dutch-organ-donor-numbers-soar.3304820.jp. Retrieved on Aug. 22, 2008.

30 Smith, paras 3–4.

31 Brown, Charles (2006). Blair Witch marketing. http://ezinearticles.com/?Blair-Witch-Marketing&id=333148. Retrieved on June 30, 2008.

32 Ibid., para. 3.

33 Product placement with a twist. Bnet.com Aug., 2002, para. 4. http://findarticles.com/p/articles/mi_pwwi/is_200208/ai_mark03045742. Retrieved on Aug. 22, 2008.

34 Study cited in Product placement with a twist.

35 Pozner, Jennifer (2004). Triumph of the shill: Part II. *Bitch Magazine*, 24, Spring: 56.

36 Ibid., p. 59.

37 Patterson, Thomas (2001). Doing well and doing good: How soft news and critical journalism are shrinking the news audience and weakening democracy—And what news outlets can do about it. The Joan Shorenstein Center for Press, Politics, & Public Policy at Harvard University.

38 Clifford, Stephanie (2008). A product's place is on the set. *New York Times*, July 22. http://www.nytimes.com/2008/07/22/business/media/22adco.html?_r=2&scp=1&sq=a%20product's%20place%20is%20on%20the%20set&st=cse&oref=slogin&oref=slogin. Retrieved on Aug. 14, 2008.

39 Ibid., para. 7.
40 Poniewozik, James (2006). How reality TV fakes it. Time.Com, Jan. 29. Retrieved on Sept. 16, 2008, at http://www.time.com/time/magazine/article/0,9171,1154194-1,00.html.
41 Cited in ibid.
42 Cited in ibid.
43 Cited in ibid.
44 Hill, Annette (2005). *Reality TV: Audiences and popular factual television.* New York: Routledge, p. 178.
45 Levak, Richard (2003). The dangerous reality of reality television. *Television Week*, Sept. 23, 14.
46 Crew, Richard (2007). The ethics of reality television producers. *Media Ethics*, 18: 2: 10, 19.
47 Cline, Austin (n.d.). Should we really watch? Posted on About.com. Retrieved on Sept. 16, 2008, at http://atheism.about.com/library/FAQs/phil/blphil_eth_realitytv.htm, para. 22.
48 Straubhaar and LaRose, *Media now*, p. 446.
49 Wiltz, Teresa (2004). The evil sista of reality television: Shows trot out old stereotypes. *Washington Post*, Feb. 25. Retrieved on July 31, 2009, at http://www.msnbc.msn.com/id/4365789.
50 Ibid.
51 Ibid.
52 Ibid.
53 Cline, Should we really watch?
54 Wiltz, The evil sista of reality television.
55 Ibid.
56 Cline, Should we really watch?
57 Straubhaar and LaRose, *Media now*, p. 446.
58 As outlined on Tourism Concern's website. Retrieved on Sept. 20, 2008, at http://www.tourismconcern.org.uk/index.php?page=the-issues.
59 Global Code of Ethics for Tourism (1999). Posted by the World Tourism Organization, para. 4. Retrieved on Sept. 20, 2008, at http://www.gdrc.org/uem/eco-tour/principles.html.
60 World Anti-Doping Agency 2003. www.wada-ama.org return.
61 Mehlman, Maxwell J. (2005). Performance enhancing drugs in sports. TheDoctorWillSeeYouKnow. com, April. Retrieved on Sept. 20, 2008, at http://www.thedoctorwillseeyounow.com/articles/bioethics/perfdrugs_10/#ref2.
62 Shermer, Michael (2008). The doping dilemma. Game theory helps to explain the pervasive abuse of drugs in cycling, baseball and other sports. *Scientific American*, March. Retrieved on Sept. 20, 2008, at http://www.sciam.com/article.cfm?id=the-doping-dilemma&page=2.
63 Mehlman, Performance enhancing drugs in sports.
64 Quinn, Ryan (date unknown). Why the silence? Athletes need to speak out about sports doping. Outsports.com. Retrieved on Sept. 20, 2008, at http://www.outsports.com/columns/2005/0209 quinndoping.htm., para. 5.
65 Elliott, V.S. (2001). Anti-doping effort looks at sports doctors. Amednews.com, Aug. 20. http:// www.ama-assn.org/amanews/2001/08/20/hlsc0820.htm. return.

Chapter 10

1   www.slate.com/id/2171430/.
2   Kilde, Jeanne H. (2002), *When church became theater.* Oxford: Oxford University Press.
3   Reported by Leo Shanahan for www.smh.com.au/. . ./2008/02/07/1202234012004.html.
4   CBA Retailers+Resources Industry Brief, June 2, 2008.
5   Matt Davis for BBC News on news.bbc.co.uk/2/hi/americas/4534835.stm.
6   Posted by Scott Eaton on worshipandthearts.blogspot.com/2008/01/religious-video-games.html.
7   http://www.media-anthropology.net.
8   www.parentstv.org/PTC/publications/reports/religionstudy06/exsummary.asp.
9   Hernandez, E.H. (2000). Lights, camera, spiritual enlightenment? A phenomenology of the TBN viewing experience. Master's thesis completed at California State University, Fullerton.
10 www.hollywoodreporter.com/hr/content_display/film/news/e3iddf6bb69274592b7f613724b4d867fa c?pn=1.
11 Berger, A. (1982). *Media analysis techniques.* Beverly Hills CA: Sage, p. 129.
12 Ibid.
13 www.economist.com/business/displaystory.cfm?story_id=10880936.
14 MacMillan for BusinessWeek.com New York posted on businessweek.com/innovate/content/nov2007/id20071114_257766.htm.
15 www.broadcastnewsroom.com/articles/viewarticle.jsp?id=416233.
16 Cashmere, Paul (2006). Universal is the biggest music company of 2005. *Undercover* (Australia), Jan. 5. Accessed on May 27, 2006, at http://www.undercover.com.au/news/2006/jan06/20060105_universal.html.

17 IFPI Report (2005, Aug.). Accessed on May 27, 2006, at: http://www.ifpi.org/site-content/publications/rin_order.html.

18 Monaco, J. (2000). *How to read a film: Movies, media, multimedia*. New York: Oxford University Press, p. 264.

19 Menand, L. (1997). The iron law of stardom. *The New Yorker*, March 24, 36–40.

20 Dyer, R. (1998). *Stars*. London: British Film Institute, p. 18.

21 Tolston, A. (1996). *Mediations: Text and discourse in media studies*. London: Arnold, ch. 5.

22 West, W. (1999). The blurred lines of heroism, villainy. *Insight on the News*, April 19, 15: 14, 48 (1).

23 Goodman, M. (1993). Where have you gone, Joe DiMaggio? *Utne Reader*, May–June, 57: 103 (2).

24 As reported in (1995) How to be great! What does it take to be a hero? Start with six basic character traits. *Psychology Today*, Nov.–Dec., 28: 6: 46 (6).

25 Cited in ibid.

26 Study referenced in ibid.

27 Ibid.

28 Ibid.

29 Fainaru-Wada, Mark and Williams, Lance (2006). *Game of shadows: Barry Bonds, BALCO, and the steroids scandal that rocked professional sports*. New York: Gotham Books.

30 Quoted in an interview with Mark Fainaru-Wada author of *Game of shadows*, posted on the UNESCO website. Accessed on June 11, 2007, at http://portal.unesco.org/en/ev.php-URL_ID=33429&URL_DO=DO_TOPIC&URL_SECTION=201.html.

31 Amos, B., Cameron, T., Mesko, J., Smith, K., and Tuinstra, K. (2001). Techno kids: An injured breed. *Grand Rapids Press*, Grand Rapids MI, June 4, B3.

Chapter 11

1 www.abc.net.au/science/news/stories/s1692920/.

2 www.media-awareness.ca/english/stereotyping/.

3 Fujioka, Y. (2005). Black media images as a perceived threat to African American ethnic identity. *Journal of Broadcasting & Electronic Media*, Dec.

4 Davis, J. and Gandy, O. (1999). Racial identity and media orientation. *Journal of Black Studies*, 29: 367–97.

5 Selznick, Barbara (2007). Religion and race in global non-fiction programming. *Global Media Journal*, Fall, 6: 11.

6 Branton, R. and Dunaway, J. (2008). English and Spanish language media coverage of immigration: A comparison. Paper presented to the Southern Political Science Association. www.allacademic.com/meta/p208258_index.html.

7 Majjar, Orayb (2007). Our north is the south *Global Media Journal*, 6: 10.

8 Havens, Timothy (2007). Universal childhood, *Global Media Journal*, 6: 10.

9 Let's go Euro (2000). *Young Consumers*, 2: 1.

10 Wolf, M.J. (1999). *The entertainment economy: How mega-media forces are transforming our lives*. New York: Random House, Times Books.

11 A history of country music. Accessed Dec. 9, 2002, at www.cduniverse.com/asp/university/cy/cy_origin.asp.

12 www.cmaworld.com/international/. Retrieved on July 29, 2008.

13 Blow, K. (1976). *History of rap: Vol. 1: The genesis* posted at http://rap.about.com/gi/dynamic/offsite.htm?site=http%3A%2F%2Frhino.com%2FFeatures%2Fliners%2F72851lin.html.

14 Cited on Davey D's Hip Hop Corner, What is Hip Hop Directory web site. Accessed Dec. 8, 2002, at www.daveyd.com/whatiship.html.

15 Erlewine, S.T. *All music guide*. Accessed Dec. 10, 2002, at www.24-7rap.com/drdre/.

16 Stroman, C. (1986). Television viewing and self concept among Black children. *Journal of Broadcast and Electronic Media*, 30: 1: 87–93.

17 Tajfel, H. (ed.) (1982). *Social identity and intergroup relations*. Cambridge: Cambridge University Press.

18 Fischoff, S., Franco, A., Gram, E., Hernandez, A., and Parker, J. (1999). Offensive ethnic clichés. Presented to the annual meeting of the American Psychological Association, Boston.

19 Luchina Fisher for ABC News; abcnews.go.com/entertainment/story?id=4991235&page=4, June 4, 2008.

20 From Tad Friends (2001). Comics from underground. *The New Yorker*, July 30, 26–9.

21 Mulkern, A.C. (2002). Feds may propel media mergers. Views differ on impact of relaxing rules. *Denver Post*, Denver, CO, Nov. 24, K01.

22 Bertelsmann receives €1.63 billion from sale of BMG Music Publishing. Press release posted on Dec. 5, 2006, at http://www.bertelsmann.com/bertelsmann_corp/wms41/bm/index.php?ci=29.

23 Patel, S.S. (2007). Writing on the wall. *Archaeology*, 60: 4.

24 Samantha Skinazi for culturenow.com, film reviewed June 16, 2008.

25 Ibid.

26 Winseck, Dwayne (2007). Media ownership and markets. *Sociology Compass*, 2: 1: 34–47.

27 Adams, K.A. and Hill, L. Jr. (1991). Protest and rebellion: Fantasy themes in Japanese comics. *Journal of Popular Culture*, 25: 1: 99–127.

28 www.thingsasian.com/stories-photos/26879/.

29 Bhattacharya, Roshmila (2007). Hanuman returns as a global superhero, *Hindustan Times*, Mumbai, Dec. From an online journal at www.virtual-china.org/2008/07/26/friendfeed-superheroes-global-iconography.

30 Hindustantimes.com/storypage/.

31 dearcinema.com/iron-man-and-the-league-of-extraordinary-superheroes/.

32 Jeffery, Lyn (2008). FriendFeed superheroes: Global iconography July 26.

33 www.german-way.com/american.html.

34 Jeffery, FriendFeed superheroes.

35 Christina Passariello's Advertising column in the *Wall Street Journal*, June 20, 2006, B1.

36 Barnard, A. (2008). Raucous Russian tabloids thrive despite narrowing of press freedom. *New York Times*, July 27, 6.

37 www.punching.com/Articl.aspx?theartic=Art2008807272514842.

38 www.nytimes.com/2008/07/28/business/media/28snoop.html.

39 www.globalhiphop.org/2008/01/20/Palestinian-hip-hop-rapped-at-sundance/.

40 Diane Garrett for *Variety Magazine*. www.varietyu.com/article/VR1117968073.htm.

41 Hofstede, Geert (1990). *Cultural consequences: International differences in work-related values*. Beverly Hills CA: Sage.

Chapter 12

1 See for review Crabb, P.B. and Goldstein, J.H. (1996). The social psychology of watching sports: From ilium to living room. In Bryant, J. and Zillmann, D. (eds), *Responding to the screen: Reception and reaction processes*. Hillsdale NJ: Lawrence Erlbaum Associates, pp. 355–71.

2 Outrageous behavior: Sportsmanship becomes a casualty of escalating violence on and off field. *The Grand Rapids Press*, Grand Rapids MI, Jan. 15, 2002, A8.

3 Crabb and Goldstein, The social psychology of watching sports.

4 Aust, Philip (2007). What is your child watching? A content analysis of violence in Disney animated films: scene. Paper presented at the annual meeting of the International Communication Association, San Francisco CA. Retrieved on Sept. 30, 2008, at http://www.allacademic.com/meta/ p171268_index.html.

5 Ansen, D. (1995). The return of a bloody great classic; *The wild bunch* still pushes our buttons about violence. *Newsweek*, March 13, 70–1.

6 From sbbfc.co.uk.

7 From Tartar, M. (1992). *Off with their heads! Fairy tales and the culture of childhood*. Princeton NJ: Princeton University Press.

8 Watson, M.W. and Peng, Y. (1992). The relation between toy gun play and children's aggressive behavior. *Early Education and Development*, 3: 370–89.

9 Lagerspetz, K.M., Wahlroos, C., and Wendeline, C. (1978). Facial expressions of preschool children while watching televised violence. *Scandinavian Journal of Psychology*, 19: 213–22.

10 Zillman, D. (1991). Television viewing and psychological arousal. In Bryant and Zillman (eds), *Responding to the screen*.

11 From Zillman, D. and Vorder, P. (eds) (2000). *Media entertainment: The psychology of its appeal*. Mahwah NJ: Lawrence Erlbaum.

12 See Zuckerman, M. (1996). Sensation seeking and the taste for vicarious horror. In Weaver, J.B. III and Tamborini, R. (eds), *Horror films: Current research on audience preferences and reactions*. Mahwah NJ: Lawrence Erlbaum, pp. 147–60.

13 See Goldstein, J.H. (ed.) (1998). *Why we watch: The attractions of violent entertainment*. New York: Oxford University Press, p. 232, Table 10.1.

14 Baron, Stanley (2004). *Introduction to mass communication: Media literacy and culture*. New York: McGraw Hill.

15 Ninety Second Congress. (1972). Hearings before the Subcommittee on Communications on the Surgeon General's Report by the Scientific Advisory Committee on Television and Social Behavior. Washington DC: U.S. Government Printing Office.

16 Paik, H. and Comstock, G. (1994). The effects of television violence on social behavior: A meta-analysis. *Communication Research*, 21: 516–45.

17 Gerbner, G., Gross, L., Morgan, M., and Signorelli, N. (1994). Growing up with television. The cultivation perspective. In Bryant, J. and Zilmann, D. (eds). *Media effects: Advances in theory and research*. Hillsdale NJ: Lawrence Erlbaum.

18 Morgan, M. and Shanahan, J. (1997). Two decades of cultivation research. In Burelson, P.R. (ed.), *Communication Yearbook 20*. Thousand Oaks CA: Sage, pp. 1–47.

19 Hirsch, P. (1980). The "scary world" of the nonviewer and other anomalies: A reanalysis of Gerbner et al.'s findings on cultivation analysis. *Communication Research*, 7: 403–56.

20 Huesmann, L.R., Moise-Titus, J., Podolski, C., and Eron, L.D. (2003). Longitudinal relations between children's exposure to TV violence and their aggressive and violent behavior in young adulthood: 1977–1992. *Developmental Psychology*, 39: 201–21.

21 Johnson, J.G., Cohen, P., Smailes, E.M., Kasen, S., and Brook, J.S. (2002). Television viewing and aggressive behavior during adolescence and adulthood. *Science*, Mar. 29: 2468–71.

22 See for review Straubhaar, Joseph, and LaRose, Robert. (2006). *Media now: Understanding media, culture and technology*. Belmont CA: Thompson.

23 Signorelli, N. (2003). *Mass media images and impact on health. A sourcebook*. Westport CT: Greenwood.

24 Wilson, B., Smith, S., Potter, W., Kunkel, D. et al. (2002). Violence in children's television programming: Assessing the risks. *Journal of Communication*, 52: 1: 5–35.

25 Anderson, C.A., Berkowitz, L., Donnerstein, E., Huesmann, L.R., Johnson, J., Linz, D., Malamuth, N., and Wartella, E. (2003). The influence of media violence on youth. *Psychological Science in the Public Interest*, 4: 81–110.

26 Liebert, R. and Sprafkin, J. (1988). *The early window*. New York: Pergamon Press.

27 Baron, M., Broughton, D., Butross, S., Corrigan, S. et al (2001). Media violence. *Pedriatrics*, 108: 5: 1222–6.

28 Anderson, J. and Meyer, T. (1988). *Mediated communication*. Newbury Park CA: Sage. Milavsky, J. Kessler, R., Stipp, H., and Rubens, W. (1982). Television and aggression: Results of a panel study. In Perarl, D., Bouthliet, I., and Lazar, J. (eds). *Television and behavior: Ten years of scientific progress and implications for the eighties*, vol. 2. Washington DC: National Institute for Mental Health.

29 Paik and Comstock, The effects of television violence on social behavior: A meta-analysis.

30 Wood, Wendy, Wong, Frank F., and Chachere, Gregory J. (1991). Effects of media violence on viewers' aggression in unconstrained social interaction. *Psychological Bulletin*, 109: 371–83.

31 Feshbeck, S. and Singer, R. (1971). *Television and aggression*. San Francisco: Jossey-Bass.

32 U.S. Department of Health and Human Services (2001). *Youth violence: A report of the Surgeon General*. Rockville MD.

33 Gonzalez, Lauren. When two tribes go to war: A history of video game controversy. *Gamespot*. Retrieved on Sept. 30, 2008, at http://www.gamespot.com/features/6090892/index.html.

34 Critics zap video games: senators urge government action to curb video-game violence. Bnet.com, Jan. 3, 1994. Retrieved on Sept. 30, 2008, at http://findarticles.com/p/articles/mi_m0EPF/is_n14_v93/ai_16809718.

35 Anderson, C.A. and Dill, K. (2000). Video games and aggressive thoughts, feelings, and behavior in the laboratory and in life. *Journal of Personality and Social Psychology*, 78: 4.

36 Ibid.

37 No easy explanation for Columbine killings. CNN.com, April 28, 1999. Retrieved on Sept. 30, 2008, at http://www.cnn.com/US/9904/28/dark.culture/.

38 Study cited in Ardent, S. (2007) Study: Kids unaffected by violent games. Wired.com. Retrieved on Sept. 30, 2008, at http://blog.wired.com/games/2007/04/study_kids_unaf.html.

39 Bensely, L. and Van Eenwyk, J. (2001). Video games and real life aggression. *Journal of Adolescent Health*, 29: 112–43.

40 See for review Williams, Ian (2007). US teen violence study exonerates video games. IT Week.com, March 6. Retrieved on Sept. 30, at http://www.computing.co.uk/vnunet/news/2184836/link-video-games-violent-teens.

41 Cited in Wright, B. (2004). Sounding the alarm on video game ratings. CNN.com, Feb. 18, para. 12. Retrieved on Sept. 29, 2008, at http://archives.cnn.com/2002/TECH/fun.games/12/19/games.ratings/.

42 Straubhaar and LaRose. *Media now*.

43 Thompson, Kimberly M. and Yokota, Fumie (2004). Violence, sex and profanity in films: Correlation of movie ratings with content. *Medscape General Medicine*, 6: 3: 3.

44 Reported in De Moraes, Lisa (2005). Television more oversexed than ever, study finds. *The Washington Post*, Nov. 10, C01.

45 Gunasekera, H., Chapman S., and Campbell, S. (2005). Sex and drugs in popular movies: An analysis of the top 200 films. *Journal of the Royal Society of Medicine*, 98: 10: 464–70; doi:10.1258/jrsm.98.10.464.

46 Pechmann, C. and Shih, C. (1999). Smoking scenes in movies and antismoking advertising before movies: Effects on youth. *Journal of Marketing*, 63: 3: 1–13.

47 Referenced in Luscombe, B. (2008). The truth about teen girls. Time.com, Sept. 11. Retrieved on Sept. 29, 2008, at http://www.time.com/time/magazine/article/0,9171,1840556,00.html.

48 Collins, Rebecca L., Elliott, Marc N., Berry, Sandra H., Kanouse, David E., Kunkel, Dale, Hunter, Sarah B.,

and Miu, Angela (2004). Watching sex on television predicts adolescent initiation of sexual behavior, *Pediatrics*, Sept., 114: 3.

49 Ibid.

50 Collins, Rebecca L., Elliott, Marc N., Berry, Sandra H., Kanouse, David E., and Hunter, Sarah B. (2003). Entertainment television as a healthy sex educator: The impact of condom-efficacy information in an episode of *Friends*. *Pediatrics*, Nov., 112: 5.

51 a.abcnews.com/. . ./Health/ is_drugs_080114_mn.jpg.

52 Cited in TV, films honored for accurate drug-use depictions. Posted at http://pn.psychiatryonline.org/cgi/content/full/36/10/5.

53 From www.msnbc.msn.com/id/14227775/.

54 For review, see Hansen, C. and Hansen, R. (2000). Music and music videos. In Zillmann and Vorderer (eds), *Media entertainment*, pp. 175–196.

55 http://www.allacademic.com/meta/p_mla_apa_research_citation/1/7/2/4/6/p172.

56 Ibid.

57 Ibid.

58 Ibid.

59 Shamlian, J. (2005). New trend in teen fiction: Racy reads. MSNBC.com, Aug. 15. Retrieved on Sept. 29, 2008, at http://www.msnbc.msn.com/id/8962686/.

60 Ibid.

61 Cited in Shamlian, New trend in teen fiction.

62 Ibid.

63 Jules Feiffer as quoted in Mitchell, E. (2000). They oughta be in pictures. *New York Times*, July 25, B1.

64 Glater, J. (July 31, 2008). Settlement over sex scenes in Grant Theft Auto Hits a snag. Retrieved on Sept. 29, 2008, at http://bits.blogs.nytimes.com/2008/07/31/settlement-over-sex-scenes-in-grand-theft-auto-hits-a-snag/.

65 Straubhaar and LaRose, *Media now*.

66 Allen, M., D'Alessio, D., and Brezgel, K. (1995). A meta-analysis summarizing the effects of pornography. Aggression after exposure. *Human Communication Research*, 22: 2: 258–83.

67 Felson, R. (1996). Mass media effects on violent behavior. *Annual Review of Sociology*, 22: 103–28.

68 Gentry, C. (1991). Pornography and rape: An empirical analysis. *Deviant Behavior*, 12: 277–88.

69 Allen, M., D'Alessio, D., and Emmers-Sommer, T. (1999). Reaction of criminal sexual offenders to pornography: A meta-analytic summary. In Roloff, M.E. (ed.) *Communication Yearbook*, 22. Thousand Oaks CA: Sage, pp. 139–70.

70 Malamuth, N., Addison T., and Koss, M. (2000). Pornography and sexual aggression: Are there reliable effects and can we understand them? *Annual Review of Sex Research*, 11: 26–91.

71 Cited in Downs, M.F. Is pornography addictive? Psychologists debate whether people can have an addiction to pornography. WebMd.com. Retrieved on Sept. 30, 2008, at http://men.webmd.com/guide/is-pornography-addictive.

72 Presented in "gambling" at *Encyclopedia Britannica Online*, www.eb.com/bol/topic, Sept. 7, 2001.

73 *Global Gaming Bulletin: 25th Anniversary Edition* (2007). Report commissioned by Global Gaming Services. Accessed on August 3, 2009, at http://www.hotelnewsresource.com/pdf/EY07090701.pdf.

74 From www.lasvegas.com/features.impact.html.

75 From Hsu, C. (ed.) (1999). *Bad bets: The inside story of the glamour, glitz and danger of America's gambling industry*. New York: Random House.

76 From www.business.com/directory/travelandleisure/casinosandgaming/profile/, March 12, 2001.

77 Becker, J. and Van Natta, D. (2008). McCain and a host of aides forged close ties to casinos. *New York Times*, Sept. 28, 1.

78 Harney, A. (2008). Macau's next gamble. *The Wall Street Journal*, Feb. 23.

79 Drape, Joe (2005). Internet site battles the fix in sports bets. *New York Times*, May 25, 11.

80 From an article by Liz Moyer for Forbes.com, Aug. 29, 2006.

81 Reported by Shafaatulla, S. (2000). Millions live in hopes of a dream ticket. *The Herald*, April 3.

82 Grodal, T. (2000), Video games and the pleasures of control. In Zillman and Vorderer (eds), *Media entertainment*, pp. 197–214.

83 From Babington, C. and Chinoy, I. (1998). Lotteries win with slick marketing. *Washington Post*, May 4, A1.

Chapter 13

1 Definitions retrieved from http://www.answers.com on Sept. 11, 2008.

2 Lee, Jae Num (1971). *Swift and Scatological Satire*. Albuquerque: University of New Mexico Press, pp. 7–22; 23–53.

3 Weisman, Ze'ev (1998). *Political satire in the Bible*. Atlanta GA: Scholar's Press.

4 Study cited in Talk-radio fans informed, but not too influential, study says. *Seattle Times*, Aug. 9, 1996.

Retrieved Sept. 7, 2008, at http://community.seattletimes.nwsource.com/archive/?date=19960809&slug=2343411.

5 Internet's broader role in campaign 2008. Report posted by The Pew Research Center for People & the Press, Jan. 11, 2008. Retrieved on Sept. 7, 2008, at http://people-press.org/report/384/internets-broader-role-in-campaign-2008.

6 The tough job of communicating with voters. Report posted by The Pew Research Center for People & the Press, Feb. 5, 2000. Retrieved on Sept. 7, 2008, at http://people-press.org/report/?pageid=243.

7 Internet's broader role in campaign 2008.

8 Cited in Winter, Kevin (2007). Campaigning in late night. Time.com, Aug. 29, para. 5. Retrieved on Sept. 11, 2008, at http://www.time.com/time/nation/article/0,8599,1657421,00.html?xid=feed-cnn-topics.

9 Cited in Tapper, Jake (2002). The salon interview: Bill Maher. The Salon.Com, Dec. 11, para. 1. Retrieved on Sept. 9, 2008, at http://dir.salon.com/story/people/interview/2002/12/11/maher/.

10 Press briefing by Ari Fleischer (Sept. 26, 2001). Posted at http://www.whitehouse.gov/news/releases/2001/09/20010926-5.html#BillMaher-Comments.

11 Littleton, Cynthia (2004). Entertainment and politics: Media are the message. *New York Times*, Oct. 26. Retrieved on Sept. 7, 2008, at http://www.hollywoodreporter.com/hr/search/article_display.jsp?vnu_content_id=1000684734.

12 Bauder, David (2008). Entertainment magazines new on campaign trail. Posted at Katu.com, Sept. 1, para. 3. Retrieved on Sept. 9, 2008, at http://www.katu.com/news/election/27734459.html.

13 Cited in ibid.

14 Nickelodeon hits the campaign trail with election-themed content, leading up to October kids' vote. Nickelodeon press release Aug. 20, 2008, para.3. Posted at Examiner.com. Retrieved on Sept. 9, 2008, at http://www.examiner.com/p-214909~Nickelodeon_Hits_the_Campaign_Trail_With_Election_Themed_Content__Leading_Up_to_October_Kids__Vote.html.

15 Top Ten Left Wing Scenes on NBC's The West Wing. Posted at http://www.mediaresearch.org/Profiles/westwing/welcome.asp. Retrieved September 9, 2008.

16 Excerpted with permission from Shaffer, Butler (2002). LewRockwell.com, May 29. Retrieved on Sept. 12, 2008, at http://www.lewrockwell.com/shaffer/shaffer19.html.

17 Cited in Littleton, Entertainment and politics, para. 7.

18 New York Times bestsellers: Paperback nonfiction. *New York Times,* July 2, 2006. Retrieved on Sep. 9, 2008 at http://www.nytimes.com/2006/07/02/books/bestseller/0702bestpapernonfiction.html?ex=1174363200&en=aa0e9c76ef010f5a&ei=5070.

19 Seeger, Pete (1985). *Carry it on!: A history in song and picture of the working men and women of America.* New York: Simon and Schuster.

20 Accessed June 5, 2007, at: http://www.lib.virginia.edu/small/exhibits/music/protest_overcome.html.

21 Seeger, *Carry it on!*

22 Unless otherwise indicated, all statistics in this section are taken from Internet's broader role in campaign 2008.

23 Cited in Davies, Frank (April 4, 2008). In 2008 campaign, the Internet packs a powerful political punch. http://www.mercurynews.com/news/ci 8793261.

24 Haney, Elissa (2006). The top 10 TV shows of the century, indeed of the millennium! Paragraph 7, http://www.infoplease.com/spot/toptv1.html. Accessed Dec. 30, 2006.

25 *Live Earth Breaks World-Wide Audience Records* (July 23, 2007). Life Earth press release circulated through Business Wire accessed on July 24, 2007, at http://home.businesswire.com/portal/site/google/index.jsp?ndmViewId=news_view&newsId=20070723006327&newsLang=en.

26 From sourcewatch.org/index.php?title=Internet_activism. Retrieved on Sept. 16, 2008.

27 Statistics cited in Lavigne, Paula (2008). Pro sports figures more invested in this political election. Espn.com, Sept. 4. Retrieved on Sept. 12, 2008, at http://sports.espn.go.com/espn/otl/news/story?id=3565666.

28 Rowe, D. (1999). *Sport culture and the media*. Philadelphia: Open University Press, p. 14.

29 Olympic pageEditor: Documented at each of the following websites accessed Dec. 19, 2002: http://www.aef2004.org/ancient_olympics/index.asp; http://www.enchantedlearning.com/olympics/printouts/Flag.shtml; http://www.wsd1.org/earlgrey/Grp3History.htm.

30 Elias, N. and Dunning, E. (1986). Folk football in medieval and early modern Britain. In Elias, N. and Dunning, E. (eds) *Quest for excitement: Sport and leisure in the civilising process*. Oxford: Basil Blackwell, p. 176.

31 Rowe, *Sport culture and the media*.

32 Ibid., p. 16.

33 Ibid., p. 22.

34 Guttmann, A. (1986). *Sports spectators*. New York: Columbia University Press, p. 149.

35 See Singer, D.G. and Singer, J.L. (eds) (2001). *Handbook of children and the media*. Thousand Oaks CA: Sage.

36 Adapted from Baran, S. (2001). *Introduction to mass communication: Media literacy and culture*. Mountain View CA: Mayfield Publishing Company. Also, Singhal, A. and Rogers, E.M. (1999).

Entertainment-education: A communication strategy for social change. Hillsdale NJ: Lawrence Erlbaum Associates.

37 Study cited in Video games stimulate learning (2002). BBC News, March 18. Retrieved on Sept. 13, 2008, at http://news.bbc.co.uk/2/hi/uk_news/education/1879019.stm.

38 Jana, Reena (2006). Microsoft: Serious gaming. Businessweek.com, March 27. Retrieved on Sept. 13, 2008, at http://images.businessweek.com/ss/07/12/1221_microsoft_esp/index_01.htm.

39 Ibid.

40 Study cited in Web worlds "useful" for children (2008). BBC News, May 23. Retrieved on Sept. 11, 2008, at http://news.bbc.co.uk/2/hi/technology/7415442.stm.

41 Glaser, Mark (2007). Virtual worlds for kids entwined with real worlds. PBS.org, June 11. Retrieved on Sept. 11, 2008, at http://www.pbs.org/mediashift/2007/06/your_take_roundupvirtual_world.html.

42 Quoted in ibid., para. 5.

43 Quoted in ibid., para. 13.

44 Speigel, Alex (2008). Old fashioned play builds serious skills. NPR.org, Feb. 21. Retrieved on Sept. 12, 2008, at http://www.npr.org/templates/story/story.php?storyId=19212514.

45 Quoted in ibid.

46 Paraphrased in ibid., para. 6.

47 Cited in ibid.

48 Quoted in ibid., para. 14.

49 Referenced in ibid., para. 6.

50 Adapted from Zirin, David (2006). Sneakers for social justice. *The Nation*, Sept. 19 (web only). http://www.thenation.com/doc/20061002/southpaw.

Chapter 14

1 Maryles, D. and Riippa, L. (2001). How they landed on top. *Publishers Weekly*, 248: 12: 31.

2 The opinion of Schickel, R. (2000). The frenzy of renown. *The Los Angeles Times Book Review*, Dec. 10, 1–2.

3 Jules Feiffer as quoted in Mitchell, E. (2000). They oughta be in pictures. *New York Times*, July 25, B1.

4 Lang, J.S. and Trimble, P. (1988). Whatever happened to the man of tomorrow? *Journal of Popular Culture*, 22: 3: 157–73.

5 Lee was quoted in Raphael, J. (2000). The invincible Stan Lee? *The Los Angeles Times Magazine*, July 16, 18–21.

6 From Tad Friends (2001). Comics from underground. *The New Yorker*, July 30, 26–9.

7 Dame Rebecca West said this as quoted in www.britannica.com.

8 As quoted in www.britannica.com.

9 Department of Labor, Bureau of Statistics.

10 Statistics from Picard, R. and Brody, J. (2000). The structure of the newspaper industry. In Greco, A. (ed.), *The media and entertainment industries*. Boston: Allyn & Bacon, p. 46.

11 Emigh, Jacqueline (2008). Analysts: Online news viewers rising as newspaper readership falls. *BetaNews*, Sept. 5.

12 Melinda Gipson at Newspaper Association of America, naa.org, July 15, 2006.

13 Encyclopedia Britannica, "Comic strip" found at www.britannica.com/bcom/eb/article/ (Dec. 8, 2000).

14 http://www.nytimes.com/2007/10/01/business/media/01paper.html?pagewanted=all.

15 From www.stateofthenewsmedia.com/narrative, July 18, 2006.

16 By Louise Story for the *New York Times*, June 13, 2005.

17 Cited in Boucher, G. (2001). The bubble pops: Radio stations are beginning to turn a cold shoulder to teen acts. *Star Tribune*, Minneapolis MN (Metro Edition), Feb. 11, 10F.

18 Bauder. David (2007). Disney rules tween scene. Newday.com, Feb. 7. Accessed on April 2, 2007, at http://www.newsday.com/features/printedition/ny-ettel5084892feb09,0,4427920.sto.

19 Gundersen, E. (1992). Hyperkinetic techno music wins dance floor raves // Blasts from Belgium // Innovators struggle to keep ahead of the clones. *USA Today*, Dec. 4, 04D.

20 Dunaway, M. (1999). James Brown is dead. *Pif Magazine* (online), 20. Accessed Dec. 5, 2002, at http://pifmagazine.com/vol20/duna.shtml.

21 Ibid.

22 Brige Ratings Press Release (June 29, 2006). Accessed May 11, 2007, at http://www.bridgeratings.com/press.06.22.06.formats.htm.

23 Ipsos press release accessed June 5, 2007, at http://www.ipsos-na.com/news/pressrelease.cfm?id=3124.

24 Podcasts and media. Accessed May 11, 2007, at http://www.pasadenatab.org/html/worship/podcasts/podcast.htm.

25 From posting accessed May 11, 2007, at http://www.podspider.com.

26 www.filmsite.org/animatedfilms7.html.

27 From Heller, S. (1994). Dissecting Disney. *The Chronicle of Higher Education*, Feb. 16, A-1.
28 Chelna Khatau for CNN at www.cnn.com/2008/TECH/09/12/future.cinema/.
29 Proclaimed in an Op-Ed column by Neal Gabler (2001). When every TV show is a rerun. *New York Times*, March 4, 15.
30 From Alessandra Stanley for the *New York Times*, Sept. 10, 2006, Arts 95.
31 Tenley Woodman for the *Boston Herald*, June 9, 2008.
32 Stated in an article by Julie Salamon in Critic's notebook for the *New York Times*, July 30, 2001, B1.
33 Patterson, Tom (2008). Is the future of television on the web? May 2. http://www.cnn.com/2008/ SHOWBIZ/TV/05/01/tv.future/index.html.

Chapter 15

1   Historical facts are based on information obtained from www.britannica.com, Nov. 2000.
2   See Zillmann, D. and Vorderer, P. (eds) (2000). *Media entertainment*. Mahwah NJ: Lawrence Erlbaum, ch. 1.
3   Alan Kozin for the *New York Times*, May 28, 2006, Arts & Leisure, 1.
4   These are the words of New York dance critic Arlene Croce as cited in an article by Chris Pasles on dance for *The Los Angeles Times*, Dec. 4, 2005, B8.
5   www.britannica.com.
6   Eakin, E. (2000). If it's funny you laugh, but why? *New York Times*, Dec. 9, A23.
7   Factual information from http://lookd.com/magic/.
8   From Jameson, M. (2000). The Houdini of the hoi polloi. *The Los Angeles Times*, Nov. 19, E1.
9   From www.magiccastle.com.
10 Furchgott, R. (2000). Taking its brand beyond the center ring. *New York Times*, March 12, B4.
11 Kimmelman, M. (2008). Bullfighting is dead! Long live the bullfight. *New York Times Sunday Magazine*, June 8.
12 Epstein, K. (2000). Sound offense, no defense: Today's pro sports events, like much entertainment, assault you with noise; some explosive moments at Redskins games can throw your hearing for a loss. *The Washington Post*, Dec. 19, Z10.
13 Hickey, J. (2000). Corporations love sports. *Insight on the News*, Nov. 13, Section: Nation: Business, p. 22.
14 Simon, M. (2001). Buying goodwill that'll stick: Big wheel could stop the stadium whining. *San Francisco Chronicle*, Dec. 13, A19.
15 Johnson, G. (2001). Some fumbles in arena name game; Marketing: A few companies with their moniker up in lights have faltered since signing the big-money deals. It's bad news for the sports franchises, too. *The Los Angeles Times*, April 20, C1.
16 Meehan, P. for the *New York Times*, June 8, 2008.
17 Cohan, J. (2008). The show must go on. www.american.com/archive/2008/march-april-magazinecontents/ the-show-must-go-on

Chapter 16

1   Horner, S. and Swarbrooke, J. (1996). *Marketing tourism, hospitality and leisure in Europe*. London: International Thomson Business Press.
2   Matley, I.M. (1976). *The geography of international tourism*. Resource Paper 76-1. Washington: Association of American Geographers.
3   Urry, J. (1990). *The tourist gaze*. Thousand Oaks CA: Sage.
4   Adapted from a list by Cohen, E. (1972). Towards a sociology of international tourism. *Social Research*, 39: 64–82.
5   See Boorstein, D. (1961). *The image: A guide to pseudo events in America*. New York: Harper & Row.
6   Ritzer, G. and Liska, A. (1997). "McDisneyization" and "post-tourism": Complementary perspectives on contemporary tourism. In Rojek, C. and Urry, J. (eds), *Touring cultures: Transformations of travel & theory*. New York: Routledge.
7   Based on a view by MacCannell, D. (1989). *The tourist: A new theory of the leisure class*. Berkeley: University of California Press.
8   From Nash, D. (1981). Tourism as an anthropological subject. *Current Anthropology*, 22: 5: 461–81.
9   Urry, *The tourist gaze*.
10 See a discussion by Pearce, P.L. (1982). *The social psychology of tourist behavior*. London: Pergamon.
11 From Dobb, E. (1998). Where the good begins: Notes of the art of modern travel. *Harper's Magazine*, 297: 1778: 59.
12 Gladstone, David (1998). Tourism urbanism in the U.S. *Urban Affairs Review*, 34: 1: 3–27.
13 MacCannell, *The tourist*, p. 41.
14 From Debra Galant (2001). Guides finger "Sopranos" sites. *New York Times*, July 22, T5.

15 From Gordon, B. (1986). The souvenir: Messenger of the extraordinary. *Journal of Popular Culture*, 20: 3: 135–46.

16 See Love, L. and Sheldon, P.S. (1998). Souvenirs: Messengers of meaning. *Advances in Consumer Research*, 25: 170–5.

17 Sayre, S. (2000). Tourism, art stars and consumption: Wyland's whales. Paper presented to the annual conference of the Association of Consumer Research, Salt Lake City.

18 From Chambers, E. (2000). *Native tours: An anthropology of travel and tourism*. Berkeley: University of California Press.

19 MacCannell, *The tourist*.

20 From Cohen, E. (1979). Rethinking the sociology of tourism. *Annals of Tourism Research*, 6: 18–35.

21 Horner and Swarbrooke, *Marketing tourism*, Ch. 16.

22 www.htrends.com/researcharticle9335.html.

23 By Justin Francis, responsibletravel.com.

24 From Schmitt, B. and Simonson, A. (1997). *Marketing aesthetics: The strategic management of brands, identity and image*. New York: The Free Press.

25 See Severin, W.J. and Tankard, J.W. Jr. (1992). *Communication theories: Origins, methods and uses in the mass media*. New York: Longman.

26 Terms used by Weiss, W. (1971). Mass communication. *Annual Review of Psychology*, 22: 309–36.

27 Horner and Swarbrooke, *Marketing tourism*, p. 98.

28 From Cook, R.A., Yale, L.J., and Marqua, J.J. (2002). *Tourism: The business of travel*. Upper Saddle River NJ: Prentice Hall.

29 Adapted from Inskeep, E. (1991). *Tourism planning: An integrated and sustainable development approach*. New York: Van Nostrand Reinhold.

30 By Eliel Sabastian at www.associatedcontent.com/article/13522/the_problems_facing_the_us_national.html?cat=58.

31 From Michael Kimmelman (2001). Museums in a quandary: Where are the ideals? *New York Times*, Aug. 26, AR2.

32 Said by art and culture critic Dave Hickey in Steven Kinzer (2001). Las Vegas's museums play to type. *New York Times*, Sept. 5, B1.

33 Smith, R. (2000). Memo to art museums: Don't give up on art. *New York Times*, Dec. 3, Arts 35.

34 Remark of art critic Hilton Kramer quoted in Puente, M. (2001). What is art? *USA Today*, Jan. 5, D1.

35 Ed Able as quoted in ibid.

36 From Ferrell, S. (2000). Famous faces, all in wax. *New York Times*, Nov. 12, TR31.

37 bizjournals.com/triangle/stories/2008/06/09/daily23.html.

38 Cited in Bonfante, P. (1999). Hooked on the edge: The old extremes aren't extreme enough for a new brand of athlete. *Boston Globe* [City Edition], Sept. 29, F1.

39 Cited in ibid.

40 Yema, J. (2000). Herd instinct. *Boston Globe* [Third Edition], July 2, BGM 5.

41 Quoted in Sullivan, J. (2000). Extreme's foothold firm in pop culture: Music, filmmaking, ads move to the edge. *San Francisco Chronicle* [Final Edition], Aug. 19, D1.

Chapter 17

1 Cited in Brown, W. and Boxer, S. (1999). Connected—Millennium issue: Entertainment. *Daily Telegraph*, London, Dec. 30, 13.

2 The phrase "sounding like a broken record" has been used to describe a person who says the same thing over and over again; the reference is to old records that would skip and repeat owing to scratch marks on the vinyl.

3 The phrase "taking an E-ticket ride" was a metaphor for a great, exciting—often whirlwind—experience; the reference was to Disney theme park's ticketing practices up until the mid-1980s. At that time, people bought individual tickets for park attractions with E-tickets, which were designated for Disney's most exciting and popular attractions, such as the Space Mountain and the Pirates of the Caribbean rides.

4 Copeland, P. (2000). Foreword to new media f@ctfile Brighton Wired Sussex. Cited in Perrons, D. (2001). Understanding social and spatial divisions in the new economy. Paper prepared for presentation at Regional Transitions. European regions and the challenges of development, integration and enlargement, Regional Studies International Conference University of Gdansk 15–18 September. Accessed Dec. 15, 2002, at http://secure.rogerbooth.co.uk/rsa/gdansk/Perrons.doc.

5 Accessed Dec. 17, 2002, at www.dabra.com/newmediaskills.pdf.

6 New Media Survey: PriceWaterhouseCoopers (1999). *Public Policy Review: A Review of Recent Policies, Regulations and Announcements*, June, 99: 6: 3 [An online publication of the Institute of Chartered Accountants of BC]. Accessed Dec. 17, 2002, at www.ica.bc.ca/pdf/june99.pdf.

7 New media: Communicating in the new media to promote teamwork. Accessed March 9, 2002, at www.lc.capellauniversity.edu/~thamilton/NewMediaSite/newmedia2.htm.

8 www.newmedia.org/articles/109/1/Prevalence-of-Digital-Reading-Electronic-Books-E-Books-and-E-Book-Readers/Page1.html.

9 Reported in Allen, K. (2000). Net used for entertainment, not info. *Advertising and Marketing*, July 28. Accessed March 9, 2002, at www.digitrends.net/ena/index_10402.html.

10 Statistics taken from the Pew Internet & American Life Project, February 15–March 7, 2007 Tracking Survey. Accessed on June 14, 2007, at http://www.pewinternet.org/trends/User_Demo_6.11.07.htm.

11 Statistics reported by Chinatoday.com. Retrieved Sept. 1, 2008, at http://www.chinatoday.com/data/data.htm.

12 Walsh, Mike (2006, July). Futuretainment: The new business of show business. *Australian Anthill Magazine*, 16, para. 1. Accessed on June 15, 2007, at http://www.australiananthill.com/main.php?page=ed_futuretainment16.

13 Ibid., para. 4.

14 Ibid., para. 12.

15 Walsh, Mark (2009). Facebook users growing up fast. *MediaPostNews*, March 26. Accessed Aug. 6, 2009, at http://www. mediapost.com/publications/?fa=Articles.showArticle&art_aid=102973.

16 Digital marketing & media fact pact, *Advertising Age*, April 23, 2007.

17 The twitter-clone-twitter-like sites collection (2007). Posted on www.thws.cn, May. Retrieved on Sept. 1, 2008, at http://www.thws.cn/articles/twitter-clones.html.

18 Some stats on China's IM services (2008). Posted on The China 2.0 Review, April 8. Retrieved on Sept. 1, 2008, at http://www.cwrblog.net/1027/some-stats-on-chinas-im-services.html.

19 Cited in Richtel, Matt and Stone, Brad (2007). Play sites offer safe fun—and lucrative advertising space. *International Herald Tribune*, June 5. Retrieved on Sept. 1, 2008, at http://www.iht.com/articles/2007/06/05/news/dolls04.4.php, para. 11.

20 Olsen, Stephanie (2007). There's about to be a boomlet in kids' virtual worlds. News.cent.com, Oct. 15. Retrieved on Sept. 1, 2008, at http://news.cnet.com/Virtual-world-makers-aim-to-hook-kids/2009-1025_3-6213355.html.

21 Cited in Olsen, Stephanie (2007). Virtual-world makers aim to hook kids. News.cnet.com, Oct. 15. Retrieved on Sept. 1, 2008, at http://news.cnet.com/Virtual-world-makers-aim-to-hook-kids/2009-1025_3-6213355.html.

22 Ibid., para. 17.

23 Hawn, Carleen (2007). Time to play, money to spend: Webkinz and Club Penguin struck gold by attracting millions of kids to their online worlds and keeping them there. What makes their sites so sticky? *Business 2.0 Magazine*, March 23. Retrieved on Sept. 1, 2008, from http://money.cnn.com/magazines/business2/business2_archive/2007/04/01/8403359/index.htm.

24 Ibid.

25 Ibid.

26 Reported in Olsen, Virtual-world makers aim to hook kids.

27 Cited in Olsen, Virtual-world makers aim to hook kids, para. 3.

28 Walsh, Futuretainment, para. 1.

29 Cited in Park, Roger (2006). Brands participate in virtual shows. Imediaconnection.com, Sept. 19. Accessed on July 2, 2007, at http://www.imediaconnection.com/ news/11266.asp.

30 Quote found on p. 74 of Steuer, J. (1992). Defining virtual reality: Dimensions determining telepresence. *Journal of Communication*, 42: 4: 73–93.

31 Haley, K. (2001). More. Better, different. [Showtime management strategy to include interactivity and expanding digital multiplex]. *Multichannel News*, July 23, 22: 30: 12A.

32 Cited in ibid.

33 Cited in ibid.

34 Vorderer, P. (2000). Interactive entertainment and beyond. In Zillmann, D. and Vorderer, P. (eds), *Media entertainment: The psychology of its appeal*. Mahwah NJ: Lawrence Erlbaum Associates.

35 www.internet-filter-review.toptenreviews.com/internet-pornography-statistics.html.

36 Arlidge, J. (2002). Focus: Naked capitalism: The dirty secret that drives new technology: it's porn. *The Observer*, London, March 3, 20.

37 Ibid.

38 Ibid.

39 Cornell, D. (1997). Edutainment and girls. *CPSR* [Computer Professionals for Social Responsibility] *Newsletter*, winter, 15: 1: 6.

40 From Poole, S. (2000). *Trigger happy: Video games and the entertainment revolution*. New York: Arcade Publishing.

41 For a comprehensive review of video game history, see Kent, S. (2000). *The first quarter: 25-year history of video games*. London: BWD Publishers.

42 From Loftus, G.R. and Loftus, E.F. (1983). *Mind at play: The psychology of video games*. New York: Basic Books.

43 Adapted from Poole, *Trigger happy*.

44 Adapted from Berger, A.A. (2000). *Video games: A popular culture phenomenon*. London: Transaction Publishers.

45 Hirschman, E. and Holbrook, H. (1982). The experiential aspects of consumption: Consumer fantasies, feelings and fun. *Journal of Consumer Research*, 9: 2: 132–40.

46 Ibid., p. 138.

47 From www.gamedev.net/reference/business/features/biologhy/page4, May 4, 2001.

48 Schiesel, Seth (2008). Resistance is futile. *New York Times*, May 25.

49 Michael Dolan for *HFM* magazine in New York City, Sept. 2006.

50 Walsh, Mike (in press). *Futuretainment: The new business of show business*. London: Phaidon Press.

51 Walsh, Mike (2006). The new business of show business. Fourth-Estate.Com. Retrieved on Sept. 1, 2008, at http://www.fourth-estate.com/2006/06/the_new_busines.html, para. 6.

52 Ibid., para. 24.

53 Walsh, Futuretainment.

54 Emuss, Peter (2006). Nike's Joga Bonito. Mansized.co.uk, Aug. 5. Retrieved on Aug. 31, 2008, at http://www.mansized.co.uk/reviews/review.phtml/204/331/.

55 Quote taken from a summary of Nike's Joga Bonito campaign in Hong Kong posted on Nike's advertising agency e-crusade's website. Retrieved on Sept. 1, 2008, at http://www.e-crusade.com/award/spikes 2007/04/nike/jogaBonito.htm#.

56 Ibid.

ILLUSTRATION CREDITS

INDEX